Evolutionary Economics and Social Complexity Science

Volume 15

The Japanese Association for Evolutionary Economics (JAFEE) always has adhered to its original aim of taking an explicit "integrated" approach. This path has been followed steadfastly since the Association's establishment in 1997 and, as well, since the inauguration of our international journal in 2004. We have deployed an agenda encompassing a contemporary array of subjects including but not limited to: foundations of institutional and evolutionary economics, criticism of mainstream views in the social sciences, knowledge and learning in socio-economic life, development and innovation of technologies, transformation of industrial organizations and economic systems, experimental studies in economics, agent-based modeling of socio-economic systems, evolution of the governance structure of firms and other organizations, comparison of dynamically changing institutions of the world, and policy proposals in the transformational process of economic life. In short, our starting point is an "integrative science" of evolutionary and institutional views. Furthermore, we always endeavor to stay abreast of newly established methods such as agent-based modeling, socio/econo-physics, and network analysis as part of our integrative links.

More fundamentally, "evolution" in social science is interpreted as an essential key word, i.e., an integrative and /or communicative link to understand and redomain various preceding dichotomies in the sciences: ontological or epistemological, subjective or objective, homogeneous or heterogeneous, natural or artificial, selfish or altruistic, individualistic or collective, rational or irrational, axiomatic or psychological-based, causal nexus or cyclic networked, optimal or adaptive, microor macroscopic, deterministic or stochastic, historical or theoretical, mathematical or computational, experimental or empirical, agent-based or socio/econo-physical, institutional or evolutionary, regional or global, and so on. The conventional meanings adhering to various traditional dichotomies may be more or less obsolete, to be replaced with more current ones vis-à-vis contemporary academic trends. Thus we are strongly encouraged to integrate some of the conventional dichotomies.

These attempts are not limited to the field of economic sciences, including management sciences, but also include social science in general. In that way, understanding the social profiles of complex science may then be within our reach. In the meantime, contemporary society appears to be evolving into a newly emerging phase, chiefly characterized by an information and communication technology (ICT) mode of production and a service network system replacing the earlier established factory system with a new one that is suited to actual observations. In the face of these changes we are urgently compelled to explore a set of new properties for a new socio/economic system by implementing new ideas. We thus are keen to look for "integrated principles" common to the above-mentioned dichotomies throughout our serial compilation of publications. We are also encouraged to create a new, broader spectrum for establishing a specific method positively integrated in our own original way.

Editors-in-Chief
Takahiro Fujimoto, Tokyo, Japan
Yuji Aruka, Tokyo, Japan

More information about this series at http://www.springer.com/series/11930

Yoshinori Shiozawa • Masashi Morioka
Kazuhisa Taniguchi

Microfoundations of Evolutionary Economics

Springer

Yoshinori Shiozawa
Osaka City University
Osaka, Japan

Kazuhisa Taniguchi
Faculty of Economics
Kindai University
Osaka, Japan

Masashi Morioka
College of International Relations
Ritsumeikan University
Kyoto, Japan

ISSN 2198-4204 ISSN 2198-4212 (electronic)
Evolutionary Economics and Social Complexity Science
ISBN 978-4-431-55266-6 ISBN 978-4-431-55267-3 (eBook)
https://doi.org/10.1007/978-4-431-55267-3

Library of Congress Control Number: 2018966133

This Springer imprint is published by the registered company Springer Japan KK part of Springer Nature.
The registered company address is: Shiroyama Trust Tower, 4-3-1 Toranomon, Minato-ku, Tokyo 105-6005, Japan

Preface to Microfoundations of Evolutionary Economics

This book explicitly provides microfoundations of evolutionary economics that have been absent thus far in evolutionary economics. The evolutionary economics continued to criticize mainstream neoclassical economics as insufficient framework of analysis, but it had no other choice than to use ideas and analytical tools of neoclassical economics implicitly or explicitly, because it lacked microfoundations of its own. It is clear that without microfoundations of its own, evolutionary economics will not become an academic discipline independent of neoclassical economics. Evolutionary economics needs theoretical foundations as fine and logically sure as Arrow and Debreu's model of competitive equilibrium (Arrow and Debreu, "Existence of an equilibrium for a competitive economy", *Econometrica* 22(3): 265–90, 1954) is, but it lacked this firm basis of analysis for a long time. This book was written in order to change this state of evolutionary economics. Although discovered by a series of studies that were not directly connected to evolutionary economics, the results we have obtained have a good chemistry with evolutionary economics and with Keynesian analysis of effective demand. We believe that our results serve as microfoundations for both evolutionary and Post-Keynesian economics.

Firstly, let me explain the reason why this book provides the microfoundations of evolutionary economics. Humans are a product of biological evolution and have many limitations as organisms. For example, we have limitations in life spans, boundedness of our rational reasoning and calculations (bounded rationality), limited range in perception and recognition (bounded or myopic sight), and limited ability in executing something planned. This is the very reason why our societies could have developed through our repeated learning and innovations. If humans were omniscient and omnipotent, our economy may have been totally different from that we have today. The limitations of human abilities are the basis of many institutions of our society. We are in a big economy which extends globally and comprises billions of people and millions of firms. We are incapable to collect relevant information and calculate solutions. One of the core issues in economics is the clarification of the mechanisms and the reasons how and why the economy as a whole functions quite well, although an enormous number of agents are acting with their limits in rationality and sight. The issue includes elucidating mechanisms that may exist in the actual economy and guarantee its smooth functioning. Of course, since the onset of economics approximately 250 years ago, the awareness of this issue has resided in the studies with a focus on the workings of the market. Adam Smith posed the problem but could not solve it except that he could barely suggest the existence of an invisible hand.

A model economy, which is studied through Chaps. 2, 3, 4, 5 and 6, forms the core of this book. It consists of many goods and services that are produced by different firms and exchanged between them. We assume a flow of final demands which are given exogenously. Our main concern is whether the economic system consisting of many producer firms with limited information (myopic sight) can follow this flow of final demands. Of course, it is impossible without conditions. Our main result is that the complex system of interconnected producers can follow the final demand flow as long as the average demand flow changes "slowly." What "slowly" means exactly is given in the main text, i.e., Chapter 2 and others. The economy we examine is very different from model economies that assume an auctioneer, and which form a long tradition in modern economics from Leon Walras to Arrow and Debreu. Our market participants, whether they are individuals or firms, conduct their activities based on their limited knowledge that they can obtain within their own perspectives. More concretely we assume that firms (or rather managers of firms) can only know the past series of sales flow of their products. In these processes, prices do not serve as mediator that brings equality of demand and supply for products. It is the producers that adjust their production flow in such a way that the supply of the product is almost equal to its demand. As firms cannot know the future demand exactly, the firms produce with an expectation, but we assume that this expectation is fulfilled in no way. Firms are obliged to hold product stocks or inventories and regulate them in order to avoid stockout situation as far as possible and keep the inventories as small as possible. As these objectives often contradict, there are no optimal solutions to these inventory control problems. We suppose firms follow rule-of-thumb solutions by adjusting the parameters of the adjustment rules. The adjustment system based on quantity changes without mediating price changes is referred to as *a quantity adjustment process (or economy)* in this book.

When prices are not primary mediators which bring equality of demand and supply, what functions do prices assume? Prices are determined in principle by producers (and by suppliers in case of the distribution industry). Price setting may have various rules but the principal method is *full-cost pricing*. In other words, the price of a product is determined as the unit cost of the product multiplied by a markup factor, namely 1 + markup rate m. In this book, we do not enter in the question how this markup rate is determined nor in the question why firms adopt this pricing policy. This is a widely observed custom and we have already a huge literature (see, for example, Frederic S. Lee, *Post Keynesian price theory*, Cambridge, Cambridge University Press, 1998). We can prove that these prices are stable in the sense that a change of demand compositions cannot influence the prices. If firms are producing by a competitive production technique, the firms cannot change to other production techniques as long as the final demands are satisfied by those productions.

This is in sharp contrast with Arrow–Debreu model. Contrary to the generally accepted (mis)understanding, Arrow–Debreu model does not guarantees the stability of prices. It only proves existence of a system of prices in which no agents want to change their behavior. The price system may stay constant at a given point of time when the market is open, but it may change in the next period when the next market takes place. Existence of futures market only proves that demand and supply of goods that will be delivered in the future are in equilibrium in the present market (Shiozawa, *Reflections on Modern Economics* [in Japanese], Tokyo, Nihon Keizai Shinbunsha, 1983, Section 2.2). In the Arrow–Debreu model, no conditions that guarantee this stability between periods are posed and there is no guarantee that prices remain stable between the present and the next periods. Chapter 2 of this book proves that prices remain constant as long as two conditions are satisfied: (1) there is enough labor power and material stocks that makes possible to produce as net product the final demands, and (2) the set of production techniques remain invariant and the markup rates remain constant. The first condition is normally satisfied if we assume that the final demands are backed by money gained one period earlier. Main arguments are obtained as what Shiozawa named *minimal price theorem*, which is in fact the dual version of Samuelson's nonsubstitution theorem. It is custom that the latter theorem is introduced as having too restricted conditions, but Shiozawa shows that it can be extended to sufficiently wide class of economies. The stability of prices provides a good base for change of production techniques which is one of main research agenda for evolutionary economics.

The main focus of this book is however everyday adjustment processes under this stable price system. If a firm can obtain enough amount of demand for its product, i.e., if the demand exceeds profit-loss point, it can get a profit. Although firms can work on markets in order to increase the demand by advertising and other marketing activities, the production unit is obliged to follow the change of the demand flow for the product. Chapters 3, 4, 5 and 6 describe and analyze in detail what happens in the interactive network of inputs and outputs. We are interested in the process how the final demand is transmitted to upstream firms through input–output relations in such a way that the total network of firms can produce final demands without causing stockouts too often. As it is already pointed out, our results are affirmative in the sense that total system of production network can follow final demands when their average moves slowly. In addition, the remarkable fact in our research is that the complex network of quantity adjustment does not necessitate unrealistic capabilities for the part of decision makers. This is the reason why we claim that our results provide the microfoundations for evolutionary economics. The new findings have the most important significance for the economics of the market economy, because this is probably the first result after Arrow and Debreu's model. It means we have found that "a social system moved by independent actions in pursuit different values (Arrow and Hahn, *General Competitive Analysis*, 1971, p.1)" can work *without* assuming the unrealistic capabilities for economic agents.

Secondly, a special mention must be added on the fact that this book examines an economy which is composed of many products. In the model, the number of products can be as big as we want. It is difficult to know the exact number of commodities (goods and services) that exist in the real world, but it surely exceeds tens of millions. It may count hundreds of millions. This bigness of number of products is an important characteristic of the modern economy. However, many standard economics models observe the single-good economy. In such an economy, there is no need of coordinating different goods. Majority of macroeconomics ignores the problems which may arise from the multiplicity of commodities. It is extremely strange that they simply assume there are no such problems. Our results in this book provide how this complicated coordination problems are solved in the real economy and where obstructions may occur. With our results, macroeconomic principle of effective demand obtains a new foundation. When firms follow the demand flow expressed for their products, the whole system of input–output links adjusts itself to produce the final demands as net production provided that each of the latter satisfies certain restrictions made explicit in this book. This provides a new foundation for Keynesian economics, because the principle of effective demand gets a new formulation based on behaviors of individual firms. Shortly stated, the principle can be reformulated at the product level. If products are differentiated by firms that produced them, the principle simply means that firms produce as much as products sell. This is what Shiozawa named *Sraffa principle* (Shiozawa, *The Revival of classical theory of values,* London, Routledge, 2015, and others). There is a strong parallelism between the firm-level principle and the economy-wide principle relative to demand and production (See Fujimoto, "Preface to Special Issue Evolution of Firms and Industries," *Evolutionary and Institutional Economics Review*, 9: 1–10, 2012).

As everybody knows, Keynes' concept of effective demand was deleted from new Keynesian economics which adopted microfoundations based on neoclassical general equilibrium theory. Its macroeconomic framework is now *Dynamic Stochastic General Equilibrium* (DSGE) model. Post-Keynesians rejected such microfoundations and they were right. But they are obliged to remain minor because they could produce no alternative theory. The present book has a power to change this state of the art, as it provides a powerful tool of analysis based in realistic human behaviors. We have not included post-Keynesian economics in the title of this book, because we believe that evolutionary economics is more comprehensive than post-Keynesian economics and the first comprises the latter as a part when a suitable analytical framework is given. Our book provides such a framework.

Thirdly, I would like to point out that, in any research field, we can built from the beginning no universal theory that can explain all the phenomena that might be relevant to the field. We should start from what can be studied with a firm base. In the economics science, the same dictum applies. It is worth emphasizing that the model economy we studied in this book only applies to the real or production economies. Evidently, it should not be applied to financial economies. We need another theory for them. We make no judgment on whether Walrasian economics is applicable to financial economies. It is well known that Walras got his image of market from Bourse de Paris (*Eléments d'économie politique pure*, 1900). No matter whether it is applicable to financial market or not, production economies and financial economies are so different with each other. We should not assume that two economies can be formulated in the same manner at the moment. The trouble with Walrasian economics started from this confusion. To avoid repeating similar mistakes again, we want to emphasize that the theory, described in this book, applies only to the production economies until some new theory appears that can unify both real and financial economies.

Fourthly, a simple note should be added on the history of our studies on quantity adjustment processes which culminated in our book. More than 30 years ago, Shiozawa was concerned why quantity adjustment process based on agents with shortsighted perspectives, or myopic agents, can function without no big troubles. The main focus of his study was on analyzing the microscopic structure of the process, run by agents with limited abilities, which was to progress step-by-step while excluding any kind of equilibrium mechanism. However, the conclusion obtained by the study of Shiozawa ("The Micro Structure of Kahn-Keynes Process (In Japanese)," *Keizaigaku Zasshi* 84(3): 48–64, 1983) was negative in the sense that the whole process of adjustment was divergent, implying that the rule-based adjustment was not sufficient to make the process to follow after the change of final demand. It meant that either some kind of price adjustment was necessary or some other adjustment rules were in reality adopted.

Taniguchi was interested in the path of economy. The starting point of his study was the "Traverse" by Hicks (*Capital and Time*, 1973). The study of "Traverse" focuses mainly on capital adjustment, and the unique point of his analysis was that the study was constructed by process analysis. Through this study, Taniguchi encountered Shiozawa's study on the microscopic structure where production was adjusted. Taniguchi ("On the Traverse of Quantity Adjustment Economies" [in Japanese], *Keizaigaku Zasshi,* 91(5): 29–43, 1991) conducted a computer-based numerical analysis to avoid suffering from the mathematical difficulties that Shiozawa faced in his study. As a result, Taniguchi discovered that a quantity adjustment economy, which consists of individual entities having their own shortsighted perspectives within a narrow range around themselves and over a short period of time in the past, has a robust convergent structure.

Morioka started his study on quantity adjustment economies with the study of *Economics of Shortage* (1980) by Kornai. He came to be interested in the analysis of the production and transaction processes in the market. Afterwards, through the study of the iteration processes of production and transactions in the markets of a capitalist economy, he explored the framework of the background theory and deepened his consideration on the history of economic doctrines. He then succeeded in showing through mathematical analysis that the quantity adjustment process can be stabilized by moderate averaging of past demands in the demand forecast formation. These achievements were published in his book *The Economic Theory of Quantity Adjustment* (in Japanese, Nihon Keizai Hyoronsha, 2005). Shiozawa later called these discoveries by Taniguchi and Morioka *the Taniguchi-Morioka theorem.*

As described above, the studies made by these three economists are separated in time and interest. Those reports were written only in Japanese, while there were no similar studies published in English as far as we know. This is the first attempt to introduce our results to English-speaking world. Through the publication of this book, we hope that the originality of our studies will be admitted and the book will get proper appreciation.

Fifthly, the followings are brief descriptions on each chapter. Readers can see how this book is organized. Chapter 1, written by Yoshinori Shiozawa, provides a theoretical perspective of evolutionary economics. First, the author discusses how our rational capability is limited, how often intractable problems exist in our lives, how restricted the range of influence of our actions is, and finally, what this implies for economics. Bounded rationality is the basis of all evolutions of economic entities of various categories, which include behavior, commodity, technology, institutions, organizations, systems, and knowledge. Because of bounded rationality, any existing entities are not optimal at any time. This is the main reason why evolution is ubiquitous and occurs successively and incessantly. Second, the author explains that the core structure of human behavior is If-Then behavior or Cognitive-Directive (CD) transformation. The author examines in detail this structure and shows how the skill of an experienced worker is built. The process analysis as an analytical framework and the concept of the micro-macro loop are also explained. This chapter is not only appropriate as an introductory chapter of this book but also a comprehensive introduction to evolutionary economics in general. It provides readers with signposts that guide them to the microfoundations of evolutionary economics.

Chapter 2, written also by Shiozawa, provides contents directly related to the quantity adjustment economy. First, a set of postulates that show how our market economy works are introduced, and the separation of price and quantity adjustment is discussed. Second, *the minimal price theorem* is proved, at first for a simple case. The theorem is then extended to various cases including fixed capital cases and the existence of labor heterogeneity, which are normally treated as the situation that the theorem does not hold. Our basic understanding on price and quantity adjustment is that they are in principle independent with each other. Thus, a change of quantities does not affect prices and vice versa, except for special cases. *The minimal price theorem* justifies the basic independence of price and quantity adjustment, because in a normal case, firms produce with the production technique which gives the minimal unit cost among alternative production techniques. This understanding, our core message, is drastically opposed to the standard price theory that assumes prices and quantities are simultaneously determined at the intersection point of the demand function and the supply function. In addition, this chapter refers to how the essence of *the minimal price theorem* can be extended to international trade economy. The economy here treated is very wide, because it is an m-country, n-commodity economy where input trade is permitted. In the final section, it is explained how the quantity adjustment process can be formulated. It gives an introduction to the quantity adjustment processes, which are main theme of the following chapters.

Chapter 3 provides the basic framework and key concepts of the economic theory of quantity adjustment and is written by Masashi Morioka. First, general characterizations of the capitalist system such as a demand-constrained economy are clarified, and the author argues that this aspect of capitalism has a profound relevance to the long-term changes of technologies and products through incessant innovations. Second, inventory shortage (stockout) avoidance behaviors by individual firms that are faced with the uncertainty of demand as a consequence of sales competition are formulated. In this way, quantity adjustments in the capitalist economy as a dynamic process generated by interactions of firms that repeat inventory shortage avoidance behaviors are outlined. In addition, Morioka describes the historical overview of earlier contributions to the analysis of the quantity adjustment that have taken the form of attempts to construct a dynamic and multisector model of the multiplier theory by Kahn–Kalecki–Keynes. This chapter introduces a quantity adjustment economy to the researchers who are unfamiliar with it. This chapter is also helpful for reading the following chapters.

Chapter 4 by Morioka includes the basic setting of the model; the author analyzes a multisector dynamic model of the quantity adjustment process in which firms determine production and material orders based on inventories and demand forecasts under fixed prices and final demands. Special attention is paid to the roles of the demand forecast by using a moving average of past demand, and the dynamic properties of the process generated through interactions among sectors are investigated. This chapter also contains a series of theorems on the stability conditions that thoroughly elucidate how the stability of the process is affected by the input structure, the extent of averaging, and the relative scale of buffer holdings. It is also shown that moderate averaging of past sales in the demand forecasts formation is indispensable for quantity adjustment stability. Otherwise, the big transition matrix would have eigenvalues outside of the unit circle. Moreover, the mechanism of stabilization through averaging in the demand forecast is closely examined. This chapter is the theoretical core of a quantitative adjustment economy in this book. Since the main parts are described with mathematical precision, it is suitable to help researchers to investigate this chapter in greater depth.

Chapter 5, also written by Morioka, provides extensions or generalizations of the model given in Chapter 4. First, the following three modifications are discussed: (1) the existence and change of work-in-process inventories, (2) the partial or delayed adjustment in the decision of production amounts, and (3) the multiplicity of firms within a single sector. Analysis of the modified models shows that these modifications do not bring fundamental change to the properties of the adjustment process. Delayed adjustment has the same effect as averaging the demand. Second, the author examines the process accompanied by occurrences of the stockout of materials and products. The stockout of a raw material causes a reduction in the production amount to the level that corresponds to the input of this raw material, and the stockout of a product causes a rationing of sales among buyers. Disturbances caused by stockout can be absorbed by buffer inventories within a certain limit. Finally, two cases that relate to the mid- and long-term changes of the final demand are investigated. It revealed that despite the temporary fluctuations, in due time, the quantity adjustment processes can follow the movement of the final demand.

Chapter 6, written by Kazuhisa Taniguchi, gives the numerical experiments of the nonlinear quantity adjustment processes based on inventory control, which is referred to as the (S, s) policy. First, the author describes the features of a contemporary society that is characterized by an enormous number of different kinds of commodities. To theoretically contemplate an economy with this many kinds of commodities, the concepts of vector space and nonlinearity are explained. Second, the (S, s) inventory control policy theory developed by Scarf ("The optimality of (S, s) policies in the dynamic inventory problem," In Kenneth J. Arrow and Samuel Karlin and Patrick Suppes, *Mathematical Methods in the Social Sciences 1959*, Stanford University Press, 1959) is explained. Since Scarf's model focuses on one kind of goods, it does not consider the movements of the entire economy. The author discusses this crucial point with respect to Scarf's model. Third, the quantity adjustment economies based on the (S, s) policy model as a whole economy are shown. The mathematical solutions of the one kind of goods and two kinds of goods models are shown, and the results of the more than three kinds of goods model are discussed, which are different from the one kind of goods and two kinds of goods models. Finally, certain results obtained by numerical experiments that were conducted by the author are explained, and the effects of the number of commodities are discussed.

Chapter 7 is also written by Taniguchi. The author considers buying and selling transactions and arbitrage based on *the Principle of Exchange* (Shiozawa, "The Present State of Complexity Economics" [In Japanese], in Shiozawa (Ed.) *The Present State of Economics*, Volume 1 History of Economic Thought, Tokyo; Nihon Keizai Hyoronsha, 2004, pp. 53–125) and the equivalence relation. Since money has emerged and price can be observed objectively, buying and selling can be conducted by referring to objective indexes. In this instance, "evaluation" has to be explicitly distinguished from prices. It is important for executing buying and selling transactions that there be a different "evaluation" formed by each buying party and selling party. Arbitrage is defined as the use of the differences in exchange rates to earn a profit. Presenting specific cases with respect to these phenomena, this chapter considers the stability and instability of prices in financial markets and product markets based on the formation of "evaluations" and the function of arbitrage. This chapter does not discuss the quantitative adjustment economy but considers buying, selling, and arbitrage as a process based on *the Principle of Exchange*. This chapter gives, we hope, the microscopic foundations of the exchange (buying and selling) economy from evolutionary point of view.

Last but not least, I want to express my deep thanks to two of my co-authors Yoshinori Shiozawa and Masashi Morioka. Shiozawa first tried to penetrate into the hard rock of quantity adjustment processes and consistently has emphasized the importance of the problem. Without his eventually failed work, we (Morioka and I) would have had no chance to attack the problem. Morioka built a firm and concrete foundation for the quantity adjustment process research by his astonishing result in estimating the Frobenius root of a large matrix which seemed for Shiozawa and me an impossible attempt. Owing to his great mathematical achievement, scholars in the field of quantity adjustment processes as well as effective demand analyses will be able to develop their researches with a firm basis.

I also would like to express my appreciation to the Project Manager at Springer, Ms. Selvaraj Ramabrabha. She patiently endured the delay of our manuscript.

Osaka, Japan
January, 2019

Kazuhisa Taniguchi

Contents

Chapter 1
Microfoundations of Evolutionary Economics

Abstract An evolutionary point of view is the best way to understand the economy and its development. This is *the central dogma* of evolutionary economics. In this chapter on the foundations of evolutionary economics, we discuss (1) why this dogma is supportable, (2) why most of economic entities evolve, (3) what are the defects of standard (or neoclassical) economic theories, and (4) ideas to reconstruct economics in an evolutionary way.

The main task of this chapter is to find the basic form of human behavior. Human being is an entity whose capability is strictly limited in (1) sight, (2) rationality, and (3) execution. How such an entity can effectively behave in a large economic system which is a network which extends worldwide. The question should be investigated from two sides. One is the structure of our behavior. We contend that all routine behavior is composed of C-D transformations or if-then rules. The other is the system characteristics which can be summarized by (1) stationarity, (2) loosely connectedness, and (3) ample margin of subsistence. Only in such a system, routine behavior is a powerful instrument of human knowledge. This two-sidedness requires the economic methodology to be reorganized from the micro-macro loop approach.

Keywords Bounded rationality · Structure of the human behavior · Micro-macro loop · If-then rule · C-D transformation · Semiotics

1.1 Introduction

Evolutionary economics lacked theoretical foundations: no theory of value, no theory of behavior, no proper tool of analysis, and no proof of how an economy works. There were some brief comments on how a market economy works and how it evolves, but few attempts had appeared[1] that try to build a theoretical foundation. Although the work of Nelson and Winter (1982) was a great achievement and helped

[1] New contributions such as Markey-Towler (2018) are now appearing.

Y. Shiozawa et al., *Microfoundations of Evolutionary Economics*,
Evolutionary Economics and Social Complexity Science 15,
https://doi.org/10.1007/978-4-431-55267-3_1

to resurrect evolutionary economics, later development was quite poor. Evolutionary economics pretends to criticize neoclassical mainstream economics, but in many of its arguments, implicitly or explicitly, it has imported the reasoning and results of neoclassical economics. Lacking a theoretical microfoundation defining the nature of human economic behaviors that is consistent with its own distinct worldview, it cannot become a differentiated branch of economics free from the neoclassical mode of thinking. This chapter and the book intend to fill this gap in the state of evolutionary economics.

An evolutionary point-of-view is the best way to understand the economy and its development. This is *the central dogma* of evolutionary economics. In this chapter, we examine the foundations of evolutionary economics and discuss (1) why this position is supportable, (2) why most economic entities evolve, (3) what are the defects of standard (neoclassical) economic theory, and (4) the ideas that are central to the reconstruction of mainstream economics according to the evolutionary view of human behavior.

The central dogma of evolutionary economics can be justified in various ways. The most conspicuous fact supporting it is that many of the important entities of the economy change or evolve. We can cite at least seven categories of such entities: (economic) behavior, commodities, technology (including production and design techniques), institutions, organizations, systems (e.g., various kinds of artificial systems, including market systems), and knowledge.[2]

An economic entity is very complex in itself. Although it is a result of human development, its overall complexity exceeds our capacity to fully understand or control completely. This observation raises the possibility of these economic entities being subject to evolutionary change. Take an example of *commodity*. A simple commodity such as a drinking cup, in its present form, is fruit of the accumulation of a huge set of human knowledge: knowledge about clay soil, the potter's wheel, techniques of treating clay, glaze-making, design, the baking oven or kiln, know-how of temperature keeping, and so on. At many points in the production process of each cup, there are also some uncontrollable factors. The present process of cup production is a crystallization of innumerable trials and errors. It incorporates elements necessary to achieving the intended output as well as those intended to ameliorate the effects of factors which cannot be completely controlled.

The seven categories identify major economic entities, each of which has a different mode of evolution. *Economic behavior* can be changed by a decision of an individual, whereas an *institution* is not changed by an individual. Even if it is a simple custom, it is required to have wide support socially that is passed from generation to generation. *Technology* is a huge network of scientific and nonscientific knowledge. It is transmitted by apprenticeships, schools, organizations, and experience. It is partially supported by a workers' skill but develops

[2]I cited four of seven categories in Shiozawa (2004). I added three others in the General Introduction to a handbook edited by Japan Association for Evolutionary Economics (2006). Seven categories are not listed for classification purpose. They are not exclusive or comprehensive.

through scientific research. The Internet is a new system that has quickly become an institution. Although its basic concepts are a result of human design, the present form of the network evolved autonomously, and no one person can completely control it. *Organization* is a new kind of human group that works as a purposeful entity. The evolution of actions, from being those of person to being those of an organization, can be compared to the transition from unicellular to multicellular organisms. *Systems* also evolve and their mode of evolution changes or evolves. When machines were typical systems, systemic evolution only occurred as a result of new design. Internet had a new property as being an evolvable system (a system open to evolution). We have observed conspicuous spontaneous development of Internet system in these 30 years. *Knowledge* may be created by a person, but a new creation is only possible with the support of long accumulated knowledge. It forms the third domain different from the objective and subjective world.[3] Openness is one of the key factors for the development of human knowledge.

The evolutionary paths taken by particular economic entities take widely varied forms. Despite this variety, we can discern three significant moments during any evolutionary process. They are *retention*, *mutation*, and *selection*. In evolutionary biology, the same moments are termed replication, mutation, and selection. The reason why we don't use the term "replication" is that many economic entities are not easily replicated or copied. Retention is a more fundamental concept than replication, because some essential features must be retained when something is replicated. However, exact analogy between the two sciences is not important. Economic evolution has its own characteristics, proper to itself. Our task is to clarify how economic entities evolve and to elucidate why they evolve.

As we have hinted above, the ubiquitous nature of evolution in an economy comes from the subtle relationship between the *complexity of our problems* and our own set of skills and *capabilities*. In Sect. 1.2, we explain how our most fundamental capabilities are bounded and how widely intractable problems are constantly percolating into our lives. Neoclassical economics, based on the maximization principle, ignores these facts, because maximization generally requires an extremely high capacity for rationality, as we will show in Sect. 1.2.1. Many economists are aware of this fact, but they cannot reformulate their frameworks of thought because they cannot abandon the maximization principle. Neoclassical economists do not know how to formulate intentional human behavior without applying the analytical framework of maximization.

Section 1.3 starts from a simple commonsense observation that we human beings are myopic, in the sense that we are short-sighted, with regard to future events. We are also myopic in the sense that we know little about the present states of different industries, areas, and activities that may be influencing the outcomes of our own actions. The third limit to our capabilities is in the limited spatial range of influence of our direct physical actions. How can an animal with these three limits (bounded rationality, myopic sight, and limited influence) behave and survive in a

[3] Karl Popper (1976, Chap. 38 World 3 or the Third World) called this the World Three.

complex world? This is the main question of Sect. 1.3. There, we present a new framework of human behavior involving patterns of actions or routine behaviors. Routine behaviors comprise 99% of our behaviors, but they each function only in a specific environment. It will be clarified that the reality of human behavior is extremely different from its conception in neoclassical economics.

Section 1.4 gives an overview of the environment created by our economic activities. Three important conditions are discussed. They are the *stationarity* of the economic process, *loose connectedness* of the system, and *slackness of subsistence* for economic agents.

Section 1.5 discusses a proper method of economic analysis. In Sect. 1.5.1, some special features of process analysis, as applied in the social sciences, are discussed: in particular, the micro-macro loop. Identifying this more precisely, although the macroeconomic process is generated by individual human actions, in aggregate these form an environment of habitual human behaviors which in turn sustains performance at the individual level. When this occurs, we can observe a kind of coevolution of macroeconomic processes and the micro behaviors of which they are comprised. This is the *micro-macro loop*. We give two instances of the micro-macro loop and consideration of the methodological questions it raises.

Section 1.5 is a preparatory section for Chap. 2. An economy is a network of routine behaviors conducted by myopic agents who see a very small part of the total economy. A great enigma in economics is why these myopic agents with bounded rationality can generate a roughly stable economy and also adapt to the changes in it. To solve some parts of this enigma is the main object of our book. We know that the market economy is a spontaneous ordering. Even if it is, it is necessary to understand how this comes about and how it works.

Readers who are not interested in the methodological aspects of evolutionary economics can go to Chap. 2 directly. They can read it independently of methodological arguments. As a market economy is a series of exchanges that are concluded by mutual agreements, the theory of prices or exchange value is crucial for any concrete understanding of the economic process. The value theory we present in Chap. 2 is in the tradition of the classical theory of value, especially that of Ricardo (Shiozawa 2016a). Readers will see how this classical theory of value can be reinstituted in modern economics in a form which competes with the modern mathematical version of general equilibrium theory. Chapter 2 is an introduction to the research to be deployed in subsequent chapters.[4]

[4]I have argued repeatedly in Japanese almost all topics treated in this Chapter (Shiozawa 1990, 2006 and others that I do not add in the reference list).

1.2 Ubiquity of Intractable Problems

Humans gained the capacity to accumulate a wide range of voluntary motor skills and can control their deployment of these actions by intelligence. Most of our actions having economic effects are taken as a result of our decision-making, and these decisions are based on our intelligence. Why should we prefer to think that there has been, and continues to be, evolution in these behaviors, instead of in our use of rational decision-making? The answer lies in considering the question of our mental capacity in relation to the difficulty of the problems we want to solve.

1.2.1 Bounded Rationality

Take as an example utility maximization, which is the most common situation that many economists suppose occurs. Let N be the number of commodities and u be the utility function. If a positive price vector $\boldsymbol{p} = (p_1, p_2, \ldots, p_N)$ and a positive budget B are given, then the problem is formulated as

$$\begin{aligned} &\text{maximize } u\left(x_1, .x_2, \ldots, x_N\right) \\ &\text{under the condition that} \\ &p_1 x_1 + p_2 x_2 + \cdots + p_N x_N \leqq B \text{ and } x_1, x_2, \ldots, x_N \geqq 0. \end{aligned} \tag{1.1}$$

When a solution or maximizer (x_1*, x_2*, ..., x_N*) exists, it is usually assumed that consumers choose a basket of goods $\mathbf{x}^* = (x_1{}^*, x_2{}^*, \ldots, x_N{}^*)$. Then we can define the demand function by

$$D\left(p_1, p_2, \ldots, p_N\right) = \left(x_1{}^*, x_2{}^*, \ldots, x_N{}^*\right).$$

There exists no problem, at first glance. Few people ask how this solution is obtained. Of course, a solution exists if utility function u has some good property such as continuity (Weierstrass theory on bounded closed set). However, the mathematical existence and the obtainability of a solution are quite different. As Neumann and Morgenstern (1953) stated, a wide range of alternating move games such as chess and the game of Go have the property that either the first player or the second player has a winning strategy.[5] If that strategy is easily identified, then these games have no fun, because the game is determined before we play. Mathematically

[5]The theorem can be stated as follows: if G is a two-person, open, alternating game and is determinable within a bounded number of moves, either the first or second player has a strategy by which one can win the game whatever the other plays. Chess and Go have a possibility of a draw (no game, stalemate in the case of chess). In that case, the theorem can be modified to assert that the first has a strategy to win or the second player has a strategy by which he or she does not loose (can gain the game or lead the game to draw). This theorem can be proved as a simple exercise of symbolic logic.

a winning strategy exists, but there is no way to find it (even by using a computer). This fact makes these games highly intellectual games and gives computer scientists a challenging task to beat professional players.

We are in the same situation as in the above games when we want to maximize a utility function under a budget constraint. Commodities are ordinarily sold by units. If a maximal solution (i.e., a combination of commodities) contains quantities that are not integer, that solution is not realizable as a basket of purchased items. If we restrict all solution variables to be integer, the maximizing problem (1) with a most simple linear function u is equivalent to a famous problem called the (unbounded) knapsack problem. It is known that this problem is NP-hard. This means that there is no algorithm that can compute the solution in a polynomial time relative to the size N of the instance (unless $\mathbf{P} = \mathbf{NP}$).[6]

A simple (but not perfect) explanation why the problem requires such a long computing time is given by restricting x_i to be either 0 or 1. Then the problem (1) reduces to knowing the subset of set $\{1, 2, \ldots, N\}$ that has the maximal value satisfying the budget condition. The set of all subsets counts 2^N. If we are to check all possibilities, it is normal that the computer requires a computing time proportional to 2^N.

In a worst case, the computing time may require a time that is proportional to 2 raised to power N. This is a very serious problem. For example, if the problem for less than 10 commodities is solved by a computer in one thousandth of a second (or a millisecond), a problem which involves 80 commodities requires computing time of about 36 billion years, which is almost the double the time that elapsed since the Big Bang until now (Shiozawa 1990, §9 and 10 or Shiozawa 1999, Table I.). However, 80, as the number of commodities, is comparatively small if we assume the problem is to make a purchase in a convenience store. A standard convenience store stocks more than 1500 items in the shop.

It is also necessary to correctly understand the meaning of the knapsack problem being NP-hard. It does not exclude that many instances of the problem can be solved rapidly. We have many algorithms which work for special subclasses of the knapsack problem. For example, if all prices are the same, the maximal solution is the top M/p commodities that have the highest utility. The combined meaning of the fundamental conjecture and the theorem that the knapsack problem is NP-hard is that there is no algorithm that solves all instances of the problem within a polynomial time.

For practical purposes, an approximate solution will do. Some approximation algorithms are very rapid. George Dantzig, the founder of linear programming, proposed an algorithm called a greedy algorithm. It seeks to find the most cost-effective set of commodities. This algorithm ends in a computing time that is proportional to the third order of N. It is not difficult to solve the problem for in instances with N more than 1000. This algorithm is guaranteed to achieve at least half of

[6]The class **P** and **NP** are defined in Sect. 1.2.3. The proposition $\mathbf{P} \neq \mathbf{NP}$ is the most basic conjecture of computing complexity theory but not yet solved.

the theoretical maximum for any given instance. We also know an approximation algorithm that has a polynomial computing time and is guaranteed to attain the value $(1-\varepsilon)\,m$, where m is the maximum and ε is any positive real number.[7]

However, this does not change the point very much. In economics we solve the maximization problem (1.1) with the purpose of defining a demand function. What we need for that is the solution, i.e., the maximizer $(x_1^*, x_2^*, \ldots, x_N^*)$, and not the maximal value $u(x_1^*, x_2^*, \ldots, x_N^*)$. Let a solution be given by an approximate computation, and let it be $(x_1^{\mathrm{a}}, x_2^{\mathrm{a}}, \ldots, x_N^{\mathrm{a}})$. If approximation is good enough, this may approximate the utility value $u\,(x_1^{\mathrm{a}}, x_2^{\mathrm{a}}, \ldots, x_N^{\mathrm{a}})$ to the maximum utility value $u(x_1^*, x_2^*, \ldots, x_N^*)$, but we cannot say that the solution $(x_1^{\mathrm{a}}, x_2^{\mathrm{a}}, \ldots, x_N^{\mathrm{a}})$ is close to $(x_1^*, x_2^*, \ldots, x_N^*)$ (see Shiozawa 1999, 2016b).

At the very basic core of neoclassical economics, there is this problem. It ignores the fact that human agents have a limited capacity for calculation. When it assumes that consumers calculate, it assumes, for all individual consumers, an infinite capacity to calculate. Human beings evolved an intelligence that is incomparably greater than other animals. However, much greater that may be, human intelligence is bounded and not perfect. Neoclassical economists ignore this basic fact.

They ignore this, either because they are simply thinking that the human capacity for computing is infinite or because they do not think that this raises a serious problem for their formulation. A prominent Japanese economist once declared that he continues to assume the maximization hypothesis, because in his opinion, economics loses all effective formulation for the behavior of consumers, if once he abandons this hypothesis. It is severely neglectful for a scientist to employ a mathematical formulation of consumer behavior for the sake of personal convenience, even though he knows very well that it is impossible that consumers behave in the manner it describes.

A general problem arises. H.A. Simon named it the problem of *bounded rationality*. In the above, we examined consumers. Simon thinks that a similar problem exists for business firms. He once declared: "If there is no limit to human rationality, administrative theory would be barren. It would consist of the single precept: Always select that alternative, among those available, which will lead to the most complete achievement of your goals" (Simon 1997, p.322). Simon contributed enormously to the recognition of the universal importance of bounded rationality. It really deserves a Nobel prize for economics. However, he made two

[7]This does not mean that any approximation problem is tractable. The Unique Games Conjecture postulates that the problem of determining the approximate value of a certain type of game, named a unique game, has NP-hard algorithmic complexity. Subhash Khot presented this conjecture in 2002. He was given the Rolf Nevalinna Prize at the World Mathematicians Congress in 2014. It is reported that Khot and his collaborators got new results in 2018, which is strong evidence for many mathematicians in this field that the conjecture is true. If the conjecture is true, even to find whether a given number is sufficient to satisfy the conditions of a problem requires more than polynomial time even if the number is not the best (or minimum) number. It means that there does exist a problem which is NP-hard even if only to find an "approximate" solution of any accuracy. See Trevisan (2012) and Klarreich (2018).

small mistakes. First, he compared economics and management science as parallel sciences and admitted that each has its own characteristics. By this unnecessary concession, he renounced the chance to reconstruct (or at least to propose to reconstruct) economics on the basis of bounded rationality. Secondly, his focus on rationality was too narrow to open a way toward the formulation of a general theory of purposeful human behaviors.

We give such a formulation in Sect. 1.3. Before attacking this problem, let us make a detour to consider the complex nature of our world.

1.2.2 Solving a Problem and Computing Complexity

Evolution of economic behavior depends much more on intelligence and learned behaviors than on hereditary characteristics. The major forces that drive change in our behaviors are rational computation, together with learning from previous decisions of self and others. Of course, the basic economic behaviors associated with physiological survival remain within a wide range of human hereditary characteristics. However, they have since evolved enormously under social influences. Behavioral evolution occurs for economic reasons and is not determined by human hereditary characteristics so long as new acquired and learned behaviors remain within the range of our physical possibilities. What then are the reasons that make evolution inevitable for almost all economic entities? To understand the true nature of an economic entity's evolution, it is necessary to consider two conditions. One is the limits of our capabilities. The other is the complexity of the decision-making.

There is no absolute criterion that determines something is complex or not. It depends on our capacity. When we got computers, many once unsolvable problems have now become solvable. The mathematics of optimization is developing everyday. Computing capacity is expanding rapidly. Despite all these manifest facts, it is ironical that mathematics is also revealing that a class of "unsolvable" or "intractable" problems exists and will persist in every corner of optimization. The class is called NP-hard. This is a very important concept in understanding the nature of the complexity that we encounter in the real world. Before entering into the discussion of NP-hard, and of computing complexity in general, we need to complete some preparations.

A problem is a set of infinitely many *instances* with an integer called *size* of the instance (there may be many different ways to measure the size of an instance). For example, a linear equation of N unknown variables is

$$\begin{aligned} &a_{11}x_1 + a_{12}x_2 + \cdots + a_{1N}x_N = b_1 \\ &a_{21}x_1 + a_{22}x_2 + \cdots + a_{2N}x_N = b_2 \\ &\cdots \\ &a_{N1}x_1 + a_{N2}x_2 + \cdots + a_{NN}x_N = b_N. \end{aligned} \tag{1.2}$$

An instance of the problem (1.2) is given, when we specify all a_{ij} and b_i. The size of this instance is, for example, N. We know that (1.2) is solvable when the determinant of the matrix of coefficients a_{ij} is not 0.

Consider an algorithm for solving (1.2). An *algorithm* is a predetermined procedure of calculation to solve the problem. How much time does it take before we get a solution? The computing time depends naturally on computing speed. In the complexity theory of computing, we normally count the number of elementary arithmetic procedures. For example, in the case of linear equations, we count the necessary number of four operations (plus, minus, multiplication, and division). This number depends of course on the design of algorithms available and varies depending on the goodness of those algorithms. Take as an example the Gaussian elimination method. A standard procedure requires

$$\left\{4N^3 + 9N^2 - 8N\right\}/6$$

operations. In this case, computing time is given by a polynomial of the size N. When we are interested in the growing length of the computing time, only the highest order term of the polynomial is relevant. In that case, we often say that the computing time is of order N^3, or use a mathematical abbreviation $O(N^3)$.

Some problems can be calculated very rapidly (if we use a computer and a good algorithm). For instance, if a sorting problem is to sort any set of integers in increasing order, then this sorting process ends by steps that are proportional to $N \log_2 N$. This means that to sort an instance of 10,000 numbers requires about 23 times more steps than sorting 1000 numbers. Many effectively soluble problems can be solved at orders 2, 3, or 4. For example, the multiplication of two matrices, or a system of linear equations, can be solved at $O(N^3)$.

Another example of a rapid algorithm is linear programming, or LP. LP covers a wide range of practical problems, and we can say that it is the most useful mathematical tool that is applicable to problems of large scale.[8] The classical simplex method runs normally in polynomial time, e.g., $O(N^3)$, but in some cases computation enters into an eternal cycle, and in some others, it requires an exponential order of time (or $O(2^N)$). The Karmarkar method (a variation of the interior method) eliminated these troubles, and it is now assured that the program runs in $O(N^\alpha)$ for any LP problem, where α is a constant between 3 and 4. In some cases, a seemingly difficult problem can be reduced to an LP problem, in which cases a problem can be solved rapidly. The reduction is drastic. The classical assignment problem is an example. With an enumeration method, computation requires $N!$ steps of a simple routine. Kuhn (1955), based on the works of Birkhoff and von Neumann, proved that it can be solved as an LP problem and the computation time can then be reduced to $O(N^3)$.[9]

[8] In some cases, we can solve problems with 1000 unknowns or more.

[9] Pak (2000) is a good illustration how LP works in the case of the classical assignment problem.

However, the lesson we should learn here is not that some problems can be solved rapidly by computers. The lesson we should learn is that there are many intractable problems. They are *intractable*, not because there is no algorithm that solves the problem, but because it takes too long a time for the computation (many years or many thousands of years). With the arrival of computers, study of the "goodness" of algorithms became urgent and important. The needs of this research led to the establishment of computational complexity theory.

1.2.3 NP-Hard Problems or Really Intractable Problems to Solve

Computational complexity theory is a part of mathematics that studies questions of how complex a problem is. *Complexity* is measured in two major ways: time complexity and space complexity. The first gives an estimate of the necessary number of operations. The second gives an estimate of the necessary memory space, or the number of places for arguments. We have seen that the time complexity of problem (1.2) is $O(N^3)$. To the astonishment of many mathematicians, computational complexity theory revealed that there are many intractable problems among the problems that we encounter in economics and industry. The NP-hard problem is one of them. To define this concept also requires some preparation.

A decision problem, in computation theory, is a problem that can be answered yes or no. The class of problems **P** is the class of decision problems that has an algorithm whose computing time is bounded by a polynomial function of the size N. In a rough description, a problem in **P** is somehow "tractable" because we can solve it in a polynomial time. Of course, even if a problem is soluble in polynomial time, it does not assure that we can effectively solve the problem. If the degree of the polynomial is as large as 6 or 7, an instance of a large size becomes difficult to solve. However, here we are concerned with those problems which are far more difficult. The majority of computer scientists believe that an NP-hard problem necessitates more computing time than any polynomial order $O(N^M)$.

A verification problem of a decision problem is the problem to verify that when a candidate of the solution is given (e.g., by chance), it is really a solution. The class of decision problems **NP** (meaning nondeterministic polynomials) is the one whose verification problem can be solved in polynomial time. Note that **P** is a subclass of **NP**, because an instance of **P** has an algorithm by which we can determine if the problem is "yes" or "no" in polynomial time.

An interesting subclass of decision problems is *NP-complete* problems. A decision problem H is NP-complete when any instance of a NP problem can be reduced to an instance of H within polynomial time. It is astonishing to know that there are such problems. In 1971, Stephen Cock proved that a problem called 3-SAT has such a property. 3-SAT is a special case of problems when we want to know if there is a set of truth values which makes a given logical formula true. Cock's result opened a new era of computational complexity theory.

After one NP-complete problem was discovered, many problems came to be known as NP-complete. An easy way to prove it was to show that we can reduce a problem to a 3-SAT problem.[10] An example of the NP-complete problem is the *subset sum problem*. Suppose we are given a set of integers of N elements. The problem is to determine if there exists a nonempty subset T such that elements of T sum up to zero. For example, if $S = \{-13, -8, -4, 2, 5, 7, 19\}$, there exists a subset $T = \{-8, -4, 5, 7\}$ which sums to zero. Then the decision problem is affirmative. Evidently this is a NP problem, because it is easy to verify (in polynomial time) that $-8-4+5+7=0$. If such a subset T is given, the verification ends with at most $N-1$ times of additions and subtractions. However, it is not easy to determine if there is a subset whose elements sum up to zero. To answer this problem by checking all possible subsets requires computing time proportional to 2^N.

When NP-complete problems were known, a new problem arose: **P** = **NP**? Since 1971 this problem has been the most challenging problem for mathematicians and computer scientists. Many challenged the problem, but no one has ever succeeded. The Cray Mathematics Institute selected this problem as one of seven Millennium Prize Problems (Cook 2000). It is promised that US$ 1,000,000 will be given to the person who is first to find a correct solution (i.e., to prove **P** = **NP** or show **P** ≠ **NP**). Although this decision problem is not yet solved and nobody knows how to approach the problem, the majority of researchers in this field believe that **P** ≠ **NP**. Thousands of NP-complete problems were found since the 1970s, but there is no known algorithm which runs in polynomial time. This is one of the reasons why the majority of researchers in this field believe that **P** ≠ **NP**.

A problem is called NP-hard, when it has an associated NP-complete decision problem. An optimization problem usually has its associated decision problem.[11] For example, the knapsack problem we have examined above is a maximization problem. The associated decision problem of a knapsack problem is the question: "Is there a 0–1 vector $\mathbf{x} = (x_i)$ which satisfies the constraint condition and whose total utility is higher than a given value?" We said that the knapsack problem is NP-hard. It is, because its associated decision problem is NP-complete. In the same way, there are as many NP-hard optimization problems as there are NP-complete decision problems which are associated with an optimization problem. Recall that an NP-complete problem is a decision problem by definition and NP-hard problems are not necessarily decision problems. This is the main difference between NP-complete and NP-hard problems.

One of most famous NP-hard problems is the traveling salesman problem. It is to find a traveling route that passes all cities in a given list and requires the least

[10]In an exact expression, this means that an instance of problem H can be reduced to an instance of 3-SAT problem in polynomial time. We use this abbreviation from now on.

[11]Optimization in mathematics and economics means to obtain a maximal or minimal solution. In engineering, optimization often means simply improvement.

cost. We cannot say that the traveling salesman problem is important in real life. However, it is intuitively understandable, and this is the reason why it is presented so often. But, there are many other problems which we do often face in real life. They are the scheduling problems. Scheduling problems appear frequently in business and industry. A *schedule* is an assignment of a set of personnel, machines, and other resources to a specific task or duty over a specific interval of time. Making a schedule is a part of everyday work for a manager.

As they appear in the most varied situations, they have many variations and have many different names. For example, they are called job-shop scheduling problems, nurse scheduling problems (or nurse rostering problems), optimal staffing problems, weighted assignment problems, general assignment problems, and others.

A job-shop scheduling problem is an optimization problem when we are given N jobs of varying time lengths, which need to be scheduled on M identical or different machines. Jobs may have sequence-order constraints. For example, job J2 should be placed after the job J1 is finished. We can take as optimizing objectives various target functions: the time span in finishing all jobs, the total cost of operating machines, the number of machines used, the time of delivery of the finished goods, and so on. We do not enter into the details of these problems, but many problems we want to solve in many of the most common situations turn out to be NP-hard.[12]

Although they are a common planning task for managers, most scheduling problems are NP-hard and intractable, if we really want an optimal solution.

Before ending this long detour into NP-hard problems, it is necessary to add one more remark. It is important to know that an NP-hard problem has many instances that can be solved in a reasonable length of time. As I have noted above, when I first introduced the knapsack problem, being an NP-hard problem does not mean that no instances can be solved rapidly. On the contrary, it is known that many (or even the majority of) instances of a NP-hard problem can be solved quite rapidly, even if they are of a large size. However, it is not well known how computing time is dispersed. A possibility is that the computing time of instances of the same size makes a landscape similar to the absolute value of a function of a complex variable. Imagine a rational function defined on a complex plane. They are finite for all points except for several poles. If the points approach to a pole, the computing time increases without limit and exceeds any predetermined one. Instances whose computing time is less than a predetermined time will be a large area with some holes. For a fixed maximum computing time, the holes become bigger and may cover almost all the area when the size of instances becomes bigger.

This fact has a serious consequence for neoclassical economics. It is based on the basic assumption that demand and supply functions exist and that they represent actual human economic behavior. Therefore, the above result implies that a demand

[12]To discern if a given problem is NP-hard or not is a delicate mathematical problem. It is hard for non-specialists to tell that this problem is NP-hard and that problem is not NP-hard. A minor modification of the problem may change NP-hard problem to a problem which can be solved in polynomial time.

function defined on the maximization assumption cannot represent actual people's demand behavior. As I have pointed out, the computing time easily exceeds any practical scale of time when the maximum computing time is proportional to 2 raised to N the number of commodities. A demand function can represent an economic agent's behavior only for an extremely small economy that counts at most a few tens of commodities.

The ubiquitous nature of NP-hard problems indicates that formulating economic behavior by a maximization principle is a bad characterization, be it a personal or organizational one. Then, how is our intellectual behavior organized? This is the question we must pose and solve. We will do it in the next section.

1.2.4 Some Economic Consequences of the Ubiquity of NP-Hard Problems

NP-hard problems appear everywhere. They are ubiquitous. Does this mean that we should abandon the rational pursuit of better solutions? By no means! In economic situations, no exactness is required. You may not attain an optimum by computation. Except in a very fortunate situation, you are obliged to satisfy by a nonoptimal feasible solution (a solution which satisfies all constraint conditions).[13]

What matters in an economic situation are the feasible solutions that you can obtain. They may result in different values for the objective function. However, you can compare their values, and if you find one solution that is the best of all, then it is sure you will choose that solution.[14]

The best solution you get is the best among the feasible solutions you can compare. That best solution may have a value which is far from the optimal value, and you may not know what that optimal value is. You cannot compare the solutions you obtained with the optimal solution. Theoretically speaking, or in the eyes of God, the value of your solution may be very bad. Your solution may give you a value that is one half of the optimal value. You can inquire in what situation you are, theoretically, but it will be a difficult mathematical problem to solve.

You can continue the search for better solutions, for example, by consuming more computing time. However, you may lose the chance to get your profit by postponing your decisions. Because of bounded rationality and the ubiquity of NP-hard problems, the majority of any existing entities are not optimal. This creates the opportunity for improvement and is the reason why evolution takes place successively and incessantly.

---

[13] Taking this fact more positively, H.A. Simon named it the *satisficing principle*.

[14] Solutions may have different effects on other aspects that are not taken in consideration. If you are a manger of a firm, you cannot ignore these points. In the above, we assumed that these side effects are all indifferent. The same remarks apply to many later discussions, but we do not repeat the same caution.

Firms are always in competition. What matters for a firm are the set of solutions you have and the sets of solutions of your competitors. Even if your firm has a solution which attains only 51% of the theoretical optimum, but your competitors have solutions which attain 49% of the optimum, your management must be satisfied with the present situation. If a firm finds a solution 53% of the optimum, managers of your firm and other competitors will become dissatisfied and will try to find a new solution.

This imaginary situation clarifies why evolution is ubiquitous in every economic category. The solution we have examined was formulated as decision problem. If the solution is adopted, it defines an action for an agent. We have already seen that the utility maximization problem is NP-hard. Consumers do not behave by finding an optimal solution for their utility maximization problem. It is simply impossible. They must behave according to some other principles, perhaps a rule of thumb and others.

Productivity of a production process is influenced by many factors. In every part of the process, there are many planning problems. One of these problems is scheduling of various kinds. Most of them are NP-hard if formulated as an optimization problem. Managers of the factory cannot wait until the optimal solution is obtained. They must continue their operations with the best knowledge they have. If they abandon optimization, a feasible solution can often be found quite easily. Every factory manager uses the Gantt chart. Visitors to a factory can see two or three Gantt charts on a wall. They show solutions of scheduling problems. The Gantt chart has continued to be used for more than a century. It was used long before any electronic computers were invented. We can construct a Gantt chart by hand (or more exactly by hands and a brain). It does not require a computer. Of course, a solution given by a Gantt chart is not optimal but is normally a good and feasible solution.

Recall also that the managers of a factory make more than 1000 small decisions every day. This is one of the most impressive reports in the now classical book of Mintzberg (Mintzberg 1973). The time to make decisions is a managers' most critical resource. Recall again that managers always have many different questions to decide. They might be related to each other, but normally managers must solve them one by one. After Goldratt's book *The Goal* (Goldratt and Cox 1984) became a best seller, many industrial consultants preached that we should seek a global optimum, not partial optimums. In this lies a misunderstanding, because in most cases a global optimum cannot be attained. We should seek a global or total optimum if possible, but we should also consider if it is possible to do so.

Complexity also intervenes in the designing of products. Don't imagine an artistic design. Take an example from one of the most common machines that of a passenger car. Think of a designing problem to encase all necessary parts in an engine compartment. This is a kind of knapsack problem but a much more complicated one, because there are many supplementary constraints. In the case of a knapsack problem, an item is specified only by weight or volume, and the unique constraint was to satisfy that the total weight or volume does not exceed a predetermined value. In the problem of encasing parts in an engine compartment, the parts have three-dimensional shape, and to pack them as dense as possible is no easy problem. In addition, some parts should be kept separated, because one part becomes too hot and the other should be kept cool. Designers must satisfy all these complicated requirements and find a solution. It is a difficult work to find even a feasible solution.

Engineers in all fields are working with similar situations. Making something requires all sorts of knowledge and skill. Designers of a consumer product should keep in mind all physical and chemical properties of major parts and components. They should know how the products are produced, because a design which can be easily machined increases productivity and by consequence lowers the cost of production. Product engineers should also know how the product is used in the household (or in a production site if the product is an industrial one). A product should be safe when it is used by children or others, but it should not be too difficult for a common person to manipulate. A good selection of various functions is an important part of the product concept, because some consumers want a function and others want some others. Forms and colors must be beautiful. Product design also requires knowledge of how the used products are disposed of. Compliance requires knowledge of laws and regulations. All these pieces of knowledge have to be combined to make a good, useful, low-priced product.

Engineers often talk about optimum designing. It expresses their desire, but what they really do is improvement. Product design often starts from examining the actual model or design. Engineers collect users' opinions or views about it. They listen to sales people. They care about specialists' opinions, including production engineers. Of course, they study new possibilities that were opened by new materials and so on. Then they make a rough concept: from this emerges a new concept and new targets to achieve. This process may solve many optimization problems, but they also care about the balance between various parts. An optimal solution may be replaced by a suboptimal solution, because the optimal solution of a problem does not provide solutions required to other problems. This is how evolution occurs in products.

Many engineer-designers know that a global optimization is impossible, and a better strategy for good designing is to make good use of evolutionary techniques. A handbook in three volumes (IEEJ 2010) was compiled by a special committee of The Institute of Electrical Engineers of Japan. It is titled *Handbook of Evolutionary Technology*: *Computation and Applications*. It covers various techniques such as genetic algorithm, machine learning, evolutionary multipurpose optimization, and many applications in various industries. As it is written in Japanese, I do not introduce it in more detail, but it represents eloquently the real nature of engineering. Evolutionary technology is becoming an indispensable tool in robotics and in other areas.

Another important lesson that we can derive from the ubiquity of complex problems is the theoretical difficulty of knowing what will happen in the future. Predictability of the future depends on having a theory of the world and the capacity for computation. Even if we have a perfect theory of the world, if we cannot compute the outcome, we cannot predict what will happen. This is the very question that Laplace posed. In the time of Laplace, we knew only Newtonian dynamics.

In it world movement is described in principle by a (huge) system of differential equations. The system is normally well posed and has a unique solution if initial conditions are given. As this is a completely deterministic world, we can know the future without any limit if the system of differential equations is solvable. However, as Laplace argued, there are two insurmountable obstacles that prevent us from knowing the future: (1) we cannot collect all the initial conditions, and (2) we cannot solve such a big system of equations. Laplace believed that this proves the necessity of probability theory. We cannot predict the future. We can only guess what will happen.

However, mainstream economics totally ignores this fact and assumes the extremely strong hypothesis that we can plan what we do in the distant future. At the root of mainstream macroeconomics lies the assumption that human agents are farsighted in time.

The dynamic stochastic general equilibrium (DSGE) model is an example. It is the core of present-day macroeconomic models for both new classical (real business cycle) and for New Keynesian economics. DSGE models contain the Ramsey model as a part of its standard formulation. We may say that the Ramsey model is one of the basic workhorse models in macroeconomics. In this model, the representative household decides how to distribute current income between consumption and saving. The model supposes that the household has an inter-temporal preference function with a constant rate of time preference and maximizes its utility through time. If the situation is in a steady state (where there is growth, but the proportions of major variables remain constant), maximization may not require perfect foresight, as the maximization problem can be solved by assuming an "invariant" solution. This assumption reduces the problem to a simple, fixed point problem. However, if the economy at any point moves off the steady-state growth path, the problem becomes much more difficult for the household. The Ramsey model's asymptotic behaviors form a saddle point, and the convergence to a steady growth relies on the capability to know the converging path (see, e.g., Solow 1990). Without assuming perfect foresight over an infinite long future, stability cannot be guaranteed.

1.3 Myopic Agents and the Structure of Human Behavior

We have talked much (maybe too much) about the limits of our rationality. As for the limits of our capacity to do things, another problem is as important as bounded rationality. It is the problem that our capacity to know what is happening now is very limited.[15] Our knowledge of the world expanded tremendously after the Scientific

[15] We think that rationality and farsightedness, i.e., the capacity to reason correctly and the capacity to collect necessary information, are very different, and it is better to treat them distinctly. H.A. Simon did not make a clear distinction between bounded rationality and bounded sight and included two of them in a single concept of bounded rationality.

Revolution of the second half of the sixteenth and seventeenth century. Even today it is enlarging rapidly, and we may confidently say that the speed of gaining new knowledge is accelerating even though the range of things we know about the actual world is very small and narrow. We know about the beginning of the universe but very little about what other people or firms are doing. In economic decision-making, what matters is not knowledge of the universe. We know very little that is relevant to our decision-making. We may confidently say that our ignorance is much greater than our knowledge.

1.3.1 Myopic Nature of Our Perception

Development of information and communication technology (ICT) does not reduce the degree of ignorance very much. What is necessary for a firm is the knowledge of what competitors are doing or trying to do. Some information may be made public, but the most important part is kept undercover by a wall of corporate secrecy. Even if there is no such barrier, as humans, our capability to know is also very limited in space and in time. We are myopic animals who know only the small part of the world we have come close to during our existence.

Mainstream macroeconomics assumes farsightedness in time. This is conspicuous. As we have argued in Sect. 1.2, the DSGE model assumes that an economic agent knows the economic theory, can predict the far future, and can take a decision after taking into consideration all of what will happen in the future. Mainstream macroeconomics assumes farsightedness in space, too. This fact is not as apparent as the farsightedness in time, because macroeconomics is based essentially on one-good models with one representative agent. Even when a model deals with different goods, the appearance of variety is only a facade. For example, the Dixit-Stiglitz utility function assumes a strong symmetry. This makes it possible to treat different goods as if there is only one good in the economy. If a model assumes different agents, they do not really intervene mutually. Assuming a one-good model is to assume that all agents have perfect foresight or the capacity to gather all relevant information in the economy.

When we reflect on real life, all goods are different and hardly substitutable. Managers of a firm can know the past series of demands for each of their products, but it is hard for them to know the competitors' exact series of demands. At the base of mainstream macroeconomics lies the assumption that human agents are farsighted in time and in space. This is of course impossible. For economics to be based on reality, it is necessary to pose ignorance and short-sightedness as the foundation of the human condition.

Short-sightedness and bounded rationality are a kind of twin. No human being can escape from these twin limits. In the next subsection, we add a third limit for our capabilities. It is the limited capability to execute something. Even if we know what we should do, our ability to do something in a certain lapse of time is limited. This third limitation was rather well incorporated in all economics including classical and neoclassical economics, because they assumed that there is a necessary number of man-hours for any production process.

These three limitations are understandable if we have once thought that humans have evolved from more primitive animals, whose capabilities were very limited by any standard. However, modern economics started to formulate human behavior as involving the maximization of an objective function and was thereby constrained to assume unlimited rationality. There is no basis to assume so, except that it was necessary for the formulation of neoclassical economics. Evolutionary economics should not start from such an absurd foundation. Instead, it should start from the opposite side. Our capacity is very limited, but step by step, we obtained more elaborated behaviors and ways of thinking. Thus there is a spectral continuity between animal and human provisioning behaviors. We can learn much by observing behaviors in less intellectually developed animals.

1.3.2 Üxküll's Biosemiotics and Human Behavior

By assuming infinite rationality and farsightedness, neoclassical economics represented the human being as an omnipotent and omniscient entity. In contrast to this, evolutionary economics takes animals as an illustrative model of our own behaviors. We have evolved from animals and not from deity. Even if we have gained high levels of behavioral capability compared to that of animals, the gap between humans and animals is small in our fundamental behaviors. The large number of acquired differences that now separate us occurred only gradually. If we cannot observe any qualitative difference in some, it is more natural to deem that our capabilities are closer to those of animals than God.

With this in mind, it is good to fix our starting point on von Üxküll's notions of "umwelt" and his idea of the functional cycle. Jakob von Üxküll (or Uexküll) is known to have been critical of Darwinism but was a good animal observer. He inaugurated a theoretical biology by asking how an animal perceives the world.[16] Animals have their own umwelt, or a surrounding sensory world, specific to a species. For example, a dog is strongly myopic but has a very good sense of smell. It is also partially color-blind and cannot distinguish yellow and green. Thus the world of a dog is very different from that of a human.

Von Üxküll studied even lower animals such as ticks and sea urchins. They have only undeveloped sense organs, but they succeeded in surviving. The egg-laying behavior of a field tick is astonishing. Ticks are blind but can feel if the world is bright or dark. They cannot jump as fleas do. A flea can jump a hundred times as high as his size. Ticks cannot run as rapidly as spiders do, but this weak animal must suck the blood of a mammal before it lays its eggs. How can it succeed in this difficult task? At this point ticks are ingenious.

---

[16] Now Jakob von Üxküll is thought to be the "starter and pioneer" of biosemiotics.

A female tick climbs to the tip of a tree twig with the help of her skin's sensitivity to light. The place becomes her watch post. She waits there for a long time, even years. She knows by the smell of butyric acid that a mammal is approaching. Butyric acid emanates from all mammals, because sweat contains it. She blindly falls when the smell reaches a certain strength and in a very fortunate case drops onto the back of her prey. She knows if she was lucky enough to have caught a mammal by the temperature because she has an organ that is precisely sensitive to that temperature. Then she searches for a less hairy spot and embeds her head in the subcutaneous tissue of her prey. She can now suck a warm stream of blood until she slowly swells to many times heavier than her original weight. If she fails to catch a mammal, she is obliged to restart her watch from the beginning.[17] The contrast between limited capabilities and the difficulty of task execution is impressive.[18] As an economic agent, we are in a similar situation. Our capability is very limited. But by combining simple operations, we can achieve an astonishingly complex and difficult task.

The secret lies in the constant relation between an animal and its environment. If mammals suddenly change into poikilotherms for some unknown reasons, or if they suddenly stop secreting butyric acid, ticks will not be able to catch mammals and lay eggs. Then, so long as they keep their egg-laying strategy, they would be destined to become extinct. This kind of extinction has occurred many times for many species. It is only the fortunate animals that have succeeded in surviving their ever-changing environments.

All species have specific relations with their environment upon which their survival depends. Üxküll studied these relations through the concept of umwelt. Each species has its own world, perceptible to it only through the various senses that are proper to it and that are meaningful for its survival. Life is an eternal process of interaction between the organic body and its environment.

Üxküll thought that an animal "grasps the world by two hands," so to speak (see Fig. 1.1). One hand, so to speak, is the *receptor* and the other is the *effector*. An animal thus receives *mark-signs* (Merkzeichen) from the world and then processes them in its central nervous system which orders it how to act. We may distinguish in this sequence three functions of the "world grasping" animal: perception, judgment, and execution. Since these functions create a cycle starting from a *mark-carrier* (an object with a mark-sign) and returning to a mark-carrier (the object to work on) through the three functions, Üxküll called the total system the *functional cycle*.

It is important that these three functions are all limited in a strong way. We can make a list in Table 1.1.

Each species has its specific functions, each of different capacities and limited in a different ways. It is notable that Üxküll thought of the information flow not simply as one of physical signals but as mark-signs, a more general term which encompasses any sensed "state change" have some "meaning" to the animal. The

[17] All this story appears in Uexküll (1992).

[18] Heiner (1983) pointed that the big C-D gap is the very condition that produces predictable behaviors (see the end of Sect. 1.3.3).

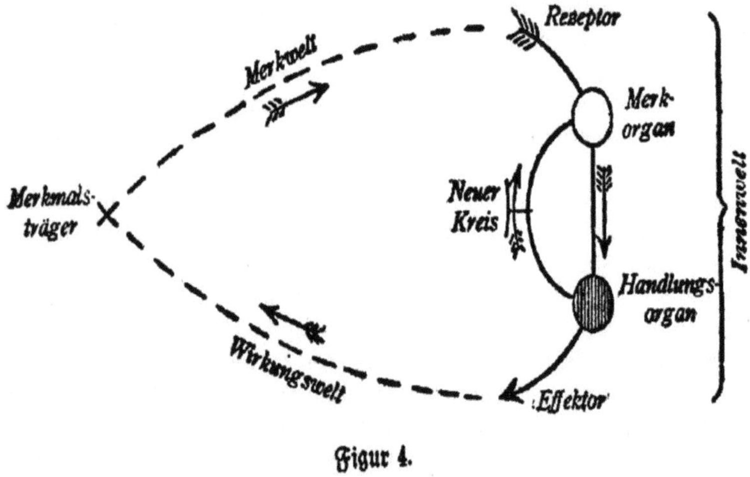

Fig. 1.1 Functional cycle with reafferent cycle (Uexkull 1920). (Reproduced from Rüting (2004, p.117))

Table 1.1 Three functions of a functional cycle and their characteristics

Function	Capability	Range of possible function
(1) Perception	Myopic sight	Limited information gathering
(2) Judgment	Bounded rationality	Simple reflective thinking
(3) Execution	Limited influence	Effects in limited space and time

functional cycle is also not simply a feedback loop, in which a single-valued quantity flows. For Üxküll, the world is not a simple set of quantities, but each object carries a sign, and animals perceive and react to these signs. He was interested in how pattern recognition works in the receptor and its relationship with the central nervous system, but it is not necessary for us to enter into such details.

Üxküll's idea of the receptor is somewhat like the garbage can model for organizational decision-making (Cohen et al. 1972). Of course, the tasks are very different, and organizational decision-making is a highly rational procedure that requires expending many resources, including information gathering and deliberation. However, the essential function of organizational decision-making is to reduce a most complicated and diversified set of information into a predefined set of conclusions. In a very primitive way, ticks and sea urchins perceive the world and by classifying the objects encountered, for example, into food, predator, sexual partner, and others, are able to select, or decide upon, their appropriate response.

1.3.3 The Structure of Animal and Human Behavior

Now let us return to our main problem. Recall the difficult task a tick had to achieve before she lays her eggs. A tick is almost blind, cannot jump, nor run fast. How can this badly conditioned animal achieve a task as difficult as catching a mammal? We now know how a tick ingeniously solved this difficult question: by a series of patterned actions. All animals, including humans, achieve difficult tasks by performing a series of actions in which each is patterned as the coupling of a stimulus and a response. Sociologist Tamito Yoshida (1990) formulated this patterned behavior as a C-D transformation. Here, C stands for cognitive meaning and D for directive meaning. Yoshida arrived at this formula after studying Charles Sanders Pierce's semiotics. In Üxküll's functional cycle, C is a sign received by the receptor, and D is a sign directed to the effector. The C-D transformation can be interpreted as a conditional directive. For example, we may interpret it as a message: if condition C is satisfied, then do D.

A similar formulation is given in evolutionary computation. John Holland (1992), the creator of the genetic algorithm, adopted if-then rules as a simple representation of behaviors and called this representation the *classifier system*. This became the tradition in almost all agent-based simulation. Holland adopted this formula, because he was thinking of using it in his evolutionary computation. The "if part" and the "then part," or conditional and directive parts, were expressed by a couple of binary codes of predetermined length.

Holland's classifier system is highly universal in the sense that any optimization problem can in principle be transformed into a genetic algorithm problem for a classifier system. Indeed, it is a simply a question of encoding. Recall that there are two parts in the classifier system: conditional and directive parts. If these parts are sets of mark-signs, as Üxküll assumed, they are finite sets, and you can encode each element into a different binary code. Then, the "optimization," transformed in an evolutionary computation, is to search for a conditional binary code whose resultant code gives you a good expected value for the objective function. However, this universality does not assure that if-then rule behavior can be a prototype of all animal or human behaviors, because the coding correspondence may be extremely complicated and may not have any practical meanings. For an animal receptor, mark-signs should be as simple as possible so that they can be recognized instinctively. A directive must also be as simple as possible so that the animal can effectively execute it. For a human being, his or her judgment may be more complicated, and a directive can be more sophisticated, but the difference is a question of degree. In humans, a mark-sign should be within the three limits to the capability of a human agent, i.e., myopic sight, bounded rationality, and limited range of execution.

In this sense, Holland's if-then rule formula is not general enough to cover all animal and human behaviors. However, it may constitute the atoms, or behavioral elements, making up more complex behaviors. Indeed, we can rightly believe that any behavior, be it animal or human, can be decomposed to a series of if-then behaviors.

This is a strong contention, and it is difficult to prove this highly universal thesis, but there is some circumstantial evidence for this.

Instead of presenting a formal proof (which may be theoretically impossible), let me talk about my own experience. How have I arrived at this idea? The story is a bit long and tortuous. It was in 1985 that I really realized that a simple utility maximization problem has within it a NP-hard problem (i.e., if it is reformulated as an integer problem). Before that, I knew that the knapsack problem is NP-hard, but I was not sure if it can be applied to the utility maximization problem. In 1985, I applied my mind and started to think about how human behaviors are organized. There were some clues. At the time, H.A. Simon was proposing the Satisficing Principle. This gave me some hints, but as a formulation of prototype behavior, this was somewhat too ambiguous. March and Simon (1958) and Cyert and March (1963) had employed the words like routine, routine behavior, and rule-based actions, but there was no precise expression as to how these rule-based actions were structured. Routine was also the key concept for Nelson and Winter (1982). The word "routine" was a big hint for me, but it seemed too ambiguous and unstructured. Instead of routine or routine behavior, I adopted the Japanese expression "teikei kōdō" which means rule-based behavior or patterned behavior. With this key word in mind, I browsed through various fields from ethology to psychology to philosophical anthropology. I did not know Holland's if-then formula. The word "routine" was doubly indicative. It signified a routine behavior but also meant a small package of computer program which served as a ready-made operational function. This reminded me of a formulation of the Turing machine that I had read in my student days.

It was in Martin Davis's book *Computability and Unsolvability* (1958). He defined a Turing machine as a set of quadruples of the form.

$$q_i S_j S_k q_l$$

To be free from contradiction, the set should not contain two quadruple with the same first two symbols.

If I omit the details, the quadruple meant this: If you are in an internal state q_i, observe if the external state is S_j and if and only if it is, do S_k to the external world and change your internal state to q_l. I thought this Turing machine parable is very good for two reasons. First, the quadruple indicates the most elementary form of behavior. Second, the fact that a set of quadruples expresses the basic operation of a Turing machine and indicates that a set of quadruples can express highly structured and complicated functions. All computable functions on a computer, or recursive functions mathematically formulated, can be computed by a Turing machine. I knew this fact when I was a high school student. I was once deeply interested in the foundations of mathematics or metamathematics.

Afterward, I came to think of humans as a kind of Turing machine. I searched for stories which reinforced the parable. There were many of them. However, Üxküll's tick story was the most impressive. I first used it in the last chapter of my book *The Science of the Market Order* (in Japanese) which was published in 1990. The book was subtitled *From Anti-Equilibrium to Complexity*. This was the first book in Japanese which carried the word complexity in its title.

My encounter with Üxküll was lucky. I did not know that he was the father of biosemiotics. The tick's egg-laying story not only impressed me, but it told me many things. When I stayed 1 year in Cambridge, UK, 1986–1987, Roberto Scazzieri taught me of the existence of Heiner (1983). This was saying that a big C-D gap (or competence-difficulty gap) conditions predictable, regular behavior. This paper was enlightening.[19] In economics, we normally assumed optimization. When we know that optimization is impossible, the second best method was to approximate the optimization. However, as I have told it above, this causes various problems for the equilibrium formulation, especially for the definition of demand functions. We had to think from the opposite direction. We had to search how an efficient behavior can be organized when we have a big gap between our competence in selecting alternatives and the difficulty of the problem. This is the way that less competent animals were successful in promoting their survival. Humans are much more competent and are capable of more complicated calculation, but, in view of the complexity of the real world, we are also in the same situation as animals. We are not sufficiently competent as to have the ability to solve any maximization problem. In this regard, we must therefore be acting in the same ways as animals do. This was really a revelation. During the following year, when I visited the USA, I went to Provo, Utah, to meet Heiner as he was working for Brigham Young University at that time.[20]

1.3.4 The Nature of Human Skilled Work

Heiner's thesis, Üxküll's tick and the Turing machine parable all fitted together in one idea. Combining and arranging elementary patterns of behaviors, we can achieve most complicated tasks. It was great. From that time on, I continued to search for other examples and kept on trying to find exceptions to my formula. I found many examples which fitted. Yoshida's C-D transformation was one of them. Holland's classifier, or if-then behavior, was another. The psychologists' framework of reflective behavior as the Stimulus-Response formulation was showing the simplest cases. Skinner's operant behavior was more complicated but at any rate was too vague an example to use as a proof of the universality of my thesis in real-life

[19]It seems that Markey-Towler (2018, Subsections 4.2 and 4.3) was also deeply impressed by Heiner (1983).

[20]Nelson and Winter (1974, p.891) had arrived at the same conclusion far before me: "The basic behavioural premise is that a firm at any time operates largely according to a set of decision rules that link a domain of environmental stimuli to a range of responses on the part of firms." But I came to know their works after I had come across the C-D transformation concept.

economics. I also found various good and persuasive examples in Nakaoka's books. Tetsuro Nakaoka is one of my personal teachers and was a colleague at Osaka City University. He is a historian and philosopher of technology.

Nakaoka (1971) is a book which investigated how the skills of workers are formed and structured. I found in this book many examples of my thesis. Examples comprised operations of a medical team, working operations in a steel making factory using an electric furnace, and clerical administrative processes in an office of a business house. In another book, Nakaoka cited books from classical Greece and also Chinese ones. These illustrated how the signs in the sky or in nature were used to inform farmers so that they might know the good time for specific tasks like sowing and cultivating. In many places, he showed that work is decomposed into a series of simple operations and a worker's skill consists in the judgment applied to each operation. He pointed out that a judgment has the form of "a symptom -> an action to take." This was just an example of Yoshida's C-D transformation and of Davis's quadruple in a simple form.

There were of course many auxiliary questions. If a behavior accompanies a judgment, how do we detect a symptom? We are conditioned by many scarcities. We have only limited thinking or computing time. We must determine how much time we should spend on an activity. The same kind of scarcity applies to our attention span and capacity. I reflected on my own mental activity and observed that the target of our attention is strictly limited to one or a small number of things. I do not know why. At any rate, this must reflect the result of our evolution. To focus attention on one or a small number of things must be the only possible way to survive for animals which have a much more restricted ability to judge what is happening around them. How do we select a target or a mark to which we will pay attention? I recalled that March and Simon (1958) used the notion "definition of the situation." Let me cite a paragraph from it. Everything was beautifully argued:

> The theory of rational choice put forth here incorporates two fundamental characteristics: (1) Choice is always exercised with respect to a limited, approximate, simplified "model" of the real situation. We call the chooser's model his "definition of the situation." (2) The elements of the definition of the situation are not "given" – that is, we do not take these as data of our theory – but are themselves the outcome of psychological and sociological processes, including the chooser's own activities and the activities of others in his environment. (Simon and March 1993[1958], p.160)

We find an astonishing coincidence with my Turing machine parable of animal and human behaviors. A quadruple is divided into two parts: conditional half and directive half. The conditional half contains two symbols: q_i and S_j. What role does q_i play? It defines the internal state. It is an "outcome" of the previous action and the environment. It defines the situation to be examined and suggests what kind of stimuli we have to observe. This is the most primitive case of the definition of the situation. If the observed result is S_j, we must do S_k to the outer world and transit to the internal state q_l. If the observed state is not S_j, it is understood to transit to the next quadruple q_i'S_j' in the set.

What seems to be very difficult can be achieved once we know each elementary behavior and the order to follow. Üxküll's egg-laying behavior of the tick can be written in the same way in a series of quadruples. Recall that all S_j and S_k are simple and restricted observations and actions. Nakaoka gives us many other more elaborate examples. Now I firmly believe that any human behavior, if it is a complex one, can always be decomposed into a series of simple behaviors.

How does our judgment and rationality work? We have to distinguish two levels.[21] The first level works in the course of a specific behavior. We must judge if we are in a state S_j. If yes, S_k is chosen instantly without substantial reflection. It may require some calculation. In some cases, S_j may contain some parameters to be observed. In that case S_k is a simple function of those parameters. The calculation is instantaneous, and this judgment is similar to the operation of instinct in animals, even though this type of activity is one of the essential skills of high-ranking workers. Recall that Mintzberg (1973) reported that a factory head makes more than a thousand decisions a day.

The second level, of judgment and rationality, works on the behaviors themselves. We have a repertoire of behavior patterns. They are classified with respect to the situations. In each situation, we have several candidates as possible behaviors. If a behavior has not produced an average result as good as we have expected, we may choose another behavior in the repertoire. In some cases, we increase the repertoire by pure invention or by learning from others. This second level judgment works mainly on observations. No complicated computation or consideration is required. What we do is to observe and compare the results. Each judgment lies within the capacity of our sight and rationality. This is essentially different from maximization by calculation. Except for an imaginary problem setting, pursuit of a better result by calculation is, on most occasions, impossible. Instead, we observe what happens if we behave this way or another. This is closer to natural selection than rational choice. Very little calculation and rationality are demanded.

I refute maximization as a principle of economic behavior, because in many cases it exceeds our capacity for calculation or judgment. This does not mean that I deny rationality when it works. This only means that we have to reconstruct, at the very foundation of economics, the theory of value and the theory of production, exchange, and consumption within a framework that does not violate our capacity for sight, rationality, and execution.

The concept of a repertoire of behaviors helps us much in understanding what is the skillfulness of a worker. We sometimes confuse dexterity with skillfulness. Of course, dexterity is a part of skillfulness, but skillfulness is not limited to the fact that a worker is dexterous. Dexterity is concerned with the quality of a behavior. A very skilled worker normally has a dexterous action of behavior. He or she has a better capacity for judgment and more exact ways of performing actions. However, this

[21] The distinction may sound similar to Kahneman's two systems (fast and slow modes of thinking and deciding) and Katona's (1951) more classical dichotomy between habitual behavior and genuine decisions. However, the second level of judgment here still lies in the first system of thinking.

skillfulness is a capability much wider than dexterity. Normally, a skilled worker also has a larger repertoire of possible actions than unskilled workers.

In good times, factory work involves the simple repetition of routines. If you have acquired a few patterns of behavior, you can work on your own. However, various unexpected events may happen: power breakdown, malfunction of a machine, repeated production of defective products, lack of parts, interaction of two independent machines, defecting of a worker (because of sudden resignation, sickness, injury, or simple absence), and so on. Some troubles happen quite frequently, for example, once or twice a week. Even a young unskilled worker can soon learn how to deal with these situations, if they happen frequently. On the other hand, we have very rare events. For example, a machine may fail with a problem which rarely occurs, say that this is every 10 years or so. An older and experienced superintendent has the knowledge required to deal with the trouble. After K. Koike (1995), this is the core intellectual skill of workers. He distinguishes usual and unusual operations.

> Workshop jobs include usual and unusual operations. Work on a mass-production assembly line does not appear to be dependent on skills and seems entirely repetitive. Only speed seems to affect efficiency. This, however, is usual operation. Observe the line closely, and you see frequent changes and problems. Dealing with these situations constitutes unusual operations. (Koike 1995, p.63)

New workers with little experience do not have the know-how to deal with these unusual operations. Of course, there are gradations between usual and unusual. One operation may be required every 2 months. Another operation is required once or twice in 10 years. Imagine, for example, the introduction of a new machine system when the older machines have been used for 5 years. When the new machine system is installed, workers whose career in the job is less than 5 years will have had no chance to experience the different tasks required, working arrangements to be accommodated and the troubles that may happen. Koike argued that the major part of the intellectual skill of workers is based on this wider experience, and its contribution to efficiency is comparable to the expertise of highly learned engineers.

We have also arrived at an important conclusion. Observing what we can do and investigating how our behaviors are organized, we found, without the intention to do so, how our own behavior evolves. Normally we have a pool of behaviors, and we choose them not by rational calculation but by observing and comparing the average result of a behavior with other comparable behaviors. This is an evolution of our behaviors. The selection of behavior works on the second level that we have examined above. Although we use minimal rationality, this selection, repeated many times, produces a result that was unimaginable at the beginning. This is the core mechanism of economic evolution.

The main purpose of this book is to show that a worldwide network of economic transactions can work with these limited assumptions. However, before we go to a concrete discussion of how the economic processes work, it is necessary to examine in what kinds of situation our behavior can be effective. This is the task of the next section.

1.4 Environment of Economic Activities

If our behavior evolves by experience and comparison, instead of by rational maximization,[22] then our economy must have various features that permit us to behave effectively by employing an appropriate behavior: a behavior that has been selected from it being the result of a long evolutionary process. For this to be possible, there are three major conditions: stationarity, decomposability, and subsistence. The core condition is the stationarity (or stationariness) of the economic process. It is possible that this expression may induce much misunderstanding. I will explain this concept in detail in Sect. 1.4.1. The second important, even vital, feature is decomposability or the loose connectedness of our economy. I explain this in Sect. 1.4.3. Before I begin explaining this most crucial feature of the economic system, I will make a deviation in Sect. 1.4.2 to argue the questions of "why" and "when" our behavior becomes effective and ineffective. The third, and least mentioned, feature is concerned with our ability to survive in a world upon which we depend in a crucial way, despite humans being severely restricted in key aspects of what intuition suggests is required: myopic sight, bounded rationality, and limited range of influences. In Sect. 1.4.4, I will argue the importance of an (ample) margin of subsistence.

1.4.1 Importance of Stationarity in the Economic Process

When we speak of an economic process, it may indicate any process from a series of transactions in a particular market to the whole network of transactions that spread worldwide. Whichever process we imagine, stationarity must be the most important feature of an economic process.

Stationarity is completely different from stability. In standard economics, two kinds of stability are argued. The first is the stability supposed in the general equilibrium framework. In this case, stability means the invariance of agents' behavior. In equilibrium, agents have no incentive to change their actions (e.g., bids for and offers of a particular security). The second meaning of stability concerns the behavior or movement of temporal equilibrium. We say that the equilibrium is stable when the economic state shifts to a fixed state when the state has been out of equilibrium.

Stationarity means only that the concerned process has some regularity or keeps constancy in some other sense. A process is stationary, when the state of the process repeats itself essentially in the same way. The qualifier "essentially" is crucial here. In a simple process in which only a single variable changes, each instance of the

[22] This is not the claim that we are irrational or behave irrationally. As we have argued in Sect. 1.2, our capacity of calculation is limited, and we are obliged to behave differently from what is assumed by maximization principle, which was long assumed in neoclassical economics.

process may follow different paths, in detail. The adverb "essentially" means the variable comes near to the same value repeatedly. In a process that comprises many variables, no same state is repeated, in the sense that all variables will not take the same value at two different points in time. Even in that case, we say the process is essentially stationary, when some variables repeatedly come near to the same combination of values.

The word "stationary" is used in stochastic process theory. The term "stationarity" here does not have such a specific meaning. It has a much wider, or a looser, meaning. A stationary process in the stochastic process theory is stationary in my meaning, but we must admit many other stochastic processes, those that are not stationary in the stochastic process theory, but which are stationary in our sense. Remember Koike's "unusual operations" in the previous section. Our concept of stationarity includes unusual states as possible states of a stationary process. Economic processes always comprise various degrees of unusualness.

Stationarity in this broad sense is the vital condition that causes an intentional human behavior to be effective.[23] We have argued in the previous two sections that our capacity for good judgment is strongly restricted either by weakness in information collecting ("myopic") or capacity for rational calculation, or both. The effectiveness of our behavior depends very much upon the evolutionary selective process by which our set of behavioral alternatives has developed.

If an economic process changes substantially, the present behavior may not be the best one even among the acquired repertoire of all our behaviors. Our actual behavior is chosen only because, in our experience, it was effective in obtaining a higher value of an objective function than its alternatives. This historical fact (knowledge) remains effective only so long as the process concerned did not change in any essential manner.

It is important to recognize that our knowledge and behaviors are deeply dependent on the stationarity of our world, or constancy over time in the patterns of everyday life. Day starts by sunrise and night comes with sunset. Years are a repetition of spring, summer, fall, and winter. Mankind has recognized in nature and invented many other patterns and rhythms for the convenience of life: a week of 7 days, a month, hours and minutes, years, decades, and centuries. All these customs or institutions help to make rhythms and provide punctuation in our everyday life. We eat breakfast, lunch and dinner in a day. Working hours start at 9 a.m. and end at 5 p.m. Firms pay wages once every week or once every month. Shops are open 6 days a week except for bank holidays. You can buy your baguette at a bakery; your macaroni and pasta at a grocery; papers, notes, and ball pens at a stationary shop; and books at a book shop. An order on a web site arrives in a day or two. You can draw your money from your bank if you have enough on deposit or if you have a credit account. At the end of a summer, you can buy an overcoat and in spring summer shirts. Almost all things necessary for your life are repeated constantly even if they are not exactly the same as 1 year ago. These are the basis of our life, and without

[23]For more details of this argument and its implications to economics, see Shiozawa (1989).

these constancies, it is very difficult for us to live. However, you easily forget this fact and believe that you are organizing your own life by your own plan and calculation. This is a very special mindset that did not exist in premodern worlds.

Modern economics conceived our economy through the looking glass of modern science. Galileo Galilei succeeded in predicting by calculation how a mass drops in a free fall. Johannes Kepler succeeded in describing how planets move around in their orbits. Pierre-Simon Laplace imagined that an omnipotent being can calculate the future state of the world by knowing the present state. If the world is governed by Newtonian dynamics, this is in principle possible, because the movement of the world can be described by a (huge) system of differential equations and because if it is well posed, it has a unique solution.

Economists, after the neoclassical revolution, imagined that a human agent behaves similarly, by using calculation. They supposed that an agent predicts what will happen in the future, calculates his or her profit or utility, and decides what he or she will do. A typical example is utility maximization under a budget constraint of a consumer. We have proved above (Sect. 1.2.1) that this simple calculation requires exorbitant computing time and it is practically impossible except for an extremely simple case of a small number of commodities. We should abandon this mode of thinking. Whether or not we really calculate or contemplate such things in our decision-making, we are helped enormously by the constancy of patterns in the occurrence of events and the processes they follow. If there are complex calculations to be done, it is the objective world that calculates them; human calculation accounts for only a small number of them. We must not overlook this fact and believe too much in our own ability to calculate and predict.

In relation to this point, it is opportune to give a few comments on G.L.S. Shackle's kaleidics. He was right to emphasize our uncertainty and ignorance regarding the future. It may serve as a good criticism of the rational expectation hypothesis and contribute to refuting what Davidson named the ergodic axiom.[24] However, I have to say that Shackle and Davidson are still within the *problématique* of future calculation or Galileo-Descartes-Newton-Laplace's *calculationist paradigm*. Galileo, Descartes, Newton, and Laplace all imagined a mechanical world. It was more dynamic than had been imagined by people in the

[24]Paul Davidson argues many times (at least 72 times in Davidson 1991, 1999, 2007) that Samuelson postulated what Davidson named the "ergodic axiom." However, in every case, he cites the same Samuelson paper (Samuelson 1969) which is a reprint of Samuelson (1968). Samuelson nowhere claimed that the "ergodic hypothesis" is "a sine qua non of economics as science" as Davidson argues (Davidson 1999, p.154, p.382). Samuelson was rather critical to the "ergodic hypothesis". He only pointed out that ergodicity is necessary if the classical dichotomy works independently of the initial distribution of money. The ergodic axiom is not an axiom of neoclassical economics but rather a scarecrow invented by Davidson. It is not accurate to say that the ergodic axiom is one of three axioms that Keynes rejected. It may be implied from his idea, but Keynes had no clear idea of the axiom. In addition, Davidson's concept of ergodicity, which inherits the definition of Samuelson (1968, 1969), does not exactly correspond to the concept of ergodicity in physics. Alvarez and Ehnts (2014) reasonably propose to use the terms stochastic and non-stochastic randomness instead of ergodicity which has an ambiguous meaning in economics.

medieval period. It involved complex clockwork, turbulent cosmic flow, a system of differential equations, and probability theory. They were all thinking it would be possible to predict the future by calculation or rational inference. This is the spirit of modern science. But, in a complex system, it is not possible to predict what will happen in the future by calculation or by any rational inference. If we can do it at all, it is only for very small parts of our world, parts which are isolated from others and comprise simple systems. If we want to calculate the movements or interactions of all elementary particles of a world, then a computer simulation would require a computer with the same weight as the universe. The question does not change much if you think of a stochastic rather than a mechanistic prediction.

Keynes (1921) and Knight (1921) were right when they argued that uncertainty excludes even the calculation of probabilities.[25] We are in a world of *non-stochastic* randomness (A'lvarez and Ehnts 2014). In this regard, we can say that Shackle and Davidson follow Keynes closely and loyally. However, we have to say that Keynes was not free from the future calculation, or world calculation *problématique*. If we really acknowledge that our capabilities are extremely limited, we must think from the opposite end. Let us imagine a lower animal with little reasoning power, Üxküll's tick, for example. The tick does not calculate or predict what will happen. She waits until the world changes to a state that the inner state dictates. It is not the tick which calculates. It is the world which evolves by itself. The tick at the tip of a branch waits until she smells butyric acid. She catches the mark-sign of the world. A mark-sign is a symptom of the world, and it is usually a special feature of a small part of the world. Even the lowest animal has some power to detect a mark-sign and deploys its series of C-D transformations. In the Turing machine parable, if the state is in S_j, we try to realize S_k. Both S_j and S_k are but two small marks of the world. The effectiveness of behavior does not depend on our rational power of prediction. It depends on the sequential constancy of the result that follows a combination (S_j, S_k). Through a long history of evolution, the tick has discovered an ingenious tactic to catch mammals. A man or a woman is not very different from a tick, a flea, or a spider. He or she mainly behaves just like the lower animals do: detect a mark-sign of the world and add a small effort to change it.

The most important target of economics is to explain how the economy, which now spreads worldwide, works. It is not our capacity of calculation and prediction that guarantees the well functioning of an economy. It is the mode of interactions that we have adopted that guarantees it. A fundamental change of paradigm is required. We need a new paradigm of thought for regarding how the complex world works and what we are individually competing for in this difficult environment. Keynes and Shackle contributed little insight to how this difficult task could be approached.

This is not to deny the modern sciences. Physical science from Galileo and Descartes to Newton and Laplace enlightened our understanding of our world. What

---

[25]This does not exclude that they denied all calculation of the probability. They knew it is sometimes possible and useful. I owe this remark to Michael Brady.

is required in economics, and human science in general, is to determine how our behaviors are organized and why they are in general effective, one way or the other. Analytical mechanics was once called rational mechanics. Newton contrasted it to practical mechanics. The latter referred to all manual arts that people practiced from olden times. Manual arts were based mainly on experience and not on theory and experiments. Modern science clarified how the physical world works. This was indeed a tremendous achievement. However, it did not make clear how our own behaviors are organized. Social scientists followed the track of rational mechanics. They imagined that human agents calculate their behaviors rationally according to their understanding of the physical. The only difference is that human agents' actions are stimulated by motivations, whereas material things had no intentions or purposes.

Fortunately for those social scientists, and unfortunately for the social sciences, analytical mechanics provided the principle of virtual displacement or virtual work. A movement of a system could be described by the variational principle. The variational method employs the minimization principle. It describes the movement of a system in such a way that the system optimizes something (e.g., minimize the virtual work). Why is it impossible to use this method for human systems? Modern economics after Walras was all based on this optimization principle. If one believes in this system, it is inevitable to assume that a human being has sufficient rational capacity to perform in this way. This was the main reason why the optimization principle was believed to be the essential factor that ensured the efficiency of the economic system. This explains why the optimization principle maintained its preeminent status in economics long after the discovery of bounded rationality.

We must change our computationist paradigm to that of the procedural paradigm illustrated by Üxküll. He has created a real revolution not only in ethology but also in the future direction of all theory of human behavior. Semiotics underlies this giant revolution. Without it, we cannot understand why we are semiotic rather than rational animals.

1.4.2 What Determines Effectiveness of Human Behavior?

Now let us return to our question. Why is our behavior so effective while our rationality plays only a minimal part? When is it effective and when does it lose effectiveness? What is the mechanism that gives us good performance from a behavior? The answer is not easy so long as we continue to think in a computationist behavioral paradigm. However, if we change our behavioral paradigm, the answer is almost completely provided by what has been written above. Nonetheless we shall look at these matters in detail.

First, reformulate the question in a more direct form. Our behavior is a series of C-D transformations. It is deployed in time. In essence, the behavior is a process. In which case, our examination is going to be organized along the time line. The simplest component of a behavior is a C-D transformation, but for the present

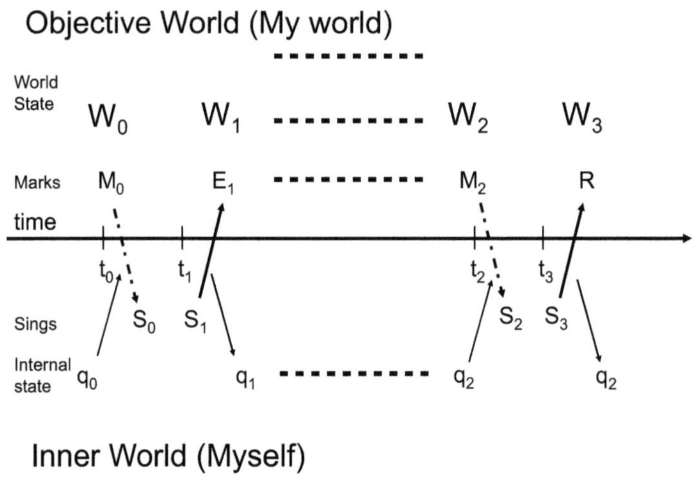

Fig. 1.2 A scheme showing how we behave in a complex world

purpose, we also need an action of collecting, or sensing, the benefit, or the result, of the first action. Consequently, our simplest series will be composed of at least two C–D transformations.

A simple scheme of interactions between an agent (myself) and the world (my world) is shown in Fig. 1.2. To clarify the sequence of events, it is more convenient to use the quadruple expression. We start from the internal state q_0. It requires me to observe the world. The world is in state W_0. *I* locate the mark $M_{0,}$ which is a small part of the world W_0. If the sign *I* sense from M_0 is S_0, *I* do an action S_1 and transit to internal state q_1. The action S_1 makes a small effect E_1 upon the world, and the world's state W_0 changes to state W_1. The world then continues to change by itself and may arrive at the state W_2. Meanwhile, *I* continue to observe the world and wait until *I* receive the sign S_2. This waiting process is described by a quadruple qSS'q where q is an order to observe the mark M_2. If *I* do not receive the sign S_2, *I* do nothing to the outer world but wait for 10 s or so (this time lapse can change conveniently) and return to internal state q_0. With this quadruple or program, I continue to observe M_2 every 10 s until *I* receive the sign S_2. S_2 is the sign of harvesting. *I* perform an action to collect the harvest's yield *G*. Then *I* will probably estimate the quantity of my gain and transit to another behavior.

During this process, the world proceeds by itself, evolving along the time line. The effect *I* added may have changed the course of the world, but in most of the cases, the effect is very small. Normally I do not know what really happens between W_0 and W_2. *I* only expect that a mark will appear in the world, but *I* do not know why or how it happens. *I* only know that if the case is q_0 and the observed sign is S_1 then if *I* act upon sign S_2, *I* have a good chance of getting the result *R*.

This view of knowing the world is not a very scientific one. "*I*" only know how to decide and act. The reason why *I* act as *I* do is based on experience. This experience may be my own or may be that of other people. *I* can learn from what other people do, and my neighbors will learn from me.[26]

When Gilbert Ryle (2009[1949]) talked about the difference between "knowing that" and "knowing how," he must have been thinking of a process similar to that which was illustrated by our question. By arguing the importance of "knowing how," Ryle mainly wanted to refute the "intellectualist legend" which inhabits most of our thinking. He defines this legend as a belief that a good intellectual performance requires one to do a bit of theory and then to do a bit of practice.

The intellectualist legend reveals a firmly embedded tradition at the roots of our way of thinking. To obtain a good performance, people think that it is necessary to have a good theory of the world. However, if we reflect on our behavior as it is formulated in Fig. 1.2, it is not the knowledge of laws of the world that gives us a good result. Even if we do not know how the world develops, if the action S_1 is taken when S_0 is observed, then it will give a good result R with good probability, and our performance is good. The knowledge of laws of the world may contribute to improving our behavior, but the effectiveness of a behavior depends in large part on our success in choosing the most effective combinations of C-D transformations.

Although his main purpose was different, Ryle's comparison between *knowing-that* and *knowing-how* was extremely valuable. In classical Greece, mathematics and astronomy were models of our intellectual accomplishments. Philosophers thought that "it was in the capacity for rigorous theory that lay the superiority of men over animals, of civilized men over barbarians and divine mind over human minds" (Ryle 2009, p.15). Then, as Ryle put it, the following understanding of rationality naturally emerged,

> To be rational was to be able to recognize truths and the connections between them. To act rationally was, therefore, to have one's non-theoretical propensities controlled by one's apprehension of truths about the conduct of life. (Ryle 2009, p.15)

The history of modern physics strengthened this belief. The great success of Newtonian physics made us believe that the world is governed by laws and, if we know these laws better, our capacity to govern the world will be extended. This was indeed true. The modern world changed much owing to this conception of it. However, despite their enormous significance, mathematics and the modern sciences can only be a small part of our intelligence. This is the sphere of knowing-that. Another part lies in the sphere of knowing-how. However great the sphere of *knowing-that* may be, the fact is that the majority of our knowledge lies in the sphere of knowing-how. Although Ryle did not emphasize this fact, this is his greatest contribution to our understanding of human behavior.

---

[26]Learning and teaching are the most effective behaviors of obtaining the knowledge on which behaviors yield the best results for each quadruple. Further behaviors can then be similarly evaluated to determine how best to transmit these "best practices" across time through the generations of a group. These behaviors evolve as knowledge and skill in their use grow. We call them social institutions. They are the bedrock of evolutionary economics. I owe this remark to Robin Jarvis.

Human behavior is organized around knowing-how. Mathematical statements and scientific laws are described by propositions. The value of a proposition is true or false. Knowing-how is described by directives. The value of a directive is not true or false, but good or bad. The mode of knowledge is fundamentally different. Even so, we have no good theory of this sphere of knowing-how. In schools we are taught through both modes, but teachers have a strong tendency to underestimate knowing-how and are given to preaching that knowing-how has no general applicability as "true knowledge." They mean by "true knowledge" the knowledge that is in the sphere of knowing-that. They are right in their statement, so far as it goes, but they do not know the true variety of all the types of knowledge nor the weight to be given to each type.

While Ryle talked long on what it means to act intelligently, he did not explain how a good performance is obtained. As I have mentioned above, a good result of a behavior (and of a decision) does not depend much on rationality or calculation but on a knowledge of the patterns of how the world changes and develops over time. In a few fortunate cases, optimization gives a better result, but we cannot think of them as typical cases.

The performance of a behavior depends on many factors: the definition of the state, the accuracy of observation, the exactness and the timing of the execution, and others. A good behavior is sometimes difficult to learn. Even if we know the rough pattern of behavior, the mark we must observe may not be well defined, and the sign we catch may depend on a delicate difference of something not well defined. Scientific research into the behavior of a skilled laborer may reveal the secret of his or her good performance, but it requires long and specialized study. Even the skilled workers themselves cannot tell others the delicate nuances of their judgments. So, the possibility of improvement always remains, and labor productivity increases with the accumulation of experience and from trial and error.

In general, experience and more focused efforts improve performance, and the improvements may be enormous. However, it is important to know that in some cases, it is the structure of the process which limits the best level of performance. A best example of this would be given by an investor who tries to outperform the stock market by technical analysis. Let the investor be a professional day trader. He has a repertoire of rules deciding the moment for buying and selling. One of such decision rules is the "golden cross." It is the moment that two different average curves cross. If he observes a golden cross for a certain brand of stock, he buys the brand. However, if we believe the weak version of the efficient market hypothesis (i.e., the irrelevance of technical analysis),[27] he cannot expect to get a profit constantly from this strategy. Stated more precisely, he cannot expect that his average return is positive.

[27]Eugene Fama's Efficient Market Hypothesis proves the information efficiency of stock markets, but this should not be interpreted as proving that a market system is efficient in a normal sense of efficiency. Stock markets are full of bubbles and crashes.

Another strategy is to place the same amount of buy and sell orders with an appropriate spread of prices at the beginning of the day. If two orders are executed and the spread of the two orders is larger than the commission of brokerage, our trader makes a profit. But this strategy has a risk. If only one of the two orders is executed, the trader must close his or her account by buying or selling contrarily, even at a loss. Taking this risk into consideration, on average the trader can make a profit with this strategy if the volatility of a brand is high enough. However, if this strategy is really profitable and many day traders employ a similar strategy, the normal volatility of the market is depressed and the strategy would lose any possibility of making profits (Shiozawa 2008, §6.4.2; 2016b, §1.4.5).

The lesson to draw here is that the performance we can expect from a behavior, a decision rule, or a strategy depends on the development of the economic process itself.

1.4.3 Loosely Connected Nature of the System

Stationarity of the economic process enables human agents to behave in a rule-based way. The process gives a cue for the action, and we draw benefits from some constancy of the process. However, as we have observed, human agents are under the yoke of three limits: myopic sight, bounded rationality, and locality of execution. If we compare the bigness of an economy and the narrowness of the range of human actions, it is a natural question to ask by what mechanism we can influence the economy.

We, mankind, live in the interface of land and atmosphere. We learned to stand up and walk vertically. This enabled us to have two free hands by which we work and manipulate everything. This must really be the basic condition enabling us to do almost everything we can do. However, human economy has a dimension that is far beyond the range that an individual man or woman can manipulate. Indeed nobody, not even a state planning agency, can manipulate or control the total economy, even if it is a small economy with only one million inhabitants.

In order that an agent with our three limitations can behave in a suitable way, the economy itself must be equipped of special characteristics. In a word, the world must be nearly decomposable (Simon 1962). It must be loosely connected, and each small part must be capable of being changed independently from other parts of the economy. H. A. Simon (1962, 1979) called this feature the "(almost) empty world assumption." In his words, "most things are only weakly connected with most other things" (Simon 1962, p.478) and "most things are not related directly to most other things" (Simon 1962, p.74). Near decomposability is really the very basis of all economic activities, but I prefer the expression "loosely connectedness" because the economy is a connected system after all (see also Weick 1976).

Components of a system are loosely connected when each component has some range of independence, or freedom of movement. They are connected because they cannot take values beyond their range of independence.

In the most abstract way, loosely connected system LC is defined to be a set that satisfies the following conditions:

1. LC is a set of entities $E_1, E_2, \ldots, E_N$ for a large integer N.
2. For all i, a vector $\mathbf{v}(i)$ in a fixed vector space is attached for each Ei.
3. For any pair of indices (i, j), a scalar $R(i, j)$ is affected. $R(i, j)$ is normally a positive real number but may take the nominal value infinity ∞.
4. A vector $v(i)$ can take arbitrary values provided that for any pair (i, j), vectors satisfy the constraints:

$$\|\mathbf{v}(i)-\mathbf{v}(j)\| \leqq R(i, j).$$

Simon gives a similar definition for his "near decomposability" by assuming that almost all entries except a few in a relation matrix are near to zero (Simon 1962, p.475). The trouble with Simon's nearly decomposable system is that it assumes (almost) linear relations. Such an assumption is necessary when we want to analyze a large-scale system. However, all variables must move simultaneously in a nearly linear decomposable system. A human agent with three limits cannot engage in influencing such a system. What we can do is to interact with a small part of the system which is relatively independent from the rest. This is possible, but when two or several components are connected tightly by the constraints like (4) with very small R_{ij}, we are sometimes incapable of controlling even a very small part of the system. These constraints are in general nonlinear. This is one of the reasons we prefer the definition above rather than Simon's nearly decomposable system. Nonlinearity is an essential feature of a loosely connected system. Of course, this is not an easy option, because analysis necessarily becomes complex and complicated.

Our main intention is to study the dynamics of a loosely connected system, and we present some concrete examples in the chapters after Chap. 2. To understand what is really happening in the economy, we need a linear analysis of large scale, but in doing so, we are obliged to exclude the cases when inventories are depleted. In such cases, we are obliged to make nonlinear operations such as taking the maximum of two variables. Even in such cases, we can use computer simulations to understand the main features of the process we are investigating. Of course, we cannot establish a theorem by such simulations. Consequently, we think both linear analysis and computer simulation are necessary and inevitable methods of analyzing loosely connected systems.[28]

In order that an economic system is a loosely connected system, the system must be equipped with specific instruments or material bases that make each part independent even within a small range. One of such universal instruments is inventory or the stock of products. Inventories exist everywhere: material inventories, work-in-process inventories, product inventories, inventories in transit

[28] This is what we do in this book. To analyze the economy-wide quantity adjustment problem, we try large-scale linear analysis in Chaps. 4, and 5 and computer simulation in Chap. 6.

(distribution), domestic stockpiles, and others. The ubiquity of inventories shows how important they are. In fact, every part of an economy is disconnected by the existence of inventories. Imagine a world with no inventories. It is like a railway system where all trains are connected rigidly to one another. Such a railway system does not function at all. In the similar way, an economy without inventories does not work either.

Another important instrument of disconnection is money. Money disconnects buying and selling. It is quite evident that a modern large-scale economy does not work without money. Money has many functions that we know from the textbooks, but few textbooks point out that money works as an instrument which makes an economy a loosely connected system.

Closely related to money, credit plays a similar role to money. Credit permits someone to procure a commodity without having enough money at that moment. Nowadays deferred payment is very common in transactions between firms. It is astonishing that selling on credit for consumers was common and popular, two centuries years ago, in the Edo period in Japan. These facts may also show the importance of the disconnecting function of the credit system.

In many kinds of organization, a different kind of loose connectedness is operational. For example, when organizations are structured in a hierarchy, a director at any level of the hierarchy is delegated power to decide by him- or herself within a certain assigned range of operational parameters. Selective delegation of authority is the sine qua non principle which makes an organization work.

1.4.4 Conditions of Subsistence

These are the most often forgotten conditions for the well functioning of an economic system. Imagine that a high percentage of the members of an economy perish for some reason, by an invasion of creatures from outer space, for example. Of course, I do not believe such nonsense, but it is easy to imagine a circumstance in which all of our existing economic networks will have broken down. In such a case, we must start again, finding a way to determine who can afford this and that and at which price and in what quantity. We will find ourselves in a crude market situation such as that which neoclassical economics presupposes.

After Josef Schumpeter (1950) advanced the concept of creative destruction, it became very popular among a wide range of people. Cox and Alm (2008) appreciated in their encyclopedic article that creative destruction "has become the centerpiece for modern thinking on how economies evolve." Nowadays we can find many books that include "creative destruction" in their titles. Creative destruction was accepted as a necessary cost of having an efficient market economy. The innovative entry of entrepreneurs is necessary for creative capitalism. Schumpeter's vision is correct. The appropriate level of destruction is crucial for capitalism to be creative. If 1% of firms per year exit by bankruptcy or through closing down, the economy can be active and prosperous. But if more than 20% of firms go bankrupt, it is disastrous for an economy. The wind of creative destruction must not blow so strong a gale as to be lethal to the system it tears through.

A sudden, widespread, and strong destruction will change the economy too rapidly and disrupt its vital quality of stationarity. Neither people nor firms can adapt quickly enough to the new situation. It takes time. A widespread unpredictable loss of stationarity among the economic markers in their environment will invalidate the very basis by which actions from their behavioral repertoire are selected, evaluated, and compared, and they will be lost as to what to do.

A considerable part of economic know-how is maintained through the existence of, and by, each team of workers. When a factory is closed, each worker from a team may retain his or her personal know-how' that may be useful in a new workplace if he or she finds employment, but for the teams dissolved by destruction of the factory, a major part of the factory's teamwork know-how will be lost, perhaps forever. Innovation is necessary, but we must not forget that creative destruction has two faces. If the destructive face is too strong, the gale of creative destruction will, by itself, kill a large part of the creativity of the people it releases back into the market. But for a healthy economy, a measure of moderate destruction should not be excluded.

The term "subsistence" may remind us of the classical economists' concept of the subsistence wage, but this subsection's remarks have little connection to the theory that wages must remain at the subsistence level, as is supposedly required by the "iron law of wages." It is doubtful if there is a sharp line that divides the level of subsistence above which the population grows and below which it will be in decline. This subsection does not suggest that a growing society existing above their subsistence level is in a so-called Malthusian trap. It only claims that an economic state that brings too many households and firms to bankruptcy or physical destruction in a short time is not sustainable as a normal economy. The existence of a sufficient buffer space for the physical survival of agents is also a necessary condition for the good working of an economy.

Readers may wonder why I emphasize these rather trivial facts. It is to avoid the misunderstanding that the evolutionary world is ruled by the "survival of the fittest" law. It is true that those species, and variations of species, when they fail to adapt appropriately to an environment, will cause them to be selected out by its stresses and will perish since they do not fit the environmental demands. But the survival of the fittest species imposes much more stringent conditions than that which is represented by the evolutionary selection of individuals. Think, for example, a situation in which several species are competing for the same niche in a common environment. Each species has the degree of fitness $f(i)$ represented by the effective rate of reproduction. This reproduction rate is much less than that of mere biological reproduction of individuals. It is the number of sexually mature and progenitorially viable offspring that the average mother produces. Suppose that the rate is measured for a unit of time that is common across all competing species. Survival of the fittest by selection means that only the variety i^* that has the maximal $f(i^*)$ will survive. We see such an account in many evolutionary game arguments. However, there is a misunderstanding here, because those species, or species variations, that have an effective rate of reproduction that is smaller than that of the fittest, but which on average is still greater than 1, will survive as well as that variety with the maximal effective rate of reproduction. By definition, those other populations will grow more slowly than that of the fittest individuals. But this smallness of each viable variants' population and their greatness in number are two important conditions in order that evolutionary selection works effectively in the long run.

Evolutionary change is "the interplay between two processes: variation and selection" (Ellerman 2014). The principle of the survival of the fittest only sees one part of the evolutionary process: the selection mechanism. Overall, the evolutionary process can be compared to climbing a very rugged and cloudy landscape (Sewall Wright). Selection is the mechanism (methodology) for climbing a hill in conditions of low visibility. What happens when the hill was low? The evolution stops there, and all viable variations begin to crowd its summit. An efficient evolutionary system must include a mechanism for continuing capacity for variation. With pressure from this mechanism, the adaptation arises in some individuals that fit them with the capacity to climb down the hill, cross the valley, and find another hill. For this to happen, genetic drift in a small group of individuals is necessary. As Ellerman (2004, 2014) pointed out, this is the scheme that guarantees the dynamic efficiency of the evolutionary selection process.

Wright was one of three collaborators who created the mathematical theory of population genetics, together with Ronald A. Fisher and J. B. S. Haldane. However, Ellerman thinks that, among many evolutionary theorists, Wright was the rare person who was interested in the variation process. He asked of himself "If selection operates to cut down variety to the survival of the fittest, what is the mechanism to increase variety in order to find a path from low to higher hills?" (Ellerman 2014, p.265). As Ellerman points out, there are many economists who have developed evolutionary theories but few who have focused on the variation process. Focus on the capacity of an environment to provide sufficient subsistence for the evolutionary process to take place is a necessary "other side of the coin" in a holistic study of evolution. Environmental capacity for subsistence must have an ample margin so that many varieties can arise and survive even in the most unfavorable environment. Therefore, a loose subsistence condition is the necessary condition for evolution to occur as effectively as we expect. This picture of an ample margin of subsistence is also in sharp contrast with the neoclassical view, which presupposes that the economy is working with the highest efficiency when it works without losses. Evolution is not possible in such an environment.[29]

[29] According to Robin Jarvis, the case of African Tribal Land management negatively illustrates the story here told.

1.5 Methodology of Analysis

Human behavior as well as animal behavior has a special time-related structure: observation, mark-sign, action, and transition to next internal state. These are deployed in time. Consequently, the core of our analysis must be sequential changes along the time axis. This kind of analysis has various names: sequential analysis, sequence analysis, period analysis, step by step method, process analysis, and others. We adopt here the term "process analysis" as the common name. In economics, equilibrium analysis was dominant for a long time. It focuses on the situation in which the overall state of a system is conserved. Process analysis adopts a very different viewpoint. It focuses on how chains (and networks) of individual activities bring about change. In Sect. 1.5.1, we will see the minimal characteristics that a process analysis must have. For practical purposes, differences of time spans are important. Section 1.5.2 discusses briefly how to reconcile different time spans and decision hierarchies. Human agents learn by experience and creation. As this learning occurs inside of the economic process, a special cycle emerges between an individuals' behavior and the total economic process. We call this cycle the "micro-macro loop." The micro-macro loop is not only important for understanding various features of economic processes, but it necessitates a new type of methodology. Section 1.5.3 is devoted to this topic.

1.5.1 Some Notes on Process Analysis

If we admit that human behavior is a pattern that follows events in time, the stage of drama for its analysis cannot be that of an equilibrium state. The analytical framework must include the time variable in a fundamental and essential way (Hahn 1984, p.53). Consequently, as has been stated, our framework of study must be process analysis.

This forces us to consider a big problem. Up until this time, the major method of economic study has been equilibrium analysis. This notion has existed from the days of classical political economy. Neoclassical economics polished up the vague ideas of the classical period and refined them through mathematical formulation. The equilibrium framework was at first adopted because it was more tractable than other methods. Even today, it is not easy to abandon equilibrium analysis and adopt another framework. This explains the conservative attitude of many economists to thoughts of abandoning equilibrium analysis. As I have noted above, there are economists who believe that we lose all our analytical tools if we oust equilibrium and maximization.

Discussing the two methods employed by Keynes, Meir Kohn (1986) pointed that the switch from process analysis to equilibrium analysis was one of the reasons for the success of *The General Theory*. In his opinion, Keynes employed process or sequence analysis in *The Treatise of Money* but then switched to equilibrium analysis in *The General Theory.* Masaaki Yoshida (1997) made the same observation. Equilibrium analysis is easier to understand. It made *The General Theory* more acceptable to a wider range of economists. However, this concession was necessarily at the cost of abandoning true monetary analysis. The equilibrium methodological framework is not consistent with true monetary analysis. For example, hoarding and forced saving contradict the static nature of liquidity preference theory (Kohn 1986, p.1218). The principle of effective demand would be another example, because it cannot be defined coherently in an equilibrium framework.

Was it then better that Keynes should have continued to be attached to the sequence analysis that he employed in *The Treatise of Money*? Kohn simply does not believe so. Sequence analysis, or the "step by step" method in Dennis H. Robertson's phraseology, is much more difficult, and with it Keynes could not have succeeded in developing and formulating his new ideas and principles that became the core of *The General Theory*. At the time, process analysis was a new method of analysis appearing among the Young Turks of economic thinking including R.G. Hawtrey, D.H. Robertson, B. Ohlin, and Keynes himself (Keyens 1979, p.270, cited in Kohn 1986, p.1201).[30] This new method was an important criterion for Keynes when he wanted to distinguish between "real-exchange economics" analysis (meaning barter economy analysis) and true monetary analysis. Thus, according to Kohn, the real revolution of *The General Theory* should have been a revolution not in contents but in method, moving from an equilibrium framework to a process-oriented analytical framework.[31] However, it would have been a more difficult and tortuous path, and he may not have succeeded in this revolution. After all, Keynes finally abandoned this revolution in method and returned to the more classical method of equilibrium analysis.

This episode illustrates well the difficulty and problems of process analysis. Keynes had enough reason to abandon sequence analysis in favor of equilibrium analysis. And yet this is the route we must take if we are to make economics a real science, both in the monetary and the evolutionary sense.

Is there any prospect of success? I dare to say "yes!" In the time of Keynes, Robertson, Hawtrey, and the Stockholm School, they had practically no tools to analyze even a little complicated process. We now have many tools. The most important and universal tool for process analysis must be computer simulation. Many varieties of agent-based simulation are now developed (Shiozawa 2016b). Other new tools comprise "bang-bang" control theory, dynamical systems theory, inventory control theory, stationary and nonstationary stochastic theory, and the nonlinear complexity sciences, besides mathematics in general.

The fact that we have many tools of analysis does not imply that our study will be organized in a good framework. We must be especially aware of risks that equilibrium framework infiltrate into our analysis and contaminate it. A typical

[30] Keynes might have named Ohlin as representative of Stockholm school economists.

[31] Kohn (1986) guesses that Keynes meant by the epithet "general" (in the title of *General Theory*) a monetary theory which he deemed more general than the real-exchange economics.

example may be J. R. Hicks's notion of a *temporary equilibrium*. This notion exists in Keynes's *The General Theory*, but it was Hicks who gave a precise concept of temporary equilibrium and the shift of the equilibrium.

Hicks elaborated the concept of temporary equilibrium in his *Value and Capital* (Hicks 1939). He considered the usefulness of this concept in his later writings. Reservations Hicks had were of three types: conception of uncertainty, assumption of perfect competition, and flexible prices (De Vroey 1999, p. 33. See also Hicks 1991). However, when building a true process analysis framework, these are not crucial issues. The main trouble with Hicks' temporary equilibrium is that it is a mixture of decision-making and negotiation without explicit description of the process. A typical example is the determination of price by demand and supply. Hicks himself worries about the flexible price assumption but does not inquire how these prices are determined. Are these prices natural phenomena? If they are not, and are determined by some agents, it is necessary to clarify how this behavioral process of price determination proceeds.

The spirit of process analysis is to clarify the time structure in which all decision-making and information transfers occur. In other words, it is to clarify how and in what order relevant variables are determined. To give effect to achieving this goal, we must adhere to two principles.

1. Never use the variables of future dates in the determination of present variables. Time order is the most important imperative that we must not violate.
2. All variables are either determined by physical relations from other variables or determined by some agent.

The assumption that prices are determined by the law of demand and supply violates the above two principles. First, how are the time orders of demand, supply, and price of a commodity sequenced? How are they determined? Standard formulation assumes that a price is announced by an auctioneer and consumers and producers react to the price. Who is an auctioneer? Except in the case of an organized market such as a stock market, no such agents exist in the economy. How can we know the total sums of demand and supply? By whom and by what means are they calculated? What happens when the demand and supply are not equal? Standard formulation assumes that the auctioneer tries again to announce a second price and consumers and producers respond to this announcement.

When does this process come to an end? Process analysis is not the method for following a virtual time series. It follows real time to explain what actually happens. Every determination must also be made within a predetermined lapse of time. Of course, some decisions can be postponed until some convenient opportunity arrives. But even in that case, the decision to postpone a decision is actually made. In the concept of temporary equilibrium, the important process of price determination remains in a black box. A time process that requires an infinite length of time is inserted in a temporary equilibrium, and few economists question this absurdity. We are too much accustomed to the mythology of Walrasian groping. Process analysis is a way to demolish this firmly established but completely misleading custom in economic thinking.

In recent days, "expectation" is the topic which appears in almost all economic arguments. This was one of the main themes of Abenomics arguments. Some economists talk about the necessity to act on the expectation of an inflation rate so that the expected interest rate is then deemed too low to stimulate investments when it became comparable with the expected inflation rate. Recent macroeconomic models have explicit variables that represent peoples' expectation, and those variables play an important role in the determination of real variables like investments and production. They may be right. However, from the evolutionary point of view, expectation cannot play such an important role. All economic agents are adaptive actors who change their expectations adaptively. In particular, people adjust their expectation each time they experience disappointment. In this adjustment, the effects of their changed expectations are then reliably included. However, if this adjustment process works, the probability of the expectation being an accurate forecast must not be very high. We are very often disappointed when we act on our expectations. Present macroeconomics ignores this fact and puts too big a weight on fragile expectations.[32]

Over reliance on expectations reveals the rationalist world view embedded in all neoclassical economics. It sees an economic process as one that is governed by the rational calculation of human agents. As we have seen in Sect. 1.2, this is an apparent misunderstanding. It is the outer objective world which "calculates," not the human agent. Section 1.3 revealed that when human agents have significant limits in three critical capabilities, they then behave just like animals do. They calculate but only frugally. Confusion exists concerning the role of expectation and what might be named *anticipated preparedness*. We prepare for future events, but normally we do not calculate the probability distribution of what may happen in the future. There are such big uncertainties, and it is not wise to act on the calculation of expected returns. In real life, we anticipate various cases that will happen and prepare for the time when one of the cases occurs. This is anticipated preparedness. If we prepare for more cases, we are safer because the chance that an anticipated case happens will be bigger. This is another form of the repertoire of behaviors. Anticipated preparedness means we possess an action plan when an anticipated case happens.

I have talked long about expectations. It is because some economists contend that expectation makes it difficult to follow the first principle of process analysis, and in view of the importance of expectation, this is therefore a fatal weakness of process analysis. This contention is based on two misunderstandings. First, expectation of what happens at time $t + F$ is a variable in the mind of someone who lives at time t. Then, expectation is a variable at the time point t. It tells the state of mind at time t about the occurrence of some events at time $t + F$. This expectation is formed from

[32]Keynes is partly responsible for the actual state of macroeconomics because of his observations on expectation in the Chapter 12 of *The General Theory*. The present arguments are forgetting the Keynes's theory on the *weight of an inference* which is an innovative core of his *Treatise on Probability*.

the experience and information which have been obtained before time t. It has no real relationship to what will happen at time $t + F$. When the expectation is betrayed, we are then disappointed. If disappointment continues, we are motivated to change (i) our expectation formation formula and (ii) the reliability or weight of expectation. There is no reason that our rational expectations are always in harmony with actual events. Expectations may well influence people's behavior, but there is no reason that expectations of people must be identical to representative agent's expectation which is but an imaginary theory of the model builder. Expectation hypothesis is but a *theoretical necessity* for equilibrium analysis. This is the reason why the rational expectation hypothesis is necessary for the equilibrium method.[33]

1.5.2 Hierarchy of Time Spans and Controls

The unit of time plays an important role in process analysis. In practice, we must use various units of time: a second, a minute, an hour, a day, a week, a quarter, and a year. The choice of time unit depends on what process we want to analyze. If we do a motion study, the second (or one tenth of a second) would be a good unit. If we are concerned with capacity investment, perhaps a quarter or a year would suit us well. In process theory, time proceeds each time an event occurs. In this sense, steps are not necessarily equal in length. For example, customers arrive at random intervals and buy this or that item. If you take a short duration like an hour it may create a Poisson point process, but the frequency may actually change from morning to afternoon and into night. If we are concerned with investment in new factories, the time span between each investment may change from a year to 10 or 20 years.

An economy is a complex system and comprises many features. We cannot include all of these in one analysis. Therefore each analysis has its purpose. For each purpose, we should take a time unit that is appropriate. If we are examining a production process in a passenger car factory, a second or a minute will be a good unit. If we are examining a supplying process of an independent small shop, a day or a week would be a good unit. In every process, a variety of events of different time scales are running. For convenience of analysis, we condense a series of events as if it is an event at a point of time. When a shop owner is calculating if it is necessary to resupply an item next day, we may condense the series of sales of the day as if the total of all sales was made at one time. What matters for the owner is the past series of sales volumes of each whole day and not the detail of the moment of each sale. The owner will calculate an average daily sale and, having checked the amount of inventory left, is then able to judge if a new supply is to be ordered or not. This procedure of condensing time is necessary if we want to make our analysis tractable. Physicists call this procedure *coarse graining*. In process analysis, if we do not know what we are doing, we are always doing coarse graining. Appropriate coarse graining is as necessary as taking an appropriate unit of time.

---

[33]For the concept of "theoretical necessity of a theory," see Shiozawa (2016b) Sections 1 and 2.

Selection of an appropriate time unit often corresponds to the time scale of decision-making. As an organization is structured in a hierarchy, the makings of decisions are arranged in a hierarchy of time spans. If individual outputs of a process are finished as they are required, then workers in a production site will make judgments as to their next action/process at each takt time. The production manager decides how many pieces the factory makes for a given day. The factory manager decides each quarter if the factory increases the production capacity of a product, or not. The top management decides perhaps each year if the firm builds a new factory, or not.

These are only a very rough description of some of the judgments and the decision-making that takes place in a firm. The time unit of analysis must be set in such a way that it corresponds to the time span (periodicity) of the decisions concerned. For example, if we want to examine if the adjustment of the quantity produced by the total process can follow a slowly changing level of final demand (as we will do in Chap. 2, Sect. 2.7 or the following chapters), then a day or a week may be a good unit because production and inventories are adjusted every day or every week. If we are concerned with investments, a year will be a good unit. Thus, the time span hierarchy of decision-making gives us an objective basis for applying an appropriate coarse graining by selecting an appropriate unit of time.

Characteristically the time span changes according to the class of behaviors under consideration. If the time span is short, the decision-making is fast and almost automatic. The behavior appears as a simple stimulus-response pair. When a decision has something big at stake, the decision-making becomes more important, and we must spend more time and resources on it. Inevitably, deliberation and discussion time then becomes longer. A manager at higher levels of a hierarchy deals with problems of wider variety and having larger financial and other implications. The time necessary for decision-making at these levels becomes longer than is required for routine decision-making. Thus, we can observe the following tendencies at different levels of a hierarchy. The lower the level of the hierarchy, the more instantaneous and automatic decision-making becomes and the narrower is the variety of decisions. The higher the level, the decision-making becomes more complicated and difficult, the stakes higher, and the variety of decisions needed to be made larger.[34]

Beer (1981) described how a hierarchical firm functions when each level of the hierarchy has autonomy and the higher levels only intervene with lower levels on an exception basis. This image helps a lot in building a model of process analysis, because in analyzing a level of decision-making, we can often assume that the processes at the levels lower to it work as an autonomic system. The necessary things in this case to keep in mind is not to disrupt the time order of events.

An economy is a large-scale complex system. In the final analysis, everything is dependent upon everything else. Walras can be interpreted as having wanted

[34]Katona (1951) distinguished routine behavior and genuine decision. Kahneman (2003, 2011) observed the two systems: fast and slow way of thinking.

to analyze these relations. He was in part right in attempting to do so. However, he was (or more correctly economists after him were) wrong in supposing that these dependencies and linkages represent simultaneously resolved relations. An economic agent can observe only a small part of the economy and can act upon only on small number of variables. The influence of this action is then transferred step by step, along the time line, to other variables, and, in the end, it propagates to the whole economy. General equilibrium theory neglects all these processes and assumes that the final possible state is the real one experienced by the agents. If all production techniques, consumers' preferences, the states of natural resources, climates, and other factors do not change for a long time, maybe we will arrive at such a state where nobody wants to change his or her actions. Then quantities and prices will be repeated day after day. However, our economy is much more dynamic and is full of changes. It is an ever-changing world. By not taking this into account, economics loses all relevance to reality.

After general equilibrium theory became the sole framework of economic analysis, people began to forget that there is no instantaneous adjustment. All the unrealistic fantasies like no involuntary unemployment, no trade conflict, and no financial instability come from this instantaneous adjustment myth. Process analysis provides a more realistic method of examination. Although it is a big challenge, process analysis has a duty to change this state of mind among economists.

Because process analysis is a new framework, it requires new methodological concepts. As an economic agent (a person or a firm) sees and acts on a tiny part of an economy, there is always a big gap between the small world that each agent occupies and sees and the whole economy which exists objectively. The time span of human actions is not very long, whereas most of the time an economic structure changes very slowly. These disparities give rise to a gap between the perceptions of the agents, who act in the contexts of their limited locations or sites, and the economists who must observe the broad processes of the economy which result from the aggregated actions of site agents. These broad processes in turn affect the perceptions and hence actions of the site agents. Many classes, or facets, of economic activity can be considered as having two similar loosely linked domains of action and reaction. Modeling the "gaps" between these linked domains necessarily requires a new methodological concept which I named the micro-macro loop. This is the subject matter of the next subsection.

1.5.3 Micro-Macro Loops and a New Methodology

The micro-macro loop extends in two dimensions: one in time and one in space. In both cases, the term *micro-macro loop* describes a loop composed of double causal links from micro to macro and macro to micro. The link from micro to macro is easy to understand. Many social sciences (economics in particular) suppose that a social process is composed of an individual's acts. This is the stance of methodological individualism. If we stand on methodological individualism, all we have to study is to examine how individuals behave and aggregate the total process from these actions. This methodological stance is quite right so far as we confine ourselves to the study of short-time duration where we can suppose that all our behaviors are given and remain constant. However, our behavior changes in the long run, and this change occurs in an evolutionary way.

Suppose our behaviors are selected just as in the natural selection of animal species. Suppose a situation where two subspecies have similar behavior patterns and one is better adapted to the environment than the other. It is normal to think that a better adapted subspecies survives and, in the end, dominates the other subspecies. However, this selection depends on the environment. If the two subspecies are adapted to different environments, it is possible that the other subspecies comes to dominate the species according to which of the two environments prevails.

Methodological individualism is constructed by ignoring this simple fact. This methodology has continued in economics for a long time because it believed that human agents are rational enough for their behavior to be objectively based and does not depend, in general, on the features of the environment. In reality, human being's rationality is bounded and its sight is myopic. As we have discussed in Sect. 1.3, our behavior is a result of a long process of selection. Selection may be intentional and conscious, but it is often an unconscious process. That is why we are not well aware of the fact that our behavior is the result of long-term selection.

Let us cite an example. When the Japanese economic miracle was still impressive, Japanese management was praised for having some of the best practices in management science. The Japanese management style comprises three established customs: (1) life-long employment, (2) seniority-based wage and promotion system, and (3) labor-management cooperation. When the Japanese economy was growing rapidly (more than 4% per year in real terms), all went well. Many commentators argued that the three customs explain the high performance of the Japanese economy. They were right, at least in the sense that the three customs contributed positively to the Japanese economy. However, this lucky combination did not continue forever. When, in and after the 1990s, the Japanese economy stagnated for a long time, it became clear that the three customs were supported by the high growth rate. For example, many enterprises could not continue a seniority-based wage and promotion system and were obliged to modify the system in order to adapt to a low growth regime. In the high growth age, a fortunate loop existed between an individual firm's behavior and the high growth rate. The firms' behavior represented by Japanese management contributed to the high performance of the Japanese economy and the high performance made Japanese management possible and rational. There was a micro-macro loop which helped high performance of the Japanese economy. If we borrow two terms from cybernetics, the micro-macro loop was *self*-rein*forcing*. When the bubble was burst, the micro-macro loop became *self-destructive* and Japanese management was forced to change a lot.

Similar relationships between macro-features and individual behaviors can be found in various fields in an economy. Another example of a micro-macro loop is more universal and explains an important feature of the modern economy. Economics talked much about higgling and haggling in the price determination process. In reality, higgling and haggling is a behavior which is seldom observed in the everyday life of a developed economy. In everyday life, prices are fixed by sellers, and we buy this and that at given prices. This "one-price policy" was declared publicly in Japan in the late seventeenth century (c. 1673) by Mitsui Takatoshi, the founder of Mitsui group, at his shop in Edo (now Tokyo). I do not know the detailed history of the fixed price system, but people in Edo welcomed this new policy, and other shops followed Mitsui, imitating this fixed price system.[35] Now this system has spread almost everywhere except, for example, some carpet shops in some parts of South Asia and elsewhere. This fixed price system is also common in trade between firms.[36] Why did this system spread widely? No laws stipulated that it must be used. Firms have the right to negotiate with customers and to fix different prices for different customers. Perhaps, one reason for adopting this policy may be a sense of fairness. For a merchant who wants to keep their shop in business for a long time, unreasonable differentiation of customers may engender anger among their customers. Another reason for a one-price policy is efficiency. The shop owner must pay the cost of negotiation time. If there are enough customers, it would be more profitable to sell quickly at a reasonably profitable fixed price than to aim for occasional windfall profits from protracted negotiation. The policy was welcomed by customers if the fixed price was as low as other shop's prices after negotiation. For busy customers, negotiation also meant a time cost. So, both sides saw merits in the one-price policy system, and this must be the reason why the one-price policy spread all over the world.

If we stop here, this is only a simple example of an evolutionary stable strategy in the economy. Let us ask more deeply the reasons why the one-price policy spread widely and ask at the same time why in some cases higgling and haggling remains. One-price policy is profitable when the commodity has some special characteristics: first, the commodity must be reproducible; second, the stability of supply is assured; and third, the procurement price is stable.[37] If these three conditions are satisfied, and if large demand is expected, the one-price policy was a good selling strategy.[38] These conditions became common after the industrial revolution and with the availability of cheap and fast transportation. Thus, the success of the one-price policy was dependent on the general change of economic conditions. It is noteworthy that a widespread one-price policy system provides the basis for other merchants and producers to adopt the same policy, because the one-price policy system guarantees the stability of prices and supplies (the minimal price theorem of Chap. 2). If we dig into the reason, we find a (self-reinforcing) micro-macro loop in this case too.

[35]See for more information Sect. 2.2 (comment to Postulate 2) of Chap. 2.

[36]Of course, there are regular negotiations on prices between the seller and the buyer, for example, once a year. But everyday transactions proceed on a predetermined fixed price.

[37]In Chap. 2, we will present the conditions under which prices remain unchanged even if the demand flow changes.

[38]We will adopt this one-price policy as one of postulates for firms' behaviors in Chap. 2.

The existence of the micro-macro loop mechanism undermines methodological individualism, because actual individual behavior is seen as being a result of a long process of selection and is conditioned by the general features of the economic processes forming the environment for their economic actions. At the same time, the micro-macro loop destroys methodological holism. Without examining behaviors and interactions between individuals (both persons and firms), we cannot analyze what happens in the economic process. The micro-macro loop approach focuses on this two-way causation. It makes clear how both methodological individualism and holism are one-sided. When we have wanted to study social phenomena, these two methodologies have been the two alternative philosophies to follow. Process analysis with the micro-macro loop approach presents a totally new method of social investigation.

The identification of micro-macro loops in real life presents a very sound reason why we need evolutionary economics.[39] It explains why the evolutionary economics methodology is unique in enabling us to understand everyday economic processes. It explains why both methodological individualism and holism are defective. Evolutionary economics stands upon a different methodology and thus escapes from the old dichotomy of individualism and holism.

As Kohn (1986) emphasized it, true monetary analysis is only possible by process analysis. Other topics, which it is possible to examine by process analysis but not by equilibrium analysis, include circular and cumulative causation (Argyrous 1996), quantity adjustment process by means of inventories (Chaps. 3, 4, 5 and 6), effective demand constraint (Chap. 2), and the economy as a dissipative structure (Chap. 2). Now it is time to depart from general methodological arguments and go to the more concrete economic analysis which is the main theme of Chap. 2.

Acknowledgment I express my special thanks to Robin Edward Jarvis, who helped me substantially in revising the earlier draft and choosing better terms and expressions. By pointing out many unclear sentences, he also forced me to make my ideas more clear. I express my special thanks to my co-authors, Kazuhisa Taniguchi and Masashi Morioka, who have continued my earlier, but failed attempt and succeeded in establishing the basic framework that permits us to analyze economy-wide quantity adjustment processes. Without the achievements of these two, I could not have advanced firmly into process analysis. The concept of micro-macro loop was a byproduct of our co-joint research. I also thank Tetsuro Nakaoka and the late Tamito Yoshida, to whose ideas I owe much in formulating the basic forms of human behavior.

References

A'lvarez, M. C., & Ehnts, D. (2014). Samuelson and Davidson on ergodicty: A reformulation. To appear in *Journal of Post Keynesian Economics.*

Argyrous, G. (1996). Cumulative causation and industrial evolution: Kaldor's four stages of industrialization as an evolutionary model. *Journal of Economic Issues, 30*(1), 97–119.

[39]Gordon (1963) emphasized a similar loop between economic behaviors and institutional conditions.

Beer, S. (1981). *Brain of the firm* (2nd ed.). Chichester: Wiley. Paperback edition 1984.

Cohen, M. D., March, J. G., & Olsen, J. P. (1972). A garbage can model of organizational choice. *Administrative Science Quarterly, 17*(1), 1–25.

Cook, S. (2000) *The P versus NP problem*. Official problem description of the Millennium Problem of the Cray Mathematical Institute. http://www.claymath.org/sites/default/files/pvsnp.pdf

Cox, W. M., & Alm, R. (2008). *Creative destruction*. An article of The Concise Encyclopedia of Economics. http://www.econlib.org/library/Enc/CreativeDestruction.html11

Cyert, R. M., & March, J. G. (1963). *A behavioral theory of the firm*. Englewood Cliffs: Prentice-Hall.

Davidson, P. (1991). *Inflation, open economies and resources* (Vol. 2). Collected Writings of Paul Davidson, Macmillan Press.

Davidson, P. (1999). *Uncertainty, international money, employment and theory* (Vol. 3). Collected Writings of Paul Davidson, Macmillan Press in UK and Saint Martin Press in USA.

Davidson, P. (2007). *Interpreting Keynes for the 21st century: Volume 4*. Collected Writings of Paul Davidson, Palgrave Macmillan.

Davis, M. (1958). *Computability and solvability*. New York: Dover Publications.

de Vroey, M. (1999). J. R. Hicks on equilibrium and disequilibrium/value and capital revisited. *History of Economics Review,**29***, 31–44.

Ellerman, D. (2004). Parallel experimentation and the problem of variation. *Knowledge, Technology & Policy, 16*(4), 77–90.

Ellerman, D. (2014). Parallel experimentation: A basic scheme for dynamic efficiency. *Journal of Bioeconomics, 16*(3), 259–287.

Goldratt, E. M., & Cox, J. (1984). *The goal: A process of ongoing improvement*. New York: North River Press.

Gordon, R. A. (1963). Institutional elements in contemporary economics. In J. Dorfman, C. E. Ayres, N. W. Chamberlain, S. Kuznets, & R. A. Gordon (Eds.), *Institutional economics: Veblen, commons, and Mitchell reconsidered* (pp. 123–147). Berkely: University of California Press.

Hahn, F. (1984). *Equilibrium and macroeconomics*. Oxford: Basil Blackwell.

Heiner, R. A. (1983). The origin of predictable behavior. *American Economic Review, 73*(4), 560–595.

Hicks, J. R. (1991). Chapter 15: The Swedish influence on value and capital. In L. Jonung (Ed.), *The Stockholm school of economics revisited* (pp. 369–376). Cambridge: Cambridge University Press.

Hicks, J. R. (1939, 2nd ed. 1946). *Value and capital: An inquiry into some fundamental principles of economic theory*. Oxford: Clarendon Press.

Holland, J. H. (1992). Genetic algorithm: Computer programs that "evolve" in ways that resemble natural selection can solve complex problems even their creators do not fully understand. *Scientific American, 267*(1), 66–73.

IEEJ. (2010). *Shinka Gijutsu Handobukk* (in Japanese; Handbook of engineering technology: Computation and applications), three volumes. Kindai Kagakusha. 2011.

Kahneman, D. (2003). Maps of bounded rationality: Psychology for behavioral economics. *American Economic Review, 93*(5), 1449–1475.

Kahneman, D. (2011). *Thinking fast and slow*. New York: Farrar, Straus and Giroux.

Katona, F. (1951). *Psychological analysis of economic behavior*. New York: McGraw-Hill.

Keynes, J. M. (1921). *A treatise on probability*. London: Macmillan.

Keyens, J. M. (1979). The general theory and after: A supplement. In D. Moggridge (Ed.), *The collected writings of John Maynard Keynes* (Vol. 29). London: Macmillan. (for Royal Econ. Soc.).

Klarreich, E. (2018). Computer scientists close in on unique games conjecture proof: First big steps toward proving the unique games conjecture. *Quanta Magazine*. https://www.quantamagazine.org/computer-scientists-close-in-on-unique-games-conjecture-proof-20180424/

Knight, F. H. (1921). *Risk, uncertainty, and profit*. Boston/New York: Riverside Press.

Kohn, M. (1986). Monetary analysis, the equilibrium method, and Keynes's "general theory". *Journal of Political Economy, 94*(6), 1191–1224.
Koike, K. (1995). *The economics of work in Japan*. LTCB International Library Foundation.
Kuhn, H. W. (1955). The Hungarian method for the assignment problem. *Naval Research Logistic Quarterly, 2*, 83–97.
March, J. G., & Simon, H. A. (1958). *Organizations*. New York: Wiley.
Markey-Towler, B. (2018). *An architecture of the mind*. Abingdon: Routledge.
Mintzberg, H. (1973). *The nature of managerial work*. Paperback: Harpercollins College Division.
Nakaoka, T. (1971). Kōjō no Tetsugaku (in Janaese, Philosophy of factories), Heibonsha. (The title is an adaptation from Ure's *Philosophy of Manufactures*).
Nelson, R. R., & Winter, S. G. (1974). Neoclassical vs. evolutionary theories of economic growth: Critique and prospectus. *The Economic Journal, 84*(336), 886–905.
Nelson, R. R., & Winter, S. G. (1982). *An evolutionary theory of economic change*. Cambridge, MA: The Belknap Press of Harvard University Press.
Pak, I. (2000). Four questions on Birkhoff polytope. *Annals of Combinatorics, 4*(2000), 83–90.
Popper, K. (1976). *Unended quest: An intellectual autobiography*. The Open Court Publishing, La Salle, Ill. Chap. 38 World 3 or the Third World.
Rüting, T. (2004). Jakob von Uexküll: Theoretical biology, biocybernetics and biosemiotics. *European Communications in Mathematical and Theoretical Biology, 6*, 11–16.
Ryle, G. (2009[1949]). *Concept of mind*. 60th anniversary version, Routledge.
Samuelson, P. A. (1968). What classical and neo-classical monetary theory really was. *Canadian Journal of Economics, 1*(1), 1–15.
Samuelson, P. A. (1969). Classical and neoclassical theory. In R. W. Clower (Ed.), *Monetary theory* (pp. 170–190). Harmondsworth: Penguin.
Schumpeter, J. A. (1950 [1942]). *Capitalism, socialism and democracy* (3rd ed.). New York: Harper and Row.
Shiozawa, Y. (1989). The primacy of stationarity: A case against general equilibrium theory. *Osaka City University Economic Review, 24*(1), 85–110.
Shiozawa, Y. (1990). Shijō no Chitsujogaku/Han-kinkō kara Fukuzatuskei e (in Japanese: *The science of market order: From anti-equilibrium to complexity*), Chikuma Shobō.
Shiozawa, Y. (1999). Economics and accounting: A comparison between philosophical backgrounds of the two disciplines in view of complexity theory. *Accounting Auditing and Accountability Journal, 12*(1), 19–38.
Shiozawa, Y. (2004). Evolutionary economics in the 21st century: A manifesto. *Evolutionary and Institutional Economics Review, 1*(1), 5–47.
Shiozawa, Y. (2006). General introduction. In Japan Association for Evolutionary Economics (Ed.), *Handbook of evolutionary economics* (In Japanese: Shinka Keizaigaku Handobukku), Kyoritsu Shuppan, pp.4–134.
Shiozawa, Y. (2008). Chapter 6: Possibility and meaning of the U-Mart. In Y. Shiozawa et al. (Eds.), *Artificial market experiments with the U-Mart system* (pp. 113–132). Tokyo: Springer.
Shiozawa, Y. (2016a). Chapter 8: The revival of classical theory of values. In Yokokawa et al. (Eds.), *The rejuvenation of political economy* (pp. 151–172). Oxon/New York: Routledge.
Shiozawa, Y. (2016b). Chapter 1: A guided tour of the backside of agent-based simulations. In H. Kita & K. Tanigichi (Eds.), *Realistic simulation of financial markets*. Tokyo: Springer.
Simon, H. A. (1962). The architecture of complexity. *Proceedings of the American Philosophical Society, 106*(6), 467–482.
Simon, H. A. (1979). Chapter 8: The meaning of causal ordering. In R. K. Merton, J. S. Coleman, & P. H. Rossi (Eds.), *Qualitative and quantitative social research: Papers in Honor of Paul F. Lazarsfeld* (pp. 65–81). New York: Free Press.
Simon, H. A. (1997[1945]). *Administrative behavior* (4th ed.). New York: The Free Press.
Solow, R. M. (1990). Reactions to conference papers, Chapter 12 of Diamond, P.A. (Ed.) 1990 *Growth, productivity, unemployment: Essays to celebrate Bob Solow's birthday*. MIT Press, pp. 221–229.

Trevisan, L. (2012). On Khot's unique game conjecture. *Bulletin (New Series) of the American Mathematical Society, 49*(1), 91–111.
von Neumann, J., & Morgenstern, O. (1953). *Theory of games and economic behavior*. Princeton: Princeton University Press.
von Uexküll, J. (1920). *Theoretische biologie*. Berlin: Verlag von Gebrüder Paetel. English translation: Theoretical Biology, New York: Harcourt, Brace & Co., 1926, p. 79.
von Uexküll, J. (1992[1934]). A stroll through the worlds of animals and men. *Semiotics, 89* (4), 317–377. Japanese translation was published in 1973 and now available in Iwanami Bunko.
Weick, K. E. (1976). Educational organizations as loosely coupled systems. *Administrative Science Quarterly, 21*(1), 1–19.
Yoshida, T. (1990). *Jiko-soshikika no Jōhō Kagaku* (in Japanese: *Information science of self-organization*), Shinyosha.
Yoshida, M. (1997). *Keynes: Rekishiteki jikan kara fukizatsukei e* (in Japanese: *Keynes: From historical time to complexity systems*), Nihon Keizai Hyoronsha.

Chapter 2
A Large Economic System with Minimally Rational Agents

Abstract Based on the idea of basic separation of price and quantity adjustments, this chapter presents a new picture on how an economy as big as the world ordinarily works by the actions of agents whose capability is limited in rationality, sight, and actions. The first part (Sects. 2.2, 2.3, 2.4, 2.5, and 2.6) is devoted to showing why prices of industrial goods are stable. It gives a reason for price stability that is completely different from the standard menu-cost explanations. Section 2.7, which is an introduction to Chaps. 3, 4, 5, and 6, explains the mechanism by which the quantity adjustment proceeds in the economy as a whole. The result obtained in this chapter (and this book) is of paramount significance for the economics of the market economy, because this is the first result after Arrow and Debreu's general competitive model that shows that "a social system moved by independent actions in pursuit of different values" can work without assuming an unrealistic capability for infinite rationality and complete information.

Keywords Price stability · Quantity adjustment · Separation of price and quantity · Process analysis · New theory of value

2.1 Introduction

In this chapter, we adopt the axiomatic method. However, when assuming postulates we do not mean that they are valid for all situations and for all times. Postulates are chosen so as to show the main mechanisms by which the modern market economy works. In this regard, we may cite Ricardo's term "strong case" (Ricardo 1952 VIII, p. 184 Letter No.363). The set of postulates is intended to show our "strong case" in order to aid our understanding of how the huge network of production and exchanges works. We know of many cases that violate some of these postulates. In Sect. 2.5 we will argue some of those cases after we have clarified the basic working of the market economy. More general cases are left for other occasions.

When we select a set of postulates in mathematics, there are three conditions to be met: consistency (no contradiction), independence (no postulate can be deduced

Y. Shiozawa et al., *Microfoundations of Evolutionary Economics*, Evolutionary Economics and Social Complexity Science 15, https://doi.org/10.1007/978-4-431-55267-3_2

from other postulates), and fecundity (can produce interesting structure). In Classical Greece, axioms and postulates are supposed to be either self-evident or plausible without proofs. However, modern mathematics has much looser criteria than self-evidence. It simply asks whether a set of postulates produces a mathematical structure that is interesting to study. For sciences other than mathematics, a set of postulates is preferably consistent and independent.[1] Unlike mathematics, which is an abstract logical entity, economics is an empirical science and has a "real-world" object of its study, i.e., economy. To use the axiomatic method in an empirical science, it is therefore necessary that postulates are also realistic, or true, within a certain range of validity. Thus, when we choose a set of postulates in economics, we should keep in mind that it must satisfy the three conditions: consistency, independence, and reality.

The reality of postulates is the first thing we should care about.[2] It may not require a long explanation. All of us know what reality is, although we may have different opinions in concrete cases. In this chapter we assume postulates are based on economic laws which are distilled from empirical observations through a long history of argumentation. We can therefore claim that they have strong links to reality. However, to ask for a postulate to be a universal truth is impractical (perhaps impossible), because an economy has such variety that a law covering all cases becomes too complicated, just like a section in some legislative law having very many clauses but which is also full of exceptions. Using a set of such complicated postulates, although very real, does not clarify the logic of how the economy works. It is that logic which is our goal, and so we have to sacrifice such completeness for the sake of tractability and comprehensiveness. Therefore, the right choices regarding the scope of a postulate's validity are of primary importance.

We cannot dispense with arguments on each postulate. Although such arguments, directly based upon empirics, are rather rare and difficult to carry out, they are an essential part of economics. This is an aspect of the discipline which has been relatively neglected, and so it is necessary to search for suitably relevant references widely, purposively, and attentively. Even so, detailed discussion of these matters would still require a whole book. We have to reject engaging with that project here, first, due the limits of publishing space and, second, by the limits of our own capabilities.

Choosing the right scope, or range, of validity for a postulate is a difficult work because it involves choices between alternatives, each of which requires making trade-offs. For this reason a simple criterion drawn directly from reality is not always a good criterion to choose when constructing postulates. The associated complexities introduced by accepting total realism tend to obscure the fundamental effects about which we seek to postulate. As an aid to this, we adopt a new criterion by which the consequences of a postulate may be judged, other than by complete accord with reality. This criterion may be called "plausibility." It is not a criterion

[1]To prove these facts would be extremely difficult. We do not attempt to do so.

[2]Obviously we are opposed to Milton Friedman's instrumentalist view of economic theory.

completely independent from reality, but, being abstracted from it, this will often allow us to come to useful conclusions and convenient judgments as we explore and develop our body of theory.

Plausibility is closely related to discussions we made in Chap. 1. We have argued that human agents and organizations composed of human agents are under three kinds of limitation to our capabilities: limited sight, limited rationality, and the limited range over which our physical actions have direct effects. Any assumptions on human behavior should satisfy these three limitations. We call behaviors that satisfy these three limitations plausible. This is the minimum requirement for a behavioral postulate to have some claim upon reality. In view of this point, maximization assumptions are in general refused because the economic situations we face in practical life do not permit us to obtain maximal solutions. Rational behaviors assumed in neoclassical economics require competence beyond human capability and therefore cannot be adopted as valid behavioral postulates. We have argued in Chap. 1 that human behavior can be better formulated as a set of C-D transformations. This is equivalent to a set of if-then rules ordinarily used in computer programs and in particular in agent-based simulation.

2.2 A Set of Postulates We Assume in This Chapter

We try to construct a theory of the modern capitalist economy. The main agents are firms comprising those that provide services to customers. We assume the following set of postulates. A brief comment is added if necessary after each postulate.

Postulate 1 (Buy and Sell)
All exchanges are made as exchange between products (goods and services) and money.

This simply means that the economy we examine is a monetary economy. In this chapter we simply assume that money exists. Theory of money requires a special theory into which we do not enter in this chapter. If necessary, readers are requested to imagine that the economy has a banking system and firms can procure the necessary amounts of money if their production and investment plan is plausible.[3]

Postulate 2 (One-Price Policy)
Firms set a price for each of their commodities and sell their commodity at the same prefixed price to all customers for a certain period of time.

[3]Theories such as endogenous money theory, circulationist theory of money, and Modern Money Theory (as proper noun) may help readers to imagine a theory of money to be connected to the present theory.

A "one-price policy" does not imply that prices are fixed. Firms can change their product price when they judge it is necessary and opportune. In some industries, the periodicity of price changes is almost fixed. In other industries, it depends how frequently and to what extent their costs change. Despite Postulate 3, small changes in unit cost are neglected, and price is changed intermittently. Although later on we use the term as if for fixed prices (or "fixprice" after Hicks), it does not mean that the prices are constant for a long time. They change when the unit cost changes.

One-price policy has a long history. In the case of Japan, it is well known that Mitsui Takatoshi publicly announced a one-price policy when he moved his shop to Surugacho in 1683.[4] No known record is left in Europe and China, but it does not mean that firms (or shopkeepers) had not adopted the one-price policy in the seventeenth century. Such a principle may have existed tacitly but was not announced publicly. At any rate, in the nineteenth century, many big shops like department stores began to adopt the one-price policy, and it became customary across a wide range of firms. Price tagging systems came after the one-price policy.

---

[4]A copy of the publicity flyer when Mitsui Takatoshi started his business in Surugacho is transmitted to our day. As I could not have found any English paper that presents it, I reproduce here my translation of the text. The original of this flyer was lost through a series of fires. The present text is a copy that was copied by the eighth chief of the house of Mitsui in the fifth year of Kaei (1852) and is now conserved in Mitsui Bunko (Higuchi and Sato 2010). From this text of the flyer, we cannot know if Echigoya used price tags from the beginning. No words like shōfuda (price tags) are used in this flyer. There exist flyers of later years that refer to a price tag system, but the starting date of the price tag system is not well known.

- Echigoya Hachirōemon in Surugachō humbly announces:
- In this new occasion, as I have started a new endeavour and am selling any clothes at a specially cheap price, please come and buy at my store. We do no sales by visiting the home of any client. As we have fully accounted for services and costs of what we put on sale, we do not ask for a price even a penny higher than what we have fixed. Consequently, we do not abate any price even if any clients ask us to do so. Of course, we accept all prices in cash. We do not sell any good on account, even for a penny.
- Cash payment, cheap price, no markups

Clothes shop

Echigoya Hachiōemon at 2-chōme Surugachō

Note: Echigoya Hachiōemon is the business name of Mitsui Takatoshi. "Markups" here means the practice to announce a higher price than the shop expects so that it can have a discount margin in the price negotiation.

The original text in Japanese (written in a Chinese-Japanese mixed style):

駿河町越後屋八郎右衛門申上候今度私工夫を以呉服物何に不依格別下値に売出し
申候間私店に御出御買可被下候何方様にも為持遣候義は不仕候尤手間割合勘定を
以売出し候上は壱銭にても空値不申上候間御直き利被遊候而も負ハ無御座候勿論
代物は即座に御払可被下候一銭にても延金には不仕候以上

呉服物現金　　駿河町弐丁目
安売無掛値　　越後屋八郎右衛門

Postulate 3 (Price Setting)
Firms set prices by the markup principle, i.e., *by the formula (price) = (1 + markup rate)· (direct unit cost) with a predetermined markup rate.*

This pricing method is called full-cost pricing or markup pricing. All administered prices are fixed by this principle (Lee 1998).[5] We do not argue how the markup rates are determined in this chapter. The essential idea is explained in Shiozawa (2016b). For more details, see Appendix to Shiozawa (2014). We emphasize here that the markup rates depend on the market state of competition for the product. Although normally fixed conventionally, the markup rate of a product may change when the market state changes substantially, for example, by the entry of new competitors.

Throughout the history of economics, the existence of two kinds of goods with different price mechanisms was acknowledged, for example, by Michał Kalecki. Indeed, he stated that "Short-term price changes may be classified into two broad groups: those determined mainly by changes in the cost of production and those determined by changes in demand" (Kalecky 1954 p. 11). The existence of two distinct systems of price formation was rediscovered by John R. Hicks (1965) and termed *flexprice* and *fixprice* systems (Robinson 1977, p. 1328; Sawyer 1985, p. 22). However, according to Morishima (1994), Hicks invented these terms first as two conjugate methods of economic analysis, and it was only in later years that Hicks used these terms as indicating different price mechanisms which operate in different sectors and commodities. This short history reveals that it has been difficult for many theorists to understand that there are two pricing mechanism systems determining prices in a modern market economy. However, the classical economists, like David Ricardo, knew that the prices of many industrial products are normally determined by the "cost-plus" principle. It is an enigma why economics has forgotten this fundamental of the classical theory of value. Although we have no time to spend upon this inquiry, it is evident that there must have been a shift of viewpoint from an economics of production to one of exchange. According to Hicks (1976), this shift of viewpoint is the true nature of the "marginal revolution" in economics. See for more detail Shiozawa (2017b).

An implication of admitting Postulates 3 and 4 is to exclude an important part of the modern economy. As a result, at this stage, we cannot handle many types of agricultural product including fishery and mining products. Another important excluded domain is the financial economy. This exclusion is required in order to make clear the basic logic of how the modern industrial economy works. Our basic assumption is that real and financial economies follow totally different logic. It is advisable not to deal with the two at the same time from the start. Although the

[5]Lee distinguishes three pricing methods: administered prices, normal cost prices, and mark up prices. These are but the historical names used by those who studied pricing principles. Their pricing principle is the same. Variance of names is a proof that full-cost pricing was discovered many times on different occasions. We may have different definitions of the "direct unit cost," and its behavior may differ according to assumptions we adopt. See also the comments on Postulate 9.

financial economy influences it, the real economy is a relatively insulated subsystem of the total system. This is the reason why we first concentrate our efforts in real economies.

Postulate 4 (Demand for Products)
Demand for a product of a firm changes through time as a non-stationary stochastic time series, which may obey certain restrictions such as aggregate demand in the economy.

We do not enter into the analysis of internal reasons of how the aggregate demand for each product (of each firm when it is differentiated) is determined. What is certain is that neoclassical formulation of the demand function is so unsatisfactory that we cannot adopt it into our theory. As we have observed in Sect. 1.2 of Chap. 1, the utility maximization formula cannot be adopted as part of our theory because it apparently contradicts human capability.[6]

We develop no theory of demand. It does not imply that theory of demand is of no importance. It simply means that further characterization of demand is not required for our analysis. Consequently, a wide variety of demand theory can be connected to the present scheme of analysis. (See also Sect. 2.3.4).

Postulate 5 (Supply Behavior)
Firms sell their products at a fixed price for all customers and for all quantities as much as they are demanded and as long as the stock of products permits.

Postulate 6 (Role of Stocks)
Differences between production and sales are adjusted by the use of product stocks.

Postulate 7 (Production Behavior)
Firms produce as much product as sells.

Postulates 5, 6, and 7 are closely related. If firms can instantaneously change the volume of production, no problem occurs for Postulates 5 and 7. However, as production takes time, it is necessary that firms keep product stock in order to respond to procurers' demand.

Although firms keep product stock, it does not imply that firms intentionally restrict their production volume aiming to raise prices. It may be a possible strategy for a firm in some specific cases, but we exclude such a behavior as rare cases. We assume instead, as Postulates 2 and 3 stipulate, that the firm follows a one-price policy and sets the prices of products sufficiently high and, further, that the firm considers it is the best policy to sell as much as possible, when demand is expressed at the price it offers. This is a big departure from the standard viewpoint

[6]Independent from the rationality argument, Sonnenschein-Mantel-Debreu theorem tells that demand function can approximately take any form as long as it satisfies the Walras law. Despite its formalistic appearance, neoclassical theory of demand requires empirical rules such as gross substitutability hypothesis in order that it becomes a workable theory. If we recognize this fact, it is much better to leave the theory vacant for the moment and simply assume Postulate 4.

of neoclassical economics where firms are price-takers and that they produce to maximize total profit.[7]

Postulate 6 has particular significance for many service products, as they are only produced face to face. In this case, firms cannot accumulate service in advance before customers arrive to be provided with their service. When customers make a queue for a service, it is a kind of stock, but the production capacity of this "stock" is very small, because firms cannot let their customers wait for a long time. Their opportunity to build and use stocks is severely limited. Even though the basic logic is the same, what they can use is a kind of "minus stocks". In other words, each firm must prepare for a certain service production capacity, with staff waiting, or working, for all their working time. Such a firm can produce its service only when it receives customers at the place of "production." When the rate at which customer service product demand arrives begins to exceed the normal operational rate of the staff who are waiting to make the product, then back orders will accumulate.

Postulate 7 is in fact ambiguous, because this only describes an approximation of how firms behave in face of uncertain demand flows. In a concrete analysis, we must stipulate in a more exact way how firms produce their products. For example, we introduce Postulate 18 in Sect. 2.7.2 and in chapters by Masashi Morioka which permits us to examine the quantity adjustment process as a linear control process. In Chap. 6, however, Taniguchi treats the nonlinear case as the main target of analyses.

The assumption that lies under Postulate 7 is that firms can quite rapidly adjust production volume per unit time. This postulate thus excludes many agricultural products because it often takes more than a year to change production quantities. We think that there are close relationships between flexprice commodities and those that need a long time to adjust their production quantity. However we have not yet elucidated the mechanism that divides these two categories of product, i.e., fixprice products and flexprice products. When this mechanism becomes clear, we may have a more complete theory of prices.

Postulate 8 (Production Takes Time)
Production of a commodity is an action (of a team of a firm) to transform a set of input into output after an interval of time.

A production is therefore a couple of a set of inputs expressed by a vector $\bar{\mathbf{a}}$ and a set of outputs expressed by a vector $\mathbf{b}$. Some readers may feel that Postulate 8 is in contradiction to the underlying assumption of Postulate 7. In reality, the two postulates are complementary. Production takes time as Postulate 8 assumes. But Postulate 7 assumes that this production time is not so long that firms cannot change

[7]We do not think it is possible for a firm to determine the so-called profit-maximizing quantity. This kind of behavior is impossible, because the cost function does not behave as the standard theory assumes. In the typical situation, the marginal cost remains constant until the production reaches full capacity. Thus the average cost is decreasing if we take into account the fixed cost. We assume the production firm operates under the law of increasing returns.

production volume within a period of time short enough to respond to changes in the demand flow.

The main implication of Postulate 8 is the requirement that we should not disturb the time order of inputs and outputs. This is in complete contradiction with Arrow and Hahn's (1971) assumption that "production and all other economic activity is timeless; inputs and outputs are contemporaneous" (p. 53). See Petri (2016, Sect. 10).

Postulate 9 (Production Technique)
A production technique is a knowledge that makes productions belonging to it possible. The set of productions belonging to a production technique is expressed by a set of nonnegative multiples of a production. Each firm has a finite set of production techniques and can choose one of them for actual production of a good.

A production technique is an abstract entity. It is all of the knowledge of the resources, processes, techniques, tools, and equipment, including the skills and experience of the firm's production team, that are available to do the production work for any of the goods the technique is capable of producing. Postulate 9 stipulates the unit of production technique and how it can be expressed. If a production $(\bar{\mathbf{a}}, \mathbf{b})$ belongs to production technique h, any nonnegative multiple $s\ (\bar{\mathbf{a}}, \mathbf{b})$ $(s \geq 0)$ belongs to the same production technique h. Thus production $(\bar{\mathbf{a}}, \mathbf{b})$ can be a representative of a production technique. In such a point of view, each entry of the vector is called input or output coefficient. Postulate 9 claims a strong concept for the nature of a production technique because it implies that all production belonging to h has a form $s\ (\bar{\mathbf{a}}, \mathbf{b})$. This signifies that two productions must belong to different production techniques when they are not proportional.

This concept of production technique is in sharp contrast with the neoclassical notion of a production technique which is expressed by a production function. Such a production function assumes that there is a continuum of production techniques in the above-defined sense. We omit this assumption because it is not at all realistic. Postulate 9 assumes that a firm (by consequence a society as a whole) possesses a finite number of production techniques. However, this part of Postulate 9 can easily be relaxed. In fact, all arguments in this chapter can be generalized when we assume that the set of production techniques is (topologically) closed, instead of assuming it to be finite. But explanations become much longer and more complicated. This is the reason why, for the time being, we simply assume that firms have a finite set of production techniques. The possibility of choice of production techniques does not necessarily imply substitution of inputs and price change. The *minimal price theorem* still holds even in the case where there is a continuum of production techniques. In the international trade situation, a similar result obtains, but we omit all these arguments on continuum of production techniques, because we do not think it important.

Postulate 10 (Production of Commodities by Means of Commodities)
Except labor, all inputs to any production are themselves products of production.

Postulate 11 (Necessity of Labor)
Labor is the only input which is not produced in a production process. It is directly or indirectly necessary for the production of any product.

The notion that labor is indirectly necessary is complex and necessitates a long exposition. This notion is necessary when we want to examine production processes like wine production which necessitates aging but without applying any labor input over long spans of time. For the details, see Shiozawa (1983a, Sect. 19). To avoid complication, we often assume in the following that labor is directly necessary for all processes, and we cite this as the strong version of Postulate 11. It means that labor input coefficients are positive for any production techniques.

From Postulates 10 and 11, input vector $\bar{\mathbf{a}}$ has a special entry which does not appear in output vector $\mathbf{b}$. It is convenient to write a production or coefficient vector as $(t, \mathbf{a}, \mathbf{b})$ instead of writing $(\bar{\mathbf{a}}, \mathbf{b})$ by explicating labor input t.

Postulates 10 and 11 stipulate the major characteristics of the system we observe. This system is usually called the *capitalist production system*. Postulate 11 assumes that we are in an economy where there is a large pool of workers who are ready to be employed as wage workers. This is the prerequisite of a capitalist production system. This state of society emerged after a long historical evolution in people's attitudes before the *industrial revolution*. De Vries called this change of society the *industrious revolution* (de Vries 2008). The "production" of a labor force is accomplished outside a capitalist production system, normally in families or households with or without the support of the society. In this sense, the labor force is the unique primary factor that a capitalist production system cannot produce. Unpaid family labor and family and social education are prerequisite conditions for the "production" of good labor force and thus of industrial capitalism.

Postulate 12 (Industrial Production)
Let T be a set of production techniques. A production $(t, \mathbf{a}, \mathbf{b})$ is *possible* by the technology T when $(t, \mathbf{a}, \mathbf{b})$ is a sum of productions which belong to a production technique in T. It is *realizable* when it is possible, stays within the limits fixed by production capacity, and when sufficient input is available.

When input prices remain constant, this postulate assures that the direct unit cost is constant. Calculation of the unit cost depends on a set of accounting rules. It is noted that the direct unit cost does not include the "contribution" of the fixed costs. If we take this into consideration, the total unit cost is normally decreasing, because the fixed cost is allocated to each product by adding average fixed cost. As the average fixed cost changes when the production volume changes, the total unit cost and the average cost are variable. This is the reason we described in Postulate 4 that prices are multiples of the direct unit cost. Only with this stipulation can product prices be constant irrespective of production volume.

Takahiro Fujimoto believes the notions of average unit cost and direct unit cost are not sufficiently good criteria to induce production staff at the production site to improve their working practices. In the case of average unit cost, an incentive operates that is more likely to produce more than necessary and to accumulate excess stocks of product. The direct unit cost does not correctly reflect the cost related to the employment of facilities (machines and installations) and does not reflect productivity improvements from reducing attributable production facility costs per unit of production. He is therefore proposing the concept of *total direct cost* by charging costs for using facilities (Fujimoto 2012). The charging rate per unit of time for facility utilization is determined by the board of directors (or a director of higher rank) in view of expected normal production volume for a period of time. Then, the total direct unit cost reflects more exactly the productivity of the production site. This is an idea that can be used for the pricing calculation. In fact, we can employ the following formula in place of the formula of Postulate 4:

$$(\text{price}) = (1 + \text{markup rate}) \cdot (\text{total direct unit cost})$$

The markup rate in the new formula must be set smaller than that used in the formula in Postulate 3. The new formula is better than the old one in the sense that it can reflect the reduction of the fixed cost more explicitly. The new formula can be interpreted as being a refined version of *normal cost pricing* (Andrews 1949; Lee 1998 Part II). All complications concerning variable unit cost can be easily treated with this idea.

Those economists who are accustomed to neoclassical economics may think that the characterization of modern industrial production in Postulate 12 is too restrictive because it neglects the possibility of input substitution. They are wrong because the possibility of input substitution is considered in the form of the choice of production techniques, which will be the major problem considered in this chapter. See Sects. 2.4, 2.5, and 2.6.

Postulate 13 (No Joint Production, or Single-Product Processes)
The net produce of a production technique is composed of a single commodity.

Postulate 14 (Homogeneous Labor)
Labor in a country is supposed to be homogeneous and has a unique wage rate.

The minimal price theorem (Sects. 2.3 and 2.4) necessitates three conditions in its primitive form: (1) lack of primary factors except labor, (2) no joint production, and (3) homogeneity of labor. These conditions are assured in turn by Postulate 10, Postulate 13, and Postulate 14.

It is often argued that no joint-production assumption excludes fixed capital goods, because they must be treated as by-product at the side of principal product. Michio Morishima (1969, 1973) and Ian Steedman (1977) emphasized that joint production is the necessary assumption in order to treat capitalist production. However, it is not necessary to assume the general form of joint production. As Piero Sraffa did in his book (1960, Chap. 10), we can reduce fixed capital to the no joint-production case. We will argue this point in Sect. 2.5.3.

Postulate 14 is put in for a similar reason. This rule is an approximate one, but it is to show a strong case. We observe quite a big disparity between wage rates among workers. However, as we are more concerned with the economic mechanism that determines the real wage level, we assume these postulates to avoid unnecessary complication of our analysis. It will be a target of this study's next stage to investigate how relative wage rates between different types of workers are determined. For the moment, we have to admit that we do not know well enough how to incorporate the wage determination mechanism into our system.

It is widely observed that relative wage rates for different categories of the workforce remain stable for relatively long periods of time. We may adopt this as a postulate instead of Postulate 14. No big problem occurs with this new postulate. We will consider this possibility when it is opportune (Sect. 2.5.4). As long as we can suppose that each skill category of the workforce is available when it is needed, there is no change of logic in the construction of our theory.

Postulate 10 excludes primary factors such as land and mines. We will argue how this assumption can be incorporated in our system in Sect. 2.5.5 where we argue for generalizations of the minimal price theorem.

Postulate 15 (Productivity)
The total set of production techniques is productive in the sense that a positive net product is possible if labor is supplied.

The word "productive" is not precisely defined here. For details see Definition 4.3 in Sect. 2.4. When we say a set of production techniques is productive, it means that the set of production techniques are productive in the extended sense of Definition 4.3.

Postulate 16 (Availability)
Except exceptional situations, firms can procure any amount of commodity at a fixed price.

These two postulates are properties of the total system. Postulate 15 is rather trivial, because the productivity of the total system is logically derived if a positive net output (for all products) is obtained.

Postulate 16 is more complicated. It depends on the working of the whole system. We will show in Sect. 2.7 that Postulate 16 is in fact assured when Postulate 17 holds. But Postulate 16 is necessary, because each firm behaves with the assumption that it can be assumed. We should better say that Postulate 16 is a part of *micro-macro loop* (see Chap. 1, Sect. 1.5.3).

Postulate 17 (Capacity Building)
If a stable increase of demand is expected from the past trend, the firm will invest to increase production capacity in such a way that demand normally remains within a certain band within that capacity.

If a firm cannot satisfy the demand for its product through lack of capacity, it is a loss for the firm and is a situation that it plans to avoid as far as possible. However, this is not an absolute imperative, because to keep too much capacity available as a buffer reduces the profit rate. Because demand growth is highly uncertain, decision-making concerning capacity building requires high-level judgment. Economic theory cannot predetermine how high-level decision-making agents behave. We must satisfy ourselves by accepting that firms try to find their capacity-building rule by trial and error.

Postulate 17 gives a new picture for firms' capacity investment behavior. We can see that interest rates (short-term and long-term) play no major role in determining the volume of investment as far as investment in industry is concerned. The converse of the contrapositive of Postulate 17 signifies that even if the interest rates are nearly equal to zero, firms do not necessarily invest in capacity building. This fact is firmly confirmed by the 5-year experience of Abenomics (2013–2018). Mr. Kuroda, appointed as governor of the Bank of Japan by Prime Minister Abe, introduced the zero interest-rate policy, but a major part of most firms' investment was occupied by replacement investment (see Sect. 2.7.6). This simple observation changes tremendously our understanding of how the macroeconomy behaves. Thus, our system of postulates presents the significant possibility of much innovation in this area of macroeconomics.

In our system of postulates, no explicit mention was made of technological change. This does not mean that our system excludes technological change. On the contrary, it gives a solid framework to examine the various effects of technological changes. To characterize technological change is no easy work. We assume no particular form of technological change or progress. But, our theory is well adapted to analyze the effects of technological changes, because our theory is valid for any set of production techniques with an arbitrarily large number of products. If once the set of products and the sets of production techniques are given, we can argue for the system of prices that emerges and tell which production techniques become competitive. If we can know the demand movements, we can argue employment and economic growth. The evolution of technology is weakly conditioned by the price system, but our theory is well organized to analyze the co-evolution between prices and production techniques. In this sense, our theory based on the above 17 Postulates has a good possibility to be a dynamic and useful theory.

2.3 Some Characteristic Features of the System

The system described by the 17 postulates in Sect. 2.2 should be interpreted in a proper way to reflect the characteristics of an economic system. It is clear that it is not a complete system, such as Hilbert's axiomatic system for Euclidean geometry. There are infinitely many economies that satisfy the 17 postulates. It is much more similar to the axioms of groups or the axioms of topological space. There are infinitely many groups, or topological spaces, that satisfy axioms of each class. However, we can study each of their instances without making special reference to any concrete instance. Our study can be divided into two aspects. We can study instances abstractly as an entity which satisfies a set of axioms. We can add supplementary assumptions on the behavior of each agent and the conditions that restrict the actions of firms and people. In fact, we did adopt a new postulate on firms' inventory policy in Sect. 2.7. We can also connect the present system to another system. For example, this chapter is exclusively concerned with production, exchange, and consumption or in short with the real economy as compared to the financial economy. It is possible that the present theory is able to be successfully connected to a theory of financial economy, although it may not be an easy task.

In this section, we present some characteristic features and underlying methodological assumptions of our system before developing theories in a more concrete way in the next sections.

2.3.1 *Separation of Price and Quantity Adjustment*

The most distinguishing feature of the new system lies in the separation of price and quantity adjustment. This does not mean that prices and quantities are unrelated. It means that prices are basically determined independently of actual quantities of demand and production. At a constant price demand for a product changes through time. This simple fact, which is observed everyday in the market economy, is neglected by the traditional theories. Prices do change through time, but for different reasons than those imagined in the standard demand and supply framework. Product prices change according to the changes in their unit cost. There are many causes that induce it. A big change in wage rates and the prices of input goods will change the unit cost. A change in productivity also changes the unit cost. On rarer occasions, a change in the competitive situation may change the markup rates.

Separation of price and quantity adjustment is not an absolute rule without any exceptions. Only in some exceptional cases may the price change due to a situation more concerned with consideration of the quantity demanded. For example, when a firm experiences a big surge of unexpected demand, and if it exceeds their production capacity, the firm has three options to take: (1) ask its customers to wait until sufficient quantity is produced, (2) ask competitors to provide some part of their products, and (3) raise the product price in order to screen out some part of the demand. The third method is always possible, but it is not certain for a firm whether this method is the best option to take. If production is limited by the shortage of primary materials, the third option will be the best. The first and second methods are measures to smooth fluctuations in demand and are not suitable when faced with a shortage of primary materials.

2.3.2 *Quantity Adjustment*

Neoclassical theory assumes that prices adjust to the demand for and supply of a product and that (near) equality of the two is obtained when prices are fixed appropriately. Our vision contrasts strongly with this view by assuming a totally different mechanism for quantity adjustment. The main logic is expressed by Postulates 5, 6, and 7. Producers adjust their production volume per unit of time so that equality of demand and supply is obtained. However, there are several obstructions to achieving this ideal. Production takes time (Postulate 8). Change in a production schedule will be reflected only after a certain period of producing the product.[8] A change of production volume per unit time often requires supplementary costs, i.e., the adjustment costs of changing the production speed. Thus, adjustment of production volume per unit of time is not sufficient to make Postulate 5 effective. It is necessary for firms (producer firms and distributors) to keep certain amounts of product stock.

Stocks or inventories are ubiquitous. An economy is a giant network of production and exchange. It is impossible to adjust all parts of the economy at one stroke. Human agents have limited capability as is argued in Chap. 1. They can each influence only a small part of the whole system, and we must admit to having only a small margin of freedom at each connection with it. Stocks of product, completed to a certain stage of production, provide the production process capacity which permits small differences between production rate and sales demand to be accommodated. At each connecting point of different production processes within a production system are needed some amount of intermediate goods in process, some of which may only be waiting for their final production process, that of delivery to their point of "final exchange." The Toyota Production System aimed to reduce these buffer stocks to the minimum, but it could not abolish the stock itself. For any big system to work, it needs to be a loosely connected system (see Chap. 1). Does such a system work as we expect? This is the theme of Sect. 2.7 (Sect. 2.7.4, in particular, and of subsequent chapters by Masashi Morioka and Kazuhisa Taniguchi).

2.3.3 Price Adjustment

We do not assume that prices play the role of equalizing demand and supply. In other words, prices are not the main agents which bring demand and supply into equality.[9] In our system, it is the function of producing firms (and selling shops) that equalize supply and demand by adjusting their production in response to the demand expressed in the market. This does not mean that prices play no function other than that they give the ratio of exchange in a market economy. On the contrary, prices play a crucially important role for the working of a capitalist economy. Prices give a unique criterion by which to judge whether a new production technique is better than existing ones. Capitalism developed rapidly by this criterion. Its efficiency does not uniquely lie in its contribution to the efficiency of resource allocation. Capitalism

[8]The concept of *production period* has a meaning here that is different from the same term in Austrian economics, in which the production period of a product means the total labor time (direct and indirect) for the production. We use it always as having the meaning of the span of time from input to output of a production process.

[9]This does not mean that we deny the near equality of demand and supply. We simply claim that the traditional formulation or interpretation of the law of demand and supply is completely misguiding.

developed by ever-evolving technological development. Through cost accounting, prices give a criterion for judging if a new production technique is better than the former ones. If the economy lacked this function of prices, it would not have developed as rapidly as we have observed in these two centuries.[10]

Prices become useful in choosing better production techniques only when they are relatively stable. The criterion for selection is that one can produce the same product more cheaply by the new production technique. If prices are volatile with large amplification, they cannot be a good criterion for any change of production techniques. For example, let us take the case of a production technique which requires building new equipment. This equipment has a lifetime of at least 5 years and sometimes of 50 years. In order that we can judge that a new production technique is better in terms of costs than the current one, it is necessary that any criterion used in this judgment remains roughly valid for more than 5 years. Stability of prices is also a prerequisite for those important activities called target costing (Monden 1995).[11] Neoclassical economics made a mistake in neglecting this crucial role of prices.

Stability of prices is important, but mainstream economics based on general equilibrium framework cannot provide a good explanation for the reason that prices do remain stable for relatively long periods.[12] In its formulation, every change in the demand changes prices. Prices remain invariant only when there is no change in demand. This means that no stability is assured since the flow of demand is always changing according to consumer whims and by various external shocks. Our system of postulates can provide a theorem by which prices do not change even when the demand structure (proportions of total demand attributed to each product) changes. This theorem is called *minimal price theory*. This theorem is explained in the next section. Its first proof is for the easier case of a closed national economy. In Sect. 2.4, it is explained that narrow assumptions can be removed to include fixed capital or durable capital goods. In Sect. 2.5, we prove that a similar theorem holds for international trade.

The theory of prices that we will develop in Sects. 2.4, 2.5, 2.6, and 2.7 has no proper name, as yet. We will call it "the new theory of value." It inherits the skeleton of the classical theory of value but contains many new aspects too (Shiozawa 2016b).[13] Therefore, it would be reasonable to give it this name.

---

[10]This is one of reasons why our theory can serve as the foundations of an evolutionary economics.

[11]Some people consider that target costing is in contradiction with full-cost pricing. They are wrong, for target costing is a series of activities before the launch of a new product, whereas the full-cost principle is applied to the production activities after the launch.

[12]Arrow-Debreu equilibrium ensures that prices have no reason to change for the markets (including futures markets) which are presently open. It tells nothing of what happens in the next market that will be open.

[13]The name "theory of value and distribution" is also often used to when referring to the "classical theory of value." But we omit the term "distribution" because our theory is a theory of value and is related to "theory of distribution" only indirectly.

2.3.4 Research Strategy

The system we describe should be understood as being a subsystem inside the total system that comprises our entire economic system. For example, we have introduced money in Postulate 1, but we have not given any specific descriptions on how money is created or controlled. From the Walrasian ideal of general equilibrium, the system should contain all aspects which are relevant to an economic system. We may pursue this ideal as a final objective of our economic research, but, as a starting point, it would be at the same time a dangerous strategy for constructing a firm scientific theory. There are big differences, in terms of clarity and tractability, between the different fields, or domains of study, existing within the total economy.

The system we have proposed in Sect. 2.2 is the system of production and exchange. It is a small part of the total economic system, which comprises financial economy, social welfare system, technology, enforcement, and others. For instance, effective enforcement assures efficiency of transactions between parties and changes the transaction costs of executing each trade. Even if we wish to consider all these aspects in a total system, it is practically impossible to do so. We have to start our economics from the firmest part of our knowledge. An attempt to wrap up all aspects of economic life in one presentation exposes the logical levels of our reasoning in its core area to being pulled down by attacks launched within areas not yet fully addressed. Our basic research strategy is to construct the firm basis of an economics from which it is possible to extend our wider knowledge and understanding of the economy. Our system is open, not only to more general fields of economy but also to new theoretical developments.

Postulates we adopted in this chapter are selected to be applicable to the most typical case. The whole set is so chosen that it reveals the fundamental logic of the working of a modern market economy. When the core theory is known, it becomes possible to adopt more complicated rules as postulates. Considering the variety of industries and the narrow range of validity of those postulates, this complexification is necessary when we want to study the economy in more detail, but it is not wise to hastily generalize from each of the postulates. We risk losing sight of the basic functioning of the economy. Our research strategy can be summarized in the following four guidelines:

Four Research Guidelines

1. *Refuse the equilibrium framework, and try to construct theories based on process analyses.*
2. *Abandon demand and supply price theory, and change over to another line of price theory called new theory of value.*
3. *Construct evolutionary analyses of behaviors, institutions, techniques, and products on the basis of the new theory of value.*
4. *Do not try to construct at once a theory that comprises all aspects of the economy. Try to find sound theories which describe specific aspects or domains of economic activity.*

Our research strategy is derived from lessons taught by the history of modern physics. Modern physics basically started with two core theories: Galileo Galilei's law of falling bodies and Johannes Kepler's laws of planetary motions. Modern physics started from these two solid results. Compared to Aristotle's all-comprising system, the starting points of modern physics were restricted to the study of two extremely special movements. However, Isaac Newton's entire system was eventually derived from these few laws.

2.4 Minimal Price Theorem (Fundamental Case)

Minimal price theorem is central to our theory of value. It is intended to represent a mechanism that great classical economists, such as David Ricardo, imagined only vaguely. It is the mechanism on which the theory is based but which they could not find. The theorem was first discovered for the differential case by Paul A. Samuelson. It was then extended to discrete cases by several economists including Tjalling Koopmans, Kenneth Arrow, and Georgescu-Roegen (Koopmans 1951). Thus this theorem started as a part of neoclassical economics. However, Samuelson and his followers did not fully appreciate the fundamental importance of their work for economics as a whole.

Some people have understood that the theorem gives the raison d'être for Leontief's input-output table.[14] Indeed, the theorem assures in certain cases that input coefficients do not change even if the final demand changes. But this is not an exact interpretation of the theorem as we shall see soon. Few heterodox economists acknowledged the importance of the theorem either, and this important theorem was forgotten after the 1960s.[15]

It is normally explained that this theorem holds when there is only one uniform primary resource and no joint production. This understanding is too restricted and ignores the possibility that this theorem can be generalized to cases where the workforce are not homogeneous and where joint production exists. Section 2.5 explains how this theorem can be extended. Section 2.6 gives a brief account of how this theorem can be extended to a form which explains international trade.

2.4.1 Historical Account

Samuelson first called his theorem the "substitution theorem" and later the "non-substitution theorem." We prefer to call it "minimal price theorem," because it

[14] Note that all four authors in Koopmans (Ed. 1951) referred to the Leontief model(s) in their titles.

[15] To be more precise, the theorem receded into the background and became seldom mentioned even in advanced microeconomics textbooks. Petri (2016, p. 18) reported that he could find no mention after 1995.

claims the existence of a system of production techniques that gives minimal prices when the wage rate is given. The system, which we call later "minimal spanning set," contains for each product a production technique that produces it. The system is chosen among the production techniques that are known to the economy. If a firm wants to change its production technique, from the one in the system to another known to the economy, it will in general increase the unit cost. The exception is the case when the two unit costs are equal. In this case, substitution of production techniques does occur, but the minimal price indicated by the system remains invariant. Thus, it is more exact to name the theorem the "minimal price theorem" than the traditional "non-substitution theorem."

The consequence of the theorem lies in the fact that prices remain constant even if demand structure (or composition of demand) changes. In addition, if the set of production techniques known to the economy remains invariant, firms have no means to efficiently switch to another production technique if minimal prices have already been attained. Because of this destructive characteristic of the minimal price theorem, neoclassical economists had a strong tendency to constrain its validity and to only use it within a limited range of economic models.

There are many economists who are against neoclassical economics and who are favorably inclined toward classical economics. Few of them clearly understood the meaning of the minimal price theorem. This is understandable because there are some clear differences between the economic visions, based upon it, that classical economists like Ricardo described and that which the theorem actually describes. In the time of Ricardo, the major part of industry was agriculture or manufactures based on agricultural production (e.g., cotton industry). Typical production periods were very long. In the case of agricultural products, the production period was 1 year. The producers could change their production plan only once a year. However, demand flow changed within the span of a year. Producers or merchants were therefore obliged to change their product prices, from month to month and more frequently, according to the fluctuations of supply and demand. Producers and intermediate merchants in the beginning of the nineteenth century were in an economy where Postulate 5 does not hold. They had to match demand and supply uniquely relying only on the use of price changes.

In this situation, classical economists had to have a two-level price theory. In the short period, it was the price that coordinated demand and supply. In the long period, production volume changed, and it reestablished the "normal price." They had two different price theories, with different adjustment mechanisms. What is important in this case is that classical economists still had an intuition that prices are in fact regulated by production costs. They knew that prices adjust demand and supply but that it is only a short-period phenomenon. They knew that there is a deeper process that regulates "normal prices" which is not a simple averaging of short-term price fluctuations taken over the long period.

A peculiarity of the history of economics is that the neoclassical revolution came about after Ricardo had already clearly established the classical theory of values. As John R. Hicks (1976) pointed out, the neoclassical revolution was a turning away from plutology (whereby economics of riches = economics of production) to catallactics (which is the economics of exchange). I have discussed this point in the comment to Postulate 3. One of the reasons (internal to economics alone) was the difficulty in extending Ricardo's theory to international trade. As I have pointed it in Shiozawa (2017b), John Stuart Mill was obliged to return to the old law of demand and supply and thus opened the way to neoclassical economics. But this difficulty has now been overcome (Shiozawa 2017a).

The minimal price theorem gives us a good interpretation of how the classical theory of values is related to our theory. It is also the key to understanding the historical development of economics.[16]

2.4.2 *The Theorem*

To state the theorem, we need some terms and their definitions.

A production technique is expressed by a couple of two vectors $(\mathbf{a}, \mathbf{b})$ where $\mathbf{a}$ is the set of input coefficients and $\mathbf{b}$ the set of output coefficients. The scale of $\mathbf{a}$ and $\mathbf{b}$ can be chosen arbitrarily, because two expressions $(\mathbf{a}, \mathbf{b})$ and $(\mathbf{a}', \mathbf{b}')$ are considered to express the same production technique when $(\mathbf{a}, \mathbf{b})$ and $(\mathbf{a}', \mathbf{b}')$ are proportional. By Postulate 10, for any production technique h, there is only one good, the net product of which is positive. If the good is numbered j, we say that it is the production technique which produces product j and denote $j = g(h)$. In other words, g is a map from the set of production techniques to the set of product numbers. In this case we can take as output coefficient vector $\mathbf{e}(j)$ the unit vector which has 1 only as the j-th entry and 0 at other places.

If we always choose $\mathbf{e}(j)$ as the output coefficient vector, a production technique which produces product j can be expressed only by a set of input coefficients. We express the set in two parts: the labor input coefficients by $u(h)$ and material input coefficients by a vector $\mathbf{a}(h)$.[17]

Each firm may have several different products and several different production techniques, each of which produces the same product. For the moment, we neglect which firm possesses which production techniques. Suppose there are in total H production techniques. Then we get a column vector $\mathbf{u}$ and a matrix A of H rows for inputs, each row of which is $u(h)$ and $\mathbf{a}(h)$, respectively.[18] We call $\mathbf{u}$ the *labor* input coefficient vector and A the *material* input coefficient matrix. The following analysis

[16]For more detailed account of the treatment of the non-substitution theorem by neoclassical economists, see Petri (2016) although I think that "long-period framework" did not help him to clarify the question. All stories should be retold in a framework of process (or sequential period) analysis.

[17]We will use a different representation in Sect. 2.6 when we argue international trade.

[18]Matrix A has H rows and N columns.

does not depend on how the product numbers are arranged. Any numbering scheme will do so long as each product number is permanently and uniquely allocated.[19]

We further assume that each product has a fixed markup rate. If the product is produced by several firms, we suppose each firm has the same markup rate for the product. When the products of the same name are produced but are differentiated by price, we suppose they are different products. In this understanding, we note $m(h)$ which is the markup rate for the product that h produces.

As we have distinguished two categories of input, we distinguish two kinds of values: (1) the wage rate and (2) the prices of products. By Postulate 14, there is only one wage rate that we denote by w. By Postulate 2, each product of a firm has a fixed price for a period, and we denote these prices by a vector $\mathbf{p} = (p_1, p_2, \ldots, p_N)$. Here we have assumed that the economy comprises N commodities (differentiating if necessary the products of different firms). The value vector is a couple of wage rate and prices. We express it as $\mathbf{v} = (w, \mathbf{p})$.[20]

The cost of production of a unit of product by production technique h is then given by

$$u(h)w + a_1(h)p_1 + \cdots + a_N(h)\ p_N.$$

We note this more simply

$$u(h)w + \langle\ \mathbf{a}(h), \mathbf{p}\ \rangle.$$

The first part is the labor cost and the second part the material cost. This is the bare unit cost as distinguished from full unit cost, which is expressed as

$$(1 + m(h))\ \{u(h)w + \langle\ \mathbf{a}(h), \mathbf{p}\ \rangle\}\ .$$

We are particularly interested in the relationship between the value of the product and the full cost of its production. When they are equal, we say that the production technique satisfies the value equation. The difference between the two is the net surplus value produced by the production technique. Thus, we can present the following definitions.

Definition 4.1 (Value Equation)
When the net surplus value is 0, we say that the production technique h satisfies the value equation. Algebraically, this means that

$$(1 + m(h))\ \{u(h)\ w + \langle\ \mathbf{a}(h), \mathbf{p}\ \rangle\} = p_{g(h)}. \tag{2.1}$$

The following terms may be foreign to many economists, but let us introduce them for the sake of brevity in expressing the theorems.

---

[19]It might be preferable to denote the labor input coefficient as a_0 or l. However, to maintain continuity with the international trade economy, we use u instead of a_0 or l. The reason to avoid l is apparent. It is confusing with 1.

[20]This expression is conveniently used when we analyze international values.

Definition 4.2 (Markup Form of a Production Technique)
An imaginary production technique $(1 + m(h))(u(h), a(h))$ *is called the markup form of the production techniques* $(u(h), a(h))$.[21] *When S is a set of production techniques* $(u(h), a(h))$, *the set* $S^{\#}$ *composed of imaginary production techniques in the markup form is called the set of production techniques in the markup form.*

Definition 4.3 (Productive in the Extended Sense)
If the set T in the markup form is productive, then T is said to be productive in the extended sense. A system of production techniques is productive if and only if there exists a subset $S = \{h\}$ *such that* $\sum_{h \in S} c(h) \cdot \{\mathbf{e}(h) - \mathbf{a}(h)\}$ *is a positive vector (a vector whose elements are all positive).*

Note that being productive in the extended sense is a stronger condition than being productive in the original sense, although this may sound contradictory to common usage.

Theorem 4.4 (Minimal Price Theorem I)[22]
Let T be the set of production techniques. When the set T is productive in the extended sense, there is a positive value vector $\mathbf{v} = (w, p_1, \ldots, p_N)$ *with a given positive wage rate w and a subset S of T, which satisfy the following conditions:*

1. *For any given product, S includes at least one production technique that produces it.*
2. *Any production techniques in S satisfy the value equation.*
3. *All other production techniques in T have the full cost which is greater than or equal to the product price.*[23]

A proof of Theorem 4.4 is given in Sect. 2.4.3. Note that the expression in Theorem 4.4 is valid for all production volumes within the available capacity. When the net output of the production is 1, then the net value is equal to the price, and the full cost is now the full unit cost.

Definition 4.5 (Spanning Set)
A set of production techniques S is said to be spanning when, for any good j, S contains at least one production technique that produces j. When S contains only one production techniques for each product, we call it a minimal spanning set.[24]

[21] Note that the output coefficient is required to be 1 even in the markup form. Shiozawa (2017a) calls this imaginary economy composed of production techniques of markup form the *equivalent economy*.

[22] This theorem assumes Postulates 3, 10, 11 (strong version), 13, and 14.

[23] In mathematical symbols, this condition is expressed by (2.6) for any production techniques *h* in *T*.

[24] The adjective "minimal" means here that the set has the minimal number of elements among the class of spanning sets.

A minimal spanning set contains as many production techniques as the number of products of the economy.

We have many variants for the minimal price theorem. A possible variant for Theorem 4.4 is to take a minimal spanning set S. For this purpose, we delete condition (1) and retain conditions (2) and (3).

Let us now select a minimal spanning set S and fix it for a while. If we restrain the vectors and matrix to rows which correspond to elements in S, we get an N-column vector $\mathbf{u} = (u(h))$ and an $N \times N$ square matrix $A = (\mathbf{a}(h))$. To make a rigorous distinction, it would be better to denote them $\mathbf{u}(S)$ and $A(S)$. But as such notations excessively complicate the symbols, we often note $\mathbf{u}$ and A by omitting (S) when it is clear that matrices are concerned with the set S.

If Theorem 4.4 holds for a minimal spanning set S, we have a matrix equation

$$(I + M)\{w\mathbf{u} + A\mathbf{p}\} = \mathbf{p}, \tag{2.2}$$

where I is a unit matrix of dimension N and M is a diagonal matrix of the same dimension whose diagonal component is $m(h)$. The vector $(w, \mathbf{p})$ defined by (2.2) is said to be associated to set S. Equation (2.2) can be transformed to equation

$$\{I - (I + M)\,A\}\ \mathbf{p} = w\,(I + M)\,\mathbf{u}. \tag{2.3}$$

The right-hand side is a positive vector, because it is greater than $w\ \mathbf{u}$ for each component (the stronger version of Postulate 11). The matrix in the left-hand side has a special form: all off-diagonal elements are zero or negative (i.e., nonpositive). It is a well-known result that such a matrix is invertible and the inverse matrix is nonnegative (nonnegative invertibility theorem).[25] Thus, we can rewrite (2.3) into the next equation:

$$\mathbf{p} = w\{I - (I + M)\,A\}^{-1}\,(I + M)\,\mathbf{u}. \tag{2.4}$$

Thus we obtain the next corollary:

Corollary 4.6 (Uniqueness of Value)
Let S be a minimal spanning set which is productive in the extended sense. Then a value vector $\mathbf{v} = (w, \mathbf{p})$ exists and satisfies condition (2) of Theorem 4.4. Such a value vector $\mathbf{v} = (w, \mathbf{p})$ is unique for a given w.

On the other hand, for a given minimal spanning set S, we can define a spanning set $S^{\&}$ composed of all production techniques that satisfy the value equation. By definition, S is a subset of $S^{\&}$, or $S^{\&}$ is a superset of S. $S^{\&}$ may include elements which do not belong to S. If the set $S^{\&}$ is not a minimal spanning set, we may

[25]This theorem is often called Hawkins-Simon theorem. A square matrix A with positive diagonals and nonpositive off-diagonal entries is nonnegatively invertible when and only when there exists a positive vector $\mathbf{u}$ such that $\mathbf{u} > \mathbf{u}\,A$. I call this theorem the "nonnegative invertibility theorem."

choose a different minimal spanning set, but the choice of the minimal spanning set does not affect the value. Whatever we choose, it gives the same vector.

The formula (2.4) is a bit complicated. If we take u and A the coefficients of production techniques in the markup form, then (2.4) can be expressed in a much simpler form:

$$\mathbf{p} = w\{I - A\}^{-1}\mathbf{u}. \tag{2.5}$$

Thus considering an imaginary economy, in the markup form, that is composed of imaginary production techniques is often helpful in calculations and for expressing theorems.

Theorem 4.4 gives a much stronger result than Corollary 4.6, because all the production techniques in T satisfy the condition (3). It is convenient to introduce a specific name to call any value vector with such a property.

Definition 4.7 (Admissible Value)
Let T be the set of production techniques known to the economy. A value vector $\mathbf{v} = (w, \mathbf{p})$ is called admissible when (1) it admits a spanning set S of competitive production techniques and (2) all production techniques h in T satisfy the condition[26]*:*

$$(1 + m(h))\,\{w\;\mathbf{u}(h) + \langle\,\mathbf{a}(h), \mathbf{p}\,\rangle\} \geqq p_{g(h)}. \tag{2.6}$$

For an admissible value $\mathbf{v} = (w, \mathbf{p})$, the set $S^{\&}$ of all production techniques that satisfy the value equation is called the set of competitive production techniques.

It is useful to note that, when a value vector $\mathbf{v} = (w, \mathbf{p})$ is admissible, the production technique which satisfies the value equation results in the minimal full cost among the production techniques producing the same product. This is easy to see. Let h and h^* be two production techniques which produce good j, and suppose h^* satisfies the value equation. Then

$$\begin{aligned}&(1 + m(h))\,\{w\;\mathbf{u}\,(h) + \langle\,\mathbf{a}(h), \mathbf{p}\,\rangle\}\\ &\quad \geqq p_{g(h)} = p_{g(h^*)} = \left(1 + m(h^*)\right)\left\{w\;\mathbf{u}(h^*) + \langle\,\mathbf{a}(h^*), \mathbf{p}\,\rangle\right\}.\end{aligned}$$

This means that h^* gives the minimal full cost among production techniques that produce product j.

Using the same nonnegative invertibility theorem, for a wage rate w, we obtain a price vector $\mathbf{p}$ for each set S by the formula (2.4) if the set is productive in the extended sense. As this price vector depends on the set S, let us write thus the defined price vector $\mathbf{p}(S, w)$. If w is fixed for the moment, we can simply express it as $\mathbf{p}(S)$.

[26]We normally assume that an admissible value possesses a spanning set of competitive production techniques. The definition 5-2 in Shiozawa and Fujimoto (2018) is not exact, because it lacks condition (1) of Definition 4.7. The true meaning of this concept becomes clear when we examine international trade situation.

The name "minimal price theorem" comes from the next theorem which is a simple corollary of Theorem 4.2.

Theorem 4.8 (Minimal Price Theorem II)
Let T be the set of production techniques which is productive in the extended sense. Then there is a spanning set S which is productive in the extended sense and the price vector* $\mathbf{p}(S^*)$ *which satisfies the condition:*

$$\mathbf{p}(S, w) \geqq \mathbf{p}(S^*, w) \tag{2.7}$$

for any minimal spanning set S which is productive in the extended sense.

Note that (2.7) is an inequality of vectors. If there is only one kind of product in our economy, Theorem 4.8 is trivial because any finite set of real numbers has a minimum. However, existence of an S^* that satisfies (2.7) defines a much stronger condition. It assures the existence of a spanning set that gives minimal prices for all goods for any spanning set which is productive in the extended sense. When S is not productive in the extended sense, we can assign infinity for some values of $\mathbf{p}(S, w)$. In this convention, we can simply say that (2.7) holds for all spanning sets.

The proof of Theorem 4.8 is easy. Let S be a spanning set which is productive in the extended sense. If S^* is the spanning set which satisfies three conditions of Theorem 4.4 and $(w, \mathbf{p}^*)$ its associated value, then, for any production technique h of S,

$$(1 + m(h)) \left\{ w \, \mathbf{u}\,(\mathrm{h}) + \langle \, \mathbf{a}(h), \mathbf{p}^* \, \rangle \right\} \geqq p*_{g(h)}.$$

If we rewrite this in the form of (2.3), this means

$$w\,(I + M)\,\mathbf{u} \geqq \{I - (I + M)\,A\}\ \mathbf{p}^*, \tag{2.8}$$

where A and M are square matrices corresponding to S. As S is supposed to be productive in the extended sense, the matrix $I–(I + M)\,A$ is nonnegatively invertible. If we apply the operator $\{I–(I + M)\,A\}^{-1}$ to both sides of (2.8) from left, we get

$$\mathbf{p}(S) = w\{I - (I + M)\,A\}^{-1}\,(I + M)\,\mathbf{u} \geqq \mathbf{p}^*.$$

This is equivalent to (2.7).

Theorem 4.9 (Covering Property)
Let T be the set of production techniques known to the economy, S be a minimal spanning set that satisfies three conditions of Theorem 4.4, and P be the production possibility set for T:*

$$P = \Big\{ \mathbf{y} = \sum\nolimits_{h \in T} s_h \, \{\mathbf{e}(h) - (1 + m(h))\,\mathbf{a}(h)\} \mid \forall \mathbf{s} = (s_h)$$
$$\sum\nolimits_{h \in T} s_h \,(1 + m(h))\ u(h) \leqq L, \mathbf{s} \geqq \mathbf{0} \Big\}.$$

Then any point **x** *in the maximal frontier of P can be produced as a net product by using production techniques h in S* and labor power L. In other words, there is a vector* $\mathbf{s} = (s_h)$ *that satisfies the conditions*

$$\sum_{h \in S^*} s_h \{\mathbf{e}(h) - (1 + m(h))\, \mathbf{a}(h)\} = \mathbf{z},\ \sum_{h \in S^*} s_h \cdot (1 + m(h))\, \mathbf{u}(h) = L, \mathbf{s} \geqq \mathbf{0}.$$

Theorem 4.9 necessitates a more delicate interpretation than usual. When we are given a set of production techniques *T*, normally we understand, by the production possibility set *P*(*T*, *L*), the set of productions to be of the form

$$P(T, L) = \left\{ \mathbf{x} = \sum_{h \in T} s_h (\mathbf{e}(h) - \mathbf{a}(h)) \mid \forall \mathbf{s} \geqq \mathbf{0} \sum_{h \in S^*} s_h \cdot u(h) \leqq L \right\}.$$

As you see by Theorem 4.9, the production possibility set defined in Theorem 4.9 is defined by using production techniques of markup form. The concept of a production possibility set depends on the set of markup rates $\{m(h) \mid h \in T\}$. If all *m*(*h*) takes the same value *m*, we can interpret *P* as a set of surplus products which can be obtained by using labor less than or equal to *L* where the surplus product is to be interpreted as net output of a proportionally growing path with growth rate *m*. Thus, in this special case, Theorem 4.4 and Theorem 4.9 show a kind of saddle point theorem. Readers not accustomed to input vectors of extended form are advised to consider first the case where *m*(*h*) is all 0 and then the uniform markup rate case.

Let us prove Theorem 4.9. For simplicity, we take an imaginary economy whose production techniques are given by those written in the markup form. Then we can assume that all markup rates are 0. If we follow the proof of Theorem 4.4 in the next subsection, there exist a positive maximal point **z** in the production possibility set *P* and a minimal spanning set *S** with labor input coefficient vector **u** and material input coefficient matrix *A* associated to *S** such that

$$\mathbf{s}^* (I - A) = \mathbf{z},\ \langle\, \mathbf{s}^*, \mathbf{u} \,\rangle = L.$$

In other expression, these equalities mean

$$\sum_{h \in S^*} s_h \{\mathbf{e}(g(h)) - \mathbf{a}(h)\} = \mathbf{z} \text{ and } \sum_{h \in S^*} s_h \{\mathbf{e}(g(h)) - \mathbf{a}(h)\} = L.$$

This is what we have to prove.

Theorem 4.9 and Theorem 4.4 signify that the change of demand has nothing to do with prices in the system and that it satisfies the postulates in Sect. 2.2. When the final demand changes, the economy can produce it as the net product of a production generated by the set *S**. Moreover, if $S^{\&}$ is the set of competitive production techniques defined by value $\mathbf{v} = (w, \mathbf{p})$ associated to *S**, then *S** is a subset of $S^{\&}$. Firms which produce good *j* have no other choice but to select a production technique in $S^{\&}$, because the production technique they employ gives the minimal full cost among all production techniques which produce *j*. If a firm tries to employ a production technique out of $S^{\&}$, then the unit cost becomes higher than to operate with a production technique in $S^{\&}$ or S^*.

We have remarked briefly on the interpretation of the minimal price theorem which suggests it gives a raison d'être for the constancy, or stability, of the input coefficients of the Leontief IO table but which is insufficiently exact. In the case where S (in Theorem 4.4) itself is a spanning set, this interpretation is exact. However, if $S \neq S^*$ or S contains more than N production techniques, firms have some degree of freedom in choosing which production technique to use. It may happen that two (or more) production techniques producing the same product have the same full cost. Of course, this can happen only by a pure coincidence. Mathematically speaking, this is a degenerated case. As a general case, we may assume that S contains only N production techniques and $S = S^*$. In this case, the minimal price theorem assures that input coefficients stay constant even if the final demand structure changes. The theorem gives assurance that input coefficients have a reasonable economic meaning. Assume that the final demand **d** changes and the production changes so as to produce **d** as the net product. Even in this case, the input coefficients remain unchanged, because the production is generated by S^*. This is important because this constancy is necessary in order that the Leontief inverse matrix and its applications have economic meanings. In an economy where input substitution is the main adjustment mechanism, as neoclassical economists assume it to be, Leontief analysis loses its significance.

2.4.3 A Brief Proof of Theorem 4.4

To simplify the description of this proof, we prove the theorem for the case where all markup rates are 0. To prove the case where $m(h)$ are positive, it is sufficient to replace **u**, A with coefficients multiplied by $1 + m(h)$.[27] In other words, take an imaginary economy composed of production techniques in the markup form, and prove the theorem for this imaginary economy. Then we get a result for the case when markup rates are positive.

[Proof of Theorem 4.4]
Let T be the set of all production techniques. Take any production technique h in T, and suppose h is expressed as a triplet of input and output coefficient vectors $u(h)$, $\mathbf{a}(h)$, and $\mathbf{e}(h)$ where $u(h)$ is by assumption a scalar. Output coefficient vector $\mathbf{e}(h)$ is taken to be the unit vector with 1 at entry $j = g(h)$. Let P be the set of net output

$$\mathbf{y} = \sum\nolimits_h s_h \{\mathbf{e}(h) - \mathbf{a}(h)\},$$

[27] In the definition of P, it is necessary to change labor input condition to $\sum h\, s_h \cdot (1 + m(h))\, u(h) \leqq L$ as we have done in Theorem 4.9.

for any nonnegative $\mathbf{s} = (s_h)$ that satisfies the labor constraint condition

$$\sum_h s_h \cdot u(h) \leqq L.$$

The summation is taken over all elements of T. The set P is a polytope in R^N. By the productivity assumption (in the extended sense), there exists a positive point $\mathbf{x}$ in P. Take a point $\mathbf{z}$ in the maximal boundary of P such that $\mathbf{z} \geqq \mathbf{x}$. By assumption, $\mathbf{z}$ is a positive vector in P. As $\mathbf{z}$ is a point of the polytope P, there exists a nonnegative vector $\mathbf{s}$ that satisfies

$$\sum_h s_h \cdot u(h) = L \quad \text{and} \quad \mathbf{z} = \sum_h s_h \{\mathbf{e}(h) - \mathbf{a}(h)\}. \tag{2.9}$$

The first relation of (2.9) holds with equality, because there would be a vector $\mathbf{z}^* \geqq \mathbf{z}$ and $\neq \mathbf{z}$ if the left-hand side of the relation is smaller than L. As $\mathbf{z}$ is a boundary point of a polytope P, a basic theorem of the theory of polytopes asserts that there exists a vector $\mathbf{p}$ (this vector may contain zero or negative entries) for a given positive number w such that it satisfies the following two conditions:

$$\langle \mathbf{z}, \mathbf{p} \rangle = w\,L \tag{2.10a}$$

and

$$\langle \mathbf{y}, \mathbf{p} \rangle \leqq w\,L \quad \text{for all } \mathbf{y} \text{ in } P. \tag{2.10b}$$

As the right constant can be an arbitrary positive number, we take it equal to $w\,L$.

From the scale vector $\mathbf{s}$ which satisfies (2.9), we define S to be the set of all production techniques h for which $s_h > 0$. For any product number j, there exists h that produces j. We prove this by contradiction. If the proposition does not hold, there is a number j, then S contains no production technique that produces product j. Then, by Postulate 10 (single-product process), the vector $\mathbf{e}(h) - \mathbf{a}(h)$ cannot be positive at the j-th entry. This contradicts that z_j is positive by definition. For any product j, as S contains at least one production technique that produces j, we can choose a minimal spanning set S^* among subsets of S. We will use the existence of S^* later.

Now let us define for all h in S,

$$\alpha_h = s_h \cdot u(h)/L.$$

Then α_h are positive. By the first equality of (2.9),

$$\sum_h \alpha_h = 1.$$

By the strong version of Postulate 11, $u(h)$ is positive. Define

$$t(h) = L/u(h). \tag{2.11}$$

Then $t(h)\,(\mathbf{e}(h) - \mathbf{a}(h))$ is an element of P and satisfies (2.10b), because $t(h)\,u(h) = L$ and satisfies the definition of P.

Let us now define

$$w(h) = \langle\, t(h)\ (\mathbf{e}(h) - \mathbf{a}(h))\,, \mathbf{p}\,\rangle\,. \tag{2.12}$$

Then, from (2.10b), for any h in P,

$$\langle\, t(h)\ (\mathbf{e}(h) - \mathbf{a}(h))\,, \mathbf{p}\,\rangle = w(h) \leqq w\,L. \tag{2.13}$$

On the other hand, from (2.10a) and the definition of $t(h)$, we have

$$\begin{aligned} \mathbf{z} &= \sum\nolimits_h s_h\,\{\mathbf{e}(h) - \mathbf{a}(h)\} = \sum\nolimits_h \{s_h u(h)/\mathrm{L}\} \cdot t(h)\,\{\mathbf{e}(h) - \mathbf{a}(h)\} \\ &= \sum\nolimits_h \alpha_h \cdot t(h)\,\{\mathbf{e}(h) - \mathbf{a}(h)\}\,. \end{aligned}$$

If we evaluate this chain equation by the positive price vector $\mathbf{p}$,

$$w\,L = \langle\, \mathbf{z}, \mathbf{p}\,\rangle = \sum\nolimits_h \alpha_h \cdot \langle\, t(h)\,\{\mathbf{e}(h) - \mathbf{a}(h)\}\,, p\,\rangle = \sum\nolimits_h \alpha_h w(h). \tag{2.14}$$

If the strict inequality (2.13) holds for at least one h in S, the right-hand side of (2.14) is strictly smaller than $w\,L$, because α_h is positive for any h in S. This is a contradiction. Thus, we have

$$w(h) = w\,L \quad \text{for all } h \text{ in } S. \tag{2.15}$$

From definition (2.11), (2.15) is equivalent to

$$\langle\, \mathbf{e}(h) - \mathbf{a}(h), \mathbf{p}\,\rangle = w\,L/t(h) = w\,u(t) \quad \text{for all } h \text{ in } S. \tag{2.16}$$

Take A and $\mathbf{u}$ as coefficient matrix and vector associated to S^*, then we get a matrix formula

$$(I - A)\ \mathbf{p} = w\,\mathbf{u}. \tag{2.17}$$

As $\mathbf{u}$ is positive, by the nonnegative invertibility theorem, $(I - A)^{-1}$ has a nonnegative inverse. Then, the price vector $\mathbf{p}$ is expressed by

$$\mathbf{p} = w\,(I - A)^{-1}\mathbf{u}. \tag{2.18}$$

Let $S^* = \mathrm{z}\,(I - A)^{-1}$. Then,

$$<\mathbf{s}, \mathbf{u}> \; = \; <\mathbf{y}(I - A)^{-1}, u> \; = \; <\mathbf{y}, (I - A)^{-1}\mathbf{u}> \; = \; <\mathbf{z}, \mathbf{p}> \; = L.$$

We have used these facts in the proof of Theorem 4.9.

Lastly, let us take any production technique $h = (u(h), \mathbf{a}(h), \mathbf{e}(h))$ in T. We have confirmed that $t(h)$ $(\mathbf{e}(h)–\mathbf{a}(h))$ is an element of P. From (2.13),

$$\langle\, t(h)\ (\mathbf{e}(h) - \mathbf{a}(h))\,, \mathbf{p}\,\rangle = w(h) \leqq wL.$$

Therefore, from (2.11),

$$\langle\, (\mathbf{e}(h) - \mathbf{a}(h))\,, \mathbf{p}\,\rangle \leqq wu(h).$$

This means that

$$wu(h) + \langle\, \mathbf{a}(h), \mathbf{p}\,\rangle \geqq \langle\, \mathbf{e}(h), \mathbf{p}\,\rangle\,.$$

Thus the condition (3) is proved for all h in T. □

2.4.4 *How Does an Economy Find Its Prices?*

The above argument in this section is concerned with the existence of a price vector with certain characteristics. In the case of the minimal price theorem, what was proved was the existence of a price vector (for a given wage rate w) and a spanning set that satisfies the conditions (1), (2), and (3) of Theorem 4.4. The next problem, naturally, is to determine how this couple of price vector and spanning set is found or established in our economy. In this subsection, we attack this problem.

The economy finds the minimal price and associated spanning set by a series of simple price adjustments. Suppose we are given an arbitrary value vector $(w, \mathbf{p}(0))$. We assume that the wage rate w is fixed throughout the series and only price vectors change. The wage rate may change, but it obscures how the price adjustment proceeds. Wage rate adjustment plays an important role when the workers' demands for a real wage rate and the markups demanded by firms are inconsistent. This inconsistency occurs when the workers are not satisfied with their wage rate relative to the price level determined by markup pricing. When workers are powerful enough to realize their demands, an endless series of wage-price adjustment spirals occurs, and the economy will be put into chronic inflation. In such a case, the real wage rate depends on the speed of wage hike realizations vis-à-vis price adjustment.[28] Here we are not concerned with such a spiral process, and we simply assume that the wage rate is constant.

The adjustment process can take two modes. One is simultaneous adjustment. The other is nonsimultaneous adjustment. The latter may be closer to reality, but we explain here how the simultaneous adjustment process proceeds. There is no

[28]See Aoki (1977) for such processes.

essential difference for the nonsimultaneous adjustment process, but it needs longer explanations, and we want to avoid that.[29]

In a simultaneous adjustment, each firm (which represents an industry) adjusts its product price assuming a price system $\mathbf{p}(n-1)$ is given. As a firm may have several production techniques that produce the same product, the firm chooses the production technique that gives the minimal cost and fixes the price by a given markup.

We use the convention that there exists a single firm that produces the product for each product. Let T be the set of production techniques and $T(j)$ be the subset of T composed of elements that produce product j. Let $\mathbf{p}(0)$ be any positive price vector. We consider a sequences of vectors $\mathbf{p}(0)$, $\mathbf{p}(1)$, ..., $\mathbf{p}(\mathrm{n})$, ... defined by the following recurrence formula. Using the markup form for the sake of simplicity, this price adjustment can be written by the formula:

$$p_j(n) = \min_{t \in T(j)} \{w\, u(t) + \langle\, \mathbf{a}(t), \mathbf{p}(n-1)\, \rangle\}.$$

When all firms make the same price adjustment, the new price vector $\mathbf{p}(n)$ is written in vector form as

$$\mathbf{p}(n) = \left(\min_{t \in T(j)} \{w\, u(t) + \langle\, \mathbf{a}(t), \mathbf{p}(n-1)\, \rangle\}\right). \tag{2.19}$$

We prove that $\mathbf{p}(n)$ tends to the minimal price $\mathbf{p}^*$ when n tends to infinity starting from any positive price vector $\mathbf{p}(0)$. In fact we have:

Theorem 4.10 (Convergence to the Minimal Price)
Let the wage rate w be fixed. If the economy is productive in the extended sense, the price adjustment process (2.19) converges to the minimal prices $\mathbf{p}^*$.

Note: In the following, we prove the case in which the number of production techniques is finite. If the set of production techniques are closed, we can get the same theorem, but it requires more complicated argument.

(Proof of Theorem 4.10)
We prove the theorem in three steps.

(First Step)
Let S be a minimal spanning set that gives the minimal price $\mathbf{p}^*$ (Theorem 4.4). Suppose we start from any positive price vector $\mathbf{p}(0)$. From the recurrence formula (2.19), all price vectors $\mathbf{p}(n)$ are positive in the sense that all elements of the vector are positive.

If t is a production technique in T, we obtain

$$p_j(n) \leqq w\, u(t) + \langle\, \mathbf{a}(t), \mathbf{p}(n-1)\, \rangle.$$

[29] A nonsimultaneous case is studied in Shiozawa (1978).

for all $t \in T(j)$. If we express by $\mathbf{u}(S)$ and $A(S)$ the vector and matrix composed of $\mathbf{u}(t)$ and $\mathbf{a}(t)$ for all t in S, then the above relations are expressed as

$$\mathbf{p}\,(n) \leqq w\,\mathbf{u}(S) + A(S)\mathbf{p}(n-1). \tag{2.19b}$$

Using the notations $\mathbf{u}(S)$ and $A(S)$, the minimal price $\mathbf{p}^*$ satisfies the following equation:

$$w\,\mathbf{u}(S) + A(S)\mathbf{p}^* = \mathbf{p}^*. \tag{2.20}$$

Then, combining the definition (2.19b) and Eq. (2.20),

$$\begin{aligned}\mathbf{p}(n) - \mathbf{p}^* &\leqq \{w\,\mathbf{u}(S) + A(S)\,\mathbf{p}\,(n-1)\} - \{w\,\mathbf{u}(S) + A(S)\,\mathbf{p}^*\} \\ &\leqq A(S)\,(\mathbf{p}\,(n-1) - \mathbf{p}^*) \leqq \ldots \leqq A(S)^n\,(\mathbf{p}(0) - \mathbf{p}^*)\,.\end{aligned}$$

As a consequence,

$$\mathbf{p}(n) \leqq \mathbf{p}^* + A(S)^n\left(\mathbf{p}(0) - \mathbf{p}^*\right). \tag{2.21}$$

The matrices $A(S)^n$ each converge to a 0 matrix when n tends to infinity.

In fact, if $\mathbf{u}(S) > 0$, Eq. (2.20) implies that $(I-A(S))$ is nonnegatively invertible and the series $I + A(S) + \ldots + A(S)^n + \ldots$ converges to $(I-A(S))^{-1}$. Then (2.21) means that the vectors $\mathbf{p}(n)$ are majorated by $\mathbf{p}^*$ with a small margin.

(Second Step)

As we have assumed that $u(t) > 0$ for all $t \in T$ (strong version of Postulate 11), there is a positive number δ such that

$$w\,u(t) \geqq \delta p_j^*. \tag{2.22}$$

for all $t \in T(j)$ and $j = 1, \ldots N$. We are assuming that T is a finite set. If we compare two sides of (2.22) for $t \in S$, δ cannot be greater than 1. In the same way, there is a positive number η for any positive vector $\mathbf{p}$ such that

$$\mathbf{p} \geqq \eta\mathbf{p}^*. \tag{2.23}$$

Without loosing generality, we can assume $\eta \leqq 1$. Remark that η depends on $\mathbf{p}$.

Let $\eta(0) = \eta$ that satisfies condition (2.23) for a given $\mathbf{p}(0)$. Define the sequence $\eta(0), \eta(1), \ldots, \eta(\mathrm{n}), \ldots$ by the recurrence formula

$$\eta(n) = (1 - \eta\,(n-1))\,\delta + \eta\,(n-1) \tag{2.24}$$

We prove the next proposition by using mathematical induction.

[Proposition].
For any positive $\mathbf{p}(0)$, let $\eta(0)$ be a positive number that satisfies estimation (2.23) for $\mathbf{p}(0)$ and δ be a positive number that satisfies condition (2.22). Then, for any $\mathbf{p}(n)$ recurrently defined by (2.19) satisfies the estimation

$$\mathbf{p}(n) \geqq \eta(n)\, \mathbf{p}^*. \tag{2.25}$$

To prove this proposition, we first confirm (2.25) holds for $n = 0$. Then assume that the estimation (2.25) is proved for $k-1$. By (2.19) and (2.25) for $n = k-1$ and for all $j = 1, \ldots, N$, we have

$$p_j\,(n) = \min_{t\in T(j)}\ \{w\ u(t) + < \mathbf{a}(t), \mathbf{p}\,(k-1) >\}$$

$$\geqq \min_{t\in T(j)}\ \left[\ (1-\eta\,(k-1))\ \ w\ u(t) + \eta\,(k-1)\left\{w\ u(t) + < \mathbf{a}(t), \mathbf{p}^* >\right\}\right]$$

$$\geqq (1-\eta\,(k-1))\ \bullet \min_{t\in T(j)}\ \{w\ u(t)\}$$

$$+\,\eta\,(k-1)\ \bullet \min_{t\in T(j)}\ \left\{w\ u(t) + < \mathbf{a}(t), \mathbf{p}^* >\right\}$$

$$\geqq (1-\eta\,(k-1))\ \ \delta \mathrm{p}^*{}_j + \eta\,(k-1)\ \ p^*{}_j$$

$$= \{(1-\eta\,(k-1))\,\delta + \eta\,(k-1)\}\ \ \mathrm{p}^*{}_j = \eta(k)\ p^*_j.$$

Thus (2.25) holds for $n = k$. By induction, the proposition holds for all n.

The recurrence formula (2.24) can be changed to the following formula:

$$1-\eta(n) = 1 - \{(1-\eta\,(n-1))\,\delta + \eta\,(n-1)\} = (1-\delta)\,(1-\eta\,(n-1))\,.$$

By induction, this signifies that

$$1-\eta(n) = (1-\delta)^n\ \ (1-\eta(0))\,, \tag{2.26}$$

for all n. Thus, $\eta(n)$ approaches to 1 when n tends to infinity. As a result, for any ε such that

$$(1-\varepsilon)\ \ \mathbf{p}^* \leqq \mathbf{p}(n)$$

when n is sufficiently big.

(Third Step)
From steps one and two, for any positive ε,
$(1-\varepsilon)\ \mathbf{p}^* \leqq \mathbf{p}(n) \leqq \mathbf{p}^* + \varepsilon 1.$

when n is sufficiently large. This means that $\mathbf{p}(n)$ tends to $\mathbf{p}^*$ when n increases infinitely. Thus we have proved that the price adjustment sequence starting any $\mathbf{p}(0)$ converges to $\mathbf{p}^*$. □

Remark 1

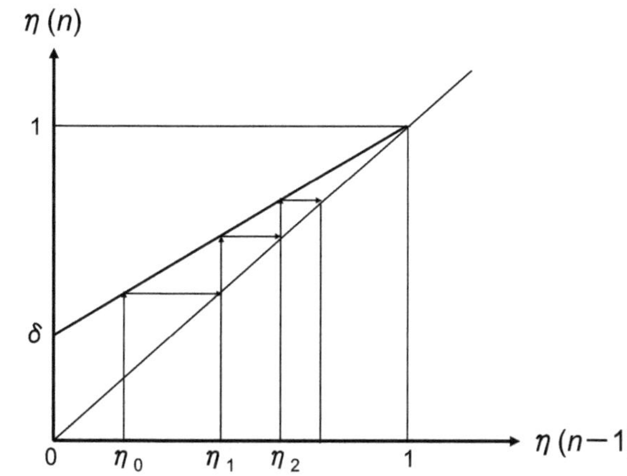

Fig. 2.1 An illustration how $\eta(n)$ tends to 1 when n increases

The behavior of the sequence can be illustrated by Fig. 2.1. Take $\eta(n-1)$ as x-axis and $\eta(n)$ as y-axis and draw a line segment $y = \delta(1-x) + x$ for $x \in [0, 1]$. Then, if we start at η_0, next η_1 is the ordinates where the vertical line $x = \eta_0$ crosses the line segment. To convert η_1 as abscissa on the x-axis, it is sufficient to take the coordinate where the horizontal line $y = \eta_1$ crosses the line $y = x$. We can continue this process recurrently. It is easy to see that η_n tends to 1 when n increases infinitely. As (2.26) shows $1-\eta(n)$ decreases by a power of $1-\delta$.

Remark 2
When the process (2.19) proceeds, it is possible to take a better δ, because we can excludes some production techniques among the possible candidates when calculating minimal (2.19). Therefore, the approximation process (2.19) accelerates than the starting points, because $\eta(n)$ defined by (2.24) can be accelerated.

2.4.5 Effects of a Change of Production Technique

The core of the new theory of value is that, in the normal situation, prices do not change with a changing flow of demand. Here a "normal situation" means that the economy satisfies three conditions, as follows:

1. Firms have enough production capacity.
2. Firms can employ a new, appropriately skilled, labor force without difficulty.
3. At constant prices, firms can purchase input goods as much as they want without delay.

In addition to these three conditions, we may add the fourth condition that there are no social or legal restrictions against an increase in production. As we are analyzing economic activities that are free from public restrictions, this condition is somewhat superfluous, so we did not add it among the list of preconditions. Condition (3) is a reconfirmation of Postulate 16.

If we observe the real economy, we can, broadly speaking, confirm that these conditions are satisfied most of the time. However, these are in sharp opposition to the conditions that are normally assumed in general equilibrium theory. The latter assumes that full employment is achieved as the normal state of the economy and that the production capacities are fully utilized. Condition (3) is supposed to be satisfied in equilibrium but under the condition that prices change to equalize demand and supply. It is ordinarily considered that without price adjustment demand and supply are not equal and in case of supply shortage firms cannot purchase input goods as much as they want. The new theory of value is constructed on the assumptions that the three conditions stated above in this Sect. 2.4.5 are satisfied. Therefore, the new theory presents an extremely different view of the normal economic state from that represented by general equilibrium theory.

However, for our assumptions to be plausible, it is not sufficient that they are observed in the real economy. Plausibility also requires the preconditions for these assumptions to be also plausible. Even so, as a theory that elucidates the mechanisms by which an economy works, this is still not sufficient. We also have to confirm why these conditions are normally expected to be satisfied. Condition (3) is especially important. How is this possible? This is the subject that we will pursue in Chaps. 3, 4, 5, and 6. Section 2.7 of this chapter is devoted to an introduction of this subject.

Condition (3) is proved on the condition that all other firms of the economy satisfy the condition (3). Thus the problem is somewhat circular. This is neither petitio principii nor circulus in probando. The task is to prove that this circular structure exists and works. To prove this *structuring structure*, the argument inevitably takes a circular form.

As far as we can assume the three conditions above, the prices do not change, even if demand changes. This conclusion is not astonishing as this is the normal situation we daily observe. The price of a product does not change for a certain span of time. Prices remain constant for 1 or 2 years for some products, but change more often for some other products. The span of time during which the price remains constant depends on various factors and we cannot say uniquely by what reason the price changes. When just one of three conditions is violated, it is always possible that there will be price changes.

There is another major reason that prices change. We have assumed that the set of production techniques are given and fixed. In a real economy, production techniques change quite rapidly. For instance, it is reported that labor productivity rises 10–15%, or more, every year, for about 3 to 5 years, whenever a firm introduces the Toyota Production System for the first time. Labor productivity rises through "learning by producing." A research study of the Boston Consulting Group claims that the cost of a product decreases almost proportionately to the reciprocal of the accumulated volume of the product's production.

This decrease of production cost occurs at constant prices. In other words, the cost changes even when the prices of input goods and wage rates remain constant. This can only happen when there is an improvement of production techniques. At least one of the input coefficients must be reduced. If the input coefficients of the new production technique are all smaller or equal to those of the old, the comparison is simple. But most often it is necessary that some input coefficients are increased in order to decrease other coefficients. For example, the processing time of a piece of work can be reduced by attaching a limit switch to a semiautomatic machine. By this device, the labor time can be reduced, but the cost to buy a limit switch increases. Thus, whether a new production technique has lower cost than that of the current one depends on the price system. If the price system changes enormously and frequently, one cannot tell whether a new production technique is an improvement or not. Thus price stability is one of the essential conditions for technical improvement to continue. However, when the production techniques are improved and costs have been reduced, prices will also be reduced, after a short delay. In a competitive economy, extra profit from cost reduction cannot be kept for a long time because competitors will also achieve similar cost savings and reduce their product prices.

This is a loop of causal chains between the price system and technical change. As we have mentioned, at the end of Sect. 2.2, they are coevolving. Prices are the criterion which tells whether a new production technique is better than the old one. The technical change induces price change, and in some rare cases the old production technique, which was once judged as high cost, becomes the cheaper technique. Even in such cases, the process shown in the previous subsection shows that the price system for a given wage rate decreases constantly whenever the set of production techniques enlarges itself adding new ones.

The efficiency of capitalist economy does not lie in the efficient allocation of scarce resources as neoclassical economists believe. Its efficiency comes from the constant technical improvement brought about by operation of the price system. The full-cost principle contributes to this total improvement system. If a monopoly firm distorts the price of a product excessively, it may slow down the innovation process, and this produces an invisible inefficiency in the economy as a whole.

2.5 Some Extensions of the Minimal Price Theorem

As noted at the beginning of Sect. 2.4, the minimal price theorem faced resistance from mainstream economists. They tried to minimize the devastating effects of the theorem. They disseminated the view that the minimal price theory holds only for an extremely restricted situation and that its theoretical significance was practically negligible. They wanted to reduce the theorem to a theoretical curiosity. However, they are wrong, as we will see in this section. Practically all major economic situations can be covered by the theorem.

Traditionally it was indicated that the minimal price theorem (or non-substitution theorem) must satisfy two crucial premises: (i) a one-factor economy and (ii) no joint production (Koopmans (Ed.) 1951, Samuelson 1961). This is true, but extensions beyond a one-factor, no joint-production economy are possible. The theme of this section is to see how the theorem can be generalized when these conditions are violated.

The first condition is violated in two different cases: (ia) nonhomogeneous labor and (ib) existence of two or more primary factors. The violation of the latter condition occurs in three different situations: (iia) co-production, (iib) multiproduct firms and industries, and (iic) fixed capital goods from which treatment joint production occurs. Arguments on each point of these problems differ greatly, and we must argue point by point. In view of the simplicity of these arguments, it is convenient to study the five problems in the following order: (1) existence of co-production, (2) multiproduct firms and industries, (3) treatment of fixed capital goods, (4) nonhomogeneous labor, and (5) multiple primary actors.

2.5.1 Co-production

When we talk about joint production, it is necessary to distinguish three different concepts of joint production:

1. By-product
2. Co-product
3. Formal treatment of fixed capital

The first two concepts are related to the physical nature of the production process, whereas the third concept derives from its formal treatment through cost accounting. We will argue on (3) in Sect. 2.5.3.

Let me explain the first two concepts. In a production process, two or more kinds of material are produced. The majority of production processes have a main product. Production volume is adjusted to follow the demand or sales volume of this main product. The materials jointly produced by the process are called by-products. They comprise various kinds of things: waste, scraps, shavings, chips, waste water, and others. Some of them can be sold at a positive value, and some others require special treatment before disposing of them into the environment. In the first case, these jointly produced materials are called by-products and have a positive market value. In the second case, the wastes have negative values. Strictly speaking, these jointly produced outputs may influence the total profit (per unit of product) positively or negatively. However, the total value of these by-products is small in comparison to the total value of the main product or even to the gross profit. They are normally neglected by "unit cost" accounting.[30]

Co-products are also materials produced by a single production process. The difference between co-products and by-products lies simply in their relative importance to the producer firm. For example, caustic soda is often produced by the electrolytic method (i.e., electrolysis of salt). This is a simple chemical process:

$$2\,\mathrm{NaCl} + 2\,\mathrm{H_2O} \rightarrow 2\,\mathrm{NaOH} + \mathrm{Cl_2} + \mathrm{H_2}.$$

Therefore, caustic soda and chlorine gas are always produced in fixed proportions. Chlorine gas was once (in the beginning of the nineteenth century) a troublesome waste, but now demand for chlorine gas is enormous. Thus for the soda-producing firms which use the electrolytic method, chlorine gas is as important as caustic soda. So caustic soda and chlorine gas are co-products. The same process produces hydrogen gas at the same time, but the total value of hydrogen gas produced is minute and it is deemed to be a by-product.

There is no absolute objective criterion by which to differentiate co-product and by-product. However, in the case of by-products, their effects upon the cost accounting determination of main product prices are negligible, and so they do not need to be treated as a subject of the minimal price theorem.

However, the case of co-products is much more damaging for the minimal price theorem. If the unit production cost remains constant, the price of each co-product may change depending on the demand. It is evident that we cannot apply the minimal price theorem to a production technique which produces co-products. We have to admit that the minimal price theorem (or more precisely stated the premises of the theorem) does not hold universally. It is not a universal law, unlike the law of universal gravitation, the law of conservation of energy (or momentum), or the second law of thermodynamics (law of increasing entropy). This nonuniversal character of the minimal price theorem does not imply that it is useless. It may be exact and useful for many cases (just like Hooke's law of elasticity). In the case of the minimal price theorem, it is important in the sense that it demonstrates the basic characteristics of the modern industrial economy. Indeed, except for some chemical industries, such as the soda industry or petroleum refining, most modern industries satisfy the two crucial premises of the minimal price theorem.

The history of co-production in economic theory is old and played an important influence on the basis of economic theory. John Stuart Mill (1848) argued "joint costs" of production in Book III, Chap. 16. The title of the chapter was "On Some Peculiar Cases of Value." Examples he pointed to there were animal husbandry cases, such as mutton and wool and also beef and hide and tallow. As for modern

---

[30] A problem remains when by-products are counted as costs or revenue in unit cost accounting. The essential question is the invertibility of matrix $B-A$ when output coefficients matrix I is replaced by B. If the total value of by-products are sufficiently small in comparison to the value of the main product, we may assume that a nonnegative matrix $(B-A)^{-1}$ exists because $B-A$ can be seen as a small perturbation of $I-A$.

industrial production, he mentioned the case of coke and coal gas, but he could cite no others. With these examples, Mill argued like this:

> Since cost of production here fails us, we must revert to a law of value anterior to cost of production, and more fundamental, the law of demand and supply. The law is, that the demand for a commodity varies with its value, and that the value adjusts itself so that the demand shall be equal to the supply. This supplies the principle of repartition which we are in quest of. (Mill 1848, III.16.5)

It is questionable if Mill really came to think that "we must revert to a law of value anterior to cost of production" just because of the existence of joint cost cases. The real issue was the problem of whether or not we should reject this core principle of Ricardian theory of value. Is Ricardian theory such a poor theory that its whole structure falls down because of a few examples of co-production? Some historians of economics took Mill's text literally. But, it is possible that Mill wanted to minimize the significance of his own drastic conversion from the one economic theory to the other.

At the beginning of his book, David Ricardo cautioned explicitly that when he spoke of laws of value, he meant always those of "such commodities only as can be increased in quantity by the exertion of human industry, and on the production of which competition operates without restraint" (Ricardo 1951, p. 12; Ch. 1, Par. 7). He knew that "there are some commodities, the value of which is determined by their scarcity alone" (ibid.; Ch. 1, Par. 5). He excluded these commodities from his theory of value, pointing that "[t]hese commodities, however, form a very small part of the mass of commodities daily exchanged in the market" (I.6). Why could not Mill also treat co-produced commodities as exceptions to the laws of value? Mill's conversion, to market-determined values, prepared the turning of economics from the classical to the neoclassical theory of value. Mill's decision was a momentous event. Examples he cited, and all other cases we can imagine, are too restricted to justify making such a grave decision. Therefore it is doubtful that Mill reverted to a law of value anterior to the cost of production just because of joint costs. It is much more plausible that his true intention was to support and camouflage his own conversion, which became necessary for him when he wanted to pursue his study of trade theory (Shiozawa 2017b).

Neoclassical economics pretends to have developed into an exact science, by adopting mathematical formulations and imitating the methodology of physics. However, we doubt if neoclassical economists have forgotten that most of the laws of physics also have strictly defined ranges of validity. Economics of the twentieth century seems to have excessively emphasized the generality of its main theory. I do not know the real reason why this has happened. It is possible that the idea of general equilibrium influenced this. It is also possible that theories like Einstein's theory of general relativity had led economists to excessively value the generality of a theory or law. If we observe the physical sciences, many of their laws have clearly restricted ranges of validity. Universal laws like the law of gravitation or law of mass and energy conservation are rather exceptional. For example, Hooke's law of elasticity is valid only, while the stress stays under the yield point. If economics is a science of real life, it is quite natural that a law or postulate admits to exceptions. Classical economists like Ricardo knew this very well. Why did neoclassical economists come to forget this important principle in the philosophy of science?

It is true that there are some important production techniques that should be treated as producing co-products, but the share they occupy in the economy is negligible. The existence of co-production cannot be a pretext to reject the validity of the minimal price theorem.

2.5.2 Multiproduct Firms and Industries

Although this is not the real problem of joint production, we add this subsection in order to avoid misconceptions among readers. The minimal price theorem assumes that the set of production techniques does not contain joint production or co-production. The fact that a firm produces many products using different production techniques causes no problem for the theorem.

When clearly considered this is the case where two different products are produced using the same production machines and installations. Even in this case, if the products can be produced at an arbitrary proportion (according to relative product demand) and production is made from a sum of inputs which is proportional to the output of each product, this can be interpreted as simple juxtaposition of two different production processes. Assignments of depreciation expenses can be done in the same way as the single product production site. This question is treated in the next subsection.

The same precautionary remark holds at the industry level. Input-output tables are now compiled by using a supply table and a use table. The numbers of industries and of commodities in those tables are normally different. Is this a reflection of the existence of joint production or simply an effect of multiproduct firms? The answer is not simple. It needs the accumulation of results from a number of empirical studies to resolve this. The point is whether inputs can be decomposed to the sum of proportional parts of each product's production volume. There may be a small number of products that we cannot decompose into single-product production (i.e., production techniques which produce a single product), but this does not reduce too much the range of validity of the minimal price theorem.

2.5.3 Fixed Capital Goods

Joint production came to be acknowledged as a matter of great importance, not because there exist production processes with co-products but because it was realized that it is necessary to use the idea of joint production to treat fixed capital goods in a formal way.

The idea is as follows. Suppose we have a fixed capital item that can be used for many years. Fixed capital as machines and equipment is an input of production.

But a peculiarity of those capital goods, as opposed to circulating capital goods, like parts and components, is that they are not totally consumed. At the end of a production period, we still have machines and equipment. Then we should consider those machines and equipment as by-products in tandem with the main product. If a fixed capital good has an eternal life and keeps its efficiency for ever, we can treat the capital we get at the end of the production period as having the same capital value as the new one had. If a fixed capital good has a finite life, we should distinguish it as having different ages. If a machine of age T is inputted, the machine we get as output is aged $T + 1$, and they should be evaluated as different products of different ages. The time unit must be taken as the same span as the unit production period.

This method was first proposed by John von Neumann (1945–1946). As indicated in the account of Postulate 13, there were at least two economists who were deeply influenced by von Neumann's treatment. One is Piero Sraffa; the other is Michio Morishima. Morishima (1969, 1974) praised this treatment of fixed capital and called this invention the *von Neumann revolution*. He claimed that what the von Neumann revolution "brought about in growth theory might be comparable with the Keynesian Revolution in static economics" (Morishima 1969, p. v). It is doubtful if von Neumann himself was aware of the significance of this treatment. The new treatment is noted in three lines as follows:

> (e) Capital goods are to be inserted on both sides of (1); wear and tear of capital goods are to be described by introducing different stages of different goods, using a separate P_i for each of these. (von Neumann 1945–1946, p. 2)

It is possible that in his understanding it was a rather trivial trick, required as a consequence of synchronizing production times which are in reality different for different production techniques. Without any comment on note (e), he only adds the next note (f):

> (f) Each process to be of unit time duration. Processes of longer to be broken down into single processes of unit duration introducing if intermediate products as additional goods. (ibid.)

The treatment proposed in (*f*) is a good method for reducing a production of long duration into a series of production techniques of unit production period. By this method, the full cost of a wine that takes 4 years for maturation instead of 1 year is counted at the time 0 as $(1 + m)^4\ c$, where c is the cost of the inputs. When we take the unit period to be a week, the full cost is calculated as $(1 + m)^{4 \cdot 52}\ c = (1 + m)^{208}\ c$ because a year contains 52 weeks.[31]

While the reduction of a long-period production process does not change it into a joint production, fixed capital equipment is only treated as joint production when it

[31] Note that markup rate is defined for a given unit production period. It changes when the unit period changes as the interest rate changes according to the time span of the period. More precisely, they must satisfy the equation $(1 + m_w)^{52} = 1 + m_a$ where m_w is the markup rate for a week and m_a for a year.

has a finite life.[32] Morishima considered that this is the only possibility for treating capital equipment in a formal way. On this understanding, Morishima thought that production techniques should necessarily include joint production. Ian Steedman also thought that testing for whether a theory of value holds for any joint-production technique is a good criterion by which to judge if the theory is general enough. Steedman (1977) criticized Marx by presenting examples in which produced values take on negative values. He showed, for example, that joint production can produce a negative labor value. Many Sraffians followed Steedman with his judgment. However, Sraffa (1960) himself seems to have taken a more moderate attitude, because he assumed that capital like a machine "works with constant efficiency throughout its life" (§75, p. 64). Here "constant efficiency" means that the input-output coefficients remain invariant despite the difference of machine age. In this case, the allowance for depreciation per unit of production period can be calculated without reference to prices other than that of the machine itself.

Indeed, suppose that a machine has a lifetime L. The prices of the machine of age h satisfy the equation

$$\begin{aligned} (1+m)\,p(0) &= p(1) + (1+m)\,d, \\ (1+m)\,p(1) &= p(2) + (1+m)\,d, \\ &\cdots \\ (1+m)\,p\,(L-1) &= p(L) + (1+m)\,d, \end{aligned} \tag{2.27}$$

where $p(0)$ is the price of the new machine, $p(h)$ the price of the machine of age h, d the cost (annuity) that should be transferred to the product price, and $p(L) = 0$ as the price of a fully depreciated machine and d is the allowance for depreciation.[33] This system of equations in (2.27) can be solved easily.

By multiplying by $(1 + m)^{L-h}$ each equation that includes $p(h)$ in the right-hand side of (2.27) and summing them up, we get

$$\begin{aligned} (1+m)^L p(0) &= (1+m)\left\{1 + (1+m) + \cdots + (1+m)^{L-1}\right\} d \\ &= \{(1+m)\,/m\}\left\{(1+m)^L - 1\right\} d. \end{aligned}$$

Rearranging,

$$d = m\,(1+m)^{L-1} / \left\{(1+m)^L - 1\right\} \cdot p(0). \tag{2.28}$$

[32] Mathematically, joint production is defined as the property of a production technique h whose net product $\mathbf{b}(h) - \mathbf{a}(h)$ has two or more than two positive entries, $\mathbf{b}(h)$ and $\mathbf{a}(h)$, being output and input vectors of the production h, respectively.

[33] Equations (2.27) are different from Sraffa's formula in §75, p. 65, because d is counted as cost at the input point of time.

Each $p(h)$ can then be calculated as

$$p(h) = \left\{(1+m)^L - (1+m)^h\right\} / \left\{(1+m)^L - 1\right\} \cdot p(0) \tag{2.29}$$

Thus we can treat the depreciation allowance of the machine as a production cost of the single main product. Even if the process uses several different machines and equipment, there is no problem. However, a more delicate problem arises when the rate of operation of equipment lies below its capacity and varies.

The operation rate of capacity is defined as volume of production in a production period divided by the full production capacity.[34] As firms change production volume according to the expected demand, actual production volume is not always equal to the planned capacity of the production site. In standard cost accounting, the cost of a machine is allocated equally across units of production produced during the accounting period. If we calculate the unit cost in this way, the unit cost varies depending on the production volume. This causes discord between Postulate 2 (one-price policy) and Postulate 3 (markup pricing). Product price must vary when the volume of production varies per period. However, there is a better procedure that we can adopt. It is to assume a normal production volume[35] for a production period (which would be ordinarily smaller than the production capacity) and allocate the machine cost among the products of the normal volume.[36] Thus the cost of a machine that should be allocated to a unit of product is

$$c = \{1/\,(\text{normal production volume})\} \cdot d \tag{2.30}$$

In this system of cost accounting, the unit cost and the product price remain constant even when the operation rate is not the normal rate. If the realized sales and production volume is different from the normal volume, the profit for the firm from the product production is not equal to the expected one, but this is a common situation in business. The questions of total profit and the rate of profit are to be discussed in Sect. 2.7.6.

If the prices of machines and equipment are determined by the formula (2.29), then the cost of using fixed machines and equipment can be calculated as if an input coefficient of the machine and equipment is

$$m\,(1+m)^{L-1}/\{(1+m)^L - 1\} \cdot \{1/\,(\text{normal production volume})\}\,.$$

[34]There is no strictly determined capacity. It is possible to operate over the standard capacity of a production line, but such an operation risks increasing unexpected machine downs and line stops.

[35]The normal production volume for a product is defined by the management taking in consideration the design, the cost, and the expected market response of the product.

[36]Professor Takahiro Fujimoto (2012) is proposing a more refined system of cost accounting that he calls "total direct cost." Unfortunately, the paper is not yet translated into English.

As these single-product imaginary production techniques are included in an economy of single-product systems, the minimal price theorem holds even when fixed capital goods are taken into consideration.

Morishima and Steedman emphasized the necessity to develop a theory of value (or prices) for any set of joint-product production techniques. If we want to determine the truncation time precisely, it is necessary to know how the "efficiency" of a machine changes.[37] This can be done, in principle, if we know the input and output coefficients for processes that use machines of different ages. However, this kind of exact accounting is not practiced in actual cost accounting. It is even impossible, because one cannot know in advance the frequencies of machine failure and malfunction (I mean before the machine life ends). Manufacturer provided failure and service/repair rates are unreliable for use in the unique conditions of each factory. Machine life is determined on the base of experience and greatly depends on the possibility of moral obsolescence. Morishima and Steedman's proposals require a level of exactness beyond what is actually possible for data collection and prediction. Firms are not operated with such exactitude, and this requirement goes beyond what can be expected from economic agents going about "the ordinary business of life" (Marshall) and removes theory far from real life. Although cost accounting can and should be changed according to the necessities of real life, expectation of excessive exactness and generality is futile. "Exactness is a fake."[38] As far as we stay near to the ordinary business of life, the joint-production problem caused by the existence of fixed capital goods brings no problem for the validity of minimal price theorem.

Here we end our arguments regarding joint-production problems. In the next subsection, we attack the multifactor problem.

2.5.4 Nonhomogeneous Labor

The second crucial premise for the minimal price theorem is the one-factor condition. Discussion of this problem is very difficult and requires a deep understanding on how the economy works. However, the question that arises from the existence of nonhomogeneous workforces is rather simple.

When there are two or more different workforces and a production technique requires these different workforces in fixed proportions, we face a multifactor problem. However, in the case in which relative wage rates are determined by

---

[37] The truncation time of a machine is the maximal number of periods that it can be used economically. This may be shorter than the physical endurance time. If the maintenance cost increases after a number of years, it may be better to buy a new machine than to continue to use the machine by repairing it.

[38] A. N. Whitehead closed his last lecture at Harvard (The Ingersoll Lecture, April 22, 1941) by saying "The exactness is a fake." See Hocking (1961, p. 516).

one reason or other, the problem can be reduced to that of a homogeneous labor economy.

In fact, suppose that there are L kinds of work forces and relative wage rates are fixed to proportions r_1: r_2: ... : r_L. Suppose also that each production technique h can be expressed as ($\mathbf{u}(h)$, $\mathbf{a}(h)$) $\Rightarrow$ $\mathbf{e}(h)$, where $\mathbf{u}(h) = (u_1(h), u_2(h), \ldots, u_L(h))$. If we put

$$u^{\#}(h) = r_1\, u_1(h) + r_2\, u_2(h) + \cdots + r_L\, u_L(h), \tag{2.31}$$

the total labor expenses for a unit production can be expressed as $w\, u^{\#}(h)$ where w is a wage rate index.[39] Then the total input cost for a unit production with h is expressed

$$w\, u^{\#}(h) + p_1\, a_1(h) + \cdots + a_N(h).$$

The value equation for a production technique now takes the form

$$(1 + m(h)) \left\{ w\, u^{\#}(h) + \langle\, \mathbf{a}(h), \mathbf{p}\, \rangle \right\} = p_{g(h)}. \tag{2.32}$$

This equation is the same as (2.1) except that $\mathbf{u}(h)$ is replaced by $u^{\#}(h)$. Then, if we take an imaginary economy E, of which the set of production techniques T are ($u^{\#}(h)$, $\mathbf{a}(h)$) $\Rightarrow$ $\mathbf{e}(h)$, this satisfies the one-factor condition. Then, if T does not contain joint-product production techniques, we can apply the minimal price theory to E, and for a given w, we have a set of production techniques S and minimal prices $\mathbf{p}$ that satisfies three conditions (1), (2), and (3) of Theorem 4.4. If we take

$$S^{\#} = \{(\, \mathbf{u}(h), \mathbf{a}(h), \mathbf{e}(h) \mid h \in \mathrm{S}\}$$

and

$$(\mathbf{w}, \mathbf{p})^{\#} = (w\, u_1, \ldots, w\, u_L;\, p_1, \ldots, p_{\mathrm{N}}),$$

this couple of the set of production techniques and the prices defined by $S^{\#}$ satisfies the three conditions of Theorem 4.4. This means that the minimal price theorem holds as long as we can assume that relative wage rates remain constant even when demand proportions vary.

As a conclusion, we can say that the minimal price theorem holds so long as relative wage rates remain constant.

Of course, we know that relative wage rates change when time passes by. However, we do not know very well how these relative wage rates are determined or how they vary. Some parts of relative wage rates are determined by convention, and

---

[39] The index w is only nominal. We can choose any index.

some parts are determined by contracts between employers and trade unions. On the other hand, we know that relative wage rates change rather slowly. We can say that the influence on changes in relative wage rates is small when we are analyzing an economy for a short period or a mid-term period. Under these conditions, it is wiser to leave the wage rate determination an open problem for the moment than to offer an uncertain, not well-founded theory hastily. As research develops in the future, we can say more on this theme.

2.5.5 Multiple Primary Factors

Existence of primary factors other than labor (workforces) requires the consideration of two questions about (1) capital goods and (2) land and exhaustible resources. The first question is simple, but the second requires a bit of controversial argument which necessitates accepting a deep change of vision regarding just how the economy works. Even under the new vision, we should admit that land and exhaustible resources can have some influence on the production economy. How to reconcile this fact, and the main theory based on minimal price theorem, provides the second question of this subsection. To get a full understanding of the problem, it is necessary to explain a new concept for economics, which is the dissipative structure. Thus, we insert a rather long discussion on the dissipative structure between arguments on how to reconcile the new theory and the theory of rent of land.

2.5.5.1 Capital Goods Are Not Primary Factors

Samuelson and others knew well that capital goods are not primary factors which may restrict the application of the minimal price theorem. Indeed, except for fixed capital, which we have explained in the previous subsection, circulating capital goods such as materials and ingredients or parts and components are the main heroes of the minimal price theorem. If there were no such circulating capital goods, the minimal price theorem becomes a trivial statement. We make this remark to avoid the misunderstanding that capital is another production factor together with labor and that the existence of capital excludes the application of the minimal price theorem. Capital goods (be it circulating or fixed capital) are production factors but are not the primary factors whose multiplicity destroys the validity of the minimal price theorem (Postulate 10).

2.5.5.2 Land and Exhaustible Resources

Modern industrial economy is not a landed economy, such as those of the medieval age whose economic base was land. In that time, land ownership determined the social and economic structure. Legal and power relations between landlords and serfs determined the main structural feature of the economy. Land now plays much more restricted roles in the modern industrial economy, and yet land ownership and rent, from the leasing of land and mining concessions, are not negligible factors even for the modern production economy.

We have to admit that land and mining concessions are actual constraints restricting the range of validity of the minimal price theorem. However, this does not mean that the essential vision based on the minimal price theorem is weakened by the existence of land and mining concessions. Firstly, rent occupies only a small part of factory production costs. Although the rent of housing occupies an important part of a consumer's expenditure, specially for consumers who live in great cities, it lies in the domain of the rent economy, which is outside the production economy with which we are concerned. For the time being, we are more concerned with the real economy rather than the financial economy, which in a wider sense includes the rent economy.[40] While the financial economy may often bring to bear pernicious effects on the real economy, our first objective remains that of establishing a solid theory of production and consumption, which is the one that supports the basic existence of each of our lives. Secondly, it is possible to build a bridge between the theory of value that we have developed in Sect. 2.4 and the theory of rent of land and mines, just as it was possible for classical economists like Ricardo. Land rent requires some modifications to the total structure of the value theory, but it does not create a contradiction that could lead to a breakdown of the theory. In order to get this understanding, it is necessary to argue for the very basic vision of just how the real economy works.

2.5.5.3 Economy as Dissipative Structure

The actual standard vision is that of neoclassical economics. This is constructed on two pillars: (1) maximization behaviors of economic agents and (2) equilibrium between various parts of the system. We have argued in Chap. 1 that the maximizing principle is not only baseless but also misleading as an understanding of human behavior. We do not repeat the same arguments here. We have also remarked on equilibrium at various places in Chap. 1 and claimed that the equilibrium framework is at the core of the present difficulties of economics. We need another fundamental principle different from that of equilibrium as our guiding concept. Here I claim it is, in addition to process, the concept of the *dissipative structure*.

The dissipative structure is not as popular as the equilibrium. The concept was first introduced by Ilya Prigogine to designate a reproducible steady-state system. Prigogine is a representative person of the Brussels School of Thermodynamics and received the 1977 Nobel Prize in Chemistry for the research that lead him to this concept. It became popular through Prigogine's popularizing books in the 1970s and

[40]Financial economy comprises FIRE, i.e., finance, insurance, and real estate.

1980s (Prigogine and Nicolis 1977; Prigogine 1980; Prigogine and Stengers 1984). The concept can even be applied to very turbulent systems, such as hurricanes or typhoons.

A dissipative structure is a macroscopic ordering of a large number of molecules which keeps its macroscopic (static or dynamic) form only by dissipating entropy out of the system. Thus a dissipative structure is always an open system. In some circumstances, a dissipative structure emerges spontaneously and keeps its structure for a certain length of time. One of the simplest examples is a lighted candle in a room (Shiozawa 1996). In a windless room, the flare of a candle keeps its lighted state as long as oxygen and heated liquid wax continues to be provided. As Prigogine emphasizes a dissipative structure can only exist far from thermodynamic equilibrium. Dissipative structures are now widely known in various complex systems, and they are in fact one of the key concepts of self-organization, emergence, and open complex systems. This kind of structure was not known before the Brussels school originated and developed non-equilibrium thermodynamics in the mid-twentieth century.

It is therefore not strange that this new concept had no chance of becoming a key concept of neoclassical economics since it was founded at the end of the nineteenth century. However, we can also point out that neoclassical economics is so deeply structured around the notion of equilibrium that the new concept could not be introduced as a part of its core theory. Even now there are few economists who consider an economy as a dissipative structure. In our opinion, this is a gross error.

There are two instances where the notion of dissipative structure is decisive: (1) when we want to analyze land and exhaustible resources and (2) when we want to analyze (involuntary or Keynesian) unemployment. We do not argue the second point here in this chapter (see Sect. 2.7.6). In this section we only consider how it is related to land use and exhaustible resources. The notion of dissipative structure plays an essential role in determining the extent of land use and the speed of exploitation of exhaustible resources.

Dissipative structure is a new mode of grasping how the economy works. In an equilibrium framework, it is customary to set boundary conditions and try to discover an optimal solution that satisfies them as constraints. If there are no binding constraints, equilibrium economists think that the economy can grow rapidly until at least one constraint becomes binding. Dissipative structure gives a picture very different from equilibrium theory.[41] Take the example of the lighted candle. The flare continues to burn as long as oxygen and liquid wax are provided. What determines the speed of combustion? Are they the total quantities of oxygen molecules and wax? No. It is the structure composed of flare, air convection, air pressure, heat radiation, volume of the pool of melted wax, and capillary attraction.

---

[41] The notion of "circular flow" (Kreislauf in German) among classical economists (see Kurz and Salvadori 1985, Chap. 13) may be an expression of their naïve ideas which tried to understand the economy as dissipative structure, although they could not clearly articulate them.

The volume of the room, its ambient temperature, and the total mass of the candle are effectively irrelevant to the speed of the burning.

If the economy is a dissipative structure, the economic system develops mainly by its own internal structures and mechanisms rather than by its boundary conditions, conditions which are in principle exogenous variables of the system. In other words, the new theory does not consider that the capitalist market economy efficiently allocates its scarce resources to the best possible uses without exceptions. This point of difference is crucial when we observe the roles that lands and mines play in the economy. Equilibrium analysis tends to assume that all resources are used efficiently. The dissipative structure view considers that it is the internal structure of the economy that determines the rates of resource usage and of the exploitation of lands and mines. Once we grasp these fundamentals, it is then easy to situate the theory of rent in the whole system of our own theory.

2.5.5.4 Theory of Rent

Economy is a dissipative structure. It is the internal cyclic relations of causation that determine the extent of land usage and the rate of exploitation of a mine. In an expression more familiar to economists, it is the level of economic activities that determines land use and the speed of mining. If we understand that, the question of rent on land and mines is not difficult to deal with.

Although the theory of rent is not as well developed as the price theory described in this chapter (Sects. 2.4, 2.5, and 2.6 in particular), it is possible to develop a theory of rent as a part of the theory of price. The first theory is the differential rent theory attempted by Ricardo. The second remarkable attempt is Sraffa (1960, Chap. 11). Christian Bidard (2010; 2013 to cite only two papers) is also energetically developing a theory of rent. The theory of differential rent is not difficult in its essence. When the total demand for corn is known, the total surface area to cultivate is determined.[42] If the total volume of economic land use activities is determined at a given time, we can know what range of land fertilities are on offer and the quantities of their respective areas. The logic of differential rent then gives how much rent the cultivators should pay for each piece of land.[43] The rent of mining obeys the same logic as far as differential rent for mines are concerned.[44]

---

[42] It is usually explained that cultivation starts from the most fertile land and shifts to less fertile land. Although theoretically this is the plausible order of cultivation, real history does not obey this rule.

[43] If the farm is cultivated by the owner of the land, the farmer obtains a virtual rent.

[44] General equilibrium theory is ambiguous about the logic of the rent. If the land is not exploited, the rule of free goods stipulates that it does not produce any rent. However, how is the total activity level determined? Neoclassical economists simply assume that there is some mechanism that makes all constraints satisfied if we admit the rule of free goods. If the economic system can be deemed as a linear programming, the rule of free goods is equivalent to the principle of complementary slackness. However, an economy is not a linear or any other type of mathematical programming system.

Another important topic concerns the problems related to exhaustible resources. In this field, Harold Hotelling's classic paper (Hotelling 1931) is still stimulating. It is true that mines are exhaustible. We see many such classical instances. Japan in the Meiji era was one of the biggest copper-producing countries. Until the mid-eighteenth century (in the Edo period), it is estimated that Japan was the biggest copper producer in the world. However, all those copper mines were closed by 1994. Domestic production of copper is now negligible. All copper production is now the by-product of other mining activity (e.g., gold mining). Hotelling showed a theory of how the price changes when the demand in physical units remains stable. Price including rent remains near to the production cost over almost all of the period of its exploitation and then rises rapidly near the exhaustion point. This hints that we should consider the exhaustible resource problem from two points of view: (1) exhaustion of a mine and (2) global exhaustion of a mineral species. In the first case, a mine is closed when the (full) cost of production becomes much higher than the cost of production of other mines. In the second case, it is necessary to find a substitute of the exhausting mineral. It is also important to note that the cost of mining and smelting changes enormously through changes in mining and smelting techniques. Copper mining revived twice in the history of Japan through the introduction of new mining and smelting techniques. Around the end of the sixteenth and beginning of the seventeenth centuries, a new smelting process (named *Nambanbuki*, meaning European process) was imported through a Chinese engineer. In the Meiji era, a new mining technology was again imported, and decreasing copper production began increasing rapidly.

All these facts are compatible with the new theory of value. Productivity of a piece of land or a mine varies as time passes by. The rent changes, but the speed of this change is slow, and the amplitude of changes is small. In addition, there is always competition between technical changes and resource exhaustion (including the shift to less fertile land). Then the questions of rent can be treated in the same way as the change in costs that arises by virtue of technical changes. Rent is a new factor for our theory of prices and requires a development of a new theory. But it is possible to incorporate rent into the new theory of value which we have developed in this chapter.

There remains another big problem which arises from the multiplicity of "primary factors." In the international economy, there are very many different countries. The workforces of different countries cannot be assumed to comprise the same primary factor. This question is increasingly important as the globalization of economy progresses. In view of its importance and the necessity of building a special theory, this subject is treated in the next section.

2.6 International Trade Situation

The main purpose of this section is to show that the main idea of the minimal price theorem can be extended to the international trade situation. To fully explain this result requires at least an independent chapter. As it is not the place here to do that, our explanations are limited to the bare minimum.[45]

As it was explained at the end of Sect. 2.5, international trade (or more basically the existence of different nations) signifies that there are as many kinds of workforce as there are countries, because the laborers of different countries have to be treated as different kinds of workforce. We have treated in Sect. 2.5.4 workers of different skills in a country as having wage rates of fixed proportions. We have argued that the multiple primary factor problems can be bypassed by assuming this. However, in the case of international trade, such a method is not applicable. Wage rate proportions are the main variables in international trade, and we cannot fix them beforehand.

The necessity to see workers of different countries as different primary factors does not come from the reason that we see them as people of different races. It comes from the fact that each country has a different set of production techniques. A different set of production techniques means different productivity and hence a different real wage for workers of each country. A worker of the same personal skill, like lathe working, is rewarded by different wage rates in different countries.

Thus international trade invites the situation in which we have many kinds of primary factors and the minimal price theory does not hold in its original form. However, we can get a similar result in the sense that there is an admissible value that we have argued in Definition 4.7 and Theorem 4.8. To get this result, it is necessary to first introduce some terms of graph theory. Thus, Sect. 2.6.1 is a short detour to graph theory. To illustrate the general result in a simpler case, we explain in Sect. 2.6.2 how the theorem can be obtained for the pure labor input case. Section 2.6.3 gives the general result. However, without giving any proofs, Sect. 2.6.4 concludes by giving how the new result can be interpreted.

2.6.1 Graph Theory

A graph is a set of vertices and edges. An edge connects two vertices. Graphical expression only indicates these connecting relations. So the places of vertices and the shapes of edges have no importance. If it is clear that an edge connects one vertex to one another, geometric exactness is not required. More formally, a graph G is a couple of a set V of vertices and a set E of edges. Each edge should be assigned exactly two vertices (including the case when two edges coincide). Normally we assume V and E are finite.

[45]This section is based on the new theory of international values. Readers are requested to refer Shiozawa (2017a) for general ideas. However, this section contains some new results which do not appear in Shiozawa (2017a). For a more detailed account of the new idea, please see Shiozawa and Fujimoto (2018).

Fig. 2.2 An example of a spanning tree

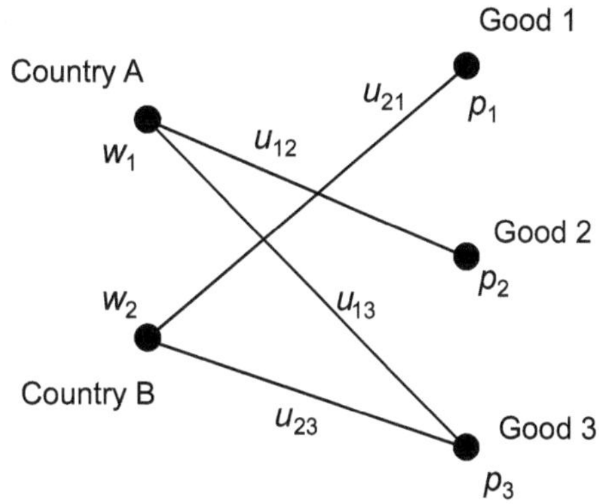

A world economy is composed of countries and goods. Let $V1$ be the set of countries and $V2$ be the set of goods and V be the union of $V1$ and $V2$. A production technique is applied to the production process of a single product in a country i which produces a good j. For each production technique, we can assign an edge which connects an element of $V1$ and an element of $V2$. Therefore, a production technique can be expressed by an edge which connects $V1$ and $V2$. If T is the set of all production techniques which is known and realizable, this state of technology can be represented by a graph $G = (V1 \cup V2, T)$, which we call a *technology graph.*

In representing a state of technology, the set of vertices is always composed of two disjoint parts $V1$ and $V2$. If a set of vertices is composed of two disjoint sets $V1$ and $V2$ and edges are always connecting an element of $V1$ and an element of $V2$, such a graph is called a *bipartite graph.* If there exists one and only one production technique for all elements of couple (i, j), all vertices of $V1$ are connected to one of the vertices of $V2$ and vice versa. Such a bipartite graph is called a *complete* bipartite graph. Two vertices of a graph are said to be connected if they can be connected by a chain of edges. A graph is *connected* when any pair of vertices is connected. A graph is called *spanning* if all vertices are connected at least by an edge. It is called *tree*, if it is connected and contains no cycles. A *cycle* here means a chain of edges which starts from a vertex and returns to the same vertex without passing the same edge. For a characterization of regular international values, we need a concept of spanning tree which is a subgraph of the technology graph.

Figure 2.2 is an example of a spanning tree for a two-country, three-good economy. A character string is used to express a graph that has no two edges which connect the same vertices (a subgraph of the complete bipartite graph). For example, for an economy of two countries A and B and three goods 1, 2, and 3, a spanning tree is expressed, for example, by A23B13, which is a set of production techniques composed of A2, A3, B1, and B3, each indicating a production technique produces a good in a country. For a two-country, three-good economy, there are in total 12 different spanning trees.

This is all we should know about graph theory.

2.6.2 Pure Labor Input Economy

Suppose we have a Ricardian pure labor input economy (R0 economy in Shiozawa 2017a).[46] Production techniques are all of the pure labor input type. Thus, they are represented by a coefficient u_{ij}. Figure 2.2 illustrates the production possibility set for an economy of two countries and three goods.

Suppose we are given a set G of production techniques which form the spanning tree A13B23 and all production techniques of G are competitive. Here, competitive means that the production technique satisfies the value equation. In other words, if production technique A2 is competitive, it means that $w_1\ u_{12} = p_2$.[47]

It is convenient to treat wage rates and prices of goods as a set. We put $\mathbf{v} = (w_1, \ldots, w_M, p_1, \ldots, p_N)$ and call it an international value. When two values are proportional, we consider they are a different expression of the same value. If we use this terminology, instead of saying that an international value is determined uniquely up to scalar multiplication, we can simply say that international value is determined uniquely.

Figure 2.2 expresses how wage rates and prices are related with each other when all techniques of spanning tree A23B13 are competitive. We can start from any vertex, say country A. Choose a positive wage rate w_1 arbitrarily. Vertex A is connected to vertices 2 and 3. As production technique A2 is competitive, we have $p_2 = w_1\ u_{12}$. In the same vein, as A3 is competitive, we have $p_3 = w_1\ u_{13}$. Thus, prices p_2 and p_3 are determined. Vertex 3 is connected to country B. If production technique B3 is competitive, then we have $w_2\ u_{23} = p_3$. Thus, wage rate w_2 is determined. As vertex B is connected to vertex 1, we have $w_2\ u_{21} = p_1$. In this way, if we choose a positive w_1 arbitrarily, we can determine all other wage rates and prices by tracking paths starting from vertex A. If competitive production techniques form a spanning tree, all vertices are connected by a unique path from the starting vertex. Tracing the path and determining values of all vertices step by step, we can determine the value of the chosen vertex. This procedure does not produce contradiction, because there are no cycles in a tree. Thus we get the following theorem.

Theorem 6.1 (Spanning Tree Determines an International Value, R0 Case) *Let U be a labor input coefficient matrix of a Ricardian trade economy with M countries and N goods. If a set G of competitive production techniques forms a spanning tree, then there is a unique international value (up to scalar multiplication) that satisfies cost-price equalities.*

---

[46] Trade economies of classes RI and RII can be reduced to R0 economy by a suitable transformation. Thus, the propositions proved for R0 economy hold for economies in the class RI or RII. Theorem 6.1 also holds for economies in RI or RII. Although R0 has an interesting mathematical structure (Shiozawa 2015), we do not enter in this topic here.

[47] Note we are using markup form coefficients.

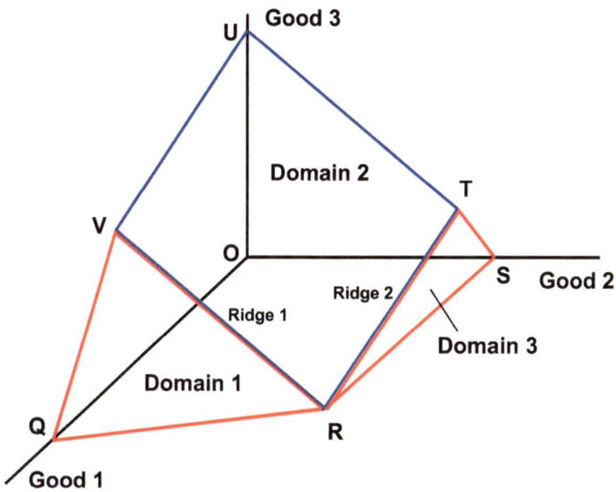

Fig. 2.3 A two-country, three-commodity trade economy

We have defined the notion of admissible value in Sect. 2.4.2. The same definition applies to international values. With this definition, we can say that, for a labor input coefficient matrix U that satisfies inequality

$$u_{11}/u_{21} < u_{13}/u_{23} < u_{12}/u_{22}, \tag{2.33}$$

the international values defined by spanning trees A1B123, A13B23, and A123B2 are admissible, whereas all other international values defined by other spanning trees are not admissible.

In Fig. 2.3, A1B123, A13B23, and A123B2 correspond to Domain 1, Domain 2, and Domain 3, respectively.[48] We see that there is a one-to-one correspondence between three kinds of things: (1) facets of the production possibility frontier,[49] (2) admissible international values that is defined by a spanning tree, and (3) spanning trees that have an admissible international value.

The correspondence between (2) and (3) is trivial. The two expressions give only a different focus on the same entity. Correspondence between (1) and (2) is more substantial. We cannot give here a detailed proof, but the rough story proceeds like this. Let us imagine a production frontier. It is a set of maximal points of a polytope like Fig. 2.3. At any point in the interior of a facet of the frontier, we have a vector **p** that is normal (perpendicular) to the facet. This vector **p** is positive in the sense that all components of the vector are positive. To this vector **p**, there is always a

[48]For the details, see Shiozawa and Fujimoto (2018).

[49]A facet of a polytope P of dimension N is a face of codimension 1, i.e., of dimension $N-1$, which is a set defined as an intersection of P and a hyperplane H when P is included in one of the half spaces divided by H.

conjugate vector **w**, and the international value $\mathbf{v} = (\mathbf{w}, \mathbf{p})$ satisfies the relations given by Theorem 3.4 in Shiozawa (2017a). The international value **v** is admissible, because the set of production techniques satisfies inequality (iii) of Theorem 3.4 in Shiozawa (2017a). As the international value is uniquely determined, there are enough production techniques that form a connected technology graph. If it is not connected, the production techniques cannot determine international value, because in that case the international value has the same degree of freedom as the number of connected components.[50] If the graph contains a cycle, it is not possible for production techniques in a general position to satisfy all the value equations. Thus the technology graph must be a spanning tree in order that prices are determined uniquely.

Consequently, we have

Theorem 6.2 (Correspondence Between Regular Values and Admissible Spanning Trees, R0 Case)
Let U and **q** *be a labor input coefficient matrix and a vector of labor powers of a Ricardian trade economy with M countries and N goods. In general,* i.e., *in the case where U is in a general position, the international value whose price vector is normal to a facet of the production frontier is admissible and equal to the international value defined by a spanning tree of production techniques and* vice versa.

See the remark after Theorem 6.5 for the notion of general position.

There are many other properties that are interesting, but we have to satisfy ourselves here by pointing out some results on the number of facets or admissible spanning trees. The number of spanning trees *s*(*M*, *N*) of (*M*,*N*)-bipartite graph is known as Scoin's formula:

$$s\,(M, N) = M^{N-1} N^{M-1}. \tag{2.34}$$

As we have seen in the case of a two-country, three-good trade economy, the number of all different spanning trees is $2^2{\cdot}3 = 12$. In the same case, the number of facets or of admissible spanning trees was 3. Let us denote by *c*(*M*, *N*) the number of facets or admissible spanning trees of an *M*-country, *N*-commodity trade economy. Is there a general formula for the number *c*(*M*, *N*)? In the case of an R0 economy in a general position, this number *c*(*M*, *N*) is known as

$$c\,(M, N) = (M + N - 2)!/\,(M - 1)!\,(N - 1)!. \tag{2.35}$$

This is the number of different (assignment) *classes*. Ronald Jones introduced this notion (1961, p. 164), although he gave no explanations of why this notion is relevant. A class of assignments or competitive patterns is the set of technology graphs that have the same number of directly connected goods for all countries.

[50]This result was already known in the 1950s. See McKenzie (1953).

As countries and goods are symmetric in technology graphs, this is the same as saying that a class is the set of technology graphs that have the same number of directly connected countries for all goods. The ratio $c(M, N)/s(M, N)$ is a decreasing function. Although $c(M, N)$ is a big number for a reasonably large M and N, the ratio decreases rapidly. For example, for a case of a three-country, five-good economy, the ratio is 15/6075 ≒ 0.0025. In a five-country, ten-good case, the ratio is approximately 0.000000037 or 1 over 30 million. Thus admissible spanning trees occupy a very small percentage among all spanning trees.

2.6.3 International Economy with Trade of Intermediate Goods

A pure labor input economy shows some typical situations which can occur in an international trade economy. However, it cannot be regarded as a general case. In recent years, in a globalized economy, we observe the rapid increase of global value chains. We can no longer consider the world economy to be a simple sum of independent national economies which are exchanging final products between them. Many commodities are produced by using parts and components processed in other countries, and those parts and components are in their turn produced by imported input goods. For some products, like smartphones produced in China, less than one third of their value added originates in the country of their final producer.

A globalized economy thus necessitates having a value theory that is constructed on the assumption that trade in input goods is normal and occupies an important role in the formation of world commodity prices. Traditional trade theories are either excluding, by assumption, any input trade or else are thinking that it is possible to get to world prices starting from each country's price data. However, when primary and intermediate goods are traded widely and extensively, the cost of production is affected much more by the cost of commodities than when they are produced totally in one country. When there is no input trade, the cost of production of the product produced in a country depends only on the wage level of the producing country. When input trade plays a big part, the cost of production now depends not only on the wage rate of the producing country of the final product but equally on the wage rates of the producing countries of the intermediate goods. Traditional trade theories cannot provide a theory to handle this except for general equilibrium theory of the Arrow-Debreu type.

Fortunately, a new theory of international values was constructed recently (Shiozawa 2017a) and is developing rapidly. In a very wide class of economy that I call Ricardo-Sraffa trade economy (or RS economy), it is now possible to analyze an international value, which is composed of wage rates for different countries and prices of commodities that are equal for all countries. This theory is constructed on the simplifying assumption of no transportation or transaction costs. It is possible to generalize this result to the case of positive transportation costs, but we confine ourselves here to the case of no transportation costs.[51]

The main result can be summarized by

Theorem 6.3 (Uniqueness of International Values)[52]
Let (E, T) be an RS economy of M countries and N goods. Let S be a subset of T, and suppose that S is in a general position and satisfies the following three conditions:

(a) *S is productive.*
(b) The technology graph *S* is a spanning tree.
(c) *A positive international value* $\mathbf{v} = (\mathbf{w}, \mathbf{p})$ *exists, and any production technique h of S satisfies the value equation.*

Let $\mathbf{u}(h)$ *and* $\mathbf{a}(h)$ *be labor input and net material input coefficient vectors, then the following two propositions hold:*

(i) *Vectors* $\{(-\mathbf{u}(h), \mathbf{a}(h)) | \forall h \in S\}$ *are linearly independent,*

and

(ii) *The international value* $\mathbf{v}$ *which satisfies condition (c) is unique up to scalar multiplications.*

Note that proposition (ii) is only a consequence of proposition (i). This uniquely determined international value $\mathbf{v} = (\mathbf{w}, \mathbf{p})$ is said to be regular when it is admissible with respect to a spanning tree *S* and satisfies value equations for all elements *h* of *S*. We propose a new definition that an international value is regular:

Definition 6.4 (Regular international value)[53]
When an international value satisfies the conditions of Theorem 6.3 and if it is admissible, we call this international value $\mathbf{v}$ *the regular value defined by the spanning tree S. S is called the associated spanning tree of the value v.*

Theorem 6.3 assures that a regular international value is unique for a given spanning tree, but it does not assure the existence of a regular value. But we have the next theorem:

Theorem 6.5 (Existence of regular international values)
For any RS trade economy (E, T), there exists at least one regular international values $\mathbf{v} = (\mathbf{w}, \mathbf{p})$. *In other words, if J is the matrix that has element 1 only at entry*

---

[51]How to extend the results obtained on the no transportation cost assumption to the positive transaction cost case (including extra transaction costs to cross the country boundary) is explained and treated in Shiozawa (2017a, Section 9).

[52]This is a new result which does not appear in Shiozawa (2017a). The esquisse is given in Shiozawa and Fujimoto (2018).

[53]The new concept of regular value is different from the one given in Definition 3.7 in Shiozawa (2017a), but is in fact equivalent.

$(h, g(h))$, there exist a positive vector $\mathbf{v} = (\mathbf{w}, \mathbf{p})$ *and a spanning tree S chosen from T such that*

$$J\,\mathbf{w} \geqq A\mathbf{p} \tag{2.36}$$

and

$$\langle\, \mathbf{u}(h), \mathbf{w}\, \rangle = \langle\, \mathbf{a}(h), \mathbf{p}\, \rangle$$

for all h belonging to S.

A key concept for Theorem 6.3 is the concept that the set of production techniques S is in a *general position*. We have used the same concept for the labor input coefficient matrix U with no explanation (Sect. 2.6.2). General position is a widely used mathematical concept but requires a definition for each case. The simplest definition of general position for a set of production techniques S whose technology graph forms a spanning tree is that the set of vectors $\{(-\mathbf{u}(h), \mathbf{a}(h)) | \forall h \in T\}$ is linearly independent. By this definition, Theorem 6.1 becomes trivial. However, in this case, it is necessary to prove that the set of spanning trees in a general position covers a dense open set in a space of input coefficients that satisfy the three conditions (a), (b), and (c).

Theorem 6.3 is totally new and does not appear in Shiozawa (2017a). Shiozawa has a written proof and is asking his colleagues to check it. As the check is not finished, it would be more correct to say that it is still a conjecture. However, as we have observed in Sect. 2.6.2, Theorem 6.1 holds for economies without input trade (trade economy of type R0 or RI), and it is strongly expected that a variant of the theorem holds if we modify sufficient conditions slightly in cases when the present theorem is not exactly correct. So, we present it as a theorem. Theorem 6.5 is a simple consequence of Theorem 3.4 in Shiozawa (2017a).

The new definition of the concept of regular international value (regular value hereafter) and Theorem 6.5 are required in order to make the new theory of international values more adaptable for the analysis of Keynesian involuntary unemployment. In the old formulation in Shiozawa (2017a), the status of regular values was ambiguous with respect to the significance that a regular value plays in the economy.

Regular values whose existence is assured by Theorem 6.5 are not unique. For example, in a Ricardian trade economy of two countries and three goods, there are in general three different regular values. The number of different regular values is given by the formula (2.35) for an (M, N) Ricardian economy. This formula is also valid for Ricardian economies of RI or RII, because RI and RII are structurally identical to R0 (see Shiozawa 2017a, p. 14). But a Ricardo-Sraffa trade economy can have a different number of regular values other than that of formula (2.35). Ogawa's example (Ogawa 2017, Fig. 5) of two countries and three goods shows that there are seven facets and regular values, whereas (2.35) gives six.

2.6.4 The Significance of Theorem 6.3 for the New Theory of Value

It is evident that the minimal price theory does not hold in the international trade economy. There are many possible regular values. But the core idea expressed by the minimal price theory is still valid in the international trade case.

Suppose a regular international value $\mathbf{v} = (\mathbf{w}, \mathbf{p})$ defined by spanning tree S. If the international value $\mathbf{v}$ holds in the economy, this value is stable in the sense that it does not change even when the final demand changes as long as it is producible by the production techniques belonging to S. Note that Theorem 6.5 gives the same necessary conditions as those of Theorem 4.4, if once the value $\mathbf{v}$ and S is given. Both theorems assure that the value is admissible and the production technique in S satisfies the value equation. The difference lies in the fact of whether Theorem 4.9 (covering property) holds or not. In the international trade economy, production techniques of the spanning tree S do not have the covering property in the form of Theorem 4.9. Theorem 4.9 assures that the maximal frontier of the production possibility set is a single simplex. In case of international trade, the maximal frontier is generally composed of many facets. A simple example is Fig. 2.3. This is the reason why we cannot have a unique admissible value in the international trade economy. But this fact is not important. What is more important is that there exists an admissible value which is determined if once a spanning tree is fixed.

In an economy in which we know only the set of production techniques T, there are no means to determine which of several different regular values is chosen. But we are in an economy where history matters. In other words, we are in an economy that is *always already given* (Althusser 1965). In the field of technical change, we customarily talk of path dependency. We are in the same situation with the international trade economy. The same economy can possess different regular values if the history were different. Suppose there are two regular values $\mathbf{v}$ and $\mathbf{v}'$ and spanning trees S and S' associated to $\mathbf{v}$ and $\mathbf{v}'$, respectively. In the economy where value $\mathbf{v}$ holds, it is impossible without the risk of incurring a loss for a firm to change the production technique h in the spanning tree S to another production technique h' in the spanning tree S', because production technique h in set S gives the minimal cost among all production alternatives that produce the same product as h.

The situation as explained above does not mean that value never changes. It does change but for reasons other than the change of demand. As we have explained in Sect. 2.4.5, the value changes when the set of production alternatives S changes. There are other reasons when the value changes. We may enumerate three cases:

1. When a country suffers from labor shortage
2. When a sudden enduring increase in demand for a product occurs and there is no sufficient production capacity and input goods to respond to the increase
3. When the prices of primary resources and the rents of lands or mines change

We will consider these cases also in Sect. 2.7 which concludes our arguments by discussing proposals for further development of our theory.

2.7 Quantity Adjustment Process

We have hitherto examined how prices are determined, what function they perform, and how they change. The fundamental assumption was the relative independence of value and quantities. We are now approaching the core problem of our book, which is to show that the quantity adjustment process works well as a consequence of the decisions of firms that can obtain only small amount of information from the economy. Managers of firms or production sites have to decide everyday how much to produce. It is a routine work, and these decisions are made almost automatically. In the words of Stafford Beer (1995), it is a part of an *autonomic reflex* or control. The task of this section is to give a rough idea how this system of quantity adjustment works, not only at the level of the firm but also for the economy as a whole. Detailed specifications of the models we use, as well as demonstrations of how they work, are provided in the subsequent chapters by Morioka and Taniguchi.

As I will argue in Sect. 2.7.5, the totally different viewpoint offered by this book is of paramount significance for the future of economics. Economy is a network of production and exchange that extends all over the world. It contains billions of people, tens of millions of firms, and hundreds of millions of commodities. The market economy is a loosely connected system, each part of which is run mainly by managers of firms. It is a highly decentralized system. In terms of information technology, it is a *distributed control system*. Managers in this decentralized system are not mythological heroes or heroines who can see the whole economy. They are entities whose capacities are bounded in sight, rationality, and actions, as we argued in Chap. 1. Even so, the economy functions as a whole in a sufficiently effective way.

Arrow and Debreu's work (1954) was a great achievement for economics. It could demonstrate how a large-scale economy works. However, it was in a sense a complete failure, because it had to assume perfectly rational agents who get price information on all goods and are able to calculate the specific combination of goods which maximizes their profit or utility. There are no such persons in the real world. All human beings are entities possessed of limited capabilities. The result we obtained in this book is significant because it demonstrated that a large-scale economic system is able to work purely by the autonomic actions of common people with bounded capabilities.

We proved that this quantity adjustment process is convergent in the sense that the process can follow the slow changes in demand as they ebb and flow. As far as we know, this is not a well-known fact. On the contrary, the quantity adjustment process as a whole was believed to be divergent under the subject of the dual stability-instability property of two adjustment processes, one being the price system and the other the quantity system. This duality has been known since Jorgenson (1960). The result here shows that the quantity adjustment process converges and relies only on each firm's capability for adjustment.

Subsection 1 gives a brief account of this fact and explains how our adjustment process is different from that of past processes. Subsection 2 explains the everyday decision-making of an individual firm. The most important part of quantity adjustment is how the total process proceeds. Subsection 3 is a brief remark on linearity and non-linearity of the adjustment process. Subsection 4 explains the essential core of the results obtained by Taniguchi and Morioka. In this examination, time order is crucial. Information that is passed within a firm and from one firm to another should not violate it. Subsection 5 emphasizes the significance of the Taniguchi-Morioka results for economics. Subsection 6 gives some remarks on problems which are to be attacked in the future.

2.7.1 Dual Stability-Instability Properties

Dale Jorgenson (1960) summarized the arguments which had continued for more than a decade before him. The question they were concerned with was the stability and instability of the Leontief dynamic input-output system. It became known before 1960 that either one of the two dual systems (i.e., prices and quantities) is unstable. As Jorgenson put it, "If the output system is stable, the dual system must be unstable and vice versa, at least for the closed system" (Jorgenson 1960, p. 892).

Our system is basically an extension of Leontief system, as we assume linear production techniques without joint productions. If Jorgenson's observations are right, the quantity adjustment process must be unstable, because our price adjustment system was quite stable as we have seen in Sect. 2.4. In spite of this rather well established understanding, we claim that the quantity adjustment process is just as stable as the price system is. This does not mean that Jorgenson and other theorems were false. They were correct, but we find that quantity adjustment develops differently than in the manner that they have assumed. Taniguchi and Morioka found the reason why Jorgenson and others' mechanism was divergent, whereas their system was convergent, as will be explained later in this section.

Before explaining the details of the quantity adjustment process, it is opportune to see what Jorgenson and others' observations meant for economics. Some economists argued that this stability-instability property signifies the inherent instability of capitalism. But the question, that of a quantity adjustment process, seems to be concerned with too basic a process of the economy to justify such a conclusion. Although we do not deny that the market economy is full of seeds of instability, it is doubtful that such an everyday process comprises a mechanism with such impact. If the argument is true, the modern economy must have collapsed at a very early stage of industrial capitalism. It must be considered as very surprising that industrial capitalism endured more than two centuries.

There were of course economists who doubted this argument and tried to prove that the market mechanism contains some unknown mechanism that makes the quantity adjustment process more stable. Masahiko Aoki was one of them. Aoki (1977) questioned if there is a mechanism in firms' modes of investment decision-making that tends to keep an economy roughly stable. Aoki pointed to the possibility that *indicative planning* may have played such a function. As almost all countries based on the market economy possess an economic agency which is engaged in forecasting, it is possible that firms may make decisions taking account the forecasting provided. Aoki argued that this may perform a virtual coordination function. We have no intention of denying this possibility, but Aoki's examination is more closely related to investment decision-making rather than the daily decision-making needed to decide how much to produce today or this week. What we will show in this section is the simultaneous stability of both the price adjustment and quantity adjustment processes.

We assume that "the investment" is made, as we have assumed Postulate 17, but such a decision is only made once or twice a year. We are concerned in Sects. 7.2 and 7.3 with everyday decisions on how much product to produce in the coming period. Based on the researches of Taniguchi and Morioka, we will show that the adjusting process of inventories is in fact stabilizing in the sense that the whole network of each firm's production decisions can easily follow the slow change of demand flows. The exact meaning of the expression "can follow the slow change of demand flows" will be become clear when Morioka's result is explained (Subsect. 2.7.4).

2.7.2 Individual Firm's Behavior

Let us first examine how each firm decides today's or tomorrow's production volume for each product. These decisions are normally made by managers of the production unit or site, say a factory or plant. Those managers know only a very small part of the economy. They surely know the sales volume history of each product. They may know the prices and changes in price of almost all input goods. They may roughly know the production trend of each client. However, they may not know how much their competitors had sold of such and such products, both competitive and substitute.

Among the various kinds of information, the most important one for them must be the sales volume of each product including its history. Suppose a manager wanted to decide how much of the product the factory produces today. At this time, he or she may not know today's sales volume of the product. However, in the age of information and communication technology, it is not difficult to know how much the product sold yesterday. The manager can also easily know the past history of sales volumes. It is easy to imagine that our manager uses this past information when he or she wants to decide the planned volume of production for tomorrow.[54]

If the sales volume is accurately constant, there is no big problem. It suffices to produce as much as the constant sales volume. However, the sales volume changes everyday. The most important work for managers is to know the sales volume of the product for today, tomorrow, and the days after tomorrow. However, accurate

[54]Expectation may play some role in the decision. But it cannot be the major determinant. It is a kind of pulling oneself up one's bootstraps.

prediction is impossible. The best method the manager can take is to assume a probability distribution for the sales volume of these days. By the past time series, the manager can know the rough probability distribution. At least, he or she can calculate the mean and variance reflecting current trends and seasonal factors. For a short run, this may be sufficient for manager to decide the production plan for today and tomorrow. But it is not assured that the mean and variance remain constant for a long time. We have to take note that firms or production units are facing ever-changing flow of demand. Therefore, demand estimation should contain an updating process to include the accumulating sales history.

As it is impossible to guess the demand even for the near future, to possess a certain amount of inventory of finished products is inevitable. The problem of finding the best decision-making method is thus transformed to that of finding the best possible and most practical inventory control policy. These problems are investigated as a theory of inventory. It is now a part of operations research or industrial management. We now have a rich stock of knowledge to guide us in this, but it is not our purpose in this section to develop the theory systematically. We only wish to show the most basic results which may thus help us to understand how the actual decisions are made.

It is well known that firms' approaches to dealing with demand fluctuation are quite varied. Many firms keep a certain amount of finished products and try to respond as quickly as possible when a purchase offer is expressed. On the other hand, some firms keep no stock of finished product. They produce the products only when a firm procurement plan is expressed by clients. The first case is called make-to-stock (MTS) production and the second case build-to-order (BTO) production. This is a widely observed fact, and we may ask what contributes to creating this difference of approaches.

A possible answer is given by Scarf (1958). He studied a case when the probability distribution is not fully known. He assumed that only the mean μ and the standard deviation σ are known. There is a continuum of probability distributions that have mean μ and standard deviation σ. Even in this case, Scarf found that the min-max solution in the following sense can be expressed in an astonishingly simple way. The min-max solution is the inventory level y that maximizes the minimal profits (or gain) for all probability distributions with μ and σ. The main part of Scarf's (1958) examination was devoted to the case of perishable goods. Perishable means that the product cannot be carried over to next production period. The producer or seller sells products as long as inventory is available. When the product remains unsold at the end of the period, the stock is destroyed without cost.

The case of durable goods is more interesting. Scarf examines this as a case of having positive salvage cost. A production period can be an interval of time of any length, but we assume it to be a day or a week. Then, almost all goods are durable goods except for rapidly perishable goods like fresh fish or newspapers. Scarf examines the positive salvage value case in Sect. 2.4. This is the result we cite here. The solution y of the min-max problem for this case is given by the formula (Scarf 1958 IV):

$$y = \begin{cases} \mu + \sigma\ f\left((c-s)\,/\,(p-s)\right) & \text{if } \left(1+\sigma^2/\mu^2\right) < (p-s)\,/\,(c-s)\,, \\ 0 & \text{if } \left(1+\sigma^2/\mu^2\right) > (p-s)\,/\,(c-s)\,. \end{cases} \quad (2.37)$$

Here, p is the price of the product, c the cost of production or purchase, and s is what Scarf called salvage value. The function f is defined as

$$f(a) = (1/2) \cdot (1-2a)\,/\sqrt{a\,(1-a)}. \quad (2.38)$$

The essence of the proof of this astonishing theorem lies in the fact that the minimum of the expected gains is achieved by a two-point distribution.

The salvage value is explained as the unit price of the unsold products when they are sold. We will interpret the salvage cost as the value of the product minus the holding cost minus the cost of deterioration, which may be difficult to evaluate. The value of the product is the unit full production cost or the unit price when it was purchased. The holding cost is the cost to carry over each unit of inventory to the next period. It comprises the interest for keeping inventory for one period and the deterioration of product by time passing. A perishable good has a deterioration rate near to 1. In other words, almost all the value is destroyed at the end of a period.

Let the interest rate be i and the deterioration rate d. Then the holding cost of a unit of unsold inventory is $(i + d)\ c$. If necessary we include other holding costs within the deterioration rate. The remaining inventory can be used as a part of inventory for the next period. If the markup rate is m, then $p = (1 + m)\ c$, and the salvage value s is $(1-i-d)\ c$. Therefore, we have

$$p - s = (m+i+d)\,c \text{ and } c - s = c - (1-i-d)\ c = (i+d)\,c.$$

Then,

$$(p-s)\,/\,(c-s) = (m+i+d)\,/\,(i+d) = 1 + m/\,(i+d)\,.$$

The first line "if" condition in (2.37) is satisfied when

$$\sigma^2/\mu^2 < m/\,(i+d)\,.$$

We show here, in the form of a theorem, Scarf's result but expressed in a slightly different form.

Theorem 7.1 (Scarf Theorem on Min-Max Solution)
Let p, c, and s be the selling price, the cost, and the salvage value, respectively. Then the initial inventory level y of the mini-max solution for all probability distributions with mean μ and standard deviation σ is given as follows:

1. *When*

$$\sigma^2/\mu^2 < m/\,(i+d)\,, \tag{2.39}$$

then

$$y = \mu + \sigma\; f\,((i+d)\,/\,(m+i+d))\,, \tag{2.40}$$

where the function f is given by (2.38).

2. *When*

$$\sigma^2/\mu^2 > m/\,(i+d)\,, \tag{2.39bis}$$

then

$$y = 0.$$

The implications of Theorem 7.1 are clear. If the product is durable, d is negligible. Normally we can expect that the markup rate m is greater than the interest rate. If not, the firms cannot gain the interest cost when they borrow operating funds from banks. We can think of it as an abnormal state. Then, the condition (2.39) is satisfied when $\sigma < \mu$. We can assume that this condition normally holds when μ is sufficiently large. When μ is small and near to 1, the order can be well approximated by a Poisson distribution. In this case, it is a well-known fact that $\sigma = \mu$. The condition $\sigma < \mu$ is not satisfied. Even in such a case, we can normally assume that m is sufficiently greater than i. Therefore, we can assume that the condition (2.39) holds for almost all durable products.

Of course, there are exceptions. A Lévy distribution has a mean, but its variation is infinite. Although we do not know a good example, if the distribution is near to this distribution, it is logically possible that σ is much greater than μ.

The condition (2.39) may not hold when the product is perishable. Suppose, for example, that $d = 1$. In this case, condition (2.39bis) holds when

$$\sigma^2/\mu^2 > m.$$

If m is 0.5, for example, the condition holds when

$$\sigma > 2.24\ \mu.$$

Even when the product is durable, if μ is very small, σ may be much greater than μ. For example, suppose that $\mu = 0.01$, i.e., the order comes once in 100 days on average. In this case,

$$\begin{aligned}\sigma^2 &= (1-0.01)^2 \cdot 0.01 + (2-0.01)\;\,2 \cdot 0.01^2 + \cdots \\ &\fallingdotseq 0.0102 \\ \mu^2 &= 0.01^2 = 0.0001.\end{aligned}$$

Then $\sigma^2/\mu^2 \risingdotseq 102$. This value may be greater than $m/(i + d)$ even if d is small. The actual short-term prime rate in Japan (as of May 2018) is 1.45% although Japan is in an extraordinary monetary easing regime. Even if the markup rate is 100%, the ratio m/i does not exceed 69.

Theorem 7.1 gives a rough idea of why some products are produced by make-to-stock principle and some others by the build-to-order principle. If the condition (2.39bis) holds for all firms which produce the same product, there are no firms which are prepared to sell the product ready-made. Then all firms that want to procure the product have to order and wait for the product to be produced. On the other hand, if the condition (2.39) holds for some firms which produce the same product, those firms offer the product ready-made and stocked. Thus, whether firms produce by the make-to-stock or the build-to-order principle depends on whether the condition (2.39) holds or not.

Theorem 7.1 gives us another interesting suggestion. When condition (2.39) holds, the formula (2.40) suggests that it is wise to prepare the initial inventory y in the form of $\mu + \sigma\, k$ where

$$k = f\left((i + d) \,/\, (m + i + d)\right). \tag{2.41}$$

As function f is given explicitly by formula (2.38), we can know its basic characteristics easily. The value $f(a)$ takes a positive value when $0 < a < 1/2$. If $m > i + d$, this condition is satisfied. It is also noteworthy that k is independent of the form of the demand distribution. If we admit that the min-max solution is a wise strategy for managers of firms to follow, it has the good property of being a solution to practical problems. The most important property that a practical solution must have is that we can calculate the solution with minimal information. The parameters m, i, and d are ordinarily used constants, although the deterioration rate is less well known generally.

As we have indicated above, the future demand for a product is the most difficult to estimate. Normally we have not enough information. Past time series may give us a rough estimate, but we cannot get accurate estimates because demand is changing over short time periods. Estimates based on a longer time series may not give more accurate results. The mean and the standard deviation are the most common parameters to estimate probability distributions. In statistics we most often suppose that the probability distribution is Gaussian or normal. However, it is doubtful if the distribution is exactly Gaussian. As Haldane (2012) emphasized, Gaussian distribution may not be normal for social phenomena despite the fact that it has the name “normal distribution.” It is normal only for purely random stochastic events. The great advantage of the Scarf theorem is that it does not assume a normal distribution for changes in demand. There are big differences between the two assumptions: one is to assume the strong limitation that the distribution is normal and the other is to assume that the distribution merely has a known mean and standard deviation. The Scarf theorem has a plausible behavioral meaning even when the distribution is not normal as when various strong social or competitive forces exist in the medium term.

The two parameters, mean and standard deviation, almost always go together. However, it is worth noting that the standard deviation is more difficult than the mean to determine accurately even if its value can be calculated. As for means, we can take a moving average of various types. In the following, the span of the moving average is five to ten. The difficulty with a standard deviation is that any degree of accuracy requires much longer series than five to ten periods. The standard deviation depends more on the occurrence of rare events than the mean and hence requires a bigger set of samples to get the same accuracy.[55]

In the following and further chapters by Morioka and Taniguchi, we most often take as the mean the moving average over every five periods. If five periods are sufficient to estimate the mean, they are surely not sufficient to get a good estimate of the standard deviation. Instead of taking a longer time series to estimate the standard deviation, it is convenient to assume that σ's proportionality to μ only changes significantly over a longer time period. If this assumption is appropriate, then the min-max solution y takes the form $(1 + K)\mu$. Indeed, if $\sigma = k' \mu$, then (2.41) gives $y = (1 + K) \mu$ if $K = k' k$.

In the following we assume the next behavior as Postulate 18.

Postulate 18 (Inventory Policy)
Firms take an inventory policy in which they aim to hold

$$y = (1 + K)\ \mu \tag{2.42}$$

as inventory at the head of a period, where μ is a moving average and K is a parameter which is adjusted by experience.

This is in fact the inventory policy that we observe on many occasions. The coefficient K is often called the buffer stock ratio (see Chap. 4 by Morioka in this book) or safety inventory ratio. There is no need to calculate K according to formula (2.40). We can start by an arbitrarily chosen K and adjust it through experience. For example, when over a short interval of time we experience two or three occasions on which inventory was insufficient, we can increase K. If large unsold stocks were left consecutively for a long period of time, we can similarly decrease K. In this way, we may converge to a suitable K without knowing the exact form of demand distribution.

On the other hand, if we can assume that the demand distribution is stable for a long time, we may calculate the mean and the variance (and the standard deviation). In such a situation, it is possible to compare two results: (1) the one

---

[55] We are accustomed to think in the world where the mean and variance exist. However, if the sequence obeys Lévy stable distribution law, the variance does not exist even when the mean exists (when $1 < \alpha < 2$ for Lévy index α). In such a case, it is evident that we cannot obtain a reasonable estimate of the variance by an observation of finite length.

which is obtained by adjusting K and (2) the one by theoretically obtained K by (2.40). However, it is not necessary that (2) is better than (1). It is possible that the customarily adjusted coefficient K is better than the theoretically calculated solution, because the assumptions of Theorem 7.1 may not have been true or the data were not sufficiently exact. The Scarf theorem is best interpreted as a thought experiment in describing what managers do in everyday decision-making.

In the inventory control theory, there is another type of control. This is named the (S, s)- or two-bin method. Its object is to prepare the initial inventory of the product according to the following rule having noted z the inventory left at the end of the previous period:

If $z < s$, prepare the initial inventory of the period to be equal to S by ordering production y.
If $z > s$, do not place a new order. In other words, let $y = 0$.

Scarf and others studied precisely the practicality of this method. See the review article by Scarf (2002). When the demand distribution is known and the gain (and loss) function can be estimated accurately, they could prove for a very wide range of situations that this is the best control method. When a big setup cost is required, this is the most often used method for actual inventory control. However, the (S, s)-method has two major inconveniences: (1) it is not easy to calculate S and s and (2) the control process is not linear.

The first inconvenience is a computational difficulty. In order to calculate S and s as a solution to the optimization problem, it is necessary to solve a recurrent equation which comprises minimization and integral operators. This is not an easy task (the reader can see some examples in Chap. 6).

The second inconvenience is no trouble for practical purposes, because it is a simple calculation when S and s are known. The trouble with (2) lies for us (i.e., researchers) when we want to know how the whole process of the economy develops. The trouble is that it is difficult to know the behavior of such a process mathematically. The process in which firms employ the (S, s)-method is analyzed empirically by numerical experiments, as the readers will know in Chap. 6 by Taniguchi. His experiments go back to Taniguchi (1991, 1997). In comparison to the (S, s)-method, the control method based on (2.42) has a much better potential for further analysis, because the process is in fact linear. Although we have to deal with extremely high-dimensional matrices, it is possible to express the total process as a linear transformation.[56] This was successfully done by Morioka (1991–1992; 2005). Their results are explained for the first time in English in the subsequent chapters.

[56] For this, it is necessary to assume that customers wait until the next period, when the demand exceeds the prepared stock. This is equivalent to assuming a negative inventory stock.

2.7.3 Linearity and Nonlinearity of the Inventory Adjustment Process

The difference between two control policies is crucial. Let us give a brief account on this point. Linearity is normally defined for operators or maps. A map f from a linear space E to a linear space F is defined to be linear when f satisfies the following property:

$$f\,(a\mathbf{x}+b\mathbf{y}) = a\ f\,(\mathbf{x}) + b\ f\,(\mathbf{y}) \qquad \forall a, b \in \mathrm{R}, \mathbf{x} \text{ and } \mathbf{y} \in E.$$

In our case, we are concerned with time series of the product demand:

$$\ldots, \mathbf{x}\,(-T)\,, \ldots, \mathbf{x}\,(-1)\,, \mathbf{x}(0), \mathbf{x}(1), \ldots. \tag{2.43}$$

The space E is the set of all these time series. An element of E is essentially transformed by a map f to a series of production volumes or procurements:

$$\ldots, \mathbf{y}\,(-T)\,, \ldots, \mathbf{y}\,(-1)\,, \mathbf{y}(0), \mathbf{y}(1), \ldots \tag{2.44}$$

First let us examine the case when the product is perishable. In that case, there is no stock of product which is transferred to the next period. In other words, the inventory $\mathbf{z}(t)$ is always 0. In this case, the production series $\mathbf{y}(y)$ defined by policy (2.41) is given by the formula:

$$\mathbf{y}(1) = (1+K)\ \left[\left(\mathbf{x}\,(-M) + \cdots + \mathbf{x}\,(-1)\right)/M\right]$$

where $\mathbf{y}(1)$ is the moving average production over M periods.

When the product is durable, we have the inventory left after the period. In this case, we should consider a series of carried-over inventories:

$$\ldots, \mathbf{z}\,(-T)\,, \ldots, \mathbf{z}\,(-1)\,, \mathbf{z}(0), \mathrm{z}(1), \ldots \tag{2.45}$$

together with the production series (2.44).

The stock $\mathbf{z}(t)$ is interpreted as the inventory which is left in the previous period and is now carried over to time point t.[57] The variable $\mathbf{x}(t)$ stands for the demand during the period $[t, t+1)$. We assume that demand for the product comes randomly like a Poisson process. The variable $\mathbf{x}(t)$ is the sum of those demands expressed in the interval $[t,\ t+1)$, which is only known at time point $t+1$. The demand is composed of final demand and endogenous demand. In the next subsection, time structure is important. It is important to distinguish the concept of time (or time point) t from the period $[t, t+1)$.

[57] The inventory $\mathbf{z}(t)$ can be interpreted in two ways. Here we have defined as inventory which is carried over to time t. Another method is to define it as stock left at the period $[t, t+1)$.

The production volume must be decided two periods earlier.[58] Thus $\mathbf{y}(2)$ is decided at $t = 0$. Necessary inputs are ordered at time 0 and prepared to be used as inputs at the time point 1. Consequently, the output $\mathbf{y}(2)$ is decided by formula:

$$\mathbf{y}(2) = (1 + K)\ \left[(\mathbf{x}(-M) + \cdots + \mathbf{x}(-1))\,/M \right] - \mathbf{z}^{\mathrm{e}}(2) \qquad (2.46)$$

while the expected inventory $\mathbf{z}^{\mathrm{e}}(2)$ is given by

$$\mathbf{z}^{\mathrm{e}}(2) = \mathbf{y}(1) + \mathbf{z}^{\mathrm{e}}(1) - \mathbf{x}^{\mathrm{e}}(1). \qquad (2.47)$$

We have written here $\mathbf{z}^{\mathrm{e}}(2)$ and $\mathbf{z}^{\mathrm{e}}(1)$, indicating estimated values, instead of $\mathbf{z}(2)$ and $\mathbf{z}(1)$, because at $t = 0$ they are not yet determined. The manager is obliged to use estimates. In our case,

$$\mathbf{x}^{\mathrm{e}}(1) = \left[(\mathbf{x}(-M) + \cdots + \mathbf{x}(-1))\,/\mathbf{M} \right], \qquad \mathbf{z}^{\mathrm{e}}(1) = \mathbf{z}(0). \qquad (2.48)$$

Replacing (2.47) by (2.48), we get the formula:

$$\mathbf{y}(2) = (2 + K)\ \left[(\mathbf{x}(-M) + \cdots + \mathbf{x}(-1))\,/M \right] - \left[\mathbf{y}(1) + \mathbf{z}(0) \right]. \qquad (2.49a)$$

If $\mathbf{y}(2)$ is determined, the inputs that are necessary to produce $\mathbf{y}(2)$ are ordered between (0, 1) and procured before $t = 1$. When $\mathbf{x}(1)$ is determined, we can calculate the actual $\mathbf{z}(1)$ by the formula:

$$\mathbf{z}(1) = \mathbf{y}(0) + \mathbf{z}(0) - \mathbf{x}(0). \qquad (2.49b)$$

Of course, this may not be equal to $\mathbf{z}^{\mathrm{e}}(1)$. In the next subsection, we show that $\mathbf{x}(0)$ can be expressed as

$$\mathbf{x}(0) = \mathbf{d}(1) + \mathbf{y}(2)\mathbf{A}. \qquad (2.49c)$$

Here $\mathbf{d}(1)$ is the final demand and $\mathbf{y}(2)\,A$ the endogenous demand for [0, 1). In this case, the transformation *f*, restricted to $t = 0$, takes a form that maps

$$\mathbf{x}(-M), \ldots, \mathbf{x}(-1), \mathbf{y}(0), \mathbf{y}(1), \mathbf{z}(0)$$

to

$$\mathbf{x}(-M + 1), \ldots, \mathbf{x}(0), \mathbf{y}(1), \mathbf{y}(2), \mathbf{z}(1).$$

[58] If firms possess material stock for input use, we can imagine a case the product is obtained only one period after the decision. Morioka uses this convention.

In view of (2.49a), (2.49b), and (2.49c), this transformation is linear. When the series $\mathbf{x}(-M+1), \ldots, \mathbf{x}(0), \mathbf{y}(1), \mathbf{y}(2), \mathbf{z}(1)$ is obtained, then we can get a new series

$$\mathbf{x}\,(-M+2)\,, \ldots, \mathbf{x}(1), \mathbf{y}(2), \mathbf{y}(3), \mathbf{z}(2)$$

by the shifted transformations (2.49a), (2.49b), and (2.49c) whose time variable t is replaced by $t+1$. We can continue in this way the transformation infinitely, and we get the total transformation f for infinite series. As shifted (2.49a), (2.49b), and (2.49c) are all linear, the total transformation f is also linear.[59]

In the case of the (S, s)-method, the decision rule (2.41) takes a different form. If we take a representative firm, it is expressed as follows:

$$\begin{aligned} y(1) &= S - z(1) \text{ if } z(1) < s, \\ y(1) &= 0 \qquad\qquad \text{if } z(1) > s. \end{aligned} \tag{2.50}$$

The map f is now discontinuous when $S > s$, because $y(1)$ is a part of the image and is discontinuous at $z(1) = s$. The map f cannot be linear. Any infinite-dimensional linear map is continuous when its domain of definition is restricted on a finite-dimensional subspace. To know the behavior described by of (2.50) is difficult to analyze. In general, an exact interpretation is impossible. The best way to understand the behavior of this kind of process is to appeal to numerical experimentation. Although we know of some exact analyses of nonlinear processes, it is often impossible to obtain a logically exact result. In the case where the setup cost is negligible, we know that $S = s$. Even in this case, the graph of map (2.50) is composed of two line segments but not linear in the sense defined above.

The analysis of nonlinear phenomenon is in general very difficult. Such a phenomenon exhibits complex behavior and often exceeds the capacity of mathematical analysis. This is one of the main reasons that we have to admit the *third mode of scientific research* (Shiozawa 2016a).

We have examined how individual firms' decisions are made. But it is not the main purpose of our investigation. An economy is a complex network of mutual interactions of different agents. What will happen if the adjustment process is extended? We will examine this problem in the next subsection.

2.7.4 Total Adjustment Process

As the details are explained in each of following chapters, here we will explain the core features of the process.

[59]In the above consideration, we have assumed that there is no beginning in our series. When we assume that the series start at a specific point of time $-T$, we must redefine the transformation f, because variables $x(-T-M)$, $x(-T-M+1)$, $\ldots$, $x(-T-1)$ are not known at $-T$.

In Sect. 2.7.2, we have observed how the producers and sellers control production volumes and product stocks. Properly speaking, how each producer and seller behaves are the problems of production control. Economics needs information on these behaviors, but the real task of economics comes after this. The question for economics is to ask what happens when each firm behaves as we have observed. This is not an easy question. A behavior of a single firm cannot be assumed to represent a behavior of the economy as a whole. Post-Keynesians criticize the concept of a representative firm or individual. They are right, because the actions of each firm are dependent on actions of other firms, and firms as organizational entities (institutions) operate differently from people. However, it seems there are only a few numbers of researchers which focus on this theme. We regret that many post-Keynesians are skipping this crucial aspect of economic analysis. This might be a side effect of the post-Keynesian objection to the new Keynesians' focus on microfoundation studies. The objection itself is correct, but it is not right to think that we can arrive at correct insights without any analyses of how the interconnections of firms work in practice and what kind of processes these produce at the macro-level.

The interactions between firms are not simple. Assume a firm F is producing a product X. To produce the product, it needs to use a variety of inputs: labor, fixed capital, parts and components, materials, and services. Except labor forces, all these inputs are products of past production processes. Thus the production of a commodity is a production by means of commodities. Moreover, these inputs are also produced by using yet other inputs. The whole network created by these chains of inputs is extremely complex. There is no simple hierarchical structure such as that which Austrian economists have usually assumed.

When a production volume is decided by a production manager, they not only communicate it to the production shop but also prepare for the supply of the material inputs required. This may not be a difficult work, because quantities necessary to produce a certain quantity of the product must have been determined in advance. The manager can give the general directive which asks their subordinates to procure the necessary quantities of parts, components, and materials from suitable producers in an appropriate time.

But what happens within this network of production and procurement chains? Suppose, for example, that all procurements are made on a build-to-order basis. Does this system work? If we analyze the time structure of the information transfer process, it turns out that this procurement system does not work at all. In fact, suppose that the decision to produce a product P at time T is made at time t. Of course, T must be after t. However, if we trace back to the inputs which have to be made N steps earlier in the chain of commodity production, the order to procure the inputs must be made at $T–N$. As N can be as big as we choose, this means that $T–N < t$ can be true for some goods. This indicates that the procurement order should have been placed before the time of the decision to make product P. This is impossible.

This contradiction is insoluble if all firms in the economy adopt the build-to-order principle. This is the reason why the build-to-order principle cannot be a universal principle for all production processes. On the other hand, the make-to-stock principle can be a universal principle, as we will soon see in the following chapters. This is the primary reason for assuming that all firms produce on the make-to-stock principle and respond to procurement orders by reducing their stocks of previously finished products. Another reason is that the make-to-stock principle is far more widely used than the build-to-order principle. For a theoretical analysis, we are required to simplify our situational setting for the sake of tractability. In a mathematical analysis, a preferable choice is to adopt a behavioral principle that can be applied uniformly to the whole economy. It is evident that this is not an imperative, but often this is a necessary simplification for the tractability and transparency of the analysis. Of course, if we do not mind complication, we can mix up several different behavioral principles. This kind of analysis is only possible when we appeal to computer simulation because of the complexity of nonlinear transformations.

Now let us proceed to a more concrete argument. We want to analyze the interdependence of production processes. In this analysis, it is necessary to avoid those behaviors of firms that might make it impossible for managers to make a decision in real-time situations. To satisfy this requirement, we assume that managers make decisions that satisfy the following three criteria:

1. No information about the future is used for the decision. Expectation is possible, but it must be made by a simple estimation rule on the basis of past information.
2. Firms use information such as orders that are revealed to them by other agents.
3. Decision rules must be simple and easily calculable ones.

Within the range that does not violate these criteria, we assume an economy and procedures whereby:

1. Firms sell at the predetermined price any amount to satisfy demand from anyone as long as the initial inventory permits.
2. We assume that a firm produces only one kind of product. Firms and products are labeled by the same index, for example, i. We assume that there are in total N different products in the economy. Production period is assumed to be equal to a time unit. This time unit can be a day or a week.
3. Each firm has an already built production capacity. Within this capacity, any amount of production is possible. To produce a unit of product i, we assume a_{ij} units of product j are to be used as inputs. By the minimal price theorem, we can assume that each firm has a fixed production technique that gives it the minimal cost.
4. Demand for a product is composed of two parts: (i) independent or exogenous demand and (ii) internal or endogenous demand. Independent demand is composed of consumer demands and investment demands (if necessary, we may include in this class the demand for exports). Internal demand is composed of inputs for the production.
5. A decision to make a product at volume y_i is made two periods earlier than the time the product is produced. Imagine that a firm i decides to produce y_i amount of the product i at time $t + 2$, the decision must be made at time t. When the

decision is made by the firm i, orders are made to each firm j. Inputs are procured during time interval $[t, t+1)$ and inputted at time $t+1$. The product comes out at time $t+2$.

6. Decision rules that a firm employs are variants of (2.49a, 2.49b and 2.49c). The demand estimation method can be replaced by other forms of moving averages.
7. We assume that the buffer coefficients are the same for all goods.

On these settings, the production process of the whole economy can be described in a matrix form. Indeed, let $\mathbf{d}(t) = (d_1(t)), \ldots, d_N(t))$ be a vector of independent demand for each product. If the production vector is $\mathbf{y} = (y_1, \ldots, y_N)$, the input vector that should be prepared is expressed as $\mathbf{y}\,A$, where A is the square matrix (a_{ij}). Suppose we are given a series of final demands:

$$\ldots, \mathbf{d}(-T), \ldots, \mathbf{d}(-1), \mathbf{d}(0), \mathbf{d}(1), \ldots \tag{2.51}$$

Then

$$\mathbf{x}(t) = \mathbf{y}(t+2)\,A + \mathbf{d}(t)$$

for all t. Then, each firm's decision generates a series of productions and procurements. In view of firms' behavior (2.49a, 2.49b and 2.49c) that we have examined in Sect. 2.7.2, vectors are determined in turn:

$$\begin{aligned}
&\mathbf{y}(t+2) = (2+K)\ [(\mathbf{x}(t-M) + \cdots + \mathbf{x}(t-1))\,/M] - [\mathbf{y}(t+1) + \mathbf{z}(t)]\,.\\
&\mathbf{x}(t) = \mathbf{y}(t+2)\,A + \mathbf{d}(t).\\
&\mathbf{z}(t+1) = \mathbf{y}(t) + \mathbf{z}(t) - \mathbf{x}(t) = \mathbf{y}(t) + \mathbf{z}(t) - \mathbf{y}(t+2)\,A - \mathbf{d}(t).
\end{aligned} \tag{2.52}$$

As a total process for the economy, this can be written as a transformation from a set of vectors

$$\{\mathbf{x}(t-M), \ldots, \mathbf{x}(t-1), \mathbf{y}(t), \mathbf{y}(t+1), \mathbf{z}(t)\}$$

to a set of vectors

$$\{\mathbf{x}(t-M+1), \ldots, \mathbf{x}(t), \mathbf{y}(t+1), \mathbf{y}(t+2), \mathbf{z}(t+1)\}$$

defined by (2.52). This process continues as long as:

1. $\mathbf{y}_j(t+2)$ stays within the capacity of the firm j.
2. $\mathbf{y}(t+2) + \mathbf{z}(t+2) > \mathbf{x}(t+2)$, i.e., there is sufficient inventory.
3. $\langle\, \mathbf{y}(t+2), \mathbf{a}_0 \,\rangle < L$, i.e., there exists sufficient labor power L in the economy. Here, column vector $\mathbf{a}_0$ is composed of labor input coefficients (Expression $\mathbf{a}_0$ is used here to avoid confusion with $\mathbf{u}(t)$ which we use later in a different meaning.).

It is possible that each of these three conditions is violated. However, if the possibility of situation (1) approaches, the firm j normally increases its capacity (Postulate 17). If the situation (2) repeats often, the buffer stock ratio will be raised. Consequently, we can assume that this situation occurs rarely. Whenever it occurs, the quantity adjustment process transgresses the rule we have examined in Sect. 2.7.2. This process is no more linear, and we are obliged to appeal to numerical simulation (see Taniguchi's chapters).

First, let us assume that the process continues without hindrances. Let $\kappa = (2 + K)/M$. We have assumed that buffer stock ratios are all the same for all products. If they are different, we have to take, instead of κ, a diagonal matrix K with $2 + K_j$ at the j-th diagonal.[60] We write Θ a big $(M + 3)\cdot N) \times (M + 3)\cdot N$ square matrix of the form[61]

$$\Theta = \begin{Bmatrix} 0 & 0 & \ldots & 0 & \kappa A & 0 & \kappa I & -\kappa A \\ I & 0 & \ldots & 0 & \kappa A & 0 & \kappa I & -\kappa A \\ 0 & I & \ldots & 0 & \kappa A & 0 & \kappa I & -\kappa A \\ \cdot & \cdot & \cdots & \cdot & \cdot & \cdot & \cdot & \cdot \\ \cdot & \cdot & \cdots & \cdot & \kappa A & 0 & \kappa I & -\kappa A \\ 0 & 0 & \ldots & I & 0 & 0 & 0 & I \\ 0 & 0 & \ldots & 0 & -A & I & -I & -A \\ 0 & 0 & \ldots & 0 & -A & 0 & -I & I - A \end{Bmatrix} \tag{2.53}$$

and $\mathbf{u}(t)$ a vector of the form

$$\{\mathbf{x}(t - M), \ldots, \mathbf{x}(t - 1), \mathbf{y}(t), \mathbf{y}(t + 1), \mathbf{z}(t)\}.$$

Then we can obtain a simple recursive equation

$$\mathbf{u}(t + 1) = \mathbf{u}(t)\,\Theta + (0\,0 \ldots \mathbf{d}(t)\;0\;0\;\text{-}\mathbf{d}(t)). \tag{2.54}$$

Suppose for the moment that $\mathbf{d}(t)$ is constant for all t. If the absolute value of all eigenvalues of matrix Θ is less than 1, $I+\Theta+\Theta^2+\cdots+\Theta^T+\cdots$ converges to a definite matrix $(I-\Theta)^{-1}$. If the exogenous demand $\mathbf{d}(t)$ is equal to a vector $\mathbf{d}$ for a long time, we can prove that $\mathbf{u}(t)$ tends to $\mathbf{u}$ that satisfies the equation

$$\mathbf{u}(I - \Theta) = (0 \ldots \mathbf{d}\;\;0\;\;0\;\text{-}\mathbf{d}).$$

This means that $\mathbf{y}(t)$ tends to produce exogenous demand $\mathbf{d}(t)$ if the latter is moving sufficiently slowly,

[60] Note that matrices K and A are no more commutative, i.e., $K\,A \neq A\,K$ in general.

[61] The matrix form and the dimensions are different from Morioka's matrices(e.g, Φ which appears in Eqs. (4.21) and (4.48)), because I have not reduced to minimum mutually dependent variables.

However, how can we estimate eigenvalues of matrix Θ? I myself tried to investigate a similar process with $M = 2$ with a predictive expectation for sales volume (Shiozawa 1983b). In this case, I found that the process was divergent. I wanted to examine other cases using a moving average over greater values of M. The hurdles seemed be too high. I could not imagine that I can estimate eigenvalues of matrices of high dimensions which still obtain a structure like Θ. To my astonishment, Morioka (1991–1992) succeeded in finding two such conditions, one necessary and another sufficient condition which are simple inequalities between M, K, and the maximal eigenvalue in absolute values of matrix A when A is diagonalizable (see later chapters by Morioka).[62] A sufficient condition was

$$\lambda < M/(M + 2K + 4).$$

If $M = 5$, $K = 0.5$, this signifies that the process is convergent (or stable) when $\lambda < 0.5$. If $M = 10$, $K = 0.5$, when $\lambda < 0.667$. For some input-output tables, the biggest eigenvalue can be as big as 0.588.[63] If we take this example, the process (2.54) is stable when we take $M = 10$ and $K = 0.5$.

Second, what happens when the process meets hindrances where one of three conditions is not satisfied. The process is no more linear, because we have to deal with operators like taking the maximum or minimum among two variables. This is the problems that Taniguchi wanted to attack. In this case, pure mathematical reasoning is not useful. We can say little about the process. This is the reason why he has appealed to simulation. To summarize Taniguchi's results is not easy. We have to ask readers to read Chap. 6. A very rough summary is this: nonlinear control processes including the (S, s)-method behave almost similar to linear cases.

Let us summarize Morioka and Taniguchi's results in a form of a theorem. As it includes the knowledge obtained from computer simulation, it is not a theorem as understood in mathematics. Perhaps it is more close to laws as employed in physics.

Theorem 7.2 (Taniguchi and Morioka)
The quantity adjustment process of firms is convergent as a whole when the span of its moving average is taken appropriately.

The meaning of convergence should be elaborated. Production of all firms tends to a state in which they produce as net product the constant levels of exogenous demand when the exogenous demand for each product tends to a constant value.

[62]Diagonalizability is not a severe condition. As it is dense in the matrices of the same dimension and the sufficient condition is given in a simple algebraic inequality, the same condition is also a sufficient condition for non-diagonalizable matrices.

[63]Eigenvalues of an input-output table's coefficients may depend on the degree of aggregation. The coefficient for manufacturing of the 14-sector table is 0.44427204. According to my computation by Mathematica, the matrix for 19 sectors from mining to miscellaneous manufacturing extracted from input coefficients (37-sector table, 2011, Japan) has the biggest eigenvalue, 0.57006. The next biggest eigenvalues are 0.435129, 0.421933, 0.382724, and 0.288406. See also Morioka's results in Chap. 4 (Subsect. 4.1.2).

This does not imply of course that the exogenous demands should be constant. Convergence means that the production system follows the changes in exogenous demand when they change slowly.

This means the following. Let the maximal eigenvalue (Frobenius root) be λ ($0 < \lambda < 1$). This depends on the input coefficient matrix A. Morioka calculates this for the input coefficient matrices of Japan for various years and various sizes (see Chap. 4 Subsect. 4.1.2 and footnote 7 there). All of them were between 0.5 and 0.55.

Let us estimate the half-life of the most simple case for the matrix Φ in Theorem 1 in Chapter 4 by Morioka. Then, the eigenvalue of Φ with maximal absolute value is given by $\{(T+2K+4)/T\}\cdot\lambda$, where λ is the Frobenius root of the input coefficient matrix A. Let us take the case M = 5, K = 0.5. If we assume that the Frobenius root of A is either 0.5 or 0.55, then the "maximal" eigenvalue is 0.75 and 0.825, respectively. Let one of them be ρ. The half-life Hl is defined by (log 1/2)/(log ρ). Then Hl = 2.4 for the first case and 3.6 for the second case. First, suppose that the system is running at a constant production volume corresponding to a constant exogenous demand. If the external demand jumps by 50% from one constant level to another, the system starts to adjust itself to a new demand. During the first few cycles, the production may overshoot the new constant level. Assume, for example, the production volume increased to double that of the original level. Then the system starts to converge to the new constant level. Let us say in this case the rate of divergence is 2/1.5 = 1.33. The half-life signifies that this rate becomes half each time the half-life passes by. In our case, the half-life was about 2.4 periods in the first case and 3.6 periods for the second case. We have assumed that one period is a day or a week. If we can assume that a period is a day, this means that the rate of divergence diminishes to half of the last divergence for each 2 and a half or 3.6 days. The rate of divergence diminishes from 33% to 15% after 2.5 or 3.6 days and then to 7% 5 or 7 days after the demand jump.

The exogenous demand changes in each period. If the variation of each period is not great, the production volume corresponds close to the average of the exogenous demand. Even if the exogenous demand is almost constant, the total demand fluctuates until the production approaches the new stable state. When the moving average does not change much for a span of two or three half-lives, the production follows the moving average within a narrow range of divergence. Small rapid fluctuations of total demand are absorbed by the ups and downs of inventory. Production as a whole responds to the moving average for two or three half-lives of constantly changing exogenous demand flows. This is the exact meaning of the expression "production follows the slow change of demand flows." Even if we talk about slowly changing demand flows, the exogenous and endogenous demands can be rapidly fluctuating with small variations.

The standard demand theory assumed that demand has a fixed value for a system of fixed prices. This kind of assumption was necessary only for the traditional demand and supply equilibrium framework. If the wage rate remains constant, our economy keeps constant prices so long as there is no change of technology or in the state of competition. But we assume as a standard situation that exogenous demand is always fluctuating and also that its moving average is changing slowly. Readers can thus clearly see the dynamic nature of our quantity adjustment process.

2.7.5 *Paramount Significance of Taniguchi and Morioka Results*

Arrow and Hahn (1971) once wrote in their introduction:

> There is by now a long and fairly imposing line of economists from Adam Smith to the present who have sought to show that a decentralized economy motivated by self-interest and guided by price signals would be compatible with a coherent disposition of economic resources that could be regarded, in a well-defined sense, as superior to a large class of possible alternative dispositions. Moreover, the price signals would operate in a way to establish this degree of coherence. It is important to understand how surprising this claim must be to anyone not exposed to the tradition. The immediate "common sense" answer to the question "What will an economy motivated by individual greed and controlled by a very large number of different agents look like?" is probably: There will be chaos. That quite a different answer has long been claimed true and has indeed permeated the economic thinking of a large number of people who are in no way economists is itself sufficient ground for investigating it seriously. The proposition having been put forward and very seriously entertained, it is important to know not only whether it *is* true, but whether it *could* be true. A good deal of what follows is concerned with this last question, which seems to us to have considerable claims on the attention of economists. (Arrow and Hahn 1971 pp. vi–vii)

According to them, "the notion that a social system moved by independent actions in pursuit of different values is consistent with a final coherent state of balance, and one in which the outcomes may be quite different from those intended by the agents, is surely the most important intellectual contribution that economic thought has made to the general understanding of social processes" (Arrow and Hahn 1971, p. 1). Frank Hahn, citing this paragraph in his inaugural lecture at Cambridge University, emphasized the importance of general equilibrium analysis (Hahn 1984 p. 64).

They may have been right when they wrote these texts. Long after them, there have been no serious attempts to go beyond Arrow and Hahn. Although there was, among mainstream economists, a big shift of interest toward more macroscopic problems, they seemed to have accepted the Arrow and Debreu framework as essentially right. Their efforts became questions of refinement, removing or introducing some or other aspect that had been neglected in the work of Arrow, Debreu, and Hahn. Questions are concerned with incomplete markets, imperfect information, monopolistic competition, sticky prices, market failure, and market-specific problems like those of the labor market and the credit market. From the 1990s to the present time, dynamical stochastic general equilibrium (DSGE) models became very popular both among new classical and new Keynesian economists. Although there emerged some new aspects of interest including rational expectations and exogenous disturbance, the names of these analysis reveal that their main framework remained the same.

The word "general equilibrium" often reduces to problems of inter-temporal coordination of a one-good economy. I doubt if their theory truly deserves the rather grand appellation of "general equilibrium." It is rather natural to assume that other mainstream economists accepted the Arrow-Debreu framework only because it was consistent with their own basic approach. However, the situation was little different among heterodox economists, who are in principle opposed to mainstream economics. Samuel Bowles was once the shining hope of American radical economists. Although he kept his social and political convictions, he seems to have accepted the Walrassian general equilibrium framework as the starting point of his evolutionary social sciences (Bowles 2003). He complains that "[t]here are four reasons for the limited applicability of the Fundamental Theorem" (Bowles 2003 p. 215). These four reasons are (1) the necessity of an auctioneer, (2) no theory on the convergence to an equilibrium, (3) the plurality of equilibria, and (4) the assumption of complete markets. But he admits that Arrow and Debreu's fundamental theorem is "a striking vindication of Adam Smith's conjecture that competitive exchange of claims on property would lead as if by 'an invisible hand to promote an end which was not part of' the participants' intentions" (ibid.). And this is for him the starting point of his research program, a program which is intended to introduce more realistic assumptions and which aims to be more suggestive of achieving a desirable society.

Another interesting example is Jean Cartelier (1991). Based on reflections that the non-tâtonnement (non-groping) research program had practically failed in France, Cartelier criticizes the general equilibrium framework in a beautiful way, even though he admits that "the fundamental problem of political economy" is the one which is concerned with how the decentralized economy functions and how the market assures the coordination of individual actions. Researches concerning general equilibrium can be classified under three big questions: (1) existence, (2) uniqueness, and (3) stability. Among these three, Cartelier points out that the first two groups had made some progress, whereas the third had produced only disappointing results and had become progressively neglected. His historical assessment is accurate, but lacks one point of detail. Although stability of the equilibrium point had been studied extensively, few researchers examined the shift from a disequilibrium state to an equilibrium state. In an attempt to remedy this state of affairs, Cartelier examines effective transactions in disequilibrium and begins to find the conditions under which a market economy works. He persuasively argues that money, the payment system, and banks are indispensable. It is a good argument, showing why a market economy needs to be supported by various institutions. At this point, he is a good institutionalist. However, the most important question remains. Although he may have detected the necessary conditions under which a market economy works, he says nothing about why, in his system, it is with money, a payment system, and banks that individual actions are coordinated successfully. He explains nothing on this crucial question. There is no sign that he is aware of this point. It seems he, quite simply, just believes that it works. But, can he then criticize neoclassical economists that they could not produce a satisfactory theory as to why the market economy is void of chaos in normal times?

Cartelier can be seen as a representative of many economists who are against the general equilibrium theory. They criticize that the Arrow-Debreu model requires various unrealistic assumptions including Bowles' four points. To them, we may add assumptions like unbounded rationality, complete information, nonexistence of money, and lack of institutions. They are frustrated with the general equilibrium theory just like Bowles and Cartelier are. But, they cannot compete with Arrow and Hahn. Arrow and Hahn knew very well that their models were unsatisfactory. They are asking economists to produce a satisfactory one if they are dissatisfied. Before Arrow and Debreu (1954), nobody could produce a logically coherent model of how a decentralized economy works. If they cannot do so, then their complaints stay in vain. When they were asked why a market economy works, they would be obliged to appeal to the parable of the general equilibrium model.

Taniguchi and Morioka's results are entirely different. The quantity adjustment process is clearly defined. Agents behave within the three limits of capabilities that we have discussed in Chap. 1. Information is transferred by activities of firms and procurers. Procurers express what quantity of which goods they want and possibly when. Among these procurers are included firms which need products as inputs to their own production. Transactions were made as an exchange between money and goods or services. Money is not a simple means of exchange. Money buys goods, but, in general, goods do not buy money. All demands are required to be backed by money. If money is not provided promptly, either suppliers should accord credit, or the procurers should get it from banks. There is no notion of equilibrium or disequilibrium. Prices are almost constant except when there is a big change in production costs. Under these relatively constant prices, demand changes constantly. If this change of demand is not very big, suppliers can provide the quantities demanded. When prices decrease, this does not normally mean that demand is decreasing or supply is excessive. Production and supply are adjusted to the fluctuation of demand within certain ranges of inventory. A price fall normally signifies that productivity increased at some point in the production process. This increase of productivity may not have necessarily occurred in the processes of the final product producer. A big improvement in the production processes of intermediate goods may have caused a decrease in their cost and so also in the price of final products using them.

The network of production and exchanges can be as big as the world. The number of goods may exceed tens of millions of items. Although information exchanged in the total system is extremely complex, what each agent is doing is simple and highly patterned. Taniguchi and Morioka's results mean that the total process works and converges to a steady state when the demand flow is sufficiently stable. The new formulation is strictly sequential and contains no process which is determined by a so-called equilibrium process. We have checked all variables so that they are decided step by step by other variables which are already known before the decision is made or else they are determined outside of the system. No agents are required to know any information outside of his or her normal range of activities and capabilities.

Hahn said in his inaugural lecture (Hahn 1973) that he wants his theory to "be sequential in an *essential* way" (Hahn, 1984, p. 53. Emphasis is by Hahn). We think his desire has been achieved in our formulation, although we did not use any concept of equilibrium. As I have argued in Shiozawa (1989), the concept of equilibrium has been an *obstacle epistémologique* (Gaston Bachelard) for a long time. Here, we have succeeded in making our theory essentially sequential because we have consciously excluded the equilibrium framework. Equilibrium has been used in economics as deus ex machina when some variables are difficult to determine step by step. This permitted economists to appeal to an easy solution which blocked them from thinking through all the difficulties (Kornai 1971, Kohn 1986).

Theorem 7.2 is comparable to Arrow and Debreu's theorem on the existence of a competitive equilibrium. But the theorem is obtained for a situation setting based on much more realistic assumptions. Although there are still many points to be improved and clarified, we think this is an achievement of paramount importance in the recent history of theoretical economics. This is particularly good news for all people who had doubts on general equilibrium theory, in the form of Walras or in the form of Arrow and Debreu. We have finally obtained a new method of economic analysis which does not rely on the general equilibrium framework.

Although Taniguchi-Morioka is a great breakthrough, we do not boast that the new theory is a *theory of everything* in economics. It is not a theory that can explain all aspects of a modern economy. The new theory is only a theory on how the modern industrial economy works. There are still vast fields of economics in which the theory can say nothing. It is evident that we need a totally different theory to investigate the financial economy. Our theory cannot be applied to the labor economy. It excludes many agricultural commodities. However, the Taniguchi-Morioka theorem is a big achievement of economics. We should remember that Newtonian mechanics started as a theory of physics in a quite restricted area. In the time of Newton, there was no theory of electromagnetics. Nuclear forces were not yet known. And yet all of modern physics developed from Newton's few insights into mechanics.

The range of validity of the new theory is narrow, at this moment, but it has the potential to change all of economics. When John R. Hicks (1976) observed revolutions in economics, he proposed to re-characterize the so-called marginalist revolution as a shift of concentration of attention. The classical political economy was originally a theory of production and distribution. The essential novelty of those economists who led the neoclassical revolution lays in their concentration on exchange. Thus Hicks proposes to rename marginalists as catallactists. If the catallactist revolution was the biggest revolution that divided economics in two (classical economics and neoclassical economics), then Arrow-Debreu theory belongs to catallactics. In comparison to this, the new theory is apparently an economics of production and therefore clearly belongs to classical economics. As such, it has the potential to refound economics on the central tenet of production economics.

This is good news for all economists who are dissatisfied with neoclassical economics. The new theory may change the total balance of power among branches of economics. Once again, the heterodox has now the chance to become mainstream, until, once more, the wheel will turn. The new theory is clearly good news to those economists who are called neo-Ricardians (or Sraffians) or those who prefer to characterize their method as the *surplus approach*. Sraffian economics has been interpreted as a theory of the long period (Kurz and Salvadori 1995), but there is no more need to restrict it to long-period analysis. The new theory stands basically on the same theory and formulation begun by Piero Sraffa and can analyze short- or medium-period questions.

The new theory is also good news for post-Keynesians. Some post-Keynesians argue that it is necessary to oust Sraffians from the group of post-Keynesians. As long as Sraffians cling to long-period analysis, they have reasons to talk like that. Long-period framework cannot be a useful tool for analyzing business cycles, involuntary unemployment, or technical change. Now, however, the new theory provides a price theory and a theory of quantity adjustment. The price theory that we presented in the first part of this chapter is the theory of value which lies in the tradition of classical economics. The minimal price theorem is much better than appealing to menu costs. Post-Keynesians can now compete with New Keynesians in the domain of microfoundations of their theory. Management scientists can also profit from the new theory, because we now have a much more firm bridge between management science and economics.

Finally, the new theory is good news for evolutionary economics. In the new theory, prices and quantities have different functions. As long as the state of market competition remains invariant, the markup rates remain constant. Prices mainly convey the state of production technology including labor productivity and transportation facilities. Supply and demand are irrelevant to price determination. This had been the major message of classical political economy. But in the eighteenth and nineteenth centuries, major products were agricultural, and their supply quantities were fixed for each crop year. In such a situation, it was prices that regulated demand and supply, but only during the time span until the supply was adjusted to the demand. Thus, although he emphasized that "[t]he opinion that the price of commodities depends solely on the proportion of supply to demand, or demand to supply, has become almost an axiom in political economy, and has been the source of much error in that science [political economy]," Ricardo had to admit that "the proportion between supply and demand may, indeed, for a time, affect the market value of a commodity" but that "this effect will be only of temporary duration" (Ricardo 1951, Chap. 30, p. 382). When the producers' capabilities increased to being able to quickly adjust their production volume to the demand, the price of commodities became much stable than before, because of the speed that supply came to be adjusted to the demand. This does not mean that demand has lost its significance. It remains as one of the most important indices for producers and for the economy as a whole, but it is now mainly transmitted more directly through the transmission of quantity information and not by the rise or fall of prices. We can say that functions of prices and quantities came to be more separated in the contemporary economy.

This separation of functions facilitates the analysis of innovations, which is one of the main targets of evolutionary economics. Discovery of a new product is reflected in the market as the emergence of a new commodity. Process innovation is mainly the improvement in production techniques and is reflected as a decrease of costs and prices. Successful development of new products is reflected by increases in demand and in production.

2.7.6 Some Supplementary Remarks

We have observed in Sect. 2.7.4 that production as a whole slowly follows the exogenous demand that is rapidly fluctuating with small variations, as long as the adjustment process satisfies three conditions[64]:

1. The production stays within the capacity of each firm j.
2. The demand is smaller than the inventory prepared for each period.
3. There is no labor shortage.

If either one of these three conditions is violated, the semiautomatic adjustment process stops, and firms are required to deal with each situation appropriately. If the labor shortage is severe, firms are obliged to take one of three reactions: (1) extend the labor time, (2) try to increase labor productivity, and (3) raise the wage rate. In case of inventory shortage, the firm may ask their customers to wait for a period or ask competitors to supply them a necessary amount of product. However, the most important issue for management is how to deal with the resulting shortage of production capacity.

Suppose a situation in which a firm is producing at about 95% of the capacity and demand is increasing. The management needs to know whether the demand increase is a temporary one or if it is the start of a stable trend. In the latter case, it is necessary to make the decision to increase capacity within an appropriate time, because to build production capacity normally requires much longer time than the product production period. This is an important decision for management, because capacity investment requires big money and the effect is irreversible. It may hold a special conference to discuss such a matter. In this decision-making, the most important variable is the future trend of product demand. To know it is a difficult task. There are so many uncertain factors. Such decisions may be affected by a kind of "animal spirits", or gut feel, of managers, but most capacity-building decision-making is based on the historical trend of product demand. After all, if the present average rate of production is 85% and annual growth rate is 5%, it would be better to wait at least one more year.

Depending on the length of capacity building, each firm must have criteria to consider when making decisions to invest in capacity. In this sense capacity investment is a rather passive decision-making process. Replacement and maintenance investment has a similar passive property. On the other hand, there are more active investment decision processes like launching new products, new market

[64] See also conditions (1), (2), and (3) in Sect. 2.4.5.

development, and research and technology development. Thus we can distinguish two kinds of investment. One is passive, autonomic investment. The other is more aggressive, non-autonomic investment.

To predict and know the trend of non-autonomic investment in a model is difficult because it depends very much on the deliberations of management. On the other hand, autonomic investment is easier to predict, because it is determined by varieties of routines and defined criteria. Of course, there must still be differences between kinds of autonomic investment. Replacement may be postponed more easily than to reduce maintenance cost. Investment to increase capacity depends mainly on the demand trend. Capacity building requires a different dimension than to simply decide "when." As there are sharp increasing returns (Whitesides 2012), managers have to decide the volume of new capacity.

We emphasize these trivial facts, because there is a strong established tradition that investment depends on the rate of interest. This tradition started with Wicksell and spread over opposing strands of economic thought including Keynes and Hayek. This tradition is often called Wicksell connection. However, there is ample evidence that investment does not depend on the rate of interest. One of two major findings of the famous Oxford Economists' Research Group was that managers do not care about the rate of interest when they examine if they should make an investment or not. Other evidence is provided by the 5-year experiment of Abenomics, or Kuroda's bold financial easing in Japan 2013–2018. The interest rate decreased below zero, but investment in increased capacity scarcely moved. Big Japanese firms accumulated retained earnings but did not invest in capacity building. The managers were, of course, behaving rationally because product demand remained depressed.

Although Keynes and Hayek bravely fought against Walrasian general equilibrium thinking, they were not free from the more general neoclassical framework. They could not see that prices and quantities are primarily independent and have different functions. They could not build a theory where quantities determine quantities. In my opinion, this is the main reason why Keynes failed in his bold attempt to build a theory of output. The new theory of quantity adjustment provides a basis on which to build a new theory of output, and hence a new theory of employment, if once a good theory of demand becomes available.

Another important consequence from our theory is given when the three conditions (1), (2), and (3) are satisfied for most periods and for a majority of firms. In this case, firms have no incentive to change their product prices. Inflation can occur only when there is a labor shortage. If in this case firms are obliged to raise wage rates, it may induce a general hike in wage rates and thus the increased cost of all products. In the traditional arguments on inflation, one talked much about the quantity of money, velocity of money, income velocity, and demand for money; however inflation does not occur as long as the three conditions (1), (2), and (3) are satisfied. Traditional arguments miss the micro-mechanism of the inflation process. Arguments on inflation must change a great deal when we review our economy from the viewpoint of our new theory of value and quantity adjustment.

Acknowledgment Special thanks are given to Robin Jarvis who has polished my poor English and made this paper readable. Of course, he has no responsibility for the errors that I may have committed in this paper. I want to dedicate this chapter to the late Masahiko Aoki, my teacher and a colleague, who by his dual stability paper (Aoki 1977) inspired me to write Shiozawa (1983b) and now this chapter some 40 years later.

References

Althusser, L. (1965). Sur la dialectique matérialiste, Dans Lous Althusser, *Pour Marx*. François Maspéro, Paris. Repropduit en 1996 avec un avant-propos d' Etinenne Balibar, Paris: La Decouverte. *For Marx*, English translation by Ben Brewster, 1969. London: Verso.

Andrews, P. W. S. (1949). *Manufacturing business*. London: Macmillan.

Aoki, M. (1977). Dual stability in a Cambridge-type model. *Review of Economic Studies, 64*(1), 143–155.

Arrow, K., & Debreu, G. (1954). Existence of equilibrium for a competitive economy. *Econometrica, 22*, 265–290.

Arrow, K., & Hahn, F. (1971). *General competitive analysis*. San Francisco: Holden-Day.

Beer, S. (1995). *Brain of the firm* (2nd ed.). Chichester: Wiley.

Bidard, C. H. (2010). The dynamics of intensive cultivation. *Cambridge Journal of Economics, 34*(6), 1097–1104.

Bidard, CH. (2014). The Ricardian rent theory: An overview. Centro Sraffa Working Papers n. 8.

Bowles, S. (2003). *Microeconomics: Behavior, institutions, and evolution*. Princeton: Princeton University Press/Boston Consulting Group.

Cartelier, J. (1991). Monnaie et système de paiement: le problème de la formation de l'équilibre. *Revue française d'économie, 6*(3), 3–37.

de Vries, J. (2008). *The industrious revolution: Consumer behavior and the household economy, 1650 to the present*. Cambridge: Cambridge University Press.

Fujimoto, T. (2012). *Kyōsōryoku Kōchiku no tame no Genka Keisan Shiron: Sekkei Jōhō Tensharon ni motozuku Zenbu Chokusetsu Genka Keisan no Kanōsei* [A preliminary note on harmonizing manufacturing (Monozukuri) management and cost accounting: A possibility of full-and-direct costing based on design-information theory of manufacturing] (MMRC Discussion Paper Series, No.410).

Hahn, F. (1973). *On the notion of equilibrium in economics* (Cambridge inaugural lecture). Cambridge: Cambridge University Press. Reproduced in F. Hahn (1984) as chapter 2, pp. 43–71.

Hahn, F. (1984). *Equilibrium and macroeconomics*. Oxford: Basil Blackwell.

Haldane, A. G. (2012). *Tails of the unexpected*. Speech given at The Credit Crisis Five Years On: Unpacking the Crisis, conference held at the University of Edinburgh Business School, 8–9 June. Available at: https://www.bankofengland.co.uk/-/media/boe/files/news/2012/june/tails-of-the-unexpected-paper-by-andy-haldane.pdf

Hicks, J. R. (1965). *Capital and growth*. New York: Oxford University Press.

Hicks, J. R. (1976). Revolution in economics. In S. J. Latsis (Ed.), *Method and appraisal in economics* (pp. 207–218). Cambridge: Cambridge University Press.

Higuchi, T., & Sato, Y. (2010). Hikifuda ni miru Kinsei-Kindai no Shakai to Bunka (in Japanese: Society and culture of early modern and modern Japan that we know through commercial copies). *Artes Liberalis (Iwate University), 86*, 40–67.

Hocking, W. E. (1961). Whitehead as I know him. *Journal of Philosophy, 58*(19), 505–516.

Hotelling, H. (1931). The economics of exhaustible resources. *Journal of Political Economy, 39*(2), 137–175.

Jones, R. W. (1961). Comparative Advantage and the Theory of Tariffs: A Multi-Country, Multi-Commodity Model. *Review of Economic Studies 28*(3), 161–175.

Jorgenson, D. (1960). Dual stability theorem. *Econometrica, 28*, 892–899.

Kalecky, M. (1954). *Theory of economic dynamics: An essay on cyclical and long-run changes in capitalist economy*. London: George Allen & Unwin.

Kohn, M. (1986). Monetary analysis, the equilibrium method, and Keynes's "general theory". *Journal of Political Economy, 94*(6), 1191–1224.

Koopmans, T. C. (Ed.). (1951). *Activity analysis of production and allocation*. Proceedings of a conference. New York: Willey. Contains chapters by Samuelson, Koopmans, Arrow and Georgescu-Roegen.

Kornai, J. (1971). *Anti-equilibrium*. Amsterdam: North-Holland Publishing Co..

Kurz, H. D., & Salvadori, N. (1995). *Theory of production: A long-period analysis*. Cambridge: Cambridge University Press.

Lee, F. S. (1998). *Post Keynesian price theory*. Cambridge: Cambridge University Press.

McKenzie, L. (1953). Specialization and efficiency in world production. *Review of Economic Studies, 21*(3), 165–180.

Mill, J. S. (1848). *Principles of political economy with some of their applications to social philosophy*. Citations are from the text in Library of Economics and Liberty.

Monden, Y. (1995). *Cost reduction systems: Target costing and kaizen costing*. Cambridge, MA: Productivity Press.

Morioka, M. (1991–1992). *Tanki Chōsei Katei no 2 Ruikei: Shijō Taipu ni yoru Zaiko no Kinō no Chigai ni tsuite* (In Japanese: Two types of short-period adjustment processes: On the difference of functions of inventories according to market types) Keizai Ronso, (1) *148*(4-5-6), 140–161 and (2) *149*(1-2-3), 79–96.

Morioka, M. (2005). *An economic theory of quantity adjustment: dynamical analysis of stock-out aversion behavior* (In Japanese: Sūryō Chōsetsu no Keizai Riron: Shinagire Kaihi Kōdō no Dōgaku Bunseki). Nihon Keizai Hyōronsha.

Morishima, M. (1969). *Theory of economic growth*. Oxford: Oxford University Press.

Morishima, M. (1973). *Marx's economics: A dual theory of value and growth*. Cambridge: Cambridge University Press.

Morishima, M. (1994). Chapter 3: Capital and growth. In Hagemann and Hamouda (Ed.), *The Legacy of Hicks* (pp. 28–44). Abingdon/Oxon: Routledge.

Ogawa, T. (2017). Analysis of production-efficient patterns of specialization allowing intermediate inputs. In O. Shiozawa & Tabuchi (Eds.), *A new construction of Ricardian theory of international values*. Tokyo: Springer.

Petri, F. (2016). *Nonsubstitution theorem, leontief model, netputs: Some clarifications* (Centro Sraffa Working Papers No.20).

Prigogine, I. (1980). *From being to becoming*. San Francisco: Freeman.

Prigogine, I., & Nicolis, G. (1977). *Self-organization in non-equilibrium systems*. New York: Wiley.

Prigogine, I., & Stengers, I. (1984). *Order out of Chaos: Man's new dialogue with nature*. London: Flamingo.

Ricardo, D. (1951). On the principles of political economy and taxation. In P. Sraffa (Ed.), *The works and correspondence of David Ricardo* (Vol. I). Cambridge: Cambridge University Press.

Ricardo, D. (1952). Letters 1819–June 1821. In P. Sraffa (Ed.), *The works and correspondence of David Ricardo* (Vol. VIII). Cambridge: Cambridge University Press.

Robinson, J. (1977). What are the questions? *Journal of Economic Literature, 15*(4), 1318–1339. Reprinted in J. Robinson, *What are the questions and other essays*. London/New York: Routledge, 1980.

Samuelson, P. A. (1961). A new theorem on nonsubstitution. In H. Hegeland (Ed.), *Money, growth, and methodology* (pp. 407–424). In Honor of Johan Åkerman. Lund: CWK Gleerup.

Sawyer, M. C. (1985). *The economics of Michał Kalecki*. Hampshire: Macmillan, Houndmills.

Scarf, H. E. (1958). A Min-Max solution of an inventory problem. In K. Arrow & Scarf (Eds.), *Studies in the Mathematical theory of inventory and production*. Stanford University Press. Working paper of 1957 is available at: https://www.rand.org/content/dam/rand/pubs/papers/2008/P910.pdf

Scarf, H. E. (2002). Inventory theory. *Operations Research, 50*(2), 186–191.

Shiozawa, Y. (1978). *Non-simultaneous mark-up pricing processes* (Kyoto Institute of Economic Research Discussion Paper No.125). Available at: https://www.researchgate.net/publication/315505189_Non-Simultaneous_Mark-up_Pricing_Processes

Shiozawa, Y. (1983a). *Sūri Keizaigaku no Kiso* (in Japanese: Elements of Mathematical Economics). Tokyo: Asakura Shoten.

Shiozawa, Y. (1983b). Kahn-Keynes Katei no Bisai Kōzō (In Japanese: The Micro Structure of a Kahn-Keynes Process). *Keizaigaku Zasshi* (Osaka City University) *84*(3), 48–64.

Shiozawa, Y. (1989). The primacy of stationarity: A case against general equilibrium theory. *Osaka City University Economic Review, 26*(1), 85–110.

Shiozawa, Y. (1996). *Economy as a dissipative structure*. A presentation made in Keihanna Prigogine Conference, organized and sponsored by Keihanna Co. and Sankei Newspaper, May 28 1996. Available at: https://www.researchgate.net/publication/236149834_Economy_as_a_Dissipative_Structure

Shiozawa, Y. (2014). *Rikādo Bōeki Mondai no Saishu Kaiketsu* (In Japanese: A final solution of Ricardo problem in international values). Tokyo: Iwanami.

Shiozawa, Y. (2015). International trade theory and exotic algebra. *Evolutionary and Institutional Economics Review, 12*(1), 177–212.

Shiozawa, Y. (2016a). Chapter 1: A guided tour of the backside of agent-based simulation. In Kita et al. (Eds.), *Realistic simulation of financial markets: Analyzing market behaviors by the third mode of science* (pp. 3–50). Tokyo: Springer.

Shiozawa, Y. (2016b). Chapter 8: The revival of the classical theory of values. In Yokokawa et al. (Eds.), *The rejuvenation of political economy* (pp. 151–172). London: Routledge.

Shiozawa, Y. (2017a). Chapter 1: The new theory of international values: An overviews. In Shiozawa et al., (2017) pp. 3–73.

Shiozawa, Y. (2017b). Chapter 7: An origin of the neoclassical revolution: Mill's "Reversion" and its consequences. In Shiozawa et al., (2017) pp. 191–243.

Shiozawa, Y., & Fujimoto, T. (2018). The nature of international competition between firms. In Fujimoto & Ikuine (Eds.), *Evolution of industries and firms – Capability building and demand creation*. Singapore: Springer.

Shiozawa et al. (Eds.). (2017). *A new construction of Ricardian theory of international values: Analytical and historical approach*. Singapore: Springer.

Sraffa, P. (1960). *Production of commodities by means of commodities: Prelude to a critique of economic theory*. Cambridge: Cambridge University Press.

Steedman, I. (1977). *Marx after Sraffa*. London: New Left Books.

Taniguchi, K. (1991). *Sūryō Chōsei Keizai ni okeru Ikō Katei ni tsuite* (In Japanese: On the traverse of quantity adjustment economies). *Keizaigaku Zasshi, 91*(5), 29–43.

Taniguchi, K. (1997). *A theory of transition process and numerical experiments* (In Japanese: Ikōkatei no Riron to Sūchi Jikken). Keibunsha.

von Neumann, J. (1945–46). A model of general economic equilibrium. *Review of Economic Studies, 13*(1), 1–9. Translated into English by G. Morgensern. Originally published in German in 1938, under the title Über ein Ökonomisches Gleichungssystem und eine Verallgemeinerung des Brouwerschen Fixpunktsatzes in K. Menger (Ed.) Ergebuisse eines Mathematischen Seminars, Vienna.

Whitesides, R. W. (2012). *Process equipment cost estimating by ratio and proportion*. https://www.pdhonline.com/courses/g127/g127content.pdf

Chapter 3
The Basic Theory of Quantity Adjustment

Abstract In this chapter, we will describe the basic framework and some key concepts of the economic theory of quantity adjustment. Section 3.1 characterizes the capitalist system as a demand-constrained economy in which firms are almost always competing to capture the demand for their products. This aspect of capitalism has a profound relevance with the long-term changes in technologies and products through incessant innovations. Section 3.2 formulates production rules for stockout avoidance behaviors by individual firms facing uncertain demand under sales competition. Here "stockout avoidance" means that firms seek to suppress their expected stockout occurrence ratio to a considerably low level by holding a certain amount of inventory. Section 3.3 outlines quantity adjustment in the capitalist economy as a dynamic process generated by the interactions of firms each of which follows production and ordering rules for stockout avoidance. An emphasis will be given to roles of inventories as buffer and information sustaining the loose stationarity of the economy. Section 3.4 provides a historical overview of preceding contributions to the analysis of quantity adjustment. After the appearance of *General Theory* by Keynes, the development in this field has been attained mainly through attempts to build dynamic and multi-sector models of the multiplier process and to clarify factors affecting the stability of this process.

Keywords Quantity adjustment · Capitalist economy · Demand-constrained economy · Sales competition · Continuous excess supply · Stockout avoidance · Decoupling · Buffer inventory · Loose stationarity · Multiplier process

---

A part of the research on this chapter was supported by JSPS Kakenhi no. 15K03386.

Y. Shiozawa et al., *Microfoundations of Evolutionary Economics*,
Evolutionary Economics and Social Complexity Science 15,
https://doi.org/10.1007/978-4-431-55267-3_3

3.1 Capitalism as a Demand-Constrained Economy

3.1.1 Predominance of Sales Competition

In a free market, every transaction is carried out based on a voluntary agreement among its participants. Over the concrete content of this voluntary agreement, two kinds of contentions may emerge. One is the confrontation between a seller and a buyer about conditions for the transaction, and the other is the struggle among buyers or sellers in order to be chosen by the other party as a trading partner. Following Kornai (1971, p. 293), we use the term "competition" in the sense of this second contention.[1]

By its definition, competition is divided into two types: one is *sales competition in which the sellers compete among each other to capture the demand*, and the other is *purchase competition in which the buyers compete among each other to capture the supply*. Sales competition arises when the total demand for a commodity at a certain price is insufficient to absorb the entire supply volume. In this case, the volume of the transaction is *constrained by demand*. Conversely, purchase competition arises when the total supply of a commodity at a certain price is insufficient to satisfy all the demand for the commodity. In this case, the volume of transaction is *constrained by supply*. In either of the competition, the competing side must struggle with its actual or potential rivals for the realization of its desirable transaction. The intensity of this struggle exerts a strong influence on *the power balance between the buyer and seller*. In a market where the sellers compete, the buyers can choose their trading partners. This choice places the buyers in an advantageous position over the sellers. Therefore, a market in which mainly the sellers are competing is called the "buyer's market."[2] Similarly, a market in which the buyers compete is called the "seller's market" because of their advantageous position over the buyers.

One of the most notable facts about capitalism is the *predominance of sales competition* in product markets. In the capitalist economy, buyers do not often compete among each other. Conversely, sellers must *almost always* compete among each other for sales of their commodities. To put it simply, *while it is easy to buy commodities as long as an individual has sufficient cash, it is difficult to sell commodities*. In this respect, capitalism can be characterized as a *demand-constrained economy*.[3] Under sales competition, the sellers must win buyer's favor

[1] Kornai (1971, p. 293) notes that, under genuine forms of competition (as defined by him), "there are some who reach goal and others who do not." The following argument in this section based on the conceptual framework of comparative economics constructed by Kornai (1971, 1980, 1992).

[2] Agents of the competing side can partially compensate their disadvantageous position by some explicit or implicit agreement limiting mutual competition. However, such cooperation is not so easy, especially when the competing side consists of many agents.

[3] The "demand-constrained economy" is an economy wherein, usually, a producer's efforts for increasing production are constrained by the buyer's demand, not by the available amount of various inputs. See Kornai (1980, pp. 26–30).

to sell their commodities.[4] In order to attract buyer's attention, firms as sellers provide actual or potential (i.e., an unspecified large number of) sellers with a vast amount of information about their commodities and themselves in the form of advertisements and promotions. This implies that costs for transactions are mostly borne by sellers. Although every transaction is mutually beneficial, it is established as a custom that the seller treats the buyers as "customers." In most product markets, sellers deal with commodities that are differentiated from other sellers' commodities. Accordingly, for buyers, the choice of commodities is inseparable from that of sellers. Besides differentiation in the quality of commodity (such as functions, design, and grade), the sellers can differentiate conditions related to a transaction (location, assortment, delivery, customer service, mode of payment, and so on). Differentiations in factors other than prices by sellers allow them to differentiate the prices of their commodities. Since all these differentiated factors affect a buyer's choice of commodities and sellers, *sales competition is contested by a wide variety of means.*

As already noted, the buyers must, though not so often, compete to buy commodities they want, and sometimes they spend a long time standing in a queue or give up on a purchase because of a stockout of their preferred commodity. Competition over a commodity may last for a certain period, especially when this commodity has no substitute and its supplies are restricted for some reason.[5] However, looking at the whole product markets, purchase competition is observed only temporarily or only for a relatively narrow range of products. Usually, shops and warehouses of the selling firm are filled with immediately sellable commodities, and the operation rate of its capacity is below 100%. Owing to this preparation by the sellers, *the buyers feel that they can buy most commodities with considerable certainty* as long as they can pay for these commodities.

It should be noted that the enduring asymmetry of the buyer-seller relationship is not observed in product markets wherein the same participant buys or sells the same kind of commodity according to circumstances. A typical example of this type of market is the resale market formed exclusively by wholesale traders. The resale market is certainly indispensable for the smooth functioning of the overall wholesale market. However, the main part of the product market consists of a chain of transactions vertically connecting production and demand. In each of this chain, the positions of firms are fixed either as buyers or sellers.

3.1.2 Continuous Excess Supply in Product Markets

In the capitalist economy, a certain part of the supplies of storable commodities is left unsold and carried over to the next period as product inventories (output stocks). While the volume of inventories fluctuates from time to time, the depletion of inventories is an exceptional phenomenon that does not last for a long period. Some

---

[4] As Kornai puts it, "the sellers court the buyers" in sales competition (Kornai 1971, p. 293).

[5] The firm might intentionally withhold to expand its supply if queuing and long waiting time serve as a signal of high reputation. Here we do not consider such a case.

part of these inventories is intentionally held for the speculative purpose. However, most product inventories are held for adaptation to the fluctuation of demand. Under sales competition, every sales opportunity is considered precious by the sellers. To ensure that they do not miss this opportunity, selling firms attempt to keep their supplies larger than the expected average demand (the supply of product is the sum of the newly produced product and initial product inventory). Consequently, *the supply of the product includes the surplus that is aimed at absorbing a portion of the demand exceeding its expected average level.* Here, the product inventory acts as a buffer between production and demand. While sales competition leads the firms to hold buffer inventory, the existence of product inventory in every seller's shop or warehouse enlarges a buyer's freedom to choose sellers and their products. The wider the buyer's choice, the more intense is the competition among sellers.[6] Thus, there is a mutually reinforcing relationship between sales competition and the holding of product inventory.

Usually, firms do not decline orders from buyers until all the product is sold out. In this respect, the product inventory can be regarded as *the unsold part of the supply* in the preceding period. Thus, the continuous carrying over of the product inventory indicates that the product market is not "cleared" and that excess supply continues to exist.[7] However, contrary to the view of the conventional (Walrasian) theory, which regards the demand-supply equilibrium as the only form of economic balance, *the constant existence of excess supply does not mean that the capitalist economy is always in an unbalanced state.* As we will see later, the balance of the capitalist product market is attained through gradual approximation to the following states: (i) *demand is equal to production* and less than supply which includes buffer inventory, and (ii) in each period, *a constant amount of product inventory is carried over to the next period.*

The seller whose commodity is perishable cannot hold product inventory. The seller who produces based on orders from the buyers need not hold product inventory. However, even these sellers, if they are producers, usually hold raw material inventories (input stocks), namely, the stocks of materials, fuels, parts, and so on. The supply of raw materials within a firm, which can be called "internal supply," consists of the sum of newly arrived raw materials and their inventories carried over from the previous period. The demand for raw materials within a firm, which can be called internal demand, is equal to their volumes that are necessary to carry out the current production plan under the given technology.[8] The uncertainty regarding the internal demand for raw materials will remain as long as the firm makes raw material order before its decision of production volume. Therefore, as is the case of the supply of the finished product, the selling firm attempts to

[6]The same can be said of surplus (unused) production capacity. Under sales competition, "every seller ... makes efforts to create surplus capacity" and thus intensifies sales competition still more "by increasing the selection possibilities of the buyer" (Kornai 1971, p. 322).

[7]Kornai (1971, p. 179) remarks that "the economic system cannot operate with an empty, 'cleared' market, without stocks and reserves."

[8]In this internal demand-supply relationship, the demander and the supplier, respectively, correspond to the production and purchase departments of the same firm.

keep its internal supplies of raw materials more than the average internal demand for them. Here, the raw material inventories acts as a buffer between the arrival and consumption of raw materials. Along with the unused productive capacities of capital equipment, raw material inventories (input stocks) make it possible for firms to promptly expand their productions in response to an increase in external demand.

The relationship between economic efficiency and the relative scale of excess supply to demand is not so simple as generally thought. It is obvious that the huge accumulation of unsold commodities and unconsumed raw materials implies a waste of enormous resources. In such a case, a considerable part of inventory might be turned to "deadstock" and eventually abandoned. On the other hand, inventory allows the firm, as a seller-producer, to quickly satisfy the buyer's orders and flexibly expand production in response to an increase in demand. The certainty of purchase, which constitutes one of the important features of capitalism, cannot be maintained without such swiftness and flexibility in the side of the seller-producer. Furthermore, as will be argued below, sales competition and the holding of inventory by sellers stimulate the demand-adaptive and demand-creative innovations. In this way, the dynamic efficiency of capitalism gets closely connected with the sustained existence of a certain level of excess supply.[9]

3.1.3 Long-Term Consequences of Sales Competition

Consequences resulting from the predominance of sales competition can be better understood by comparing this situation with the predominance of purchase competition. This comparison is not a mere thought experiment because the humanity experienced the predominance of purchase competition over several decades in former socialist economies including the Soviet Union, Eastern European countries, and pre-reform China. Contrary to the official principle of the planned economy, individual state-owned firms in the socialist economy had a certain degree of autonomy in their daily operations. Such firm-level autonomy reflected the intrinsic limit of any centralized control over a large-scale economy.[10] Since the allocation of production goods by the central government organs was far from perfect, the firms had to procure some part of production goods independently. Horizontal transactions of raw materials between two socialist firms shared a common feature with the transactions in free markets, at least, in that they were based on mutual consent. Concerning consumption goods, considerable parts of their distribution

[9]This book does not deal with the labor market. However, it should be noted that the above argument on sales competition can be, at least partly, applied to the competition among workers (suppliers of labor forces) in the labor market. Sales competition in the labor market is inseparable from the continuous existence of a surplus labor population which Marx called "the industrial reserve army" (Marx 1990, pp. 781–794). As Marx depicted, this reserve army enables firms flexible expansion of production and effective control over workers in workplaces.

[10]This limit was precisely foreseen by Leroy-Beaulieu (1908) originally published in 1883, and then further elaborated by von Mises (1935), Brutzkus (1935), and Hayek (1935) based on the experiences of the Russian Revolution.

were entrusted to legal and semilegal markets, except for the period of rationing, although private commerce was largely prohibited.[11]

Product markets in the socialist economy were characterized by the predominance of purchase competition. Under purchase competition, *it was easy to sell commodities, but it was difficult to buy commodities even if the buyer had sufficient money.* Quite often the buyers in the socialist economy must wait for a long time to obtain a commodity. As a result, they are frequently forced to buy commodities other than those they initially wanted to buy. Competition among the state-owned firms revolves mainly around obtaining raw materials and capital goods from allocative organs or other firms producing the required production goods. Under chronic shortage, firms and households tend to buy as many commodities as they can whenever they get a chance to buy them. This "hoarding" tendency further exacerbates the shortage and thereby strengthens purchase competition.[12] On the other hand, owing to the technological complementarity, which is especially rigid in the short term, the shortage of certain necessary raw materials directly constrains the scale of production. An accumulation of several raw materials fails to compensate the shortage of other raw materials. Consequently, there exist a surplus as well as a shortage of raw materials in the same factory.[13]

In both sales and purchase competitions, those who compete among each other make an effort to realize their desirable transaction under the pressure of competition. However, there is a fundamental difference between both types of competition. This relates to long-term consequences that competition exerts on commodities. If a firm wants to take a leading position in sales competition, then a certain part of its activities must be directed toward improving existing commodities or introducing new commodities. Efforts in this direction are unavoidable even for a less ambitious firm that merely aims to survive in the market. Furthermore, the ease of purchase under the predominance of sales competition allows firms to concentrate their efforts on measures to make their commodities more attractive to buyers. In the long run, *these efforts by the firms as producers and sellers improve qualities of products, raise productivity, and diversify items.*[14]

Circumstances are quite different under purchase competition. The buyers standing in a long queue cannot make strong requests about the quality of their preferred commodity. Even if a courageous buyer complains about the quality of the provided commodity, the seller can simply dismiss the complaint. Concerning the supply side, an enduring shortage forces firms to allocate a large part of their efforts to the procurement of raw materials and capital goods. As a result, there remains little room for firms to focus on the qualities of their products. Even when

---

[11]Regarding the actual functioning of the Soviet-type economy outside of the official framework, refer to Campbell (1963), Kornai (1980) and Nove (1980).

[12]The hoarding of raw material inventories within firms was one of the notable features of the socialist economy. See Table 3.1 in Sect. 3.3. Socialist firms also had to compete to ensure labor forces. From the viewpoint of workers, chronic labor shortage partly compensated for the lack of independent trade unions (Kornai 1980, 1992).

[13]This coexistence of surplus and shortage is emphasized by Kornai (1980).

[14]On this aspect of the capitalist economy, see also Kornai (2014).

the firm conceives of an idea about a new commodity and gets the permission from the government, it must overcome an additional difficulty of securing the necessary material resources to realize this idea. In this way, *the predominance of sales competition becomes more favorable for innovative changes in commodities than the predominance of purchase competition.* The history of twentieth century socialism distinctly confirmed this proposition. It should be noted that here we are concerned with innovations that aim to effectively satisfy the buyer's demand. While the socialist firms also undertook numerous innovations, many of them were intended to satisfy their own needs and therefore related to the substitution or self-supply of lacking raw materials.

The economic failure of the socialist economy is often explained by the lack of competition. This explanation is adequate only when "competition" is understood as sales competition. As already mentioned, firms and households in the socialist countries had to compete to obtain products. For households, this competition sometimes took very severe forms such as queueing before dawn. The ease of sales resulting from this permanent purchase competition *liberated the firms as sellers from the necessity to innovate commodities to satisfy the buyer's demand in an effective manner.* Therefore, the true problem is not whether competition exists, but *which of the buyers and sellers compete.*[15]

The difference in the type of competition also influences the long-term relationship between production and wants. In the capitalist economy, production swiftly adapts to demand through sales competition. At the same time, the sellers try to influence the buyer's wants through advertisements and promotions using various channels. Furthermore, newly emerging commodities reveal potential wants or rather create them. Concerning the short term, the consumers (users) can behave as "sovereigns" in each market transaction. In the long run, the wants of these consumers are gradually transformed through the continuous emergence of new products. Conversely, consumers in the socialist economies are forced to adapt their wants to production. This does not imply that their wants are completely neglected. However, under the predominance of purchase competition, the adaptation of production to demand takes place only indirectly and very slowly.

3.1.4 Sales Competition and Property System

What makes sales competition predominant in product markets of the capitalist economy? It is not easy to answer this question in a purely deductive manner. Still, the property system undeniably has a strong relevance in this matter for the reasons described below.

---

[15]In the field of scientific and technological discoveries, socialist countries (especially the Soviet Union) have made many excellent records. Nevertheless, economic systems in these countries lacked the mechanism bridging these discoveries with the introduction of new commodities in the market. Concerning this point, refer to Kornai (1971, pp. 288–289).

The essence of the institution of private ownership is the *economic independence of individual owners from each other and from the political power.* According to this criterion, state- and community-owned firms can be regarded as a variation of private firms if they have substantial independence in their market activities. The economic independence of owners implies that they are placed under budget constraints. Every independent economic organization cannot ignore the profitability of its activity in the market as long as it intends to continue its activity and it has no significant nonmarket source of income. To avoid the risk of insolvency, firms must be cautious with the formation of their demand, especially when they decide on their capital investment.

This self-regulation of demand might be insufficient to generate chronic excess supply in the product markets. However, it is certainly a necessary condition. In fact, during the two world wars, even the capitalist countries experienced an overall shortage of products (and labor forces) due to the extraordinary expansion of direct and indirect military demands.[16] Once the wars ended, military demands rapidly shrunk to the level of peacetime, and the predominance of sales competition was reestablished after a short transition period that was full of turmoil.

In the socialist economy where the main part of the means of production is nationalized, the state-owned firms are substantially liberated from budget constraints. While individual state-owned firms are instructed to focus on the profitability of their production, the plan of capital investment is decided based mainly on political considerations. Once an investment project is authorized, the firm carrying out this project is not required to express concern about the payment. In the current production, also, the pursuit of the quantity goal of the plan weakens a firm's concern for profitability. On the other hand, managers and administrators have a natural propensity to strengthen their powers through the expansion of factories and sectors under their control. Besides the indifference to profitability, this urge for expansion inflates the demand of firms to such a high level that shortage spreads to the markets of most products. Since a considerable part of production goods are used to produce consumption goods or are consumed by households in their daily lives, a shortage cannot be restricted to production goods markets. Moreover, as described above, once purchase competition becomes predominant, shortage is reinforced by the hoarding behavior of buyers. In this way, purchase competition under chronic shortage becomes a daily phenomenon of the socialist economy.

Can a peacetime capitalist economy be compatible with the predominance of purchase competition? Or, can sales competition become predominant in a socialist economy? At a purely abstract level, we cannot exclude such possibilities. However, accumulated empirical facts clearly suggest that the predominance of sales competition is inseparable from the institution of private ownership. To avoid possible misunderstandings, we would like to emphasize that here we have no intention of providing a comprehensive explanation of the innovations in the capitalist economy.

[16]Keynes (1940) vividly describes this conversion in the United Kingdom that was caused by the start of the Second World War.

While sales competition is an essential condition for facilitating demand-adaptive or demand-creative innovations, the actual briskness of innovative activities also depends on other factors. Besides, the predominance of sales competition does not presuppose laissez-faire capitalism. Sales competition has its own detrimental side effects including exaggerated advertisements, excessive services, long and intense working hours, and increasing arrogance of buyers. Partial regulations of sales competition for the protection of human health and dignity do not reverse the basic tendencies of the demand-constrained economy.[17]

3.1.5 Reconsideration of the Concept of Competition

The existence of demand constraint in the capitalist product market has been referred to in economic literature from its very early days. The famous chapter of Say's *Treatise on Political Economy*, which contains the description about the so-called Say's law, starts with the following description: according to most entrepreneurs, "their difficulty lies not in the production, but *in the disposal of commodities*; that products would always be abundant, if there were but a ready demand, or market for them" (Say 1964, p. 132, emphasis added). However, Say himself rejected this assertion as a superficial observation and claimed that overall excess demand was impossible because the aggregate supply of products necessarily coincides with their aggregate demand.[18] Despite the criticism by Sismondi and Malthus, the "Say's law" received a strong support from Ricardo and was widely acknowledged as one of the basic dogmas of political economy. Marx (1990, p. 200) pointed out the fundamental asymmetry of sales and purchase and emphasized the difficulty of sales using the phrase "salto mortale" (a deadly leap). Nevertheless, even Marx implicitly accepted Say's law when he examined the mechanism of capitalist reproduction. As a result, the problem of demand constraint did not receive theoretical attention, which it deserved until the 1920s.

In the 1870s to 1890s, Walras and Marshall established models of the market under perfect competition in which all firms produce commodities on the precondition that *they can sell as much as they want under the given prices and production conditions* (Walras 1954; Marshall 1920). Although Marshall made a lot of cautious reservations on the validity of his model, these reservations were not explicitly related to the lack of demand constraint. After Walras and Marshall, the economic theory of production and market developed toward the elaboration and refinement of their models.

[17]It should be noted, furthermore, that the property right is a bundle of partial rights each of which takes various forms. This complexity of private property is itself one of the causes of the regional and historical variety of capitalism. On this point, see Hodgson (1988).

[18]Say's assertion can be correct only when there is no saving and all the production factors are fully employed.

The theoretical concern on the demand constraint was activated by the well-known criticism of Marshall by Sraffa (1926). He writes:

> The chief obstacle against which they [business persons] have to contend when they want gradually to increase their production does not lie in the cost of production—which, indeed, generally favors them in that direction—but in *the difficulty of selling the larger quantity of goods* without reducing the price, or without having to face increased marketing expenses (Sraffa 1926, p. 543, emphasis added).[19]

The question raised by Sraffa captured the attention of several prominent economists. Among such reactions was a celebrated model by Hotelling (1929) on the distribution of demand among the sellers located in particular points of the considered space. Chamberlin (1933) and Robinson (1933), respectively, presented models of a market in which each competing firm was faced with a downward-sloping demand curve. Robinson's theory of "imperfect competition" is substantially a revival of Cournot's model of the seller's monopoly developed almost a century ago. While Chamberlin paid more attention to the concrete aspects of sales competition than Robinson, his theory of "monopolistic competition" is not significantly different from Robinson's theory in its basic framework. Their models of imperfect or monopolistic competition have notable merit in that *they eliminate the assumption that each firm can sell its commodity as much as it wants.* However, neither Robinson nor Chamberlin sufficiently explored the problem of how a firm knows or estimates the demand curve for the product it produces. Profit maximization based on a subjective estimation of demand curve does not guarantee optimization in the objective sense.[20] Precisely, optimization in the objective sense is impossible (or indefinable) when the firm is under demand constraint and cannot know the exact relationship between the price it sets and the demand for its product. This implies that the behaviors of firms cannot be uniquely deduced only based on the assumption that they want to maximize profit. If this is the case, then the behaviors for profit maximization can take various forms depending on the ways of simplification that the firm adopts to find a certain concrete guidance.

In *General Theory* (1936), Keynes formulated the principle of effective demand and incorporated the multiplier theory formulated by Kahn into this principle. Unfortunately, Keynes did not provide a proper expression of his sound insight that production in the capitalist economy is constrained by demand. As argued later, one of the reasons behind this failure is that he assumed perfect competition wherein the firms are not required to think about demand constraint. Due to this assumption,

[19]Just before this passage, Sraffa (1926, p. 543) describes the thinking of entrepreneurs as follows: "Business men, who regard themselves as being subject to competitive conditions, would consider absurd the assertion that the limit to their production is to be found in the internal conditions of production in their firm, which do not permit of the production of a greater quantity without an increase in cost."

[20]As Arrow (1959, p. 46) points out, "Any estimate of the demand curve to a single entrepreneur involves a guess as to both the supply conditions and prices of other sellers, as well as some idea of the demand curve to the industry as a whole."

Keynes's theory was regarded as a special theory applicable to a world in which prices are fixed for some reason.[21]

Thirty-five years after the "Keynesian revolution," Kornai in his *Anti-Equilibrium* (1971) distinctly described that capitalist firms usually compete to capture demand. He clarified that the predominance of sales competition, which he called "pressure," is closely connected with the two essential features of capitalism: the short-term "consumer sovereignty" and the long-term changes in demand through continuous innovations. He put it:

> Every humanist will subscribe to the idea that the production of material goods should serve the satisfaction of human wants; production should adapt to men's needs, and men's needs should not be forced to conform to any pattern of production. However, fulfilment of this humanistic norm is not served by an economy in a strict state of equilibrium. ... *It is only in the case of pressure that the seller is compelled to adapt to the buyer's requirements; it is only in that case that the consumer is 'sovereign.'* (Kornai 1971, pp. 309–310)

Kornai formed this recognition through his direct observations of the Hungarian economy. As we have already mentioned, competition also existed in the socialist economy, but the predominant form of competition in this economy was purchase competition. In other words, firms had to compete to obtain raw materials and capital goods, and households had to compete to obtain consumption goods. Despite its severity and fierceness, purchase competition did not contribute toward the improvement of products.

In the context of the reconsideration of the socialist calculation debate, Lavoie (1985) introduced "rivalry" in place of "competition" as the term expressing the clash of interests among the market participants. Rivalry is the struggle in the market fought among rival firms. This depiction of rivalry by Lavoie agrees with Kornai's conception of competition. However, Lavoie did not make a clear distinction between rivalry among sellers and rivalry among buyers. He took it for granted that rivalry in the capitalist economy is contested mainly by sellers.

Perfect competition presupposes that all the product markets are uniformly organized and all the selling and purchasing orders are concentrated at one point. The situation in which every agent is a price-taker is possible only when (tentative) prices are presented by a third party acting in the name of "the market." In other words, *perfect competition is a special institution that liberates firms from direct demand constraint.* Auction in the form of *the tâtonnement* process completes this liberation. However, the liberation of sellers from the demand constraint is attained at the expense of their freedom to bid prices or to conclude a transaction without waiting that an overall equilibrium is established.

For the transaction of a single commodity, a tâtonnement-type auction, which is called "*itayose*" (gathering orders) in Japanese, is quite exceptional in the organized

[21] Upon the modeling of Keynes's theory, several economists replaced the assumption of perfect competition with the assumption that the firm attempts to adapt productions to demands under constant prices. Development in this direction will be described in Sect. 3.4.

markets like the stock and commodity exchanges.[22] The most conventional way of trading in the existing organized markets is continuous trading, which is called "*zaraba*" (a common place) in Japanese. Continuous trading prioritizes the speedy closing of transactions over the attainment of market equilibrium. It also allows participants to designate the upper limit of the buying price or the lower limit of the selling price. The fact that continuous trading is dominant in organized markets indicates that traders place great significance on the speed of transactions.

From the viewpoint of the conventional equilibrium theory, transactions under disequilibrium are inefficient in that they must be accompanied with "rationing" in some way or another. This negative evaluation of "rationing" reflects a natural aversion toward queueing and the rationing system. It is true that the rationing of consumption goods leads to strong dissatisfaction and serious inconveniences. However, *rationing can occur among sellers*. In the capitalist economy, demand for a commodity is almost always "rationed" by buyers among sellers, *and this rationing is accomplished in the manner that buyers freely choose sellers and their commodities within their income*. If all types of "rationing" are equally inefficient, then we can say that capitalism is a quite inefficient economic system. However, in truth the dynamic efficiency of capitalism is sustained by the rationing of demand among sellers through the free choice by buyers.

3.2 Stockout Avoidance in Short-Term Decisions by Individual Firms

3.2.1 Inevitability of Unintended Inventory Fluctuations

As described in the previous section, in a product market where sales competition is predominant, the firm as a seller attempts to hold an adequate amount of product and raw material inventories to ensure that it can satisfy orders from buyers as certainly as possible. In this section, we will elaborate on several concrete forms of such inventory holding.

Let us think about the circumstances under which a firm is forced to refuse a part of its received orders or ask for an extension of the delivery date. In an ordinary, unorganized product market, each firm determines its production volume based on the forecasted demand or the received orders. In the case of make-to-stock production, the firm is faced with demand uncertainty for its product. Since the demand forecast cannot be accurate, the fluctuation in product inventory almost always includes an unintended component. When the actual demand exceeds the

[22] "*Itayose*" was adopted by the Tokyo Grain Exchange until 2013 (after which it was dissolved). "*Itaawase*" is carried out at the opening and the closing time of the market in most Japanese exchanges. However, it is not a way of attaining market equilibrium. In this method, the price is determined to ensure that the amount of contract satisfying the presented orders is maximized.

supply (the sum of product inventory and newly produced product), a stockout occurs, leaving a part of the demand unsatisfied. Thus, the inevitability of unintended inventory fluctuation is obvious in the case of make-to-stock production. What about the case of make-to-order production? Certainly, the firm does not have to hold product inventory if it starts production after the receipt of orders. An individual firm can dispense with the inventory by placing orders for raw materials that are exactly necessary to satisfy received orders. However, since any production takes a certain length of time and requires an input of various kinds of raw materials, production without inventory is possible for some firms *only when the other firms hold inventory*. This is apparent if we assume a situation in which all firms start production after the receipt of orders. In this case, a certain amount of raw materials must be produced *before* the production for final demand. Moreover, the production of these raw materials must be preceded by the production of raw materials necessary as inputs for these raw materials. Since this regression continues on infinitely, production never starts.

Make-to-order production is possible when firms hold raw material inventories. However, the holding of raw material inventories cannot eliminate the uncertainty of demand. To clarify this point, let us suppose the following situation: (i) each firm places orders for raw materials at the beginning of each period and subsequently starts production to satisfy the received orders, and (ii) production initiated at the beginning of period t is finished at the beginning of period $t + 1$. Subsequently, the product is swiftly delivered to buyers. Under this assumption, orders made at the beginning of period t are not satisfied *until* the beginning of period $t + 1$. Therefore, it is impossible to use raw materials obtained from these orders for production in period t. Firms must place the raw material orders *before* knowing the precise amount of product that should be produced from these raw materials. In this way, if all firms simultaneously determine the amounts of production based on received orders, then they have to determine the raw material orders *based on the forecast of future orders*. This system can be called "make-to-stock order." As in the case of make-to-stock production, "make-to-stock order" is inevitably accompanied by unintended fluctuations in raw material inventories. When the required input of a specific kind of raw material (internal demand) exceeds the sum of inventory and the new arrival of this raw material (internal supply), stockout occurs, and consequently, a part of the production plan cannot be carried out.

3.2.2 Typical Production Rule for Stockout Avoidance

What happens when a buyer places an order to a seller (or goes to a seller's shop) but this seller cannot provide the commodity that the buyer wants to buy? In this case, the following reactions are conceivable on the buyer's side: (i) to simply give up the purchase, (ii) to buy another commodity that the seller provides as a substitute, (iii) to wait until the commodity arrives, and (iv) to place new orders to another seller. *All these reactions impose certain additional costs on the buyer.* Therefore, the buyers consider the relative certainty of purchase upon the choice of sellers. Under lasting sales competition, firms as sellers also compete by ensuring buyers the certainty of purchase. Because of the uncertainty of external and internal demand, firms cannot control the actual stockout occurrence rate. Still, they can control the subjective probability of a stockout based on the estimation of the probability distribution of demand. They attempt to avoid stockout as much as possible by setting this expected stockout occurrence rate at a low level at which buyers can be convinced of the rapid fulfillment of their demands. *Stockout avoidance* in this sense is peculiar to firms in a capitalist economy.

However, a mere possibility of the occurrence of a stockout does not provide a sufficient reason for a firm to avoid it. Profit-seeking firms hold a buffer inventory beyond the average demand only when frequent occurrences of stockout might cause a great loss and the cost of storing product is not so significant. In the following, we will examine this point through a formal model of the decision about production (or ordering).

Let us suppose that a firm produces and sells a single product. The firm regards that demands for the product in each period $d(t)$ ($t \in \{1, 2, \ldots\}$) are independently and identically distributed random continuous variables, and f denotes its probability density function. Let $y(t)$ be this firm's supply of product in period t and F be the cumulative density function of f; then, $F(y(t))$ represents the planned satisfaction rate (the subjective probability of the non-occurrence of stockout) corresponding to $y(t)$. Therefore, $\phi(y(t)) = 1 - F(y(t))$ represents the planned stockout occurrence rate corresponding to $y(t)$. A production rule that directs the firm to set this rate at a sufficiently low level can be used as a guide for practicing stockout avoidance.

Since F is an increasing function, $\phi(y(t))$ is lower as $y(t)$ is larger. The precise estimation of the probability distribution of the unknown stochastic variables is practically a difficult task. However, if it can be roughly approximated by a known distribution, then the firm would only be required to estimate its means and variance. If f is a normal density function with mean μ and standard deviation σ, then

$$\phi(\mu) = 0.5, \phi(\mu + \sigma) = 0.159, \phi(\mu + 2\sigma) = 0.023.$$

Therefore, in this case, the planned stockout occurrence rate is reduced to 2.3% by setting the buffer twice as large as the standard deviation.[23] In reality, most firms produce multiple kinds and types of products, and the determination of the production volume of each product is closely related to the determination of the assortment (product mix). Furthermore, the cycle or timing of determining the production volume might itself be adjustable. However, for simplicity, we assume that the component of products is fixed and set our focus on the problem of how a firm determines the production volume of a single storable commodity.

The setting of the model is as follows. First, the price of the product is temporarily fixed. This implies that *the revision of price is made at a longer interval*

[23] Since the demand is nonnegative, normal distribution can be used only as an approximation.

than the adjustment of the production volume.[24] Second, the actual volume of sales is equal to the smaller side of the supply and demand.[25] While an excess supply is carried over as an increase in product inventory, excess demand is simply cancelled. Third, the supply in each period consists of the initial product inventory and the newly produced product. In each period, the firm can know the demand for its product *only after* it decides on the production volume. Finally, the firm supposes that the conditions about cost and demand remain unchanged. This assumption simply implies that the firm does not have sufficient information to believe any change in the cost and demand in the near future.

The costs of the firm comprise the production cost, storage cost of inventory, and penalty cost of a stockout (the production cost can be replaced by the ordering cost in the case of distribution firms). In addition to the loss of the opportunity of sales, a stockout may cause the payment of late charges and reduce the future demand *if disappointed buyers turn to other sellers*. Since it is difficult for the firm to estimate the loss caused by a stockout, the penalty cost function would reflect the firm's recognition of the severity of sales competition. It is assumed that the firm determines its production volume to maximize the expected present value of the stream of profit in an infinite number of future periods. It must be noted that the assumption of an infinite planning period does not imply that the firm seriously thinks about its activities in the distant future. It simplifies the problem by eliminating the influence of the terminal value of the inventory left at the end of the final period.[26]

Let $z(t)$ be the product inventory at the end of period t, $x(t)$ be the production in period t, $y(t)$ be the supply in period t, $s(t)$ be the actual sale in period t, and $d(t)$ be the demand in period t. As long as the time for production of the commodity remains sufficiently short, it holds

$$y(t) = z(t-1) + x(t). \tag{3.1}$$

Product inventory $z(t)$ changes by

$$z(t) = y(t) - s(t). \tag{3.2}$$

Sale $s(t)$ is determined by the short-side rule

$$s(t) = \min\{y(t), d(t)\}. \tag{3.3}$$

[24] According to Blinder (1994), out of approximately 200 American firms representing various industries, 50% change prices once or less than once a year, while less than 15% change the price at least once a month. According to Mizuho Sogo Kenkyusyo (2011), out of 120 Japanese firms, 68% consider the revision of prices once or less than once a year.

[25] This so-called short-side rule was introduced by Arrow et al. (1951) in a research of the optimal inventory policy.

[26] If the planning periods are finite, then the firm must evaluate the inventory that will remain until the end of the planning period in a certain arbitrary manner.

Let p be the price of the product, C be the production cost function, H be the storage cost function, L be the penalty cost function, and α be the discount factor ($0 < \alpha < 1$). C, H, and L are all increasing functions and take zero for any non-positive argument. The expected profit in period t is the gap between the sales revenue $ps(t)$ and the sum of three kinds of cost $C(x(t)) + H(z(t)) + L(d(t) - s(t))$. The firm solves the problem of finding $x(t)$ which maximizes the expected value of

$$\Pi \equiv \sum_{t=1}^{\infty} \alpha^{t-1} \left(ps(t) - C\left(x(t)\right) - H\left(z(t)\right) - L\left(d(t) - s(t)\right)\right),$$

subject to the constraints (3.1) to (3.3) and $x(t) \geq 0$.

An increase in supply $y(1)$ has the following effects: (i) to raise the expected value of sales revenue $ps(1)$, production cost $c(x(1))$, and storage cost $H(z(1))$, (ii) to raise the expected value of storage cost $H(z(1))$, (iii) to reduce the expected value of penalty cost $L(d(1) - s(1))$, and (iv) to change the expected present value of the profit obtained from the next period. Since the probability distribution of demand and the penalty cost depend on the firm's subjective estimation, the maximization of Π is merely a subjective maximization.

Due to the dynamic nature of the problem, it would be difficult to perform a concrete calculation of the (subjectively) optimal solution. Generally, it is necessary to solve complex function equations. However, the solution takes a relatively simple form when the unit cost of the production is constant, that is, $C(x) = cx$ ($c > 0$). In this case, if the parameters and the functions satisfy certain conditions, then there would exist a positive critical value y^*. The optimal rule is given by the following form: if $z(0) \leq y^*$, then it produces up to y^*; if $z(0) > y^*$, then it does not produce (Arrow et al. 1958, pp. 135–139). This rule can be written as

$$x(1) = \max\left\{y^* - z(0), 0\right\} = \begin{cases} y^* - z(0) & z(0) \leq y^* \\ 0 & z(0) > y^* \end{cases}. \tag{3.4}$$

We can further simplify this result in the following manner.

Theorem 1
Assume that the problem has a solution, the density function satisfies $f(\xi) > 0$ for any $\xi > 0$, all the cost functions are linear, namely, $C(x) = cx$, $H(x) = hx$, $L(x) = lx$ ($c,\ h,\ l > 0$), and the unit production cost c is less than price p. Then, the optimal production rule of the above problem is given by (3.4), and the critical values y^* are calculated by

$$\phi\left(y^*\right) = \frac{h + (1-\alpha)c}{p + h + l - \alpha c}. \tag{3.5}$$

Proof: See Appendix 1.

The optimal stockout ratio $\phi(y^*)$ in (3.5) becomes lower as the unit storage cost h is smaller and the unit penalty cost l is larger. Assume $\alpha \cong 1$, then

$$\phi\left(y^*\right) \cong \frac{h}{p+h+l-c},$$

Therefore, $\phi(y^*) < 1/n$ for any $n \geq 1$ satisfying $p + l > c + (n - 1)h$. For example, if $p + l > c + 4h$, then the planned stockout rate would be less than 20%. As long as $p + l - c$ is considerably larger than h, the adjustment based on production rule (3.4) can be regarded as a form of stockout avoidance behavior.

Let f_0 be the probability density function of $\frac{d(t)-\mu}{\sigma}$ and F_0 be its cumulative density function. Let us assume, furthermore, that the standard deviation of demand is proportional to its mean, namely, mean μ and standard deviation σ satisfy the relationship $\sigma = b\mu$ $(b > 0)$. Then, from

$$F_0\left(\frac{y^*-\mu}{\sigma}\right) = F\left(y^*\right) = 1-\phi\left(y^*\right) = \frac{p+l-c}{p+h+l-\alpha c},$$

we have

$$y^* = \mu\left(1+k\right), \qquad k \equiv bF_0^{-1}\left(\frac{p+l-c}{p+h+l-\alpha c}\right).$$

Therefore, production rule (3.4) can be rewritten as

$$x(1) = \max\left\{(1+k)\,\mu - z(0), 0\right\}. \tag{3.6}$$

Coefficient k represents the desirable buffer inventory ratio. If f is a normal density function and the planned stockout occurrence ratio is 10%, then $k = 1.28b$. Therefore, the desirable buffer inventory ratio is 12.8% for $b = 0.1$ and 25.6% for $b = 0.2$.

Production rule (3.6) is a typical example of programs to practice stockout avoidance. It can also be applied to raw material ordering. As we will see in Sect. 3.4, rule (3.6) has been assumed in a number of models of the quantity adjustment process. Our analysis indicates that it is possible to derive this rule from subjective profit maximization based on the forecast of demand (and penalty cost).

3.2.3 Variations in Production Rules for Stockout Avoidance

The solution to subjective optimization depends on the shapes of cost functions. For example, if the marginal production cost is increasing, namely, $C''(x) > 0$, then rule (3.4) is modified as follows.

Fig. 3.1 Dependence of optimal supply on initial inventory

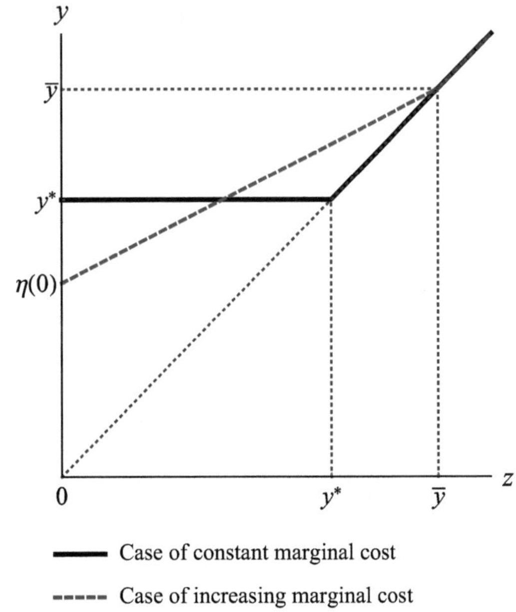

Theorem 2
(i) Assume that the storage cost and the penalty cost are linear, but the marginal production cost is increasing, then the optimal production rule is given by

$$x(1) = \eta\,(z(0)) - z(0),$$

where $\eta(z)$ is a function such that

$$\begin{cases} z < \eta(z) < \overline{y},\ 0 < \eta'(z) < 1 & z \leq \overline{y} \\ \eta(z) = z & z > \overline{y} \end{cases} \tag{3.7}$$

and $\overline{y}$ is a certain critical value.

(ii) Let $c = C'(0)$ and y_* be the values satisfying (3.5), then

$$\eta(0) < y^* < \overline{y}. \tag{3.8}$$

Proof: See Appendix 2.

This theorem shows that the (subjectively) optimal supply $\eta(z(0))$ increases from $\eta(0)$ up to $\overline{y}$ as $z(0)$ increases from 0 up to $\overline{y}$, and then switches to $z(0)$ for $z(0) \geq \overline{y}$ (the firm halts production). The optimal level of supply is less than y_* (the value in the case of linear production cost) when the initial inventory is very small, but larger than y_* as the initial inventory gets close to $\overline{y}$. Figure 3.1 indicates this relationship.

Function $\eta(z)$ and critical value $\overline{y}$ are determined by complicated functional equations. However, considering (3.8), they might be approximated by

$$\overline{y} = \left(\frac{1}{r} + k\right)\mu, \quad \eta(z) = (1 + rk)\,\mu + (1 - r)\,z \ \text{ for } \ 0 < z \leq \overline{y},$$

where $0 < r < 1$. In fact, let $y_* = (1 + k)\mu$, then,

$$\eta(0) = (1 + rk)\,\mu < y^* < \left(\frac{1}{r} + k\right)\mu = \overline{y} = \eta\left(\overline{y}\right), \quad 0 < \eta'(z) = 1 - r < 1.$$

In this case, the production rule is simplified into

$$x(1) = \max\left\{\mu + r\left(k\mu - z(0)\right), 0\right\}. \tag{3.9}$$

Rule (3.9) corresponds to the "partial adjustment" for the smoothing of production. In other words, the firm intends to fill only a part of the necessary inventory investment $k\mu - z(0)$. Under increasing marginal production cost, it is advantageous for the firm to flatten the production at each period. If $r = 1$, then rule (3.9) is reduced to rule (3.6). Thus, the coefficient r is presumed to be close to unity if the upward slope of the marginal cost curve is not very steep.

A well-known rule in the practice of inventory control is derived when a fixed setup cost is necessary for any positive production. In fact, if $C(0) = 0$ and $C(x) = cx + c_0$ for $x > 0$ $(c, c_0 > 0)$, then the optimum production is given by

$$x(1) = \begin{cases} S - z(0) & z(0) < s, \\ 0 & z(0) \geq s, \end{cases} \tag{3.10}$$

where s and S are critical values such that $s < y_* < S$.[27] Rule (3.10) is called the S-s method. Rule (3.6) can be regarded as a special case of this rule in which $s = y_* = S$ holds. The gap $S - s$ reflects the existence of the setup cost. Similar to the case of increasing marginal production cost, precise calculation of s and S is an extremely difficult task.[28]

Rules (3.9) and (3.10) are more complicated variations of the rules for stockout avoidance. Complications resulting from nonlinearity of the production cost do not eliminate the necessity to maintain the stockout rate at a low level. Given the difficulty in conducting a concrete calculation of optimal solutions, firms might simplify these solutions by a linear approximation and an empirical setting of parameters. Such simplifications can provide practically satisfactory solutions to complicated problems. It is worth noting that an adherence to the calculation of the

[27] As to the proof of this theorem, see Scarf (1959, 1963) and Morioka (2005, pp. 268–269).

[28] Quantity adjustment by this method will be examined in Chap. 6.

exact optimal solution is not rational in the procedural sense, especially when the premises of optimization include subjective expectations.

3.2.4 Premises for Stockout Avoidance

Until now, we have assumed that an unsatisfied part of demand is not carried over to the future and that the product is storable. Rule (3.6) is modified if one of these assumptions does not hold. First, let us consider the case in which buyers pay for the unsatisfied part of their demand and sellers record this part as a backlog, with the payment of the delay charge. In this case, the firm maximizes the expected value of

$$\Pi \equiv \sum_{t=1}^{\infty} \alpha^t \left(pd(t) - C\left(x(t)\right) - H\left(z(t)\right) - L\left(d(t) - s(t)\right)\right),$$

subject to the constraints $x(t) \geq 0$, $z(t) = z(t-1) + x(t) - s(t)$. Here, $z(t)$ can take a negative value and $-z(t)$ represents the backlog for $z(t) < 0$. If all the cost functions are linear, then the optimal production is given by $x(1) = \max\left\{\tilde{y} - z(0), 0\right\}$, where[29]

$$\phi\left(\tilde{y}\right) = \frac{h + (1-\alpha)\,c}{h + l} < \frac{h + (1-\alpha)\,c}{p + h + l - \alpha c} = \phi\left(y^*\right)$$

Thus, the possibility of carrying over the backlog raises the planned stockout occurrence rate when compared to the case of a simple cancellation. If $\alpha \cong 1$, then $\phi\left(\tilde{y}\right) \cong h/(h+l)$, which depends only on the ratio of the unit penalty cost to the unit storage cost.[30]

Second, if the product cannot be stored due to its characteristics, then its supply will always equal to its production. Furthermore, if the unsold products can be disposed of for free, then the firm would maximize the expected value of

$$\Pi \equiv \sum_{t=1}^{\infty} \alpha^t \left(p \min\left\{d(t), x(t)\right\} - C\left(x(t)\right) - L\left(d(t) - x(t)\right)\right),$$

subject to the constraint $x(t) \geq 0$. This is a static maximization problem. If all the cost functions are linear, then the optimal production supply would be determined by $\phi\left(x(1)\right) = c/(p+l)$, and $x(1) < y*$ holds if $c > \alpha^{-1}h$. Therefore, the planned stockout occurrence rate of the product which cannot be stored is higher than that of

[29]Regarding its proof, see Morioka (2005, pp. 271–272).

[30]If $l = 0$, then this maximization problem does not have a solution. This is because the firm can infinitely prolong production without any loss as long as the cost functions of production and storage are both linear.

the storable product. The cause of this rise is that an increase in the present supply ceases to reduce the expected value of the future production cost.

However, even in these cases, the planned stockout rate is set low if the unit penalty cost is sufficiently large in relation to other costs. Short-term production or ordering rules have the property of stockout avoidance as long as the firm assumes that frequent occurrences of stockout can lead to customer dissatisfaction and thereby cause considerable losses in the future.

Rules for stockout avoidance formulated in this chapter presuppose that firms can flexibly change the production amount in a fixed short cycle (day, week, or month). This flexible adjustability further requires that (i) each firm specializes in certain partial stages of the entire production process and organizes these stages within its factory or workshop in a parallel manner, and (ii) a solid regularity is established between the input of raw materials and the output of product. These two conditions are satisfied in many fields of the manufacturing industry. Meanwhile, the situation is quite different in agriculture. Its production processes are strongly bounded by seasonal cycles, and its harvest is considerably influenced by weather and other natural conditions. These circumstances substantially narrow the room for specialization and simultaneous parallel processing. As a result, agricultural producers are less likely to have an inclination toward stockout avoidance. Moreover, it will not be essential for agricultural producers to directly consider the risk of a stockout if they entrust the sales of their products to brokers who sell an entire day's supply in an organized wholesale market. Thus, the tendency to avoid a stockout can spread widely only when the manufacturing industry acquires dominance through the industrial revolution. Industrialization itself weakens the seasonality of agricultural production through the rapid development of transportation and preservation technologies.[31]

Concerning the recent rapid growth of service sectors, currently, this change has not thwarted the predominance of sales competition in capitalist product markets. In addition to the holding surplus productive capacities, the firms of service sectors can practice stockout avoidance with respect to their raw material inventories for the flexible adjustment of production.

3.2.5 Significance of Routines for Short-Term Decisions

In a large-scale economy, the external environment that surrounds individuals and organizations is sufficiently complicated in relation to their available attention and concern. As Simon (1978) emphasized, the human mind is one of the scarce

[31] Today, retail sellers of agricultural products adjust their supplies to avoid frequent occurrences of a stockout.

resources of the economy.[32] Considering the limit of time and energy that is available for decision-making, it is neither possible nor necessary to formulate a single integrated problem by incorporating all the related factors simultaneously. Instead, they set a series of partial problems belonging to different fields and time horizons and solve them in a sequential manner. From the viewpoint of the efficient utilization of the mind, allocating a considerable amount of time for a trivial problem would be unwise. Rationality, in the practical sense, requires a balance between the input of intellectual resources and the relative importance of the considered problem. This balance is not always easy to attain because an adequate allocation of intellectual resources among problems of varying importance is itself a task requiring a considerable amount of intellectual resources.

Intellectual resources for decision-making can be greatly economized by setting practicable routines which require only limited and readily available information.[33] The saving effect gained from setting such routines is substantially large as for behaviors repeated at short intervals. In decision-making by organizations (firms), these routines often take the form of an explicitly formulated program derived from subjective optimization. However, in the case of individuals, it is common that routines take a form of an unconscious habit.

Parallel to the short-term decisions about current production and transactions, firms make various mid- and long-term decisions, including price setting, capital investment, introduction of new commodities or technologies, and fund raising. The decisions about these activities are far more complex than short-term decisions, and therefore, require very careful consideration. By following easily practicable programs for short-term decisions, firms can spare intellectual resources for mid- and long-term decisions while attaining satisfactory results in their short-term activities.[34] Decision rule (3.6) is an example of such programs. While it might occasionally give a wrong decision, the savings effect of setting a simple program for short-time decisions would be sufficiently larger than the potential loss caused by restricting the scope of attention. Of course, the firm can choose a program, revise it, and replace it with a new program. However, even if the firm attempts a thorough consideration of every kind of available information, it cannot precisely estimate the (probability distribution of) demand and the loss caused by a stockout. Since several key variables cannot be known in advance, there is no objective criterion to define the best program. Many decision rules, including those not taking a form of optimization, can be equally rational from a practical viewpoint.

---

[32]"The scarce resource is computational capacity – the mind. The ability of man to solve complex problems and the magnitude of the resources that have to be allocated to solving them, depend on the efficiency with which this resource, mind, is deployed." (Simon 1978, pp. 12–13).

[33]"The decision maker's model of the world encompasses only a minute fraction of all the relevant characteristics of the real environment." (Simon 1959, p. 272).

[34]"We must surrender the illusion that programmed decision-making is a process of discovering the 'optimal' course of action in the real, complex world. ... We should view programmed decision-making as a process making choices within the framework set by highly simplified models of real-world problems" (Simon 1958, pp. 57–58).

It should be noted that the programming of behavior does not imply that the firm would blindly follow the directive given by the adopted program. As mentioned above, the purpose of simplification in the programming of behaviors lies in economizing intellectual resources for collecting and processing information. If the firm receive some reliable information related to changes in the cost or demand, then it would temporarily set aside the given program and consider these changes in its short-term decisions.

Routinized short-term decisions have an autonomous nature in that they are relatively independent from higher (namely, mid- and long-term) decisions requiring careful consideration. The stockout avoidance behaviors by individual firms, embodied in certain production and ordering rules, shape the autonomous functions of the capitalist economy. Their working depends on the properties of the dynamic process generated by the interactions of individual behaviors. As we will see in the next chapter, this process has stability under certain plausible conditions. The stationarity of the autonomous functions ensures the reproduction of the capitalist economy at the most daily level.[35]

3.3 Quantity Adjustment Process and Dual Functions of Inventories

3.3.1 Quantity Adjustment as a Dynamic Process

Generally, any analysis of the economic process must make clear the distinction between the intentions of individual agents and the actual results of their actions. Even if a firm hopes to keep its stockout occurrence rate at a low level, *this intention is not automatically realized*. Actual stockout frequency depends on the movement of the demand for its product, and the latter is affected by the interactions with other firms. The demand for a product appears as a random variable to the seller(s) of this product. Or, more precisely, seller firms are forced to consider demand as a random variable. However, from the viewpoint of the whole economy, demands for products are determined as the sum of intermediate and final demands. The volumes of raw materials ordered by each firm depend on their plans of production and volumes of raw material inventories. Each firm's production plans depend on its demand forecast and the levels of its product inventory. If each firm's demand forecast depends on its actual quantities of sales in past periods, then changes in production plans can lead to changes in intermediate demands, and the latter again

[35]Concerning the concept of autonomous and higher functions of the economy, refer to Kornai (1971). He wrote in that book that "the features of the autonomous functions do not depend on the political and ownership relations of the system" (Kornai 1971, p. 185). However, Kornai (1980) withdrew this view and admitted that the autonomous functions have significantly different features under the socialist and capitalist system.

lead to changes in production plans through revisions of demand forecasts. These series of interdependencies constitute a complicated dynamic system. *The quantity adjustment to be explored in this book is a dynamic process in which production demand and inventory fluctuate through interactions among the firms connected by the input-output relationships.*

The dynamic properties of the quantity adjustment process depend on parameters related to firms' behaviors and technologies. It is worth emphasizing that the constancy of final demand does not automatically guarantee the stability of this process. In fact, variables can move unstably even under constant final demand if parameters do not satisfy the stability condition. In this case, eventually the firms will be faced with an excessive accumulation of inventories, a shortage of raw materials, or capacity constraints. On the other hand, if a stockout of a product occurs, a certain form of the rationing of demand among buyers becomes inevitable. Comprehensive analysis of the dynamic properties of the quantity adjustment process will be conducted in the next chapter. As will be indicated there, under certain plausible conditions, the quantity adjustment process can gradually establish a balance between production and demand.

From the viewpoint of daily, weekly, or monthly activities, *the economy can mostly be regarded as a loosely stationary system with autonomous repetitions of productions and transactions*. Here, "loose stationarity" means that the economy is always moving, but most of its short-term changes are within such a range that allows individual agents to keep their respective routines.[36] Stationarity in this loose sense is one of the preconditions for the proper functioning of prices. Actually, price changes of some commodities can serve as a useful guide for adapting to changes in situations that have caused these price changes, *only if prices of most commodities remain constant or fluctuate in quite narrow ranges*. In a world where prices of all the commodities change simultaneously in an unpredictable manner, no guidance for adaptation can be derived from those price changes. Thus, the stability of prices is crucial for any individual and organization to develop a more or less consistent plan for future economic activities.

Routine behaviors by firms and households presuppose a widely shared belief that a large part of the present situation will also continue in the near future. The most solid foundation of this belief is the fact that, in many cases, the economy is actually repetitive. However, *this broadly shared expectation of continuity does not directly guarantee an actual repetition of the whole process*. In any large-scale economy, the reproduction of the whole economy is attained through complex interactions among multiple agents.[37] The question of whether an economy can be

[36]Loose stationarity of the economy might be temporarily lost by serious events like a financial crisis, hyperinflation, shortage of a critical fuel, large-scale war, and natural disaster. The turmoil caused by these events obstructs the normal progression of the autonomous economic process on the established orbit. However, sooner or later, the looped relation between routine behaviors and stationary process can be reconstructed on a new orbit corresponding to the changed conditions.

[37]This point is related to the following question raised by Simon: "what is it that maintain the stability of the pattern of behavior in groups of interacting persons?" He adroitly notes that "We

repetitive depends on the dynamic properties of these interactions. Our analysis of the quantity adjustment process elucidates *the looped relation in which individual routine behaviors presupposing loose stationarity actually maintain this loose stationarity through their interactions.*

3.3.2 Decoupling Function of Inventories

The amount of a product that the firm as a producer-seller can sell is ultimately restricted by its production. However, if the firm holds the product inventory of this product that is carried over from the previous period, then it can sell more than the newly produced product within the limit of this inventory. In other words, the *product inventory temporarily decouples production and sales.* A similar argument can be applied to raw material inventories. The volumes of raw materials that the firm as a producer-buyer can consume in the production process are ultimately restricted by its purchase of raw materials. However, if the firm holds inventories of these raw materials, then it can consume more than the newly arrived raw materials within the limit of these inventories. In other words, *raw material inventory temporarily decouples purchase and consumption.*[38] If the volume of finished product can be adjusted in the middle of the production process, then the work-in-process inventory would act as a buffer, temporarily decoupling the production of semifinished products and their inputs to produce finished products.

Let us suppose that firm A declines (a part of) firm B's raw material order because this raw material is temporarily sold out. This failure to purchase will not affect firm B's production if firm B has sufficient inventory of this raw material (or if it can purchase it from other firms). However, if this condition is not satisfied, and the original amount of firm B's order is precisely equal to the amount of this raw material necessary to carry out its production plan, then the stockout in firm A would directly lead to a shortage of raw materials in firm B. Consequently, firm B will be forced to modify its production plan downward. If firm B has sufficient product inventory, then this failure in production will not affect firm B's sales. However, if this condition is not satisfied, and firm B's original production plan is precisely equal to the forecasted demand, then the stockout in firm A will directly lead to a stockout in firm B when firm B's forecast is realized. Again, this stockout of firm B's product may affect the production of firm C, which usually buys a raw material from firm B. In this manner, *if product and raw material inventories held by firms*

do not need a theory of revolution so much we need *a theory of the absence of revolution*" (Simon 1958, p. 60, emphasis added).

[38] As noted above, unused capacities of capital equipment also enhance the flexibility of production. Since it takes a significantly longer time to construct and install equipment than to purchase raw materials, the smooth progress of the quantity adjustment process would require that the production capacity of equipment be set in advance. It would also be essential to consider *a certain slack* over the expected average demand.

Table 3.1 Component of inventories in Hungary and Japan in the 1970s to 1980s

	Hungary				Japan			
	1971	1976	1981	1986	1971	1976	1981	1986
Raw materials	70.9	70.2	72.1	72.8	15.3	16.7	17.0	12.4
Work-in-process	17.2	17.9	15.8	15.2	30.2	28.0	29.7	29.8
Products	11.9	11.9	12.1	12.0	54.8	55.4	53.3	57.8

Source: Hunyadi (1988) and Ministry of Finance Japan, *Financial Statements Statics of Corporation by Industry*

are small, then a stockout in one firm would easily spread to other firms through the input-output relationships. The economy can avoid such a spread of stockout only when firms hold a certain volume of product or raw material inventories.

From the viewpoint of the whole economy, the *smooth expansion of production reacting to an increase in final demand would require a certain scale of buffer inventories*. Here, "smooth" means that all the demand is satisfied at each period after an increase in final demand. In fact, if there is neither product nor raw material inventory, the transition of the economy to a new orbit of reproduction corresponding to this increase would be achievable only when a part of final demand is curtailed for several periods. This curtailment is necessary to enlarge the production of raw materials (it must be noted that the economy inevitably shrinks due to lack of raw materials if final demand is prioritized).[39]

As we have already argued, in the capitalist economy, sales competition leads firms to hold product inventories enough to respond to an increase in demand. Product inventories held by firms as a seller considerably increases the certainty of purchases for buyers. Since each firm feels the success of its purchases of raw materials is almost certain, there would be little need to hold raw material inventories as long as the interval from ordering to delivery is considerably short. Therefore, the main reason behind holding raw material inventories is attributed to the fact that either the time of processing orders or the delivery time is not negligible. These reasons reveal that *product inventory is very crucial and predominant in the capitalist economy*. A quite different situation was observed in the socialist economy, characterized by the predominance of purchase competition. Since purchases were almost always difficult, socialist firms had a motivation to accumulate deficient raw materials to the maximum extent possible.[40] Such a hoarding tendency shortened the average time in which newly produced products stayed at the warehouses of producers. Consequently, a large part of inventories was occupied by raw material inventories. Nevertheless, since various raw materials are mutually complementary, a hoarding of several kinds of raw materials could not prevent a halt in production arising from a shortage of other raw materials. Table 3.1

[39]Concerning a formal analysis of this point, see Morioka (2005, pp. 83–86).

[40]"In markets, where overdemand prevails, inventories are mainly held in order to protect the firm against shortages of raw materials or merchandise. In such a market which is typical in Hungary, a firm's operations require a relatively high level of input inventories and a low level of work-in-process and finished goods inventories" (Hunyadi 1988, p. 183).

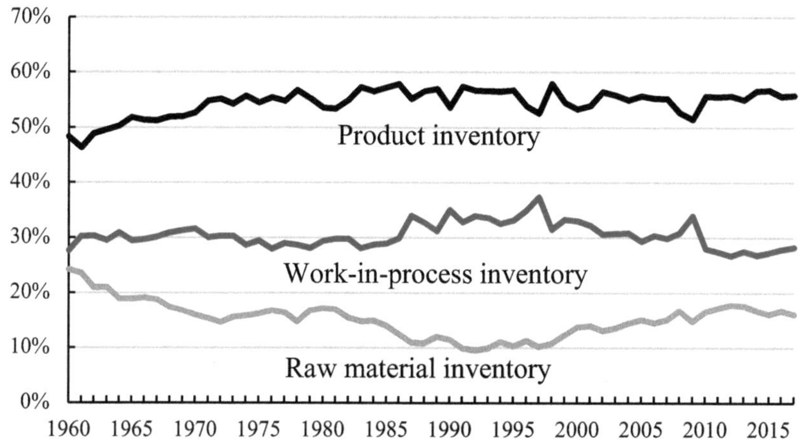

Fig. 3.2 Changes in the composition of aggregate inventory in Japan (1960–2017)
Source: Ministry of Finance Japan, *Financial Statements Statics of Corporation by Industry*

compares the composition of the aggregate inventory in Japan and socialist Hungary in the 1970s–1980s, thereby confirming the aforementioned difference.

Figure 3.2 indicates the long-term trend of the composition of aggregate inventory in Japan since the 1960s. In most of the period, the ratio of the product and raw material inventories fluctuated within a quite narrow range (50–60% and 10–20%, respectively). It is remarkable that the composition of aggregate inventories has been considerably stable for more than half a century. Naturally, the inventory composition significantly differs by sectors. Table 3.2 shows inventory compositions of various sectors at the end of 2017 in Japan. The product inventory accounts for 56% of the total inventory in all industries (except for finance and insurance) and 40% in manufacturing. In the wholesale and retail trade, product inventory accounts for more than 90% of the total inventory. In the construction industry, which is characterized by a long production period, work-in-process inventory accounts for approximately 70% of the total inventory. Work-in-process inventories are the dominant form of inventory also for transport and postal activities which always hold a large amount of freight.

Let us see the actual relative scales of inventories and their changes. Along with the progress in communication and transportation technologies and the improvement in inventory control techniques, the ratio of inventories to the weekly or monthly sales can be reduced. Figure 3.3 indicates the long-term changes in the ratios of three types of inventories to the average monthly sales in postwar Japan. The ratio of the raw material inventory to the average monthly sales had steadily decreased until the end of the 1990s, except for the years of the first oil shock. Conversely, ratios of product and work-in-process inventories to the monthly average sales had shown no sign of decrease in this period. A rapid fall in these

Table 3.2 Inventory composition by industry in Japan (End of 2017)

	Products (%)	Works-in-process (%)	Raw materials (%)	Share of this industry's inventory (%)
All industries[a]	55.7	28.2	16.0	100.0
Manufacturing	40.3	29.7	29.9	36.9
Wholesale and retail trade	92.3	2.7	5.0	29.7
Real estate and goods rental	56.6	38.3	5.1	12.8
Construction	25.3	68.2	6.5	10.3
Services	38.0	40.0	22.0	3.2
Transport and postal activities	7.5	81.2	11.3	3.1
Information and communications	37.6	37.2	25.2	1.6
Electricity	5.3	3.2	91.5	0.6

Source: Ministry of Finance Japan, *Financial Statements Statics of Corporation by Industry*
[a]except for Finance and Industry

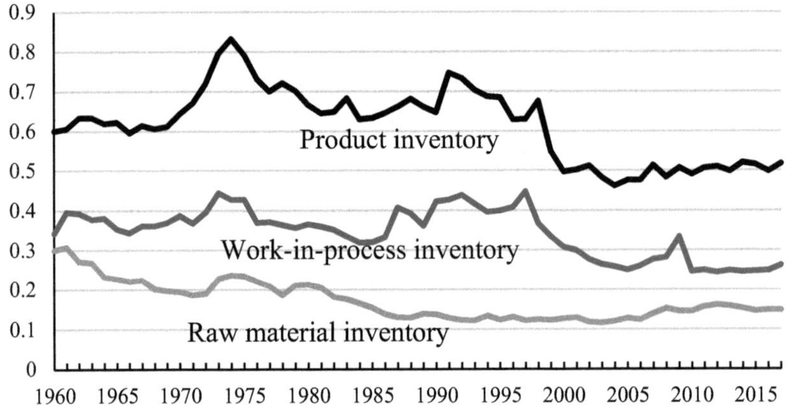

Fig. 3.3 Changes in ratios of inventories to average sales per month (1960–2017)
Source: Ministry of Finance Japan, *Financial Statements Statics of Corporation by Industry*

ratios was observed at the turn of the century, though they have remained mostly unchanged in recent years.

The ratio of the total inventory to the average monthly sales is also different by industry. Generally, this ratio is lower in the non-manufacturing than in the manufacturing sectors. As Fig. 3.4 indicates, the gap in this ratio between manufacturing and non-manufacturing industries was reduced until the 1990s and subsequently widened after the 1990s. It is important to take several cautionary measures to evaluate the sector-level inventory ratios. First, the product inventory is supposed to include old commodities that are practically difficult to sell at reasonable prices.

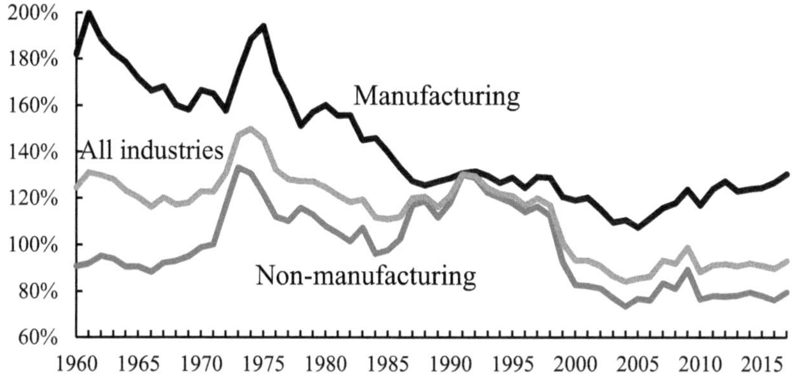

Fig. 3.4 Changes in ratios of total inventories to the average monthly sales (manufacturing and non-manufacturing, 1960–2017)
Source: Ministry of Finance Japan, *Financial Statements Statics of Corporation by Industry*

Unfortunately, no data about the share of such "dead stock" is recorded in the product inventory. However, it is highly probable that a considerable part of the product inventory ceases to be the object of reproduction and does not affect current production decisions. Second, an adequate unit period to measure the relative scale of inventory differs by sector. The average interval of the decision on production or ordering depends on technological conditions, especially on adjustability of the production volume. If we take two months as the unit period, then the ratios in Table 3.2 is halved. With these cautions, we can say that, at present, there is no indication that the significance of the buffer function of inventories is diminishing.[41]

3.3.3 Information Function of Inventories

As already mentioned, the capitalist firm attempts to hold certain volumes of product and/or raw material inventories. However, there is no assurance of the fulfillment of these intentions. As long as the sales quantity is determined by the demand of buyers, *the firm cannot directly control the ex-post amount of product inventory.* Similarly, as long as the raw material orders are made before their necessary volumes are finally determined, *the firm cannot directly control the ex-post volumes of raw material inventories*. In this way, the fluctuations in inventories almost always reflect errors in the demand forecast or changes in the production plan. Therefore, levels of inventories provide firms new information on the changes in demands for products and consumptions of raw materials.

[41]Concerning the level, change, and trends of inventories in countries other than Japan, refer to a comprehensive comparative study by Chikán et al. (2018).

In addition to demands for products, volumes of inventories comprise the most basic information that firms consider for their short-term production and ordering decisions. These quantity data are *available within firms* providing that the firms accurately record their activities. Broadly speaking, "excessive" product inventory tends to restrain production, and "insufficient" product inventory tends to stimulate production. Similarly, "excessive" raw material inventory tends to restrain ordering, and "insufficient" raw material' inventory tends to stimulate ordering.[42] These principles constitute a very simple but important guide for an economy. As already argued, a concrete rule (program) for the determination of the production volume and raw material orders can take various forms, corresponding to concrete conditions and ways of simplification.

Regarding the significance of quantity adjustment and roles of inventories in this adjustment, Simon states:

> Price provides only one of the mechanisms for coordination of behavior, either between organizations and within them. *Coordination by adjustment of quantities is probably a far more import mechanism from day to day standpoint, and in many circumstances will do a better job of allocation than coordination by prices.* For example, inventory control systems record the amounts of inputs for the organizations activities, and place order when quantities fall below specified level. The orders, recorded by the control systems of supplies, initiate the scheduling of new prediction and used to adjust aggregate production level as well. From a conceptual standpoint, it is entirely feasible to construct economies in which prices are based on costs and final demands are limited wholly by budget constraints, with demand vectors that are otherwise insensitive to prices. *Quantities of goods sold and inventories, not prices, provide the information for coordinating these systems.* ... Many observers of business scheduling and pricing practices have claimed that (with the possible exception of the agricultural and mining sectors) models that use quantities as signals approximate first-world national economies more closely than do models in which prices are the principal mechanisms of coordination. ... *Quantity adjustment plays a very large role in the real world in equilibrating the operations of different organizations and different parts of organizations.* (Simon 1991, p. 40, emphasis added)

One of the purposes of this book is to establish a theoretical basis of this Simon's view through analyzing the dynamic properties of a process that emerges from the interactions among individual firms guided by quantity signals.[43] For this purpose, in the next chapter, we will first construct a multi-sector model of the quantity adjustment process to get explicit descriptions of interactions among sectors; subsequently, using this model, we will demonstrate that, under certain plausible

[42]As Kornai puts it, "*changes in stocks yields outstandingly important information of non-price character. They are signals that are most economical of information and they can be observed within the firm*" (Kornai 1971, p. 179).

[43]Stiglitz also makes a similar comment. According to him, the conventional understanding that "economic relations in capitalist economies are governed primarily by prices" is a "myth." One of the reasons why this is a myth is that "it ignores the many non-price sources of information used by firms." Actually, "firms look at quantitative data—like what is happening to their inventories and inventories of other firms" (Stiglitz 1994, pp. 249–250).

conditions, a sequential adjustment of production and ordering by individual firms, based on the quantity information, can generate a stable process in which production and demand can be gradually equilibrated.

3.4 An Overview of Preceding Analyses

3.4.1 Contributions Before the General Theory

Although not having attracted much attention until now, the economic theory of quantity adjustment has its own history.[44] In this section, we will trace the development of this theory by surveying preceding significant contributions.

One of the first serious theoretical considerations about the roles of inventory in the capitalist economy was provided by the second volume of Marx's *Capital* (its manuscripts were written in the 1860s). Marx grasped the activities of individual capitalist firms as a process consisting of three stages, namely, the purchase of raw materials and labor forces, the production of commodities, and the sales of commodities. By examining conditions for the smooth transition of these consecutive stages, Marx focused on the fact that, at any time, there exists a considerable amount of inventory in the form of raw materials and finished products. In his view, "*It is only by way of this stock formation that the permanence and continuity of the circulation process is ensured, hence that of the reproduction process which includes the circulation process*" (Marx 1992, p. 224, emphasis added). Recognizing that necessary volumes of raw material inventories depend on the extent of the certainty of purchases, Marx wrote that the holding of a "great store of coal" becomes "superfluous," along with the expansion of domestic coal production and the development of transport (Marx 1992, p. 219). Furthermore, he clearly described the intentional formation of product inventory exceeding the average demand by firms as sellers under sales competition in the following words:

> The commodity stock must have a certain volume in order to satisfy the scale of demand over given period. ... Moreover, *it must be greater in scale than the average scale or the average demand*, otherwise excessive above this average could not be satisfied. ... The producer himself attempts to have an inventory adequate for his average demand, *in order not to directly dependent on production, and to secure himself a constant circle of customers.* (Marx 1992, p. 223, emphasis added)

Unfortunately, Marx's insightful remarks about the functions of inventories were not carefully interwoven with other parts of his theory.

Hawtrey shed light on the role of inventory as information guiding economic behaviors. In *Currency and Credit*, first published in 1919, Hawtrey described

[44] A possible reason behind this weak theoretical interest in inventory is the lack of statistical data about quantity variables (including inventories) in the nineteenth and early twentieth century.

a mechanism in which an increase in demand for commodities stimulates the enlargement of production through a reduction of inventories held by merchants (Hawtrey 1950). While Hawtrey was mainly concerned with the movement of prices and interest rates, his theory must be mentioned here because it focused on *the economic process accompanied by the fluctuation in inventories*.

The modeling of the quantity adjustment process starts from the multiplier theory. The idea of cumulative interactions between production and demand was already suggested in Marshall's *Principle* (Marshall 1920). However, an explicit formulation of this idea was first made by Kahn (1931). In this paper, Kahn observes that during a depression "the supply curve is likely to be very elastic" because "nearly all industries have at their disposal *a large surplus of unused plant and labor*" (Kahn 1931, p. 182, emphasis added). Under such a situation, he asserts, a creation of additional demand by the public sector leads to a significant increase in production (and employment) and a small rise in prices. Kahn constructed a simple model of this increase in production based on the assumptions that production is perfectly elastic and any additional income yields a proportional increase in consumption demand. From this model, he derived a famous formula indicating the multiplier effect by an increase in independent demand. Although Kahn recognized that an expansion of production is a time-consuming process, he simply set aside "the question of this time lag" (Kahn 1931, p. 183). In a paper published in 1933 in Poland, Kalecki found a formula similar to that of Kahn (Kalecki 1971). In the same year, Keynes used Kahn's theory in his article "The means to prosperity" to advocate the expansion of public investment as a stimulus for production (Keynes 1933). However, neither Kalecki nor Keynes paid due attention to the process of expansion.

3.4.2 The General Theory and Quantity Adjustment

In the history of the economic theory of quantity adjustment, Keynes' *General Theory* occupies a very important but somewhat singular position. Its principal message is that the level of production and employment is usually constrained by the demand for products, and therefore an increase in demand leads to an expansion in production and employment until the full employment is achieved. In *General Theory*, Keynes rejected Say's law and assumed that the aggregate investment demand is determined by firms, independent of the aggregate savings. While the introduction of an independent investment function causes an overdetermination of variables in the system of the general equilibrium,[45] Keynes solved this problem

[45]This problem was raised by Morishima (1977). In the latter half of the 1970s, Morishima turned from an admirer of Walras to a radical Keynesian and began to emphasize the significance of quantity adjustment in industrial sectors.

by allowing that a part of the labor force is not employed and a part of the capital equipment is not utilized.

By explicitly rejecting Say's law and recognizing the permanent existence of unemployment and unused capacities in the capitalist economy, Keynes made a significant contribution to the theory of quantity adjustment. Subsequent developments in the model analyses in this direction owed much to the stimulus provided by *General Theory*. At the same time, *General Theory* contained several factors contradicting its own central message, among which the assumption of perfect competition in product markets was especially problematic. Under perfect competition, each firm determines its supply on the premise that *it can sell as much as it wants at given prices*. There is no demand constraint, and the supply of the firm is constrained by the rise of marginal cost up to the selling price. On the other hand, Keynes writes that "the volume of employment is *determined by the estimates of effective demands* made by entrepreneurs" (Keynes 1936, p. 78, emphasis added). Although this seems to imply that the firm adapts its production and employment to the estimated demand, there is no need for such adaptation under perfect competition.[46]

As we have seen, Kahn pointed out that the marginal cost of production is constant or rather decreasing as long as the firm still has surplus productive capacity. A similar contention was made by Sraffa and Kalecki. After the publication of *General Theory*, Keynes admitted the constancy of the marginal cost under the usual level of the operation rate.[47] Though Keynes stuck to the point that the marginal cost "eventually turns upwards" as production gets close to the capacity, the shape of the marginal cost curve is not the true problem. Perfect competition presupposes that the market is organized in a centralized manner and that every participant follows the same procedure to find the market-clearing price. Therefore, *the true problem is whether a well-organized market should be regarded as the most representative type of product markets*. Our view on this point is that well-organized markets are quite exceptional in the entire product markets. Most product markets are dispersive in the sense that every transaction can be made only by a mutual consent between the buyer and the seller. The predominance of dispersive markets is rooted in the very nature of the market as a collection of free transactions.

In *General Theory*, Keynes (like Kahn) ignored the lag between an increase in demand and the subsequent expansion of production. However, this lag is not mere friction that can be eliminated without affecting our understanding about the multiplier effect. Since production takes time, firms must start production or place raw material orders before knowing the actual demand. It seems that Keynes did not have any doubt about the stability of this process. The fact that this process can be

[46]In the formal model of *General Theory*, the equilibrium of the aggregate product market is attained through a change in the real wage rate. Therefore, it cannot be regarded as a model of quantity adjustment.

[47]"If we start from a level of output very greatly below capacity, so that even the most efficient plant and labor are only partially employed, marginal real cost may be expected to decline with increasing output or, at the worst, remain constant" (Keynes 1939, p. 44).

unstable under particular rules or particular values of parameters was discovered by a series of studies that we will take up in the following subsections.

3.4.3 Dynamic Analyses of the Multiplier Process

In the year following the publication of *General Theory*, Eric Lundberg's *Studies in the Theory of Economic Expansion* (written in Swedish) took the first important step in performing a dynamic analysis of the quantity adjustment process. Under strong influence of Wicksell's theory of the cumulative process and the impact of Keynes' principle of effective demand, Lundberg applied the method of "a sequence analysis of the total development" to the fluctuation of production caused by a change in demand (Lundberg 1964, p. 5). His main purpose was to build a model with an explicit consideration of the fact that the reaction of production to a change in demand entails a certain amount of time. His model was also intended to be a description of the "'*quantitative*' *reaction pattern of entrepreneurs*" to an increase in final demand (Lundberg 1964, p. 106, emphasis added).

The basic setting of Lundberg's model is as follows.[48] Time is divided into discrete periods and the unit period corresponds to "a reaction interval, measuring the average distance between the rise in demand and the subsequent increase in production activity" (Lundberg 1964, p. 187). The aggregate firm starts (the final process of) the production at the beginning of the period and obtains the finished product at the end of the period. The product demand is determined immediately after the determination of production and realized at the end of the period. The firm hopes to set the production volume equal to the demand while keeping the price constant. However, the firm cannot know the precise demand before it determines the production volume. Thus, the firm sets the production volume equal to the expected demand, that is,

$$Y(t) = S^e(t), \tag{3.11}$$

where $Y(t)$ is the production volume determined at the beginning of period t and obtained at the end of period t, and $S^e(t)$ is the expected demand that should be satisfied at the end of period t. The actual demand consists of the consumption demand, which is proportional to the production, and the exogenously given investment demand. That is,

$$S(t) = C(t) + I, \quad C(t) = cY(t) \ (0 < c < 1), \tag{3.12}$$

[48]Lundberg (1964) made a distinction between the consumption goods sector and the investment goods sector. However, since the activities of the former are assumed to be constant except for inventory investment we can regard his model as a single-sector macro model.

where $S(t)$ is the actual demand, $C(t)$ is the consumption demand, c is the marginal propensity to consume, and I is the exogenously given aggregate investment demand. Concerning the method of expectation, Lundberg assumes the static expectation, that is,

$$S^e(t) = S(t-1), \tag{3.13}$$

with a remark that this is "certainly only one assumption out of an infinite number of possible alternatives" (Lundberg 1964, p. 154).

(3.11) to (3.13) constitute a simple model of the quantity adjustment process. They are summarized into the following difference equation:

$$Y(t) = cY(t-1) + I. \tag{3.14}$$

The stationary point of this system is

$$Y^* = S^* = S^{e*} = \frac{1}{1-c}I,$$

which is identical with the equilibrium of the corresponding static model. Since $0 < c < 1$, this system is globally asymptotically stable, that is, $Y(t)$, $S(t)$, and $S^e(t)$ all converge to Y^* with the lapse of periods. In this respect, this model describes "how, i.e., *through what sequence, this state of equilibrium is reached*" (Lundberg 1964, p. 195, emphasis in original).

In this model, production $Y(t)$ can be different from demand $S(t)$ and the gap between them is absorbed by an unintended change in product inventory.[49] Let $Z(t)$ be the product inventory at the end of period t, then it changes by

$$Z(t) = Z(t-1) + Y(t) - S(t). \tag{3.15}$$

Lundberg implicitly supposes that there exists enough product inventory to absorb the excess demand whenever demand exceeds production. That is, the condition

$$Z(t-1) + Y(t) \geq S(t). \tag{3.16}$$

is always satisfied. Since $Z(t-1) + Y(t)$ is the supply in period t, (3.16) implies that *the economy is in a situation of continuous excess supply*. If (3.16) does not hold, then demand $S(t)$ must be distinguished from the actual sales

$$\tilde{S}(t) = \min\{Z(t-1) + Y(t), S(t)\},$$

[49] Like Hawtrey, Lundberg had a clear idea about the roles of inventories. In a reference to activities by retail traders, he writes that inventories held by these traders "act as *a buffer* that take up the discrepancies between supply and demand" (Lundberg 1964, p. 106, emphasis added).

and accordingly, (3.15) must be replaced by

$$Z(t) = Z(t-1) + Y(t) - \tilde{S}(t).$$

However, Lundberg did not pay attention to the nonnegativity constraint on the inventory (this problem will be addressed in Chap. 5).

Let us assume that $Y(0) = S(0) = S^e(0) = \frac{1}{1-c}I$ and the exogenous investment demand expands from I to $I + \Delta I$, from period 1 onward. Then, as long as (3.16) is satisfied, we have

$$Y(1) = Y(0),\ Y(t+1) = Y(0) + \sum_{i=0}^{t-1} c^i \Delta I,$$

$$Z(t) = Z(0) - \sum_{i=0}^{t-1} c^i \Delta I \quad (t \geq 1).$$

Hence, $Y(t)$ and $Z(t)$ converge to $Y^* = \frac{1}{1-c}(I + \Delta I)$ and $Z^* = Z(0) - Y(0)\frac{\Delta I}{I}$, respectively. Therefore, to ensure that $Z(t) \geq 0$ is satisfied for any $t \in \{1, 2, \ldots\}$, it must hold $Z(0)/Y(0) > \Delta I/I$, that is, the initial inventory-output ratio must be larger than the growth rate of investment.

Lundberg extended his analysis to the case in which the firm seeks to maintain a certain "normal" level of product inventory under the assumption that this normal level depends on the expected demand. In his second model, $Z^d(t)$, the normal or desired level of product inventory at the end of period t, is proportional to the expected demand (Lundberg 1964, p. 199), that is,

$$Z^d(t) = kS^e(t) \ (k > 0). \tag{3.17}$$

Coefficient k can be regarded as the buffer inventory ratio. The firm determines the production volume to ensure that the actual end-of-period inventory is equal to this desirable inventory when its expectation of demand is correct, that is,

$$Z(t-1) + Y(t) - S^e(t) = Z^d(t). \tag{3.18}$$

From (3.17) and (3.18), we have

$$Y(t) = (1+k)\, S^e(t) - Z(t-1). \tag{3.19}$$

As long as $Z(t-1) \leq (1+k)S^e(t)$, (3.19) coincides with (3.6), a typical production rule for stockout avoidance, except for the difference of notation.

Lundberg's second dynamic model is constructed from (3.12), (3.13), (3.15), and (3.19). These are summarized into

$$Y(t) = c\,(2+k)\,Y\,(t-1) - c\,(1+k)\,Y\,(t-2) + I. \tag{3.20}$$

The stationary point of this dynamic system is

$$Y^* = S^* = S^{e*} = \frac{1}{1-c}I, \quad Z^* = kY^* = \frac{k}{1-c}I.$$

Lundberg investigated the nature of this process by a numerical calculation. Mathematically, system (3.20) is stable if and only if

$$c\,(1+k) < 1. \tag{3.21}$$

Hence, an increase in the buffer coefficient narrows the bound of the consumption propensity for stability.[50] In this model, $c < 1$ is no more sufficient for stability if $k > 0$. Furthermore, if system (3.20) is stable, then the movement of variables would be accompanied by damped cyclical oscillations.[51] Thus, system (3.20) can be regarded as a model of inventory cycle. Figure 3.5 illustrates the movements of $Y(t)$ and $Z(t)$ when the initial values and parameters are set as $Y(0) = S(0) = 250$, $Z(0) = 100$, $c = 0.6$, $k = 0.4$ and $I = 100$ $(t = 0)$, $I = 110$ $(t > 1)$. Under these values of parameters, $Y(t)$ and $Z(t)$ converge to $Y^* = 275$ and $Z^* = 110$, respectively, with a cyclical oscillation.[52]

In this way, while the introduction of planned inventory investment in the model does not affect the stationary value of production and demand, it significantly changes the stability condition and the dynamic nature of the process.

Metzler's article "The Nature and Stability of Inventory Cycle" (1941) is eminent for its classical model analysis of inventory cycle. His purpose was almost the same

[50]In his numerical calculation, Lundberg assumes that $c = 0.9$ and $k = 0.5$. Although this pair of values does not satisfy $c(1+k) < 1$, his calculation shows the convergence of the process (Lundberg 1964, p. 201). The reason behind this convergence lies in Lundberg's implicit assumption that a planned inventory investment cannot be negative. This implies that $Y(t)$ is determined $Y(t) = S^e(t) + \max\,\{kS^e(t) - Z(t-1), 0\}$. However, it is difficult to find a reason justifying this assumption.

[51]The characteristic equation corresponding to system (3.20) is $\xi^2 - c(2+k)\xi + c(1+k) = 0$. It can be easily shown that the dominant root of this equation is less than unity if and only if $c(1+k) < 1$. Furthermore, $c(1+k) < 1$ implies that this equation has a pair of conjugate complex roots.

[52]Concerning classical empirical studies on inventory cycle, refer to Metzler (1947) and Abramowitz (1950). While inventory cycles is now called "Kitchin's cycle," Kitchin (1923), which detected a trade cycle of 40 months in average, made no mention of inventory.

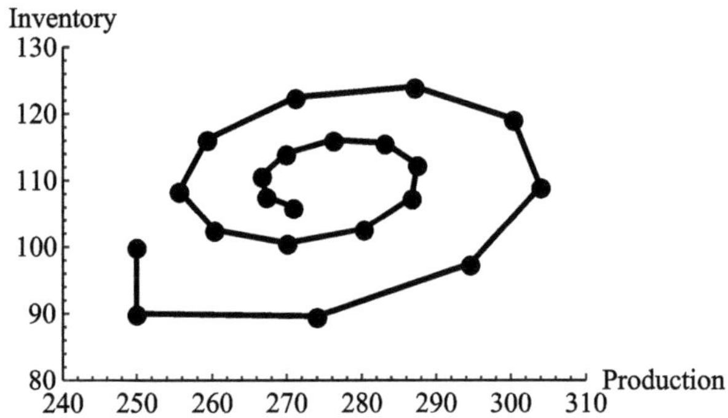

Fig. 3.5 Movement of production and inventory in Lundberg's model

as Lundberg's, that is, the construction of a model that can explain "*how* the system moves from one equilibrium to another and *why* it tends to approach equilibrium at all." Metzler quite distinctly pointed out that Keynes' *General Theory* lacked "a description of *the time sequence of events by which an increase of net investment produces a rise of income*" (Metzler 1941, p. 113, emphasis added). Concerning the buffer role of inventories, Metzler observed that "Entrepreneurs have adequate inventories so that *any discrepancy between output and consumer demand may be met by inventory fluctuations rather than price changes*" (Metzler 1941, p. 117, emphasis added).

In our notation, the most complicated model in Metzler (1941) consists of (3.12), (3.15), (3.19), and the expectation of demand by the method

$$S^e(t) = S(t-1) + \eta(S(t-1) - S(t-2)) \quad (-1 \leq \eta \leq 1). \tag{3.22}$$

This method is based on Metzler's consideration that "expectations of future sales may depend not only upon the past *level* of sales, but also upon the *direction of changes* of such sales" (Metzler 1941, p. 119). The right-hand side of (3.22) is a weighted average of sales in the past two periods such that the weight for $S(t-1)$ is always nonnegative, but the weight for $S(t-2)$ can be negative (for $0 \leq \eta < 1$). If $\eta = 0$, then (3.22) would be reduced to the static expectation.

(3.12), (3.15), (3.19), and (3.22) are summarized into

$$Y(t) = c((1+\eta)b + 1)Y(t-1) - bc(2\eta + 1)Y(t-2) + bc\eta Y(t-3) + I, \tag{3.23}$$

where $b \equiv 1 + k$. This is a third-order difference equation, and, naturally, its stability condition takes a much more complicated form. In fact, system (3.23) is stable if and only if

$$c < \begin{cases} c_1(\eta, k) & \beta(k) < \eta \leq 1 \\ c_2(\eta, k) & -1 \leq \eta \leq \beta(k). \end{cases} \tag{3.24}$$

where $\beta(k) \equiv -(3+2k)/(3+3k)$ and

$$c_1(\eta, k) \equiv \frac{1 + 2\eta - \sqrt{1 + 4\eta^2 - 4\eta/(1+k)}}{2(k+2)\eta}, \quad c_2(\eta, k) \equiv \frac{-1}{1 + (k+1)(1+2\eta)}$$

Thus, an increase in c or k always lowers the possibility that (3.24) holds.[53] However, the effect of the change in η is not monotonic. As η increases, the upper bound of c for stability increases for $-1 \leq \eta \leq \beta(k)$ and decreases for $\beta(k) \leq \eta \leq 1$; hence, it takes the maximum value at $\eta = \beta(k)$ (in this case, the stability condition is $c < 3/(3+2k)$. Therefore, the demand expectation *positively* projecting the trend of change in the past two periods (the case $0 < \eta \leq 1$) might destabilize the system which is stable under the static expectation. For example, let $k = 0.4$, then the stability condition is $c < 0.714$ for $\eta = 0$ (the case of static expectation) and $c < 0.659$ for $\eta = 0.2$. Hence, if $c = 0.7$, then the system (3.23) would lose stability by an increase in η from 0 to 0.2.

3.4.4 Microfoundation of Stockout Avoidance Behavior

Production rule (3.15) assumed by Lundberg and Metzler was considerably different from those in the models of perfect competition. The theoretical foundation of this rule was given by studies on the operations research or, more precisely, those of the optimal inventory policy in the 1950s. A pioneering paper on the optimal inventory control by Arrow et al. (1951) strongly stimulated the development of this field. They sought to focus on "the major questions that have actually risen in the practice of business and non-profit organizations" about inventory holding. Therefore, they excluded "speculative inventories" from consideration by assuming *constancy of the situation,* and introduced, in their model, "the penalty cost of stock depletion" caused by the loss of customers (Arrow et al. 1951, pp. 251–252)[54]. The central premises of their model are that the firm is under a demand constraint and regards demand in each period as a random variable.

Mills (1954) highlighted the relevance of this paper to models of Lundberg and Metzler. He argued that the Lundberg-Metzler type production rule "can be derived as a special case of maximal behavior," by applying the method of Arrow et al. This is because they shared the assumption that "the firm is uncertain as to future sales

[53]Concerning the derivation of this condition, see Appendix 9, Chap. 4.

[54]According to Arrow, the penalty cost is "the loss of the customer's goodwill and his possible future unwillingness to do business with the firm." He notes, furthermore, that "Such a penalty cost is real but may be very hard to measure in any precise case" (Arrow et al. 1958, p. 21).

and holds inventory to *avoid the risk of disappointing customers*" (Mills 1954, p. 15, emphasis added). Arrow and his collaborators compiled their findings on inventory models into a book titled *Studies in the Mathematical Theory of Inventory and Production* (Arrow et al. 1958). In this book, Scarf presented a common framework for the model analysis on the production and ordering rule, which could treat various cases corresponding to different types of cost functions. As already shown in Sect. 3.2, rule (3.19) can be derived from this framework by assuming that all kinds of costs are linear and the standard deviation of demand is proportional to its mean.

In the introduction of the above book, Arrow observed that the "economic theory has had remarkably little to say about inventories" and "the usual textbook has only the most scattered references to the motives for the holding of inventories" (Arrow et al. 1958, p. 3). A little earlier, Hicks expressed similar dissatisfaction on the state of the economic theory. Critically reconsidering the method adopted in his *Capital and Values*, Hicks (1956, p. 145) admitted that "A model in which quantities bear the brunt of disequilibrium fits most of the facts distinctly better."[55] In order to ensure that quantities absorb the gap between demand and supply while continuing to allow the freedom of choice to buyers, sufficient volumes of product inventories must be held by sellers. Even though this issue was raised by two prominent economists, Kornai (1971, p. 179) still had to lament that "economic theory has become separated entirely from the branch of operations research dealing with stock building."[56]

The term "quantity adjustment" was used in the 1960s by economists engaged in the research of optimal planning theory founded by Arrow and Hurwitz (1960). They adopted this term to characterize the type of planning process in which every production unit (firm) was placed under the quantity constraints of available productive resources, and the central planning organ revised these constraints based on the comparison of shadow prices of each resource reported by each production unit. Kornai and Lipták (1965) is one of representative models of such a type of adjustment. In their model, the object of adjustment by the central organ is certainly the quantity constraints. However, "quantity adjustment" in this sense is quite different from the one we have argued in this chapter in that there is no demand constraint and the changes in quantities are made in a centralized manner. At least, it cannot be regarded as a description of capitalist product markets.[57]

---

[55] Concerning prices, Hicks (1956, p. 145) observed that "both the manufactures and the retailer are, for the most part, 'price makers' rather than 'price takers'; they fix prices and let the quantities they sell be determined by demand."

[56] Although nearly half a century has passed since then, this situation has barely changed. The buffer function of product and raw material inventory cannot be integrated into any economic theory that disregards the demand constraint on production and the successive nature of adjustment.

[57] Interestingly, Aoki (1978) attempted to bridge the gap between these different concepts of quantity adjustment. Having built a model of centralized successive allocation in which the central organization assigns each firm the gross output that it should produce, he transformed it into a model of decentralized quantity adjustment, in our sense, by interpreting this constraint as the perception (or forecast) of demand by the firm. See Morioka (2018).

3.4.5 Incorporation of the Input-Output Analysis

The framework of input-output analysis built by Leontief (1941) provided a powerful analytical tool to examine the interactions among sectors that Lundberg and Metzler had eliminated from their models. Using this tool, Goodwin (1949) and Chipman (1950) constructed very similar multi-sector models of the multiplier process. In their models, the economy consisted of n sectors each of which produced a single commodity. Let $x_i(t)$ denote the production volume of sector i in period t, a_{ji} denote the amount of product i required per unit output of product j, and d_i denote the final demand, which is assumed to be constant.[58] The production of sector i is determined by

$$x_i(t) = \sum_{j=1}^{n} x_j(t-1)\,a_{ji} + d_i. \tag{3.25}$$

In matrix notation, (3.25) can be written as

$$x(t) = x(t-1)\,A + d, \tag{3.26}$$

where $x(t)$ and d are $1 \times n$ vectors of $x_i(t)$ and d_i, respectively, and $A = [a_{ij}]$ is an ordinary input matrix.

According to Goodwin and Chapman, (3.25) describes make-to-order production such that production is determined to precisely satisfy the total demand that consists of intermediate and final demand. Owing to the Perron-Frobenius Theorem, input matrix A has at least one nonnegative eigenvalue, and the largest real eigenvalue is equal to the spectrum radius (the largest eigenvalue measured by absolute value) of A. If the economy is able to produce net products, in other words, if there is a semi-positive vector y such that $y - yA$ is semi positive, then the spectrum radius of matrix A is less than unity.[59] In this case, the matrix $I - A$ (I is the identity matrix of size n) is invertible to a nonnegative matrix, and system (3.26) has a unique stationary point $x^* = d(I - A)^{-1}$. Furthermore, the (gross) production vector $x(t)$ converges to x^* over time. The Leontief inverse matrix $(I - A)^{-1}$ can be regarded as the multiplier in matrix form that indicates the relationship between the final demand vector and the production vector.

[58] In Goodwin (1950), input coefficients are defined in monetary terms, that is, they denotes the value of the good required per production of the unit value of the commodity. However, this does not affect the following argument.

[59] Concerning this theorem, refer to Hawkins and Simon (1949) and Nikaido (1961).

The introduction of an input matrix by Goodwin and Chipman was a great step in the analysis of the quantity adjustment process. However, in their models, the sequence of decisions and actions were not clearly formulated. Owing to this obscurity, they did not pay due attention to *the necessity of raw material inventories* in their models. To clarify this point, let us assume the following sequence: (i) Sector i receives orders at the beginning of period t and instantaneously starts production $x_i(t)$ to satisfy this order. (ii) Production $x_i(t)$ is completed and delivered at the beginning of period $t+1$.

Owing to the simple fact that time is irreversible, inputs for production $x(t)$ cannot be obtained from $x(t)$ itself. Under the above sequence, inputs $x_i(t)a_i \quad (a_i = [a_{i1}, \ldots, a_{in}])$ necessary for production $x_i(t)$ are obtained from the internal supply of raw materials at the beginning of period t. Let $v_{ij}(t)$ be the raw material inventory of product j held by sector i at the end of period t. In period t, it increases as a result of the arrival of ordered raw material $x_i(t-1)a_{ij}$ and decreases by its productive consumption $x_i(t)a_{ij}$. Thus, we have

$$v_{ij}(t) = v_{ij}(t-1) + x_i(t-1)\,a_{ij} - x_i(t)a_{ij},$$

which implies that sector i can carry out production $x_i(t)$ only if

$$v_{ij}(t-1) + x_i(t-1)\,a_{ij} \geq x_i(t)a_{ij}$$

for any j. In this way, process (3.26) presupposes that there exist enough raw material inventories to satisfy the above constraint.

Lovell (1962) presented a multi-sector model in which a Lundberg-Metzler type behavior is attributed to individual firms. In accordance with Lundberg and Metzler, Lovell assumed that, under constant prices and "incomplete knowledge of future sales," firms hold product inventories "*as buffer stocks in order that unanticipated demand may be satisfied.*" At the same time, he departed from their approach in that he considered "the implications of a *multitude* of interacting firms all attempting to adjust inventories to a level deemed appropriate in the face of incomplete knowledge of future market conditions" (Lovell 1962, p. 267, emphasis added). Lovell's approach was also different from that of Goodwin-Chipman in that "a crucial role is explicitly assigned to errors of expectations and inventory stocks" (Lovell 1962, p. 268)[60].

Lovell's model consisted of the following equations:

$$x_i(t) = s_i^e(t) + r_i\left(s_i^e(t)k_i - z_i(t-1)\right) \tag{3.27}$$

$$s_i^e(t) = s_i(t-1) \tag{3.28}$$

$$z_i(t) = z_i(t-1) + x_i(t) - s_i(t) \tag{3.29}$$

---

[60]Lovell's investigation of inventory cycle was supervised by Leontief (Lovell 1962, p. 267). This fact suggests that there was an interesting link between the multi-sector analysis of quantity adjustment and Leontief's input-output analysis.

$$s_i(t) = \sum_{j=1}^{n} x_j(t+1)a_{ji} + d_i, \tag{3.30}$$

where $s_i(t)$ and $s_i^e(t)$ are the actual and anticipated demands for product i in period t, respectively, $z_i(t)$ is the product inventory held by sector i at the end of period t, k_i is the buffer stock coefficient of sector i, and r_i is the coefficient of inventory adjustment ($0 \leq k_i, 0 < r_i \leq 1, i \in \{1, \ldots, n\}$). Concerning the determination of the production volume, Lovell assumed that firms attempt to fill the ratio r_i of $s_i^e(t)k_i - z_i(t-1)$, that is, the gap between the desirable and actual levels of inventory. If $r_i = 1$, (3.27) is simplified into

$$x_i(t) = (1+k_i)s_i^e(t) - z_i(t-1), \tag{3.31}$$

which is identical with (3.19) except for the difference of notation. (3.30) represents that the demand for good i is the sum of intermediate demands derived from productions $x_1(t+1), \ldots, x_n(t+1)$ and final demand d_i. Hence, $s_i(t)$ is decided after $x_i(t+1)$ is decided. However, according to (3.27) and (3.28), $x_i(t+1)$ is decided based on $s_i(t)$. This loop in the decisions of $s_i(t)$ and $x_i(t)$ is reflected in the following matrix difference equation:

$$x(t) = x(t)A(I+R+RK) + x(t-1)(I-R-A(I+RK)) + dR,$$

where K and R are diagonal matrices of buffer coefficient k_i and adjustment coefficient r_i, respectively. From this equation, Lovell derives a recursive equation

$$x(t) = x(t-1)(I-R-A(I+RK))B^{-1} + dRB^{-1} \tag{3.32}$$

under the assumption that $B = I - A(I+R+RK)$ is a regular matrix. The stationary point of this system is $x^* = s^* = d(I-A)^{-1}$, $z^* = x^*K$. In order to calculate $x_i(t)$ by (3.32), sector i must know other firms' buffer coefficients, adjustment coefficients, and input coefficients. However, such sharing of internal information among firms obviously contradicts the basic premise of the model that the adjustment proceeds in a decentralized manner.

One possible way out of this contradiction is to replace (3.30) with

$$s_i(t) = \sum_{j=1}^{n} x_j(t)a_{ji} + d_i. \tag{3.33}$$

(3.27) to (3.29) and (3.33) are summarized into[61]

$$\begin{aligned} x(t) = {} & x(t-1)\left(A\left(I+R+RK\right)+I-R\right) \\ & - x(t-2)\,A\left(I+RK\right)+dR. \end{aligned} \tag{3.34}$$

In this case, sector i's material orders $x_i(t)a_{i1}, \ldots, x_i(t)a_{in}$ are delivered *after* the same amount of inputs are consumed for production $x_i(t)$. This implies that sector i determines raw material orders so that the consumption of raw materials in production is precisely replenished. Another option to maintain the consistency of the time sequence is to replace (3.27) with

$$x_i(t+1) = s_i^e(t) + r_i\left(k_i s_i^e(t) - \left(z_i(t-1) + x_i(t) - s_i^e(t)\right)\right) \tag{3.35}$$

where $s_i^e(t)$ denotes the expected demand for the good i *per period* from period t onward. In other words, at the beginning of period t, sector i determines $x_i(t+1)$, not $x_i(t)$, to ensure that it fills the expected gap between the desirable and the expected actual product inventory at the end of period t, under the assumption that the demand is realized as expected. In this case, raw material order $x_i(t+1)a_{ij}$ is promptly delivered from supply $x_i(t) + z_i(t-1)$, which already exists at the beginning of period t. (3.28), (3.29), (3.30), and (3.35) are summarized into

$$\begin{aligned} x(t) = {} & x(t-1)\left(A\left(I+2R+RK\right)+I-R\right) \\ & - x(t-2)\,A\left(I+R+RK\right)+dR. \end{aligned} \tag{3.36}$$

This coincides with (3.34), if K is replaced with $I + K$.

Returning to Lovell's original model, he correctly indicated that, under the simplifying assumption $R = rI$ and $K = kI$, system (3.32) is stable if and only if $\lambda^{\mathrm{F}}(A) < (2-r)/(2+r+2rk)$ (Lovell 1962, pp. 286, 292–295). According to this condition, the stability of system (3.32) does not depend on A's eigenvalues other than the Frobenius root. However, this independence of stability from the input structure cannot be generalized. If Lovell had examined (3.34) or (3.36) in place of (3.32), he would have found that its stability depends on the whole input structure, that is, on the distribution of A's eigenvalues on the complex plane.[62]

[61] Similar to the models of Goodwin and Chipman, the system (33) presupposes that there are enough raw material inventories.

[62] Concerning the stability of (3.34) and (3.36), see Sect. 5.1.2, Chap. 5. As will be shown there, if A has $-\lambda^{\mathrm{F}}(\mathrm{A})$ as its eigenvalue, the necessary and sufficient conditions for the stability of (3.34) and (3.36) in the case of $R = rI$ and $K = kI$ are $\lambda^{\mathrm{F}}(A) < \frac{2-r}{2+r+2rk}$ and $\lambda^{\mathrm{F}}(A) < \frac{2-r}{3+2r+2rk}$, respectively. Both conditions are not necessary if A does not have negative or complex eigenvalues.

3.4.6 Development of Multi-sector Dynamic Analyses

Foster (1963) assumed make-to-order production and built models focused on the buffer function of the raw material inventories. The most important contribution of this article is that it exhibited that a multi-sector dynamic system "might well become unstable because of interactions among industries" (Foster 1963, p. 418). One of the models by Foster consisted of the following equations:

$$x_i(t) = s_i(t) = \sum_{j=1}^{n} m_{ji}(t) + d_i \tag{3.37}$$

$$m_{ij}(t) = s_i^e(t)a_{ij} + r_i\left(l_i s_i^e(t)a_{ij} - v_{ij}(t-1)\right) \tag{3.38}$$

$$v_{ij}(t) = v_{ij}(t-1) + m_{ij}(t-1) - a_{ij}x_i(t) \tag{3.39}$$

$$s_i^e(t) = s_i(t-1) + \eta_i\left(s_i(t-1) - s_i(t-2)\right) \tag{3.40}$$

where $m_{ij}(t)$ is the raw material order placed by sector i to sector j at the beginning of period t, l_i is the buffer material inventory coefficient of sector i, and η_i is the coefficient projecting the increase in demand in the past two periods ($0 \leq \eta_i \leq 1$). In this model, sector i determines production $x_i(t)$ equal to demand $s_i(t)$, and the latter is equal to the sum of raw material orders from other sectors $m_{1i}(t) + \cdots + m_{ni}(t)$ and final demand d_i. Therefore, sector i cannot know $s_i(t)$ *before* it determines its raw material orders $m_{i1}(t), \ldots, m_{in}(t)$. These orders are decided in a manner similar to that of (3.27). The raw material inventory increases by the arrival of the previous order at the beginning of the period and diminishes by the productive consumption during the period.[63] For simplicity, Foster assumed that r_i, l_i, and η_i are equal to r, l, and η for any i, respectively.

If $r = 0$, then $v_{ij}(t)$ would be disconnected from the loop of interdependencies in this dynamic system. In this case, (3.37) to (3.40) are summarized to

$$s(t) = (1+\eta)\, s(t-1)\, A - \eta s(t-1)\, A + d, \tag{3.41}$$

where $s(t)$ is a vector of $s_i(t)$. The stationary point of this system is $x^* = s^* = d(I-A)^{-1}$, $m_{ij}^* = x_i^* a_{ij}$ $(i, j \in \{1, \ldots, n\})$.

A necessary and sufficient condition for asymptotic stability of this system is that the dominant root of the equation $\xi^2 - (1+\eta)\,\lambda_i\xi + \eta\lambda_i = 0$ is less than unity for any $i \in \{1, \ldots, n\}$, where $\lambda_1, \ldots, \lambda_n$ are the eigenvalues of matrix A. By numerical computation, Foster indicated that while "positive roots [eigenvalues] up to one are acceptable" for stability, "negative and complex roots are much more severely

[63] While Foster also assumes a method of sales expectation $s^e(t) = x(t-1)A + d$, which he calls "customers demand's forecast," here we pick up only the case of the Metzler type expectation.

restricted" (Foster 1963, p. 308). In fact, let $\overline{\xi}(\lambda_i, \eta)$ be the dominant root of the above equation and $\overline{\lambda}$ be the Frobenius root of A, then $\overline{\xi}\left(\overline{\lambda}, \eta\right) < 1$ holds if and only if $\eta\overline{\lambda} < 1$, which always holds as long as $\overline{\lambda} < 1$. However, these conditions cease to be sufficient if A has complex or negative eigenvalues. Especially, $\overline{\xi}\left(-\overline{\lambda}, \eta\right) < 1$ holds if and only if $(1 + 2\eta)\,\overline{\lambda} < 1$.[64]

If $r = 1$, then (3.37) to (3.40) are summarized into

$$x(t) = \big((1+\eta)\,b + 1\big)x\,(t-1) - (1+2\eta)\,bx\,(t-2)\,A + \eta bx\,(t-3)\,A + d, \tag{3.42}$$

where $b \equiv 1 + l$. This is a matrix version of system (3.23). In this case, the stationary value of raw material inventory $v_{ij}(t)$ is $l_i x_i^* a_{ij}$. This system will be stable if and only if the dominant root of the cubic equation

$$\xi^3 - ((1+\eta)\,b + 1)\,\lambda_i\xi^2 + b\,(1+2\eta)\,\lambda_i\xi - b\eta\lambda_i = 0$$

is less than unity for any $i \in \{1, \ldots, n\}$. Again, by numerical computation, Foster illustrates that even in this system, the upper bound of $|\lambda_i|$ for stability becomes severer if λ_i is negative or complex[65].

Negative and complex eigenvalues of the input matrix reflect the interdependencies between sectors through input-output relationships. Thus, based on the above results, Foster concludes that "*the most important consequence arising from disaggregation is that interindustry relations can amplify movements of final demand to such an extent as to destabilize an otherwise stable cycle*" (Foster 1963, p. 418, emphasis added).[66]

As an embodiment of the theoretical vision described in *Anti-Equilibrium*, Kornai and Martos edited *Non-Price Control*, a collection of models describing "control mechanisms, which rely exclusively on a system of non-price signals and

---

[64]Let $\lambda_i = \mu e^{i\theta}$ and assume $0 < \theta < 2\pi$, $|\eta| \leq 1$, then $\overline{\xi}(\lambda_i, \eta) < 1$ holds if and only if

$$\frac{(1-\eta\mu)^2\,(1-\mu)\,(1+\mu\,(2\eta+1))}{2\eta(1+\eta)^2\mu^3} + \cos\theta < 1.$$

The value of μ equalizing both sides of this inequality in $0 < \mu < 1$ decreases from 1 to $1/(2\eta + 1)$ as θ increases from 0 to π. Concerning the proof of this proposition, see Appendix 5 in Chap. 4.

[65]Especially, for negative λ_i, $|\xi| < 1$ is equivalent to $|\lambda_i| < 1/\left(2b\,(2\eta+1)+1\right)$.

[66]In his attempt to treat final consumption demands as endogenous variables, Foster assumed that these demands are derived from the productions in the same period (Foster 1963, p. 405). Similar to Lovell, by this assumption, Foster introduced a loop of the sequence of events in his model. Foster thought that a simultaneous determination of two sets of variables can be attained, "presumably a re-contracting process," in which "every industry keeps modifying its orders for inputs, and in turn receives changed order for outputs, until mutual consistency is achieved" (Foster 1963, p. 417). However, the obligation to participate in such an organized adjustment significantly impairs the merit of the quantity adjustment process in which every transaction can be carried out simply by the consent between the buyer and the seller.

which are, at the same time, decentralized" (Kornai and Martos 1981, p. 41)[67]. A common idea of these models is "decentralized economic control by means of norms" (Kornai and Martos 1981, p. 26), which was first formulated in Kornai and Martos (1973). They assumed continuous time in which firms decide to increase rates per time of productions and raw material orders. Let $\dot{x}_i(t) = dx_i(t)/dt$, among others, then the model of Kornai and Martos consisted of the following equations:

$$\dot{x}_i(t) = \dot{s}_i(t) - \alpha_i \dot{z}_i(t) + \beta_i\left(\overline{z}_i - z_i(t)\right) \tag{3.43}$$

$$\dot{m}_{ij}(t) = \dot{x}_i(t)a_{ij} - \gamma_{ij}\dot{v}_{ij}(t) + \delta_{ij}\left(\overline{v}_{ij} - v_{ij}(t)\right) \tag{3.44}$$

$$\dot{z}_i(t) = x_i(t) - s_i(t), \quad \dot{v}_{ij}(t) = m_{ij}(t) - x_i(t)a_{ij} \tag{3.45}$$

$$s_i(t) = \sum_{j=1}^{n} m_{ji}(t) + d_i, \tag{3.46}$$

where $\alpha_i > 0$ and $\beta_i > 0$ are sector i's coefficients of reaction to a change in and a shortage from the norm of the product inventory, respectively; $\gamma_i > 0$ and $\delta_{ij} > 0$ are sector i's coefficients of reaction to a change in and a shortage from the norm of raw material inventory of good i, respectively; $\overline{z}_i$ is the norm of a product inventory of good i; $\overline{v}_{ij}$ is the norm of raw material inventory of good j held by sector i ($i, j \in \{1, \ldots, n\}$). This system can be decomposed to the following $n(1 + n)$ second-order difference equations:

$$\ddot{z}_i(t) + \alpha_i \dot{z}_i(t) - \beta_i\left(\overline{z}_i - z_i(t)\right) = 0,$$

$$\ddot{v}_{ij}(t) + \gamma_{ij}\dot{v}_{ij}(t) - \delta_{ij}\left(\overline{v}_{ij} - v_{ij}(t)\right) = 0.$$

Therefore, $z_i(t)$ and $v_{ij}(t)$ converge to $\overline{z}_i$ and $\overline{v}_{ij}$, respectively, both $x(t)$ and $s(t)$ converge to $x^* = s^* = d(I - A)^{-1}$, and $m_{ij}(t)$ converges to $m_{ij}^* = x_i^* a_{ij}$. This remarkable simplicity is not preserved if, for example, $\dot{s}_i(t)$ is eliminated from the right-hand side of (3.43)[68]. It should be noted that, in Kornai-Martos' model, the control reacting to a change in the state variable plays a more important role than the "control by norms."

Kornai and Martos admitted that "operating properties of dynamic systems are qualitatively modified by the introduction of time lags into the system" (Kornai and Martos 1981, p. 41–42). However, modifying Kornai-Martos' continuous time model into a discrete time model is not an easy task. A mechanical replacement of

[67]"The models in this volume illustrate ... at *micro level*, 'quantitative adaptation' in an economic system with n participants, with decentralized decision and information" (Kornai and Martos 1981, p. 44).

[68]On this point, see Martos (1990, p. 105) and Morioka (2005, p. 200–201).

$\dot{x}_i(t)$ with $x(t) - x(t-1)$ or $x(t+1) - x(t)$ causes inconsistency in the time sequence of events[69]. Generally speaking, dynamic models assuming continuous time tend to obscure the time sequence of events.

Shiozawa (1983) constructed a multi-sector dynamic model of quantity adjustment with a consistent time sequence of events. Like Lovell and Foster, he sought to explore the multiplier effect "through the process in which it exhibits" and "in interactions between multiple firms" (Shiozawa 1983, p. 48). His model consisted of (3.28) to (3.30) and

$$x_i(t+1) = (2 + k_i)\, s_i^e(t) - z_i(t-1) - x_i(t). \tag{3.47}$$

Since (3.35) is reduced to (3.47) when $r_i = 1$, Shiozawa's model is a special case of the second modification of Lovell's model. Thus, the equation summarizing this system is obtained by substituting $R = I$ into (3.36), that is,

$$x(t) = x(t-1)\, A\, (3I + K) - x(t-2)\, A\, (2I + K) + d. \tag{3.48}$$

Since the stability of this system requires that the Frobenius root of A is less than $1/(2+k)$, Shiozawa (at that time) presumed that the process following (3.48) was likely to be unstable.

In models from Lundberg to Shiozawa, the number of past demands used by firms for the formation of demand forecast is two at the most. While firms may use a larger number of past demands, an increase in the number of past demands used for forecast heightens the order of the corresponding difference equation. Taniguchi (1991) investigated the stability of the process in which each firm forms its demand forecast by the simple moving average of its demands in past τ_i periods:

$$s_i^e(t) = \tau_i^{-1}\left(s_i(t-1) + \cdots + s_i(t-\tau_i)\right). \tag{3.49}$$

Under simplifying assumptions $\tau_i = \tau$ and $k_i = k$ for all i, the difference equation summarizing (3.29), (3.30), (3.47), and (3.49) is

$$x(t) = \left(\frac{2+k}{\tau} + 1\right) x(t-1)\, A - \frac{2+k}{\tau} x(t-\tau-1)\, A + d. \tag{3.50}$$

The stability of this system depends on the eigenvalues of an $n(\tau+1) \times n(\tau+1)$ matrix. Specifying matrix A and buffer coefficient k, Taniguchi numerically computed the spectrum radius of this matrix for various values of τ and discovered that it "rapidly diminishes until τ increases to around 7 and after that remains to be almost constant" (Taniguchi 1991, p. 39). More concretely, for a particular A whose largest eigenvalue is 0.535 and $k = 1$, system (3.50) is unstable for $\tau < 5$ and stable for $\tau \geq 6$. In this case, system (3.50) gets stability by increasing averaging

[69] The model by Dancs et al. (1981) contained this kind of inconsistency.

period τ to a value larger than five. Therefore, the averaging of past sales in demand forecast exhibits a strong stabilizing effect. The discovery of the stabilizing effect of averaging by Taniguchi was a further important progress in the investigation of the quantity adjustment process.[70] It indicated that an instability in the quantity adjustment process under the static expectation arises mainly from the very method of expectation and that this instability can be eliminated by averaging an adequate number of past demands.

Morioka (1991–1992, 1988) examined how the stability of the quantity adjustment process depends on the way and the extent of averaging in demand forecast and demonstrated several theorems on stability corresponding to the forecast by the simple moving average and geometric moving average. They also expounded that the effect of averaging in demand forecast is influenced by the input structure in a complex manner. Simonovits (1999) reconsidered the Metzler-Lovell-type control from the viewpoint of a more general control theory.[71] The model presented by Simonovits has common dynamic properties with system (3.34) or (3.36). Simonovits contrived an ingenious method to find the stability conditions without assuming the uniformity of parameters among sectors. While Simonovits supposes a partial adjustment, his method can be applied for averaging in demand forecast. Morioka (2005) attempted to integrate and further develop these preceding contributions in a coherent theoretical framework. Its result will be shown in the next chapter with refinement and generalization.

3.5 Conclusions

The capitalist system is considered a demand-constrained economy in which firms are placed under ceaseless sales competition. As long as firms can flexibly adjust their production volumes, sales competition would urge firms to avoid frequent occurrences of stockout. For this purpose, they set their stockout occurrence ratios at a certain low level. In setting the desirable stockout occurrence ratio, the firms consider, besides the costs of production and storage, the loss which a stockout might bring by disappointing buyers. Stockout avoidance behaviors can be regarded as a form of subjective profit maximization that is adapted to the environment of sales competition within the bounds of available intellectual resources. It takes a form of certain simple programs (routines) and, in that respect, constitutes the autonomous functions of the capitalist economy.

[70]This result was implicitly anticipated by Metzler (1941). This is because, for $\eta = -0.5$, (3.22) represents $S^e(t) = \frac{1}{2}(S(t-1) + S(t-2))$, namely, a forecast by the simple moving average of sales in the past two periods. Let $k = 0.4$, then the upper bound of c for stability corresponding to $\eta = -0.5$ is 0.771, while this bound corresponding to $\eta = 0$ (namely, to the static expectation) is 0.714. However, Metzler did not explicitly point out this stabilizing effect of averaging.

[71]Simonovits was one of Kornai's collaborators in *Non-Price Control*.

Individual stockout avoidance behaviors generate the quantity adjustment process that proceeds with the flow of time. As long as this process is stable, quantity adjustment can gradually lead the economy to the state characterized by the balance of production and demand and the constant existence of product and raw material inventories. Loose stationarity of the entire economy kept by quantity adjustment is an essential precondition for its higher functions. In fact, it would ensure that firms follow simple rules in their short-term decisions and thereby concentrate on the mid- or long-term activities requiring deliberation. In the quantity adjustment process, inventories function as a buffer decoupling production and demand or purchase and consumption, on the one hand, and, as basic information for short-term decisions of production and ordering, on the other.

Although the relationship between quantity adjustment and *General Theory* is not straightforward, a rigorous analysis of the quantity adjustment process has been developed through attempts to construct dynamic and multi-sector models of Kahn-Keynes' multiplier theory. These preceding studies clarified that the stability of the process depends on the method of demand forecast and the technological interdependence between sectors.

Appendix

1. Proof of Theorem 1

First, we consider the case of the finite planning period. Let

$$\Pi_n \equiv \sum_{t=1}^{n} \alpha^{t-1} \left(ps(t) - cx(t) - hz(t) - l\left(d(t) - s(t)\right)\right),$$

and $z(0) = z$, $y = x(1) + z$, $q = p + l$. Then, from (3.1) to (3.3), we have

$$\Pi_1 = \begin{cases} (p+h)d(1) - c\,(y-z) - hy & d(1) \le y \\ qy - c\,(y-z) - ld(1) & d(1) > y \end{cases}$$

Let $E_{n,\,z}(y)$ be the expected values of Π_n and $R_n(y) \equiv E'_{n,z}(y) + c \;\; (y \ge z)$, then

$$E_{1,z}(y) = P(y) - c\,(y-z),$$

$$P(y) \equiv \int_0^y \left((p+h)\xi - hy\right) f(\xi)\,\mathrm{d}\xi + \int_y^\infty (qy - l\xi)\, f(\xi)\,\mathrm{d}\xi,$$

$$R_1(y) = P'(y) = q - (q+h)\,F(y).$$

Let $\eta^* \equiv F^{-1}\left(\frac{q-c}{q+h-\alpha c}\right)$, $R(y) \equiv P'(y) + \alpha c F(y)$, then we obtain

$$R\left(\eta^*\right) = P'\left(\eta^*\right) + \alpha c F\left(\eta^*\right) = q - (q + h - \alpha c)\, F\left(\eta^*\right) = c,$$

$$R_1(0) - c = q - c > 0, \quad R_1\left(\eta^*\right) - c = -\alpha c F\left(\eta^*\right) < 0.$$

Therefore, there exists a unique η_1^* such that $0 < \eta_1^* < \eta^*$, $R_1\left(\eta_1^*\right) = c$.

Let $\eta_n(z)$ be the optimal y and $g_n(z) \equiv E_{n,\,z}(\eta_n(z))$ be the corresponding expected profit when the number of planning period is n. From the above results, we have

$$\eta_1(z) = \eta_1^*, \quad g_1(z) = -c\left(\eta_1^* - z\right) + P\left(\eta_1^*\right), \quad g_1'(z) = c, \quad g_1''(z) = 0.$$

for $z \leq \eta_1^*$, and

$$\eta_1(z) = z, \quad g_1(z) = P(z), \quad g_1'(z) = P'(z) < c, \quad g_1''(z) = P''(z) < 0.$$

for $\eta_1^* < z$.

Next, we shall prove that the same results hold for any n and η_n^* increases with n, by mathematical induction. Assume that, for a certain n, there exists a unique η_n^* such that

$$R_n\left(\eta_n^*\right) = c, \quad \eta_{n-1}^* < \eta_n^* < \eta^*\left(\eta_0^* = 0\right),$$

$$\eta_n(z) = \begin{cases} \eta_n^* & z \leq \eta_n^* \\ z & \eta_n^* < z \end{cases}, \quad g_n'(z) \begin{cases} = c & z \leq \eta_n^* \\ < c & \eta_n^* < z \end{cases}, \quad g_n''(z) \leq 0.$$

Since the maximal expected future profit obtained from periods 2 onwards is equal to the expected value of $\alpha g_n(z)$, we have

$$E_{n+1,z}(y) = P(y) - c\,(y - z) + \alpha Q_n(y),$$

$$Q_n(y) \equiv \int_0^y g_n\,(y - \xi)\, f\,(\xi)\, \mathrm{d}\xi + g_n(0)\,(1 - F(y)) \quad (Q_0 = 0)\,,$$

$$Q_n'(y) = \int_0^y g_n'\,(y - \xi)\, f\,(\xi)\, \mathrm{d}\xi$$

By definition, $R_{n+1}(y) = P'(y) + \alpha Q_n'(y)$. If $y \leq \eta_n^*$, then the assumption $g_n'\,(y - \xi) = c$ for $0 < \xi < y$ leads to $Q_n'(y) = cF(y)$ and

$$R_{n+1}(y) = P'(y) + \alpha c F(y) = R(y).$$

Since $R'(y) = -(q + h - \alpha c) f(y) < 0$ and $\eta_n^* < \eta^*$, we obtain

$$R_{n+1}\left(\eta_n^*\right) = R\left(\eta_n^*\right) > R\left(\eta^*\right) = c.$$

If $y \geq \eta_n^*$, then again by the assumption, we have

$$Q_n'(y) = \int_0^{y-\eta_n^*} g_n'(y-\xi) f(\xi)\,\mathrm{d}\xi + c\int_{y-\eta_n^*}^{y} g(\xi)\,\mathrm{d}\xi < cF(y).$$

This implies $R_{n+1}(y) < R(y)$, therefore

$$R_{n+1}\left(\eta^*\right) < R\left(\eta^*\right) = c.$$

From $g_n'(0) = c$ and $g_n''(z) \leq 0$, it follows

$$Q_n''(y) = cf(y) + \int_0^y g_n''(y-\xi)\,\varphi(\xi)\,\mathrm{d}\xi \leq cf(y),$$

and consequently, $R_{n+1}'(y) \leq -(q+h-\alpha c)\,f(y) < 0$. Therefore, there exists a unique η_{n+1}^* such that

$$\eta_n^* < \eta_{n+1}^* < \eta^*, \quad R_{n+1}\left(\eta_{n+1}^*\right) = c$$

It can easily be confirmed that η_{n+1}^* satisfies

$$\eta_{n+1}(z) = \begin{cases} \eta_{n+1}^* & z \leq \eta_{n+1}^* \\ z & \eta_{n+1}^* < z \end{cases}, \quad g_{n+1}'(z) \begin{cases} = c & z \leq \eta_{n+1}^* \\ < c & \eta_{n+1}^* < z \end{cases}, \quad g_{n+1}''(z) \leq 0.$$

Finally, let us move to the case of the infinite planning period. Since η_n^* is smaller than η^* and strictly increases with n, it converges to a certain limit value y^* as n infinitely increases. y^* is the optimal supply in the case of a positive production. Since $E_{\infty,z}(y) = E_{1,z}(y) + \alpha Q_\infty(y)$, we have

$$E_{\infty,z}'(y) = R_1(y) - c + \alpha\int_0^y g_\infty'(y-\xi) f(\xi)\,\mathrm{d}\xi = R(y) - c$$

for $z < y \leq \eta^*$. Therefore, $E_{\infty,z}'(\eta^*) = R(\eta^*) - c = 0$, hence $\eta^* = y^*$, this implies that y^* satisfies (3.5).

2. Proof of Theorem 2

It is sufficient to describe the points differing from the proof of Theorem 1. Let $\eta_n(z)$ be the optimal supply when the number of planning periods is n. Since

$$E_{1,z}(y) = P(y) - C(y-z),$$

there exist unique $\overline{y}_1$ such that $P'(\overline{y}_1) = C'(0) \equiv c$. When $z < \overline{y}_1$, $\eta_1(z)$ is a function satisfying $P'(\eta_1(z)) = C'(\eta_1(z) - z)$. In this interval, $\eta_1(z)$ also satisfies $z < \eta_1(z) < \overline{y}_1$, $0 < \eta_1'(z) < 1$ because

$$P'(0) = q > c, \quad \eta_1'(z) = \frac{C''(y-z)}{C''(y-z) - P''(y)}.$$

Since $g_1(z) = -C(\eta_1(z) - z) + P(\eta_1(z))$, we have

$$g_1'(z) = C'(\eta_1(z) - z) < q, \quad g_1''(z) < 0.$$

When $z > \overline{y}_1$, then the firm halts production, that is, $\eta_1(z) = z$; hence $g_1(z) = P(z)$, and consequently,

$$g_1'(z) = P'(z) = R_1(z) < c < q, \quad g_1''(z) < 0.$$

Assume that, for a certain n, the following propositions hold: (i) there exists a unique $\overline{y}_n$ such that $R_n(\overline{y}_n) = c$. (ii) $\eta_n(z)$ satisfies

$$R_n(\eta_n(z)) = C'(\eta_n(z) - z), \quad z < \eta_n(z) < \overline{y}_n, \quad 0 < \eta_n'(z) < 1$$

for $z < \overline{y}_n$, and $\eta_n(z) = z$ for $z \geq \overline{y}_n$. (iii) $g_n'(z) < q, \quad g_n''(z) < 0$. (iv) $\overline{y}_{n-1} < \overline{y}_n$, $\eta_{n-1}(z) < \eta_n(z)$ for $z < \overline{y}_n$. (v) $g_{n-1}(z) < g_n(z)$ for $z < \overline{y}_n$ ($\overline{y}_0 = 0, g_0 = 0$).

Because of (iii), it follows $Q_n''(y) < qf(y)$, hence we have

$$R_{n+1}'(y) = -(q(1-\alpha) + h) F(y) < 0$$

Using this, (i) to (iv) are easily confirmed for $n+1$. When $y \leq \overline{y}_n$, then (v) leads to $Q_n'(y) < Q_{n+1}'(y)$, and therefore,

$$c = R_n(\overline{y}_n) < R_{n+1}(\overline{y}_n),$$

$$C'(\eta_n(z) - z) = R_n(\eta_n(z)) < R_{n+1}(\eta_n(z)) \quad \text{for } z \leq \overline{y}_n.$$

These imply $\overline{y}_n < \overline{y}_{n+1}$ and $\eta_n(z) < \eta_{n+1}(z)$ for $z \leq \overline{y}_n$, respectively.

Using the latter inequality, and considering $g_{n+1}'(z) = C'(\eta_{n+1}(z) - z)$ for $z < \eta_{n+1}(z)$, we have

$$g_{n+1}'(z) \begin{cases} > C'(\eta_n(z) - z) = g_n'(z) & z < \eta_n(z) \\ > c \geq R_n'(z) = g_n'(z) & \eta_n(z) \leq z < \eta_{n+1}(z) \end{cases}.$$

Since $R_n'(y) < P'(y) + \alpha F(y)$, it follows $\overline{y}_n < F^{-1}\left(\frac{q-c}{q+h-\alpha q}\right)$ for any n; hence $\overline{y}_n$ and $\eta_n(z)$ converge to $\overline{y}$ and $\eta(z)$ satisfying

$$q - (q+h) F(\overline{y}) + \alpha \int_0^{\overline{y}} C'\big(\zeta(\overline{y} - \xi)\big) f(\xi)\, \mathrm{d}\xi = c,$$

$$q - (q+h) F\big(\eta(z)\big) + \alpha \int_0^{\eta(z)} C'\big(\zeta(\eta(z) - \xi)\big) f(\xi)\, \mathrm{d}\xi = C'(\zeta(z)),$$

respectively, where $\zeta(z) \equiv \eta(z) - z$. By observing that $C'(\zeta(\overline{y} - \xi)) > C'(0) = c$ for $\xi < \overline{y}$ and $C'(\zeta(\eta(0) - \xi)) < C'(\eta(0))$ for $\xi < \eta(0)$, we have

$$q - (q + h - \alpha c) F(\overline{y}) < c,$$

$$q - (q + h - \alpha C'(\eta(0)))F(\eta(0)) > C'(\eta(0)),$$

which implies $\eta(0) < y^* < \overline{y}$.

References

Abramowitz, M. A. (1950). *Inventory and business cycles, with special reference to manufacture's inventories*. New York: National Bureau of Economic Research.

Aoki, M. (1978). *Model analysis of the firm and the market* [In Japanese: Kigyo to shijo no mokei bunseki]. Tokyo: Iwanami Syoten.

Arrow, K. J. (1959). Toward a theory of price adjustment. In M. A. Abramowitz et al. (Eds.), *The allocation of economic resources* (pp. 41–51). Stanford: Stanford University Press.

Arrow, K. J., Harris, T., & Marschak, J. (1951). Optimal inventory policy. *Econometrica, 19*(3), 250–272.

Arrow, K. J., & Hurwicz, L. (1960). Decentralization and computation in resource allocation. In R. W. Pfouts (Ed.), *Essays in economics and econometrics* (pp. 34–104). Chapel Hill: The University of North Carolina Press.

Arrow, K. J., Karlin, S., & Scarf, H. (1958). *Studies in the mathematical theory of inventory and production*. Stanford: Stanford University Press.

Blinder, A. S. (1994). On sticky prices: Academic theories meet the real world. In N. G. Mankiw (Ed.), *Monetary policy* (pp. 117–150). Chicago: University of Chicago Press.

Brutzkus, B. D. (1935). *Economic planning in Soviet Russia*. London: George Routledge and Sons.

Campbell, R. W. (1963). *Accounting in soviet planning and management*. Cambridge, MA: Harvard University Press.

Chamberlin, E. H. (1933). *The theory of monopolistic competition*. Cambridge, MA: Harvard University Press.

Chikán, A., Kovács, E., Matyusz, E., Magdolna, S., Sass, M., & Vakhal, P. (2018). *Inventory in national economy: A cross-country analysis of mactro economic data*. London: Springer.

Chipman, J. S. (1950). The multi-sector multiplier. *Econometrica, 18*(4), 355–374.

Dancs, I., Hunyadi, L., & Sivak, J. (1981). Discrete-time control with time lags. In J. Kornai and B. Martos (Eds.), *Non-Price Control* (pp. 131–147). Amsterdam: North-Holland.

Foster, E. (1963). Sales forecasts and the inventory cycle. *Econometrica, 31*(3), 400–421.

Goodwin, R. (1949). The multiplier of matrix form. *Economic Journal, 59*, 537–555.

Goodwin, R. (1950). Does the matrix multiplier oscillate? *The Economic Journal, 60*, 764–770.

Hawkins, D., & Simon, H. (1949). Note: Some conditions of macro economic stability. *Econometrica, 17*(3–4), 245–248.

Hawtrey, R. G. (1950[1919]). *Currency and credit*. London: Longman.

Hayek, F. A. (Ed.). (1935). *Collectivist economic planning*. London: George Routledge and Sons.

Hicks, J. R. (1956). Methods of dynamic analysis. In *25 economic essays in honour of Erik Lindahl* (pp. 139–151). Stockholm: Ekonomisk Tidskrift.

Hodgson, J. M. (1988). *Economics and institutions*. London: Polity Press.

Hotelling, H. (1929). Stability of competition. *Economic Journal, 39*, 41–57.

Hunyadi, C. (1988). Inventory regulation in Hungary. In A. Chikán & M. C. Lovell (Eds.), *The economics of inventory management* (pp. 183–193). New York: Elsevier.

Kahn, R. (1931). The relation of home investment to unemployment. *The Economic Journal, 41*, 173–198.

Kalecki, M. (1971). *Selected essays on the dynamics of the capitalist economy*. Cambridge: Cambridge University Press.
Keynes, J. M. (1933). *The means to prosperity*. London: Macmillan.
Keynes, J. M. (1936). *The general theory of employment, interest and money*. London: Macmillan.
Keynes, J. M. (1939). Relative movements of real wages and output. *Economic Journal, 49*, 34–51.
Keynes, J. M. (1940). *How to pay for the war*. London: Macmillan.
Kitchin, J. (1923). Cycles and trends in economic factors. *Review of Economic Statistics, 5*(1), 10–16.
Kornai, J. (1971). *Anti-equilibrium: On economic systems theory and the tasks of research*. Amsterdam: North-Holland.
Kornai, J. (1980). *Economics of shortage*. Amsterdam: North-Holland.
Kornai, J. (1992). *The socialist system: The political economy of communism*. Princeton: Princeton University Press.
Kornai, J. (2014). *Dynamism, rivalry, and the surplus economy*. Oxford: Oxford University Press.
Kornai, J., & Lipták, T. (1965). Two level planning. *Econometrica, 33*(1), 141–169.
Kornai, J., & Martos, B. (1973). Autonomous functioning of the economic system. *Econometrica, 41*(3), 509–528.
Kornai, J., & Martos, B. (Eds.). (1981). *Non-price control*. Amsterdam: North-Holland.
Lavoie. (1985). *Rivalry and central planning. Socialist calculation debate reconsidered*. Cambridge: Cambridge University Press.
Leontief, W. (1953[1941]). *Studies in the structure of American economy*. New York: Oxford University Press.
Leroy-Beaulieu, P. (1908[1884]). *Collectivism: A study of some of the leading social questions of the day*. London.
Lovell, M. C. (1962). Buffer stocks, sales expectations and stability: A multi-sector analysis of the inventory cycle. *Econometrica, 30*(2), 267–296.
Lundberg, E. (1964[1936]). *Studies in the theory of economic expansion*. New York: Kelly and Millman.
Marshall, A. (1920[1890]). *Principles of economics*. London: Macmillan.
Martos, B. (1990). *Economic control structures: A non-Walrasian approach*. Amsterdam: North-Holland.
Marx, K. (1990). *Capital* (Vol. 1). London: Penguin Books.
Marx, K. (1992). *Capital* (Vol. 2). London: Penguin Books.
Metzler, L. A. (1941). The nature and stability of inventory cycle. *The Review of Economic Statistics, 23*(3), 113–129.
Metzler, L. A. (1947). Factors governing the length of inventory cycles. *The Review of Economic Statistics, 47*(1), 1–15.
Mills, E. S. (1954). Expectations, uncertainty and inventory fluctuations. *The Review of Economic Studies, 22*(1), 15–22.
Mizuho Sogo Kenkyusyo. (2011). *Research and analysis on the price revisions by firms* (In Japanese: Kigyo no Kakaku Kaitei Kodo nikansuru Chosabunseki).
Morioka, M. (1991–1992). Two types of the short-term adjustment processes (in Japanese: Tanki choseikatei no niruikei). *Keizai Ronso (Kyoto University), 148*(4–6), 140–161, *149*(1–3), 79–86.
Morioka, M. (1998). Input-output structure, Buffer inventory and sales forecast (in Japanese: Tounyu sansyutsu kozo, kansho zaiko, hanbai yosoku). *Keizai Ronso* (Kyoto University), *161*(1), 108–132.
Morioka, M. (2005). *The economic theory of quantity adjustment: Dynamic analysis of stockout avoidance behavior* (In Japanese: Suryo chosei no keizai riron). Tokyo: Nihon Keizai Hyoronsya.
Morioka, M. (2018). From the optimal planning theory to the theory of the firm and the market: A quest in Masahiko Aoki's early works. *Evolutionary and Institutional Economic Review, 15*(2), 267–288.

Morishima, M. (1977). *Walras' economics: A pure theory of capital and money*. Cambridge: Cambridge University Press.
Nikaido, H. (1961). *Linear mathematics for economics* (In Japanese: Keizai no tameno Senkei Sugaku). Tokyo: Baihukan.
Nove, A. (1980). *The soviet economic system*. London: Allen and Unwin.
Robinson, J. (1933). *The economics of imperfect competition*. London: Macmillan.
Say, J. B. (1964). *A treatise on political economy*. New York: Kelley.
Scarf, H. E. (1959). The optimality of (*S,s*) policies in the dynamic inventory problem. In K. J. Arrow, S. Karlin, & P. Supples (Eds.), *Mathematical methods in the social sciences* (pp. 196–202). New York: Stanford University Press.
Scarf, H. E. (1963). A survey of analytic techniques in inventory theory. In H. E. Scarf, D. M. Gilford, & M. W. Shelley (Eds.), *Multi-stage inventory models and techniques* (pp. 185–225). Stanford: Stanford University Press.
Shiozawa, Y. (1983). The micro structure of a Kahn-Keynes process (In Japanese: Kahn-Keynes Katei no Bisai Kozo). *Keizaigaku Zasshi, 84*(3), 48–64.
Simon, H. A. (1958). The role of expectations in an adaptive or behavioristic model. In M. J. Brown (Ed.), *Expectations, uncertainty and business behavior* (pp. 49–68). New York: Social Science Research Council.
Simon, H. A. (1959). Theories of decision making in economics and behavioral science. *American Economic Review, 49*(3), 253–283.
Simon, H. A. (1978). Rationality as process and as product of thought. *American Economic Review, 68*(2), 1–16.
Simon, H. A. (1991). Organizations and markets. *Journal of Economic Perspectives, 5*(2), 25–44.
Simonovits, A. (1999). Linear decentralized control with expectations. *Economic Systems Research, 11*(3), 321–329.
Sraffa, P. (1926). The laws of returns under competitive conditions. *Economic Journal, 36*, 535–550.
Stiglitz, J. E. (1994). *Wither socialism?* Cambridge, MA: The MIT Press.
Taniguchi, K. (1991). On the traverse of quantity adjustment economies (In Japanese: Suryo Chosei Keizai ni okeru Iko Katei nit suite). *Keizaigaku Zashi, 91*(5), 29–43.
von Mises, L. (1935[1920]). Economic calculation in the socialist common wealth. In: Hayek (1935) pp. 87–130
Walras, L. (1954). *Elements of pure economics*. London: Allen and Unwin.

Chapter 4
Dynamic Properties of Quantity Adjustment Process Under Demand Forecast Formed by Moving Average of Past Demands

Abstract In this chapter, we shall analyze a family of multi-sector dynamic models of the quantity adjustment process in which firms determine their productions and raw material orders based on inventories and demand forecasts under constant prices and final demands. Special attention is paid to the role of demand forecast by a moving average of past demands. Section 4.1 describes the assumptions common to all the models and explains how and in what sequence firms determine productions and raw material orders. For the demand forecast method, we assume the simple moving average and the geometric moving average. Sections 4.2 and 4.3 investigate the dynamic properties of the process generated through the interactions between sectors under the above two demand forecast methods. A series of theorems will elucidate how the stability of the process depends on the input structure, the extent of averaging, and the buffer inventory coefficients. It will be shown that averaging of past demands in the demand forecast formation is essential for stability if the input matrix has negative or complex eigenvalues reflecting the interactions between sectors. Section 4.4 closely examines the mechanism of stabilization by averaging of past demands in forecast formation. Stability conditions corresponding to the forecast by the finite geometric moving average will indicate that stability depends on the allocation of weights to each past demand in addition to the number of past periods referred for averaging.

Keywords Sequence · Input structure · Product inventory · Raw material inventory · Demand forecast · Averaging · Simple moving average · Geometric moving average · Dynamic stability

4.1 Sequence of Decisions and Actions

4.1.1 Common Setting of the Model

The assumptions common to models in this chapter are as follows. The economy consists of n sectors and each sector has multiple firms producing a single

Y. Shiozawa et al., *Microfoundations of Evolutionary Economics*,
Evolutionary Economics and Social Complexity Science 15,
https://doi.org/10.1007/978-4-431-55267-3_4

homogenous product by a Leontief-type technique. The product produced in sector i is called product i. Firms belonging to the same sector have the same parameters set in their activities. This assumption allows us to *aggregate firm-level variables by sectors* and thereby develops a *sector-level analysis*. Hereafter, "firm i" represents a collective body of firms belonging to sector i. Later (in the next chapter), we will indicate that, under certain conditions, our sector-level analysis can be extended to the case in which firms belonging to the same sector are not homogenous.

Let A be an ordinary $n \times n$ input coefficient matrix. Its (i,j) element a_{ij} represents the input of the product j required per unit output of product i. Matrix A satisfies the condition for reproducibility (viability) of the economy, that is, for any semi-positive $1 \times n$ vector ξ, there exists a semi-positive $1 \times n$ vector η such that $\eta = \eta A + \xi$. Let $\lambda^{\mathrm{F}}(A)$ be A's Frobenius root, that is, the largest real eigenvalue of a nonnegative square matrix. By the Frobenius theorem, $\lambda^{\mathrm{F}}(A)$ is equal to A's spectrum radius, that is, the largest eigenvalue measured by absolute value.[1] Using this notation, the condition for reproducibility (viability) can be written as $\rho(A) = \lambda^{\mathrm{F}}(A) < 1$.

Firms make both short- and long-term decisions. Short-term decisions cover a weekly period, while long-term decisions refer to a quarterly scale. It should be noted that the week/quarter pair is merely an example. Alternatively, day/month or month/year scales can be chosen. What is important here is that there are two groups of decisions belonging to different time horizons. Short-term decisions include adjustment of production volumes and raw material orders. Long-term decisions comprise price setting, choice of technique, capital investment, and fund raising. The direct subject of our model analysis is the *short-term process*, that is, the process generated by each firm's weekly decisions about production and raw material orders. Therefore, in addition to production techniques and capital investment demand, prices of products are also given in our model. By keeping prices constant, firms respond to fluctuations of demand by changing production and raw material orders. However, *this does not imply that prices are completely irrelevant to quantity adjustment*. Quantity adjustment can work as a short-term balancing mechanism of the economy only when prices satisfy the following requirement: (i) Producers of each product can gain at least positive gross profit from the sales of product (otherwise, some of the producers might suspend production). (ii) The balance of production and demand is attained within the limit of the capacity and labor force (otherwise, expansion of production would be blocked by the shortage of equipment or labor force).

The demands for products consist of final demands (sum of the demand for capital investment and final consumption) and intermediate demands (demand for raw materials). We assume that the multiplier process is stratified into two levels

[1] Since A is a nonnegative square matrix, its spectrum radius is equal to its Frobenius root (Nikaido 1961). The reproducibility condition is also equivalent to $I - A$ satisfying the Hawkins-Simon's condition (Hawkins and Simon 1949).

belonging to different time horizons: one is a weekly process in which intermediate demands change under fixed final demands, and the other is a quarterly process in which the final demands themselves fluctuate. While a part of consumption demands may depend on income during the previous quarter, this dependence does not affect the weekly adjustment process (effects of the derivation of consumption demand will be considered in the next chapter). Thus, intermediate demands arising from raw material orders constitute the only variable part of demands in our model.

The cycles of production and raw material orders by individual firms are synchronized to the unit period (week). Common to all the sectors, production of the product and processing of the received orders take 1 week, respectively. Each firm (i) starts production at the beginning of week t *after* the arrival of raw materials ordered at the beginning of week $t-1$, (ii) completes production at the end of week t, and (iii) delivers the newly produced product to buyers on the first day of week $t+1$. In parallel with them, each firm also (iv) places orders for raw materials at the beginning of week t and (v) receives these raw materials at the beginning of week $t+1$.

Variables in our mode are listed below.

$s_i(t)$: sales volume of product i in week t, which is to be delivered to buyers at the beginning of week $t+1$

$s_i^e(t)$: forecasted demand for product i per week from week t onward

$x_i(t)$: production volume of product i that firm i starts at the beginning of week t and completes at the beginning of week $t+1$

$z_i(t)$: product inventory held by firm i at the *end* of week t

$m_i(t) = [m_{i1}(t), \ldots, m_{in}(t)]$: the vector of raw material orders that firm i places at the beginning of week t and delivers at the beginning of week $t+1$ (hence scalar $m_{ij}(t)$ denotes orders by firm i to firm j)

$v_i(t) = [v_{i1}(t-1), \ldots, v_{in}(t-1)]$: the vector of raw material inventories held by firm i at the *end* of week t (hence $v_{ij}(t)$ denotes raw material inventory of product j held by firm i)[2]

At the beginning of week t, the newly produced product $x_i(t-1)$ is added to the initial product inventory $z_i(t-1)$, and then, the shipment of sales $s_i(t-1)$ is subtracted from the supply $z_i(t-1) + x_i(t-1)$. Therefore, each firm's product inventory changes by:

$$z_i(t) = z_i(t-1) + x_i(t-1) - s_i(t-1). \tag{4.1}$$

Similarly, at the beginning of week t, the vector of newly arrived raw materials $m_i(t-1)$ is added to the vector of initial material inventories $v_i(t-1)$, and $x_i(t)a_i$ is consumed from $v_i(t-1) + m_i(t-1)$ to produce $x_i(t)$, where $a_i \equiv [a_{i1}, \ldots, a_{in}]$ is

[2]As described in Subsect. 3.4.6 of the previous chapter, the buffer function of raw material inventories was first modelized by Foster (1963).

the i-th column of the input matrix A. Therefore, each firm's vector of raw material inventory changes by:

$$v_i(t) = v_i(t-1) + m_i(t-1) - x_i(t)a_i. \tag{4.2}$$

Sales $s_i(t-1)$ cannot exceed supply $z_i(t-1) + x_i(t-1)$. Similarly, inputs $x_i(t)a_i$ cannot exceed available raw materials (their internal supplies) $v_i(t-1) + m_i(t-1)$. In other words, product inventory scalar $z_i(t)$ and raw material inventory vector $v_i(t)$ cannot be negative.

4.1.2 Decisions on Production and Raw Material Orders

Every week, firm i forms demand forecast $s_i^e(t)$ and determines the production volume $x_i(t)$ and raw material orders $m_i(t)$. The method of demand forecast will be discussed later. In this subsection, we explain how each firm decides the production volume and raw material orders based on its demand forecast. By (4.1), firm i can calculate in advance the weekend product inventory $z_i(t)$ at the beginning of week t. It determines production $x_i(t)$ so that $z_i(t) + x_i(t)$, which is supply available at the beginning of week $t+1$, is equal to the sum of forecasted demand in week t and the buffer part. Firm i's desirable level of buffer product inventory is k_i-times its demand forecast ($k_i > 0$). Thus, $x_i(t)$ is determined by

$$x_i(t) = (1 + k_i)\, s_i^e(t) - z_i(t) \tag{4.3}$$

as long as $z_i(t) \leq (1 + k_i)\, s_i^e(t)$. This rule is what we called "a typical example of programs to practice stockout avoidance" in Subsect. 3.2.2 of the previous chapter (rule (3.6)). We derived it from subjective profit maximization under the assumption that all the related costs are linear and the standard deviation of demand is proportional to its expected value. As already explained there, each firm's buffer coefficient of product inventory depends on the price, production cost, storage cost of inventory, penalty cost of stockout, and (subjective) probability distribution of demand.

Similarly, using (4.2) and (4.3), firm i can calculate in advance the weekend raw material inventories $v_i(t)$ at the beginning of week t. To determine the vector of raw material orders $m_i(t)$, firm i must consider the amount of raw materials necessary for production of $x_i(t+1)$, which is to be started at the beginning of week $t+1$. However, since $x_i(t+1)$ is not yet determined at the beginning of week t, firm i must instead rely on $x_i^e(t+1)$, the forecast of $x_i(t+1)$ at the beginning of week t corresponding to $s_i^e(t)$. Let $z_i^e(t+1)$ be the forecast of $z_i(t+1)$ at the beginning of week t corresponding to $s_i^e(t)$, and then from (4.1) and (4.3), we have

$$z_i^e(t+1) = z_i(t) + x_i(t) - s_i^e(t) = ks_i^e(t+1),$$

and accordingly,

$$x_i^e\,(t+1) = (1+k_i)\,s_i^e(t) - z_i\,(t+1) = s_i^e(t).$$

That is, the forecast of $x_i(t+1)$ at the beginning of week t is equal to the demand forecast $s_i^e(t)$. Based on this relation, firm i determines its raw material order $m_{ij}(t)$ so that internal supply $v_{ij}(t) + m_{ij}(t)$ at the beginning of week t is equal to the sum of necessary input and buffer raw material inventory. Firm i's desirable levels of buffer inventories of each raw material are l_i-times its necessary inputs. Therefore, the vector of raw material orders $m_i(t)$ is determined by

$$m_i(t) = (1+l_i)\,s_i^e(t)a_i - v_i(t). \tag{4.4}$$

Thus, in our model, firms follow the typical (Lundberg-Metzler type) rule for stockout avoidance for both production and raw material orders.[3] Let $m^i(t)$ be the sum of each firm's intermediate demand for product i, that is:

$$m^i(t) \equiv m_{1i}(t) + \cdots + m_{ni}(t),$$

and let d_i denote the final demand for product i per week. Then, the total demand for product i is equal to $m^i(t) + d_i$. Figure 4.1 illustrates the sequence of events described above. Dashed lines in this figure indicate the processes via transactions with other sectors.

It should be noted that order $m_i(t-1)$ in (4.2) represents the *actual delivery of materials* at the beginning of week t. It coincides with order $m_i(t-1)$ determined by (4.4) at the beginning of week $t-1$ only when the raw material orders made at the beginning of week $t-1$ are completely fulfilled. In other words, (4.2) holds only when the constraint

$$z_j\,(t-1) + x_j\,(t-1) \geq m^j(t) + d_j \tag{4.5}$$

is satisfied. This constraint implies that a stockout of product j does not occur. Furthermore, $x_i(t)$ in (4.2) represents the volume of *actually started production* at the beginning of week t. It coincides with $x_i(t)$ determined by (4.3) only when firm i has the required materials to produce it at the beginning of week t. For this, the constraint

$$m_i\,(t-1) + v_i\,(t-1) \geq x_i(t)a_i \tag{4.6}$$

[3]For simplicity, we assume here that the buffer inventory coefficients for various raw materials are uniform within the firm.

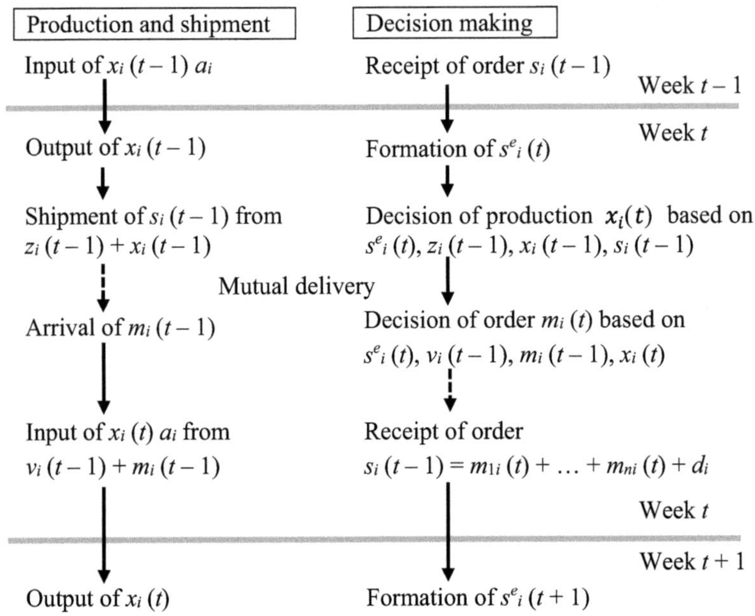

Fig. 4.1 Sequence of actions and decisions

must be satisfied. This constraint expresses that a stockout of raw materials does not occur. In this chapter, we assume that constraints (4.5) and (4.6) are always satisfied for any i, j. In the next chapter, we will explore the process in which a stockout actually occurs and firms are forced to respond to it by rationing among buyers or revising their production plans.

In matrix notation, (4.1) to (4.4) are, respectively, written as

$$z(t) = z(t-1) + x(t-1) - s(t-1), \tag{4.7}$$

$$v(t) = v(t-1) + m(t-1) - x(t)A, \tag{4.8}$$

$$x(t) = s^e(t)(I+K) - z(t), \tag{4.9}$$

$$m(t) = s^e(t)(I+L)A - v(t), \tag{4.10}$$

where $z(t)$ is the vectors of $z_i(t)$, $x(t)$ of $x_i(t)$, $s(t)$ of $s_i(t)$, and s^e of $s_i^e(t)$; K is the diagonal matrix of k_i, L of l_i; I is the $n \times n$ identity matrix; and

$$v(t) \equiv v_1(t) + \cdots + v_n(t), \; m(t) \equiv m_1(t) + \cdots + m_n(t).$$

$m(t) = [m^1(t), \ldots, m^n(t)]$ represents the vector of aggregate raw material orders for each product. As long as (4.5) holds, the sales of product i is equal to its demand, that is, the sum of intermediate and final demand:

$$s_i(t) = m^i(t) + d_i.$$

In matrix notation, it can be written as

$$s(t) = m(t) + d, \tag{4.11}$$

where d is the vector of d_i.

From (4.7) to (4.10), we have

$$x(t) = \Delta s^e(t)(I + K) + s(t-1), \tag{4.12}$$

$$m(t) = \Delta s^e(t)(I + L)A + x(t)A, \tag{4.13}$$

where $\Delta s^e(t) = s^e(t) - s^e(t-1)$. By substituting (4.12) and (4.13) into (4.12), we obtain the following summarized equation:

$$s(t) = \Delta s^e(t)(2I + K + L)A + s(t-1)A + d. \tag{4.14}$$

Hereafter, the sum of firm i's buffer coefficients for product inventory and raw material inventory, $k_i + l_i$, is simply referred to as its buffer coefficient.

If each firm's demand forecast is a constant, namely, if $s_i^e(t) = \overline{s}_i^e$, then (4.12) and (4.13) are simplified into $x(t) = s(t-1)$ and $m(t) = x(t)A$, respectively. These equations imply that each firm adjusts its production and raw material orders so that newly produced products and newly delivered raw materials *precisely replenish* the reduction in product and raw material inventories caused by shipment and productive consumption during the period, respectively. In this case, (4.14) is simplified into

$$s(t) = s(t-1)A + d. \tag{4.15}$$

Consequent to the assumption that the spectrum radius of A is less than unity, system (4.15) is globally asymptotically stable, that is, vector $s(t)$ converges to the stationary point $s^* = d(I - A)^{-1}$ for any initial value $s(0)$. Production $x(t)$ and aggregate raw material orders $m(t)$ also converge to $x^* = s^*$ and $m^* = s^*A$, respectively.[4] Accordingly, if the system consists of (4.14) and the equation on the

[4]The corresponding stationary values of product and raw material inventories are $z^* = \overline{s}_i^e(1 + k_i) - x_i^*$ and $v_i^* = \left((1 + l_i)\overline{s}_i^e - x_i^*\right)a_i$, respectively. Note that the convergence to these values requires that $\overline{s}_i^e \geq x_i^*(1 + k_i)^{-1}$ and $\overline{s}_i^e \geq x_i^*(1 + l_i)^{-1}$ are satisfied for any i. If one of these conditions do not hold, convergence is hindered by the depletion of inventories.

revision of demand forecast, *the source of instability must be found in the method by which individual firms form and revise their demand forecasts.*[5]

Since productions $x(t)$ are determined base on forecasts $s^e(t)$ and actual demands $s(t)$ are derived from $x(t)$ through raw material orders $m(t)$, firms can not know $s_i(t)$ before their decision on $x_i(t)$. Therefore, *perfect foresight of demand is impossible under the sequence of events in our model.* However, it is of some interest to examine the properties of a process in which $s(t) = s^e(t)$ holds every week. By inserting this into (4.15) and assuming that matrix $\Omega = I - (2I + K + L)A$ is regular, we have

$$s^e(t) = -s^e(t-1)(I + K + L)\Omega^{-1} + d\Omega^{-1}. \tag{4.16}$$

If $\lambda^{\mathrm{F}}(2I + K + L)A < 1$, then Ω^{-1} is a nonnegative matrix. In order to calculate $s_i^e(t)$ according to (4.16), firm i must know all of the parameters concerning behaviors of other firms. Therefore, the ex-post "perfect foresight" in the form of (4.16) requires sharing entire information about individual firms. Asymptotical stability of the stationary point of system (4.17) is equivalent to $\lambda^{\mathrm{F}}((I + K + L)\Omega) < 1$. Let $\kappa = \min_i(k_i + l_i)$, then by the assumption we have $\lambda^{\mathrm{F}}(A) < 1/(2 + \kappa)$ and

$$\lambda^{\mathrm{F}}\left((1+\kappa)A(I-(2+\kappa)A)^{-1}\right) = \frac{(1+\kappa)\lambda^{\mathrm{F}}(A)}{1-(2+\kappa)\lambda^{\mathrm{F}}(A)} \leq \lambda^{\mathrm{F}}(\Omega)$$

---

[5]The (S, s) policy, which was referred to in Subsect. 3.2.3 of the previous chapter, can be regarded as a way of adjustment based on a fixed forecast. When each firm follows this policy in its decision on the production, (4.3) is replaced by

$$x_i(t) = Q_i - z_i(t) \text{ if } z_i(t) < q_i \text{ and } x_i(t) = 0 \text{ if } z_i(t) \geq q_i,$$

where Q_i and q_i correspond to S and s, respectively. Let Q and q be the vectors of Q_i and q_i, and for simplicity, let us assume, in place of (4.4), that the raw material orders are simply determined by $m_i(t) = x_i(t)a_i$. Then, in matrix notation, it holds $s(t) = x(t)A + d$. In this case, *as long as* $z_i(t) < q_i$ *holds for any sector and in any period*, we have

$$x(t) = Q - z(t) = x(t-1)A + d.$$

Therefore, if $x(0) = d(I - A)^{-1}$ and $z(0) < q$, then the system is stable against a small perturbation of final demand d. It should be noted that Taniguchi's model in Chap. 6, Subsect. 6.3.3 of this book, is based on different assumptions about the time sequence of events. Under those assumptions, the production is determined by

$$x_i(t) = Q_i - z_i(t-1) \text{ if } z_i(t-1) < q_i \text{ and } x_i(t) = 0 \text{ if } z_i(t-1) \geq q_i,$$

and (4.1) is modified to $z_i(t) = z_i(t-1) + x_i(t-1) - s_i(t)$. Accordingly, we have

$$x(t+1) = x(t)(I + A) - x(t-1) + d.$$

As Taniguchi remarks, this system is unstable if the economy consists of more than three sectors. A cause of such instability lies in that firm i does not consider $x_i(t-1)$, which is already known at the beginning of period t, in its decision on $x_i(t)$.

Therefore, the asymptotic stability of system (4.16) requires[6]

$$\lambda^{\mathrm{F}}(A) < \frac{1}{3 + 2\min(k_i + l_i)}.$$

Considering that the values of $\lambda^{\mathrm{F}}(A)$ calculated from the actual input-output tables are around 0.5 to 0.55, system (4.16) is almost certainly unstable.[7] This implies that the quantity adjustment process is brought to divergence under the successive coincidence of the actual and forecasted demands. Thus, *errors in demand forecast cannot be deemed as the fundamental cause of instability.*

4.1.3 Demand Forecast by Moving Average of Past Demands

Forecast of weekly demand belongs to what Keynes calls "short-term expectation" in his *General Theory*. Keynes characterizes the essence of short-term expectation in that "the most recent results play a predominant role" (Keynes 1936, p. 51). Two factors justify focusing attention on the most recent results: first, the need to economize thinking and, second, such expectation usually leads to a satisfying performance unless external conditions do not change drastically.[8] Since short-term expectation is formed by a projection of the recent past, "revision of short-term expectation is a gradual and continuous one, carried largely in the light of realized results." Therefore, "expected and realized results run into and overlap one another in their influence" (Keynes 1936, p. 50).

Our usage of the term "forecast" is based on Brown (1959). According to Brown, forecast means "the projection of the past into the future." This definition of forecast coincides with the above definition of short-term expectation by Keynes. Brown distinguishes "forecast" from "prediction" which means "anticipation of changes of new factors affecting demand" (Brown 1959, p. 3). Forecast is formed by a certain simple mechanical rule using data of the recent past.[9] In contrast, making predictions is a complicated process in which all available information related to the subject is collected and examined. An important role of forecast is

[6]Lovell obtained a similar result (1962, p. 274–275).

[7]The Frobenius roots calculated from the input-output tables of the Japanese economy in 1995-2011 are 0.5242 (93 sectors, 1995), 0.5230 (104 sectors, 2001), and 0.5527 (190 sectors, 2005).

[8]"It would be too complicated to work out the expectation de novo whenever a productive process was being started; and it would, moreover, be a waste of time since *a large part of the circumstances usually continues substantially unchanged from one day to the next*" (Keynes 1936, p. 51, emphasis added).

[9]Simon (1959, p. 269) suggests that forecasts formed by the assumption that "the next period will be a weighted average of recent past periods" are sufficiently satisfactory from a practical perspective. He further adds, "The elaboration of the models [of expectations] beyond the first few steps of refinement does not much improve prediction."

to give entrepreneurs sufficient time to make predictions for long-term decisions. It should be noted that agents who make short-term decisions based on forecasts (short-term expectations) do not actually presume that the current situation will last permanently. However, if there are no plausible reasons to believe that the current situation will change drastically, it is rational (in a practical sense) for firms to assume a continuance of the recent past state in their short-term decisions.

Following Brown, we assume two practicable ways for such a forecast. One is the simple moving average, and the other is the exponential smoothing. *The simple moving average* is a forecast by

$$s_i^e(t) = \tau_i^{-1}\left(s_i(t-1) + \cdots + s_i(t-\tau_i)\right), \tag{4.17}$$

where τ_i is a positive integer. Hereafter τ_i is referred to as firm *i*'s *averaging period*. *The exponential smoothing* is a forecast by

$$s_i^e(t) = s_i(t-1) + \gamma_i\left(s_i^e(t-1) - s_i(t-1)\right), \tag{4.18}$$

where γ_i is a constant such that $0 < \gamma_i \leq 1$. Hereafter γ_i is referred to as firm *i*'s *smoothing constant*. By applying (4.18) repeatedly to $s_i^e(t-1), s_i^e(t-2), \ldots$, we have

$$s_i^e(t) = \sum_{u=1}^{\infty} \gamma_i(1-\gamma_i)^{u-1} s_i(t-u), \quad \sum_{u=1}^{\infty} \gamma_i(1-\gamma_i)^{u-1} = 1$$

Thus, the exponential smoothing is the moving average of an infinite number of past demands such that the weight for $s_i(t-u)$ are given by $\gamma_i(1-\gamma_i)^{u-1}$. In statistics, this is called *the geometric moving average* because the weights constitute a geometric sequence.[10] An obvious merit of the exponential smoothing is that it "does not require keeping a long historical record in the active file and thus cuts down on the data-processing time required" (Brown 1959, p. 46). Moreover, while averaging period τ_i can change only discretely, the smoothing constant γ_i can change continuously from 0 to 1. In the case $\tau_i = \gamma_i = 1$, the above two forecasting methods are reduced to the static expectation $s_i^e(t) = s_i(t-1)$. From the perspective of averaging, this forecasting method may be characterized as "zero-averaging."

[10] In economic literature, this forecasting method is usually called "adaptive expectation." Regarding detailed properties of the exponential smoothing or the geometric moving average, refer to Muth (1960) and Hines (2004).

4.2 The Case of Demand Forecast Formed by the Simple Moving Average

4.2.1 Dynamic Stability Conditions

In the following two sections, we shall analyze the dynamic properties of the quantity adjustment process modeled in the previous section. In matrix notation, (4.17) can be rewritten as

$$s^e(t) = s(t-1)\,U_1 + \cdots + s(t-\tau)\,U_\tau, \tag{4.19}$$

where $\tau \equiv \max_i \tau_i$ and

$$U_\upsilon \equiv \begin{bmatrix} u_{1\upsilon} & \cdots & 0 \\ \vdots & \ddots & \vdots \\ 0 & \cdots & u_{n\upsilon} \end{bmatrix} \ (\upsilon = 1, \ldots, \tau), \quad u_{i\upsilon} \equiv \begin{cases} 1/\tau_i & \upsilon \le \tau_i \\ 0 & \upsilon > \tau_i \end{cases}.$$

For example, if $n = 2$, $\tau_1 = 3$, and $\tau_2 = 4$, then

$$U_1 = U_2 = U_3 = \begin{bmatrix} \frac{1}{3} & 0 \\ 0 & \frac{1}{4} \end{bmatrix}, \quad U_4 = \begin{bmatrix} 0 & 0 \\ 0 & \frac{1}{4} \end{bmatrix}.$$

By substituting (4.19) into (4.14), we have a complete system of difference equations:

$$\begin{aligned} s(t) &= s(t-1)(U_1B + I)A + s(t-2)(U_2 - U_1)BA \\ &\quad + \cdots + s(t-\tau)(U_\tau - U_{\tau-1})BA + s(t-\tau-1)\,U_\tau A + d, \end{aligned}$$

where $B \equiv 2I + K + L$ is the diagonal matrix of $b_i \equiv 2 + k_i + l_i$. This system can be written as

$$[s(t), \ldots, s(t-\tau)] = [s(t-1), \ldots, s(t-\tau-1)]\,\Phi + [d, 0, \ldots, 0], \tag{4.20}$$

$$\Phi \equiv \begin{bmatrix} (U_1B + I)A & I & \mathrm{O} & \cdots & \mathrm{O} \\ (U_2 - U_1)BA & \mathrm{O} & I & \cdots & \mathrm{O} \\ \vdots & \vdots & \vdots & \ddots & \vdots \\ (U_\tau - U_{\tau-1})BA & \mathrm{O} & \mathrm{O} & \cdots & I \\ -U_\tau BA & \mathrm{O} & \mathrm{O} & \cdots & \mathrm{O} \end{bmatrix},$$

where Φ is an $n(\tau + 1) \times n(\tau + 1)$ matrix, 0 is the $1 \times n$ zero vector, and O is the $n \times n$ zero matrix. Therefore, (4.20) represents a difference system of order $n(\tau + 1)$. Let us call this system SMA (simple moving average) to focus on the method of demand forecast.

The stationary point of SMA is $s^* = d(I - A)^{-1}$. The corresponding stationary values of (the vectors of) the other variables are as follows:

$$x^* = s^{e*} = s^*, \quad z^* = x^* K = \left[k_1 x_1^*, \ldots, k_n x_n^*\right],$$

$$m_i^* = s_i^* a_i = \left[s_i^* a_{i1}, \ldots, s_i^* a_{in}\right], \quad v_i^* = l_i m_i^* = \left[l_i m_{i1}^*, \ldots, l_i m_{in}^*\right].$$

The stationary values of actual demand, production, and forecasted demand are identical and equal to the product of the final demand vector and the Leontief inverse matrix. At the stationary point, firm i's product inventory z_i^* is k_i-times its production x_i^*, and its raw material inventories v_i^* are l_i-times its raw material orders m_i^*.

Dynamic properties of SMA depend on the transitive matrix Φ. Let $\rho(P)$ denote the function giving the spectral radius of any square matrix P. Subsequently, $\rho(\Phi) < 1$ is necessary and sufficient for the asymptotic stability of SMA. Thus, examining the stability of this system requires an evaluation of all the eigenvalues of matrix Φ.

Theorem 1

(i) Let T be the diagonal matrix of T_i, then SMA is asymptotically stable if

$$\lambda^{\mathrm{F}}\left(\left(2T^{-1}B + I\right)A\right) < 1, \tag{4.21}$$

(ii) If A has an eigenvalue μ such that

$$\mu = \omega\lambda^{\mathrm{F}}(A), \quad \omega^{\tau_1} = \cdots = \omega^{\tau_n} = -1, \tag{4.22}$$

then SMA is asymptotically stable *if and only if* (4.21) is satisfied.

Proof: See Appendix 1.

Statement (ii) indicates that (4.21) becomes a necessary and sufficient condition for the stability under a particular set of τ_i and A that satisfies (4.22). This condition means that A has an eigenvalue $\lambda = |\lambda|\mathrm{e}^{\mathrm{i}\theta}$ such that each of $\theta\tau_i$ is odd times π (e denotes the basis of a natural logarithm, and i denotes the imaginary unit). Therefore, (4.21) cannot be loosened any more without supplementary assumptions on the structure of the input matrix.

$(2T^{-1}B + I)A$ is a nonnegative square matrix and its (i,j) element is $\left(2\tau_i{}^{-1}b_i + 1\right)a_{ij}$; hence, $\lambda^{\mathrm{F}}((2T^{-1}B + I)A)$ is an increasing function with respect to any of τ_i^{-1}, b_i, and a_{ij}. Especially, if A is indecomposable, that is, if all kinds of products are *directly or indirectly* necessary as inputs to produce any product, $\lambda^{\mathrm{F}}((2T^{-1}B + I)A)$ is a *strictly* increasing function with respect to these parameters (note that $(2T^{-1}B + I)A$ and A have an identical distribution of positive elements).[11] Hence, the smaller are τ_i^{-1}, b_i, and a_{ij}, the more likely that inequality (4.21) will be satisfied. Moreover, once (4.21) is satisfied, SMA does not lose stability by any change in parameters toward the above directions. Since averaging period τ_i affects stability *through its inverse number*, any increase in τ_i is presumed to have a considerably strong stabilizing effect when it is small. Later, we will see that this conjecture is basically correct, though not always.

Let $\tau_i = 2^{\alpha_i}\beta_i$ (β_i is an odd number) and $\alpha = \max \alpha_i$, then (4.22) is satisfied if and only if A is a cyclic matrix of cycle $2^{\alpha+1}$. Thus, if all the τ_i's are odd, then (4.22) is satisfied when A is a two-cyclic matrix. In this case, $-\lambda^{\mathrm{F}}(A)$ belongs to A's eigenvalues and directly affects stability. Similarly, if some τ_i are even numbers but indivisible by 4, then (4.22) is satisfied when A is a four-cyclic matrix. In this case, $\mathrm{i}\lambda^{\mathrm{F}}(A)$ and $-\mathrm{i}\lambda^{\mathrm{F}}(A)$ belong to A's eigenvalues and directly affect stability.

Cyclic matrices, or *imprimitive matrices*, are a specific type of nonnegative indecomposable square matrix.[12] In terms of an economic interpretation, the input matrix A is a cyclic matrix of cycle c when the set of sectors $N = \{1, \ldots, n\}$ can be divided into mutually disjoint subsets $N_1, \ldots, N_c$ such that sectors belonging to N_{i+1} use only products produced by sectors belonging to N_i ($i = 1, \ldots, c$; $N_{c+1} = N_1$). These groups of sectors constitute a loop of input relations: $N_1 \to N_2 \to \cdots \to N_c \to N_1$. It is known that if A has cycle c, then any of its divisors (except for 1) also form A's cycle. Moreover, let $\omega = \mathrm{e}^{2\mathrm{i}\pi/c}$, then all of $\omega\lambda^{\mathrm{F}}(A), \ldots, \omega^{c-1}\lambda^{\mathrm{F}}(A)$ are eigenvalues of A. For orders 2 and 3, the two-cyclic matrix takes the form $\begin{bmatrix} 0 & + \\ + & 0 \end{bmatrix}$ and $\begin{bmatrix} 0 & 0 & + \\ 0 & 0 & + \\ + & + & 0 \end{bmatrix}$, respectively.

Now let us assume that both averaging periods τ_i and buffer coefficients $k_i + l_i$ are uniform between all the firms, that is,

$$\tau_i = \tau, \quad k_i + l_i = k + l \quad (i = 1, \ldots, n). \tag{4.23}$$

In this case, (4.19) is simplified into

$$s^e(t) = \tau^{-1}\left(s(t-1) + \cdots + s(t-\tau)\right).$$

[11] For more on the indecomposable matrices, refer to Nikaido (1961, pp. 80-89).

[12] For the properties of cyclic (or imprimitive) matrices, refer to Nikaido (1961, pp. 103–113).

Accordingly, transitive matrix Φ is simplified into

$$\Phi' = \begin{bmatrix} \left(\frac{b}{\tau}+1\right)A & I & \mathrm{O} & \cdots & \mathrm{O} \\ \mathrm{O} & \mathrm{O} & I & \cdots & \mathrm{O} \\ \vdots & \vdots & \vdots & \ddots & \vdots \\ \mathrm{O} & \mathrm{O} & \mathrm{O} & \cdots & I \\ -\frac{b}{\tau}A & \mathrm{O} & \mathrm{O} & \cdots & \mathrm{O} \end{bmatrix},$$

where $b \equiv 2 + k + l$. Let us call this system SMA(u) ("u" represents the uniformity of buffer coefficients and averaging periods). It is a simplified version of SMA by assumption (4.23). Concerning the stability of SMA(u), we can prove the following theorem.

Theorem 2

(i) Let $\overline{\phi}(\mu, \theta, \tau, b)$ be the dominant root of the equation

$$\phi^{\tau+1} - \left(\frac{b}{\tau}+1\right)\mu e^{i\theta}\phi^{\tau} + \frac{b}{\tau}\mu e^{i\theta} = 0. \tag{4.24}$$

Subsequently, the necessary and sufficient condition for asymptotic stability of SMA(u) is $\overline{\phi}(\mu, \theta, \tau, b) < 1$ for any A's eigenvalue $\lambda = \mu e^{i\theta}$ $(0 \le \mu)$.

(ii) $\overline{\phi}(\mu, \theta, \tau, b) = \overline{\phi}(\mu, \theta + 2\pi/\tau, \tau, b) = \overline{\phi}(\mu, 2\pi/\tau - \theta, \tau, b)$.

(iii) Assume $0 \le \theta \le \pi/\tau$, then $\overline{\phi}(\mu, \theta, \tau, b) < 1$ holds if and only if $\mu < \mu^*(\theta, \tau, b)$, where $\mu^*(\theta, \tau, b)$ is a unique μ satisfying $\overline{\mu} \equiv \tau/(2b+\tau) \le \mu < \sqrt{(\tau+2)/(\tau+2b)}$ and

$$\tau \arctan \frac{\sqrt{(1-\mu^2)(\mu^2-\overline{\mu}^2)}}{\mu^2+\overline{\mu}} + \arctan \frac{\mu^2\left(1+2b^2\tau^{-2}\overline{\mu}\right)-\overline{\mu}}{\sqrt{(1-\mu^2)(\mu^2-\overline{\mu}^2)}} + \tau\theta = \frac{\pi}{2} \tag{4.25}$$

on the condition that the range of function arctan is $[-\pi/2, \pi/2]$.

(iv) $\mu^*(\theta, \tau, b)$ is strictly increasing with respect to θ in $0 \le \theta \le \pi/\tau$.

(v) A necessary condition for the stability of SMA(u) is given by

$$\lambda^F(A) < \mu^*(0, \tau, b), \tag{4.26}$$

and particularly,

$$\mu^*(0, 1, b) = \frac{1}{b}, \quad \mu^*(0, 2, b) = \frac{2}{\sqrt{2b(b+1)}}$$

(vi) $\mu_*(\theta,\tau,b)$ satisfies the following inequalities:

$$\mu^*(\theta,\tau,b) < \mu^*\left(\frac{\tau}{\tau+1}\theta,\tau+1,b\right); \mu^*(0,\tau,b) < \frac{\tau+1}{2b+\tau-1} \quad \text{for } \tau \geq 2.$$

(vii) $\mu_*(\theta,\tau,b)$ is strictly increasing with respect to b.

Proof: See Appendix 2.

Statement (ii) means that $\overline{\phi}$ is a periodic function of period $2\pi/\tau$ with respect to θ and a symmetric function with respect to $\theta = \pi/\tau$. Thus, we can derive the stability condition for any value of θ from statements (ii) and (iii). Statement (iv) indicates that an increase in argument θ in interval $[0, \pi/\tau]$ tightens the constraint on μ. The constraint for stability becomes most restrictive when $\theta = \pi/\tau$ or, more generally, $\theta = (2\nu - 1)\pi/\tau$. This shows that the stability of SMA(u) depends on the input structure of the economy, especially on intersectoral relations.

According to statements (v), the stability of SMA(u) implies $\lambda^F(A) < 1/b$ for $\tau = 1$ and $\lambda^F(A) < 2/\sqrt{2b(b+1)}$ for $\tau = 2$. While (4.26) cannot be rewritten in such explicit forms for lager values of τ, statement (vi) guarantees that an increase in τ raises $\mu_*(0,\tau,b)$.[13] In fact, this statement shows that an increase in averaging period τ loosens the constraint on μ *if argument* θ *is adjusted so that product* $\theta\tau$ is kept constant. Especially, for $\theta = 0$ we obtain

$$\mu^*(0,\tau,b) < \mu^*(0,\tau+1,b).$$

Meanwhile, because of statements (i), (iii), (v), (vi), and (viii), a necessary condition for the stability of SMA(u) is given by

$$\lambda^F(A) < \frac{\tau+1}{2b+\tau-1}, \tag{4.27}$$

which is simpler but slightly looser than (4.26). Thus, stability requires that the spectrum radius of the input matrix must be less than a certain value that is less than unity. On the other hand, from statements (i) and (vi), we have

$$\frac{\tau}{2b+\tau} = \overline{\mu} = \mu^*\left(\frac{(2\nu-1)\pi}{\tau},\tau,b\right) \leq \mu^*(\theta,\tau,b)$$

for $\nu \in \{1,\ldots,\tau\}$. Therefore, SMA(u) is stable if

$$\lambda^F(A) < \frac{\tau}{2b+\tau}, \tag{4.28}$$

[13] In fact, for $\tau = 3$, (4.26) is equivalent to $\mu < \mu_1$, where μ_1 is the only positive root of $\mu(3b + b^2\mu + b(3+2b)\mu^2) < 9$ $(\mu = \lambda^F(A))$.

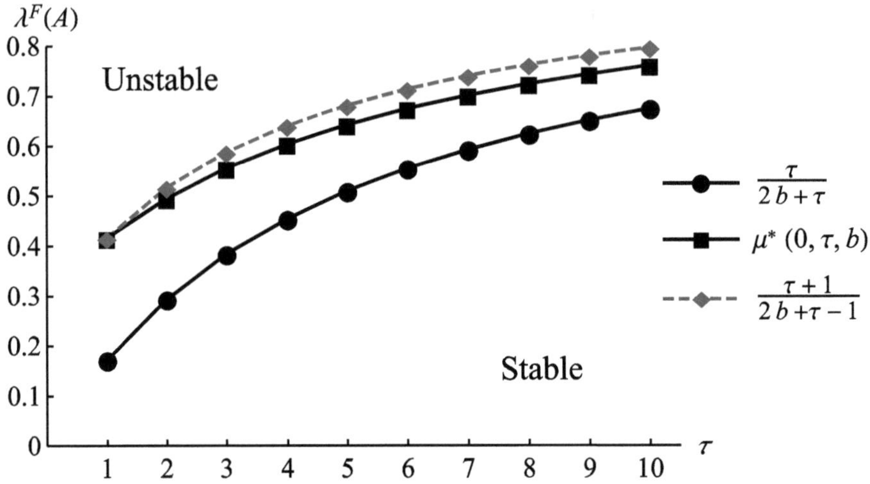

Fig. 4.2 Dependence of stability on $\lambda^F(A)$ and τ

and this is also necessary when A has $\lambda^F(A)\ e^{((2\nu-1)/\pi)i}$ as one of its eigenvalues.[14] The same proposition can be also directly derived from (4.21). Finally, statement (vii) means that an increase in buffer coefficient b tightens the constraint on μ for stability.

Figure 4.2 illustrates how stability depends on τ and $\lambda^F(A)$, for $k + l = 0.4$ ($b = 2.4$). The line graph of $\mu^*(0, \tau, b)$, which is upward sloping with respect to τ, is drawn by numerical computations. If the pair (τ, $\lambda^F(A)$) lies in the region over the line marked by squares, SMA(u) is unstable. If it lies in the region under the line marked by circles, SMA(u) is stable. However, if it lies in the intermediate region between these lines, stability of SMA(u) depends on the input structure, that is, the distribution of A's eigenvalues on the complex plane. An increase in buffer coefficient $k + l$ leads to a downward shift of both curves and, thereby, makes the constraint on τ and $\lambda^F(A)$ for stability more restrictive.

Under the static expectation ($\tau = 1$), $\lambda^F(A)$ must be less than 0.4167 for stability. Even when $k + l = 0$ ($b = 2$), $\lambda^F(A)$ still must be less than 0.5. As long as $\lambda(A)$ is around 0.5 to 0.55, quantity adjustment with the static expectation is likely to be unstable. With the increase in τ from 1 to 2, this bound is loosened to 0.4951. Let $\lambda^F(A) = 0.55$, then SMA(u) is unstable for $\tau \leq 2$ and stable for $\tau \geq 6$. Therefore, SMA(u) can be stabilized by a moderate increase in the averaging periods. For τ=3, 4, and 5, stability depends on the input structure. For instance, when A has a negative eigenvalue λ such that $|\lambda| \geq 5/(2b + 5) = 0.5102$, then the system is unstable for τ=5 due to the non-Frobenius eigenvalue even if $\lambda^F(A) < \mu^*(0, 5, 2.4) = 0.6431$.

[14] This proposition was first proved in Morioka (1991–1992).

Condition (4.22) in Theorem 1 presupposes that the economy consists of interdependent multiple sectors. If we aggregate all the sectors into a single sector, the input matrix is degenerated into a scalar. In this case, (4.28) is the necessary and sufficient condition for the stability of the macro version of SMA. Therefore, aggregation into a single-sector macro model substantially widens the range of parameters ensuring stability. In other words, our multi-sector model has dynamic features *peculiar to the existence of interactions among sectors*. These features deserve more detailed examination.

4.2.2 Detailed Analysis of the Effect of Parameters

To explicate the effects of various parameters on the stability of SMA(u), we must closely examine how $\overline{\phi}(\mu, \theta, \tau, b)$ depends on its arguments. Since solutions of any algebraic equation are continuous with respect to its coefficients, $\overline{\phi}(\mu, \theta, \tau, b)$ is a continuous function with respect to any of its arguments. For $\mu = 0$, all the roots of Eq. (4.24) are reduced to zero irrespective of θ, τ, b. For a positive μ, we can prove that $\overline{\phi}(\mu, \theta, \tau, b)$ has the following properties.

Theorem 3

(i) $\overline{\phi}(\mu, \theta, \tau, b)$ is strictly increasing with respect to μ.
(ii) $\overline{\phi}(\mu, \theta, \tau, b)$ is strictly increasing with respect to θ for $0 \le \theta \le \pi/\tau$.
(iii) If $\left(\frac{b}{b+\tau}\right)^{\frac{1}{\tau}} \le \overline{\phi}(\mu, \theta, \tau, b)$, then $\overline{\phi}\left(\mu, \frac{\tau}{\tau+1}\theta, \tau+1, b\right) < \overline{\phi}(\mu, \theta, \tau, b)$.
(iv) $\overline{\phi}(\mu, \theta, \tau, b)$ is strictly increasing with respect to b.

Proof: See Appendix 3.

Statement (i) shows that an increase in μ has a destabilizing effect. However, $\lambda^{F}(A)$ does not always affect stability because $\rho(\Phi')$ may be given by $\overline{\phi}(\mu, \theta, \tau, b)$ corresponding to eigenvalues other than the Frobenius root. Figure 4.3 illustrates how $\overline{\phi}$ depends on μ for $\theta = 0, \pi$ and τ=1, 5 ($b = 2.4$). To set focus on the effect of μ, let us write $\overline{\phi}$ as $\overline{\phi}(\mu; \theta, \tau)$. The graph of function $\overline{\phi}(\mu; \theta, \tau)$ shifts by changes in argument θ and averaging period τ. Furthermore, for $\theta = 0$, the graph of $\overline{\phi}(\mu; 0, \tau)$ curves steeply at the point where the solution giving the dominant root of (4.24) switches from a pair of conjugate complex numbers to a positive real number.

Because of statement (ii) and Theorem 2, $\overline{\phi}(\theta; \tau)$ takes the minimum values at $\theta = 0, 2\pi/\tau, 4\pi/\tau, \ldots, 2(\tau-1)\pi/\tau$ and takes the maximum value at $\theta = \pi/\tau, 3\pi/\tau, \ldots, (2\tau-1)\pi/\tau$. Thus, for fixed $\mu = |\lambda|$, b, and τ, $\overline{\phi}$ always takes the minimum value when λ is a positive real number. Input matrix A has negative or complex eigenvalues only when the economy consists of multiple sectors, and input relations across sectors have considerable weight in comparison with those

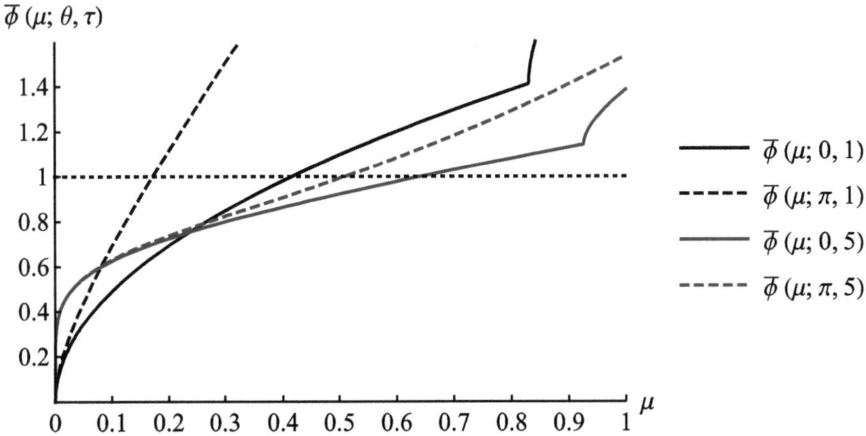

Fig. 4.3 Graphs of $\overline{\phi}(\mu; \theta, \tau)$

within each sector.[15] Therefore, we can state that *the interdependence between sectors connected by input relations is itself a potential destabilizing factor in the quantity adjustment process.* Figure 4.4 illustrates how $\overline{\phi}$ depends on argument θ, for various values of τ ($\mu = 0.55$ and $b = 2.4$). Roughly speaking, the graphs of $\overline{\phi}(\theta; \tau)$ corresponding to various values of τ shift downward along with an increase in averaging period τ. However, since an increase in τ reduces the cycle of $\overline{\phi}(\theta; \tau)$ and changes the values of θ maximizing $\overline{\phi}(\theta; \tau)$, the relation between $\overline{\phi}(\theta; \tau)$ and $\overline{\phi}(\theta; \tau + 1)$ is not so simple. The graph of $\overline{\phi}(\theta; 2)$ crosses the graph of $\overline{\phi}(\theta; 3)$ around $\theta = \pi$, and the latter crosses the graph of $\overline{\phi}(\theta; 4)$ around $\theta = 2\pi/3, 4\pi/3$.

Statement (iii) of the theorem indicates that an increase in averaging period τ decreases $\overline{\phi}(\tau; \theta)$, providing that $\overline{\phi}(\tau; \pi/\tau)$ is larger than a certain value and θ is adjusted so that its ratio to $2\pi/\tau$ (hence, the product $\theta\tau$) is kept constant. Since $\overline{\phi}(\tau; \theta)$ converges to one from below when τ increases infinitely,[16] the precondition cannot be eliminated from this statement. Under a very large averaging period, changes of $s^e(t)$ and $s(t)$ are almost separated, and consequently, the system gets close to (4.15). In such a case, $s(t)$ converges to its stationary point with a speed corresponding to $1/\lambda^F(A)$.

Figure 4.5 illustrates how $\overline{\phi}$ depends on averaging period τ, for $\theta = 0, \pi/\tau, \pi$ ($\mu = 0.55$ and $b = 2.4$). $\overline{\phi}(\tau; \pi)$ is equal to $\overline{\phi}(\tau; \pi/\tau)$ when τ is odd and equal to $\overline{\phi}(\tau; \theta = 0)$ when τ is even. While both $\overline{\phi}(\tau; 0)$ and $\overline{\phi}(\tau; \pi/\tau)$ slope downward,

[15] Matrix $\begin{bmatrix} a_{11} & a_{12} \\ a_{21} & a_{22} \end{bmatrix}$ has a negative eigenvalue when $a_{11}a_{22} < a_{12}a_{21}$. This condition implies that the coefficients corresponding to the intersectoral input-output relationship are relatively large in comparison with the ones corresponding to self-consumption.

[16] This is shown from $\left(\frac{b\mu}{\tau}\right)^{\frac{1}{\tau+1}} < \overline{\phi} < 1$ for $\tau > \left(\frac{2b}{\tau} + 1\right)\mu$ and $\lim_{\tau\to\infty}\left(\frac{b\mu}{\tau}\right)^{\frac{1}{\tau+1}} = 1$.

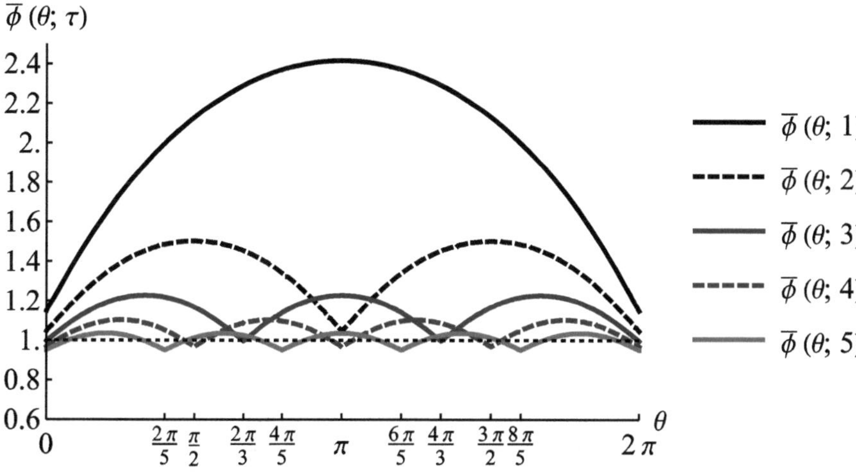

Fig. 4.4 Graphs of $\overline{\phi}\,(\theta;\tau)$

$\overline{\phi}\,(\tau;\pi)$ describes a zigzag line in which $\overline{\phi}\,(\tau;\pi) < \overline{\phi}\,(\tau+1;\pi)$ holds only for even τ. Let

$$A = A_1 \equiv \begin{bmatrix} 0 & 0.55 \\ 0.55 & 0 \end{bmatrix},$$

then eigenvalues of A_1 are ± 0.55 and the negative eigenvalue -0.55 satisfies (4.22) for odd τ. It follows from statement (ii) that $\rho(\Phi') = \overline{\phi}\,(0.55, \pi, \tau, 2.4)$; hence, the zigzag line in Fig. 4.5 shows the changes in $\rho(\Phi')$ due to the increase in τ. $\rho(\Phi')$ is equal to 1.228 for $\tau = 3$, 0.967 for $\tau = 4$, 1.036 for $\tau = 5$, and 0.967 for $\tau = 6$. Thus, there are cases where the system *loses stability* by an increase in τ. As noted above, this reverse effect of averaging is caused by the change in $2\pi/\tau$, the cycle of $\overline{\phi}\,(\theta;\tau)$.

Figure 4.6 indicates, on the complex plane, the bounds on A's eigenvalues for the stability of SMA(u) for various values of τ. The inside of each bound constitutes a stable region corresponding to a particular value of τ. As expected from the above argument, each bound has bulges (or kurtosis) toward the arguments $\theta = 2\alpha\pi/\tau$ (α is an integer). Therefore, for $\tau \geq 3$, each boundary takes the form that is close to a τ-sided polygon. Along with an increase in τ, the stable region expands outward *as a whole*. However, the stable region corresponding to $\tau + 1$ does not entirely enclose the region corresponding to τ. When one of A's eigenvalues exists in the stable region corresponding to τ but not belongs to that corresponding to $\tau + 1$, an increase in τ destabilizes the system. Thus, in the case of demand forecast by the simple moving average, the influence of the input structure upon stability depends on the averaging period in a somewhat complicated manner.

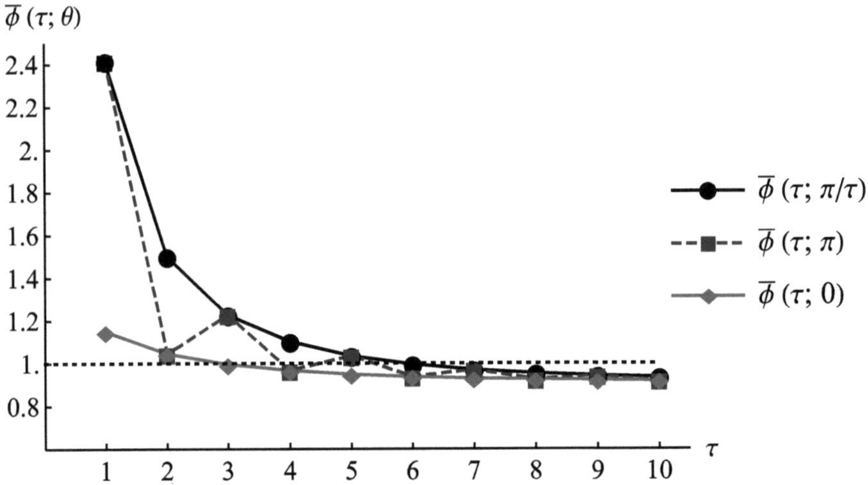

Fig. 4.5 Graphs of $\overline{\phi}(\tau;\theta)$

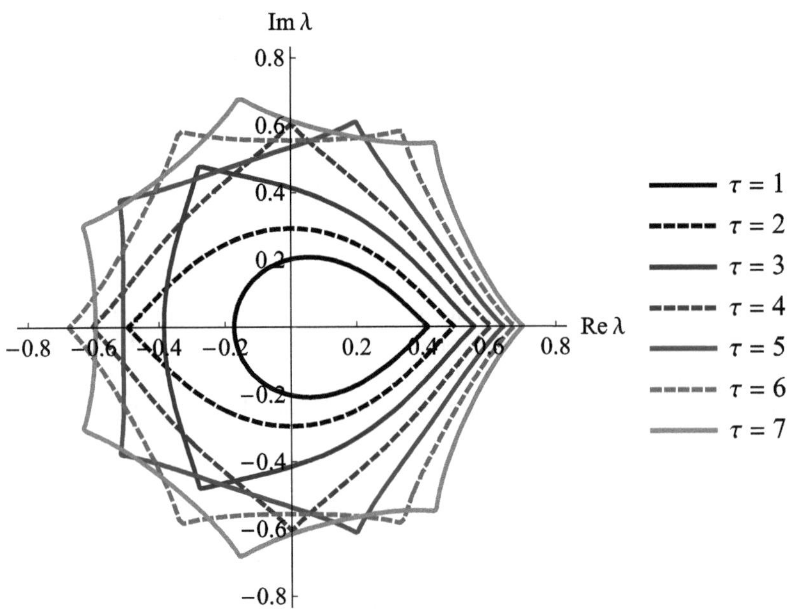

Fig. 4.6 Bounds on eigenvalues of A for stability of SMA(u)

Similar cases can occur also in SMA where each firm's averaging period is not uniform. Figure 4.7 shows how $\rho(\Phi)$ in a two-sector economy changes by increases in τ_1, for $\tau_2 = 2, 3, 4$; $A = A_1$, $b = 2.4$. According to Theorem 1, a sufficient condition for stability under this input matrix is

$$0.55^2\left(\frac{2b}{\tau_1}+1\right)\left(\frac{2b}{\tau_2}+1\right) < 1,$$

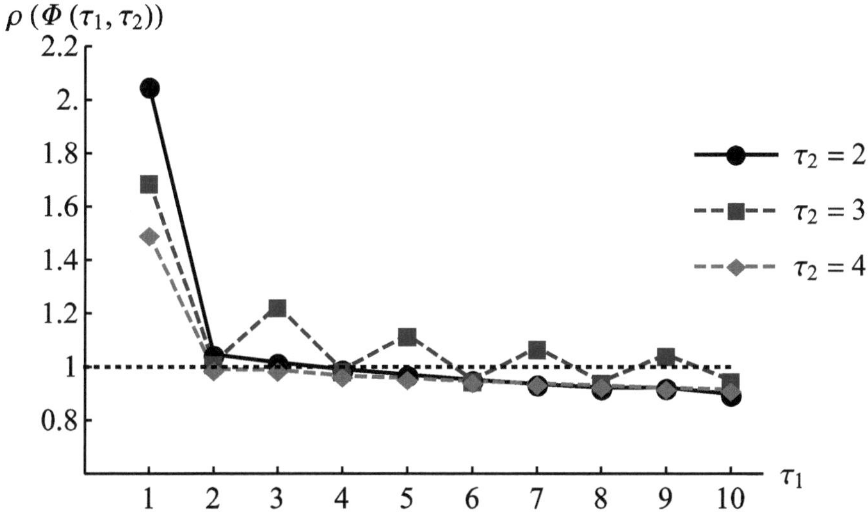

Fig. 4.7 Graphs of $\rho(\Phi(\tau_1;\tau_2))$

and it becomes necessary if both τ_1 and τ_2 are odd. However, it is not necessary if one of them is even. This difference causes complications. In fact, when $(\tau_1, \tau_2) = (4, 3)$, $(6, 3)$, or $(8, 3)$, an increase in τ_1 makes a stable system unstable. Furthermore, when τ_1 and τ_2 simultaneously increase from $(\tau_1, \tau_2) = (4, 2)$, $(6, 2)$, or (8, 2), the system again loses stability. Notably, this is one of the cases in which the stabilizing effect of averaging is strongly disturbed by the interactions between sectors. However, it should be remarked that the occurrence of these reversals depends on the property of the input matrix. In fact, under the input matrix

$$A = A_2 \equiv \begin{bmatrix} 0.15 & 0.4 \\ 0.4 & 0.15 \end{bmatrix},$$

SMA never loses stability by an increase in τ_i as long as it is already stable. This simplicity is explained by the fact that A's nonpositive eigenvalues is small in comparison with its Frobenius root (A_2 has eigenvalues of 0.55 and -0.25, and the latter does not affect the stability).

Finally, statement (iv) shows that an increase in buffer inventory coefficient $k + l$ always has a destabilizing effect. Unlike averaging period τ, the relationship between an increase in buffer coefficient $k + l$ and an increase in $\overline{\phi}$ is almost linear. Figure 4.8 indicates this near linearity ($\mu = 0.55$). Therefore, a small change in the buffer coefficient does not exert substantial effect on stability.

While buffer coefficient $k + l$ must not be too large for stability, it should be recalled that stability is not the only condition guaranteeing smooth progress of the quantity adjustment process. As already noted, (4.20) is obtained under the assumption that nonnegativity and other constraints on variables are always satisfied. Even if $\rho(\Phi')$ is less than unity, a very small buffer coefficient is likely to cause frequent stockout occurrences, which may temporary halt production. A

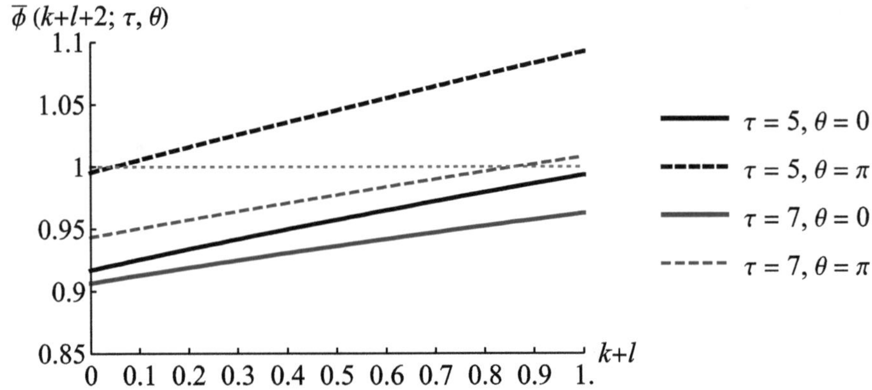

Fig. 4.8 Graphs of $\overline{\phi}\,(k + l + 2;\, \tau, \theta)$

stable and uninterrupted progress of the process requires that the buffer coefficient should be in a certain adequate range. This remark is also applicable also to the case of nonuniform buffer coefficients. The relationship between the buffer coefficients and the frequency of stockout occurrences will be examined in the next chapter.

4.3 The Case of Demand Forecast Formed by the Geometric Moving Average

4.3.1 Dynamic Stability Conditions

In matrix notation, (4.18) can be rewritten as

$$s^e(t) = s^e\,(t-1) + \left(s\,(t-1) - s^e\,(t-1)\right)\Gamma \tag{4.29}$$

where Γ is a diagonal matrix of γ_i. Substituting (4.33) into (4.15), we have a complete system of difference equations:

$$\left[s(t), s^e(t)\right] = \left[s\,(t-1)\,, s^e\,(t-1)\right]\Psi + [d, 0]\,, \tag{4.30}$$

$$\Psi \equiv \begin{bmatrix} (I + \Gamma B)\,A & \Gamma \\ -\Gamma B A & I - \Gamma \end{bmatrix},$$

where Ψ is a $2n \times 2n$ square matrix. Let us call this system GMA (geometric moving average) to emphasize the method of demand forecast. The stationary point of GMA is identical with that of SMA. Like the case of SMA, the necessary and sufficient condition for the stability of GMA is equivalent to $\rho(\Psi) < 1$.

Theorem 4

(i) GMA is asymptotically stable if

$$\lambda^{\mathrm{F}}\left(\left(2\Gamma B(2I-\Gamma)^{-1}+I\right)A\right) < 1 \tag{4.31}$$

(ii) $-\lambda^{\mathrm{F}}(A)$ is one of A's eigenvalues; GMA is asymptotically stable *if and only if* the inequality (4.31) holds.

Proof: See Appendix 4.

As argued in the previous subsection, the premise in statement (ii) is satisfied when A is a cyclic matrix with the cycle of an even number. Since matrix $(2\Gamma B(2I - \Gamma)^{-1} + I)A$ is a nonnegative square matrix and its (i,j) element is $\left(2\gamma_i b_i (2-\gamma_i)^{-1}+1\right)$, $\lambda^{\mathrm{F}}((2\Gamma B(2I - \Gamma)^{-1} + I)A)$ is an increasing function (a strictly increasing function if A is indecomposable) with respect to γ_i, k_i, l_i, and a_{ij}. Therefore, the smaller γ_i, $k_i + l_i$, and a_{ij} are, the more likely that inequality (4.31) will be satisfied.

Now let us assume that smoothing constant γ_i and buffer coefficient $k_i + l_i$ are uniform between all the firms, that is,

$$\gamma_i = \gamma, \quad k_i + l_i + 2 = b \quad (i = 1, \ldots, n)\,. \tag{4.32}$$

In this case, the transitive matrix Ψ' is simplified to

$$\Psi' = \begin{bmatrix} (1+\gamma b)\,A & \gamma I \\ -\gamma b A & (1-\gamma)\,I \end{bmatrix}.$$

We call this system GMA(u). It is a simplified version of GMA with the uniformity assumption (4.32). Concerning the stability of GMA(u), the following theorem holds.

Theorem 5

(i) Let $\overline{\psi}\,(\mu,\theta,\gamma,b)$ be the maximum solution (measured by its absolute value) of the equation

$$\psi^2 - \left((\gamma b+1)\,\mu e^{i\theta} + 1 - \gamma\right)\psi + (1-\gamma+\gamma b)\,\mu e^{i\theta} = 0. \tag{4.33}$$

Then, the necessary and sufficient condition for the asymptotic stability of GMA(u) is $\overline{\psi}\,(\mu,\theta,\gamma,b) < 1$ for any of A's eigenvalue $\lambda = \mu e^{i\theta}$.

(ii) $\overline{\psi}\,(\mu,\theta,\gamma,b) = \overline{\psi}\,(\mu, 2\pi-\theta,\gamma,b)\,.$

(iii) $\overline{\psi}(\mu, \theta, \gamma, b) < 1$ holds if and only if $\mu < \mu^*(\theta, \gamma, b)$, where $\mu^*(\theta, \gamma, b)$ is a unique μ such that $\mu \leq 1/(1 + \gamma(b-1))$ and

$$\frac{(1-\mu)(1-\mu(1-\gamma+\gamma b))^2(2-\gamma+\mu(2-\gamma+2\gamma b))}{2\mu(2-\gamma+\gamma b)\left(\mu^2(1-\gamma+\gamma b)(1+\gamma b)-(1-\gamma)\right)} + \cos\theta = 1.$$

(iv) $\mu^*(\theta, \gamma, b)$ is strictly decreasing with respect to θ in $0 \leq \theta \leq \pi$, and

$$\mu^*(0, \gamma, b) = \frac{1}{1+\gamma(b-1)}, \quad \mu^*(\pi, \gamma, b) = \frac{2-\gamma}{2+(2b-1)\gamma}. \tag{4.34}$$

(v) A necessary condition for stability of GMA(u) is

$$\lambda^F(A) < \frac{1}{1+\gamma(b-1)}. \tag{4.35}$$

(vi) $\mu^*(\theta, \gamma, b)$ is strictly decreasing with respect to γ.
(vii) $\mu^*(\theta, \gamma, b)$ is strictly decreasing with respect to b.

Proof: See Appendix 5.

Statement (ii) implies that $\overline{\psi}$ is a symmetric function about $\theta = \pi$. Statement (iv) indicates that an increase in argument θ in interval $[0, \pi]$ tightens the constraint on μ. The constraint for stability becomes most restrictive when $\theta = \pi$. This shows that the stability of GMA(u) depends on the intersectoral input-output relationship. From (i), (ii), and (iv), we have $\mu^*(\pi, \gamma, b) \leq \mu^*(\theta, \gamma, b)$. Consequently, GMA(u) is stable if

$$\lambda^F(A) < \frac{2-\gamma}{2+(2b-1)\gamma}, \tag{4.36}$$

and this condition is also necessary when A has $-\lambda^F(A)$ as its eigenvalue.[17] Sufficient condition (4.36) of GMA(u) coincides with sufficient condition (4.32) of SMA(u) when $\gamma = 2/(\tau + 1)$. In this relation, for example, $\gamma = 0.5$ corresponds to $\tau = 3$, $\gamma = 0.25$ to $\tau = 7$, and $\gamma = 0.2$ to $\tau = 9$. Statement (viii) and (ix) show that an increase in either smoothing constant γ or buffer coefficient b tightens the constraint on μ to ensure stability.

Figure 4.9 illustrates how stability depends on γ and $\lambda^F(A)$ for $k + l = 0.4$. If the pair $(\gamma, \lambda^F(A))$ lies in the region above the upper curve, the system is unstable. If it lies in the region below the lower curve, the system is stable. However, if it lies in the intermediate region in which (4.35) holds but (4.36) does not hold, stability depends on the input structure, that is, the distribution of A's eigenvalues on the complex plane. An increase in buffer coefficient $k + l$ leads a downward shift of both curves and, thereby, makes the constraint on γ and $\lambda^F(A)$ for stability more restrictive. These curves move downward as the buffer coefficient increases.

[17] This proposition is first proved in Morioka (1992–1992).

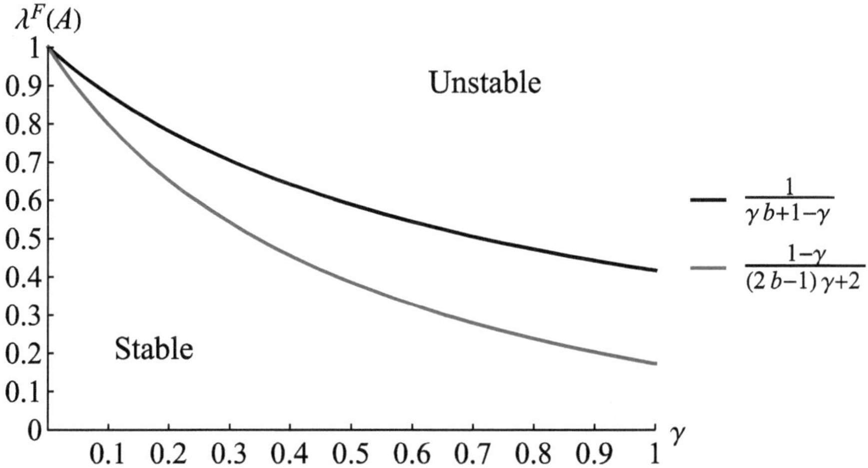

Fig. 4.9 Dependence of stability on $\lambda^F(A)$ and γ

Let $\lambda^F(A) = 0.55$ and $b = 2.4$; the system is unstable for $\gamma > 0.5894$ and stable for $\gamma < 0.2910$. Therefore, the system can be stabilized by a moderate decrease in the smoothing constant. For $0.2910 < \gamma < 0.5894$, stability depends on the input structure. When A has a negative eigenvalue such that $\lambda < -\mu^*(\pi, 0.3, 2.4) = -0.5102$, then the system is unstable for $\gamma = 0.3$ due to this negative whether or not $\lambda^F(A)$ is less than $\mu^*(0, 0.3, 2.4) = 0.7042$.

4.3.2 *Detailed Analysis of the Effect of Parameters*

Let us examine how $\overline{\psi}(\mu, \theta, \tau, b)$ depends on its arguments. For positive μ we can prove that $\overline{\psi}(\mu, \theta, \tau, b)$ has the following properties.

Theorem 6 Let $\mu_0(\gamma, b) \equiv (1-\gamma)/(1+\gamma b)$ and assume $\mu_0 \leq \mu$. Then,

(i) $\overline{\psi}(\mu, \theta, \gamma, b)$ is strictly increasing with respect to μ.
(ii) $\overline{\psi}(\mu, \theta, \gamma, b)$ is strictly increasing with respect to θ in $0 \leq \theta \leq \pi$ for $\mu_0 < \mu$, whereas $\overline{\psi}(\mu_0, \theta, \gamma, b)$ is constant with respect to θ.
(iii) $\overline{\psi}(\mu, \theta, \gamma, b)$ is strictly increasing with respect to γ.
(iv) $\overline{\psi}(\mu, \theta, \gamma, b)$ is strictly increasing with respect to b.

Proof: See Appendix 6.

Since $\mu_0 = \frac{1-\gamma}{1+\gamma b} < \frac{2-\gamma}{2+(2b-1)\gamma}$, the premise $\mu_0 < \mu$ is satisfied as long as $\overline{\psi}$ can be larger than unity depending on θ. Statement (i) indicates that an increase in μ has a destabilizing effect like the case of SMA(u). Figure 4.10 illustrates how $\overline{\psi}$ depends on μ, for $\theta = 0, \pi$ and $\gamma = 0.25, 1$ ($\mu = 0.55, b = 2.4$). The graph of $\overline{\psi}(\mu; \theta, \gamma)$ shifts significantly along with changes in argument θ and smoothing constant γ.

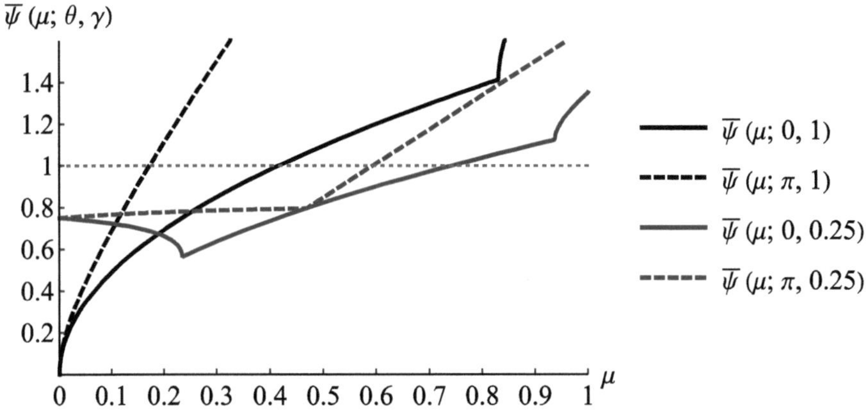

Fig. 4.10 Graphs of $\overline{\psi}\ (\mu;\theta,\gamma)$

Furthermore, because of statement (ii), $\overline{\psi}$ is symmetric around $\theta = \pi$ and takes the minimal value at $\theta = 0$ and the maximum value at $\theta = \pi$. Differing from the case of SMA(u), the value of θ maximizing $\overline{\psi}\ (\theta)$ does not depend on γ. Thus, providing that μ, b, and γ are fixed, $\overline{\psi}$ always takes the minimum value when λ is a positive real number. Accordingly, the interdependence between sectors is a potential destabilizing factor also in the case of GMA(u).

Figure 4.11 shows how $\overline{\psi}$ depends on θ, for $\gamma = 0.3, 0.5, 1$ ($\mu = 0.55, b = 2.4$). As γ decreases, the graph of $\overline{\psi}\ (\theta;\gamma)$ shifts downward. When γ decreases to the level satisfying $\mu = \mu_0(\gamma, b)$, that is, to

$$\gamma = \gamma_0\,(\mu, b) \equiv \frac{1-\mu}{1+b\mu} = 0.194,$$

the graph for $\overline{\psi}\ (\theta;\gamma)$ becomes perfectly flat at

$$\overline{\psi}\left(\theta;\frac{1-\mu}{1+b\gamma}\right) = \sqrt{\frac{b\mu+\mu^2}{b\mu+1}} = 0.836.$$

Since $\mu_0(\gamma, b) < \mu$ is equivalent to $\gamma_0(\mu, b) < \gamma$, statement (iii) indicates that $\overline{\psi}$ is an increasing function with respect to γ in the range $\gamma_0\,(\mu, b) < \gamma \le 1$. As long as γ remains in this range, the graphs of $\overline{\psi}\ (\theta;\gamma)$ corresponding to different values of γ never cross each other. Therefore, in case of demand forecast by the geometric moving average, an increase in the weights for demands during periods of more distant past does not cause destabilization. This lack of reversal is the most remarkable difference from the case of SMA(u).

Figure 4.12 shows how $\overline{\psi}$ depends on γ, for $\theta = 0, \pi$ ($\mu = 0.55$, $b = 2.4$). The graph of $\overline{\psi}\ (\gamma;0)$ bends at the point $\gamma = \gamma_0(\mu, b)$ where the solution giving the dominant root of (4.32) switches from a pair of conjugate complex numbers to a positive real number. The graph for $\overline{\psi}\ (\gamma;\pi)$ bends at the point where the

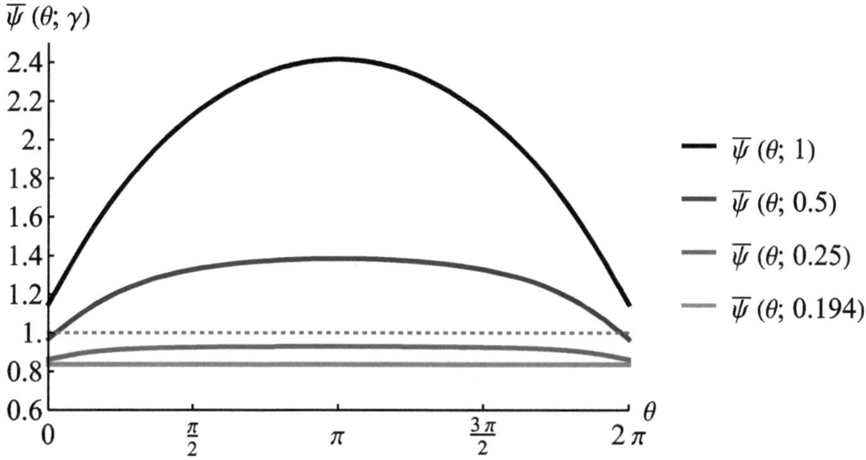

Fig. 4.11 Graphs of $\overline{\psi}(\theta; \gamma)$

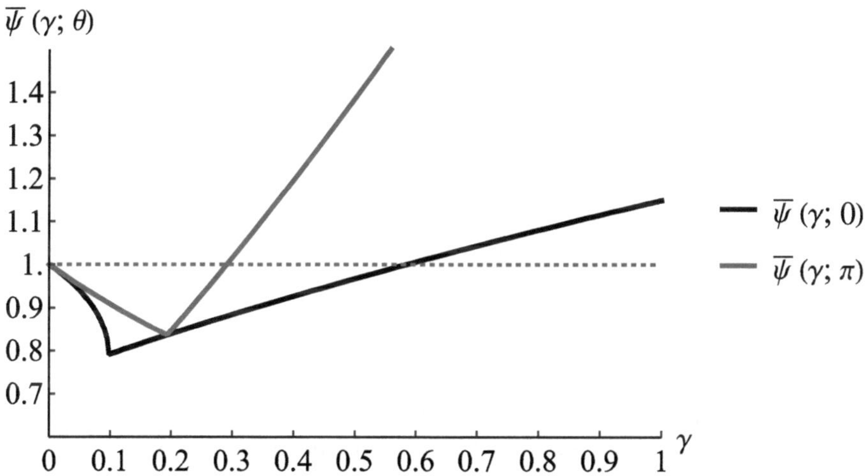

Fig. 4.12 Graphs of $\overline{\psi}(\gamma; \theta)$

solution giving the dominant root of (4.32) switches from a positive to a negative real number. $\overline{\psi}$ converges to 1 when γ reduces to 0. In fact, when $\gamma = 0$, then (4.33) is reduced to $\psi^2 - (\lambda + 1)\psi + \lambda = (\psi - 1)(\psi - \lambda) = 0$.

Like the case of SMA(u), this convergence reflects virtual separation of the movement of $s(t)$ from that of $s^e(t)$. If $A = A_1$, then it follows from Theorem 5 and statement (ii) that $\rho(\Psi') = \overline{\psi}(0.55, \pi, \gamma, 2.4)$. Hence, the graph of $\overline{\psi}(\gamma; \pi)$ in Fig. 4.12 represents the change in $\rho(\Psi')$ with respect to γ. From this figure we can see that the relation between γ and $\overline{\phi}$ is nearly linear in the range affecting stability.

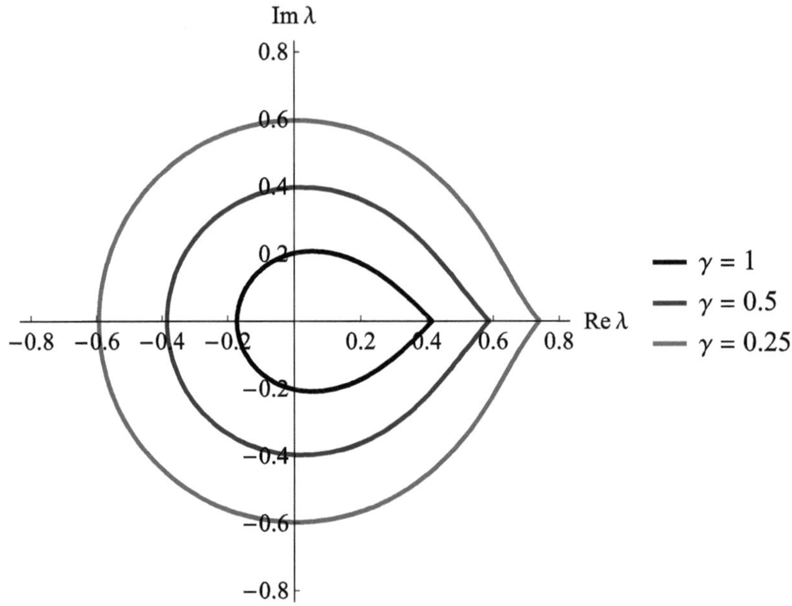

Fig. 4.13 Bounds on eigenvalues of A for stability of GMA(u)

Figure 4.13 indicates the bounds on A's eigenvalues compatible with the stability of GMA(u) on the complex plane for various values of γ. The inside of each boundary constitutes the stable region corresponding to the particular value of γ. As γ decreases, the stable region expands outward *in all directions*. Thus, *in the case of demand forecast by the geometric moving average, the input structure does not disturb the stabilizing effect of averaging*.

This simplicity seems to be maintained also in GMA, where each firm's smoothing constant is not uniform. Further more, by Theorem 4, the necessary and sufficient condition for the stability of SMA corresponding to $A = A_1$ is

$$0.55^2 \left(\frac{2 + (2b - 1)\,\gamma_1}{2 - \gamma_1} + 1 \right) \left(\frac{2 + (2b - 1)\,\gamma_2}{2 - \gamma_2} + 1 \right) < 1.$$

As shown in Fig. 4.14, if we replace A_1 with A_2, the bound for stability moves higher right, and thereby, the restriction on (γ_1, γ_2) is considerably loosened.

The effect of the buffer coefficient on stability is almost the same as the case of forecast by the simple moving average. Figure 4.15 indicates that an increase in the buffer coefficient causes a nearly proportional increase in $\overline{\phi}$ ($\mu = 0.55$).

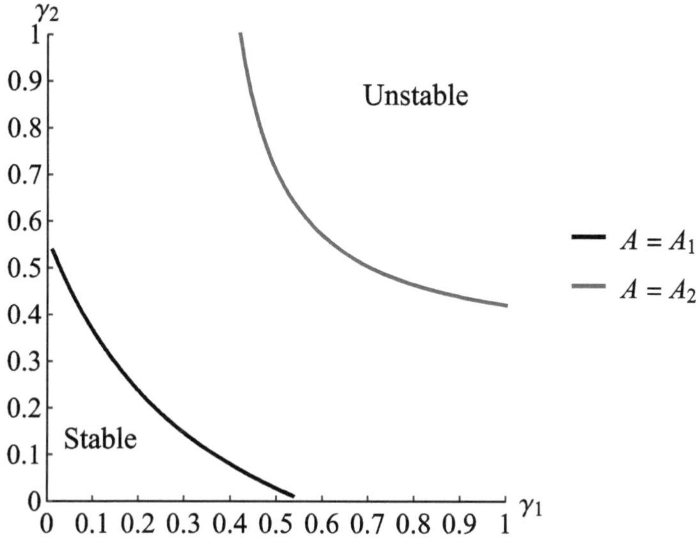

Fig. 4.14 Bounds on (γ_1, γ_2) for stability

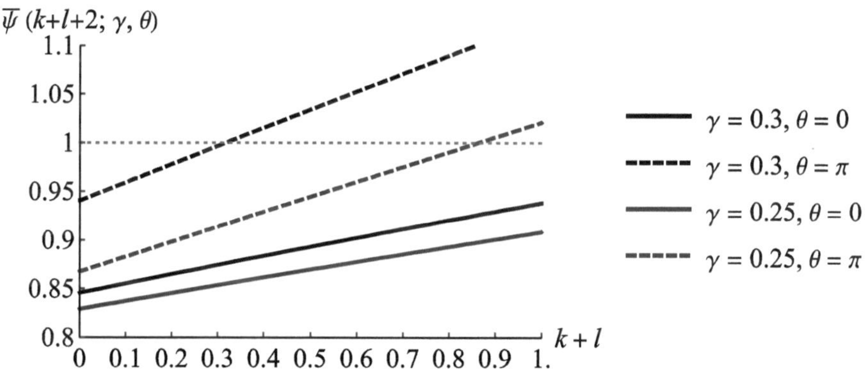

Fig. 4.15 Graphs of $\overline{\phi}\,(b; \gamma, \theta)$

4.4 Mechanism of Stabilization Through Averaging of Past Demands in Forecast Formation

4.4.1 Generalization of the Forecasting Method: The Finite Geometric Moving Average

As seen in the preceding two sections, stability of quantity adjustment with the demand forecast by moving average of past demands depends on, among other factors, *the extent of averaging*. The static expectation, which corresponds to the case of $\tau_i = \gamma_i = 1$, is an extreme case where the extent of averaging is minimized. This forecasting method is likely to make the system unstable under plausible values of the parameters. Another extreme case is a fixed forecast corresponding to the case of $\tau_i = \infty$ or $\gamma_i = 0$. In this case, changes in production and demand are close to those of the case where each firm simply replenishes its sales and raw material consumption. The stability conditions derived in the previous sections indicate that the system can be stable under a variable forecast, if the averaging period takes a certain large value (around 6 to 7) or the smoothing constant takes a certain small value (around 0.2 to 0.3). That is, *averaging to a certain degree* suffices in order that the quantity adjustment process can have stability.

Both the simple moving average and the geometric moving average are special cases of a forecast by

$$s_i^e(t) = \frac{s_i(t-1) + r_i s(t-2) + \cdots + r_i^{\tau_i - 1} s(t-\tau_i)}{1 + r_i + \cdots + r_i^{\tau_i - 1}}, \tag{4.37}$$

where r_i is a nonnegative constant. In fact, the right-hand of (4.37) represents the simple moving average when $r_i = 1$ and the geometric moving average when $0 \le r_i < 1$ and $\tau_i = \infty$ (in the latter case the smoothing constant is $\gamma_i = 1 - r_i$). It is a moving average of demands in the past τ_i weeks whose weights form a geometric progression with a geometric ratio r_i. Hereafter, we will refer to this forecasting method as *the finite geometric moving average.*[18]

In matrix notation, (4.37) can be rewritten as

$$s^e(t) = s(t-1)U_1 + \cdots + s(t-\tau)U_\tau \tag{4.38}$$

where $\tau = \max_i \tau_i$ and U_υ ($\upsilon \in \{1, \ldots, \tau\}$) is the diagonal matrix of

$$u_{i\upsilon} = \begin{cases} \frac{r_i^{\upsilon-1}}{1+r_i+\cdots+r_i^{\tau_i-1}} & \upsilon \in \{1, \ldots, \tau_i\} \\ 0 & \upsilon > \tau_i \end{cases}.$$

By substituting (4.38) into (4.14), we have a complete system of difference equations:

$$[s(t), \ldots, s(t-\tau)] = [s(t-1), \ldots, s(t-\tau-1)]\,\Phi + [d, 0, \ldots, 0], \tag{4.39}$$

[18]If $\tau_i = 2$ and r_i can take a negative value equal to or larger than $-1/2$, then (4.37) covers the method of the demand forecast assumed in Metzler (1941) and Foster (1963).

$$\Phi \equiv \begin{bmatrix} (U_1 B + I)\, A & I \; O \cdots O \\ (U_2 - U_1)\, BA & O \; I \; \cdots O \\ \vdots & \vdots \; \vdots \; \ddots \; \vdots \\ (U_\tau - U_{\tau-1})\, BA & O \; O \cdots \; I \\ -\, U_\tau BA & O \; O \cdots O \end{bmatrix},$$

where Φ is an $n\,(\tau + 1) \times n\,(\tau + 1)$ matrix. As before, focusing on the method of demand forecast, we call this system FGMA (finite geometric moving average). The stationary point of (4.39) is same as those of (4.20) or (4.30). On the stability of FGMA, we can prove the following theorem.

Theorem 7

(i) FGMA is asymptotically stable if

$$\lambda^{\mathrm{F}}\left((2HB + I)\, A\right) < 1, \tag{4.40}$$

where H is the diagonal matrix of

$$\eta\,(\tau_i, r_i) \equiv \frac{1 + r_i^2 + \cdots + r_i^{2(\tau_i - 1)}}{\left(1 + r_i + \cdots + r_i^{\tau_i - 1}\right)^2}.$$

(ii) If $-\lambda^{\mathrm{F}}(A)$ is one of A's eigenvalues and all τ_i are odd numbers, then FGMA is asymptotically stable *if and only if* (4.40) holds.

Proof: See Appendix 7.

Note that $\eta(\tau_i,\ \gamma_i)$ is *the sum of squares of the weights allocated to sales of past τ_i periods* in the finite geometric moving average (this point will be discussed later). Further, (4.40) coincides with (4.22) when $r_i = 1$ for any i and with (4.35) when $r_i < 1$ and $\tau_i = \infty$ for any i.

Let us assume that all the parameters of forecast and the buffer coefficients are uniform between sectors, namely, $r_i = r,\ \ \tau_i = \tau$, and $b_i = b$ for all i. In this case, Φ is simplified into

$$\Phi' \equiv \begin{bmatrix} (uB + I)\, A & I \; O \cdots O \\ -\, u\,(1 - r)\, BA & O \; I \; \cdots O \\ \vdots & \vdots \; \vdots \; \ddots \; \vdots \\ -\, u\left(r^{\tau-2} - r^{\tau-1}\right) BA & O \; O \cdots \; I \\ -\, ur^{\tau-1} BA & O \; O \cdots O \end{bmatrix},\ u \equiv \frac{1}{1 + r + \cdots + r^{\tau-1}}.$$

We call this system FGMA(u). Because of Theorem 7, FGMA(u) is stable if

$$\lambda^{\mathrm{F}}(A) < \frac{1}{2b\eta\,(\tau, r) + 1}. \tag{4.41}$$

Observing

$$\eta(\tau, 0) = \eta(1, r) = 1, \eta(\tau, 1) = \frac{1}{\tau}, \ \eta(\infty, r) = \eta\left(\infty, \frac{1}{r}\right) = \frac{|1-r|}{1+r},$$

it is easily confirmed that (4.41) coincides with (4.28) when $r = 1$ and with (4.36) when $0 < r = 1 - \gamma < 1$ and $\tau = \infty$. This condition guarantees that the dominant solution of the equation

$$\phi^{\tau+1} - (bu+1)\,\mu e^{i\theta}\phi^{\tau} + bu\mu e^{i\theta}\left((1-r)\sum_{\upsilon=0}^{\tau-2} r^{\upsilon}\phi^{\tau-1-\upsilon} + r^{\tau-1}\right) = 0 \quad (4.42)$$

is less than the unity for any A's eigenvalues $\lambda = \mu e^{i\theta}$ and $\tau \geq 2$.

4.4.2 *Effect of Averaging Period and Allocation of Weights*

Let us examine the effects of the averaging period and the allocation of weights to past demands on the stability condition under the assumption that the input matrix is two-cyclic. In this case, (4.40) is the necessary and sufficient condition for the stability of FGMA.

Theorem 8

(i) $\eta(\tau+1, r) < \eta(\tau, r)$
(ii) With respect to r, $\eta(\tau, r)$ is strictly decreasing for $0 < r < 1$ and strictly increasing for $r > 1$.

Proof: See Appendix 8.

Therefore, FGMA can be stabilized by, in addition to an increase in averaging period τ_i, a decrease in $|r_i - 1|$. This decrease implies that *the weights given to past demands becomes more even.* Under fixed τ_i, FGMA is most likely to be stable when $r_i = 1$, namely, when each past sale has the same weight. To put it differently, *the stabilizing effect of referring to demands in larger number of past periods is diminished by giving them weights biased to either the recent past or the distant past.* The reason that an increase in smoothing constant γ_i stabilizes GMA lies in that it brings about a more even allocation of weights.

If $s_i(t)$ is an independent and identically distributed random continuous variable with variance σ^2, the variance of $s_i^e(t)$ in (4.37) is equal to $\eta(\tau_i, r_i)\,\sigma_i^2$. In other words, $\eta(\tau, r)$ represents *the ratio of the variance of averaged demands to the variance of one-time demand.* Therefore, we can infer that the extent of the stabilizing effect by averaging depends on the extent that the variance of averaged demands (the right-hand side of (4.37)) becomes smaller. The variance of averaged

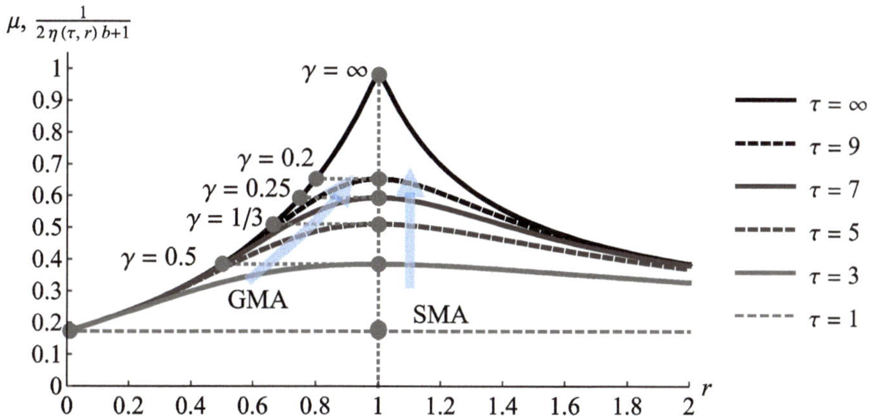

Fig. 4.16 Effects of geometric ratio r on stability

demands is minimized when $r = 1$, that is, when weights are evenly allocated to each past period.[19] Since

$$\eta(\tau, 1) = \frac{1}{\tau} = \eta\left(\infty, \frac{\tau - 1}{\tau + 1}\right),$$

the simple moving average with averaging period τ and the geometric moving average with smoothing constant

$$\gamma = 1 - \frac{\tau - 1}{\tau + 1} = \frac{2}{\tau + 1}$$

reduce the variance of averaged demands to the same extent. In this respect, they have equivalent stabilizing effects as long as stability depends on (4.40).

Figure 4.16 describes how $1/(2b\eta(\tau, r) + 1)$ changes when the geometric ratio r increases from 0 to 2 for various values of averaging period τ $(k + l = 0.4)$. The closer r to 1 and the larger τ, the slacker the constraint on $\lambda^{F}(A)$ (that is, the system is more likely to be stable). The horizontal shift at $r = 1$ corresponds to the stabilization by increasing τ in SMA. The upward slope of the graph in $0 < r \leq 1$ corresponds to the stabilization by decreasing $\gamma(= 1 - r)$ in GMA. The stabilizing effect by an increase of averaging period is enhanced as r gets close to 1.

When $r = \infty$, (4.37) represents

$$s_i^e(t) = s_i(t - \tau), \tag{4.43}$$

that is, the forecast referring to only the demand τ weeks before. Since $\eta(0, \tau) = \eta(\infty, \tau) = 1$, stability condition (4.41) corresponding to (4.43) is the same as

[19] For any $w_1, \ldots, w_\tau$ such that $w_1 + \ldots + w_\tau = 1$, the sum of squares $w_1^2 + \cdots + w_\tau^2$ is minimized when $w_1 = \cdots = w_\tau = 1/\tau$. Therefore, the variance of averaged demand is minimized by equal allocation of weights among past demands.

the case of the static expectation. Therefore, *the reason that the static expectation is likely to bring instability lies not in its "myopic" nature, but rather in its "narrowness of sight" in that it considers demand only in one particular period.* In other words, *the stabilizing effect in demand forecast comes from referring to demands during the past consecutive multiple periods.* "Far-sighted" demand forecast would, if its sight is constrained to one particular period, cause instability no less than the static expectation.

Hitherto, we have assumed that $-\lambda^{\mathrm{F}}(A)$ is one of A's eigenvalues and τ_i are all odd. We will now examine the effect of the averaging period and allocation of weights in more general cases in which these conditions are not satisfied. For simplicity, however, we restrict our analysis to the case of FGMA(u).

Let $\overline{\phi}\,(\tau, r, \mu, \theta, b)$ be the dominant root of equation (4.42). If $\tau = 1$, then r becomes irrelevant ((4.37) is reduced to $s_i^e\,(t) = s_i\,(t-1)$), and because of Theorem 4, the stability condition gets more restrictive as θ increases from 0 to π. If $\tau = 2$, then (4.42) becomes a cubic equation

$$\phi^3 - \left(\frac{b}{1+r} + 1\right)\mu e^{i\theta}\phi^2 + \frac{1-r}{1+r}b\mu e^{i\theta}\phi + \frac{r}{1+r}b\mu e^{i\theta} = 0.$$

Regarding this case, the following theorem holds.

Theorem 9

(i) $\overline{\phi}\,(2, r, \mu, 0, b) < 1$ holds if and only if

$$\mu < \begin{cases} \mu_1\,(r, b) & 0 \le r \le \beta(b) \\ \mu_2\,(r, b) & \beta(b) \le r \end{cases}, \tag{4.44}$$

where $\beta\,(b) \equiv (2b+1)\,/\,(b-1)$ and

$$\mu_1\,(r, b) \equiv \frac{r-1+\sqrt{1+2r+5r^2+4r\,(1+r)\,/b}}{2r\,(1+b)}, \quad \mu_2\,(r, b) \equiv \frac{1+r}{2b\,(r-1)-(1+r)}.$$

(ii) $\overline{\phi}\,(2, r, \mu, \pi, b) < 1$ holds if and only if

$$\mu < \begin{cases} \mu_3\,(r, b) & 0 \le r \le \delta\,(b) \\ \mu_4\,(r, b) & \delta\,(b) \le r \end{cases}, \tag{4.45}$$

where $\delta\,(b) \equiv (3b+1)\,/\,(5b-1)$ and

$$\mu_3\,(r, b) \equiv \frac{1+r}{2b\,(1-r)+1+r}, \quad \mu_4\,(r, b) \equiv \frac{1-r+\sqrt{1+2r+5r^2+4r\,(1+r)\,/b}}{2r\,(1+b)}.$$

Proof: See Appendix 9.

In order that FGMA(u) with $\tau = 2$ is stable, $\lambda^{F}(A)$ must satisfy condition (4.44).[20] If matrix A has $-\lambda^{F}(A)$ as its eigenvalue, then for stability $\lambda^{F}(A)$ must also satisfy the condition (4.45). With respect to r, $\mu_1(r,b)$ is increasing for $r \leq \beta(b)$ and $\mu_2(r,b)$ is decreasing for $\beta(b) \leq r$.[21] At $r = \beta(b)$, they take the common value $\mu^*(b) \equiv 3/(2b+1) > \mu_1(1,b) = 2/\sqrt{2b(b+1)}$.

Similarly, $\mu_3(r,b)$ is increasing for $r \leq \delta(b)$ and $\mu_4(r,b)$ is decreasing for $\delta(b) \leq r$. At $r = \delta(b)$, they take the common value $\mu^{**}(b) \equiv 2/(b+1) > 3/(2b+1)$. Condition (4.45) is more restrictive than (4.44) except for the range

$$r_1(b) \equiv \frac{2(b+1)(2b+1)}{5b^2+b-2+b\sqrt{17b^2+30b+17}} < r < 1.$$

If $b = 2.4$ $(k+l = 0.4)$, then

$$\beta = 4.142, \quad \mu^* = 0.517; \quad \delta = 0.745, \quad \mu^{**} = 0.588; \quad r_1 = 0.636.$$

The value of r under which the constraint on μ for stability becomes loosest is larger than 1 for $\theta = 0$ and less than 1 for $\theta = \pi$. The constraint on positive eigenvalues becomes loosiest when the demand forecast is formed by

$$s_i^e(t) = \frac{b-1}{3b}s_i(t-1) + \frac{2b+1}{3b}s_i(t-2), \tag{4.46}$$

not by the simple moving average. For $b = 2.4$, this represents $s_i^e(t) = 0.194s_i(t-1) + 0.806s_i(t-2)$. Moreover, since

$$\mu_1(0,b) = \frac{1}{b} > \mu_2(\infty,b) = \frac{1}{2b-1},$$

the forecast $s_i^e(t) = s_i(t-2)$ (the case of $r = \infty$) sets a stricter constraint on positive eigenvalues than the forecast $s_i^e(t) = s_i(t-1)$. As we have already seen, when r increases from 0 to 1, the direction in which the constraint for stability becomes most restrictive changes from $\theta = \pi$ to $\theta = \pm\pi/2$. Figure 4.17a illustrates the bounds on μ satisfying $\overline{\phi}(2, r, \mu, \theta, b) < 1$ for $\theta = 0, \pm\pi/2$, and π $(b = 2.4)$. The bound corresponding to $\theta = \pm\pi/2$ is located below that corresponding to $\theta = \pi$ unless r is nearly zero or very large, and touches $1/(2b\eta(2,r)+1)$ only at $r = 1$.

If $\tau = 3$, (4.42) becomes a quadratic equation. In this case, the stability condition corresponding to $\theta = 0$ cannot be expressed in such an explicit manner as (4.44). However, because of Theorem 8, the stability condition corresponding to $\theta = \pi$ is

[20] This is identical with the stability condition of Metzler's model (inequality (3.24) in the previous chapter) if μ is replaced by c, r by $-\eta/(1+\eta)$, and $1+k$ by b (Metzler 1941).

[21] Theorem 9 can be extended for $-1/2 \leq r < 0$. Since $\mu_2(-1/2,b) < \mu_2(0,b)$, demand forecast by $s_i^e(t) = s_i(t-1) + h(s_i(t-1) - s_i(t-2))$ $(0 < h < 1)$ is more likely to cause instability than the static expectation.

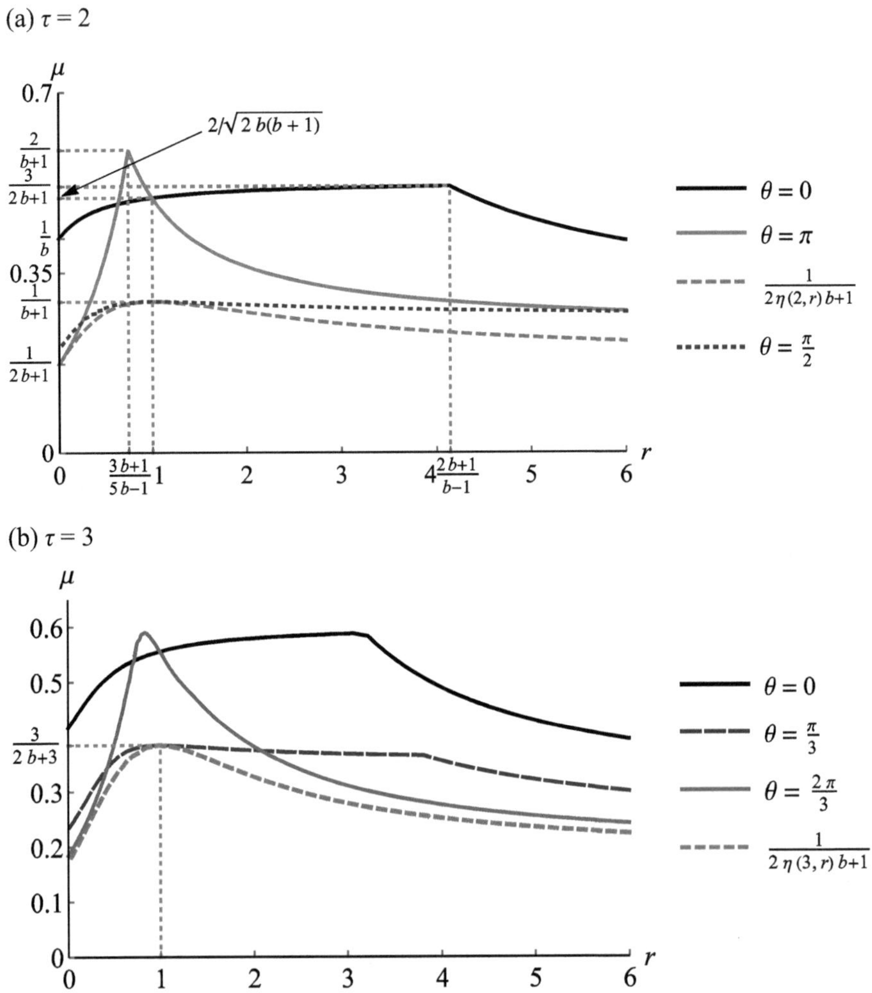

Fig. 4.17 Effect of geometric ratio r on stability

$\mu < 1/(2b\eta\,(3, r) + 1)$, and it is more restrictive than those corresponding to other values of θ. Figure 4.17b illustrates the bounds on μ satisfying $\overline{\phi}\,(3, r, \mu, \theta, b) < 1$ for $\theta = 0, \pm\pi/3, \pm 2\pi/3$, and π $(b = 2.4)$. Like the case of $\tau = 2$, the value of r under which the constraint on μ for stability becomes loosest is larger than 1 for $\theta = 0$. The constraint corresponding to $\theta = \pm\pi/3$ coincides with the constraint corresponding to $\theta = \pi$ only at $r = 1$.

Figure 4.18 shows how the stable region of A's eigenvalues on the complex plane shifts when r increases under a fixed averaging period ($\tau = 2, 3$). When $\tau = 2$, as r increases from 0 to 1, the stable region first expands in all directions but slightly shrinks nearby $\theta = \pi$ as r gets close to 1. As shown by Theorem 9, on the negative

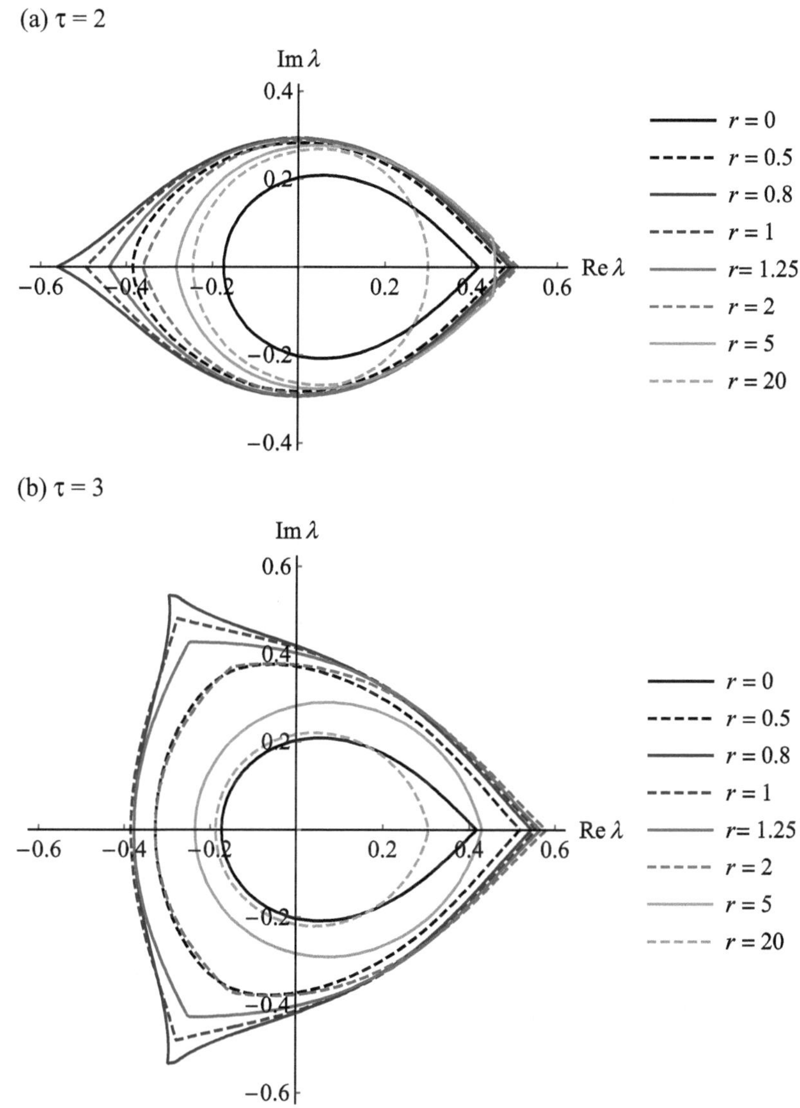

Fig. 4.18 Bounds on eigenvalues of A for stability of FGMA

part of the real axis, this contraction occurs for $(3b + 1)/(5b - 1) < r < 1$. However, this does not substantially affect stability because before this contraction starts, the stable region becomes narrower nearby the positive real axis than nearby the negative real axis. When r increases over 1, the stable region expands slightly nearby the positive real axis up to $r = (2b + 1)/(b - 1)$ (demand forecast by (4.46) corresponds to this value). However, it shrinks in most other directions, especially nearby the negative real axis. Further increases in r contract the stable region in all directions, including the nearby positive real axis.

When $\tau = 3$, the direction in which the constraint for stability becomes most restrictive remains $\theta = \pi$ irrespective of r. Apart from this point, a shift in the stable region could have a similar property as the case $\tau = 2$. As r increases from 0 to 1, the stable region expands except for small reversals which occur nearby the directions of $\theta = 2\pi/3$ and $\theta = 4\pi/3$ only when r is very close to 1. As r increases over 1, the stable region shrinks except for small reversals, which occur nearby the positive ax only when r is not so far from 1. Almost the same argument applies for a larger τ. Thus, despite certain exceptions nearby the directions of $\theta = 2k\pi/\tau$, the stable region widens overall as r gets closer to 1 from either the upper or lower side. Thus, we can conclude that *the more evenly the weights are assigned to past periods, the more likely it is that the system is stable.*

Next, we consider the effect of averaging period τ under a fixed geometric ratio r. Figure 4.19 illustrates how the stable region shifts by changes in τ for $r = 0.75$ and $r = 10$. When $r < 1$, as τ increases from a small value, the stable region expands overall, though partial reversals occur along with the shift of the directions in which the stable region becomes locally most narrow. As τ increases toward infinity, the stable region of FGMA approaches to that of GMA with smoothing constant $\gamma = 1 - r$. This convergence proceeds rapidly when r is small. The stable region of GMA contains that of FGMA with the same geometric ratio and a finite averaging period. Therefore, FGMA cannot be stabilized by any increase in τ if GMA with $\gamma = 1 - r$ is unstable.

When $r > 1$, forecast (4.37) does not converge to the exponential smoothing. As long as r is close to 1, the shifting of the stable region has similar properties to the case $r < 1$. However, as r moves far away from 1, increase in the averaging period τ does not have stabilizing effect anymore. In fact, when $r = 10$, the stable region shrinks in all the directions when τ increases from 2 to 3, and its hardly moves by its further increases. This near immobility of the stable region to changes in τ larger than 3 is common in cases where r is very or infinitely large (recall that $r = \infty$ corresponds to the forecast $s_i^e(t) = s_i(t - \tau)$). Thus, we can conclude that looking back the distant past, in itself, does not stabilize the process.

4.5 Conclusions

In the general equilibrium theory, the *tâtonnement*-type price adjustment process is supposed to play the role of leading the economy toward market equilibrium. Notable basic assumptions common to models of this *tâtonnement* process are centrally organized markets, lack of buffer inventories, and unlimited intellectual resources. In comparison with these models, our models of the quantity adjustment process have three important characteristics. First, both the buyer and seller have the freedom to carry out the transaction they have just concluded based only on their mutual consent, *without awaiting the establishment of an overall equilibrium*. In this

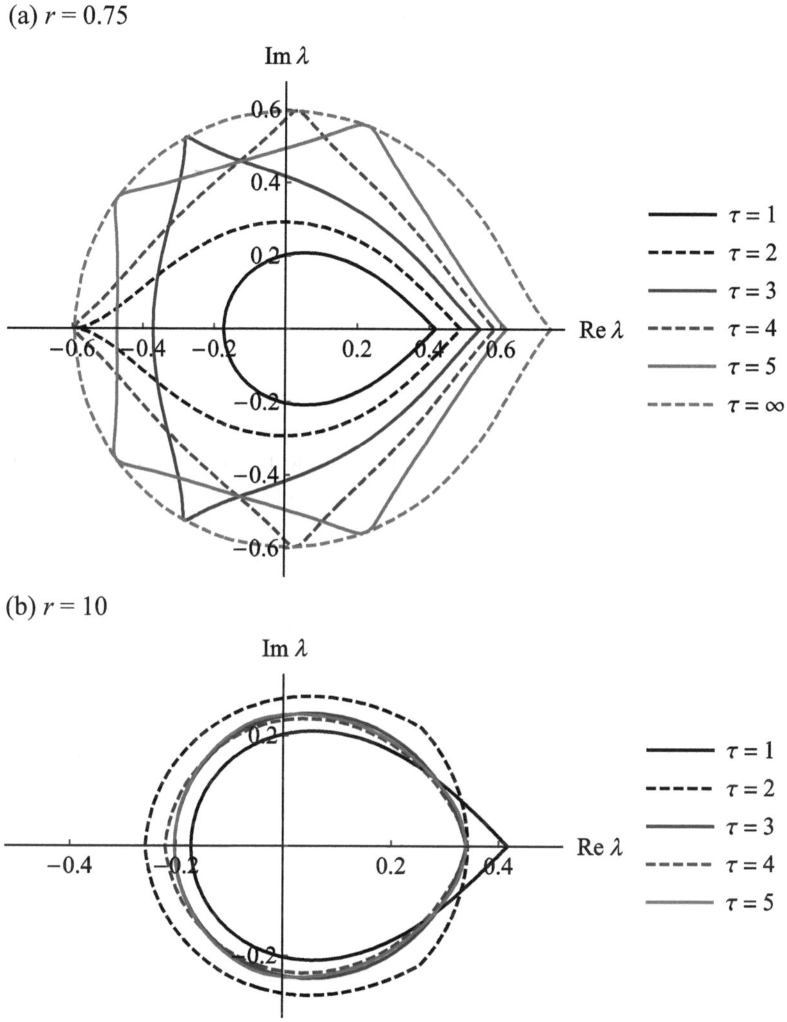

Fig. 4.19 Bounds on eigenvalues of A for stability of GMA

sense, in quantity adjustment, not only individual production and ordering decisions but also individual transactions are *decentralized*. Second, quantity adjustment can attain the balance of production and demand through *the successive process* where firms change their *actual* productions and raw material orders repeatedly in order to hold adequate scales of buffer inventories. In this process, the gap between supply and demand (or purchase and consumption) is absorbed by product (or raw materials) inventories. Third, for any firm, production and ordering rules for avoiding frequent stockout occurrences are *fully practicable with several easily obtainable quantity signals and simple calculations using them*. Since short-term decisions take the form of automated routines, firms can secure time to deliberate on middle- and long-term decisions.[22]

The quantity adjustment process is stable if each firm simply replenishes sold product and consumed raw materials, or uses a fixed demand forecast. Potential instability arises from succesive corrections in demand forecast based on the actual demand, as well as setting desirable levels of inventories. Since the process with "perfect foresight" is likely to be unstable, it is wrong to attribute instability to the inaccuracy in forecasting. In both the simple moving average and the geometric moving average, which are two typical forecasting methods based on demands recorded in the past periods, the stability of the process depends on the following factors: input matrix, each firm's parameters representing the extent of averaging (the averaging period or the smoothing constant), and each firm's buffer coefficients for product and raw material inventories. An increase in the Frobenius root of input matrix and an increase in any of buffer coefficients narrow the range of other parameters for stability. In the case of the simple moving average, the stability condition becomes most restrictive when input matrix is cyclic with a particular cycle corresponding to the set of each firm's averaging period (two-cyclic if all averaging periods are odd). In the case of the geometric moving average, the stability condition becomes most restrictive when the input matrix is two-cyclic. Since negative and complex eigenvalues of the input matrix reflect intersectoral input-output relationship, these complexities indicate that the interactions between sectors can influence stability.

Whereas it is highly probable that the static expectation causes instability, it is possible to eliminate this instability by averaging demands during past periods in the formation of demand forecast, that is, by increasing the averaging period or decreasing the smoothing constant. The stabilizing effect of increasing the extent of averaging in demand forecast is especially strong when the extent of averaging before the change is very small. Interestingly, in the case of the simple moving average, an increase in the averaging period could destabilize the stable system under specific conditions. This destabilization occurs by a shift in the directions on the complex plane where the constraint on stability becomes most restrictive (such reversals never occur in the case of the geometric moving average). However, despite certain exceptional cases, *moderate averaging in the formation of demand forecast is sufficient to ensure the stability of the quantity adjustment process.*[23]

The above two forecasting methods are special cases of the finite geometric moving average. In this method, the extent of averaging is measured by each firm's averaging period and allocation of weights among past periods. When the input matrix is two-cyclic and each firm's averaging period is odd, the necessary and

---

[22]Assumptions in our models about decisions by individual firms satisfy the following three prerequisites set by Simon (1959, p. 275): "(1) The models must be formulated so as to require for their application only data that are obtainable. ... (2) The models must call only for practicable computations. ... (3) The models must not demand unobtainable forecast information."

[23]As remarked in the previous chapter, this fact was first discovered by Taniguchi (1991) using numerical computations.

sufficient condition for stability is loosened by giving past demand more uniform weights, as well as by increasing the averaging period. Under a given averaging period, the process is most likely to be stable in the case of demand forecast by the simple moving averaging. This implies that stabilization by averaging is the mixed result of (i) r*eferring to a larger number of past periods* and (ii) *allocating weights more evenly among past periods*. A decrease in the smoothing constant corresponds to the second change. Although partial reversals could occur in general cases, more even allocation of weights usually contributes to stabilization.

Appendix

1. Proof of Theorem 1[24]

(i) Let $\phi \neq 0$ be an eigenvalue of Φ, and let $\xi = [\xi_\tau, \xi_{\tau-1}, \ldots, \xi_1, \eta]$ be an associated eigenvector, where ξ_i and η are $1 \times n$ vectors. Then, from $\phi\xi = \xi\Phi$ we obtain

$$\xi = \left[\phi^\tau \eta, \phi^{\tau-1}\eta, \ldots, \phi\eta, \eta\right], \quad \phi\eta = \eta Q(\phi) A,$$

$$Q(\phi) \equiv (\phi - 1)\left(\phi^{-1}U_1 + \cdots + \phi^{-\tau}U_\tau\right) B + I.$$

Therefore, ϕ is also an eigenvalue of $Q(\phi)A$. Conversely, if ϕ is an eigenvalue of $Q(\phi)A$ and η is the corresponding eigenvector, then it is also an eigenvalue of Φ and the above ξ is the corresponding eigenvector. Consequently, $\phi \neq 0$ is an eigenvalue of Φ *if and only if* ϕ is an eigenvalue of $Q(\phi)A$.

To prove the contraposition, assume $\rho(\Phi) \geq 1$ and ϕ is an eigenvalue of Φ such that $\phi \geq 1$. Then, from the above fact, it follows $1 \leq \rho(Q(\phi)A)$. Let q_i be the i-th diagonal element of matrix $Q(\phi)$, then

$$|q_i| = \left|\left(1 - \frac{1}{\phi^{\tau_i}}\right)\frac{b_i}{\tau_i} + 1\right| \leq \frac{2b_i}{\tau_i} + 1 \tag{4.47}$$

Let C^+ denote a matrix obtained from a matrix C by replacing its elements with their absolute values. It is known that $\rho(C) \leq \lambda^{\mathrm{F}}(C^+)$ holds for any complex square matrix C.[25] Since $Q(\phi)$ is diagonal and A is nonnegative, (4.47) leads to

$$(QA)^+ \leq Q^+A \leq \left(2T^{-1}B + I\right)A.$$

[24]The method of proof used here is based on Simonovits (1999). The theorem itself was first proved in Morioka (2005).

[25]On this theorem, see Nikaido (1961, p. 114).

Since ϕ is an eigenvalue of QA, these inequalities lead to

$$1 \le \rho(QA) \le \lambda^{\mathrm{F}}\left((QA)^{+}\right) \le \lambda^{\mathrm{F}}\left(Q^{+}A\right) \le \lambda^{\mathrm{F}}\left(\left(2T^{-1}B+I\right)A\right).$$

(ii) To prove the contraposition, assume that $\omega\lambda^{\mathrm{F}}(A)$ is an eigenvalue of A satisfying (4.22) and $\lambda^{*} = \lambda^{\mathrm{F}}((2T^{-1}B+I)A) \ge 1$. Let $\phi \ne 0$, $\Psi = \omega^{-1}\phi$, and $\tilde{A} = \omega^{-1}A$; then since $\omega^{\tau_i} = -1$ for any i, ϕ is an eigenvalue of Φ if and only if Ψ is an eigenvalue of $F(\psi)\tilde{A}$, where

$$F(\psi) = \begin{bmatrix} 1+\psi^{-\tau_1} & \cdots & 0 \\ \vdots & \ddots & \vdots \\ 0 & \cdots & 1+\psi^{-\tau_n} \end{bmatrix} T^{-1}B + I.$$

For any $\Psi > 0$, matrix $F(\Psi)A$ is a nonnegative and identically cyclic with matrix A; hence $\omega\lambda^{\mathrm{F}}(F(\Psi)A)$ is an eigenvalue of $F(\Psi)A$, and hence $\lambda^{\mathrm{F}}(F(\Psi)A)$ is an eigenvalue of $F(\psi)\tilde{A}$. Let

$$h(\psi) = \psi - \lambda^{\mathrm{F}}(F(\psi)A) \text{ for } \psi > 0,$$

then $h(\Psi)$ is an eigenvalue of $\psi I - F(\psi)\tilde{A}$; hence $h(\Psi) = 0$ implies that $\phi = \omega\Psi$ is an eigenvalue of Φ. It follows from $F(\lambda^{*}) \le F(1)$ that $\lambda^{\mathrm{F}}(F(\lambda^{*})A) \le \lambda^{\mathrm{F}}(F(1)A) = \lambda^{*}$;hence

$$h(1) = 1-\lambda^{\mathrm{F}}(F(1)A) = 1-\lambda^{*} \le 0,\ h(\lambda^{*}) = \lambda^{\mathrm{F}}(F(1)A)-\lambda^{\mathrm{F}}(F(\lambda^{*})A) \ge 0.$$

Since polynomial h is continuous with respect to Ψ, there exists an α such that

$$1 \le \alpha \le \lambda^{\mathrm{F}}\left(\left(2T^{-1}B+I\right)A\right),\quad h(\alpha) = \alpha - \lambda^{\mathrm{F}}(F(\alpha)A) = 0;$$

hence $\alpha\omega$ is an eigenvalue of Φ. Therefore,

$$\rho(\Phi) \ge |\alpha\omega| \ge 1.$$

2. Proof of Theorem 2

(i) The characteristic equation of Φ' is

$$F(\phi) = \left|\phi^{\tau+1}I - \phi^{\tau}\left(\frac{b}{\tau}+1\right)A + \frac{b}{\tau}A\right| = 0.$$

Let Λ be the Jordan normal form of matrix A, then there exists a regular matrix X satisfying $XAX^{-1} = \Lambda$ and

$$\begin{aligned} F(\phi) &= \left|X\left(\phi^{\tau+1}I - \phi^{\tau}\left(\tfrac{b}{\tau}+1\right)A + \tfrac{b}{\tau}A\right)X^{-1}\right| \\ &= \prod_{i=1}^{\nu}\left(\phi^{\tau+1} - \phi^{\tau}\left(\tfrac{b}{\tau}+1\right)\lambda_i + \tfrac{b}{\tau}\lambda_i\right)^{\kappa_i}, \end{aligned}$$

where ν is the number of A's different eigenvalues and κ_i is the multiplicity of an eigenvalue $\lambda_i = \mu_i e^{i\theta_i}$ (thus $\kappa_1 + \cdots + \kappa_n = n$). Thus, $\rho(\Phi') < 1$ is equivalent to $\overline{\phi}(\mu_i, \theta_i, \tau, b) < 1$ for any $i \in \{1, \ldots, \nu\}$.

(ii) Let $\xi e^{i\omega} = \xi(\cos\omega + i \sin\omega)$ $(\xi \geq 0)$ be a root of (4.24). Then, it satisfies

$$f(\xi, \omega, \theta) \equiv \xi^{\tau+1} e^{i(\tau+1)\omega} - \left(\frac{b}{\tau} + 1\right) \mu e^{i(\tau\omega+\theta)} \xi^{\tau} + \frac{b}{\tau} \mu e^{i\theta} = 0.$$

Let $\theta' = \theta + 2\pi/\tau, \omega' = \omega + 2\pi/\tau, \theta'' = 2\pi/\tau - \theta, \omega'' = 2\pi/\tau - \omega$, then

$$f\left(\xi, \omega', \theta'\right) = e^{2i\frac{\pi}{\tau}} f(\xi, \omega, \theta) = 0, \;\; f\left(\xi, \omega'', \theta''\right) = e^{2i\frac{\pi}{\tau}} f(\xi, -\omega, -\theta) = 0.$$

The second equation is obtained by observing that $f(\xi, -\omega, -\theta)$ is the conjugate of $f(\xi, \omega, \theta)$. Therefore, when $\mu e^{i\theta}$ rotates by $2\pi/\tau$ radians on the complex plane, each of the solutions of (4.24) also rotates by $2\pi/\tau$ radians. Furthermore, if θ_1 and θ_2 are symmetric on the complex plane about the direction π/τ, two sets of the roots of (4.24) corresponding θ_1 and θ_2 are also symmetric about this direction.

(iii) This statement is obvious for $\mu = 0$, so let us assume $\mu > 0$. Let

$$g_+(\xi; \tau, b, \mu) \equiv -e^{-i\frac{\pi}{\tau}} f\left(\xi, \frac{\pi}{\tau}, \frac{\pi}{\tau}\right) = \xi^{\tau+1} - \xi^{\tau}\left(\frac{b}{\tau} + 1\right)\mu - \frac{b}{\tau}\mu,$$

and $\phi_+(\mu, \tau, b)$ be the unique positive ξ such that $g_+(\xi; \tau, b, \mu) = 0$.[26] By a theorem about the upper bound on roots of an algebraic equation[27], it follows $\overline{\phi}(\mu, \theta, \tau, b) \leq \phi_+(\mu, \tau, b)$, where the equality sign holds if and only if $\theta = \pi/\tau$. Hence, $\overline{\phi}(\mu, \pi/\tau, \tau, b) < 1$ holds if and only if

$$g_+(1; \tau, b, \mu) = (2b + \tau)(\overline{\mu} - \mu) > 0,$$

where $\overline{\mu} \equiv \tau/(2b + \tau)$. Therefore, $\overline{\phi}(\overline{\mu}, \pi/\tau, \tau, b) = 1$ and

$$\overline{\phi}(\mu, \theta, \tau, b) \leq \overline{\phi}(\mu, \pi/\tau, \tau, b) < 1 \text{ for } \mu < \overline{\mu}.$$

Let $\alpha \equiv -(b/\tau + 1)\mu, \beta \equiv b\mu/\tau$, then $1 - \alpha > \beta$. According to Schur's condition,[28] a necessary and sufficient condition for $\overline{\phi}(\mu, \theta, \tau, b) < 1$ is that all the following inequalities hold:

$$C_u \equiv \begin{vmatrix} I_u + \alpha e^{i\theta} J_u & \beta e^{i\theta} I_u \\ \beta e^{-i\theta} I_u & I_u + \alpha e^{-i\theta} J_u^{\mathrm{T}} \end{vmatrix} > 0 \;\; (u \in \{1, \ldots, \tau\}),$$

[26]By Descartes' rule of signs, a real algebraic equation whose coefficients change their signs from plus to minus only once has one and only one positive root. See Takagi (1965, p. 101)

[27]Concerning this theorem, refer to Takagi (1965, p. 104–105).

[28]Concerning Schur's condition, refer to Takagi (1965, pp. 373–376).

$$\tilde{C}_{\tau+1} \equiv \begin{vmatrix} I_{\tau+1} + \alpha e^{i\theta} J_{\tau+1} & \beta e^{i\theta} I_{\tau+1} + \alpha e^{i\theta} K_{\tau+1} \\ \beta e^{-i\theta} I_{\tau+1} + \alpha e^{-i\theta} K_{\tau+1}^{T} & I_{\tau+1} + \alpha e^{-i\theta} J_{\tau+1}^{T} \end{vmatrix} > 0, \tag{4.48}$$

Where I_u is the unit matrix of order u, $J_u \equiv \begin{bmatrix} 0 \; I_{u-1} \\ 0 \; 0_{u-1} \end{bmatrix}$, $K_{\tau+1} \equiv \begin{bmatrix} 0 \; O_{\tau} \\ 1 \; 0_{\tau} \end{bmatrix}$ (0_u is the zero row vector of order u, O_τ is the zero matrix of order τ), and T denotes transposition. Let $C_0 = 1, \delta \equiv 1 + \alpha^2 - \beta^2$. Then, since

$$C_u = \left| \delta I_u + L_u - \alpha^2 \begin{bmatrix} O_{u-1} & 0 \\ 0_{u-1} & 1 \end{bmatrix} \right|, \quad L_u \equiv \alpha e^{i\theta} J_u + \alpha e^{-i\theta} J_u^T,$$

C_u satisfies the following recursion formula:

$$C_u = \delta C_{u-1} - \alpha^2 C_{u-2}. \tag{4.49}$$

Similarly, from

$$\tilde{C}_{\tau+1} = \left| \delta I_{\tau+1} + L_{\tau+1} - \alpha^2 \begin{bmatrix} 1 & 0_{\tau-1} & 0 \\ 0_{\tau-1}^T & O_{\tau-1} & 0_{\tau-1}^T \\ 0 & 0_{\tau-1} & 1 \end{bmatrix} - \alpha\beta \left(K_{\tau+1} + K_{\tau+1}^T \right) \right|,$$

we have

$$\tilde{C}_{\tau+1} = \left(1 - \beta^2\right) C_\tau - \alpha^2 \left(1 + \beta^2\right) C_{\tau-1} - \alpha^2\beta^2 D_{\tau-1} + 2\left(-\alpha\right)^{\tau+1} \beta \cos \tau\theta,$$

$$D_0 = 0, \, D_u \equiv \begin{vmatrix} \delta I_{u-1} + L_{u-1} & 0 \\ 0 & \alpha^2 \end{vmatrix}.$$

It can be shown that D_u satisfies the same recursion formula as that of C_u. Let $C_{-1} = 1, D_{-1} = -1$, and

$$E_\tau \equiv \left(1 - \beta^2\right) C_\tau - \alpha^2 \left(1 + \beta^2\right) C_{\tau-1} - \alpha^2\beta^2 D_{\tau-1},$$

then $\tilde{C}_{\tau+1}$ can be written as

$$\tilde{C}_{\tau+1} = E_\tau + 2\left(-\alpha\right)^{\tau+1} \beta \cos \tau\theta, \tag{4.50}$$

where E_u satisfies the recursion formula:

$$E_0 = 1 - \alpha^2 - \beta^2, \quad E_1 = \left(1 - \beta^2\right)^2 - \alpha^2\left(1 + \beta^2\right), \quad E_u = \delta E_{u-1} - \alpha^2 E_{u-2}.$$

Assume $\mu > \overline{\mu}$, then $-\alpha + \beta = \mu/\overline{\mu} > 1$, hence

$$\delta^2 - 4\alpha^2 = \left((1+\alpha)^2 - \beta^2\right)\left((1-\alpha)^2 - \beta^2\right) < 0.$$

Let $\varepsilon = \alpha^2 + \beta^2 - 1$, $\eta = \sqrt{4\alpha^2 - \delta^2}$. From (4.49) and (4.50), we have[29]

$$C_u = 2\beta(-\alpha)^{u+1}\eta^{-1}\cos F(\mu, u, b) \ \ (u \in \{1, \dots, \tau\}),$$
$$\tilde{C}_{\tau+1} = 2\beta(-\alpha)^{\tau+1}(\cos G(\mu, \tau, b) + \cos \tau\theta)$$

where

$$F(\mu, u, b) \equiv u \arctan\ (\eta/\delta) + \arctan\ (\varepsilon/\eta),$$
$$G(\mu, \tau, b) \equiv \tau \arctan\ (\eta/\delta) + \arctan\ (\varepsilon/\eta) + \pi/2 = F(\mu, \tau, b) + \pi/2.$$

and arctan takes values in interval $[-\pi/2, \pi/2]$. Under the assumption $0 \le \theta \le \pi/\tau$ and $\overline{\mu} < \mu$, C_τ and $\tilde{C}_{\tau+1}$ can be simultaneously positive if and only if

$$\begin{aligned} F(\mu, \tau, b) = \tau \arctan \frac{\sqrt{(1-\mu^2)(\mu^2-\overline{\mu}^2)}}{\mu^2+\overline{\mu}} \\ + \arctan \frac{\mu^2(1+2b^2\tau^{-2}\overline{\mu})-\overline{\mu}}{\sqrt{(1-\mu^2)(\mu^2-\overline{\mu}^2)}} < \frac{\pi}{2} - \tau\theta. \end{aligned} \tag{4.51}$$

Note that $F(\overline{\mu}, \tau, b) = -\pi/2$, $F(1, \tau, b) = \pi/2$. Since

$$-\pi/2 \le F(\mu, 1, b) < F(\mu, 2, b) < \cdots < F(\mu, \tau, b),$$

(4.51) guarantees $C_1 > 0$, $C_2 > 0$, $\dots$, $C_{\tau-1} > 0$. Thus, providing that $\mu > \overline{\mu}$ and $0 \le \theta < \pi/\tau$, (4.48) holds if and only if

$$-\pi/2 < F(\mu, \tau, b) < \pi/2 - \tau\theta.$$

---

[29] When the characteristic equation of a second-order linear difference equation has a pair of conjugates roots $\{\lambda, \overline{\lambda}\}$, its solution is written as

$$x(t) = |\lambda|^t \frac{\sqrt{x^2(0)|\lambda|^2 - 2x(0)x(1)\operatorname{Re}\lambda + x^2(1)}}{|\operatorname{Im}\ \lambda|}\cos(t\theta + \omega),$$

$$\tan\theta = \frac{\operatorname{Im}\lambda}{\operatorname{Re}\lambda}, \tan\omega = \frac{x(0)\operatorname{Re}\lambda - x(1)}{x(0)\operatorname{Im}\lambda},$$

where $x(0)$ and $x(1)$ are initial values.

Let $\mu^{\dagger} \equiv \sqrt{\frac{\tau+2}{\tau+2b}}$, then $\mu^{\dagger 2} - \overline{\mu}^2 = \frac{2(1+b\overline{\mu})}{2b+\tau} > 0$. Thus, differentiating F with respect to μ, we have

$$F_{\mu}(\mu, \tau, b) = \frac{\tau\left(\mu^{\dagger 2} - \mu^2\right)}{\mu\sqrt{\left(1-\mu^2\right)\left(\mu^2 - \overline{\mu}^2\right)}} > 0$$

for $\overline{\mu} < \mu < \mu^{\dagger}$. Since $F(\mu, \tau, b)$ increase from $-\pi/2$ to $F\left(\mu^{\dagger}, \tau, b\right) > \pi/2$ as μ increases from $\overline{\mu}$ to $\mu^{\dagger}$, there exists a unique μ such that

$$\overline{\mu} < \mu < \mu^{\dagger}, \quad F(\mu, \tau, b) = \pi/2 - \tau\theta.$$

Let us denote this unique μ by $\mu^{*}(\theta, \tau, b)$, then (4.51) is equivalent to $\mu < \mu^{*}(\theta, \tau, b)$ for $0 \leq \theta < \pi/\tau$. When $\theta = \pi/\tau$, (4.51) is never satisfied, and from the above-mentioned fact, (4.48) is equivalent to $\mu < \overline{\mu}$. However, by definition we have $F\left(\mu^{*}(\pi/\tau, \tau, b), \tau, b\right) = -\pi/2$, hence, $\mu^{*}(\pi/\tau, \tau, b) = \overline{\mu}$, and consequently, (4.48) is equivalent to $\mu < \mu^{*}(\theta, \tau, b)$ for $0 \leq \theta \leq \pi/\tau$.

(iv) For $0 \leq \theta < \theta' < \pi/\tau$, it holds

$$F\left(\mu^{*}\left(\theta', \tau, b\right), \tau, b\right) = \pi/2 - \tau\theta' < \pi/2 - \tau\theta = F\left(\mu^{*}(\theta, \tau, b), \tau, b\right),$$

which implies $\mu^{*}(\theta', \tau, b) < \mu^{*}(\theta, \tau, b)$.

(v) The first part of this statement directly follows from statement (iii). As for the second part, $\mu^{*}(0, 1, b)$ and $\mu^{*}(0, 2, b)$ can be directly calculated from (4.48).

(vi) Let $\mu_1 \equiv \sqrt{\frac{\tau(1+\tau)}{2b^2+(2b+\tau)(\tau-1)}}$ and $\xi_1 \equiv \left(\frac{b\tau+b}{\tau+b}\right)^{\frac{1}{\tau}}$, then we have

$$\begin{aligned} F(\mu_1, \tau, b) &= \pi/2 - \arctan\sqrt{\xi_1^{2\tau} - 1} + \tau \arctan \tau^{-1}\sqrt{\xi_1^{2\tau} - 1} \\ &\geq \pi/2 \geq \pi/2 - \tau\theta = F\left(\mu^{*}(\theta, \tau, b), \tau, b\right), \end{aligned}$$

here we used the fact that $x \arctan a/x \geq \arctan a$ holds for any $x \geq 1$ and $a > 0$. Hence $\mu_1(\tau, b) \geq \mu^{*}(\theta, \tau, b)$, where the equality sign holds if and only if $\tau = 1$, $\theta = 0$ (note that $\mu_1 < \mu^{\dagger}$). Treating τ as a continuous variable and differentiating F with respect to τ, for $\overline{\mu} < \mu < 1$ we obtain

$$\begin{aligned} F_{\tau}(\mu, \tau, b) &= \frac{-(1-\mu^2)(1+b\overline{\mu})}{(b+\tau)\sqrt{(1-\mu^2)(\mu^2-\overline{\mu}^2)}} + \arctan\frac{\sqrt{(1-\mu^2)(\mu^2-\overline{\mu}^2)}}{\overline{\mu}+\mu^2} \\ &< \sqrt{\frac{1-\mu^2}{\mu^2-\overline{\mu}^2}}\frac{\left(2b^2+(2b+\tau)(\tau-1)\right)\left(\mu^2-\mu_1^2\right)}{(b+\tau)(2b+\tau)(\overline{\mu}+\mu^2)}. \end{aligned}$$

Here we used the fact that $\arctan x < x$ for $x > 0$. Assume $0 \le \theta < \pi/\tau$, then $\mu_1 > \mu^* > \overline{\mu}$, hence $F_\tau < 0$ at $\mu = \mu^*$. If $\mu^*(\theta, \tau, b) < (\tau+1)/(2b+\tau+1)$, then $\mu^*(\theta, \tau, b) < \mu^*(\pi/(\tau+1), \tau+1, b) \le \mu^*(\tau\theta/(\tau+1), \tau+1, b)$. Otherwise, since μ_1 is increasing with respect to τ, we have

$$F\left(\mu^*(\theta, \tau, b), \tau+1, b\right) < F\left(\mu^*(\theta, \tau, b), \tau, b\right) = \frac{\pi}{2} - \tau\theta$$

$$= \frac{\pi}{2} - (\tau+1)\frac{\tau\theta}{\tau+1} = F\left(\mu^*\left(\frac{\tau}{\tau+1}\theta, \tau+1, b\right), \tau+1, b\right).$$

Thus, $\mu^*(\theta, \tau, b) < \mu^*(\tau\theta/(\tau+1), \tau+1, b)$, and this holds also for $\theta = \pi/\tau$.

Next, let $\mu_2(\tau, b) \equiv (\tau+1)/(\tau+2b-1)$. Note that $F(\mu_2(1,b), 1, b) = \pi/2$ holds because $\mu^*(0, 1, b) = 1/b = \mu_2(1, b)$. Since

$$F(\mu_2, \tau, b) = \tau \arctan \frac{2\sqrt{(b-1)\left(b+2b\tau+\tau^2\right)}}{1+2b\tau+\tau^2} + \arctan \frac{b+2b\tau+2\tau^2-b\tau^2}{2\tau\sqrt{(b-1)\left(b+2b\tau+\tau^2\right)}},$$

$$F_\tau(\mu_2, \tau, b) = -\sqrt{\frac{b-1}{b+2b\tau+\tau^2}}\frac{2\left(\tau+2b-1+\tau^2+b\tau\right)}{(\tau+2b-1)(\tau+1)} + \arctan \frac{2\sqrt{(b-1)\left(b+2b\tau+\tau^2\right)}}{1+2b\tau+\tau^2},$$

$$F_{\tau b}(\mu_2, \tau, b) = \sqrt{\frac{b-1}{b+2b\tau+\tau^2}}\frac{(\tau-1)\left(3\tau^2+2\tau+1\right)+2\left(b\left(3\tau^2+\tau-1\right)+1\right)}{\left(b+2b\tau+\tau^2\right)(\tau+2b-1)^2} > 0,$$

we have $F_\tau(\mu_2(\tau, b), \tau, b) \ge F_\tau(\mu_2(\tau, 2), \tau, 2) > 0$ (the last inequality sign can be confirmed by some mechanical calculation). Therefore,

$$\pi/2 = F(\mu_2(1, b), 1, b) < F(\mu_2(\tau, b), \tau, b),$$

which implies $\mu_2(\tau, b) > \mu^*(0, \tau, b)$ for $\tau > 1$

(vii) Differentiating F with respect to b, we have

$$F_b(\mu, \tau, b) = \sqrt{\frac{1-\mu^2}{\mu^2-\overline{\mu}^2}}\frac{\tau(1+b\overline{\mu})}{b(b+\tau)} > 0$$

for $\overline{\mu} < \mu < 1$. Hence, if $b < b'$, then

$$F\left(\mu^*\left(\theta,\tau,b'\right),\tau,b'\right) = F\left(\mu^*\left(\theta,\tau,b\right),\tau,b\right) < F\left(\mu^*\left(\theta,\tau,b\right),\tau,b'\right),$$

which implies $\mu^*(\theta,\tau,b') < \mu^*(\theta,\tau,b)$.

3. Proof of Theorem 3

(i) By virtue of Theorem 4.2(ii), we can assume $0 \le \theta \le \pi/\tau$ without losing generality. Let $\overline{\psi}_m(\mu,\theta,\tau,b)$ denote, for $m > 0$, the dominant root of the equation:

$$\psi^{\tau+1} - \left(\frac{b}{\tau}+1\right)m^{-1}\mu e^{i\theta}\psi^{\tau} + \frac{b}{\tau}m^{-(\tau+1)}\mu e^{i\theta} = 0. \qquad (4.52)$$

Obviously, Ψ is a solution of (4.52) if and only if $m\Psi$ is a solution of (4.24), therefore, $\overline{\psi}_m(\mu,\theta,\tau,b) \lesseqgtr 1$ is equivalent to $\overline{\phi}(\mu,\theta,\tau,b) \lesseqgtr m$. Let

$$B \equiv b+\tau,\ M \equiv m^{\tau},\ \alpha \equiv -\frac{B\mu}{\tau m},\ \beta \equiv \frac{b\mu}{\tau m M},\ X \equiv \frac{b}{B},\ \xi_0 \equiv X^{\frac{1}{\tau}},$$

$$Y \equiv X(1+\tau),\quad \mu' = \frac{\tau m M}{BX},\quad \mu_- \equiv \frac{\tau m M}{B(M-X)},\quad \mu_+ \equiv \frac{\tau m M}{B(M+X)},$$

$$\tilde{\mu} \equiv \frac{mM}{B}\sqrt{\frac{\tau(\tau+2)}{M^2-X^2}},\quad \mu_0 \equiv \frac{m(1+\tau)}{B},\quad \mu_1 \equiv \frac{m\tau M}{B\sqrt{M^2-Y^2}}.$$

Note that $X < 1 < Y = (b+b\tau)/(b+\tau)$. Define E_τ similarly to the case of $m=1$, then $\overline{\psi}_m < 1$ requires

$$0 < 1-\beta^2,\quad 0 < E_\tau + 2(-a)^{\tau+1}\beta\cos\tau\theta \le E_\tau + 2(-a)^{\tau+1}\beta.$$

By induction, it can be shown that $E_\tau + 2(-a)^{\tau+1}\beta$ is a product of

$$(1+\alpha+\beta)(1-\alpha\pm\beta)\,q_\tau(\alpha,\beta)^2,$$

where $q_\tau(\alpha,\beta)$ is a τ-th order polynomial of α, β and the double sign corresponds to odd τ and even τ in this order. Since $1-\alpha\pm\beta > 0$ for $\beta < 1$, $\overline{\psi}_m < 1$ implies

$$1-\beta = 1-\mu/\mu' > 0,\quad 1+\alpha+\beta = 1-\mu/\mu_- > 0$$

By the Gauss' theorem about the bound on the solution of an algebraic equation[30], $\overline{\psi}_m < 1$ also requires $\mu < \mu_0$. Since $\mu_- - \mu_0 = m(M - Y)/(B(M - X))$, μ_0 becomes more restrictive than μ_- when $\xi_0 < \xi_1 < m$.

Like the case of $\overline{\phi}(\mu, \theta, \tau, b)$, if $\mu < \mu_+$, then $1 + \alpha - \beta > 0$, which ensures $\overline{\psi}_m < 1$. If $\mu_+ < \mu < \mu_-$, then $1 + \alpha - \beta < 0$, and $\overline{\psi}_m < 1$ holds if and only if $1 + \alpha + \beta > 0$ and $-\pi/2 < F^m(\mu, \tau, b) < \pi/2 - \tau\theta$ (hence $\theta < \pi/\tau$), where

$$F^m(\mu, \tau, b) = \tau \arctan H/G_1 + \arctan G_2/H, \quad G_1 \equiv 1 + \alpha^2 - \beta^2 > 0,$$

$$G_2 \equiv \alpha^2 + \beta^2 - 1, H \equiv \sqrt{-\left((1+\alpha)^2 - \beta^2\right)\left((1-\alpha)^2 - \beta^2\right)} > 0.$$

Note that $\mu_+ < \mu'$ and $F^m(\mu_+, \tau, b) = \pi/2$ for any $m > 0$. Let F^m_μ be the partial derivative of F^m with respect to μ. If $M \leq X$, then $1 + \alpha + \beta > 0$, $F^m(\mu', \tau, b) \geq \pi/2$, and

$$F^m_\mu(\mu, \tau, b) = \frac{m^2\tau(\tau + 2)M^2 - B^2\left(M^2 - X^2\right)\mu^2}{\mu\tau m^2 M^2 H} > 0.$$

If $M > X$, then $1 + \alpha + \beta > 0$ is equivalent to $\mu < \mu_-$, and by definition, we have $\tilde{\mu}^2 - \mu_+^2 = \frac{2\tau m^2 M^2 (M+Y)}{B^2(M+X)^2(M-X)} > 0$. Accordingly,

$$F^m_\mu(\mu, \tau, b) = B^2\left(M^2 - X^2\right)\left(\tilde{\mu}^2 - \mu^2\right)/\left(\mu\tau m^2 M^2 H\right) > 0$$

for $\mu_+ < \mu' < \tilde{\mu}$. Since $G_2(\mu_-) = \frac{2MX}{(M-X)^2} > 0$, we have $F^m(\mu_-, \tau, b) = \pi/2$. Therefore, there exists a unique μ such that $\mu_+ \leq \mu \leq \mu'$ for $M \leq X$, $\mu_+ \leq \mu \leq \min\{\mu_-, \tilde{\mu}\}$ for $X < M$, and

$$F^m(\mu, \tau, b) + \tau\theta = \pi/2.$$

Let us denote this unique μ by $\mu^*_m(\theta, \tau, b)$, then $\mu^*_m(\pi/\tau, \tau, b) = \mu^+$; therefore, like the case of $m = 1$, $\overline{\psi}_m(\mu, \theta, \tau, b) < 1$ is equivalent to $\mu < \mu^*_m(\theta, \tau, b)$.

Because of the continuity of $\overline{\psi}_m$ with respect to its arguments, $\mu = \mu^*_m(\theta, \tau, b)$ is equivalent to $\overline{\phi}(\mu, \theta, \tau, b) = m$. Assume $\mu < \mu' < 1$ and $\overline{\phi}\left(\mu', \theta, \tau, b\right) = m$, then $\mu < \mu' = \mu^*_m(\theta, \tau, b)$, which implies $\overline{\phi}(\mu, \theta, \tau, b) < m = \overline{\phi}\left(\mu', \theta, \tau, b\right)$.[31]

[30] The maximum solution (measured by absolute value) of an algebraic equation is not smaller than that of its derivative function. On this theorem, see Takagi (1965, pp. 102–104).

[31] This result can be shown also by differentiating $\overline{\phi}(\mu, \theta, \tau, b)$ with respect to μ. In fact, $\overline{\phi}$ is differentiable with respect to any of its arguments except at $\theta = 0$, $\mu = (1 + \tau)Y^{1/\tau}/B$. However, it is a tedious work to prove this and to examine the sign of the derivatives. See Morioka (2005, pp. 280–282).

(ii) Assume $0 \leq \theta < \theta' \leq \pi/\tau$ and $\overline{\phi}\left(\mu, \theta', \tau, b\right) = m$. Then, since

$$F^m(\mu, \tau, b) = \pi/2 - \theta'\tau < \pi/2 - \theta\tau,$$

we have $\overline{\phi}(\mu, \theta, \tau, b) < m = \overline{\phi}\left(\mu, \theta', \tau, b\right)$.

(iii) Assume $m > \xi_0$ $(M > X)$ and $Z \equiv X\sqrt{2\tau + 1}$. Note that $X < Z < Y$. Differentiating F^m with respect to τ, we have

$$F_\tau^m(\mu, \tau, b) = \frac{K_1 + BK_2 \log m}{m^2\tau^2 M^2 BH} + \arctan\frac{H}{G_1},$$

$$K_1 \equiv \mu^2\left((1+b)B^2M^2 - b^2(1+\tau+B)\right) - (B+b+b\tau)\tau m^2 M^2,$$

$$K_2 \equiv B^2\left(M^2 - Z^2\right)\mu^2 - m^2\tau^2 M^2.$$

First, we consider the case $X < M < Y$. If $M \leq Z$, then $K_2 < 0$. Assume $Z < M < Y$, then since $\mu_1^2 - \mu_-^2 = \frac{2\tau^2 m^2 M^2 (Y-M)}{B^2(M-X)^2(M^2-Z^2)} > 0$,we have

$$K_2 = B^2\left(M^2 - Z^2\right)\left(\mu^2 - \mu_1^2\right) < 0$$

for $\mu < \mu_-$. Therefore, in these cases, we have

$$F_\tau^m(\mu, \tau, b) < \frac{K_1}{m^2\tau^2M^2BH} + \frac{H}{G_1} = -\frac{L_1\left(\mu^2 - \mu_2^2\right)\left(\mu^2 - \mu_3^2\right)}{m^4\tau^4M^4G_1H},$$

$$L_1 \equiv B\left((\tau-1)BM^2 + b^2(1+\tau)\right)\left(M^2 - X^2\right) > 0,$$

$$\mu_2 \equiv \frac{\tau m M\sqrt{\tau+1}}{\sqrt{(\tau-1)B^2M^2 + b^2(\tau+1)}},\ \mu_3 \equiv \frac{mM\sqrt{\tau(b+B)}}{B\sqrt{M^2-X^2}}.$$

Because $\mu_0^2 - \mu_2^2 = \frac{(\tau+1)m^2B^2(Y^2-M^2)}{(\tau-1)M^2B^2+b^2(\tau+1)}$, $\mu_3^2 - \mu_0^2 = \frac{m^2((Y^2-M^2)+2M^2\tau(b-1))}{B^2(M^2-X^2)}$, and $\mu_0 - \mu_- = \frac{m(M-Y)}{B(M-X)}$, we obtain $\mu_2 < \min\{\mu_-, \mu_3\}$, hence $F_\tau^m < 0$ for $\mu < \mu_2$. On the other hand, since

$$F^m(\mu_2, \tau, b) = \frac{\pi}{2} + \tau\arctan\frac{\sqrt{Y^2-M^2}}{\tau M} - \arctan\frac{\sqrt{Y^2-M^2}}{M},$$

we have $F^m(\mu_2, \tau, b) > \pi/2 \geq \pi/2 - \tau\theta = F^m\left(\mu_m^*(\theta, \tau, b), \tau, b\right)$, which implies $\mu_m^*(\theta, \tau, b) < \mu_2$. Therefore, $F_\tau^m(\mu, \tau, b) < 0$ at $\mu = \mu_m^*(\theta, \tau, b)$.

Next, we turn to the case $Y < M$. In this case, it follows that $\mu_1 \le \mu_- \le \mu_0 \le \mu_2$. If $\mu < \mu_1$, then $K_2 < 0$ because $Z < Y \le M$, hence $F_\tau^m < 0$. If $\mu_1 \le \mu < \mu_-$, then $K_2 \ge 0$ and $0 < \log m \le m - 1$ because $1 < Y \le M$. Thus,

$$F_\tau^m < \frac{K_1 + (m-1) B K_2}{m^2 \tau^2 M^2 B H} + \frac{H}{G_1} = \frac{L_2(\mu)}{m^2 \tau^2 M^2 G_1 H},$$

$$L_2(\mu) \equiv -L_1 \left(\mu^2 - \mu_2^2\right)\left(\mu^2 - \mu_3^2\right) + (m-1) G_1 K_2.$$

Since $\mu_3^2 - \mu_-^2 = \frac{2b\tau m^2 M^2 (M-1)}{B^2(M^2-X^2)(M-X)^2}$, we have $\mu_1 \le \mu_- < \min\{\mu_2, \mu_3\}$. Therefore, $L_2(\mu)$ is increasing in $\mu_1 \le \mu < \mu_-$. Hence,

$$L_2(\mu) \le L_2(\mu_-) = -\frac{4b\tau m^2 M^3 (m^\tau - m\tau + (\tau - 1))(M - Y)}{B(M-X)^3} \le 0,$$

where the second inequality sign holds because

$$m^\tau - m\tau + (\tau - 1) = (m-1)^2 \sum_{j=1}^{\tau-1} j m^{\tau-1-j} > 0$$

for $m > 1, \tau \ge 2$. Consequently, $F_\tau^m < 0$ holds for any $\mu < \mu_-$. Hence, in this case also $F_\tau^m(\mu, \tau, b) < 0$ at $\mu = \mu_m^*(\theta, \tau, b)$.

In sum, $F_\tau^m(\mu, \tau, b) < 0$ at $\mu = \mu_m^*(\theta, \tau, b)$ for any $m > \xi_0$, and it also holds for any $\mu < \mu_2$ (when $X < M < Y$) and $\mu < \mu_-$ (when $Y \le M$). Let $\overline{\phi}(\mu, \theta, \tau, b) = m > \xi_0$. Then, since $\mu = \mu_m^*(\theta, \tau, b)$ and both μ_2 and μ_- are increasing with respect to τ in their relevant ranges, we have

$$F^m(\mu, \tau + 1, b) < F^m(\mu, \tau, b) = \frac{\pi}{2} - \tau\theta = \frac{\pi}{2} - (\tau + 1)\frac{\tau\theta}{\tau + 1},$$

which implies $\overline{\phi}(\mu, \tau\theta/(\tau+1), \tau+1, b) < m = \overline{\phi}(\mu, \theta, \tau, b)$.

(iv) Differentiating F^m with respect to b, we have

$$F_b^m(\mu, \tau, b) = P(\mu)/(bB\tau m^2 M^2 H), \quad P(\mu) \equiv N_1 + \mu^2 N_2,$$

$$N_1 \equiv \tau m^2 M^2 (B + b\tau + b), \quad N_2 \equiv -(1+b) B^2 M^2 + b^2 (B + \tau + 1).$$

Considering that the sign of $\mu_0 - \mu_-$ is equal to that of $M - Y$, and

$$P(\mu_+) = 2b\tau m^2 M^2 (1 + M)(M + Y)/(M + X)^2 > 0,$$

$$P(\mu_0) = -(1 + \tau + B) m^2 \left(M^2 - Y^2\right),$$

$$P(\mu_-) = 2b\tau m^2 M^2 (M - 1)(M - Y)/(M - X)^2,$$

$F_b^m > 0$ holds for $\mu_+ < \mu < \min\{\mu_0, \mu_-\}$. Let $\overline{\phi}\left(\mu, \theta, \tau, b'\right) = m$, then since $\mu = \mu_m^*(\theta, \tau, b')$ and both μ_2 and μ_- are increasing with respect to τ in their relevant ranges, we have

$$F^m(\mu, \tau, b) < F^m\left(\mu, \tau, b'\right) = \pi/2 - \tau\theta,$$

which implies $\overline{\phi}(\mu, \theta, \tau, b) < m = \overline{\phi}\left(\mu, \theta, \tau, b'\right)$.

4. Proof of Theorem 4

(i) To prove the contraposition of statement (i), let us assume $\rho(\Psi) \geq 1$. Let Ψ be an eigenvalue of Ψ such that $|\Psi| \geq 1$ and $\xi = [\xi_{\mathrm{I}}, \xi_{\mathrm{II}}]$ be an associated eigenvector, where both ξ_{I} and ξ_{II} are $1 \times n$ vectors. Then, from $\Psi\xi = \xi\Psi$ we obtain

$$\xi = \left[\xi_{\mathrm{I}}, \xi_{\mathrm{I}}\Gamma(\psi I - (I - \Gamma))^{-1}\right], \quad \psi\xi_{\mathrm{I}} = \xi_{\mathrm{I}} Q(\psi) A$$

$$Q(\psi) \equiv (I + \Gamma B) - \Gamma(\psi I - (I - \Gamma))^{-1}\Gamma B.$$

Therefore, Ψ is also an eigenvalue of matrix $Q(\Psi)A$, hence $1 \leq |\Psi| \leq \rho(Q(\Psi)A)$. Let q_i be the i-th diagonal element of matrix $Q(\Psi)$, then

$$|q_i| = \left|1 + \gamma_i b_i - \frac{\gamma_i^2 b_i}{\psi - (1 - \gamma_i)}\right| = (1 + \gamma_i b_i)\left|\frac{\psi - \frac{1 - \gamma_i + \gamma_i b_i}{1 + \gamma_i b_i}}{\psi - (1 - \gamma_i)}\right| \leq \frac{2 - \gamma_i + 2\gamma_i b_i}{2 - \gamma_i}.$$

Since Q is diagonal and A is nonnegative, we have

$$(QA)^+ \leq Q^+ A \leq \left(2\Gamma B(2I - \Gamma)^{-1} + I\right) A.$$

Because ψ is an eigenvalue of QA, these inequalities imply

$$\begin{aligned} 1 \leq \rho(QA) &\leq \lambda^{\mathrm{F}}\left((QA)^+\right) \leq \lambda^{\mathrm{F}}\left(Q^+ A\right) \\ &\leq \lambda^{\mathrm{F}}\left(\left(2\Gamma B(2I - \Gamma)^{-1} + I\right) A\right) \end{aligned}$$

(ii) To prove the contraposition of statement (ii), assume that $-\lambda^{\mathrm{F}}(A)$ is an eigenvalue of A and $\lambda^* = \lambda^{\mathrm{F}}((2\Gamma B(2I - \Gamma)^{-1} + I)A) \geq 1$. Let $\Psi \neq 0$, then Ψ is an eigenvalue of Ψ if and only if

$$|\psi I - Q(\psi) A| = 0.$$

For any $\Psi > 0$, matrix $Q(-\Psi)A$ is nonnegative and identically cyclic with matrix A. Hence, $-\lambda^{\mathrm{F}}(Q(-\Psi)A)$ is an eigenvalue of $Q(-\Psi)A$. Let

$$h(\psi) \equiv \psi - \lambda^{\mathrm{F}}(Q(-\psi) A)$$

for $\Psi > 0$, then $h(\Psi)$ is an eigenvalue of $\Psi I + Q(-\Psi)A = -((-\Psi)I - Q(-\Psi)A)$. Hence, $h(\Psi) = 0$ implies that $-\Psi$ is an eigenvalue of Ψ. Since $Q(-\lambda^*) \leq Q(-1)$, we obtain $\lambda^{\mathrm{F}}(Q(-\lambda^*)A) \leq \lambda^{\mathrm{F}}(Q(-1)A) = \lambda^*$. Consequently,

$$h(1) = 1 - \lambda^{\mathrm{F}}(Q(-1)A) = 1 - \lambda^* \leq 0,$$

$$h(\lambda^*) = \lambda^* - \lambda^{\mathrm{F}}\left(Q(-\lambda^*)A\right) \geq 0.$$

Because of the continuity, there exists an α such that

$$1 \leq \alpha \leq \lambda^*, \quad h(\alpha) = \alpha - \lambda^{\mathrm{F}}(Q(-\alpha)A) = 0.$$

Therefore, $-\alpha$ is an eigenvalue of Ψ, hence $\rho(\Psi) \geq 1$.

5. Proof of Theorem 5

(i) Like the case of Φ', the characteristic equation of Ψ' is

$$\prod_{i=1}^{\nu}\left(\psi^2 I - \psi\left((\gamma b + 1)\lambda_i + (1-\gamma)\right) + (1 - \gamma + \gamma b)\lambda_i\right)^{\kappa_i} = 0,$$

where ν is the number of A's different eigenvalues and κ_i is the multiplicity of an eigenvalue $\lambda_i = \mu_i e^{i\theta_i}$. Therefore, $\rho(\Psi') < 1$ is equivalent to $\overline{\psi}(\mu_i, \theta_i, \gamma, b) < 1$ for any $i \in \{1, \ldots, \nu\}$.

(ii) Let $\xi e^{i\omega} = \xi(\cos\omega + i\sin\omega)$ $(0 \leq \xi, 0 \leq \omega < 2\pi)$ be a root of (4.33), then

$$\xi^2 e^{2i\omega} - \left((\gamma b + 1)\mu e^{i\theta} + (1-\gamma)\right)\xi e^{i\omega} + (1 - \gamma + \gamma b)\mu e^{i\theta} = 0.$$

Let $f(\xi, \omega, \theta)$ be the left-hand side of this equation; then $f(\xi, -\omega, -\theta) = 0$, because it is the conjugate of $f(\xi, \omega, \theta)$. Therefore, $\overline{\psi}(\mu, \theta, \gamma, b) = \overline{\psi}(\mu, -\theta, \gamma, b)$.

(iii) From Schur's condition, $\overline{\psi}(\mu, \theta, \gamma, b) < 1$ holds if and only if

$$E_1 \equiv \begin{vmatrix} 1 & D\mu e^{i\theta} \\ D\mu e^{-i\theta} & 1 \end{vmatrix} = 1 - D^2\mu^2 > 0,$$

$$E_2 \equiv \begin{vmatrix} 1 & -\left(B\mu e^{i\theta} + C\right) & D\mu e^{i\theta} & 0 \\ 0 & 1 & -\left(B\mu e^{i\theta} + C\right) & D\mu e^{i\theta} \\ D\mu e^{-i\theta} & -\left(B\mu e^{-i\theta} + C\right) & 1 & 0 \\ 0 & D\mu e^{-i\theta} & -\left(B\mu e^{-i\theta} + C\right) & 1 \end{vmatrix} > 0, \tag{4.53}$$

where $B \equiv 1 + \gamma b$, $C \equiv 1 - \gamma$, $D \equiv 1 - \gamma + \gamma b$. Note that

$$B - CD = \gamma(B + C) > 0, \quad BC - D = -\gamma^2 b < 0,$$

$$B - C = \gamma(b + 1) > 0, \quad B - D = 1 - C = \gamma, \quad 1 - D = -\gamma(b - 1) < 0,$$

and $E_1 > 0$ is equivalent to $D\mu = (1 - \gamma + \gamma b)\mu < 1$. Let

$$\mu_1 = \sqrt{\frac{C}{BD}}, \mu_2 = \frac{1+C}{B+D} = \frac{2-\gamma}{2-\gamma+2\gamma b}, \mu_3 = \frac{1}{D} = \frac{1}{1-\gamma+\gamma b},$$

then $\mu_1 < \mu_2 < \mu_3$ because

$$\mu_2^2 - \mu_1^2 = \frac{\gamma^3 b\,(B+C)}{BD(B+D)^2} > 0, \mu_3 - \mu_2 = \frac{\gamma\,(D+1)}{D\,(B+D)} > 0.$$

By direct calculation, we have

$$E_2 = F\,(\mu) - (1-\cos\theta)\,G\,(\mu)\,,$$

$$F\,(\mu) = \gamma D^2\,(1-\mu)\,(\mu_3 - \mu)^2\,(1 + C + \mu\,(B+D)) \geq 0,$$

$$G\,(\mu) = 2\mu\left(BD\mu^2 - C\right)(B - CD) = 2\gamma\mu\,(B+C)\,BD\left(\mu^2 - \mu_1^2\right).$$

Let $H\,(\mu) = F\,(\mu)\,/G\,(\mu)$, then $H\,(\mu_2) = 2, H\,(\mu_3) = 0$. Differentiating H with respect to μ, we have

$$H_\mu = \frac{\left(\mu_3^2 - \mu^2\right)K\,(\mu)}{2\mu^2 B^2 \left(\mu^2 - \mu_1^2\right)^2 (B+C)},$$

$$K\,(\mu) \equiv BD\,(B+D)\,\mu^4 - (3D - BC)\,(B+C)\,\mu^2 + C\,(1+C)\,.$$

Since $G\,(\mu)$ has the same sign as that of $\mu - \mu_1$, $E_2 > 0$ is equivalent to either $\mu \leq \mu_1$ or $\mu_1 < \mu, H\,(\mu) > 1 - \cos\theta$. $K\,(\mu)$ is a quadratic expression of μ^2 and

$$K\,(\mu_1) = -2b\gamma^2 C\,(B+C)\,/(BD) < 0, \quad K\,(\mu_3) = -\gamma\,(b-1)\,P/D^3 < 0,$$

where $P \equiv (B+C)\,(B+2D+CD)$. Thus, $H\,(\mu)$ is decreasing in $\mu_1 < \mu < \mu_3$. Hence, there exists a unique μ such that $\mu_2 \leq \mu \leq \mu_3$ and $H\,(\mu) = 1 - \cos\theta$. Let $\mu^*\,(\theta, \gamma, b)$ be this unique μ, then (4.53) is equivalent to $\mu < \mu^*\,(\theta, \gamma, b)$.

(iv) From the above results, for $0 < \theta < \theta' \leq \pi$ we have

$$H\left(\mu^*\,(\theta, \gamma, b)\right) = 1 - \cos\theta < 1 - \cos\theta',$$

which implies $\mu^*\left(\theta', \gamma, b\right) < \mu^*\,(\theta, \gamma, b)$. The latter part of the statement directly follows from $H\,(\mu_2) = 2, H\,(\mu_3) = 0$.

(v) This statement directly follows from statement (iii).

(vi) Assume $\gamma < \gamma' < 1$. Differentiating H with respect to γ, we have

$$H_\gamma = \frac{\left(1-\mu^2\right)\left(\mu_3^2-\mu^2\right)L\left(\mu\right)}{2\mu(B+C)^2B^2\left(\mu^2-\mu_1^2\right)},\ L\left(\mu\right) \equiv P_1 - \mu^2 P_2,$$

$$P_1 = 2\left(b-2\right) - \left(b-1\right)\gamma\left(4-\gamma\right),$$

$$P_2 = 2\left(b-2\right) + 4\gamma(b-1)^2 + \gamma^2\left(b-1\right)\left(1+2b\left(b-1\right)\right) > 0,$$

Note that the sign of H_γ is the same as that of $L(\mu)$ for $\mu_2 < \mu < \mu_3$. From

$$L\left(\mu_3\right) < L\left(\mu\right) < L\left(\mu_2\right) = -\frac{2\gamma b\left(B+C\right)\left((\gamma-2)^2+\gamma b\left(4-\gamma\right)\right)}{(B+D)^2} < 0,$$

we have $H_\gamma < 0$ for $\mu_2 < \mu < \mu_3$. Assume $\mu = \mu^*(\theta,\gamma,b)$ and $0 \le \theta < 2\pi$. If $\mu_3(\gamma') = 1/(1-\gamma'+\gamma' b) < \mu$, then $\mu^*(\theta,\gamma',b) \le \mu^*(0,\gamma',b) \le \mu^*(\theta,\gamma,b)$. Otherwise, since

$$1-\cos\theta = H\left(\mu,\gamma,b\right) > H\left(\mu,\gamma',b\right),$$

we have $\mu*(\theta,\gamma,b) = \mu > \mu*(\theta,\gamma',b)$, and this also holds for $\theta = 0$.

(vii) Differentiating H with respect b, we have

$$H_b = \frac{\gamma\left(1-\mu^2\right)\left(\mu_3^2-\mu^2\right)M(\mu)}{2\mu(B+C)^2B^2\left(\mu^2-\mu_1^2\right)},\ M\left(\mu\right) \equiv Q_1 - \mu^2 Q_2,$$

$$Q_1 \equiv \left(\gamma-1\right)\left(\gamma-2\right),\quad Q_2 \equiv 2 + (1+4b)\gamma + (2b^2+2b-3)\gamma^2 + (b-1)^2\gamma^3.$$

Considering that

$$M\left(\mu_2\right) = -\frac{\gamma(2-\gamma)(B+C)\left((\gamma-2)^2+\gamma b\left(4-\gamma\right)\right)^2}{(B+D)^2} < 0,$$

we can apply the same argument as the case of (vi).

6. Proof of Theorem 6

(i) B, C, and D are the same as those in the proof of the previous theorem, and let $\overline{\phi}_m\left(\mu,\theta,\tau,b\right)$ be the dominant root of the equation:

$$\phi^2 - m^{-1}\left(B\mu e^{i\theta} + C\right)\phi + m^{-2}D\mu e^{i\theta} = 0.$$

Then, it follows that $\overline{\psi}(\mu,\theta,\gamma,b) = m\overline{\phi}_m(\mu,\theta,\gamma,b)$. Let

$$\psi_0 \equiv \sqrt{\frac{CD}{B}},\quad \mu_0 \equiv \frac{C}{B} = \frac{1-\gamma}{1+b\gamma},\quad \mu_{\mathrm{I}} \equiv m\sqrt{\frac{C}{BD}},$$
$$\mu_{\mathrm{II}} \equiv \frac{m(m+C)}{mB+D},\quad \mu_{\mathrm{III}} \equiv \frac{m^2}{D},\quad \mu_{\mathrm{IV}} \equiv \frac{m(m-C)}{mB-D}$$

As before, by Schur's condition, $\overline{\phi}_m(\mu,\theta,\gamma,b) < 1$ holds if and only if

$$\begin{aligned}
&\mu < \mu_{\mathrm{III}},\quad F^m(\mu) - (1-\cos\theta)\,G^m(\mu) > 0,\\
&G^m(\mu) \equiv 2\mu m^{-6}B^2D\left(m^2-\psi_0^2\right)\left(\mu^2-\mu_{\mathrm{I}}^2\right),\\
&F^m(\mu) \equiv m^{-8}D^2\left(m^2B^2-D^2\right)(\mu_{\mathrm{III}}-\mu)^2(\mu_{\mathrm{II}}+\mu)(\mu_{\mathrm{IV}}-\mu)
\end{aligned}\tag{4.54}$$

By the assumption $\mu \geq \mu_0$, it is sufficient to consider the case $m \geq \sqrt{\mu_0 D} = \psi_0$. Assume $m > \psi_0$ and let $r(m) \equiv Bm^2 - CD$, $s(m) \equiv m^2B^2 - D^2$, then from

$$\mu_{\mathrm{I}}^2 - \mu_0^2 = \frac{Cr(m)}{BD} > 0,\quad \mu_{\mathrm{II}}^2 - \mu_{\mathrm{I}}^2 = \frac{m^2\gamma^2br(m)}{BD(mB+D)^2} > 0,$$

$$\mu_{\mathrm{III}} - \mu_{\mathrm{II}} = \frac{mr(m)}{D(mB+D)} > 0,\quad \mu_{\mathrm{IV}} - \mu_{\mathrm{II}} = \frac{2m^2\gamma^2b}{s(m)},$$

$$\mu_{\mathrm{IV}}^2 - \mu_{\mathrm{III}}^2 = -\frac{m^2r(m)q(m)}{D^2(mB-D)^2},\quad q(m) \equiv m^2B - 2mD + CD,$$

we have $\mu_0 < \mu_{\mathrm{I}} < \mu_{\mathrm{II}} < \mu_{\mathrm{III}}$. If $\mu \leq \mu_{\mathrm{I}}$, $mB > D$, then $\mu < \mu_{\mathrm{I}} < \mu_{\mathrm{II}} < \mu_{\mathrm{IV}}$. If $\mu \leq \mu_{\mathrm{I}}$, $mB < D$, then $\mu_{\mathrm{IV}} < 0$. Hence, (4.54) holds when $\mu \leq \mu_{\mathrm{I}}$.

Assume $\mu > \mu_{\mathrm{I}}$, then $G^m(\mu) > 0$. Since $q(0) > 0$ and $q(D/B) = -\gamma^2bD/B < 0$, equation $q(m) = 0$ has two positive roots. Let ψ_{I} be its larger root, then $D/B < 1 < \psi_{\mathrm{I}}$ because $q(1) = -(b-1)\gamma^2 < 0$. Observe that $q(\psi_0) = 2D(C-\psi_0) < 0$; $\mu_{\mathrm{III}} < |\mu_{\mathrm{IV}}|$ for $\psi_0 < m < \psi_{\mathrm{I}}$; and $\mu_{\mathrm{II}} < \mu_{\mathrm{VI}} < \mu_{\mathrm{III}}$ for $\psi_{\mathrm{I}} < m$. Let $H^m(\mu) = F^m(\mu)/G^m(\mu)$, then

$$H^m(\mu_{\mathrm{II}}) = 2,\quad H^m(\mu_{\mathrm{III}}) = H^m(\mu_{\mathrm{VI}}) = 0.$$

Differentiating H^m with respect to μ, we have

$$H_\mu^m = \frac{\left(\mu_{\mathrm{III}}^2 - \mu^2\right)K(\mu)}{2m^2\mu^2B^2\left(\mu^2-\mu_{\mathrm{I}}^2\right)^2 r(m)},$$

$$K(\mu) \equiv BDs(m)\mu^4 - m^2(3D-BC)\,r(m)\mu^2 + m^4C\left(m^2-C^2\right).$$

Let $p(m) \equiv m^2B + 2mD + CD$. $K(\mu)$ is a quadratic expression of μ^2, and

$$K(\mu_{\mathrm{I}}) = -2b\gamma^2 m^4 Cr(m)/(BD), \quad K(\mu_{\mathrm{III}}) = m^4 r(m)p(m)q(m)/D^3,$$

$$K(\mu_{\mathrm{IV}}) = -2b\gamma^2 m^4 (m - C)\, r(m)q(m)/(mB - D)^3.$$

Hence, if $\psi_0 < m < \psi_{\mathrm{I}}$, then $\mu_{\mathrm{I}} < \mu < \mu_{\mathrm{III}} < |\mu_{\mathrm{IV}}|$ and $K_m(\mu) < 0$ in $\mu_{\mathrm{I}} < \mu < \mu_{\mathrm{III}}$; if $\psi_{\mathrm{I}} < m$, then $\mu_{\mathrm{I}} < \mu < \mu_{\mathrm{IV}} < \mu_{\mathrm{III}}$ and $K_m(\mu) < 0$ in $\mu_{\mathrm{I}} < \mu < \mu_{\mathrm{IV}}$. Thus, $H^m_\mu < 0$ in $\mu_{\mathrm{I}} < \mu < \min\{\mu_{\mathrm{III}}, |\mu_{\mathrm{IV}}|\}$, so there exists a unique μ such that

$$\mu_{\mathrm{II}} \le \mu \le \min\{\mu_{\mathrm{III}}, |\mu_{\mathrm{IV}}|\},\ H^m(\mu) = 1 - \cos\theta.$$

Let us denote this unique μ by $\mu^*_m(\theta, \gamma, b)$, then, it satisfies

$$\mu^*_m(0, \gamma, b) = \begin{cases} \mu_{\mathrm{III}} & \psi_0 < m \le \psi_{\mathrm{I}}, \\ \mu_{\mathrm{IV}} & \psi_{\mathrm{I}} < m \end{cases}, \quad \mu^*_m(\pi, \gamma, b) = \mu_{\mathrm{II}},$$

and (4.54) is simplified into $\mu < \mu^*_m(\theta, \gamma, b)$.

Assume $\mu_0 < \mu < \mu' < 1$. Let $m = \overline{\psi}\left(\mu', \theta, \gamma, b\right)$ then $m > \psi_0(\gamma, b)$, hence $\mu' = \mu^*_m(\theta, \gamma, b)$, which implies $\overline{\psi}(\mu, \theta, \gamma, b) < m = \overline{\psi}\left(\mu', \theta, \gamma, b\right)$.[32]

(ii) If $m = \psi_0$, then $\mu_0 = \mu_{\mathrm{I}} = \mu_{\mathrm{II}} = \mu_{\mathrm{III}}$ and $\overline{\psi}(\mu, \theta, \gamma, b) < \psi_0$ is equivalent to $\mu < \mu_0$, which implies that $\psi = \psi_0$ holds irrespective of θ when $\mu = \mu_0$.

Assume $\mu_0 < \mu, 0 \le \theta < \theta' \le \pi$, and $\psi\left(\mu, \theta', \gamma, b\right) = m$.
Then, it follows that

$$H^m(\mu, \gamma, b) = H^m\left(\mu^*_m\left(\theta', \gamma, b\right), \gamma, b\right) = 1 - \cos\theta' > 1 - \cos\theta,$$

which implies $\overline{\phi}(\mu, \theta, \gamma, b) < m = \overline{\phi}\left(\mu, \theta', \gamma, b\right)$.

(iii) Differentiating H^m with respect γ, we have

$$H^m_\gamma = -\frac{\left(\mu^2_{\mathrm{III}} - \mu^2\right) L(\mu)}{2\mu m^2 B^2 r^2(m)\left(\mu^2 - \mu^2_{\mathrm{I}}\right)^2}, \quad L(\mu) \equiv S_1\mu^4 + 2S_2 m^2\mu^2 + S_3 m^4,$$

$$S_1 \equiv (b-1)\, B^4 m^4 - 2BD^2(bB - 1)\, m^2 + D^3(bB - C),$$

$$S_2 \equiv -B\Big(B(b-1) - \gamma b\Big)\, m^4 + BC(b-1)(3D - BC)\, m^2 - CD^2(b - C),$$

$$S_3 \equiv (bC - B)\, m^4 - 2C(bC - D)\, m^2 + C^4(b-1).$$

---

[32] Like the case of $\overline{\phi}(\mu, \theta, \tau, b)$, this result can be shown also by differentiating $\overline{\psi}(\mu, \theta, \gamma, b)$ with respect to μ. In fact, $\overline{\psi}(\mu, \theta, \gamma, b)$ is differentiable with respect to any of its arguments unless $\theta = 0, \gamma = (1-\mu)/\sqrt{b\mu \pm 1}$. See Morioka (2005, pp. 283–284).

Note that $L(\mu)$ is a quadratic expression of μ^2. Since

$$L(\mu_{\rm II}) = -2b^2\gamma^2 m^4(1+m)^2 r^2(m)p(m)/(mB+D)^4,$$

$$L(\mu_{\rm III}) = (b-1)\,m^4 r^2(m)p(m)q(m)/D^4,$$

$$L(\mu_{\rm IV}) = -2b^2\gamma^2 m^4(m-1)^2 r^2(m)q(m)/(mB-D)^4,$$

$H^m_\gamma < 0$ holds for $\mu_{\rm II} < \mu < \min\{\mu_{\rm III}, |\mu_{\rm IV}|\}$. Assume $\mu_0(\gamma, b) \le \mu, \gamma < \gamma' \le 1$, and let $\overline{\psi}(\mu, \theta, \gamma', b) = m$, that is $\mu = \mu^*_m(\theta, \gamma', b)$. Then, applying the same argument as in the proof of Theorem 5(vi), we have

$$1 - \cos\theta = H^m(\mu, \gamma', b) < H^m(\mu, \gamma, b),$$

which implies $\overline{\phi}(\mu, \theta, \gamma, b) < m = \overline{\phi}(\mu, \theta, \gamma', b)$.

(iv) Differentiation H^m with respect to b, we have

$$H^m_b = \frac{-\gamma\left(\mu^2_{\rm III} - \mu^2\right)M_m(\mu)}{2\mu m^2 B^2 r^2(m)\left(\mu^2 - \mu^2_{\rm I}\right)^2}, \quad M_m(\mu) \equiv T_1\mu^4 + T_2 m^2\mu^2 + T_3 m^4,$$

$$T_1 \equiv B^4 m^4 + BD^2(\gamma B - 2D)m^2 + CD^3(B+\gamma)$$

$$T_2 \equiv -B(2D + \gamma B)m^4 + 2BC(3D - BC)m^2 - C^2D^2(2+\gamma),$$

$$T_3 \equiv Cm^4 - C^2(C+1)m^2 + C^4.$$

Note that $M(\mu)$ is a quadratic expression of μ^2. From

$$M(\mu_{\rm II}) = -2b\gamma^2 m^4(1+m)(m+C)\,p(m)r^2(m)/(mB+D)^4 < 0,$$

$$M(\mu_{\rm III}) = m^4 r^2(m)p(m)q(m)/D^4,$$

$$M(\mu_{\rm IV}) = -2b\gamma^2 m^4(m-1)(m-C)\,r^2(m)q(m)/(mB-C)^4,$$

we have $H^m_b < 0$ for $\mu_{\rm II} \le \mu < \min\{\mu_{\rm III}, |\mu_{\rm IV}|\}$. Thus, we can repeat a similar argument to the case of (iii).

7. Proof of Theorem 7

(i) Let Ψ be the transitive matrix of FGMA and ϕ be one of its eigenvalues such that $|\phi| \ge 1$. Then, like the case of GMA, ϕ is also an eigenvalue of QA, where Q is an $n \times n$ diagonal matrix whose i-th diagonal element is

$$q_i = \frac{1}{1+\cdots+r_i^{\tau_i-1}} \frac{\phi-1}{\phi-r_i}\left(1-\frac{r^{\tau_i}}{\phi^{\tau_i}}\right) b_i + 1.$$

Let $\Psi = \phi^{-1}$, then

$$\frac{\phi-1}{\phi-r_i}\left(1-\frac{r^{\tau_i}}{\phi^{\tau_i}}\right) = (1-\psi)\left(1+r\psi+\cdots+(r\psi)^{\tau_i-1}\right).$$

Let us denote this polynomial of Ψ by $F(\psi)$. Since $F(\psi)$ is a complex integer expression, for any complex number α and $\epsilon > 0$, there exists a complex number β such that $|\beta-\alpha| < \epsilon, |F(\beta)| > |F(\alpha)|$.[33] Therefore, under the constraint $|\phi| \leq 1$, $F(\psi) = F(1/\phi)$ takes the maximum value at a certain ϕ satisfying $|\phi| = 1$. In this case, observing

$$\left|\frac{\phi-1}{\phi-r_i}\right| \leq \frac{2}{1+r_i}, \quad \left|1-\frac{r^{\tau_i}}{\phi^{\tau_i}}\right| \leq 1+r_i^{\tau},$$

we have $F(1/\phi) \leq 2\left(1+r_i^{\tau}\right)/(1+r_i)$. Consequently,

$$|q_i| \leq \frac{2(1+r^{\tau_i})\, b_i}{\left(1+\cdots+r_i^{\tau_i-1}\right)(1+r_i)} + 1 = \frac{2\left(1+r^2+\cdots+r_i^{2(\tau_i-1)}\right)}{\left(1+\cdots+r_i^{\tau_i-1}\right)^2} b_i + 1$$

which implies $1 \leq \rho(QA) \leq \lambda^{\mathrm{F}}\left(Q^{+}A\right) \leq \lambda^{\mathrm{F}}((2HB+I)A)$.

(ii) This can be shown in a similar manner to the proof of Theorem 4(ii).

8. Proof of Theorem 8

(i) By definition, it follows that

$$\eta(\tau, r) - \eta(\tau+1, r) = \frac{2r^{\tau}}{(1+r)\left(\sum_{\upsilon=0}^{\tau-1} r^{\upsilon}\right)\left(\sum_{\upsilon=0}^{\tau} r^{\upsilon}\right)} > 0$$

(ii) Differentiating $\eta(\tau, r)$ with respect to r, we have

$$\eta_r(\tau, r) = \frac{2f(\tau, r)}{(1+r)^2(1-r)^2\left(\sum_{\upsilon=0}^{\tau-1} r^{\upsilon}\right)^2}, \quad f(\tau, r) \equiv r^{2\tau} - 1 + \tau r^{\tau-1}\left(1-r^2\right).$$

[33] Concerning this point, refer to Takagi (1965, pp. 48–49)

Since $f(1, r) = 0$ and

$$f(\tau + 1, r) - f(\tau, r) = r^{\tau-1}(r+1)(r-1)^3 \sum_{\upsilon=1}^{\tau} \upsilon r^{\tau-\upsilon},$$

$\eta_r(\tau, r)$ can be written as:

$$\eta_r(\tau, r) = \frac{2(r-1)\sum_{\upsilon=1}^{\tau-1} r^{\upsilon-1} \sum_{u=1}^{\upsilon} u r^{\upsilon-u}}{(1+r)\left(\sum_{\upsilon=0}^{\tau-1} r^{\upsilon}\right)^2}.$$

9. Proof of Theorem 9

(i) By Schur's condition, the dominant root of a cubic equation with real coefficient $x^3 + \alpha x^2 + \beta x + \gamma = 0$ is less than unity if and only if

$$|\gamma| < 1, \quad \left(1 - \gamma^2\right)^2 > |\beta + \alpha\gamma|^2, \quad |1 + \beta|^2 > |\alpha + \gamma|^2.$$

Therefore, $\overline{\phi}(2, r, \mu, 0, b) < 1$ holds if and only if

$$\begin{gathered} |Rr\mu| < 1, \quad \left(1 - R^2 r^2 \mu^2\right)^2 > \left((1-r)R\mu + r\mu^2 R(R+1)\right)^2, \\ (1 + (1-r)R\mu)^2 > ((r-1)R - 1)^2 \mu^2, \end{gathered} \tag{4.55}$$

where $R \equiv b/(1+r)$. Let $\beta(b) \equiv (2b+1)/(b-1)$ (do not confuse this β with the secondary coefficient of the above equation). Then, the pair of first two inequalities are equivalent to $\mu < \mu_1$ for $0 < r < \beta$, and

$$\mu < \nu(r, b) \equiv (1+r)\frac{1 - r + \sqrt{5r^2 - 6r + 1 - 4r(1+r)/b}}{2r(b(r-1) - (1+r))}$$

for $\beta \leq r$. The third inequality is equivalent to $\mu < \mu_2$ for $(b+1)/(b-1) < r$. Since $\mu_2 < \nu$ for $\beta < r$ and $\mu_1(\beta, b) = \mu_2(\beta, b) = \nu(\beta, b) = 3/(2b+1)$, these conditions are summarized into (4.44).

(ii) By replacing μ in (4.55) by $-\mu$, we have

$$\begin{gathered} |Rr\mu| < 1, \quad \left(1 - R^2 r^2 \mu^2\right)^2 > \left(-(1-r)R\mu + r\mu^2 R(R+1)\right)^2, \\ (1 - (1-r)R\mu)^2 > ((r-1)R - 1)^2 \mu^2. \end{gathered}$$

as the necessary and sufficient condition for $\overline{\phi}(2, r, \mu, \theta, b) < 1$. (4.45) can be derived from these condition in the similar way to (4.44).

References

Brown, R. G. (1959). *Statistical forecasting for inventory control*. New York: McGraw-Hill.

Foster, E. (1963). Sales forecasts and the inventory cycle. *Econometrica, 31*(3), 400–421.

Hawkins, D., & Simon, H. (1949). Note: Some conditions of macro economic stability. *Econometrica, 17*(3-4), 245–248.

Hines, W. G. S. (2004). Geometric moving average. In *Encyclopedia of statistical sciences* (Vol. 4, 2nd ed., pp. 2784–2788). New York: Wiley-Interscience.

Keynes, J. M. (1936). *The general theory of employment, interest and money*. London: Macmillan.

Lovell, M. C. (1962). Buffer stocks, sales expectations and stability: A multi-sector analysis of the inventory cycle. *Econometrica, 30*(2), 267–296.

Metzler, L. A. (1941). The nature and stability of inventory cycle. *The Review of Economic Statistics, 23*(3), 113–129.

Morioka, M. (1991–1992). Two types of the short-term adjustment processes (in Japanese: Tanki choseikatei no niruikei). *Keizai Ronso (Kyoto University), 148*(4-6), 140–161, 149(1–3), 79–96.

Morioka, M. (2005). *The Economic Theory of Quantity Adjustment: Dynamic analysis of stockout avoidance behavior* (in Japanese: Suryo chosei no keizai riron). Tokyo: Nihon Keizai Hyoron-sya.

Muth, J. F. (1960). Optimal properties of exponentially weighted forecasts. *Journal of American Statistical Association, 55*, 299–360.

Nikaido, H. (1961). *Linear Mathematics for Economics* (in Japanese: Keizai no tameno senkei sugaku). Tokyo: Baihukan.

Simon, H. A. (1959). Theories of decision making in economics and Behavioral science. *American Economic Review, 49*(3), 253–283.

Simonovits, A. (1999). Linear decentralized control with expectations. *Economic Systems Research, 11*(3), 321–329.

Takagi, T. (1965). *Lectures on Algebra* (In Japanese: Daisugaku kogi). Kyoritsu Shuppan.

Taniguchi, K. (1991). On the traverse of quantity adjustment economies (in Japanese: Suryo chosei keizai ni okeru iko katei nitsuite). *Keizaigaku Zashi 91*(5):29-43.

Chapter 5
Extensions of Model Analysis of the Quantity Adjustment Process in Several Directions

Abstract In this chapter, we will extend the model of the quantity adjustment process presented in Chap. 4 in several directions. Section 5.1 examines the models considering work-in-process inventory, partial adjustment of production volume, and heterogeneity of firms within a sector. It will be shown that, under certain conditions, the stability conditions of these models are given in similar forms to those in Chap. 4, and thus, the introduction of the above factors into the model does not change the basic dynamic properties of the process. Section 5.2 traces the process with stockout, rationing, and bottleneck. A stockout of product inventory leads to a rationing of sales volume among buyers, whereas a stockout of raw material inventory leads to a reduction in the production volume due to bottleneck. Numerical computations will highlight the buffer role of inventories in the adaptations of the whole economy to a one-time increase or random fluctuations in final demand. Finally, Sect. 5.3 investigates the effects of mid- and long-term changes in final demand. It will be confirmed that, while quantity adjustment can follow the gradual movement of final demand accompanied by the inducement of consumption demand from past income, it cannot suppress the oscillations caused by unstable movements of final demand itself.

Keywords Work-in-process inventory · Partial adjustment · Firm-level model · Stockout · Rationing · Bottleneck · Induced consumption demand

5.1 Work-in-Process Inventory, Partial Adjustment, and a Firm-Level Model

5.1.1 Work-in-Process Inventories

In the previous chapter, we dealt with only product inventory and raw material inventory. However, if the cycle from the input of raw materials to the output of product is longer than the decision-making cycle for production, each firm also carries over the work-in-process inventories to the next period, in addition

Y. Shiozawa et al., *Microfoundations of Evolutionary Economics*, Evolutionary Economics and Social Complexity Science 15,
https://doi.org/10.1007/978-4-431-55267-3_5

to the inventories of product and raw materials. The work-in-process (semi-product) inventory decouples the production of work-in-process and its productive consumption. To build a model of quantity adjustment incorporating work-in-process inventory, we shall modify a part of the assumptions so far in the following manner.[1]

It takes two weeks from the input of raw materials to the output of products. Every week, two stages of the production process proceed in parallel. In the first process of firm i, ν_i kinds of works-in-process are produced from (at most) n kinds of raw materials. These works-in-process are consumed in the second process as inputs to produce the product, i. Let us assume that the two processes proceed in parallel. Let C_i be a $\nu_i \times n$ matrix whose (h,j) element $c_{i,\,hj}$ represents the input of raw material j required per unit output of work-in-process h in the production process of firm i; and b_i be a $1 \times \nu_i$ vector whose h-th element b_{ih} represents the input of work-in-process h required per unit output of product i. In this model, the input matrix is written as

$$A = \begin{bmatrix} a_1 \\ \vdots \\ a_n \end{bmatrix} = \begin{bmatrix} b_1 C_1 \\ \vdots \\ b_n C_n \end{bmatrix}, \quad a_{ij} = \left[b_{i1} c_{i,1j} + \cdots + b_{i\nu_i} c_{i,\nu_i j} \right].$$

Figure 5.1 illustrates these two stages of production stated above.[2]

Let $y_i(t)$ be a $1 \times \nu_i$ vector of the production volumes of the works-in-process for product i that starts at the beginning of week t and finishes at the beginning of week $t + 1$ and $w_i(t)$ be a $1 \times \nu_i$ vector of firm i's work-in-process inventories at the end of week t. If it is technically difficult to change the production volume that has already begun, $y_i(t)$ is automatically determined by the production plan made at the beginning of week $t - 1$. In this case, buffer inventory of work-in-process is unnecessary. However, here we shall consider the case where $y_i(t)$ is flexibly adjustable based on newly obtained information about demand at the beginning of week t.

First, let us assume that each firm applies the typical stockout avoidance rule to the decision on the productions of works-in-process. Under the forecast that demand per week from week t onward is $s_i^e(t)$, each firm plans to adjust its product and work-in-process inventories to their respective desirable levels at the end of week t. If this forecast is correct, the firm keeps its productions of finished product and semi-products equal to $s_i^e(t)$ and $s_i^e(t)b_{ij}$, respectively, from week $t + 1$ onwards.[3] The internal supplies of works-in-process at the beginning of week $t + 1$ are equal

[1] The model described below was first presented in Morioka (1992).

[2] If additional raw materials are necessary in the second stage, input matrix A is replaced by $A + A'$, where A' is the matrix of inputs additionally required to produce a unit of product i in the second stage. This point does not affect the essence of the following argument.

[3] See the argument on the production and ordering decisions in Subsect. 4.1.2, Chap. 4.

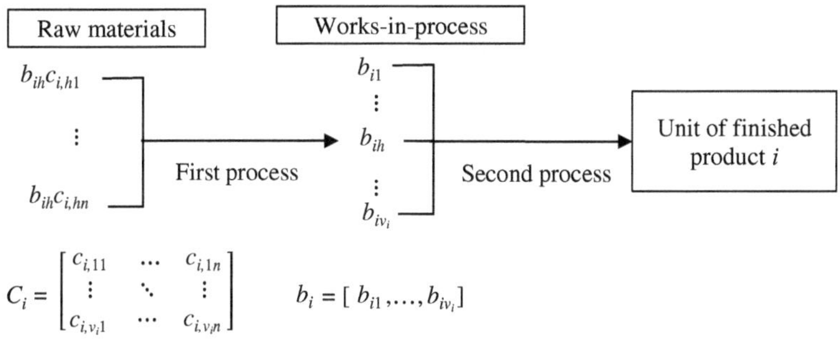

Fig. 5.1 Flow chart of two stages of production

to the sum of newly produced works-in-process $y_i(t)$ and their inventories $w_i(t)$. The internal demands for works-in-process at the beginning of week $t + 1$ are, under the above assumptions, equal to $s_i^e(t)b_i$.

Let h_i be the buffer work-in-process inventory coefficient of sector i. Then, the firm sets its internal supplies of works-in-process equal to $(1 + h_i)$-times their forecasted internal demand, namely,

$$y_i(t) = (1 + h_i)\, s_i^e(t)b_i - w_i(t). \tag{5.1}$$

Similar to the cases of product and raw material inventories, firm i's buffer coefficient of work-in-process inventories, h_i, is set by considering the storage cost and the loss caused by stockout of work-in-process. The vector of work-in-process inventories $w_i(t)$ changes by

$$w_i(t) = w_i\,(t - 1) + y_i\,(t - 1) - x_i(t)b_i, \tag{5.2}$$

where $x_i(t)$ is the production volume of the final product that starts at the beginning of week t and finishes at the beginning of week $t + 1$. Similarly, the vector of raw material inventories $v_i\,(t)$ at the end of week t changes by

$$v_i(t) = v_i\,(t - 1) + m_i\,(t - 1) - y_i(t)C_i, \tag{5.3}$$

where $m_i(t)$ is the vector of raw material orders placed at the beginning of week t and delivered at the beginning of week $t + 1$. In other respects, the model is unchanged from those of the previous chapter. That is, the production and orders are determined by the following equations:

$$x_i(t) = (1 + k_i)\, s_i^e(t) - z_i(t), \tag{5.4}$$

$$m_i(t) = (1 + l_i)\, s_i^e(t)b_iC_i - v_i(t), \tag{5.5}$$

where k_i and l_i are the buffer coefficients of product and raw material inventory, respectively, and $z_i(t)$ is the product inventory at the end of week t. Product inventory $z_i(t)$ changes by

$$z_i(t) = z_i(t-1) + x_i(t-1) - s_i(t-1), \tag{5.6}$$

where $s_i(t)$ is the sales volume of product i in week t (delivery is made at the beginning of week $t+1$). As before, the demand for product i, that is equal to its sales volume except in the case of stockout of finished products, consists of the sum of raw material orders and independent demand for this product. Thus,

$$s_i(t) = \sum_{i=1}^{n} m_i(t) + d_i. \tag{5.7}$$

Figure 5.2 illustrates the sequence of events described above.

From (5.4) and (5.6), we obtain

$$x_i(t) = (1 + k_i)\, \Delta s_i^e(t) + s_i(t-1), \tag{5.8}$$

where $\Delta s_i^e(t) = s_i^e(t) - s_i^e(t-1)$.

From (5.1), (5.2), and (5.8), we obtain

$$y_i(t) = (2 + k_i + h_i)\, \Delta s_i^e(t) b_i + s_i(t-1)\, b_i. \tag{5.9}$$

From (5.3), (5.5), and (5.9), we obtain

$$m_i(t) = (3 + k_i + h_i + l_i)\, \Delta s_i^e(t) a_i + s_i(t-1)\, a_i. \tag{5.10}$$

In matrix form, (5.7) and (5.10) are summarized as

$$s(t) = \Delta s^e(t)\,(3I + K + H + L)\, A + s(t-1)\, A + d, \tag{5.11}$$

where K, H, and L are the diagonal matrices of k_i, h_i, and l_i, respectively. (5.11) is obtained by replacing $K + L$ in (4.15) in Chap. 4 with $I + K + L + H$. The increase in the integer part from 2 to 3 in (5.11) reflects that the same demand forecast, $s_i^e(t)$, is used to decide on *three* sets of variables[4]: (i) product production $x_i(t)$, (ii) raw material orders $m_i(t)$, and (iii) works-in-process productions $y_i(t)$. This *increase in the number of decisions using the same demand forecast has a destabilizing effect.* We can apply similar argument to the case where one cycle of production takes more

[4]In other words, $s_i^e(t)$ is used to forecast *three* variables: sales in week t, (i) production in week $t+1$, *and* production of works-in-process in week $t+1$.

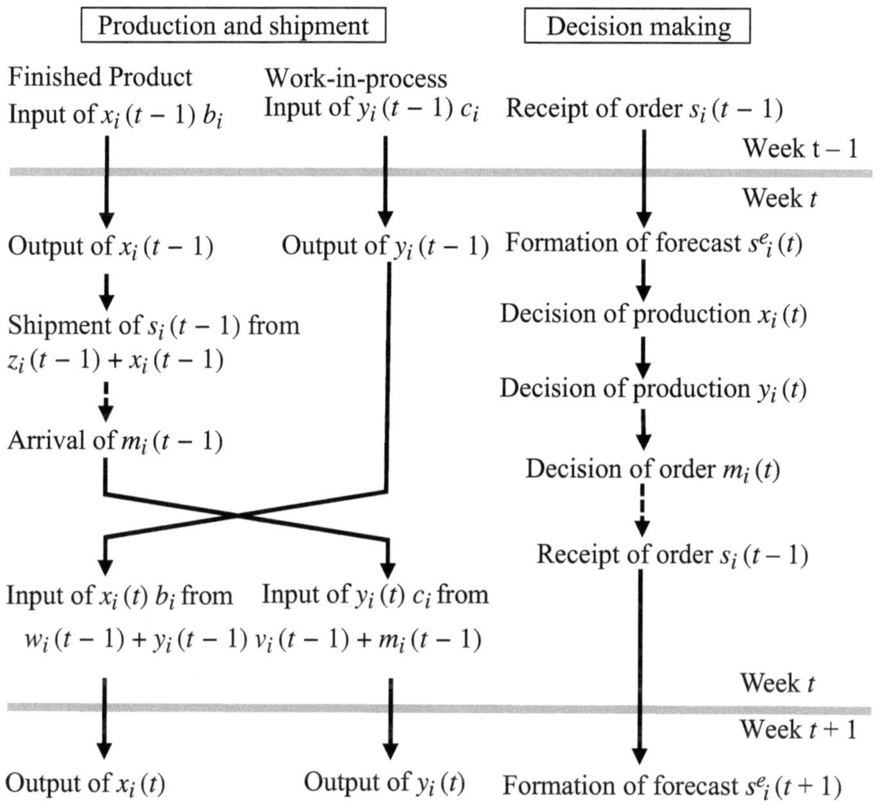

Fig. 5.2 Sequence of actions and decisions

than 3 weeks and the production of works-in-process at each stage is determined by a common demand forecast.

We refer to the system comprising (5.11) and the demand forecast by SMA (the simple moving average):

$$s_i^e(t) = \tau_i^{-1}\left(s_i(t-1) + \cdots + s_i(t-\tau_i)\right)$$

as SMA(w), and the system comprising (5.11) and the demand forecast by GMA (the geometric moving average):

$$s_i^e(t) = s_i^e(t-1) + \gamma_i\left(s_i(t-1) - s_i^e(t-1)\right)$$

as GMA(w), where "w" expresses that these models include work-in-process inventory. Note that τ_i is a positive integer and $0 < \gamma_i \leq 1$.

The dynamic properties of SMA(w) and GMA(w) are the same as those of SMA and GMA, respectively, except for the above replacement. The theorems in Chap. 4 indicate that the constraints for the stability of SMA(w) and GMA(w) are stricter than those of SMA and GMA, respectively, because of the addition of $I + H$. While the stability of GMA with $K = L = 0.2I$ and $\Gamma = 0.25I$ requires $\lambda^{F}(A) < 0.7407$, the stability of GMA(w) with $K = L = H = 0.2I$ and $\Gamma = 0.25I$ requires $\lambda^{F}(A) < 0.6060$. The corresponding sufficient condition, which is also necessary when $-\lambda^{F}(A)$ belongs to A's eigenvalues changes from $\lambda^{F}(A) < 0.5932$ to $\lambda^{F}(A) < 0.4930$.

Let us assume, secondly, that the firm determines $y_i(t)$ to simply recover the decreases in work-in-process inventories. In this case, (5.1) is replaced by

$$y_i(t) = x_i(t)b_i. \tag{5.12}$$

Accordingly, (5.11) is replaced by

$$s(t) = \Delta s^e(t)\,(2I + K + L)\,A + s\,(t-1)\,A + d.$$

This is the same as (4.14) in Chap. 4. Therefore, *as long as the productions of works-in-process at each stage are determined in a purely replenishing manner, an increase in the number of parallel processes does not affect stability*. It is worth emphasizing that buffer work-in-process inventories are necessary even when the decision is made by (5.12), because the input of works-in-process for $x_i(t)$ is made not from $y_i(t)$, but from $w_i(t-1) + y_i(t-1)$. Production $x_i(t)$ is feasible only when the constraint $w_i(t-1) + y_i(t-1) \geq x_i(t)b_i$ is satisfied. Otherwise, the firm must curtail its production plan to the level corresponding to the actual availability of raw materials.

The averaging of past demands in demand forecast cannot eliminate the destabilizing effect caused by increase in the number of decisions using the same demand forecast. However, it would be unlikely that the firm makes forecast-based decisions in all of their short-term adjustments. *The adoption of the pure replenishing rule by the firm in some part of its production and ordering decisions significantly contributes to the stability of the quantity adjustment process, especially when the production process consists of several partial processes and each process is adjustable.*

5.1.2 Partial Inventory Adjustment

In economic literature on investment, partial or delayed adjustment is sometimes assumed. Partial adjustment is the manner of adjustment by which firms fill only a part of the gap between actual and desirable inventory or capital stock. As we have already seen in Chap. 3, this type of adjustment can be regarded as an approximation of the production rule under increasing marginal production cost. In introducing partial adjustment to our model, let us simplify a part of the assumptions as follows.

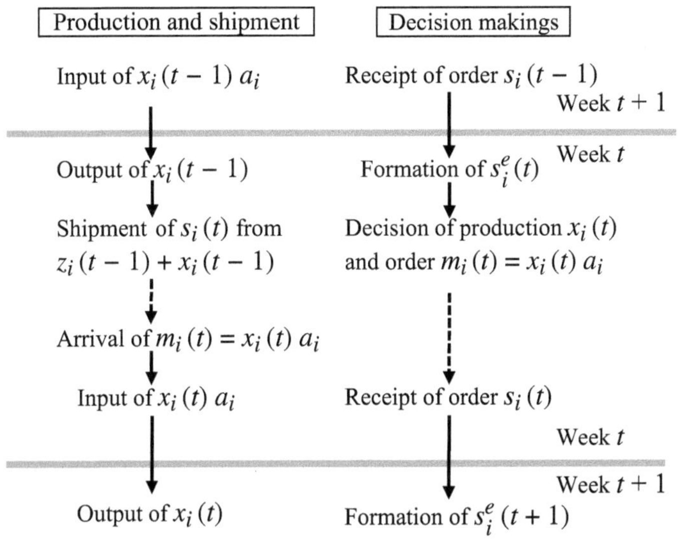

Fig. 5.3 Sequences of actions and decisions

The raw material orders made at the beginning of each week are *instantaneously processed and delivered.* Under this modified assumption, firms do not have to hold buffer raw material inventories because they can at once obtain raw materials as much as exactly required to carry out their production plans. Accordingly, ordering rule (5.5) is replaced by

$$m_i(t) = x_i(t)a_i, \tag{5.13}$$

and product inventory changes not by (5.6), but by

$$z_i(t) = z_i\,(t-1) + x_i\,(t-1) - s_i(t). \tag{5.14}$$

Figure 5.3 illustrates the sequence of events corresponding to these modifications. Because of (5.14), the product inventory at the end of week t is unknown at the beginning of week t.

Under the forecast that demand per week from week t onward is $s_i^e(t)$, the desirable level of product inventory at the end of week t is $k_i s_i^e(t)$, where k_i is the buffer product inventory coefficient. Let $z_i^e(t)$ be the forecasted level of product inventory at the end of week t corresponding to the demand forecast $s_i^e(t)$, namely:

$$z_i^e(t) = z_i\,(t-1) + x_i\,(t-1) - s_i^e(t). \tag{5.15}$$

On the production rule, we assume partial adjustment. More concretely, each firm determines its production volume $x_i(t)$ so that $x_i(t) - s_i^e(t)$ fills the gap between the desirable and the forecasted level of product inventory at a rate of r_i $(0 < r_i < 1)$.[5] That is,

$$\begin{aligned} x_i(t) &= s_i^e(t) + r_i\left(k_i s_i^e(t) - z_i^e(t)\right) \\ &= (1 + r_i + r_i k_i)\, s_i^e(t) - r_i\left(z_i(t-1) + x_i(t-1)\right). \end{aligned} \tag{5.16}$$

From (5.13) and $s_i(t) = \sum_{j=1}^{n} m_{ji}(t) + d_i$, we have

$$s_i(t) = \sum_{j=1}^{n} x_j(t) a_{ji} + d_i \tag{5.17}$$

In matrix notation, (5.14), (5.16), and (5.17) are written as

$$z(t) = z(t-1) + x(t-1) - s(t), \tag{5.18}$$

$$x(t) = s^e(t)\left(\mathrm{I} + R + RK\right) - \left(x(t-1) + x(t-1)\right) R, \tag{5.19}$$

$$s(t) = x(t)A + d, \tag{5.20}$$

respectively, where R is the diagonal matrix of r_i.

As for the demand forecast, we simply assume the static expectation:

$$s^e(t) = s(t-1). \tag{5.21}$$

That is, the firm makes partial adjustment, whereas it does not average past demands in its demand forecast.

(5.18) to (5.21) constitute a complete system of linear difference equations, which can be written in matrix form as:

$$[x(t), x(t-1)] = [x(t-1), x(t-2)]\,\Omega + [dR, 0], \tag{5.22}$$

$$\Omega \equiv \begin{bmatrix} A(I + BR) + (I - R) & I \\ -A(I - R + BR) & \mathrm{O} \end{bmatrix}, \; B \equiv 2I + K.$$

[5]In Lovell (1962), $x_i(t)$ is determined so that $x_i(t) + z_i(t-1)$ covers $s_i(t)$, and therefore, partial adjustment takes the form $x_i(t) = s_i^e(t) + r_i\left(k_i s_i^e(t) - z_i(t-1)\right)$. Meanwhile, here we assume that $x_i(t)$ is determined so that $x_i(t) + z_i(t)$ covers $s_i(t+1)$. Note that, in our model, both $s_i(t+1)$ and $z_i(t)$ are unknown at the beginning of week t.

We shall refer to system (5.22) as PSE, which expresses partial adjustment and the static expectation. PSE is the same as Lovell's second modified models mentioned in Chap. 3 (Eq. (3.36)).

By applying the method that we used in Theorem 4 in Chap. 4, we can prove a proposition that PSE is asymptotically stable if

$$\lambda^{\mathrm{F}}\left(A\left(I+2BR(2I-R)^{-1}\right)\right)<1, \tag{5.23}$$

and this condition is necessary for stability if A has $-\lambda^{\mathrm{F}}(A)$ as its one of eigenvalues.[6]

Inequality (5.23) is very similar to the corresponding stability condition of GMA:

$$\lambda^{\mathrm{F}}\left(\left(2\Gamma B(2I-\Gamma)^{-1}+I\right)A\right)<1. \tag{5.24}$$

In fact, (5.23) is perfectly identical to (5.24) if $R=\Gamma=rI$ and $B=bI$. In this case, since it holds $A(I+2BR(2I-R)^{-1})=(2\Gamma B(2I-\Gamma)^{-1}+1)A=\left(\frac{2rb}{2-r}+1\right)A$, (5.23) is simplified into

$$\lambda^{\mathrm{F}}(A)<\frac{2-r}{2-r+2br}. \tag{5.25}$$

Furthermore, a necessary condition for the stability of PSE is given by

$$\lambda^{\mathrm{F}}(A)<\frac{1}{1-r+br}. \tag{5.26}$$

---

[6]Let $\omega\geq 1$ be an eigenvalue of Ω and $\xi\equiv[\xi_1,\xi_2]$ (both ξ_1 and ξ_n are $1\times n$ vectors) be the corresponding eigenvector. Then, it follows

$$\omega\xi_1=\xi_1AQ(\omega),\quad Q(\omega)=(\omega(I+BR)-(I-R+BR))(\omega I-(I-R))^{-1},$$

hence ω is also an eigenvalue of $AQ(\omega)$, thus $\rho(AQ(\omega))\geq 1$. Let q_i be the i-th diagonal element of $Q(\omega)$, then

$$|q_i|=\left|\frac{\omega(1+b_ir_i)-(1-r_i+b_ir_i)}{\omega-(1-r_i)}\right|=(1+b_ir_i)\left|\frac{\omega-\frac{1-r_i+b_ir_i}{1+b_ir_i}}{\omega-(1-r_i)}\right|\leq\frac{2-r_i+2b_ir_i}{2-r_i}.$$

Hence, $1\leq\rho(AQ)\leq\lambda^{\mathrm{F}}(AQ^{+})\leq\lambda^{\mathrm{F}}(A(I+2BR(2I-R)^{-1})$. Therefore, (5.23) implies $\rho(\Omega)<1$. The same result can be directly obtained by rewriting (4.30) in Chap. 4 as

$$X(t)=X(t-1)\Theta+[d,0]\,,\ \Theta\equiv\begin{bmatrix}(I+\Gamma B)A+(I-\Gamma) & I\\ -(I-\Gamma+\Gamma B)A & \mathrm{O}\end{bmatrix}.$$

where $X(t)\equiv[\xi(t),\xi(t-1)]$, $\xi(t)\equiv s^e(t)\Gamma^{-1}$. If $R=\Gamma$, then Θ and Ω are different only in the direction of muttiplying A.

Conditions (5.25) and (5.26) correspond to conditions (4.36) and (4.35) in the previous chapter, respectively.

Thus, in this case, partial adjustment by reaction coefficient r has the same stabilizing effect as demand forecast by the geometric moving average with smoothing constant r.[7] The equivalence between partial adjustment and averaging of past demands also holds under the same time sequence as in Chap. 4 if firms apply partial adjustment only to raw material orders. In fact, by this assumption, (4.10) in Chap. 4 is replaced by

$$m(t) = s^e(t)\, A\,(I + RL) - v(t)R. \tag{5.27}$$

By combining (5.21) and (5.27) with (4.7) to (4.9) and (4.11) in Chap. 4, we have a complete system of linear difference equations:

$$[s(t), s\,(t-1)] = [s\,(t-1)\,, s\,(t-2)]\,\Omega + [dR, 0]\,. \tag{5.28}$$

Obviously, this system has the same dynamic properties as PSE (and therefore, as GMA) if reaction coefficients and buffer coefficients are uniform among sectors. While such a perfect equivalence does not generally hold, the above two cases clearly indicate that *partial adjustment could contribute to the stabilization of quantity adjustment through a similar mechanism as averaging past demands in the demand forecast formation.*[8]

5.1.3 A Multi-firm Model with Constant Share Coefficients

So far, we have assumed that the firms belonging to the same sector are homogeneous in the sense that their parameters are uniform. This assumption enabled us to aggregate firm-level variables to sector-level ones. In this subsection, we extend

[7]This similarity in the stabilizing effect between partial inventory investment and forecast formation by the geometric moving average was first shown in Morioka (2005). While the partialization of inventory investment is related to increasing marginal cost (see the argument in Sect. 3.2.3, Chap. 3), averaging of past demands is not directly related to the conditions of production.

[8]Blinder and Maccini (1991) reported that estimates of the reaction coefficient (r in our model) obtained by econometric analyses were usually very small. For example, the estimate concerning manufactures that Lovell (1961) gave based on US economic data for 1948–1955 was 0.1521. However, an estimate of the reaction coefficient in partial adjustment can also be interpreted as that of the smoothing constant in demand forecast by the geometric moving average. If firms make their demand forecasts by the geometric moving average, it is not surprising that this rate takes a small value around 0.15 to 0.3. The observed slowness of adjustment likely reflects the gradual nature of the revision of demand forecast.

our model to the case where firms belonging to the same sector are not totally homogeneous. For this purpose, the assumptions of the model are modified in the following manner.

Let ν_i be the number of firms belonging to sector i (i.e., producing product i), and let N be the total number of firms, that is, $N = \nu_1 + \cdots + \nu_n$. Hereafter, we refer to the j-th firm of sector i as firm (i,j). Thus, we can arrange N firms in the following order:

$$\underbrace{(1,1),\ldots,(1,\nu_1)}_{\text{sector } 1};\ldots;\underbrace{(i,1),\ldots,(i,\nu_i)}_{\text{sector } i};\ldots;\underbrace{(n,1),\ldots,(n,\nu_n)}_{\text{sector } n}.$$

The firms belonging to the same sector produce products that could, while perfectly substitutable from the technological viewpoint, be different in other respects such as prices, delivery terms and services. Firm (i,j) and firm (k,h) $(i \neq k)$ can be different production units (factories) of the same firm. The essential premise for the analysis below is that the decisions made by individual "firms" on production and raw material orders are *mutually independent*. The input coefficient vector of firm (i,j) is denoted by

$$a_{ij} = \left[a_{ij,1},\ldots,a_{ij,n}\right],$$

where $a_{ij,k}$ is the input of product k required *by the techniques of firm* (i,j) per unit output of product i. The production techniques of firms belonging to the same sector are not necessarily uniform.

Let δ_{ij}^{kh} be the relative share of firm (k,h) in firm (i,j)'s purchase of product k as one of raw materials (do not confuse these k, h with buffer coefficients). By definition,

$$\sum_{h=1}^{\nu_k}\delta_{ij}^{kh} = 1 \ \ (k \in \{1,\ldots,n\}, h \in \{1,\ldots,\nu_i\}).$$

The share coefficients δ_{ij}^{kh} are determined by various factors related to the competition among sellers. We assume that *these coefficients remain constant in the short-term.*

Let $\delta_{ij}^{k} = \left[\delta_{ij}^{k1},\ldots,\delta_{ij}^{k\nu_k}\right]$, a $1 \times \nu_k$ vector, and

$$A \equiv \begin{bmatrix} A_{11} & \ldots & A_{1n} \\ \vdots & & \vdots \\ A_{n1} & \ldots & A_{nn} \end{bmatrix}, A_{ij} = \begin{bmatrix} a_{i1,j}\delta_{i1}^{j} \\ \vdots \\ a_{i\nu_i,j}\delta_{i\nu_i}^{j} \end{bmatrix} = \begin{bmatrix} a_{i1,j}\delta_{i1}^{j1} & \cdots & a_{i1,j}\delta_{i1}^{j\nu_j} \\ \vdots & \ddots & \vdots \\ a_{i\nu_i,j}\delta_{i\nu_i}^{j1} & \cdots & a_{i\nu_i,j}\delta_{i\nu_i}^{j\nu_j} \end{bmatrix},$$

where A is an $N \times N$ matrix and A_{ij} is a $\nu_i \times \nu_j$ matrix.

We call $\delta_{ik}^{jh} a_{ik,j}$ an "order coefficient" from firm (i,k) to firm (j,h). Let, for example, $N = 4$, $\nu_1 = \nu_2 = 2$, and

$$a_{11} = [0, 0.5], a_{12} = [0, 0.6], a_{21} = [0.4, 0], a_{22} = [0.5, 0].$$

Then, from the above definition, A is given by

$$A = \begin{bmatrix} 0 & 0 & 0.5\delta_{11}^{21} & 0.5\left(1 - \delta_{11}^{21}\right) \\ 0 & 0 & 0.6\delta_{12}^{21} & 0.6\left(1 - \delta_{12}^{21}\right) \\ 0.4\delta_{21}^{11} & 0.4\left(1 - \delta_{21}^{11}\right) & 0 & 0 \\ 0.5\delta_{22}^{11} & 0.5\left(1 - \delta_{22}^{11}\right) & 0 & 0 \end{bmatrix}$$

The productivity of the overall economy depends both on the technology of each firm and the share coefficients.[9]

Let p_{ij} be the price of product i produced by firm (i,j). As already mentioned, the prices of products produced by firms belonging to the same sector need not be identical. However, they are assumed to be strictly greater than the unit cost of any firm producing this product, that is,

$$p_{ij} > \left(\sum_{h=1}^{\nu_1} p_{1h}\delta_{ij}^{1h}\right) a_{ij,1} + \cdots + \left(\sum_{h=1}^{\nu_n} p_{nh}\delta_{ij}^{nh}\right) a_{ij,n}$$

for $j \in \{1, \ldots, \nu_i\}$, $i \in \{1, \ldots, n\}$. This assumption guarantees that $I - A$ is nonnegatively invertible (I is the unit matrix of order N). If $p_{i1} = \cdots = p_{i\nu_i} = p_i$ for any i, then the above inequality is reduced to $p_i > p_1 a_{ij,1} + \cdots + p_n a_{ij,n}$. Note that the unit cost depends on the order coefficients if prices are not uniform among firms belonging to the same sector.

As before, final demand (capital investment and final consumption) per week is exogenously given and denoted by $d = [d_1, \ldots, d_n]$. Let δ_{ij} be the relative share of firm (i,j) in the final demand for product i. Then, the final demand for the product of

[9] In this numerical example, firm (1,1) is more technologically efficient than firm (1,2). Thus, the larger δ_{21}^{11} and δ_{22}^{11} are, the more efficient the economy becomes. Similarly, since firm (2,1) is more technologically efficient than firm (2,2), the larger δ_{11}^{21} and δ_{12}^{21} are, the more efficient the economy becomes. On the Frobenius root of A, it holds

$$\frac{1}{\sqrt{5}} = \lambda^{\mathrm{F}}\left(\begin{bmatrix} 0 & 0.5 \\ 0.4 & 0 \end{bmatrix}\right) < \lambda^{\mathrm{F}}(A) < \lambda^{\mathrm{F}}\left(\begin{bmatrix} 0 & 0.6 \\ 0.5 & 0 \end{bmatrix}\right) = \sqrt{\frac{3}{10}}.$$

However, it should be noted that, in more general cases, the relative efficiency of each technique depends on the relative prices.

firm (i,j) is $d_{ij} = \delta_{ij} d_i$. Each firm's decision about production and raw material orders is the same as before. At the beginning of week t, firm (i,j) decides on its production $x_{ij}(t)$ and (the vector of) raw material orders $m_{ij}(t)$ based on the following equations:

$$x_{ij}(t) = \left(1 + k_{ij}\right) s_{ij}^{e}(t) - z_{ij}(t), \tag{5.29}$$

$$m_{ij}(t) = \left(1 + l_{ij}\right) s_{ij}^{e}(t) a_{ij} - v_{ij}(t), \tag{5.30}$$

where the variables and constants with subscript (i,j) correspond to those with subscript i in the models of Chap. 4. Each component of firm (i,j)'s raw material orders vector $m_{ij}(t) = [m_{ij,1}(t), \ldots m_{ij,n}(t)]$ is divided into firm-level orders by the relative share coefficients. Of the total purchase of product k as an input, firm (i,j) buys $\delta_{ij}^{kh} m_{ij,k}(t)$ from firm (k, h). Therefore, the sum of raw material orders that firm (i,j) receives is given by

$$m^{ij}(t) = \sum_{k=1}^{n} \sum_{h=1}^{\nu_k} \delta_{kh}^{ij} m_{kh,i}(t). \tag{5.31}$$

The product inventory $z_{ij}(t)$ and (the vector of) raw material inventories $v_{ij}(t)$ change, by the following equations:

$$z_{ij}(t) = z_{ij}(t-1) + x_{ij}(t-1) - s_{ij}(t-1), \tag{5.32}$$

$$v_{ij}(t) = v_{ij}(t-1) + m_{ij}(t-1) - x_{ij}(t) a_{ij}. \tag{5.33}$$

Thus, the total demand directed to firm (j, h) is

$$s_{ij}(t) = m^{ij}(t) + d_{ij} = \sum_{k=1}^{n} \sum_{h=1}^{\nu_k} \delta_{kh}^{ij} m_{kh,i}(t) + \delta_{ij} d_i. \tag{5.34}$$

Let $s(t)$ be the vector of firm-level demand $s_{ij}(t)$, that is,

$$s(t) = \left[s_{11}(t), \ldots, s_{1\nu_1}(t), \ldots, s_{n1}(t), \ldots, s_{n\nu_n}(t)\right].$$

Likewise, let $s^e(t)$ be the vector of firm-level demand forecast $s_{ij}^{e}(t)$, and d be the vector of firm-level final demand d_{ij}. Equations (5.29) to (5.34) are, in matrix form, summarized as

$$s(t) = \left(s^e(t) - s^e(t-1)\right) BA + s(t-1) A + d, \tag{5.35}$$

where B is the diagonal matrix of $2 + k_{ij} + l_{ij}$. This is the multi-firm version of (4.14) in the previous chapter. We can close this system by the assumption on the method of demand forecast. The multi-firm version of SMA consists of (5.35) and demand forecast by the simple moving average:

$$s_{ij}^{e}(t) = \tau_{ij}^{-1}\left(s_{ij}\left(t-1\right) + \cdots + s_{ij}\left(t-\tau_{ij}\right)\right), \tag{5.36}$$

where τ_{ij} is a positive integer. The multi-firm version of GMA consists of (5.35) and demand forecast by the geometric moving average:

$$s_{ij}^{e}(t) = s_{ij}^{e}\left(t-1\right) + \gamma_{ij}\left(s_{ij}\left(t-1\right) - s_{ij}^{e}\left(t-1\right)\right), \tag{5.37}$$

where $0 < \gamma_{ij} \leq 1$. The stationary point of both systems is

$$s^{*} = s^{e*} = s(I-A)^{-1}.$$

Differing from sector-level models, *this stationary point depends on the share coefficients*. A rise in the relative share of firm (i,j) in the intermediate and final demand for product i causes the expansion of its production at the stationary state. We can directly apply to this model the theorems on the dynamic properties of SMA and GMA shown in Chap. 4. By Theorem 1, the system comprising (5.35) and (5.36) is stable if

$$\lambda^{\mathrm{F}}\left(\left(2T^{-1}B + I\right)A\right) < 1, \tag{5.38}$$

where T is the diagonal matrix of τ_{ij}. This condition is also necessary for stability if A has an eigenvalue, $\mu = \omega\lambda^{\mathrm{F}}(A)$ such that $\omega^{\tau_{ij}} = -1$ for any $i \in \{1, \ldots, N\}$ and $j \in \{1, \ldots, \nu_i\}$. Similarly, by Theorem 4 in Chap. 4, the system comprising (5.35) and (5.37) is stable if

$$\lambda^{\mathrm{F}}\left(\left(2\Gamma B(2I-\Gamma)^{-1} + I\right)A\right) < 1, \tag{5.39}$$

where Γ is the diagonal matrix of γ_{ij}. This condition is also necessary for stability if A has $-\lambda^{\mathrm{F}}(A)$ as one of its eigenvalues. Conditions (5.38) and (5.39) indicate that the effect of parameters τ_{ij},γ_{ij} and b_{ij} on stability is the same as the case of sector-level models. In particular, *the averaging of past demands in demand forecast formation (an increase in the averaging period or a decrease in the smoothing constant) also has a stabilizing effect in the firm-level model.* Thus, so long as the share coefficients can be stable in the short term, the heterogeneity of firms within a single sector does not undermine the basic validity of our sector-level analysis.

While both stability conditions depend on the share coefficients, it is possible to find a stability condition that is more restrictive but independent from the share coefficients. Let $a_{ij}^{*} \equiv \max_{k\in\{1,\ldots,n_i\}} a_{ik,j}$, and

$$A_0^* \equiv \begin{bmatrix} a_{11}^* & \cdots & a_{1n}^* \\ \vdots & \ddots & \vdots \\ a_{n1}^* & \cdots & a_{nn}^* \end{bmatrix}, A^* \equiv \begin{bmatrix} a_{11}^* D_{11} & \cdots & a_{1n}^* D_{1n} \\ \vdots & \ddots & \vdots \\ a_{n1}^* D_{n1} & \cdots & a_{nn}^* D_{nn} \end{bmatrix}, D_{ij} \equiv \begin{bmatrix} \delta_{i1}^j \\ \vdots \\ \delta_{i\nu_i}^j \end{bmatrix}.$$

Then, $A \leq A^*$, hence $\lambda^{\mathrm{F}}(A) \leq \lambda^{\mathrm{F}}(A^*)$. Let ξ be the right-hand Frobenius vector of A_0^*, and let η be the $N \times 1$ vector formed by arraying ν_1 number of $\xi_1, \ldots, \nu_n$ number of ξ_n, where ξ_i is i-th element of vector ξ. By definition of the share coefficients, the sum of any row of matrix D_{ij} is equal to 1. Hence, $A^*\eta = \lambda^{\mathrm{F}}\left(A_0^*\right)\eta$.

If A^* is indecomposable, then η is positive and $\lambda^{\mathrm{F}}\left(A_0^*\right)$ is also the Frobenius root of A^*. If A^* is decomposable, then the same can be said of its indecomposable principal submatrix.[10] Consequently, we have $\lambda^{\mathrm{F}}\left(A_0^*\right) = \lambda^{\mathrm{F}}(A^*)$. Therefore,

$$\lambda^{\mathrm{F}}\left(\left(2T^{-1}B + I\right)A\right) \leq (2b/\tau + 1)\,\lambda^{\mathrm{F}}\left(A_0^*\right),$$

$$\lambda^{\mathrm{F}}\left(\left(2\Gamma B(2I - \Gamma)^{-1} + I\right)A\right) \leq (2\gamma b/(2-\gamma) + 1)\,\lambda^{\mathrm{F}}\left(A_0^*\right),$$

where $2b/\tau = \max\ 2b_{ij}/\tau_{ij}$, $2\gamma b/(2-\gamma) = \max 2\gamma_{ij}b_{ij}/(2-\gamma_{ij})$. Hence, the system comprising (5.35) and (5.36) is stable if $\lambda^{\mathrm{F}}\left(A_0^*\right) < \tau/(2b+\tau)$, while the system comprising (5.35) and (5.37) is stable if $\lambda^{\mathrm{F}}\left(A_0^*\right) < (2-\gamma)/(\gamma\,(2b-1)+2)$. These conditions do not depend on the allocation of orders by buyers among sellers.

5.2 Quantity Adjustment Accompanied by Stockout, Rationing, and Bottleneck

5.2.1 Assumptions on Firms' Reaction to Stockout

The analysis of the quantity adjustment process in the previous chapter was restricted to the case in which productions and transactions were not hindered by stockout. When a stockout of product inventory occurs in a firm producing a particular product, a part of (or all) the orders received by this firm cannot be satisfied. If each buyer firm of this product has sufficient inventory of this raw material, then the occurrence of a stockout does not affect its production. However, if one of these buyer firms cannot compensate the (partial) failure of purchase by its raw material inventory, then this firm is forced to curtail its production to the level corresponding to the available amount of the input which becomes bottleneck. Such

[10]Concerning this point, refer to Nikaido (1961, pp. 85–89). Here we assume that technologies of firms producing the same product are not significantly different. If this is not the case, then it would be meaningless to think about matrix A^*.

unintentional curtailment of production could affect the productions of other firms by way of raw material shortage. Thus, by tracing the process *after* the occurrence of a stockout, we can deepen our understanding of the function of quantity adjustment and its limitations. To avoid excessive complication, in this section we once again return to the sector-level model.

When a stockout occurs, *we must make a clear distinction between intentions and their actual results*. Let $\tilde{s}_i(t)$ be the actual sales volume of product i, which is equal to *the short side* of demand $s_i(t)$ and supply $x_i(t) + z_i(t)$. That is,

$$\tilde{s}_i(t) = \min\ \{s_i(t), x_i(t) + z_i(t)\}\,. \tag{5.40}$$

As before, the total demand for product i is the sum of raw material orders and the final demand:

$$s_i(t) = \sum_{j=1}^{n} m_{ji}(t) + d_i\,. \tag{5.41}$$

If $s_i(t) > x_i(t) + z_i(t)$, a stockout of product i occurs. In this case, the actual purchase of each product depends on *the rationing rule*, that is, on *how the firm assigns its sales volume to buyers*. There are several typical rationing rules, including sales on a first-come-first-served basis, random selection, and setting an upper limit of the purchase volume. Furthermore, sellers may have reasons to prioritize some buyers over others.[11] However, for simplicity, we assume that the demands are satisfied *proportionally* to their volume. This rationing rule requires that each firm decides the assignment of its sales volume *after* the receipt of orders in that week from all the buyers.

Let $\tilde{m}_i(t)$ be the vector of the *fulfilled* part of the raw material orders; and $\tilde{d}(t)$ be the vector of the *fulfilled* part of final demand. Then, under the above assumptions, they are determined by the following equations:[12]

$$\tilde{m}_{ij}(t) = m_{ij}(t)\frac{\tilde{s}_j(t)}{s_j(t)} = \frac{m_{ij}(t)}{m_{1j}(t) + \cdots + m_{nj}(t) + d_j}\tilde{s}_j(t), \tag{5.42}$$

$$\tilde{d}_j(t) = d_j\frac{\tilde{s}_j(t)}{s_j(t)} = \frac{d_j}{m_{1j}(t) + \cdots + m_{nj}(t) + d_j}\tilde{s}_j(t), \tag{5.43}$$

Unfulfilled demands (orders) may be recorded and carried over to the next week by sellers as backlog. In this case, the backlog would play the role of "negative

[11] As we have argued in Chap. 3, this priority often plays a significant role under the predominance of purchase competition. In a market characterized by chronic shortage, buyers must make various efforts to win the favor of sellers.

[12] Here we do not consider the possibility that the firm intentionally inflates its raw material orders to get more under this rationing rule. On such customs, which were widely observed in the socialist economies, refer to Kornai (1980, 1992).

inventory," so to speak, and as such, might affect decisions on production and demands.[13] However, again for the sake of simplicity, we assume that *unfulfilled orders are simply cancelled.* This assumption implies that the decision on production and raw material orders does not depend on past unfulfilled demands. Instead, we shall consider the non-negativity constraints of these variables explicitly. The precise expressions of production rule (4.3) and ordering rule (4.4) are as follows:

$$x_i(t) = \max\left\{(1+k_i)\, s_i^e(t) - z_i(t), 0\right\}, \tag{5.44}$$

$$m_{ij}(t) = \max\left\{(1+l_i)\, s_i^e(t)a_{ij} - v_{ij}(t), 0\right\}. \tag{5.45}$$

Note that $x_i\,(t)$ represents firm i's intended production volume and $m_{ij}\,(t)$ represents firm i's intended purchase of raw material j.

Let $\tilde{x}_i(t)$ be the *actual* production volume and $M_{ij}\,(t) \equiv v_{ij}\,(t) + m_{ij}\,(t)$. Then, under a Leontief-type technology,

$$\tilde{x}_i(t) = \min\left\{x_i(t), M_{in}\,(t-1)\,/a_{i1}, \ldots, M_{in}\,(t-1)\,/a_{in}\right\}, \tag{5.46}$$

where $\tilde{x}_i(t) = x_i(t)$ holds if and only if $v_{ij}\,(t-1) + m_{ij}\,(t-1) \geq a_{ij}x_i(t)$ holds for any j. If this condition is not satisfied concerning one of raw materials, it becomes a *bottleneck* of production.

The change in product inventory is equal to the gap between the *actual* production and *actual* sales. Similarly, the change in raw material inventories is equal to the gap between the *actual* purchase of raw materials and their *actual* consumption. That is,[14]

$$z_i(t) = z_i\,(t-1) + \tilde{x}_i\,(t-1) - \tilde{s}_i(t)\,(t-1)\,, \tag{5.47}$$

$$v_i(t) = v_i\,(t-1) + \tilde{m}_i\,(t-1) - \tilde{x}_i(t)a_i. \tag{5.48}$$

On the demand forecast, we assume GMA (the geometric moving average):

$$s_i^e(t) = s_i^e\,(t-1) + \gamma_i\left(s_i\,(t-1) - s_i^e\,(t-1)\right) \quad (0 < \gamma_i \leq 1)\,. \tag{5.49}$$

(5.40) to (5.49) constitute a system of nonlinear difference equations. Let us examine the movement of this system by numerical computations. Let

$$A = \begin{bmatrix} 0 & 0.5 & 0.25 \\ 0.5 & 0 & 0.15 \\ 0.15 & 0.15 & 0 \end{bmatrix}, \qquad d = [88 \;\; 112 \;\; 132]\,,$$

[13]In order to describe the short-term adjustment process in the socialist system, Kornai and Simonovits (1981), Martos (1990) and Morioka (1991–1992) developed models in which each firm adjusts productions and sales based on the deviations of the backlog of unfulfilled orders from their normal levels.

[14]As in the previous chapter, $\tilde{s}_i(t)$ is assumed to be delivered at the beginning of week $t+1$.

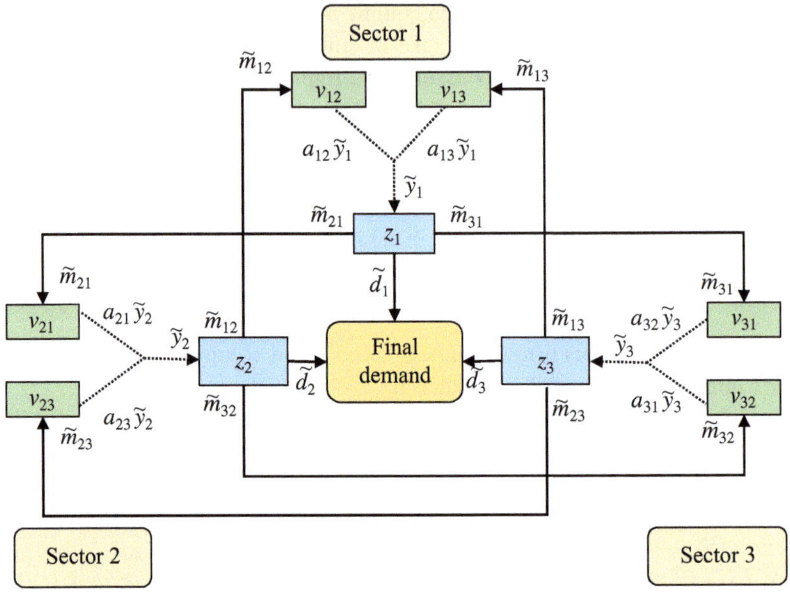

Fig. 5.4 Flow of product between three sectors

and $k_i = k, l_i = l, \gamma_i = \gamma, d' = (1+g)d$. Suppose that in week 0, all the variables take the stationary values corresponding to final demand d. That is,

$$s(0) = s^e(0) = x(0) = d(\mathrm{I} - A)^{-1} = [264, 280, 240]\,,$$

$$z(0) = kx(0), \quad m_i(0) = x_i(0)a_i, \quad v_i(0) = lm_i(0) \quad (i \in \{1, 2, 3\})\,.$$

The set of the eigenvalues of A is $\{0.6, -0.5, -0.1\}$. By virtue of Theorem 5 in Chap. 4, the necessary and sufficient condition for the stability of GMA(u) with the above parameters is given by $\gamma < 2/(2k + 2l + 5)$.

Figure 5.4 illustrates the flow of products through production and transaction in the economy consisting of three sectors. The arrows connecting the inventory variables represent the routes by which a stockout in one sector might propagate to other sectors. A depletion of raw material inventory directly affects the production process using this raw material but does not necessarily affect the sales of finished products. Product inventory can absorb, within a certain range, the impact of contraction of decrease production volume caused by the shortage of raw materials. Similarly, a depletion of product inventory causes rationing of this product but does not necessarily affect the productions of other firms using this product as a raw material. Raw material inventory can absorb, within a certain range, the impact of a decrease in the available raw materials caused by the failure of purchase.

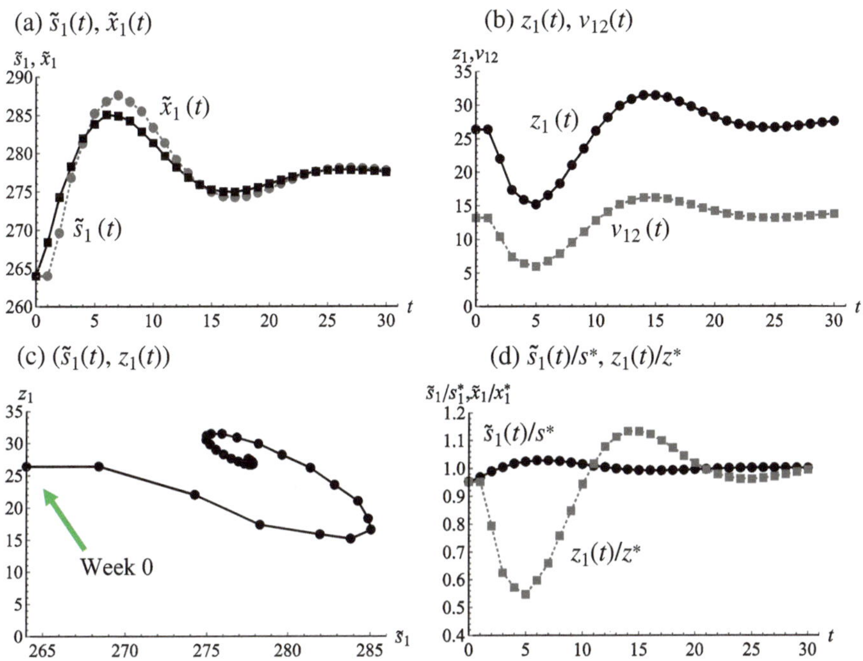

Fig. 5.5 Movement of variables when the stability condition is satisfied

5.2.2 *Adaptation to an Increase in the Final Demand*

Let us assume that $k = l = 0.1$, $\gamma = 0.25$, and $g = 0.05$. In this case, the above stability condition is satisfied. When the weekly final demand increases from d to $d' = 1.05d$ since week 1, the variables gradually converge to a new stationary point corresponding to d'. The new stationary point of demand and production is

$$d'(\mathrm{I} - A)^{-1} = [277.2, 294, 252] .$$

Although this convergence is accompanied by cyclical oscillations, product and raw material inventories can absorb the increases in demands and necessary inputs caused by 5% increase in final demand.

Figure 5.5 shows the change in the variables of sector 1 from week 0 to week 30.[15] The pattern of change in production $\tilde{x}_1(t)$, denoted by the dashed line in Fig. 5.5a, is similar to that of sales $\tilde{s}_1(t)$ except for a small delay. The pattern of change in raw material inventory $v_{12}(t)$, denoted by the dashed line in Fig. 5.5b, is similar to that of the product inventory $z_1(t)$. As shown in Fig. 5.5c, $(\tilde{s}_1(t), z_1(t))$

[15] Since in this case the increases rates of final demand are uniform among sectors, patterns of changes of the variables belonging to different sectors do not show any considerable differences.

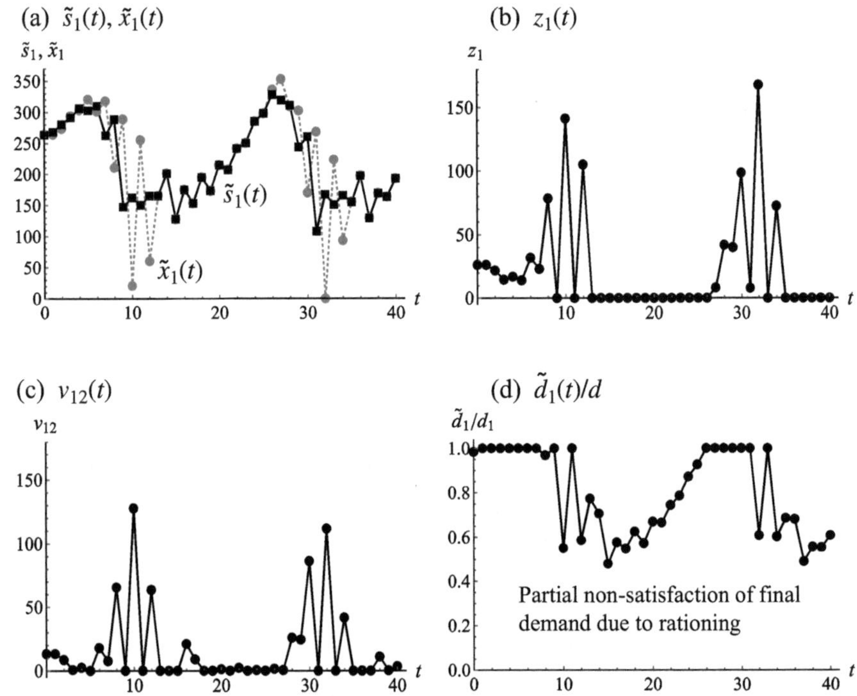

Fig. 5.6 Movement of variables when the stability condition is not satisfied

approaches the new stationary point on the $\tilde{s}_1$-z_1 plane counterclockwise. Figure 5.5d indicates that the relative oscillation of product inventory is much larger than that of sales.

What happens when the values of the parameters do not satisfy the stability condition? As an extreme case, let us assume that $\gamma = 1$ (the static expectation). In this case, the GMA is unstable. However, it should be noted that the instability of the linear process ignoring nonnegative constraints on the variables does not directly imply an explosive divergence of the nonlinear process subject to this constraint.[16]

Figure 5.6 shows changes in the variable of sector 1 for 40 weeks when final demand increases from d to 1.05 d since week 1 ($k = l = 0.1$). At a first glance, the movement of $\tilde{s}_1(t)$ seems to resemble a limit cycle with a large amplitude. However, the center of its fluctuation is considerably smaller than its stationary value. The fluctuation in production $\tilde{x}_1(t)$, denoted by the dashed line in Fig. 5.6a, is much larger than that of $\tilde{s}_1(t)$. From week 31 to week 33, $\tilde{x}_1(t)$ suddenly dips from 269 to 0 and again jumps to 224. Product inventory $z_1(t)$ first shows extreme oscillations, and then remains at zero (i.e., stockout continues) for forteen weeks, and then, these

[16]Here the term "linear process"is an abridged expression of a process following a linear difference equation.

Table 5.1 Occurrences of stockout under one-time increase in final demand

(i) Product inventories

		g (growth rate of final demand, %)									
		2	4	6	8	10	12	14	16	18	20
k, l (buffer coefficients, %)	2	0	37	60	78	87	87	87	87	87	87
	4	0	0	21	36	47	57	66	75	84	87
	6	0	0	0	14	27	34	43	50	57	63
	8	0	0	0	0	7	20	27	34	40	46
	10	0	0	0	0	0	6	15	24	29	34
	12	0	0	0	0	0	0	4	14	20	26
	14	0	0	0	0	0	0	0	3	11	17
	16	0	0	0	0	0	0	0	0	2	7
	18	0	0	0	0	0	0	0	0	0	2
	20	0	0	0	0	0	0	0	0	0	0

(ii) Raw material inventories

		g (growth rate of final demand, %)									
		2	4	6	8	10	12	14	16	18	20
k, l (buffer coefficients, %)	2	10	39	60	78	87	87	87	87	87	87
	4	0	10	26	39	49	57	66	75	84	87
	6	0	0	10	23	29	40	46	51	57	63
	8	0	0	0	10	23	27	33	36	43	49
	10	0	0	0	0	10	15	25	30	32	36
	12	0	0	0	0	0	10	17	21	27	29
	14	0	0	0	0	0	0	10	18	21	26
	16	0	0	0	0	0	0	0	10	19	23
	18	0	0	0	0	0	0	0	2	10	14
	20	0	0	0	0	0	0	0	0	2	10

patterns are roughly repeated alternately. The movement of raw material inventory $m_{12}(t)$ shows a similar pattern. As shown in Fig. 5.6d, the continuous stockout of product inventory significantly hinders the satisfaction of the final demand. The sufficiency rate of final demand through 40 weeks is less than 80%, and even drops to approximately 50% at particular periods.

These persistent and strong oscillations are common in the case where final demand shrinks. Although the non-negativity constraints suppress explosive movements, *this suppression does not guarantee the approximation of the economy toward the new stationary point.* Adaptation to an increase in final demand requires the satisfaction of the stability condition. However, even if the stability condition is satisfied, the frequent occurrences of stockouts are inevitable when the growth rate of final demand is considerably high. Let us return to the case with $\gamma = 0.25$ and give various values to the buffer coefficients and the rate of increase in final demand. Table 5.1 indicates how the occurrence frequency of stockout depends on the buffer inventory coefficients and the growth rate of final demand under the

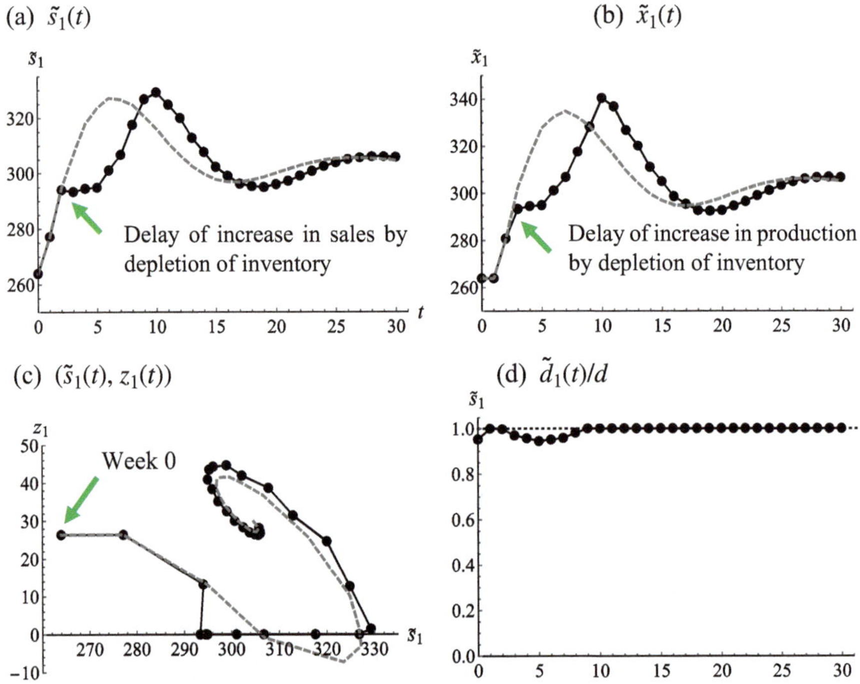

Fig. 5.7 Adaptation to a large increase in final demand

above assumption. The numbers written in the table are total occurrences of stockout in 3 sectors for 30 weeks. The possible maximum of product stockout occurrences is $3 \times 29 = 87$, and the possible maximum of raw material stockout occurrences is $6 \times 29 = 174$ (by the assumption about the initial situation, stockout never occurs in week 1). However, because of the rationing, available raw materials are not proportional to their unit inputs. Therefore, a shortage of one of raw materials is usually accompanied with a surplus of the other raw material. Considering these circumstances, the actual maximum of raw material stockout occurrences is 87.

According to this table, transition to the new stationary point without the occurrence of product stockout is possible if the rate of increase in final demand is not greater than the buffer inventory ratio. While the depletion of raw materials occurs for several weeks when g is equal to k $(= l)$, product inventories can absorb the disturbing effects caused by modification of the production plan.

Let us examine more closely the process when final demand increases by a rate higher than the buffer coefficient. Assume that $k = l = 0.1$ and $g = 0.15$. Under these parameters, product stockout occurs from week 2 to week 8 in sector 1 and sector 3, and from week 3 to week 8 in sector 2. Figure 5.7 illustrates *how the movements of variables are modified by the nonnegative constraint on inventory*. The dashed lines indicate the movement of corresponding variables when inventories can take negative values. Owing to the stockout of product, sector 1 is forced to delay its adaptation to the increase in final demand. The kinks in the curve in Fig. 5.7a reflect the exhaustion of the product inventory. Product inventory $z_1(t)$ is soon depleted and remains at zero for seven weeks. During this period, the production and sales gradually increase with a slight curtailment in the realized final demand. From week 9, variables finally start an ordinary movement to the new stationary point. A stockout in the early weeks would somewhat reduce the satisfaction of buyers.[17]

As shown in Table 5.1, the larger the extent by which the rate of increase in final demand exceeds the buffer coefficient, the greater the occurrence frequency of stockouts, and the greater the extent by which the final demand is not realized. So long as the growth rate of final demand is not so large in relation to the buffer coefficient, the unrealized part of final demand due to rationing is limited, and the exhaustion of product inventory does not last very long. However, *if the rate of increase in final demand is far greater than the buffer coefficient, then large-scale and long-lasting rationing is inevitable*. In such cases, quantity adjustment by itself cannot perform the task of balancing demand and production; thus, *restraint of excessive final demand is possible only by a considerable change in relative prices* (including wage rate and rate of interests).[18] This is a limit of quantity adjustment.

We have so far ignored the constraint imposed on the production volume by the capacity of fixed equipment. If the production volume cannot exceed a certain limit, then this constraint might affect the movement of various variables. Let $\overline{x}_i$ represent the upper limit of production under the current fixed equipment of sector i. Then, (5.46) must be modified to

$$\tilde{x}_i(t) = \min\{x_i(t), M_{in}(t-1)/a_{i1}, \ldots, M_{in}(t-1)/a_{in}, \overline{x}_i\}, \tag{5.50}$$

to ensure that $\tilde{x}_i(t) \leq \overline{x}_i$. For numerical computations, let us assume, in addition to the previous set of parameters ($\gamma = 0.25, k = l = 0.1, g = 0.15$), that the capacity constraint is given by

$$\overline{x} = (\overline{x}_1, \overline{x}_2, \overline{x}_3) = 1.2d(\mathrm{I} - A)^{-1} = [316.8, 334, 288].$$

This assumption implies that the initial operation rate is 5/6.

Figure 5.8 illustrates how this constraint affects the movement of sales and production. The dashed lines show the changes in these variables when production takes any positive value. From the comparison between the solid and dashed lines, we can see that the production capacity constraint hinders a rapid increase in sales and production volumes. Production $x_1(t)$ reaches its upper limit in week 8 and sticks to this limit till week 16. Similar to the non negativity constraint, *the capacity constraint on production somewhat suppresses oscillation*.

[17] If the final demand is highly prioritized over the intermediate demand in the rationing at the time of stockout, then the economy continues to shrink because of the shortage of raw materials.

[18] A decline in the demand for capital investment requires a raise in real interest rates, while a decline in the demand for consumption goods requires a reduction in real wage rates.

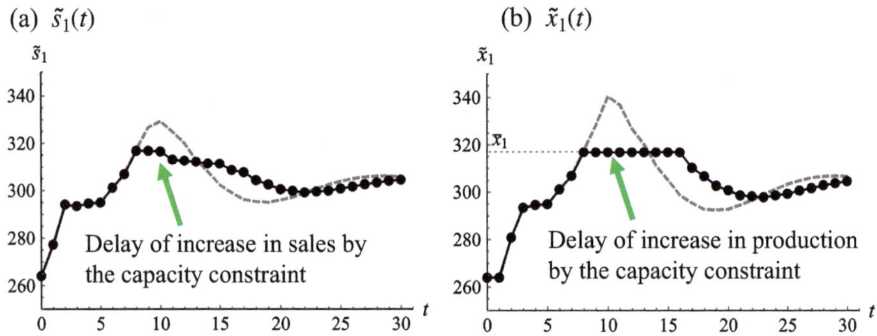

Fig. 5.8 Adaptation under the capacity constraint

If the new stationary point corresponding to the increased final demand exceeds the capacity constraint, then the economy cannot achieve the transition to this new stationary point. The achievability of the transition depends on the final demand for each product, as well as on the scale of each sector's capacity. The structure of final demand, in turn, depends on relative prices. A prompt transition is possible only when relative prices lie in the range ensuring that the production levels of each product at the corresponding stationary point are within the production capacities. Thus, smooth functioning of quantity adjustment presupposes that prices are adequately set in the sense that they satisfy the above condition.

5.2.3 *Adaptation to Random Changes in the Final Demand*

In the previous subsection, we supposed that final demand is kept constant after a one-time increase. This supposition reflects our recognition that changes in intermediate demand and final demand belong to different time horizons. However, at least a part of final demand will be exposed to accidental fluctuations for various reasons. Even if the average final demand per week is constant, buffer inventory is indispensable to absorb the disturbances caused by such accidental fluctuations. In order to clarify this point, we assume that final demand for each week independently follows an identical normal distribution. More concretely, let

$$d(t) \equiv \left[(1 + \sigma \xi_1(t))\, d_1, \ldots, \left(1 + \sigma \xi_n(t)\right) d_n \right],$$

where $\xi_i(t)$ follows the normal distribution with an average value of 0 and a standard deviation of 0.01. Thus, σ is the standard deviation of $\sigma \xi_1(t)$ measured by percentage.

Table 5.2 Occurrences of stockout under random fluctuations in final demand

(i) Product inventories

	σ (standard deviation of final demand, %)											
k, l (buffer coefficient, %)	1	2	3	4	5	6	7	8	9	10	11	12
2	0	1	10	15	22	29	42	49	59	60	64	66
4	0	0	0	1	6	10	14	15	18	23	26	28
6	0	0	0	0	1	1	6	7	9	14	14	15
8	0	0	0	0	0	0	1	1	5	6	9	9
10	0	0	0	0	0	0	0	0	1	1	4	6
12	0	0	0	0	0	0	0	0	0	0	1	1
14	0	0	0	0	0	0	0	0	0	0	0	1
16	0	0	0	0	0	0	0	0	0	0	0	0
18	0	0	0	0	0	0	0	0	0	0	0	0
20	0	0	0	0	0	0	0	0	0	0	0	0

(ii) Raw material inventories

	σ (standard deviation of final demand, %)											
k, l (buffer coefficient, %)	1	2	3	4	5	6	7	8	9	10	11	12
2	0	10	28	39	49	62	67	71	69	73	72	74
4	0	0	4	10	23	28	33	39	42	49	55	59
6	0	0	0	2	6	10	16	25	30	33	33	39
8	0	0	0	0	0	4	8	10	16	23	27	30
10	0	0	0	0	0	0	2	4	10	10	16	20
12	0	0	0	0	0	0	0	2	4	6	10	10
14	0	0	0	0	0	0	0	0	2	4	4	8
16	0	0	0	0	0	0	0	0	0	0	4	4
18	0	0	0	0	0	0	0	0	0	0	0	2
20	0	0	0	0	0	0	0	0	0	0	0	0

Table 5.2 indicates how the occurrence frequency of stockouts depends on the buffer raw material and product inventory coefficients and the standard deviation of final demand for a particular sample set $\xi_i(t)$ (30 weeks, $\gamma = 0.25$). While the result shown in this table depends on the chosen sample set $\xi_i(t)$, the basic tendency does not change by a replacement of samples. When σ takes a large value in relation to k $(= l)$, stockouts occur frequently, and continuous rationing becomes inevitable. Therefore, *an increase in the buffer inventory coefficient enhances the adaptability of the economy to random fluctuations of final demand.*

Figure 5.9 illustrates the movement of variables of sector 3 for 30 weeks when $k = l = 0.08$ and $\sigma = 9$. Production tends to follow sales with delay and overshoot. During this period, product inventory $z_3(t)$ is depleted twice, and raw material inventory $v_{31}(t)$ is depleted four times ($z_3(22)$, $v_{31}(15)$, and $v_{31}(17)$ are barely larger than zero). This can be regarded as a case in which the impact of random fluctuations is absorbed by the buffer product and raw material inventories in a reasonably satisfactory manner. The stability of the process also plays an essential role in this case. If the stability condition is not satisfied, then the movement of variables is dominated by such oscillations as we have seen in Fig. 5.6.

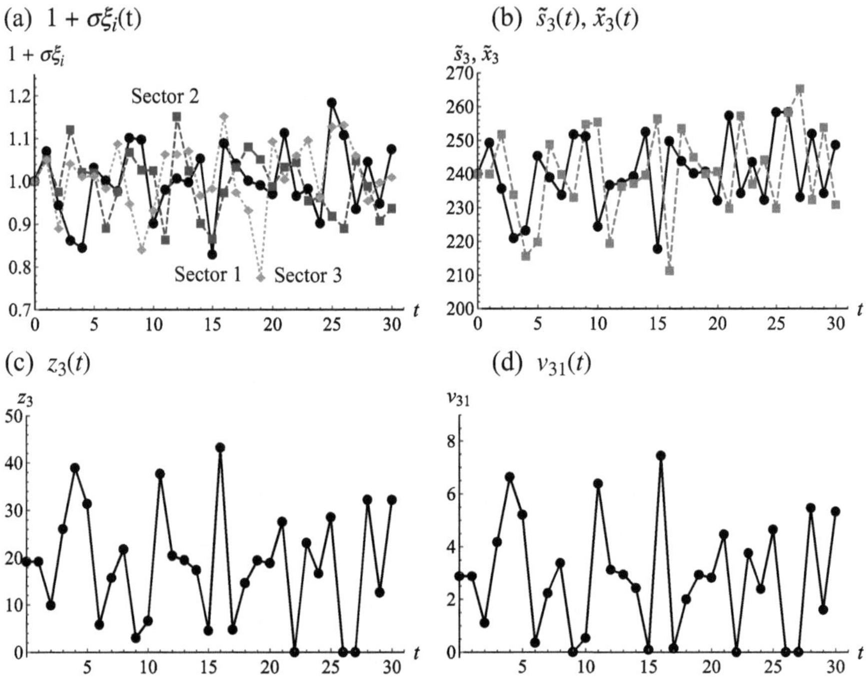

Fig. 5.9 Adaptation to random changes in final demand

5.3 Mid- and Long-Term Changes in Final Demand

5.3.1 Inducement of Consumption Demand

We have shown that the quantity adjustment process proceeds stably and smoothly through moderate averaging of past demands in the demand forecast formation and moderate holding of buffer inventory. However, this does not imply that quantity adjustment guarantees the stability of the whole economy. In fact, the stability of quantity adjustment merely implies *that the economy can adapt to the mid- and long-term changes in final demand by maintaining the short-term balance between production and demand.* In this section, we will confirm these points through several numerical examples.

First, we shall consider a case in which a part of consumption demand is induced from average income during a certain preceding period. Let us assume that a part of consumption demand changes every 12 weeks (quarterly) based on the average income during the previous quarter. Let p be $1 \times n$ the price vector, then gross income per week measured from the production side is

$$y(t) = \tilde{x}(t)\,(\mathrm{I} - A)\,p, \quad \tilde{x}(t) = \left[\tilde{x}_1(t), \ldots, \tilde{x}_n(t)\right].^{19}$$

Let ε_i be the rate of gross income spent for product i, in other words, the Engel coefficient of the product i. The sum $\varepsilon_1 + \ldots + \varepsilon_n$ represents the overall average propensity to consume. Let $c(t)$ be the vector of consumption demand per week $c_i(t)$. According to the above assumption, $c(t)$ during quarter $T + 1$ (from week $12T+1$ to week $12T+12$) is determined by the following equation:

$$c\,(12T + t) = \frac{1}{12}\sum_{u=1}^{12} y(12(T-1) + u)\varepsilon \ (t \in \{1, 2, .., 12\}), \tag{5.51}$$

where $\varepsilon = [\varepsilon_1/p_1, \ldots, \varepsilon_n/p_n]$. For example,

$$c(13) = \cdots = c(24) = (y(1) + \ldots + y(12))\varepsilon/12,$$

$$c(25) = \cdots = c(36) = (y(13) + \ldots + y(24))\varepsilon/12,$$

and so on. Let d be the vector of final demand other than $c(t)$. Then, the total demand per week is the sum of intermediate demand, derived consumption demand, and the residual independent part of final demand. That is,

$$s(t) = \sum_{i=1}^{n} m_i(t) + c(t) + d. \tag{5.52}$$

Although vector d can include various kinds of demand, hereafter we simply call it fixed capital investment.

Under these assumptions, *two multiplier processes belonging to different time horizons* proceed in parallel. The first is a weekly process in which intermediate demand is derived from gross production; the second is a quarterly process in which a part of consumption demand is derived from income.[20] If the independent part of final demand remains constant, then the stationary point of the second process is defined as $s^* = x^* = x^*A + x^*(\mathrm{I} - A)p\varepsilon + d$. Since $\varepsilon_1 + \cdots + \varepsilon_n < 1$, this equation gives (a vector of) nonnegative stationary values of production and demand:

$$x^* = d(I - p\varepsilon)^{-1}(I - A)^{-1}.$$

The vector multiplications by $(I - A)^{-1}$ and $(\mathrm{I} - p\varepsilon)^{-1}$ correspond to the derivation of the intermediate and consumption demand, respectively. The capacity constraint

[19]This gross income includes $(s^e(t) - s(t))p$ of the (aggregate) unintended product inventory investment and $(s^e(t) - s(t))Ap$ of the (aggregate) unintended raw material inventory investment.
[20]Here, we do not consider the effect that income distribution between wage and profit might exert on consumption demand.

is satisfied at the stationary point only when the relative prices lie within a particular range.[21]

Now we shall examine the dynamic properties of the quantity adjustment process comprising (5.40), (5.42) to (5.49), (5.51), and (5.52) by numerical computations. Let

$$p = [1, 1, 1], \quad \varepsilon = [0.2, 0.2, 0.35], \quad d = \begin{bmatrix} 21.6 \; 45.6 \; 15.8 \end{bmatrix},$$

and assume that parameters are the same as before. Initially, the economy is in the stationary state corresponding to these parameters, and

$$c(0) = c(1) = \cdots = c(12) = [66.4, 66.4, 116.2].$$

Figure 5.10 illustrates how the 5% change (increase and decrease) in fixed capital investment since week 1 causes a change in the variables. In this case, the movement of the variables generates a chain of small waves each of which restarts every quarter. If the multiplier process is completed instantaneously, then the demand vector in week t is equal to $(c(t) \pm 1.05d)(\mathrm{I} - A)^{-1}$. The dashed lines in Fig. 5.10 indicate changes of $\tilde{s}_1(t)$ and $z_1(\mathrm{t})$ in this case. The discrepancy between the marked and dashed lines reflects the delays and overshoots in adjustment caused by the necessity of time and raw material inputs in the production process.[22]

The independence of consumption demand from weekly changes in production plays an important role in maintaining the stability of the process. What if consumption demand changes *weekly* based on the income of the previous week? In this case, consumption demand is determined by

$$c(t) = \varepsilon y(t-1). \tag{5.53}$$

Figure 5.11 illustrates the movement of variables in the process consisting of (5.40), (5.42) to (5.49), (5.52), and (5.53) for 48 weeks. In this case, the movement of the variables generates far bigger waves than those in the case where consumption demand changes only quarterly (compare the marked line with the dashed line in Fig. 5.11a). From the oval-shaped movement of the pair of sales and product inventory in Fig. 5.11b, we can see that the values of the parameters are close to

[21]Let $\overline{x}$ be the vector of production capacities, then constraint $x^* \leq \overline{x}$ can be rewritten as $(\beta_i - d_i)p_i - \varepsilon_i(\beta_1 p_1 + \cdots + \beta_n p_n) \geq 0$ for any i, where β_i is the i-the element of vector $\overline{x}\,(I - A)$. These linear inequalities restrict the range of relative prices.

[22]In the following analysis, prices and production conditions are assumed to remain unchanged. Certainly, the longer the considered period is, the less plausible the assumption of the constancy of these factors becomes. Nevertheless, our analysis would have some significance for understanding the way through which the multiplier process proceeds under variable consumption demand, as long as prices and production conditions changes gradually.

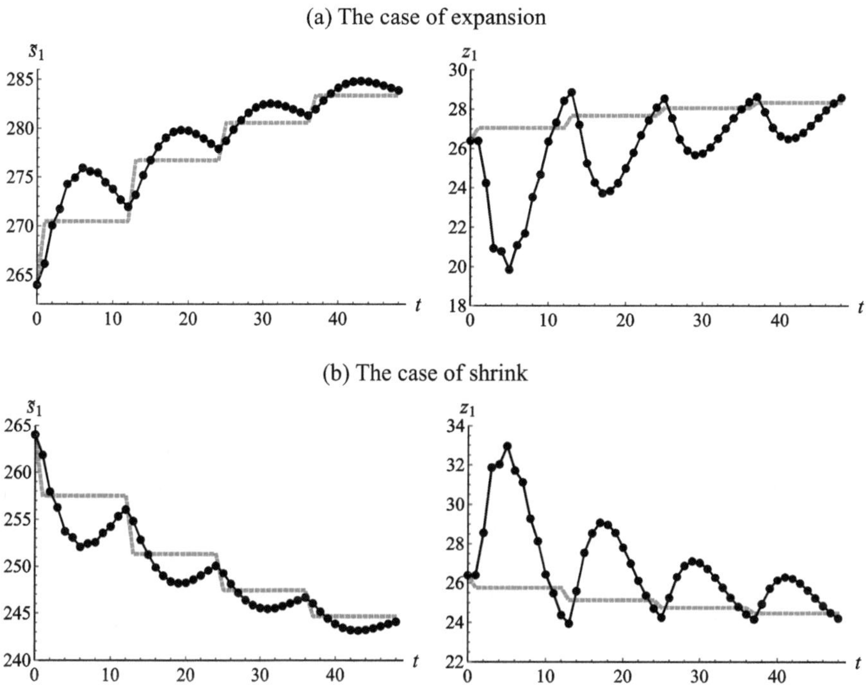

Fig. 5.10 Weekly and quarterly multiplier process

the boundary for stability. If the propensity to consume takes larger values, then the process may lose stability.[23]

Consumption demand has persistency and is affected by habitual factors.[24] What if consumption demand depends not on the income during the immediately preceding period but on a moving average of incomes over a number of past weeks? Let us assume that consumption demand $c(t)$ is determined by,

$$c(t) = \varepsilon y^p(t),\ y^p(t) = y^p\,(t-1) + \alpha\left(y\,(t-1) - y^p\,(t-1)\right), \tag{5.54}$$

where $y^p(t)$ is "the permanent income" and α is the parameter corresponding to the smoothing constant in the geometric moving average ($0 < \alpha \leq 1$). When $\alpha = 1$, (5.54) is reduced to (5.53). Permanent income $y^p(t)$ is a moving average of an infinite number of past incomes such that the weight for $y(t - u)$ is equal to

[23] Equation (5.51) presupposes that there is a 1-week lag from gaining of income to its spending. If income is spent instantaneously, it is replaced by $c(t) = y(t)\varepsilon$, and the process corresponding to this consumption function is unstable under the above parameters.

[24] Concerning this point, refer to Duesenberry (1949).

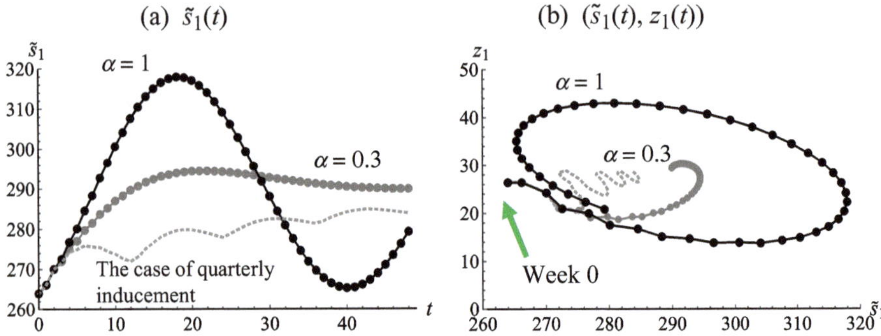

Fig. 5.11 Movement of variables when consumption demand changes weekly

$\alpha(1-\alpha)^{u-1}$. Averaging past incomes reflects the habitual nature of consumption.[25] The marked gray lines corresponding to $\alpha = 0.3$ in Fig. 5.11 show how fluctuation is damped by the reduction of coefficient α, that is, by more averaging in the calculation of the permanent income ($y^p(0)$ is assumed to be equal to $y(0)$). Thus, *while the dependence of consumption demand on income intensifies the oscillation, this destabilizing effect could be partially weakened by averaging the income that consumers refer to in their formation of demand.*

5.3.2 Stable Adjustment Under Unstable Movements of Final Demand

In the previous subsection, we assumed that the capital investment demand remained constant after its initial increase. Now we consider a case where the investment demand changes every quarter. Let us assume that $d(t)$ during quarter T is given by

$$d\,(12\,(T-1)+t) = (1+g_T)\,d(0)\ (t \in \{1, \cdots, 12\}). \tag{5.55}$$

More concretely, for example,

$$d(1) = \cdots = d(12) = (1+g_1)\,d(0), \quad d(13) = \cdots = d(24) = (1+g_2)\,d(0),$$

and so on. Here we do not argue about how the quarterly growth rate is determined. Our purpose is to trace the fluctuation caused by exogenous changes in capital investment demand.

[25] In an attempt to estimate the consumption function, Friedman (1957) defined "permanent income" as a moving weighted average of incomes in past periods.

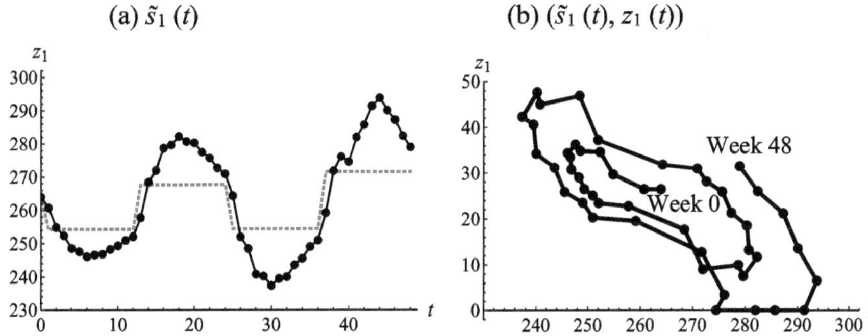

Fig. 5.12 Fluctuation by unstable movement of investment

Figure 5.12 illustrates the simulated movement of the variable in the process comprising (5.40), (5.42) to (5.49), (5.51), (5.55), and

$$s(t) = \sum_{i=1}^{n} m_i(t) + c(t) + d(t), \tag{5.56}$$

provided that $d(0) = \begin{bmatrix} 21.6 & 45.6 & 15.8 \end{bmatrix}$ and $g_1 = -0.15,\ g_2 = 0.20, g_3 = -0.25, g_4 = 0.3$. The dashed line in Fig. 5.12a represents the level of sales if the short-term multiplier effect works instantaneously. This is the case in which the capital investment demand repeats a sharp drop and a sharp rise at increasing rates. As a combined effect of the decrease in product inventory at the end of the third quarter and the considerable rise in the final demand in quarter 4, the stockout of product 1 occurs for four weeks in this quarter. Although there is a steady tendency to move toward the stationary point corresponding to the level of final demand in that quarter, this converging movement is discontinued by the quarterly changes in this level itself. Therefore, *the quarterly movements of variables could be unstable despite the stability of the week-level movements.*

In this manner, mid- and long-term trends in the overall economy are determined by the movement of independent final demand. Nevertheless, our analysis of the short-term fluctuations of intermediate demand (and of derived consumption demand) does not lose its significance by this dominance of independent final demand. This is because the very fact of *the dominance of independent final demand presupposes that production can be gradually adjusted to demand through a genuinely dispersive process in which each firm repeatedly adjusts its production and raw material orders using its own internal information.* In contrast, in conventional Walrasian economics, the function equilibrating production and demand has been almost exclusively attributed to changes in prices. However, in our view, *the main balancing factor in the short-term (daily, weekly, or monthly) process is the adjustment in the quantities of productions and raw material orders in response to changes in demand and inventory.* At the same time, quantity adjustment can perform its balancing function only when relative prices lie within a certain range. In this sense, quantity adjustment can be seen as "fine-tuning" of productions and purchasing orders under the adequate setting of prices and the given independent final demand. While we have no intention of insisting that prices are irrelevant to the balance of production and demand, their role in the short-term process is more limited than that presumed in conventional economic theory. One of the essential functions of quantity adjustment is that it makes frequent revisions of prices unnecessary. *The loose constancy of prices supported by quantity adjustment in productions and purchasing orders is the basis of both rational and innovative economic behaviors.*

5.4 Conclusions

When a firm holds work-in-process inventories and adjusts its production of works-in-process in the same manner as production of final products and raw material orders, the stability condition becomes more restrictive owing to the increase in the number of decisions using the common demand forecast. However, if the firm adjusts its production of works-in-process in a purely replenishing manner, the holding of work-in-process inventory does not affect the stability of the process.

The partialization of planned inventory investment has a similar stabilizing effect as the averaging of past demands by the geometric moving average in forecast formation. In special cases, the process under partial inventory investment and static expectation and the process under the demand forecast by the geometric moving average have the same dynamic properties. Therefore, partial inventory adjustment is an alternative method of stabilizing a process made unstable by the static expectation.

Provided that each firm allocates its purchasing orders for a particular product among sellers according to certain fixed shares, our sector-level model can be extended to the case in which each sector consists of multiple heterogeneous firms. Theorems on the stability of the sector-level model and their economic interpretations are valid also in this firm-level model if the input matrix is replaced by the order-coefficient matrix reflecting allocation of orders by buyers among sellers.

To trace the process in which stockouts actually occur, we must clearly distinguish actual results from intentions. Since both the rationing of sales volumes and the bottleneck (the raw material shortage or the capacity constraint) in production bring complex nonlinearities into the model, the analysis of this process requires numerical calculations. When the stability condition of the linear process is not satisfied, stockouts occur frequently and spreads rapidly to other sectors. Furthermore, even if this stability condition is satisfied, continuous occurrence of stockouts is inevitable so long as the growth rate or the standard deviation of final demand is significantly high with respect to the buffer coefficient. In general, the higher the growth rate or the volatility of final demand, and the lower the buffer coefficient, the more frequent the occurrences of stockout.

Stability of the quantity adjustment process implies that the economy can follow mid- and long-term movements of final demand. A part of consumption demand usually depends on average income of recent past periods. If this average income is constant at least in the short-term, the inducement of consumption and intermediate demands constitute two multiplier processes belonging to different time horizons. Even if this average income is revised every period, moderate averaging is sufficient to offset the destabilizing effect through the inducement of consumption demand. Since quantity adjustment is always passive to changes in independent final demand, it is obvious that the short-term stability of quantity adjustment does not exclude mid- and long-term instabilities in the economy. The role of quantity adjustment lies in providing a solid foundation for higher economic activities that have their own and far more complex mechanisms.

References

Blinder, A. S., & Maccini, L. J. (1991). Taking stock: A critical assessment of recent research on inventories. *Journal of Economic Perspective, 5*(1), 73–98.

Duesenberry, J. S. (1949). *Incomes, saving, and the theory of consumer behavior*. Harvard: Harvard University Press.

Friedman, M. (1957). *A theory of the consumption function*. Princeton: Princeton University Press.

Kornai, J. (1980). *Economics of shortage*. Amsterdam: North-Holland.

Kornai, J. (1992). *The socialist system: The political economy of communism*. Princeton: Princeton University Press.

Kornai, J., & Simonovits, A. (1981). Control by order signals. In Kornai & B. Martos (Eds.), *Non-price control* (pp. 267–280). Amsterdam: North-Holland.

Lovell, M. C. (1961). Manufacturers' inventories, sales expectations, and acceleration principle. *Econometrica, 29*(3), 293–314.

Lovell, M. C. (1962). Buffer stocks, sales expectations and stability: A multi-sector analysis of the inventory cycle. *Econometrica, 30*(2), 267–296.

Martos, B. (1990). *Economic control structures: A non Walrasian approach*. Amsterdam: North-Holland.

Morioka, M. (1991–1992). Two types of the short-term adjustment process (in Japanese: Tanki choseikatei no niruikei). *Keizai Ronso* (Kyoto University), 148(4–6):140–141, 149(1–3):79–96.

Morioka, M. (1992). "The autonomous control by inventory stocks" (In Japanese: Zaiko stokku ni motozuku jiritsuteki seigyo). *Kyoto Daigaku Keizai Ronsyu, 5*, 45–59.

Morioka, M. (2005). *The economic theory of quantity adjustment: Dynamic analysis of stockout avoidance behavior* (in Japanese: Suryo chosei no keizai riron). Tokyo: Nihon Keizai Hyoron-sya.

Nikaido, H. (1961). *Linear mathematics for economics* (In Japanese: Keizai no tameno Senkei Sugaku). Tokyo: Baihukan.

Chapter 6
Significance of Nonlinearity and Many Goods Models

Feasibility of the (S, s) Inventory Control Policy in the Economy as a Whole

Abstract This chapter examines what economic consequences can be induced in the entire economy when many different enterprises in the economy implement production based on inventory control, which is referred to as the (S, s) policy.

The first section describes the features of a contemporary society that is characterized by an enormous number of different kinds of commodities. To theoretically contemplate an economy with these many kinds of commodities, the concepts of vector space and nonlinearity are explained in the Introduction. The second section of this paper explains the (S, s) inventory control policy theory developed by Scarf (The optimality of (S,s) policies in the dynamic inventory problem. In: Arrow KJ, Karlin S, and Suppes P (eds) Mathematical methods in the social sciences 1959. Stanford University Press, Stanford, 1959). Since Scarf's model is a model that focuses on one kind of goods, it does not consider the movements of the entire economy. We discuss this crucial point with respect to Scarf (The optimality of (S,s) policies in the dynamic inventory problem. In: Arrow KJ, Karlin S, and Suppes P (eds) Mathematical methods in the social sciences 1959. Stanford University Press, Stanford, 1959) and develop the Scarf model into a many kinds of goods model. The sequence of events and the determinant processes of our model are precisely explained. Next, the third section shows the quantity adjustment processes based on the (S, s) policy model. The mathematical solutions of a one kind of goods and two kinds of goods models are shown, and next, the results, which are different results from the one kind of goods and the two kinds of goods, by the more than three kinds of goods model are discussed. In the fourth section, certain of the results obtained by numerical experiments conducted by the author are explained, and the effects of the number of commodities are discussed.

Keywords Many kinds of goods · Vector space · Nonlinearity · Inventory shortage · Numerical experiments · (S · s) Policy model

---

I would like to express my thanks to the co-authors, Yoshinori Shiozawa and Masashi Morioka, who read this chapter and gave me helpful comments.

Y. Shiozawa et al., *Microfoundations of Evolutionary Economics*,
Evolutionary Economics and Social Complexity Science 15,
https://doi.org/10.1007/978-4-431-55267-3_6

6.1 Introduction

6.1.1 Many Kinds of Goods and Vector Space

The number of goods and services or the kinds of commodities surrounding us have increased as our economy has developed. In contemporary society, for example, even at one average-sized convenience store in Japan, there are approximately 2,000 to 2,500 kinds of goods. A standard-sized car equipped with a gasoline engine contains approximately 20,000 to 30,000 automobile parts. Although the number of parts in an EV car without an internal combustion engine is much smaller than the number of parts in a car with a gasoline engine car, an EV car still contains approximately 10,000 parts. Of course, the number itself is dependent on how the items are counted; nevertheless, enormous kinds of goods are prevalent in a modern society of production and consumption. However, there were only a small piece of bread and dishes on the meal table in Michelangelo's "Last Supper" painting. We can see only few items on the table. Alternatively, if you look at Vermeer's "The Milkmaid," drawn approximately 360 years ago, you will notice that the kinds of goods in the room at that time were surprisingly few. Most of the goods surrounding us in our daily life are those that did not exist 360 years ago (Fig. 6.1). Since the economy has developed and many kinds of goods or commodities have emerged,

Fig. 6.1 Vermeer, "The Milkmaid," 1658–1660, Rijksmuseum Amsterdam

in an economic analysis, it is natural to explicitly focus on an enormous number of different kinds of goods.

Moreover, the number of the kinds of goods has important implications for economic theories because a difference in the number of the kinds of goods can result in different conclusions. For example, in this chapter, a periodic solution is obtained for the one kind or two kinds of goods model, but a divergence appears for three or more kinds of goods model. This fact is described in Sect. 6.3 after the economy with which the model is concerned is introduced. In general, this point is an important focus in this book.

The use of the concept of vectors is helpful when dealing theoretically with many kinds of goods. Assuming there are n kinds of goods in the economy, each kind of goods is numbered $1, 2, \ldots, n$. Then, the quantity of goods is defined as x_j by defining its measuring method and unit. The index $j\,(j = 1, 2, \ldots, n.)$ at the lower right of x_j is a number representing the kind of goods. In this way, the kind and quantity of goods are expressed as follows:

$$(x_1, x_2, \ldots x_n).$$

Using this methodology, even if the number of kinds of goods is dozens, thousands, or millions, the mathematical expression will be the same. It is also possible to express all kinds and quantities of goods with one character x:

$$x = (x_1, x_2, \ldots x_n).$$

The character x is called a vector, and each $x_j(j = 1, 2, 3, \cdots, n)$ is called an element or component of the vector. The number of elements of one vector is called the degree. It is a three-dimensional vector when the number of goods n is 3 and is a n-dimensional vector in the case of n. The space vector is a three-dimensional vector with the size and orientation in a geometric space. In economics, as we must represent a large number of goods, that is, n kinds, it is generally a n-dimensional vector. Additionally, the vector's elements are real numbers because they represent the quantity of goods. When the set of all real numbers is expressed by R, the set of all vectors is a real space R^n of the n dimension.[1]

[1]The origin of the word "vector" comes from the Latin vehere (carrying). A vector is often indicated by a bold character $\boldsymbol{x}$ or $\vec{x}$ with an arrow over the character, but this chapter uses the normal character x.

6.1.2 *The Axiom of Vector Space and Linearity*

A vector space is also called a linear space. Important operations, such as linear mappings, are defined on a vector space. Next, we introduce the axioms of vector space.

6.1.2.1 The Axiom of Vector (or Linear) Space

A nonempty set of vectors is called a vector space when two operations are defined and satisfy the following axioms.

1. (Commutative law) For all vectors x and y, $x + y = y + x$.
2. (Associative law for addition) For all vectors x, y, and z, $(x+y)+z = x+(y+z)$.
3. (Existence of a zero) There exists an element that satisfies $x + 0 = x$ for all vector x.
4. (Existence of inverse elements) There exists a vector y that satisfies $x + y = 0$ for any vector x.
5. (Distributive law I) For all vectors x and y and for all real number a, $a(x + y) = ax + ay$.
6. (Distributive law II) For all vectors x and for all real numbers a and b, $(a+b)x = ax + bx$.
7. (Associative law for scaler multiplication) For all vectors x and real numbers a and b, $(ab)x = a(bx)$.
8. (Existence of identity element) The real number 1 satisfies the equation $1x = x$ for all vectors x.

Axioms 1–4 are related to addition, and Axioms 5–8 are related to scalar multiplication.

A mapping (or a map) from a vector space E to a vector space F (the same or another) is called linear when it conserves these linear operations. In other words, a mapping $f : E \to F$ is linear when it satisfies the following two conditions:

Condition (1) For any vectors x and y in E, $f(x + y) = f(x) + f(y)$.
Condition (2) For any vectors x in E and for any real number c, $f(cx) = cf(x)$.

The following are some examples of linear mapping. Where the set of real numbers R is considered to be a vector space, the mapping $f(x) = ax$ (a is constant real number) is a linear mapping. Indeed, for any real numbers, x, y, a, and c, the mapping satisfies conditions (1) and (2) as follows:

$$f(x + y) = a(x + y) = ax + ay = f(x) + f(y).$$

$$f(cx) = acx = cax = cf(x).$$

Another example is a definite integration. Let E be the vector space composed of all real valued continuous functions over the interval $[a, b]$. Then, the operation

$$f(\phi) = \int_a^b \phi(x)dx$$

is a linear mapping from E to a vector space R. It is easy to confirm that the map f satisfies the above two conditions (1) and (2).

A third example is an operation of a matrix. Let E be a vector space of dimensions m and F a vector space of dimensions n. Then, a (n, m) matrix A maps a vector x in E to a vector y in F:

$$y = Ax.$$

If we think of this operation as a mapping of f, it also satisfies the conditions (1) and (2). We will often use matrix operations later.

6.1.3 Nonlinearity and Nonlinear Economic Phenomena

The term nonlinearity indicates an object that is literally not linear. For example, where the set of real numbers R is a vector space, the mapping $f(x) = x^2$ for any value of $x \in R$ takes the shape of a parabola on a two-dimensional plane. This mapping does not satisfy the condition (1). Indeed,

$$f(x + y) = (x + y)^2 = x^2 + 2xy + y^2 \neq x^2 + y^2 = f(x) + f(y)$$

when x and y are not zero. The graph of a linear mapping f is always a straight line through the origin when it can be expressed in a two-dimensional plane. When it does not pass through the origin, the mapping is not linear. For example, the mapping $f(x) = ax + b$ for two constants a and b is not linear when $b \neq 0$. In this way, the distinction between linear and nonlinear depends on whether two conditions (1) and (2) are satisfied or not.

In economics, the input-output relations $f : x \to f(x)$ are not linear when the laws of diminishing or increasing returns are valid. When the laws of constant returns hold, the mapping is piecewisely linear but not linear in the strict sense as it will be explained later. Even when a mapping is not linear, if it is a linear mapping plus a constant (vector), the tools of linear mapping can be applied with small modifications. Such a mapping is called *affine*.

Figure 6.2 illustrates a linear mapping from a vector space E to a vector space F. It is only an illustration, as E and F have in general a larger dimension than 1. However, this illustration in the figure helps us to intuitively understand high-dimensional relations. Figure 6.3 is the graph of a map (indeed a function) defined by the formula

$$f(x) = \min\{ax, b\}$$

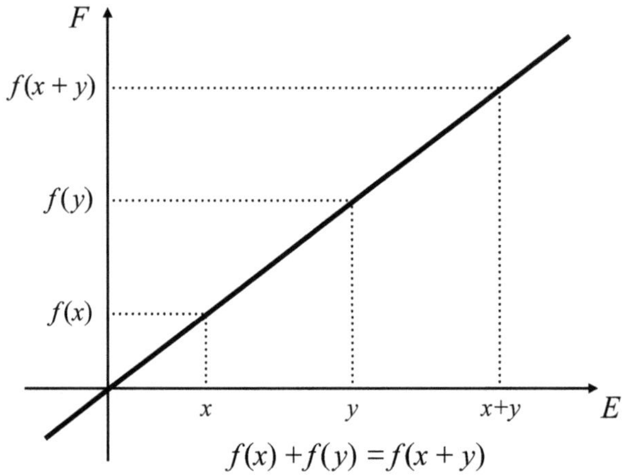

Fig. 6.2 Linear mapping $f : E \to F$ (x, y, and $x + y \in E$, $f(x)$, $f(y)$, and $f(x + y) \in F$)

Fig. 6.3 Nonlinear mapping $f : x \to f(x)$ ($f(x) = \min[ax, b]$)

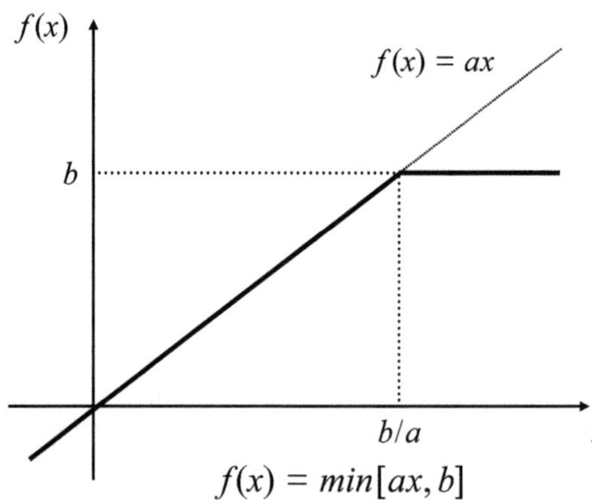

for two constants $a(\neq 0)$ and b. This can be expressed also as

$$f(x) = \begin{cases} ax \text{ when } x < b/a, \\ b \text{ when } x \geq b/a. \end{cases}$$

The graph is piecewise linear, but the map is not linear because it does not satisfy the condition (1). All mappings that include operations *min* (minimum) and *max* (maximum) operations are effectively not linear. Mappings that have different expressions in different cases are also in general nonlinear.

Most economic phenomena can be said to be nonlinear because economic variables in general do not take negative values. As all linear mappings satisfy the relation $f(-x) = -x$, they must take a negative value in some elements of a vector. For example, an input element of production cannot take a negative value.

Important economic variables, such as national income or national population, do not take negative values. Negative values may be considered in financial operations. Borrowing can be expressed as negative lending, but these cases are very limited. Another mechanism by which nonlinearity intervenes is the existence of upper limits. For example, there is an upper limit for a production scale because the scale cannot exceed the capacity of the capital equipment. When input-output relations satisfy the law of constant returns to scale, the graph is partially linear, but it is not linear as a mapping because there is an upper bound for the production scale.

Linear models are most often used in economics because they are tractable, even in a high-dimensional case. Matrix operations can be usefully applied in these cases. However, in a strict sense, almost all economic phenomena are nonlinear. The trouble with nonlinear mapping is that it is often very difficult to see how it behaves for different inputs. The only way to avoid this difficulty is to appeal to numerical experiments. This is one important reason why we need agent-based simulation in economics.[2]

6.2 Scarf's Inventory Theory and Our Search Focuses

6.2.1 (S, s) *Inventory Control Policy Theory by Scarf*

Studies regarding optimum inventory policy has started with the study of Arrow et al. (1951), and achievements in this area were collected in Arrow et al. (1958). In this section, the optimum inventory control system based on the (S, s) policy proposed by Scarf (1959, 2002) is introduced.

This ordering method is an enormously simple method that places orders by using the following rules at each period:

1. Order an $S - z$ amount of product when the inventory level z is less than s.
2. Order nothing when the inventory level z is greater than or equal to s.

As this control process includes a *max* operation, this is a nonlinear control process.[3] Scarf (1959) demonstrated that under certain conditions, this method was an optimum inventory control policy.

At first, Scarf (1959) defined the function $L(z)$ as the expected loss at the end of the period, which is charged by holding the inventory level z as follows:

$$L(z) = \int_0^z h(z - \xi)\phi(\xi)d\xi + \int_z^\infty p(\xi - z)\phi(\xi)d\xi, \quad z \geq 0 \tag{6.1}$$

[2]See Shiozawa (2016).

[3]The relation that z is greater than or equal to s can be expressed as the case $z = \max\{z, s\}$.

$$L(z) = \int_0^{\infty} p(\xi - z)\phi(\xi)d\xi. \quad z < 0 \tag{6.2}$$

Here, h indicates the function of the holding cost charged by holding inventory excessively: it is a function of the excess supply over demand at the end of the period; p indicates the function of the shortage cost charged due to inventory shortages: it is a function of excess of demand over supply at the end of period; ξ indicates demand, and ϕ indicates the function of the density of the demand distribution. The first term of Eq. (6.1) expresses the expected holding cost charged when demand (sales) falls below inventory in the current period, while the second term expresses the expected penalty cost charged when demand (sales) exceeds inventory in the current period. Equation (6.2) does not include the expected holding cost because inventory is negative, while the expected loss consists only of the expected penalty cost. Negative inventory defined in Eq. (6.2) means goods that cannot be shipped due to shortages. In accounting, the amount of these nonshipped goods may not be recorded in the books.

Where the inventory holding period is n periods and where the initial inventory starts with z_0, the expected cost $C_n(z_0)$ during the period n is expressed by the equation below.

$$C_n(z_0) = \min_{z \geq z_0}\{c(z - z_0) + L(z) + \alpha \int_0^{\infty} C_{n-1}(z - \xi)\phi(\xi)d\xi\} \tag{6.3}$$

Here, z is an inventory level, z_0 is an initial inventory level, and c is the function of a purchasing (or ordering) cost, which is described in the following. If z_n is the minimizing value of z in Eq. (6.3), then $z_n - z_0$ represents the optimum initial purchasing quantity. Here, α indicates the discount rate, which is expressed as $0 < \alpha < 1$.

Scarf (1959) was demonstrated by referring to Karlin's paper (chapters 8 and 9) contained in Arrow et al. (1958), which shows that the optimum inventory policy is determined to be two numbers, (S, s), where the ordering cost function c satisfies the following conditions:

$$If \quad x = 0, \quad \text{then } c(x) = 0,$$
$$if \quad x > 0, \quad \text{then } c(x) = K + cx.$$

K is described as the reorder cost, and x is the amount purchased.

The conclusion of Scarf (1959) was already mentioned earlier: where the holding cost function and the penalty cost of shortage are linear or, more generally, where the expected loss function $L(z)$ is convex, if $z_0 < s$, $S - z_0$ amount of orders are placed, and if $z_0 > s$, no orders are placed. This conclusion is based on the consideration of the following function expressed below.

$$G_n(z) = cz + L(z) + \alpha \int_0^\infty C_{n-1}(z-\xi)\phi(\xi)d\xi$$

Under the condition of $G_n(z_0) > K + G_n(z)$, if and only if there is z greater than z_0, orders are placed until the amount of inventory reaches z from z_0. In addition, if orders are placed from z_0, orders are placed until the amount of inventory reaches $z(> z_0)$, which minimizes $G_n(z)$. At that time, $G_n(z)$ decreases to the minimum value, $G_n(S_n)$, and increases subsequently afterward. If the minimizing value of z is denoted by S_n and if s_n is defined by the following equation

$$G_n(s_n) = G_n(S_n) + K, \tag{6.4}$$

then the policy defined by (S_n, s_n) is optimum. In other words, in an optimum inventory, the cost charged by maintaining the smaller inventory level s_n is equal to the sum of the cost charged by the larger inventory level S_n and the ordering cost. Since there is a penalty cost here, holding a large amount of inventory can eliminate the payment of a penalty cost due to inventory shortages. By introducing *K-convex*, Scarf (1959) demonstrated the case where goods are shipped immediately after orders are placed and the case where shipping is delayed temporally.

Next, a more intuitive understanding based on the assumption of an extremely simple linear function in a mere single period is described. First, the holding cost function and the function of penalty due to inventory shortages are expressed as linear functions, as shown below.

$$h(z-\xi) = z - \xi$$
$$p(\xi - z) = \xi - z$$

Second, the density distribution of demand is also expressed as the following simple uniform distribution.

$$\phi(\xi) = 1/a \quad (0 \le \xi \le a, \quad a \ne 0)$$

At this time, based on Eq. (6.1), the expected loss function $L(z)$ is expressed as follows: the first term represents the expected holding cost, and the second term represents the expected penalty cost.

$$L(z) = \frac{z^2}{2a} + \frac{(z-a)^2}{2a}$$

Therefore, where $z = a/2$, L takes the minimum value $a/4$. Here, since a is the maximum amount of demand, the expected loss takes the minimum value when half of the demand is held as an inventory. Now, where the ordering cost function is linear, the expected cost function is expressed by the following equation.

$$C(z) = cz + \frac{z^2 + (z-a)^2}{2a}$$

Since the expected loss function is *convex*, there exists a z that gives the expected cost $C(z)$ a minimum value. When the value z is set to S, a value smaller than S is s. At this time, $C(S) - C(s)$ provides the ordering cost.

As described above, the focus by Scarf (1959) is placed on the existence of the optimum inventory level and how it is determined. The inventory level is determined so as to minimize the cost of the expected loss. This situation remains unchanged even in a static model or a dynamic model. However, it is difficult to obtain the values of S and s that determine the specific inventory level, from the discussion developed by Scarf (1959). To do so, for example, the density function of demand needs to be identified. However, when there is an inventory shortage, decision made by the ordering agent changes. As a result, demand function varies. Therefore, although the demand function can be expressed as a probability density function, this probability cannot be identified and predetermined.

6.2.2 Inventory in the Economy as a Whole and Inventory Shortage

As we have seen in the previous section, Scarf (1959) showed that inventory control based on the (S, s) policy is optimal; however, there is only one kind of good in Scarf's model economy. Since there is only a single type of good, it is difficult to consider the existence of another type of enterprise. The enterprises in the Scarf's model economy buy or order goods, and the purchased quantity itself becomes the inventory quantity of the enterprise. Then, the purchased goods themselves are resold.[4] Since there is only one kind of good, discrimination between raw materials required for production and production goods is not considered in Scarf's model. From this viewpoint, all these enterprises seem to belong only to the distribution industry.

Therefore, the following problems are not addressed. Since there is only one kind of good, even if a certain enterprise cannot ship due to lack of inventory, other enterprises can compensate for the shortage. It represents in Scarf's model there are many complete substitution of goods. Therefore, when the concerned enterprise pays the penalty and records the unshipped orders in the account book, the inventory shortage problem is resolved. As there are substitute goods, the out-of-inventory problem is not serious for the whole economy. Therefore, the movements of the whole economy are not the focus of the analysis. The problem addressed here is the concerned enterprise costs, and the focus of discussion is only the minimization of the expected loss. The whole economy is taken as a given to those

[4] Scarf (1959) p.197.

enterprises that implement inventory control. Enterprises are isolated in the given economic environment: they resemble isolated islands in the ocean and decide their optimum inventory levels. For a discussion of contemporary society's economy, which is characterized by an enormous number of different kinds of goods, that is, a production economy, Scarf's one kind of goods model needs to be developed into a many kinds of goods model.

In the economy, there are many kinds of goods for which no substitute goods are available. Even if the enterprise pays the penalty cost, it is impossible to resolve the inventory shortage problem without considering its influence on the whole economy. In the case of an inventory shortage, crucial problems can arise that affect the whole economy. For example, an inventory shortage causes a reduction or suspension in the production activities of enterprises that require the shortage goods as raw materials. The reduction or suspension of one enterprise's production activities causes chain reactions and affects the whole economy. This will result in discontinuity in the operations of the whole economy. A lack of substitute goods can cause suspension of the whole economy, and the economy may seriously collapse and finally may disappear.

6.2.3 The Relation Between Enterprises and the Sequence of Events

As there is only one kind of good in Scarf's model, it is impossible to observe the relation between different kinds of goods. Regarding the time structure of the model, Scarf (1959) discussed the current period and the subsequent following period. For example, when the arrivals of goods ordered are delayed, shipping is postponed to the next period or to several periods later. However, ordering itself is conducted within the same current period to minimize the expected loss cost. The influence of decisions made within the current period can be realized in the next period, two periods later, and even later periods. In this way, the enterprises have to minimize their costs in every period.

Since there are many kinds of goods in our model, we can consider the existence of many kinds of enterprises. In addition to the problems of inventory shortage, which affect the whole economy, the relations between enterprises, that is, the relation between cause and effect, can be observed by our model. The relation between enterprises means the sequence of events of all decision-making and information transfers. For example, in the economy, the input and output sequence should be clearly distinguished: a crucial point when considering the whole economy is that there is output after input. Many kinds of goods models have the capability to clearly consider these types of points.

One of our concerns is what happens over the time process. To clearly consider the relation between enterprises and the sequence of events, the concept of "process analysis," which is described in Sect. 6.2.5, is helpful.[5] Process analysis shows that determinations proceed along a passing time flow. In other words, since the relationships of decisions are considered along with a time path, decision-making that determines the quantity of the production in each period varies depending on the past decisions made, namely, the past quantity of production. To explicitly express that output goods by other enterprises are input goods for our own enterprises, we consider a time lag between the time required to purchase the goods from other enterprises and the time at which the goods are used for production.[6] Therefore, based on the production plan $y_i^p(t+1)$ formulated in the beginning of the this period, raw materials $y_i^p(t+1)a^i$ are purchased during this period, and production $y_i(t+1)$ is carried out in the next period.[7] Therefore, the production of goods, which is planned at the beginning of this period, is completed in next period.

6.2.4 *The Kinds and Functions of Inventory*

In general, there are three kinds of motives for holding inventory. Arrow, K. J. wrote as follows:

> Firms and individuals ordinarily hold stocks of money, even though they could be invested to earn interest. Though there are many controversies in this area, it is broadly agreed that there are three motives for holding cash, referred to by Keynes as the transaction, precautionary, and speculative motives. ...... Since most (though not all) of the elements in the determination of the level of inventories can be brought under one of these three head, we shall organize our discussion about them. (Arrow et al. (1951) pp.3–4.)

Money is a general current means of exchange, namely, an abstract commodity; therefore, money also has a function of inventory. The holding of money means having "goods to sell" as inventory. Keynes distinguished three motives for a liquidity preference, that is, a preference for holding cash, and the three motives are defined as the transactions motive, the precautionary motive, and the speculative motive.[8] This distinction between the liquidity preference motives can apply to the motives for holding commodity inventories.

The discrimination between the raw materials and production goods is taken into consideration in this chapter. The enterprises belong to the production industry, not the distribution industry. In general, there are the three following types of inventory involved in production: the raw material inventory, the goods-in-process inventory, and the finished goods inventory. As described in Sect. 6.3.1, the inventory level does not affect the equilibrium output level, while it plays an important role in the feasibility of the production process. This is not a situation in which the function

[5]Regarding the "process analysis," see Chap. 1, Sect. 5, "Methodology of Analysis."

[6]See Eq. (6.7).

[7]See Table 6.1.

[8]Keynes (1936) pp.195–6.

of holding inventory is a speculative one. Here, the focus is on transactions and on inventory functioning as a buffer. When the focus on the function of inventory is on its role as a buffer, it is normal for ordering agents, having only partial knowledge, to disassociate the expected inventory quantity from the actual inventory quantity. Inventory viewed as a buffer serves a joint function between agents in a "loosely connected system" in the whole economy.[9] Due to an enterprise holding inventory, during short periods of time, dependent variables that mutually depend on each portion of the whole economy can be treated as independent variables. Although ordering agents have a limited range of knowledge, they can interfere independently with the whole economy.

Therefore, the motives for holding inventory focused on here are the transactions motive and the precautionary motive. The speculative motive is not considered. In addition, since the focus here is on the function of inventory as a buffer, only finished goods inventory is considered as inventory, while raw material inventory and goods-in-process inventory are not considered in this chapter.

With regard to the decision of production quantity, there are two types of decision methods: make-to-stock (MTS) production and make-to-order (MTO) production. The inventory types depend on each individual decision method. Resulting in holding inventory in the form of finished goods, MTS production is a typical decision method of production quantity in a demand-restricted market. If the whole economy adopts and conducts the MTS production method, raw materials are easily obtained. In principle, therefore, there is no need to hold raw material inventory. MTO production, a typical decision method in a supply-restricted market, is not based on a prediction of the sales quantity. Therefore, in principle, a finished goods inventory is not necessary. If MTO production is viewed as a method in which raw materials are obtained only after orders are placed, then it may not be necessary to have raw material inventory. However, if all enterprises start their production from the stage of preparing raw materials after receiving orders, some enterprises will not be able to complete their goods by the production deadline. If this type of production is conducted as a whole, the economy cannot be maintained. In an economy in which production requires time, even if it is a short time, if a certain delivery period exists, raw material inventory has to be held, even for the MTO economy.[10]

Ordering methods are divided into the fixed quantity ordering method and the periodic ordering method. The fixed quantity ordering method is a method in which a constant predetermined amount of orders are irregularly placed when the amount of inventory falls below a certain value. Ordering intervals are not determined previously, while the determined amount of orders is not frequently changed. In order to determine the amount of orders in advance, the unit price, holding cost, ordering costs, and the past quantity of goods shipped are taken into consideration. Generally, those goods with more storage charges and those with expensive ordering

[9]Regarding the "loosely connected system," see Chap. 1, Sect. 4, "Environment of Economic Activities."

[10]Refer to Kornai and Martos (1981) and Morioka (2005).

costs are ordered less frequently. Consideration of the past quantity of goods shipped assumes that there exists a certain relationship between the future quantity of goods shipped and the past quantity of goods shipped. This fixed quantity ordering method is simpler when compared with the periodic ordering method because there is no need to predict the quantity of goods shipped during each period. In the long run, however, the quantity of orders may change based on forecasts. Therefore, this is not to say that this method makes no predictions at all. The periodic ordering method is a method to place orders periodically by predicting the future sales quantity (or the quantity of goods shipped). Prediction methods include the moving average method, the adaptive method, the exponential smoothing method, and so on. These methods require a certain amount of time to develop the predictions; however, the inventory level is often maintained properly when compared to the fixed quantity ordering method.

As the inventory control economy based on the (S, s) policy is an MTS production economy and a kind of fixed quantity ordering method economy, there is no periodic ordering in this type of economy. A single period, however, is referred to in this chapter; a single period means a unit production period. While the length of a production period varies depending on the type of the good, production periods are synchronized.

According to the optimum inventory theory proposed by Arrow et al., the relevant prices in each period are referred to in order to determine the amount of inventory. Here, however, a price change in the concerned period is not considered. Therefore, when the level of S and s is determined, prices may be referred in the determination, but the determined prices are not revised during the period concerned. This means that the unit period for revision of S and s differs from that of production and sales. Therefore, a demand change is adjusted based on a quantity change, not a price change.[11] During the concerned period, the production capacity and workforces do not reach their upper limits, while consumption demand changes as an exogenous shock.

6.2.5 Building Our Model Based on (S, s) Inventory Control Policy

In our model economy, each individual enterprise purchases the goods of other enterprises as raw materials for their own production, and each of these enterprises produces their unique single good. In other words, while raw materials are distinguished from finished goods, many types of enterprises exist. Joint production is out of consideration. These enterprises are closely associated with each other, similar

[11] See Chap. 2, Sect. 3, "Some Characteristic Features of the System."

to a mesh, and this dependent relationship is represented by the input coefficient matrix A.[12]

In addition, our inventory adjustment model described here has the following characteristics. These points show evolutionary features.[13]

- Economic agents only know about the sale of their own goods. No agent knows the activity level of the whole economy.
- Economic agents only have the right to decide about their own production quantity. Decentralized decision-making is done.
- Each enterprise interferes with the other enterprises by sales and purchases in markets.
- Each enterprise conducts the economic activities, such as prediction, purchases, production, and sales, repeatedly parallel and retrospectively.

The meaning of each character in our model is described below. The production goods quantity vector y, the finished goods inventory quantity vector z, the sales (= shipping) quantity vector x, and the final demand quantity vector f are n-dimensional nonnegative vertical vectors. The final demand f is given as an exogenous variable. The input coefficient is $A = [a^i_j](i, j = 1, \cdots, n)$. Each x_i, y_i, z_i, and f_i is the ith element of each vector and indicates the ith good. The sign shown in parentheses indicates the time in which the event happens. The right shoulder p of y^p means that the y^p is the planned (not yet fulfilled) quantity.

Now, let us describe the sequence of events, namely, the order of decisions, of a certain enterprise, for example, the ith enterprise. In our model, it is essential to understand what happens in the time sequences. Table 6.1 shows the details of this

Table 6.1 The sequence of events: The order of decision occurs as follows: (1) plan for next period's production → order (ordered) for next period's production → arrival (shipment) for next period's production and simultaneously or with parallel (2) input by previous period's order → output of this period → shipment ($\min\{ordered, inventory\ by\ previous\ period + output\ of\ this\ period\}$) for next period's production → inventory of this period

	$t-1$ period	t (this) period	$t+1$ period
Plan	$y_i^p(t)$	$y_i^p(t+1)$	$y_i^p(t+2)$
Order	$y_i^p(t)a^i$	$y_i^p(t+1)a^i$	$y_i^p(t+2)a^i$
Arrival	$y_i(t)a^i$	$y_i(t+1)a^i$	$y_i(t+2)a^i$
Input	$y_i(t-1)a^i$	$y_i(t)a^i$	$y_i(t+1)a^i$
Output	$y_i(t-1)$	$y_i(t)$	$y_i(t+1)$
Ordered	$x_i(t-1)$	$x_i(t)$	$x_i(t+1)$
Shipment	$\min\{x_i(t-1),$ $z(t-2)+y_i(t-1)\}$	$\min\{x_i(t),$ $z(t-1)+y_i(t)\}$	$\min\{x_i(t+1),$ $z(t)+y_i(t+1)\}$
Inventory	$z_i(t-1)$	$z_i(t)$	$z_i(t+1)$

[12]Regarding the multiple enterprises model, see Pasinetti (1977, 1981).

[13]Regarding the evolutionary features, see Chap. 1, Sects. 1, 2, and 3.

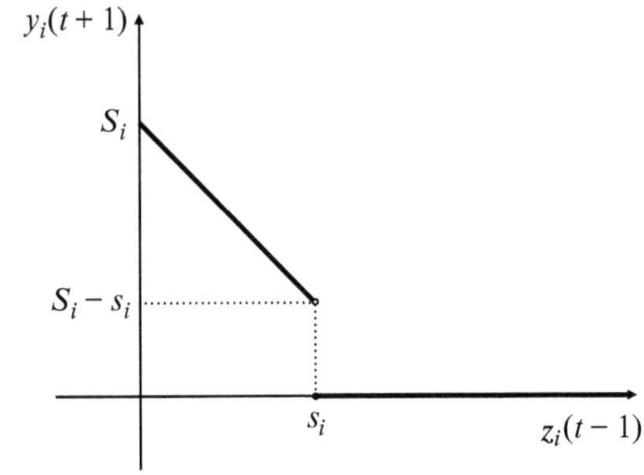

Fig. 6.4 $y_i(t+1), z_i(t-1) \geq 0$ and $if\ z_i(t-1) < s_i$, then $y_i(t+1) = S_i - z_i(t-1)$, $if\ z_i(t-1) \geq s_i$, then $y_i(t+1) = 0$.

process. Suppose that our ith enterprise is now at the beginning of the t period. This enterprise holds the following production goods in its warehouse for shipping: the good $y_i(t-1)$ that was produced during the $t-1$ period and the inventory $z_i(t-1)$. The quantity $y_i^P(t)$ has already been decided, according to the plan established at the beginning of the $t-1$ period. Raw materials $y_i^P(t)a^i$ were ordered at the $t-1$ period in accordance with the goods quantity $y_i^P(t)$. These raw materials $y_i(t)a^i$ arrive at the beginning of the t period if they are supplied without a shortage. By using these raw materials $y_i(t)a^i$, the production of $y_i(t)$ starts from the beginning of the t period and then is finished in the t period.

Now, the ith enterprise has to determine the quantity $y_i^P(t+1)$ that is produced in the $t+1$ period. This quantity is determined by comparing the inventory quantity $z_i(t-1)$ at the end of the $t-1$ period with the inventory level s_i which was predetermined as follows:

$$if\quad z_i(t-1) < s_i,\quad \text{then}\quad y_i(t+1) = S_i - z_i(t-1), \tag{6.5}$$

$$if\quad z_i(t-1) \geq s_i,\quad \text{then}\quad y_i(t+1) = 0. \tag{6.6}$$

According to Eqs. (6.5) and (6.6), this inventory-production relation is displayed in Fig. 6.4.

In the whole economy, each enterprise builds their plan as described above, and after that, the orders to purchase raw materials starts. Goods, which were ordered in the $t-1$ period by each enterprise, are also shipped by the beginning of t period and production starts. For the ith enterprise, the amount of goods to be shipped is determined by the following equation.

$$x_i(t) = \sum_{j=1}^{n} y_j(t+1)a_i^j + f_i \tag{6.7}$$

Thus, the quantity $x_i(t)$, namely, the demanded quantity, to be ordered by the ith enterprise is determined.

Production requires time, and there are n enterprises in our model. The raw materials that are inputted at the beginning of the current t period are completed as finished goods in the current t period. In the current t period, it is assumed that the output quantity $y(t)$, for which production starts at the beginning of the current t period, can be shipped for the order $x(t)$ that is received in the current t period. The inventory quantity $z_i(t)$ at the end of the current t period is the inventory quantity $z_i(t-1)$ at the end of the previous $t-1$ period plus the production quantity $y_i(t)$ in the current t period minus the shipped quantity $x_i(t)$ in the current t period. The amount ordered may exceed the capacity of shipment. As it is impossible to ship the goods over the capacity, the inventory becomes zero. Therefore, the inventory $z_i(t)$ generated at the end of the t period can be expressed as follows:

$$z_i(t) = \max\{z_i(t-1) + y_i(t) - x_i(t), 0\}. \tag{6.8}$$

In the beginning of the $t+1$ period, the production quantity $y_i^p(t+2)$ is planned, while the inventory quantity $z_i(t)$ at the end of the t period is referred to. It is the beginning of a new period.

Here, the following point should be emphasized: after the production quantity of all enterprises $y(t+1)$, which is produced in the next period, is planned and determined at the beginning of the t period, the received orders $x(t)$ at the t period are known to all enterprises as the sum of the intermediate demand $y(t+1)A$ and the final demand f. Before the production plan is determined, the order of raw materials is not placed by the ordering enterprises, that is, the orders $x(t)$ are not received. Therefore, the quantity $z(t)$ is not determined before the production plan is determined. In other words, as $z(t)$ is unknown at the beginning of the current t period, the enterprise has to plan the productive quantity by using the $z(t-1)$ instead of $z(t)$. It is shown clearly in the Eqs. (6.5) and (6.6).

6.3 The Periodic Production Model and the Difference in the Number of the Kinds of Goods

The inventory economy controlled by (S, s) policy is a nonlinear model economy. In this section, however, we assume that periodic production is executed, that is, whatever the amount of inventory is, production is conducted periodically. This periodic production model, which is modified from the nonlinear (S, s) model, is introduced in order to compare (S, s) policy model with this model and to examine the consequences of differences in the number of kinds of goods. This model is not linear, but affine.

In the case of the periodic production model, the production goods quantity, the inventory quantity, and the sales (or shipping) quantity can take any real number. Therefore, this periodic production model is constructed by the following three equations.

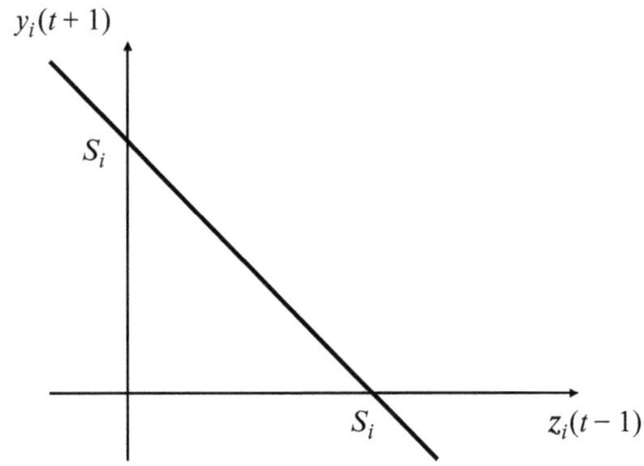

Fig. 6.5
$y_i(t+1) = S_i - z_i(t-1)$

$$y_i(t+1) = S_i - z_i(t-1) \tag{6.9}$$

$$x_i(t) = \sum_{j=1}^{n} y_j(t+1)a_i^j + f_i \tag{6.10}$$

$$z_i(t) = z_i(t-1) + y_i(t) - x_i(t) \tag{6.11}$$

Since the inventory quantity can take on a negative value, the production volume can take on any large value. It is assumed that there is no limit on the production capacity. These transformation are represented in a form which maps

$$[y(t), x(t-1), z(t-1)]$$

to

$$[y(t+1), x(t), z(t)]$$

according to Table 6.1. According to Eq. (6.9), the inventory-production relation of the periodic production is displayed in Fig. 6.5.

6.3.1 Equilibrium State in the Inventory Control Economy

We describe the case where the inventory control economy based on the (S, s) type policy remains in an equilibrium state. Since a certain activity level continues, each production amount y, the inventory amount z, and the shipping amount x remain the same. Therefore, each of Eqs. (6.9), (6.10), and (6.11) can be expressed as follows:

$$y^* = S - z^*$$
$$x^* = Ay^* + f^*$$
$$z^* = z^* + y^* - x^*$$

where each constant amount is expressed with the $*$ mark in the upper right of each vector. The following two equations are obtained by the above three equations.

$$y^* = Ay^* + f^* \tag{6.12}$$

$$S = y^* + z^* \tag{6.13}$$

The production amount y^* is expressed as $y^* = (I - A)^{-1} f^*$ based on Eq. (6.12), which can be determined if the final demand f and the input coefficient A are given. As shown by Eq. (6.13), in such an economy, inventory can or may exist; however, it could be zero. When a certain constant production level continues in an inventory adjustment economy, the role of the inventory as a buffer fades. In other words, when an inventory adjustment economy is in an equilibrium, the concept of inventory itself becomes unnecessary. In this way, it turns out that the inventory does not play any role in the equilibrium state.

6.3.2 *The Case of One Kind and Two Kinds of Goods Periodic Production Model*

What will happen when there is only one kind of goods or when there are two kinds of goods in a periodic production model economy?

6.3.2.1 One Kind of Goods Model

The following equations are derived based on the equations of (6.9), (6.10), and (6.11).

$$y(t+1) = S - z(t-1) \tag{6.14}$$

$$x(t) = ay(t+1) + f \tag{6.15}$$

$$z(t) = z(t-1) + y(t) - x(t) \tag{6.16}$$

where a is the input coefficient. The following equation is derived by substituting Eqs. (6.14) and (6.15) into Eq. (6.16).

$$y(t+2) - (1+a)y(t+1) + y(t) = f \tag{6.17}$$

This is a second-order inhomogeneous differential equation. We find the general homogeneous solution of Eq. (6.17). Where the characteristic root takes μ, the following characteristic equation is established:

$$\mu^2 - (1+a)\mu + 1 = 0$$

This equation can be solved in the following:

$$\mu = \frac{1 + a \pm \sqrt{(1+a)^2 - 4}}{2}.$$

The input coefficient a is productive, that is, $0 < a < 1$; the characteristic root μ is inevitably a complex root. By putting this characteristic root μ_1 and μ_2, the general solution can be expressed:

$$y(t) = C_1\mu_1^t + C_2\mu_2^t$$

where C_1 and C_2 are a given constant values. In the case in which the equation is inhomogeneous, the right-hand f is a constant value, and the characteristic root is not 1. Therefore, where the special solution is expressed as $y^*(t) = y^*$, the following equation is derived.

$$y^* = \frac{f}{1-a}$$

Based on this, the general solution is obtained as follows:

$$y(t) = C_1\mu_1^t + C_2\mu_2^t + \frac{f}{1-a}$$

The characteristic roots μ_1 and μ_2 are complex numbers and conjugate to each other and the absolute value of two eigenvalues are 1; therefore, the general solution is a periodic solution.

6.3.2.2 Two Kinds of Goods Model

The two kinds of goods model are not very difficult to handle mathematically since the characteristic equation for A is quadratic. Where A is productive, the two eigenvalues of A take on the real numbers whose absolute value of eigenvalues is smaller than 1. Suppose that A is expressed as the following productive matrix.

$$A = \begin{pmatrix} a & b \\ c & d \end{pmatrix}$$

With this matrix, where the eigenvalue is λ, the following characteristic equation is obtained.

$$\lambda^2 - (a+d)\lambda + ad - bc = 0,$$

and the root is expressed by the following equation:

$$\lambda = \frac{a + d \pm \sqrt{(a-d)^2 + 4bc}}{2}$$

Inside the square root is $(a - d)^2 \geqq 0$ and $bc \geqq 0$, which is nonnegative; therefore, all eigenvalues λ are real numbers. A is a productive matrix, so that the eigenvalue is $\lambda < 1$. The other eigenvalue, which is not a Frobenius root, is also a real number, whose absolute value is smaller than 1.

Based on the Eqs. (6.9), (6.10), and (6.11), the following equations are established.

$$y(t+1) = S - z(t-1) \tag{6.18}$$

$$x(t) = Ay(t+1) + f \tag{6.19}$$

$$z(t) = z(t-1) + y(t) - x(t) \tag{6.20}$$

Variables are column vectors. The following equation is obtained by using Eqs. (6.18) and (6.19) in Eq. (6.20):

$$y(t+2) - (I + A)y(t+1) + y(t) = f \tag{6.21}$$

Therefore, the convergence or divergence of the model, that is, the value of $y(t)$, is independent from the values of S or s.

By putting ${}^{T}u(t) = (y(t), y(t-1))$, Eq. (6.21) can be expressed as a simultaneous differential equation that uses the following partitioned (block) matrices.

$$u(t+2) = \Phi u(t+1) + \Psi \tag{6.22}$$

where the following block matrices are used:

$$\Phi = \begin{pmatrix} I + A & -I \\ I & 0 \end{pmatrix}$$

and

$$\Psi = \begin{pmatrix} f \\ 0 \end{pmatrix}.$$

Therefore, the convergence or divergence of $y(t)$ is dependent on the maximum eigenvalue of Φ. The input coefficient A is a 2×2 matrix. If it is productive, the eigenvalues and the eigenvectors do exist within the real-number range. However, the eigenvalue of Φ does not always exist within the real-number range.

Now, the eigenvalue of Φ is considered here. Since the input coefficient A is a 2×2 matrix, Φ is a 4×4 matrix. Suppose that A is productive and that the eigenvalue $\lambda \in R$ is given with the eigenvector $u \in R^2$.

$$Au = \lambda u$$

The matrix Φ is composed of the matrix A and the identity matrix I. Now, based on the partitioned matrix type of Φ, let us consider a 2×2 matrix ϕ as shown below.

$$\phi = \begin{pmatrix} 1+\lambda & -1 \\ 1 & 0 \end{pmatrix}$$

Notice that this ϕ is a 2×2 matrix. Where the eigenvalue of ϕ is $\nu \in C$ and its eigenvector is ${}^T(\alpha, \beta) \in C^2$, the following equation is established:

$$\phi \begin{pmatrix} \alpha \\ \beta \end{pmatrix} = \nu \begin{pmatrix} \alpha \\ \beta \end{pmatrix}. \tag{6.23}$$

Then, we consider the following vector, which has complex numbers α and β as coefficients:

$$\begin{pmatrix} \alpha u \\ \beta u \end{pmatrix} \in C^4.$$

When we multiply this vector in the right side of matrix Φ, the following expressions can be developed:

$$\begin{aligned} \Phi \begin{pmatrix} \alpha u \\ \beta u \end{pmatrix} &= \begin{pmatrix} I+A & -I \\ I & 0 \end{pmatrix} \begin{pmatrix} \alpha u \\ \beta u \end{pmatrix} \\ &= \begin{pmatrix} \alpha I u + \alpha A u - \beta I u \\ \alpha I u \end{pmatrix} \\ &= \begin{pmatrix} \{\alpha(1+\lambda) - \beta\} u \\ \alpha u \end{pmatrix}. \end{aligned}$$

Based on Eq. (6.23), the following equations are obtained:

$$\begin{aligned} \alpha(1+\lambda) - \beta &= \nu\alpha \\ \alpha &= \nu\beta. \end{aligned}$$

Therefore, using these two equations, the following equation is obtained.

$$\Phi \begin{pmatrix} \alpha u \\ \beta u \end{pmatrix} = \nu \begin{pmatrix} \alpha u \\ \beta u \end{pmatrix}$$

The maximum eigenvalue of Φ is ν, while the eigenvector that belongs to this value is ${}^T(\alpha u, \beta u)$.

The characteristic equation for the matrix ϕ is expressed below:

$$\nu^2 - (1 + \lambda)\nu + 1 = 0$$

Therefore, the eigenvalue ν is expressed as the equation below:

$$\nu = \frac{1 + \lambda \pm \sqrt{(1 + \lambda)^2 - 4}}{2}$$

Here, since $0 < \lambda < 1$ is established, the eigenvalues ν of the matrix Φ are a conjugated complex number. Therefore, the absolute value of ν is 1. Therefore Φ is the periodic solution. According to Eqs. (6.21) and (6.22), $y(t)$ is a periodic orbit.

In a model where the number of the kinds of goods is one or two, the input coefficient A does exist within the real-number range. Therefore, the absolute value of the eigenvalue for the partitioned block matrix is 1, and the production amount and the inventory amount of the model show a periodic orbit.

6.3.3 *The Case of Many Kinds of Goods Periodic Production Model*

In case of more than three kinds of goods model, the input coefficient A becomes more than a three-dimensional matrix. The equations that constitute the many kinds of goods model, however, are the same form as the equations of the two kinds of goods model (6.18), (6.19), and (6.20). The input coefficient A is productive and a nonnegative irreducible square matrix, so it has a real-number eigenvalue (Frobenius root) of which the absolute value is the maximum. As we can see in Sect. 6.3.2, in the case of the quadratic matrix A, the eigenvalues exist within the real-number range; however, when the kind of goods exceeds or equals three kinds, some eigenvalues of the input coefficient A can be found to be complex numbers. Even though the absolute values of the eigenvalue of A are smaller than the Frobenius root, when the eigenvalues of A are conjugated, the absolute value of the eigenvalue of Φ could be greater than 1.[14]

For example, let the input coefficient table A be the 13 industrial sectors' table of the input-output table of Japan in the year 2005. We can find that the eigenvalue of the input coefficient matrix A takes on the following five real numbers and eight complex numbers (which are rounded off to three significant figures, as below): 0.549, 0.212, 0.119, -0.056, -0.003, $0.076 \pm 0.023i$, $0.036 \pm 0.055i$, $0.006 \pm 0.039i$, and $-0.005 \pm 0.034i$. The absolute value take on the following nine numbers

[14]See the Theorems 1 and 2 in Chap. 4 and Morioka (2005).

in order as follows: 0.549, 0.212, 0.119, 0.056, 0.003, 0.080, 0.067, 0.040, and 0.034.

Additionally, the following 26 eigenvalues of Φ can be obtained when the input coefficient matrix A in the year 2005 is used for our model[15]: $0.535 \pm 0.884i$, $0.515 \pm 0.884i$, $0.507 \pm 0.885i$, $0.546 \pm 0.855i$, $0.559 \pm 0.829i$, $0.498 \pm 0.867i$, $0.775 \pm 0.632i$, $0.606 \pm 0.796i$, $0.472 \pm 0.882i$, $0.531 \pm 0.831i$, $0.488 \pm 0.851i$, $0.492 \pm 0.845i$, and $0.501 \pm 0.828i$. The absolute value takes on the following values in order: 1.033, 1.033, 1.023, 1.023, 1.020, 1.020, 1.014, 1.014, 1.000, 1.000, 1.000, 1.000, 1.000, 1.000, 1.000, 1.000, 1.000, 1.000, 0.986, 0.986, 0.980, 0.980, 0.977, 0.977, 0.968, and 0.968.

Since the eigenvalues of Φ takes on the absolute value that is greater than 1 as shown above, the production amount y diverges from Eq. (6.22). This is the crucial different point between the one kind, two kinds, and more than three kinds of goods model. From this viewpoint, in general, we need to investigate not only the one or two kinds model but also the many kinds of goods models.

6.4 Numerical Experiments for the (S, s) Policy Model with Many Kinds of Goods

6.4.1 The Nonlinear Inventory Model and Numerical Experiments

Nonlinear phenomena are generally treated with linear models by using first-order approximations. Previous studies have actually obtained exact solutions by using linear models that are based on the assumption that inventories can be increased unlimitedly or on the assumption that negative inventory can be managed as a backlog.[16] The (S, s) inventory policy model based on Scarf (1959) is a nonlinear model because there are an upper limit S and a lower limit s of inventory quantity.

Even though exact solutions are impossible to obtain in a mathematical sense, numerical experiments can provide us with a picture of the phenomenon in question to a certain degree. Among the numerical experiments, there is an experiment that is referred to as an agent-based simulation or a multiagent-based simulation. These simulations are conducted with a number of agents with an internal structure, where each individual agent makes independent decisions internally while recognizing the external environment. An entire situation is emerged as the result of the mutual interference of the multiple agents. The analysis conducted in Sect. 6.4 of this chapter is also deemed as one of these multiagent-based simulations.

[15]Since A is a 13×13 matrix, Φ is a 26×26 matrix.

[16]See Chaps. 3, 4, and 5.

One of the important concerns of this chapter is what kind of economic consequences can be induced when many different enterprises implement production based on a (S, s) inventory control policy. In other words, our research focus is as follows: if each enterprise adopts the inventory control system based on the (S, s) policy, what are the consequences for the whole economy? Regarding Scarf's discussions, the point that should be investigated is the movement of the whole economy, which is constituted by many kinds of enterprises.

Our model economy comprises the four Eqs. (6.5), (6.6), (6.7), and (6.8). When the economy is at a certain constant level of activity, $x(t)$, $y(t)$, and $z(t)$ are always constant, and the economy repeats the same production amount. Suppose the final demand f suddenly increases to $f + \Delta f$ for some reason, for example, a sudden change in consumption demand at time $t = 1$. Our model economy is struck by the change in the exogenous demand. As already described in Sect. 6.2.5, each enterprise determines the production amount of the next term $y(2)$ by recognizing the inventory amount $z(-1)$ at $t = 1$ according to Eqs. (6.5) and (6.6). At this time, the amount ordered $x(1)$ in the present term is unknown. This is an essential structure in economies where a multiple number of enterprises appear. According to Eqs. (6.7) and (6.8), each enterprise, which cannot recognize the entire change of demand, perceives the change of $x(1)$ through the market, and as a result, a change of the inventory level $z(1)$ occurs. Therefore, each enterprise can decide the new production level according to Eqs. (6.5) and (6.6) at the next term $t = 2$.

As individual enterprises change their production level in this way, where does our model economy will reach as a whole? To investigate the traverse path, at first, we assume the economy is in stationary state, that is, the steady state values are given to the initial values $y(0)$ and $z(-1)$. Let the economy be at state 1 ($t \leq 0$), and the exogenous demand increase suddenly at $t = 1$. In the numerical experiments, an increase of final demand by 5% ($\Delta f = 0.05f$) is assumed. Receiving the shock, our economy starts to traverse according to the four Eqs. (6.5), (6.6), (6.7), and (6.8) ($t \geq 1$). If the economy reaches the new stationary state, the economy is considered to be at state 2 ($t \geq 1$). The state 2 does not necessarily indicate an equilibrium state.

If inventory is managed properly, production can continue overall in the economy. However, when some enterprises cannot respond to a demand due to an inventory shortage, the shortage of products by these enterprises become a bottleneck that results in suspending the activities of the entire economy. However, it is not always true that holding a large amount of inventory can make the economy continue. To avoid an inventory shortage, the upper limit S needs to be increased. However, a large amount of inventory causes a low frequency of the production process, which increases the production amount per production process. As a result, this also increases the order amount of raw materials for one production term, and enterprises that receive the orders of raw materials for this one production term may not be able to respond to this large increased amount of orders.

The relation below is introduced with regard to the upper-limit inventory S and the lower-limit inventory s in the (S, s) policy for convenience.

$$s = \rho S \quad (0 \le \rho \le 1) \tag{6.24}$$

For the economy at state 1 to traverse toward state 2 without suffering from inventory shortages, in what range should S and s (namely, ρ) exist? Alternatively, if an inventory shortage occurs, how frequently does it occur and for what range of values of S and s? What multiple of the standard deviation of demand fluctuations of the inventory should be used to determine the amount of inventory that should be held? Then, instead of determining the optimum values of (S, s), what value should ρ take in an economy where production is appropriately continued based on the appropriate amount of inventories held?

The following simply describes the economic data that was used in order to build the model. The input coefficient table used represents the 13 industrial sectors table of the input-output table of Japan in the year 2005. Since we assume that one industry sector in this input coefficient table is one enterprise, there are 13 enterprises in the model economy in which each individual enterprise makes decisions as described in Sect. 6.2.5. The following revisions were added to this input-output table. The real Japanese economy incorporates overseas trade. Since the mining industry sector in Japan can only supply 5% of the necessary amount of products in Japan, many mining products are imported. However, our model represents a single-country model economy that does not consider overseas trade. Therefore, we must add slight adjustments to the data for convenience sake so that all goods could be covered by domestic production. As a result, the GDP of the modified model economy was increased by approximately 6% when compared to the actual Japanese GDP in the year 2005. The GDP of the modified economy is approximately 538 trillion yen, and the final demand plus intermediate demand is approximately 1,043 trillion yen.

6.4.2 Results, Analysis, and Evaluation of Numerical Experiments

When an economy at a certain production level traverses to a different production level due to a change in the exogenous final demand, the initial inventory amount plays an important role in this traverse path. In an economy with zero inventory, the real consumption level needs to be lowered, and a surplus has to be kept. Postulating that the initial inventory amount would be around a 0.2 to 4.0 of the production amount y^* of the economy at an initial stable status, we examined the traverse paths over this range. In other words, we examined the traverse paths from status 1 to status 2 in all 20 points by changing the initial inventory amount to the range between 0.2 and 4.0 of the production amount within the range of the parameter $\rho = 0.3 \sim 0.9$. The terms examined were 100 terms (namely, 100 terms for each of 13 industrial sectors, 1,300 points in total), including 1,000 terms depending on the sector. Table 6.2 shows the results, including the ratio of how many times the

Table 6.2 The ratio of zero production within 1,300 points

The ratio of zero production ($y = 0$)						
		$z(0)/y(0)$				
		0.2	1.0	2.0	3.0	4.0
s/S	0.9	0.000	0.004	0.038	0.095	0.224
	0.7	0.000	0.162	0.467	0.562	0.596
	0.5	0.023	0.504	0.607	0.672	0.722
	0.3	0.406	0.588	0.677	0.741	0.778

Table 6.3 The ratio of negative inventory within 1,300 points

The ratio of negative inventory ($z < 0$)						
		$z(0)/y(0)$				
		0.2	1.0	2.0	3.0	4.0
s/S	0.9	0.050	0.002	0.000	0.000	0.000
	0.7	0.050	0.078	0.037	0.014	0.002
	0.5	0.068	0.256	0.110	0.041	0.035
	0.3	0.348	0.275	0.175	0.120	0.079

production amount becomes zero (ratio of $y_i = 0, i = 1, \cdots 13$ to appear within 1,300 points), and Table 6.3 shows the results, including the ratio of how many times negative inventory appears (ratio of $z_i < 0, i = 1, \cdots 13$ to appear within 1,300 points).

The range of parameters in which no inventory shortage of the model economy would occur even if the amount of production is zero in the period is limited. Table 6.2 shows that this range is only where $\rho = 0.9$ is established, when the initial inventory amount is 2.0, 3.0, and 4.0 times the production amount. The ratio of zero production is 0.038, 0.095, and 0.224, respectively. Therefore, the amount of inventory that needs to be held is about two times the production amount. The lower limit for the inventory s needs to be kept approximately 0.9 times the upper limit for the inventory S. Namely, the production plan needs to be formed within a range where enterprises do not come closer to the potential inventory shortage level. At this level, the inventory control quantity adjustment economy based on the (S, s) type policy can arrive at an economy with a different production level.

Next, for example, where the initial inventory amount is equivalent to the production amount (i.e., $z(0)/y(0) = 1.0$), the percentage of inventory shortage to occur at $\rho = 0.9$ is 0.2%, while at $\rho = 0.7$, it is 7.8% (see Table 6.3). The ratio of zero production when $\rho = 0.9$ and $\rho = 0.7$ is 0.004 and 0.162, respectively (see Table 6.2). Therefore, inventory shortages do not occur when ρ takes a greater value. Namely, bringing the lower limit for inventory s closer to the upper limit for inventory S can prevent inventory shortages. Inventory shortages could occur as ρ decreases. At the same time, inventory is not exhausted as the initial inventory amount becomes larger. Understandably, the most stable status is attained when the inventory level fluctuates less and the production amount is kept constant as much as possible.

To what extent can we validate the shortage range of the inventory in this numerical experiment? Alternatively, how should we evaluate these results as a realistic decision? Let us consider this adequacy based on some assumptions in the present model. Suppose that there is a possibility that other companies, such as subcontractors, have the corresponding substitute goods. If 13 enterprises perform production activities through 100 terms while an inventory shortage of 5% is allowable (on average each enterprise can allow their inventory run short 5 times during 100 terms, namely, 65 times of all 1,300 points), they do not suspend their production in about half of the simulation experiments. Of course, this inventory shortage range depends on the extent of the economic shock. In this experiment, the increase of final demand by 5% is assumed. We can easily understand that the economy can traverse from the state 1 to state 2 without the shortage of inventory when the increase of final demand is less than 5%. Alternatively, we can manage the inventory shortage by proportionally partitioning the excess demand. In this case, the production level decelerates; however, our economy is able to continue without being forced to halt production.[17]

According to this numerical experiment, to what extent should inventory be held for demand distribution fluctuations? For example, Fig. 6.6 shows the frequency

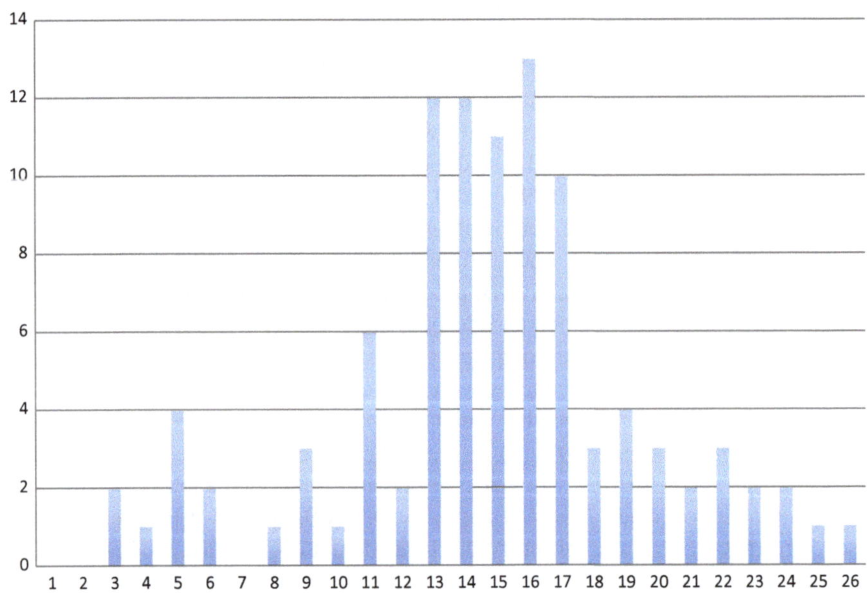

Fig. 6.6 The distribution of demand ($\rho = 0.7$, $z_1(0) = y_1(0)$. Horizontal axis, trillion yen; vertical axis, occurrence times)

[17]In this chapter, we did not perform experiments regarding the traverses with different growth rates and cases where demand is partitioned due to inventory shortages.

distribution of the demand that the first industry sector of the 13 industrial sectors receives. This is based on the scenario in which the initial inventory amount $z_1(0)$ is equivalent to the production amount $y_1(0)$ at $\rho = 0.7$. The ratio of negative inventory is 0.078. At this point, the average demand amount is approximately 14.2 trillion yen, while the standard deviation σ is approximately 4.71 trillion yen. In experiments, inventory ran short 14 times for 100 demand fluctuations. Of those 14 times, the inventory ran short 6 times when the range of the demand fluctuation was within the average value $\pm\sigma$. The inventory ran short six times when the range of the demand fluctuation was greater than the average value $\pm\sigma$ and less than the average value $\pm 2\sigma$. Of the 14 times, the inventory ran short twice when the range of the demand fluctuations was greater than the average value $\pm 2\sigma$.

What would happen if these enterprises had tried to respond to this situation by raising the initial inventory amount or the value of the lower limit of inventory level s? For example, where ρ is set to 0.9 and the initial inventory amount is deemed as four times the production amount, inventory shortages do not occur within this range. The average of the demand amount at this time reached approximately 17.0 trillion yen, while the standard deviation is approximately 2.83 trillion yen. Naturally, the standard deviation decreases. Every enterprise confronts the demand that has a small standard deviation under this situation; therefore, no one needs to maintain a greater ρ. If enterprises decide as described above and lower the inventory level, inventories run short again, and the demand fluctuates greatly.

This issue is such an interesting phenomenon. From the viewpoint of an interdependent relationship, we can see that a micro-macro loop works.[18] Setting a large range where an inventory shortage does not occur at a certain level and trying to prevent inventory from running short causes a new demand fluctuation that has a smaller standard deviation. Thus, although each enterprise begins the production after the inventory level corresponding to the new demand fluctuation is determined, as a result, the inventory corresponding to the demand may run short again. To extend this research for this phenomenon, the parameter ρ needs to be made endogenous.

Taniguchi (1991) showed that even though each individual enterprise makes decentralized decisions while referring to the past order amount (production amount), the whole economy can traverse to a new area previously unknown by each enterprise, namely, a stationary production level. In Taniguchi (1991), each individual enterprise determines the production amount by using methods, such as the weighted average method; therefore, the production amount y_i is determined endogenously. In the inventory control economy model based on this (S, s) policy, the production amount y_i is determined endogenously; however, the lower-limit inventory s and the upper-limit inventory S are given exogenously. The economy sometimes reaches a new production level without suffering from an inventory shortage. For example, in the one example case described below, the economy is on a periodic orbit. In reality, the values of s and S should be modified, while the economy proceeds. However, these values of s and S are constant in this model.

---

[18] Regarding the "micro-macro loop," see Chap. 1, Sect. 5, "Methodology of Analysis."

Furthermore, alternative goods also exist. Therefore, although supply chains are disconnected, other channels work, and the economy is still in progress, even though in reality it may be delayed.

6.4.3 *One Example: Inventory Does Not Run Short, Although the Production Amount Becomes Zero*

When each individual enterprise puts the initial inventory amount equal to two times the initial production amount at $\rho = 0.9$, no enterprise suffers from inventory shortages. Figure 6.7 shows the product amounts of the 13 industrial sectors during 21 terms between the 250th term and the 270th term after the increase of final demand, where zero appears in the production amount. To observe these amounts in more detail, Fig. 6.8 shows the production amount y_1, the inventory amount z_1, the upper-limit inventory S_1 (indicated as SB in the figure), the lower-limit inventory s_1 (indicated as sa in the figure), and the order amount received x_1 of the first industrial sector during 21 terms between the 250th term and the 270th term, in the same level plane. Figure 6.9 shows the gross production amount $\Sigma_i y_i$ of the entire economy at this time. The axis indicates the amount of money (in trillion yen), while the horizontal axis indicates the term. Over 500 terms, no enterprise

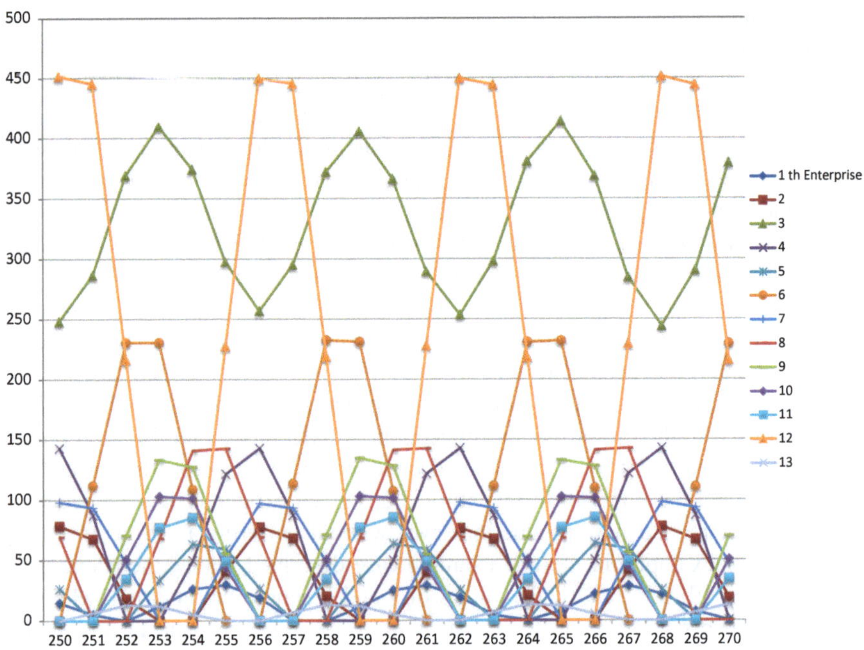

Fig. 6.7 Production amount of each enterprise y_i ($\rho = 0.9$, initial inventory is twice the initial production amount)

experiences inventory shortages. The economy continues to fluctuate based on the new production level in about the first 90 terms. As we have discussed in Sect. 6.3.3, the production amount diverges in the case of the many kinds of goods periodic production model. However, in this nonlinear model, the fluctuation range gradually declines, and the economy enters a new periodic orbit from around the 200th term.

6.5 Conclusions

In this chapter, in the numerical experiments conducted based on the nonlinear model, there are a wide variety of parameters that indicate economic conditions. Points that should be understood from the experimental results become vague if the search objects as goals are not clearly indicated. In other words, when evaluating the experimental results, we sometimes might be confused by attempting to determine whether the factors that critically influence the experimental results can truly be found in the model itself or in the parameters of the model. This shows us somewhat interesting and troublesome things that coexist in numerical experiments. There is probably no way to ascertain these factors other than by undertaking a patient effort to examine what is needed. Therefore, the numerical experiments conducted in this chapter may have only touched the surface in the examination of a nonlinear quantity adjustment economy.

It should be stressed that the difference in the number of the kinds of goods, that is, one kind, two kinds, or more than three kinds of goods, caused a crucial difference in the research results. Namely, the conclusion of this chapter is that divergence can occur in economies with many kinds of goods, including those with more than three kinds of goods, although the periodic solution was derived for a situation in which the number of the kinds of goods was one or two. Since the eigenvalues of A could be complex in cases in which there are three or more kinds of goods, the conclusions derived in the case with one kind or two kinds of products are different from those derived in a situation involving three or more kinds of goods. The parameter representing the number of entities in the model is significant here. In theoretical economy models, in many cases, only one kind of good is assumed. However, this could make us miss important conclusions and run the risk of losing an understanding itself about the real economy. Moreover, in cases with multiple goods, however, divergence could not occur, due to the appearance of the nonlinear characteristic of the (S, s) type policy.

Studies on models in which an economy progresses while absorbing inventory and demand fluctuations were already started by Shiozawa (1981) and Yoshinori (1983), while Taniguchi (1991, 1995, 1997) conducted related analyses. Morioka (2005) also reported organized analytical results. Most of them have been published in Japanese, while important portions have also been presented in English.

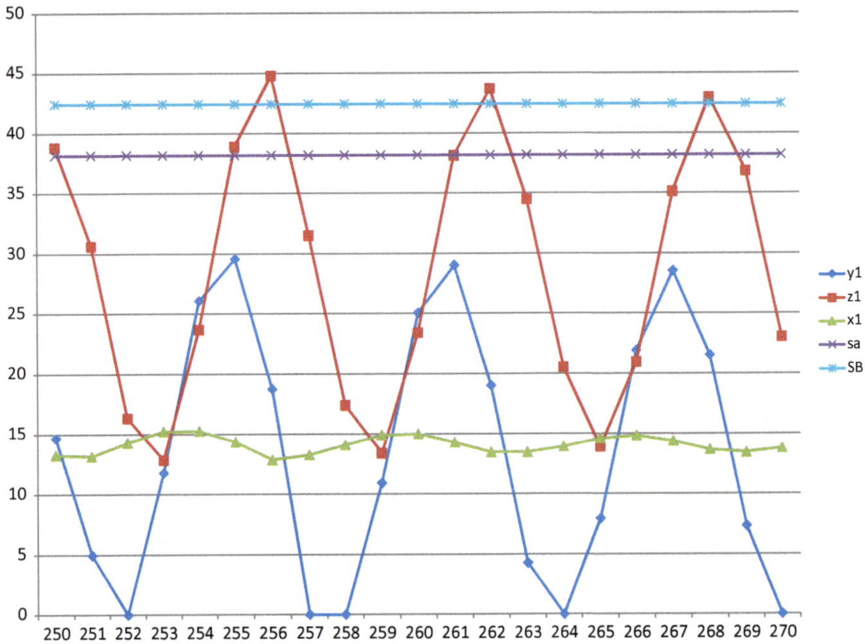

Fig. 6.8 Production amount y_1, inventory amount z_1, the inventory level S_1, and s_1 of the first industrial sector ($\rho = 0.9$, initial inventory is twice the initial production amount)

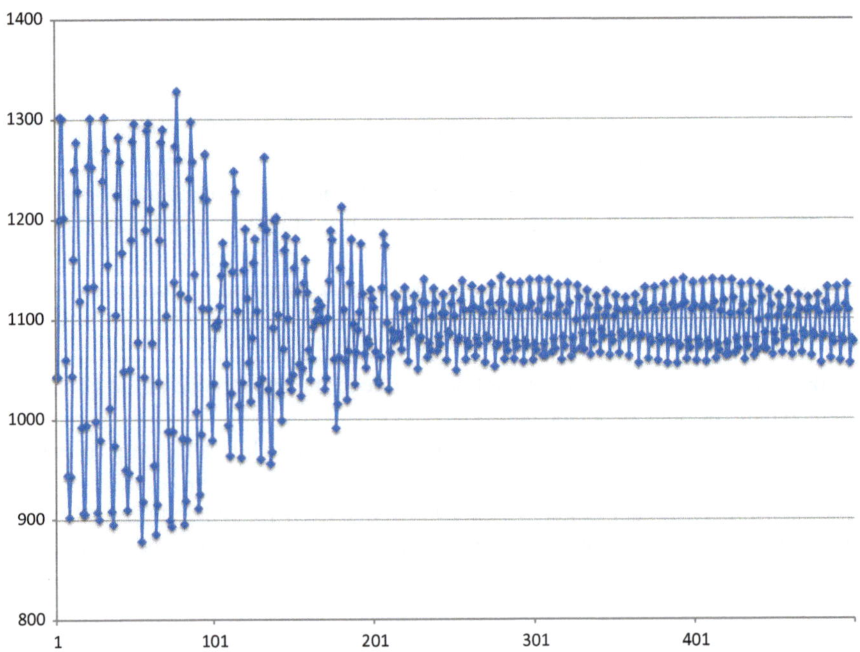

Fig. 6.9 Gross production amount $\Sigma_i y_i$ ($\rho = 0.9$, initial inventory is twice the initial production amount)

References

Arrow, K. J., Harris, T., & Marschak, J. (1951). Optimal inventory policy. *Econometrica, 19*, 250–272.

Arrow, K. J., Karlin, S., & Scarf, H. (Eds.). (1958). *Studies in the mathematical theory of inventory and production*. Stanford: Stanford University Press.

Keynes, J. M. (1936). *The general theory of employment, interest and money*. The Collected Writings of John Maynard Keynes Vol. 7 (1973). London: Macmillan.

Kita, H., Taniguchi, K., & Nakajima, Y. (Eds.). (2016). *Realistic simulation of financial markets – analyzing market behaviors by the third mode of science*. Tokyo: Springer.

Kornai, J., & Martos, B. (Eds.). (1981). *Non-price control*. Amsterdam: North-Holland Publishing Company.

Morioka, M. (2005). *The economic theory of quantity adjustment (In Japanese)*. Nihon Keizai Hyouronnsya. (Japanese Title; *Suuryou Tyousei no Keizai Riron*).

Pasinetti, L. L. (1977). *Lectures on the theory of production*. New York: Columbia University Press.

Pasinetti, L. L. (1981). *Structural change and economic growth*. Cambridge/New York: Cambridge University Press.

Scarf, H. (1959). The optimality of (S,s) policies in the dynamic inventory problem. In K. J. Arrow, S. Karlin, & P. Suppes (Eds.), *Mathematical methods in the social sciences 1959*. Stanford: Stanford University Press.

Scarf, H. E. (2002). Inventory theory. *Operations Research, 50*(1), 186–191.

Shiozawa, Y. (1981). *Foundations of mathematical economics (In Japanese)*. Asakura Shoten. (Japanese Title; *Suuri Keizaigaku no Kiso*).

Shiozawa, Y. (2016). A guide tour of the backside of agent-based simulation, chapter 1. In H. Kita, K. Taniguchi, & Y. Nakajima (Eds.), *Realistic simulation of financial markets*. Tokyo: Springer.

Taniguchi, K. (1991). On the traverse of quantity adjustment economies (In Japanese). *Journal of Economics (The Keizaigaku Zasshi), 91*(5), 29–43. The Economic Society of Osaka City University.

Taniguchi, K. (1995). On a complex adaptive system in short-run quantitative adjustment economies. In N. Aoki, K. Shiraiwa, & Y. Takahashi (Eds.), *Proceedings of the international conference on dynamical systems and chaos*. Singapore: World Scientific.

Taniguchi, K. (1997). *Theories and numerical experiments of traverse (In Japanese)*. Keibunsha, Kyoto. (Japanese Title; *Ikoukatei no Riron to Suuchijikken*).

Yoshinori, S. (1983). The micro structure of Kahn and Keynes multiplier process (In Japanese). *Journal of Economics (The Keizaigaku Zasshi), 84*(3), 48–64. The Economic Society of Osaka City University.

Chapter 7
Exchange and Arbitrage

Price, Evaluation, and the Principle of Exchange

Abstract This chapter considers buying and selling transactions and arbitrage based on *the Principle of Exchange* and the Equivalence Relation. Since money has emerged and price can be observed objectively, buying and selling can be conducted by referring to objective indexes. In this instance, "evaluation" has to be explicitly distinguished from prices. It is important for executing buying and selling transactions that there be a different "evaluation" formed by each buying party and selling party. Arbitrage is defined as the use of differences in exchange rates to earn a profit. Presenting specific cases with respect to these phenomena, this chapter considers the stability and instability of prices in financial markets and product markets based on the formation of "evaluations" and the function of arbitrage.

Keywords The principle of exchange · Money · Price · Arbitrage · Equivalence relation · Buy and sell · Exchange

7.1 Money, Price, and the Equivalence Relations

7.1.1 The Emergency of Money and Price

There is an object that does not exist in the natural world but has special significance only to humans. It is money. Money is independent from the subjective states of mind of humans, such as pain or satisfaction. In this sense, money is an objective existence. Although money is an objective existence, it is able to really exist only because humans exist. Therefore, money is different from other natural phenomena, such as a stone or a tree. Money makes sense only to humans. For humans, money is a critically important objective existence.[1]

[1] "The third category" was asserted in Friedrich (1967, 1973) p.20. See Taniguchi (2012).

Y. Shiozawa et al., *Microfoundations of Evolutionary Economics*,
Evolutionary Economics and Social Complexity Science 15,
https://doi.org/10.1007/978-4-431-55267-3_7

Historically, barter existed prior to the emergence of money.[2] Three notions – property, justice, and liberty (in a sense that one can dispose of one's possessions as one wishes) – appeared almost simultaneously in the human history.[3] These simultaneous emergences gradually made it possible to barter goods. Barter was then expanded, and a wide variety of types of barter were enacted and executed concurrently at certain locations. This expansion generated a marketplace. The emergence of the marketplace must have activated trade further. Each good had its own marketability and the marketability differed. Therefore, a highly marketable good autonomously became a general current means of exchange: this marketable good is called money. Although money is abstract, the fact that it is one of the commodities still remains.[4] Money was born, and exchange became a type of intermediated exchange using money, namely, the process of buying and selling. Prices, serving as exchange rates for money, also appeared. When bartering was conducted, the types and volumes of goods to be exchanged were negotiation targets. When money appeared, however, it began to serve as the one-of-a-kind exchange target of goods. Because of this, the exchange rate with money (namely, price) consciously became a more important index. When exchange with money was conducted more widely, competition that had not yet been observed also appeared. Significant differences have emerged between the price, which serves as the exchange rate with money, and the exchange rate used in bartering. It is the emergence of the competition not between buyers and sellers but among buyers and among sellers. For example, in bartering, when individual A who possesses good X desires good Y, no matter how much individual B, who does not possess good Y but possesses good Z, desires to obtain good X, individual B cannot be a negotiation target for individual A. If good Y and good Z become a general current means of exchange, this individual B can become one of individual A's negotiation targets.[5] Exchange represents a relation between humans. Price also represents relations between humans, not the relation between an object and a human. This fact imposes a very strong restriction on prices, which is discussed in Sect. 7.1.2.

7.1.2 The Exchange Rate and the Equivalence Relation

The exchange rate in bartering is expressed in the ratio of goods that are exchanged. Since this value is determined depending on the exchanged unit, the exchange rate has a dimension. When the kinds of goods to be exchanged increase, the exchange rate is expressed in a continued ratio.

---

[2]According to Hayek, exchange originates in donation. He presumes that exchange was started by placing a gift on the border between the domains of mutual parties. See Hayek (1973) p.82.

[3]See Hayek (1988) Chap. 2.

[4]Marketability includes exchange easiness, separation easiness, easiness in quality preservation, and scarcity. See Menger (1923) Chapter.9.

[5]See Menger (1923) Chapter.9.

Suppose, for instance, three goods A, B, and C are exchanged. Let the quantity x [e.g., weight (g)] of the good A, the quantity y [e.g., length (m)] of the good B, and the quantity z [e.g., volume (l)] of the good Z be exchanged by the ratio of these good's quantity a(g): b(m): c(l), which can be expressed as

$$x : y : z = a : b : c.$$

This continued ratio gives the following two equations:

$$\frac{x}{a} = \frac{y}{b} = \frac{z}{c} \tag{7.1}$$

where each term has no dimension.

Next, we can also express the exchange rate by considering how many units of a certain good is exchanged for another good in which the good's unit acts as the reference. We call the other good the standard good. In other words, when the inverse of each value of the continued ratio is multiplied by a specific amount of the one standard good that is selected, each value of the continued ratio obtained can indicate that the exchange is conducted with how many units of the standard good. When a certain good, M, is set as the standard good, where the quantity m of M is multiplied by the inverse of the continued ratio, m/a, m/b, and m/c are obtained in sequence. This is the relative index based on the good M as the standard. This provides the continued ratio:

$$\frac{m}{a} : \frac{m}{b} : \frac{m}{c}.$$

To consider buying and selling, let us explicitly include money into the exchange target. We can obtain the following continued ratio:

$$\frac{a}{a} : \frac{a}{b} : \frac{a}{c}$$

where the good A is money. In this ratio, each of a/a, a/b, and a/c is the price determined by money, while the money price is always 1 because a/a is measured by money. The price of money has no dimension. Therefore, we obtain

$$\boldsymbol{p} = (1, a/b, a/c), \tag{7.2}$$

where the price vector $\boldsymbol{p}$ expresses the exchange rate with money.

Since the quantity of the goods to be exchanged has a mathematical relationship given by Eq. (7.1), we can define the following binary relationship given by

$$xRy \overset{def}{\Longleftrightarrow} \frac{x}{a} = \frac{y}{b}$$

to the exchange quantity. This definition then makes this binary relation R *an equivalence relation*. Therefore, this definition derives the following conditions:

1. According to this definition, xRx means $x/a = x/a$. Therefore, this satisfies the *reflexive law*. In terms of exchange, this means that the quantity x of the good A is exchanged with the quantity x of the good A.
2. We can obtain $y/b = x/a$ by $x/a = y/b$. Then,

$$xRy \Longrightarrow yRx$$

is derived, and this satisfies the *symmetric law*. This means that if the quantity x of the good A is exchanged with the quantity y of the good B, the quantity y of the good B is exchanged with the quantity x of the good A.
3. We can acquire $x/a = z/c$ by $x/a = y/b$ and $y/b = z/c$. Therefore,

$$xRy \quad and \quad yRz \Longrightarrow xRz$$

is obtained, and this satisfies the *transitive law*. This means that where three goods are exchanged and where the quantity x of the good A is exchanged with the quantity y of the good B and the quantity y of the good B is exchanged with the quantity z of the good C, the quantity x of the good A is exchanged with the quantity z of the good C.

As shown above, the binary relation between the goods to be exchanged satisfies the reflexive law, the symmetric law, and the transitive law, which becomes *an equivalence relation.*

When the quantities of the goods to be exchanged have an equivalence relation, there is only one kind of exchange rate. Therefore, there is only one straight line that indicates the exchange rate within the exchanged product space. We could also say that this equivalence relation can be expressed only by using one straight line. Where three goods are exchanged, we can obtain the following equation:

$$G(R) = \{(x, y, z)|\frac{x}{a} = \frac{y}{b} = \frac{z}{c}\} \tag{7.3}$$

according to Eq. (7.1).

7.2 Why Do We Exchange?

7.2.1 The Exchange Vector and the Invariability of the Amount of Value

The exchange rate and the equivalence relation were discussed in the previous section. However, the establishment of an equivalence relation does not mean the execution of an exchange. In this section, the reason why we exchange must be considered.

Goods that are bought and sold are called commodities. To distinguish the various commodities, each different commodity is numbered, and commodity vector $\boldsymbol{q}$ is defined as representing each amount of this numbered commodity, namely, $\boldsymbol{q} = (q_1, q_2, \ldots, q_n)$. Next, in order to show the goods given or the goods taken through exchange in this commodities vector, a possessed vector and an exchange vector are defined as follows: Where an exchange is conducted by two persons A and B, let A and B's goods that are possessed before the exchange be vectors $\boldsymbol{a_1}$ and $\boldsymbol{b_1}$, respectively, and, after the exchange, be vectors $\boldsymbol{a_2}$ and $\boldsymbol{b_2}$, respectively. Therefore, A's obtained and lost goods by exchange are expressed by the exchange vector $+\boldsymbol{e} = \boldsymbol{a_2} - \boldsymbol{a_1}$. B's obtained and lost goods by this exchange are quite the revers of A's goods, that is, $-\boldsymbol{e} = \boldsymbol{b_2} - \boldsymbol{b_1}$.

Next, price vectors, that is, the exchange rates between unit quantities of various goods and the quantities of money, which correspond to the exchange vectors, are considered. As *Money is considered to be an abstract commodity, and buying and selling is the exchange of goods and money, the exchange vector includes money as one element. Therefore, the price vector also includes the rate of money measured by money as one element.* As mentioned in Sect. 7.1.2, the exchange rate between money and money is obtained by measuring the money by the money, so that the value is 1, while the unit is a dimensionless number.

As already mentioned, this chapter regards the money as the first element of the exchange vector and the price vector. Therefore, the first element of the price vector is always 1, as in Eq. (7.2). Next, we define *an amount of value as a product of a good quantity and a price, namely, the scalar product* $< \boldsymbol{p}, \boldsymbol{q} >$. *The measurement unit of this value is the amount of money.*

Now, let person A be a seller, and let person B be a buyer. Where the exchange column vector $+\boldsymbol{e}$ expresses the increase and decrease in the amount of goods of seller A, the exchange column vector $-\boldsymbol{e}$ expresses the increase and decrease in the amount of goods of buyer B. The amount of money is shown as the first element $\pm e$ of the exchange vectors. In buying and selling, one of the exchange targets is an abstract commodity, which is money. Therefore, let the price vectors be row vectors $\boldsymbol{p}$; then, the first element is 1, as mentioned. The obtained amount minus lost amount of value by the seller is the scalar product $< \boldsymbol{p}, +\boldsymbol{e} >$, and the obtained amount minus lost amount of value by the buyer is the scalar product $< \boldsymbol{p}, -\boldsymbol{e} >$.

When the amount of value is invariable, an exchange is executed. The amount of value of possession remains the same before and after buying and selling. Sellers and buyers neither suffer loss nor gain a profit. In other words, the scalar product of the price vector and the exchange vector $< \boldsymbol{p}, \pm\boldsymbol{e} >$ is 0. Since this scalar product is 0, these two vectors are orthogonal, which is illustrated in Fig. 7.1. In principle, it is impossible to plot those with different unit systems in the same space. Plotting them in the same space requires the introduction of different unit coordinate systems for descriptive purposes. Since prices and goods exist in different spaces, we cannot define the distance. If the distance cannot be defined, we cannot define the angle.

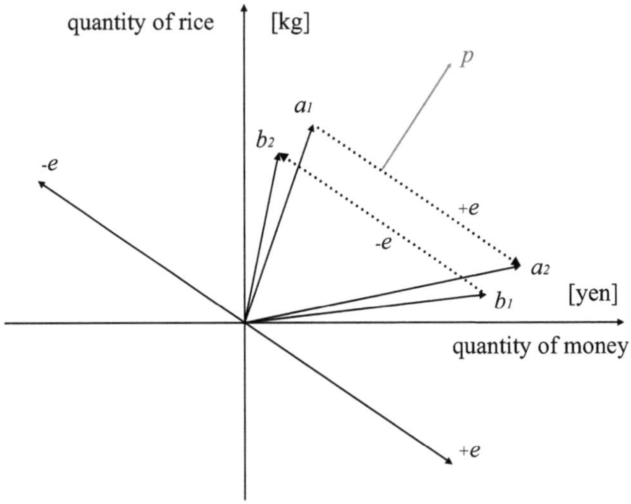

Fig. 7.1 Example of buying and selling

Therefore, these vectors are orthogonal, with no strictly geometric significance, except in a broad sense that the scalar product is 0.

For example, in our case of buying and selling rice, suppose that the Japanese yen is used as currency and that the unit for buying and selling rice is a kilogram. Here, the unit of currency is the *yen*, while the unit of rice is the *kg*. Where seller A has 2,000 yen and 14 kg of rice, the initial vector possessed by seller A is ${}^T\boldsymbol{a_1} =$ (2,000 yen, 14 kg).[6] Where buyer B has 7,000 yen and 2 kg of rice, this buyer's initial vector is ${}^T\boldsymbol{b_1} =$ (7,000 yen, 2 kg). Let us say 10 kg of rice is bought and sold at 6,000 yen. The possession vector of each party after this trade is ${}^T\boldsymbol{a_2} =$ (8,000 yen, 4 kg) and ${}^T\boldsymbol{b_2} =$ (1,000 yen, 12 kg). The exchange vector viewed from seller A is expressed as ${}^T + \boldsymbol{e} =$ (+6,000 yen, −10 kg), and the exchange vector viewed from buyer B is expressed as ${}^T - \boldsymbol{e} =$ (−6,000 yen, +10 kg). The price vector is $\boldsymbol{p} =$ (1 [yen/yen], 600 [yen/kg]). Figure 7.1 shows this buying and selling on a two-dimensional plain. The horizontal axis indicates the amount of the money, and the vertical axis indicates the amount of the commodity.

7.2.2 The Evaluation Vector and the Principle of Exchange

Next, why were goods bought and sold? Why did the buyer and the seller agree to exchange a certain good for the amount of value $< \boldsymbol{p}, \boldsymbol{q} >$? Why did this buyer

[6] T placed on the left shoulder of the vector symbol ${}^T\boldsymbol{a}$ indicates the transpose of the vector a with this mark.

decide to pay this amount? Alternatively, why did this seller accept to release the good he possessed at this amount of payment?

Let us consider buying and selling by using evaluation value vectors or, simply, evaluation vectors, $\boldsymbol{v}$. Here, in order to explain exchange, we define *an evaluation value vector as follows: evaluation vectors, which represent an evaluation of various commodities, correspond to exchange vectors. The evaluation value may be subjective or objective. As different individuals evaluate these commodities, the evaluation value itself will naturally differ.*

We normalize the evaluation of money as being 1, similar to the price of money. Therefore, the first element of the evaluation vector is always 1. As is the case with the definition of an amount of value, a product of an evaluation and quantity, namely, the scalar product $< \boldsymbol{v}, \boldsymbol{q} >$, is defined as an amount of evaluation value. The reason the amount of value measured by the price vector and the amount of evaluation value measured by the evaluation vector are different is, as Fig. 7.2 shows, observed because the evaluation vector, which is possessed by the trading parties, is separated by a hyperplane including the price vector. For this reason, the amount of evaluation value of both exchange parties increases after buying and selling. As the price and the evaluation value of money is always 1, the horizontal length of the price vector and the evaluation vector is always 1 in Fig. 7.2. Giving us a clear description of this point, *the Principle of Exchange* means that the exchange of two goods is executed because the evaluation vectors possessed by the exchange parties differ. This has been proved by Shiozawa (2004) with a common form in which nonnegative n goods were exchanged.

The concept of evaluation value is almost the same as the value in use or the utility concept, and *the Principle of Exchange* is the contraposition of Pareto opti-

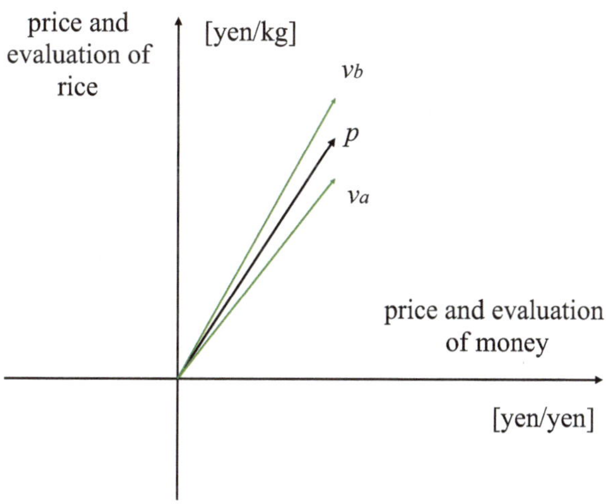

Fig. 7.2 Price vector $\boldsymbol{p}$ and evaluation vectors $\boldsymbol{v}_a$, $\boldsymbol{v}_b$

mality.[7] The proposition of *the Principal of Exchange* is the same mathematically as the Pareto optimality theory; however, it is different from the Pareto optimality theory with respect to buying and selling situations. Pareto optimality represents the finished situation of buying and selling. In contrast, *the Principal of Exchange* refers to the situation before buying and selling. This principle describes the process of buying and selling up to the moment of execution of the trade, by showing the reason why buying and selling are conducted.

The direction of two evaluation vectors coincide with each other after Pareto optimality is attained. However, after Pareto optimality is attained, there is no reason to buy and sell. If buying and selling are not conducted, there is no reason for the market to exist. For the market to continue to exist, the evaluation vector must be different, or a different evaluation vector must appear. *The Principle of Exchange* asserts this simple situation.

7.2.3 The Evaluation Vectors in Financial Markets and Product Markets

The differences of the evaluation vectors between financial markets and product markets are considered in this section.

7.2.3.1 Evaluation Vectors in Financial Markets

In financial markets, the persons concerned with buying and selling can symmetrically participate in the market: they can easily change their position as a buyer or seller. In addition, it is easy to observe quotes for both the desired selling and buying price.[8] Therefore, we consider the evaluation vectors referring to quotes in the financial markets.

Now, making a limit order, a trader buys or sells a certain stock for a buying or a selling price.[9] Let the trading volume be one, the selling quote p_s, the buying quote p_b, the contracted price p_c, the evaluation by seller v_s, and the evaluation by buyer v_b. For example, let us consider that our trader tries to sell a certain stock. It may be a certain enterprise's stock that was purchased in an earlier trade, and

[7] See Shiozawa (2004).

[8] There are some unique terms that express the conditions or characteristics of financial markets. Most of them are not usually used for describing product markets. Bull and bear, liquidity, spread, board thickness, resilience, and quotes are examples of these types of terms. Quotes indicate the asking prices of buying and selling orders appearing on the board.

[9] According to *Guide to TSE Trading Methodology* (Tokyo Stock Exchange 2004): Limit orders are orders at specific prices, meaning that investors have stated that they want to "buy at not more than XX yen, or sell at not less than XX yen." In other words a limit order represents the lowest/highest price at which the investor is willing to sell/buy (p.8).

our trader, forecasting that the stock price will decline, tries to sell it on the present day, before the price falls. Alternatively, it may be index futures: he will try to sell it short today and will buy it back in the future. Therefore, today, he evaluates the stock as being lower than the selling price, or he thinks that he can sell the stock at a higher price than the evaluation. Therefore, let $\delta_s(>0)$ be the discrepancy between the selling quote p_s and the evaluation v_s, and the following can be defined as the seller's evaluation:

$$v_s = p_s - \delta_s.$$

Since the selling quote p_s means that the stocks are sold higher than or equal to the quoted price (including the quotes price), the quoted price may become the contacted price p_c. On the other hand, our buyer has an opposite position. Let the trader buy a stock. The trader forecasts the stock price that she wants to buy will rise in the future, or she hopes to short sell the futures indexes that she buys today. Therefore, she forms an evaluation that is higher than the buying price today. Alternatively, she thinks that she can buy them at a price lower than the evaluation. Therefore, let the buyer's evaluation be v_b and $\delta_b(>0)$ be the discrepancy between the quote and the evaluation, and the buyer's evaluation can be defined as follows:

$$v_b = p_b + \delta_b.$$

Since the buying quote p_b means that the stocks are bought at a price lower than or equal to the quoted price, the quoted price may become the contacted price p_c. Hence, the inequality $v_s < p_s \leq p_c \leq p_b < v_b$ is established.

When buying orders and selling orders are matched, the contracted price p_c is established. Since the contracted volume is 1, the seller's exchange vector is $^T+\boldsymbol{e} = (p_c, -1)$, the buyer's exchange vector is $^T-\boldsymbol{e} = (-p_c, +1)$, and the contracted price vector is $\boldsymbol{p_c} = (1, p_c)$. The seller's evaluation vector is $\boldsymbol{v_s} = (1, v_s) = (1, p_s - \delta_s)$, and the buyer's evaluation vectors is $\boldsymbol{v_b} = (1, v_b) = (1, p_b + \delta_b)$. The changes in the amount of value are $< \boldsymbol{p_c}, +\boldsymbol{e} >= 0$ by the seller and $< \boldsymbol{p_c}, -\boldsymbol{e} >= 0$ by the buyer; therefore, there is no augmentation of the amount of value, but the amount of the evaluation value is changed. The seller's amount of evaluation value rises as follows:

$$< \boldsymbol{v_s}, +\boldsymbol{e} >= p_c - p_s + \delta_s.$$

Since the selling is accomplished, the contacted price p_c and the selling quote p_s satisfy $p_c \geq p_s$. Therefore, the amount of the evaluation value increases by $p_c - p_s + \delta_s$. The greater the difference between the contracted price p_c and the quoted price p_s is, the more the amount of the evaluation value. Similarly, the buyer's amount of evaluation value rises as follows:

$$< \boldsymbol{v_b}, -\boldsymbol{e} >= -p_c + p_b + \delta_b.$$

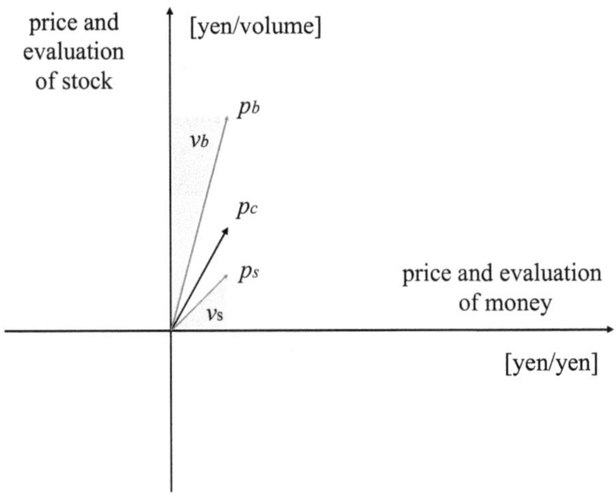

Fig. 7.3 Price vector, quotes, and evaluation vectors

Since the buying is accomplished, the contracted price and buying quote satisfy $p_b \geq p_c$. Therefore, the amount of evaluation value increases by $p_b - p_c + \delta_b$.

Figure 7.3 shows the examples of the price vector, the quotes, and the evaluation vectors. The buyer can buy a stock at a price lower than the buying quote p_b, and the seller can sell it at the price higher than the selling quote p_s. The evaluation vectors v_b and v_s exist in the shadow area. When the trader cannot find the opposite trader, that is, the selling or buying quote cannot be matched to the opposite trade, the trader will change the quote. For example, the seller will lower the quote within the δ_s, to secure a price in the range $\delta_s > p_s - p_c$. Similarly, the buyer will raise the quote within the δ_b, securing a price in the range $\delta_b > p_c - p_b$.

7.2.3.2 Evaluation Vectors in Product Markets

We consider the evaluation in product markets. The persons who participate in the market and want to buy something or to sell something do not easily change positions as buyers or sellers: the role of buyer and seller is not changed.

Therefore, regarding consumption goods, it can be easy to observe the seller's desired price because the seller must put the price tags on the goods in order for the goods to be purchased. However, it is difficult to observe the buyer's desired price because the buyer will choose to buy only if he is satisfied with the selling price that is shown on the price tags: the buyer will not buy if the selling price is unacceptable. Evaluations of consumption goods used by individuals in their daily lives are habitually formed based on each individual's propensities.

When seeing a product and its price, for example, the price of vegetables, gasoline, or electrical appliances, individuals feel the product is expensive or inexpensive because they already have formed their own conscious or unconscious evaluations. The evaluation of each individual for a certain product is not strictly determined: it keeps on changing based on the situation and condition at that time. If individuals frequently change their evaluations of consumption goods, however, due to their emotions, they feel frustrated and psychologically stressed in their daily buying and selling activities. Such stress probably prevents them from performing daily activities. When producers procure materials as inputs to produce the commodities for the market, they form evaluations regarding the inputs' cost, which are required for production. Since the production methods may have to be modified in response to changes in the cost of raw materials, the frequent cost changes are not good for production. Therefore, the evaluations of raw material costs need to be stable.

When buying and selling is executed, the buyer will consider how much he/she can spend for purchasing a certain good as a maximum, and the seller will consider the lowest price that can be set for selling a certain good. Let's consider the buying and selling evaluations. In this instance, following the example in Sect. 7.2.1, when the seller thinks that he can sell 1 kg of rice for 500 yen and the buyer thinks that he can pay 700 yen for 1 kg of rice, the evaluation vector of the seller is $\boldsymbol{v_a} = (1\ [\text{yen/yen}], (500 - \delta_s)\ [\text{yen/kg}])$, and the evaluation vector of the buyer is $\boldsymbol{v_b} = (1\ [\text{yen/yen}], (700 + \delta_b)\ [\text{yen/kg}])$, where $\delta_s > 0$, $\delta_b > 0$. According to the evaluation vectors, we can see here how much the evaluation value increased by buying and selling. As the exchange vector is measured by the evaluation vector, the seller's increased evaluation value is $< \boldsymbol{v_a}, +\boldsymbol{e} >= 1{,}000[\text{yen}] + 10\delta_s[\text{yen}]$, and the buyer's increased evaluation value is $< \boldsymbol{v_b}, -\boldsymbol{e} >= 1{,}000[\text{yen}] + 10\delta_b[\text{yen}]$.

7.3 Why Do We Practice Arbitrage?

The selling price and the buying price of a certain good could differ because of transaction costs, such as transportation, storage, and charges. If the differences in the exchange rate are originated only in the transaction costs, there is no room for conducting an arbitrage transaction. The aim of the arbitrage transaction is to gain profit. Therefore, the arbitrage transaction is conducted when there are differences in the exchange rates exceeding the transaction costs, while it is continued until these differences no longer produce a profit. Therefore, the exchange rates converge within a certain range in an economic system in which arbitrage transactions are conducted repeatedly. This "certain range" depends on the transaction costs. If the transaction has no costs, the selling price matches the buying price: the exchange rate becomes one value. To simplify the point that we are considering here, let us assume that there are no transaction costs.

7.3.1 Arbitrage Transactions and Out of Equivalence Relations

An arbitrage transaction, also referred to as arbitrage trading, usually indicates a buying and selling transaction that aims to gain profit by taking advantage of the differences in prices in markets. In other words, arbitrage means using differences in prices to earn a profit margin. While arbitrage assumes buying and selling, that is, paying money to get money, we here have a broad interpretation of a type of bartering, as transactions that are conducted to gain surplus by using differences in the exchange rate are also arbitrage transactions.

An arbitrage transaction is conducted when a binary relation that is not in *an equivalence relation* is established. Judging from three conditions that indicate *the equivalence relation*, we can see that there exist three kinds of arbitrage transactions.

7.3.1.1 When the Reflexive Law is Broken

When the reflexive law is not satisfied, we can gain $x/a \neq x/a$ in xRx. This means that the quantity x of the good A is not exchanged with the quantity x of the good A. This also means that the quantity x of the good A can be exchanged with the quantity $x'(\neq x)$ of the good A. Using the exchange rate in which the reflexive law is not satisfied can increase the possessions more than before the exchange. This shows that arbitrage works.

7.3.1.2 When the Symmetric Law is Broken

When the symmetric law is not satisfied, we cannot derive yRx from xRy. Therefore, we obtain $y/b \neq x/a$ by $x/a = y/b$. This means that if the quantity x of the good A is exchanged with the quantity y of the good B, the quantity $y'(\neq y)$ of the good B is exchanged with the quantity x of the good A. Hence, we can conduct an arbitrage transaction by taking advantage of the differences in the exchange rate.

For example, suppose that white sugar is sold at a more expensive price in Tokyo than in Osaka. Since the symmetric law is not satisfied between these cities, where the price of one unit of white sugar in Tokyo being p_t and the price in Osaka being p_o, $p_t > p_o$ is satisfied, which means buying white sugar at the unit quantity in Osaka and selling it in Tokyo can enable suppliers to gain a profit of $p_t - p_o$. This makes it possible to provide a profit by arbitrage between two cities. Alternatively, the suppliers in Osaka will try to sell their white sugar in Tokyo, not Osaka. At the same time, the purchasers in Tokyo will try to buy white sugar in Osaka, not Tokyo.[10]

---

[10]See Morishima (1984), Chapter 2.

7.3.1.3 When the Transitive Law Is Broken: Triangular Trading in History

When the transitive law is not satisfied, we cannot derive xRz from xRy and yRz. In other words, we obtain $x/a \neq z/c$, according to $x/a = y/b$ and $y/b = z/c$. This also means that where the quantity x of the good A is exchanged with the quantity y of the good B and the quantity y of the good B is exchanged with the quantity z of the good C, the quantity x of the good A is exchanged with the quantity $z'(\neq z)$ of the good C.

Therefore, where $z > z'$, we can make a profit not by directly exchanging the good A with the good C but by exchanging the good A with the good B first and then exchanging the good B with the good C. Where $z < z'$, exchanging the good A with the good C without exchanging it with the good B can provide a greater profit.

The triangular trade known as the slave trade conducted between the seventeenth and the eighteenth centuries is one of the arbitrage transaction examples that was conducted because the transitive law was not satisfied. Weapons, rum, and textile goods were brought to West Africa from Western Europe, slaves (black cargo) were brought to the West Indies from West Africa, and sugar and cotton (white cargo) were brought to Western Europe from the West Indies. This trade created huge profits for the merchants. Another triangular trade, which provided the cause of the Opium War in the nineteenth century, brought tea to Britain from Qing, China, cotton fabrics to India from Britain, and Opium to Qing from India.

7.3.2 *The Emergence of Money and a Quotient Set*

7.3.2.1 Arbitrage Transactions by the Emergence of Money

In case of the barter exchange, the number of exchange rates for a certain good is the same as the number of the kinds of good that are bartered for a certain good. If each good is exchangeable for every other good and the number of goods is n, the number of exchange rates is the combination number ${}_nC_2$. If we have 10 kinds of goods, the number of combinations, ${}_{10}C_2$, is only 45, and if we have 100 kinds of goods, the number of combinations, ${}_{100}C_2$, is 4,950. Additionally, if we have 10,000 kinds of goods, the number of combinations, ${}_{10{,}000}C_2 = 49{,}995{,}000$.

To conduct an arbitrage, there must be different exchange rates between the same trade, and these rates must be found by the trader. The more the number of exchange rates of goods are, the more difficult it is to find the different exchange rates between the same trade and to conduct arbitrage, even in the same marketplace. Moreover, if the exchange is conducted in a different place and time, the more the number of exchange rates of goods there are, the more difficult it is to find the different rates of exchange of each barter exchange. Therefore, the arbitrage trading was conducted with very limited goods.

However, when money emerged, this situation changed drastically. Many specific exchange rates were unified as a single unique exchange rate for money. As the exchange of goods with money developed, various exchange rates by barter trade became the only exchange rate with money. To be more precise, since money separates the exchange itself into buying and selling, for the various exchange rates of barter trading, this separation produced the two monetary exchange rates: the selling price and the buying price.

This is the price system in the economy. As many types of exchange rates converged into one kind of exchange rate, namely, price, the number of exchange rates was the number of the goods in the whole economy. Accordingly, the number of exchange rates decreased significantly with the emergence of money. For example, when the number of goods is ten thousand, the number of prices is also ten thousand, which is one five thousandth ($1/5{,}000$) of the number of prices there would be in a barter exchange. When money emerged and the exchange rate was acknowledged as price, the exchange rate of goods was easy to compare accurately, and arbitrage was conducted more actively.

7.3.2.2 Classification Based on Differences in the Exchange Rate: A Quotient Set

No arbitrage transaction is conducted when the exchange relation is an equivalence relation. Conversely, if an arbitrage transaction is conducted, the exchange relation is not an equivalence relation. This means that this exchange relationship is not included in a subset of the same equivalence relation. Suppose, we create a subset based on the equivalence relation R, where the entire set in which transactions are conducted is W. Namely, we assort (classify) equivalence classes based on R and define the set of all the equivalence classes as the quotient set based on R while expressing this as W/R. Within the assorted quotient set, defining one element determines all the values that are equivalent to the element defined. For instance, where this element is defined as 1,000 yen, the quantity of all goods that are exchanged with 1,000 yen will be autonomously determined.

7.3.3 Two Examples of Arbitrage

First, the arbitrage of index futures trading in financial markets as an example of arbitrage generated due to difference in exchange rates in temporally different regions is described. When arbitrage trading is conducted between the spot and future market in financial markets, the volatile movement of the price becomes gradually stable. Arbitrage trading plays an important role in stabilizing sudden price changes. Second, the point described here is the arbitrage discussed by the Ricardian trade theory. It is an example of arbitrage generated due to the difference in exchange rates in spatially different regions. When arbitrage trading is conducted between geographically and spatially different regions, the merchants play an active role in trading to make a profit. Both types of arbitrage are conducted when the symmetric law is broken.

7.3.3.1 Arbitrage in the Index Futures Markets

Let us consider a futures market where indexes are transacted. Arbitrage is conducted based on index futures that fluctuate due to difference in the futures period (trading period) in the futures market. Considering the situation in which one unit of index futures is traded, suppose that the first exchange vector is expressed as $\pm\boldsymbol{e_1}$, the price established in this trading is p^1, the second exchange vector is $\pm\boldsymbol{e_2}$, and the price at that time is p^2. When a trader A sells one unit of indexes at p^1 in the first trading session, this trader A's exchange vector is $+\boldsymbol{e_1} = (+p^1, -1)$. The exchange vector of a trader B as a buyer, who conducts buying and selling in reverse, is expressed as $-\boldsymbol{e_1} = (-p^1, +1)$. In the second buying and selling session, where the trader A repurchases what he sold in the previous session and where the trader B sells what he bought, the exchange vector of the trader A is $-\boldsymbol{e_2} = (-p^2, +1)$, while that of the trader B is $+\boldsymbol{e_2} = (+p^2, -1)$. The price vector in the first session of buying and selling is $\boldsymbol{p^1} = (1, p^1)$, while that in the second session is $\boldsymbol{p^2} = (1, p^2)$. Therefore, where $p^1 > p^2$ is established, the amount of value, namely, the amount of money, possessed by the trader A, who bought and sold $+\boldsymbol{e_1} - \boldsymbol{e_2}$, increases by $p^1 - p^2$, while the amount of value, the amount of money, possessed by the trader B, who bought and sold in reverse $-\boldsymbol{e_1} + \boldsymbol{e_2}$, decreases by $-p^1 + p^2$ reflecting a loss.

As the total volume of index futures of both traders does not change, there is no increase or decrease in the index futures. For the scalar product of the exchange vectors and price vectors, $< \boldsymbol{p^1}, +\boldsymbol{e_1} >=< \boldsymbol{p^1}, -\boldsymbol{e_1} >= 0$ and $< \boldsymbol{p^2}, +\boldsymbol{e_2} >=< \boldsymbol{p^2}, -\boldsymbol{e_2} >= 0$ are established. Therefore, there is no change in the amount of value before and after each of the first and the second sessions of buying and selling. However, the amount of value changes between the first session and the second session of buying and selling: there is a different amount of value between the first session and the second session, as the trader A obtains a gain $p^1 - p^2$, while the trader B suffers a loss $-p^1 + p^2$. Figure 7.4 shows this arbitrage.

Trading is conducted even in a zero-sum game because the buying and selling parties have different evaluation vectors. Their evaluation vectors differ because they have different predictions. Before the first session of buying and selling, trader A predicted a fall in the index futures price, and trader B predicted an increase in this price. The evaluation vectors based on these predictions existed on both sides of the price vector. For this reason, at first, trader A decided to sell and trader B decided to buy. This resulted in establishing buying and selling. Buying and selling is conducted because different predictions exist and evaluation vectors based on these predictions differ, which makes it possible to conduct arbitrage trading. As a result, gains and losses appear due to arbitrage trading. Further new predictions are formed, and arbitrage trading is conducted again. This process continues. If prices

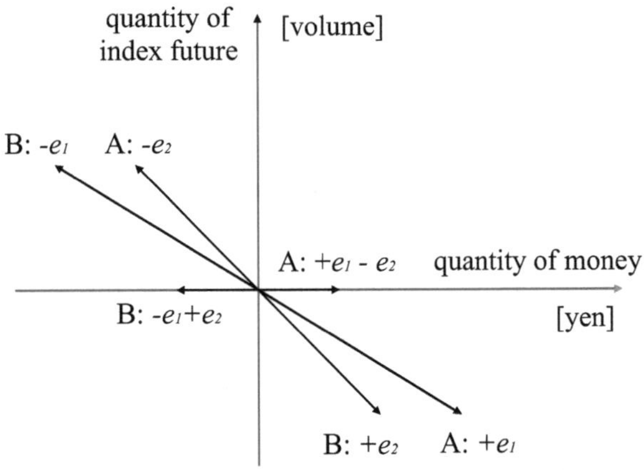

Fig. 7.4 Arbitrage in the index futures markets

stop changing in the index futures market and traders start to predict that prices will remain the same, the traders will have fixed evaluation vectors. As a result, arbitrage trading is not conducted. Traders lose their reasons for remaining in the market, and soon, no one is participating in the market.

7.3.3.2 Arbitrage in the Ricardian Trade Theory

Between two countries, the profit of commerce trading must be distinguished from that of arbitrage trading between two countries, in the Ricardian trade theory. The profit obtained by commerce means that commerce done between two countries with different technical levels can increase the real earnings, enhance the consumption level, reduce the real price, and reduce hours of labor. These profits are the equivalent mathematically and are gained during one session of commerce. On the other hand, the profit due to arbitrage is realized just because the exchange rate (the price proportion) differs between two goods which are exchanged (traded). Therefore, profit can continuously be obtained by repeating this process as long as the exchange rate differs.[11]

In the Ricardian trade theory, wool and wine are traded between England and Portugal. Arbitrage is transacted because the exchange rate between these two goods differs in each country. Table 7.1 shows labor quantities necessary for producing a unit quantity of wool and wine in England and Portugal, as described by Ricardo.

Where the wage rates of England and Portugal are w_e and w_p, while the markup rates are r_e and r_p, respectively, the value and the unit of the wage rates are different in the two countries. The markup rate also differs. In England, where wool is the first good and wine is the 2nd good, the price of wool is expressed as $p_e^1 = 100w_e(1+r_e)$

[11] See Shiozawa (2017).

Table 7.1 Labor quantities necessary for producing a unit quantity of wool or wine

	Labor quantities for a unit of wool	Labor quantities for a unit of wine
England	100 persons	120 persons
Portugal	90 persons	80 persons

and the price of wine is expressed as $p_e^2 = 120w_e(1 + r_e)$, as nominal monetary amount. Similarly, in Portugal, the price of wool is expressed as $p_p^1 = 90w_p(1+r_p)$, and the price of wine is expressed as $p_p^2 = 80w_p(1 + r_p)$.

In this instance, in England, merchant A purchases one unit of wool from merchant B at a monetary amount of $100w_e(1+r_e)$ which A possesses. Merchant A then exports this wool to Portugal and sells it to merchant C and obtains a monetary amount of $90w_p(1 + r_p)$. Next, when merchant A purchases wine from merchant D in Portugal by spending the monetary amount of $90w_p(1 + r_p)$, merchant A can obtain wine in units represented by the ratio $90w_p(1 + r_p)/80w_p(1 + r_p) = 9/8$. When exporting all of this wine to England and selling it to merchant E in England, merchant A can obtain the monetary amount $120w_e(1+r_e) \times 9/8 = 135w_e(1+r_e)$. This means that the monetary amount possessed by merchant A actually increases 1.35 times the amount merchant A possessed in the beginning. As long as the exchange rates of wool and wine differ in both of these two countries, continuing this arbitrage enables merchant A to increase his monetary amount. The wool exported to Portugal is not exchanged directly with wine in Portugal. It is exchanged once into Portugal's currency (Real), and next, this exchanged money is spent for purchasing wine in Portugal. In England, the money that was possessed in the beginning (Pound) was exchanged for wool, while through selling, the wine imported from Portugal is exchanged into currency in England (Pound). The exchange of wool with wine within the country is performed through the intermediary of money. Therefore, this is considered to be buying and selling. The transportation cost of goods is not considered here, and there is no cost for the commerce trading itself. Money appears only in the trading performed domestically, and it has nothing to do with commerce trading between two countries. When bartering is conducted, not buying and selling, domestically, the same arbitrage can be established: Merchant A, who possesses one unit of wool (Point I in Fig. 7.5) in England, moves to Portugal and exchanges it for 9/8 of a unit of wine (Point II in Fig. 7.5) possessed by the merchant F. The merchant A then moves this 9/8 of a unit of wine to England and exchanges it with 1.35 units of wool (Point III in Fig. 7.5) possessed by merchant G. The amount of wool possessed by the merchant A has increased 1.35 times. Once again, merchant A transports this wool to Portugal and exchanges it for the wine and can gain more from the exchange of the wine (Point IV in Fig. 7.5). Using the process considered above makes the concept of the arbitrage in the Recardian trade theory easier to understand.

The amount of the arbitrage-based gain is defined by the exchange rate of goods. The exchange direction in order to obtain a gain is also defined by this exchange rate. In other words, the amount of wool possessed in the beginning increases by trading in England; however, the amount of wine does not increase by this

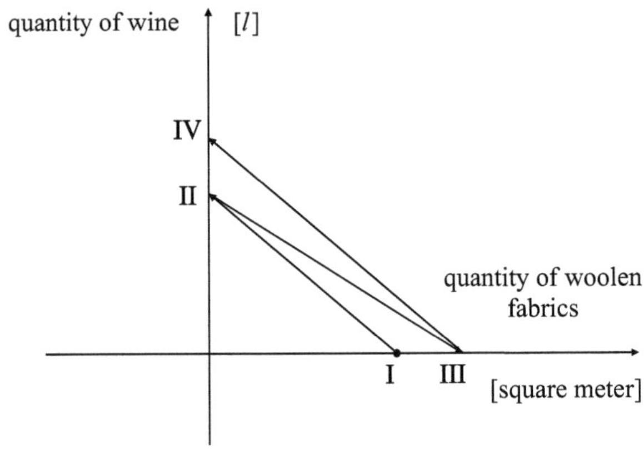

Fig. 7.5 Arbitrage in Ricardian trade

trading. In Portugal, however, the amount of wine that is possessed in the beginning can increase, while it is impossible to increase the amount of wool. Figure 7.5 graphically shows this fact. Wool increases along the horizontal axis, while wine increases along the vertical axis.

For this trading to be executed, all of these six merchants need to have evaluation vectors that are different from the merchant A and their evaluation vectors must be placed on both of the different sides of the hyperplane, including the price (exchange rate) for each good. If merchants have the same evaluation vector or if they have different evaluation vectors that exist on the same side of this hyperplane, buying and selling of these merchants cannot be established. No merchants conduct transactions while knowing that transactions can reduce their evaluation values. The intention of merchant A, who aims to an obtain arbitrage-based gain, collapses. Where wool and wine are the only goods transacted in both countries during a limited trading period (or a limited number of trades), this arbitrage transaction is considered to be a zero-sum game. Merchant B through the merchant G suffers losses due to this trading. However, if trading is continued while they know that the relevant trading is a zero-sum game, it is because the trading parties possess different evaluation vectors.

7.4 Buying-Selling and Arbitrage in Financial Markets and Product Markets

7.4.1 The Difference Between Buying-Selling and Arbitrage

Buying and selling transactions and arbitrage are conducted for different reasons, which must be distinguished. In buying and selling, the amount of value obtained is equivalent to the amount of value released. Therefore, it is impossible to increase the amount of value in only one execution of buying and selling. *The Principle of Exchange* describes what happens in a single exchange session. If we seek an increase in the amount of value, we need to execute buying and selling at least two times. A gain or loss by these multiple executions should not be confused with the gained or lost amount of evaluation value. Where the exchange rate differs in goods that are exchanged (bought and sold) in two spatially (geographically) or temporally different locations, performing more than two sessions of exchange (buying and selling) by utilizing differences in this exchange rate can increase the amount of possession, namely, the amount of value initially possessed. Note that there needs to be an exchange that happens at least two times, not a single exchange. A transaction with the aim of obtaining this gain by an exchange that occurs more than two times is referred to as an arbitrage transaction or as arbitrage trading.

We, however, execute buying and selling continuously, even though the amount of value does not increase. This is because the exchange parties have different evaluation values. To understand buying and selling, the value measured by the price vector needs to be distinguished from the evaluation value measured by the evaluation vector.

7.4.2 The Properties of Price and the Formation of Evaluation

The formation or creation of evaluation depends on the character of markets and goods. Let us consider the evaluation of the commodities that were demanded in financial markets. Prices and evaluations of those commodities bought and sold in financial markets always fluctuate. To obtain funds, enterprises issue bonds and stocks in the financial market. This is an essential role of the financial market. To support the activities of the enterprises, the purchasers will hold the bonds and stock for an extended period of time. Keynes wrote the following approximately 80 years ago:

> The spectacle of modern investment markets has sometimes moved me towards the conclusion that to make the purchase of an investment permanent and indissoluble, like marriage, except by reason of death or other grave cause, might be a useful remedy for our contemporary evils. For this would force the investor to direct his mind to the long-term prospects and to those only. (Keynes (1936) p.160.)

Accordingly, it is not necessary to buy and sell in the short period. Today, however, dealings are performed 1,000 times in 1 second, such as in the arrowhead system in the Tokyo Stock Exchange.[12] This ultrahigh-speed method for transaction processing has been an effective response to the demand of traders, and the financial market has affirmatively accepted it. As these transactions are conducted frequently, the evaluations change frequently. With various different evaluations, many traders participate in these transactions. As a result, the contracted executed prices fluctuate

[12] This system has started since 2015.

sharply and wildly. Moreover, evaluations will change. In this way, these frequent changes of evaluations and prices are repeated, and the transactions of financial markets become more active.

In contrast, in product markets, the consumer's evaluation of the goods are formed habitually and are stable, as stated in Sect. 7.2.3.2. Except for market sensitive commodities, such as agricultural products, the prices in the product markets are comparatively stable, and buying and selling can proceed under stable evaluations and prices. This is one of the reasons why production activities can be continued. If the price of a commodity changes and it contradicts the transitive law, arbitrage trading is conducted, and the price will converge within a certain range based on the transportation cost: The stability of the price and the evaluations will be strengthened.

7.4.3 The Properties of Goods and Arbitrage

Why are there differences between the financial markets and the product markets? This is because the existing purpose and reason for goods are different in the financial markets and the product markets. The purpose of goods in the financial markets is the augmentation of the amount of value, which can be said to be a self-multiplication objective. This augmented value in the financial market may be exchanged sooner or later for goods, which are produced for use in product market. A part of the funds that are gained in the financial market may be spent to increase fixed capital formation in the products market. The purpose of investment, however, in the financial market is the augmentation of the value itself. The frequent trading itself is evidence of this. There may even be speculation in the barter economy: the purpose of most barter exchanges is to use the exchanged goods. Many monetary commodities have emerged after money became the primary means of exchange. The purpose of the transactions involving most of these commodities is to increase the amount of value: this is also a self-multiplication objective. In the last 30 years, the monetary assets became more than three times compared to the GDP in the world. This is because there is a great deal of pressure to increase the amount of value itself in the financial market. To increase the amount of value, traders have to repeat the arbitrage activity. In order to conduct arbitrage, prices must change. Even if through arbitrage, prices start to follow the transitive law, new prices that disrupt the transitive law will appear again. In other words, different evaluations are generated by the many different predictions of traders who participate in the trading, and these evaluations will be changed again by other predictions. These frequent changes in evaluations create opportunities for arbitrage for many economic agents.

In contrast, in the product market, transacted commodities are produced for use: the final purpose of the commodities is use. When the product commodities are sold, they become objects to use not to sell. The commodity that is produced to sell finishes its role as a commodity and becomes a good to use. The purpose of the commodity is accomplished completely. The purpose of the trading is not to increase the amount of value but to enjoy the convenience by using the goods itself. Therefore, the purpose of gaining goods is to obtain the materials for production or consumption. Of course, arbitrage trading may be conducted for the purpose of increasing value, even in product markets; however, as the price system satisfies the transitive law, there is no need to conduct arbitrage again. One of the differences between the two kinds of markets is that it is easy to observe the performance of the arbitrage trading. The purpose of arbitrage is the augmentation of the amount of value. The economic consequences of the trading are different in the two kinds of markets because the purpose of the goods in the two markets is different. By arbitrage trading, a stable price is created in the product market; however, the fluctuation of the price is created again in the financial markets. If we are not able to conduct arbitrage, there will be no reason to trade in the financial market, and the market will vanish because there will be no trade, which is the reason why price changes occur frequently in the financial market.

7.5 Conclusion

Humans acquired the concept of possession and then came to be able to exchange goods, and exchange rates came into existence. Exchange then developed, and the general current means of exchange, namely, money, which is unique to each community or region, appeared. The advent of money resulted in buying and selling. Prices also appeared as a result of the existence of buying and selling. For buying and selling to be conducted, the relevant buying and selling parties needed to form an evaluation toward the goods to be traded and their evaluations had to be different. Therefore, evaluations for the goods to be traded would habitually be formed, while the prices that appeared as a result were referred to. Over many generations, as members of communities or regions, humans have gradually formed such evaluations along with other customs, through learning and growth. Money has emerged, and the trading by money, namely, buying and selling, developed. Buying was conducted for selling, not for using: this is speculation. Markets developed, and capital was accumulated. This produced financial markets. The purpose of buying and selling in financial markets is to obtain gains. Therefore, price fluctuations are an essential condition for markets to exist.

We have to avoid equating the characteristics related to the prices in product markets with those in the financial markets. Evolutionary economics actually recognizes that habitually formed behavioral rules play an important role in human behavior and the human decision-making process. Microscopic viewpoints of the stability of habitually formed evaluations and the stability of prices are inescapably tied to the entire concept of evolutionary economics.

References

Hayek, F. A. (1967). The results of human action but not of human design. In F. A. Hayek (Ed.), *Studies in philosophy, politics and economics* (pp. 96–105). Chicago: The University of Chicago Press.

Hayek, F. A. (1973). *Law, legislation and liberty, volume 1 – rules and order*. Chicago: The University of Chicago Press.

Hayek, F. A. (1988). *The fatal conceit – The errors of socialism*. Chicago: The University of Chicago Press.

Keynes, J. M. (1936). *The general theory of employment, interest and money*. The Collected Writings of John Maynard Keynes Vol. 7 (1973). London: Macmillan.

Menger, C. (1923). *Grundsäetze der Volkswirtschaftslehre, Zweite Auflage*. Wien: Hölder-Pichler-Tempsky A. G./Leipzig: G. Freytag G. M. B. H.

Morishima, M. (1984). *The economics of industrial society*. Cambridge: Cambridge University Press.

Shiozawa, Y. (2004). The present of economics of complexity. In Y. Shiozawa (Ed.), *The present of economics 1*. Tokyo: Nihon Keizai Hyoronsya (In Japanese).

Shiozawa, Y. (2017). The new theory of international values: An overview. In Y. Shiozawa, T. Oka, & T. Tabuchi (Eds.), *A new construction of Ricardian theory of international values*. Tokyo: Springer.

Taniguchi, K. (2012). Price, price formation and transmittance of price information. Presented in 16th annual conference of the European society for the history of economic thought, Saint Petersburg state university, Saint Petersburg, May 2012.

Tokyo Stock Exchange. (2004). *Guide to TSE trading methodology* (3rd ed.). Tokyo: Tokyo Stock Exchange.

MIX
Papier aus verantwortungsvollen Quellen
Paper from responsible sources
FSC® C105338

If you have any concerns about our products,
you can contact us on
ProductSafety@springernature.com

In case Publisher is established outside the EU,
the EU authorized representative is:
Springer Nature Customer Service Center GmbH
Europaplatz 3, 69115 Heidelberg, Germany

Printed by Libri Plureos GmbH
in Hamburg, Germany